JUVENILE

DELINQUENCY

A Sociological Approach

Jack E. Bynum
Oklahoma State University

William E. Thompson
Emporia State University

Allyn and Bacon
Boston · London · Sydney · Toronto

To our mothers—Frances Bynum and Flora L. Thompson—and to the memory of our fathers—Jack E. Bynum, Sr. and Edwin N. Thompson—who through their precepts and examples helped us become the authors of this book and not the subjects.

Managing Editor: Mylan Jaixen
Series editor: Karen Hanson
Production/editorial services: Editing, Design & Production, Inc.
Production administrator: Peter Petraitis
Text design: Editing, Design, & Publication, Inc.
Cover coordinator: Linda Dickinson
Composition buyer: Linda Cox
Manufacturing buyer: Tamara McCracken

Library of Congress Cataloging in Publication Data

Bynum, Jack E.
    Juvenile delinquency: A sociological approach / Jack E. Bynum, William E. Thompson.
        p.   cm.
    Includes index.
    ISBN 0-205-11774-0
    1. Juvenile delinquency—United States. I. Thompson, William E. (William Edwin), 1950- . II. Title.
HV9104.B9 1988
364.3'6'0973—dc19   88-19077
                                                      CIP

Printed in the United States of America
10 9 8 7 6 5 4 3 2   93 92 91 90 89

Photo Credits:

H. Armstrong Roberts xx, 7, 18, 42, 62, 98, 114, 176, 214, 238, 257, 281, 310, 327, 346, 375, 400, 418, 473 Zefa, 475
Comstock Photos 98, 143, 214 Skip Barron, 231, 310, 383
Taurus Photos 98, 168, 184, 214, Spencer Grant, 264 Eric Kroll, 310, 318, 350, 414, 423, 447
UPI/Bettmann Newsphotos 129, 293, 400
Marilyn R. Thompson 36, 109
Cartoon 196 From *Sense and Nonsense About Crime: A Policy Guide* by S. Walker. Copyright © 1985 by Wadsworth Inc. Reprinted by permission of Brooks/Cole Publishing Co. Pacific Grove, CA 93950

Contents

Part II
Causes of Juvenile Delinquency   99

Part III

Collective Behavior and Juvenile Delinquency 215

Part IV

Confrontation: Society and the Juvenile Delinquent   311

Part V

Control: Strategies for Dealing with Juvenile Delinquency   401

List of Figures

List of Tables

Preface

Juvenile delinquency is one of the most complex, interesting, and challenging phenomena in American society. Newspapers, television, and radio bombard us with accounts of juvenile misbehavior and crime which range from truancy to first degree murder. Consequently, youths who violate the law receive considerable attention from law enforcement officials, social agencies, criminologists, and social and behavioral scientists.

This book is guided by the basic premise that juvenile delinquency is inherently social in nature. It is a social concept, part and product of the society in which it occurs. Thus, any meaningful discussion of delinquency must be couched in a sociological framework which views it relative to the normative processes and societal responses which define it. More specifically, this book approaches delinquency as it relates to and emerges from the youth's family, neighborhood, school, peer group, social class, and overall cultural and social environment.

Rather than aligning this analysis to any particular theoretical perspective, we utilized an eclectic sociological approach which integrates elements of functionalist, conflict, and symbolic interactionist theories. Thus, we have attempted to present delinquency in its broadest sociological context. This approach should give the reader a growing awareness of and sensitivity to the social nature of human behavior whether it be socially adjudged as conforming or nonconforming, normative or deviant, acceptable or unacceptable, good or bad, or some paradoxical mixture of these seemingly antithetical evaluations.

This sociological work has been enhanced by the inclusion of some important past and present contributions of psychologists, social workers, criminologists, and other specialists who have sought to understand, explain, control, and prevent juvenile delinquency. The reader will note that each section of the book is carefully grounded in knowledge and research and unified by the sociological theme that delinquency must be viewed within its social context.

The book is organized in a format that guides the reader through an unfolding sequence of five interrelated dimensions of the study of juvenile delinquency: conformity, causes, collective behavior, confrontation, and control. Each part begins with a brief introduction which includes basic sociological concepts and ideas related to the topical theme of that section. For example, in **Part I CONFORMITY, DEVIANCE, AND JUVENILE DELINQUENCY,** before addressing the problem of juvenile delinquency, we offer a brief introduction to sociology and the sociological perspective. Then, an overview of the normative system of society, and the concepts of conformity and deviance are introduced and explained. In **Part II CAUSES OF JUVENILE DELINQUENCY,** students are first introduced to the nature of scientific theory and the theory building process. Then, they are presented with specific theories which attempt to explain the causes of delinquency. **Part III**

COLLECTIVE BEHAVIOR AND JUVENILE DELINQUENCY begins by looking at the nature of social groups and their impact upon individuals. It then proceeds to explore the influence of family, youth values, and peers on juvenile behavior. **Part IV CONFRONTATION: SOCIETY AND THE JUVENILE DELINQUENT** introduces the concept of social arena, and look at the three major social arenas in which the juvenile delinquent interacts: school, streets, and court. **Part V CONTROL: STRATEGIES FOR DEALING WITH JUVENILE DELINQUENCY**, first describes the basic elements of social control which exist in virtually every society, before going on to detail specific strategies for the treatment and prevention of juvenile delinquency. It ends with a final chapter which reiterates the social nature of delinquency and challenges the reader to rethink the basic social issues related to juvenile delinquency as a social problem.

Each of the five parts is divided into three topically related chapters. Each chapter begins with a list of Reading Objectives for that particular unit of content. These alert the readers in advance to the specific learning expectations for that chapter so that they may identify, extrapolate, and integrate major concepts while proceeding through the chapter. The learning objectives are reemphasized at the end of the chapter through the use of Questions and Topics for Study and Discussion which are designed to help prepare students for examinations and to stimulate class discussion. Each chapter also includes a Concept Application which allows the student to identify and apply abstract concepts in some type of concrete example.

This book provides a basic sociological foundation for the study of juvenile delinquency. We encourage the reader to build upon this foundation.

While the authors assume final responsibility for the book, as with any other work of this magnitude, numerous people made significant contributions for which we are indebted. Special thanks go to Deanna Applegarth, Virginia Cunningham, Jan Fitzgerald, Jean Kay, Debi Lutke, Jean Ryan, and Vicki Thornton for their "behind the scenes" work. We also appreciate the support and encouragement received from our colleagues. We are indebted to the staff of Allyn and Bacon for their help and technical assistance, especially Bill Barke, Karen Hanson, and Alicia Reilly. We are very grateful for the insightful suggestions and comments from reviewers Benedict S. Alper at Boston College, Billy Hu at Central Missouri State University, and Robert M. Regoli at the University of Colorado, Boulder. Finally, our most heartfelt thanks and love go to Margaret Bynum, and Marilyn, Brandon, and Mica Thompson for their love, support, and encouragement throughout this entire project.

Jack E. Bynum
Stillwater, Oklahoma

William E. Thompson
Emporia, Kansas

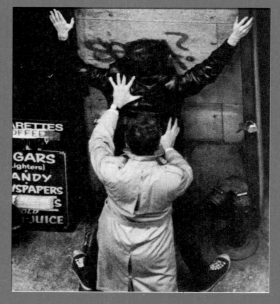

Part I
Conformity, Deviance, and Juvenile Delinquency

Part I

Introduction: The Sociological Perspective and Focus on Juvenile Delinquency

There are several reasons why most readers will identify with the subject of this book. For one thing, the book is about young people—in many cases, not much younger than most of the college students who will be reading the book. Moreover, you may experience a powerful empathy for American youths in general as we explore and explain the frustrations and marginality of being adolescent—a situation and status shared by nearly everyone who grows up in the United States.

Additionally, as the thoughtful reader gains insight into the deviant and disruptive behavior of juvenile offenders, personal youthful escapades may be recalled that, if discovered or reported, might have resulted in an adversarial confrontation with society and adjudication as a juvenile delinquent. The reader probably will be surprised to learn that most illegal acts committed by young people do not apply to adults and are only against the law if the offender happens to be a minor.

Part I explains the **sociological perspective** for the study and understanding of juvenile delinquency. From the sociological viewpoint, delinquency must be viewed within the social context in which it occurs. Within the sociological perspective, there are three overriding theoretical approaches to the study of delinquency: the functionalist approach, conflict approach, and the interactionist approach. The **functionalist approach** *views society as a social system comprised of a network of interrelated and interdependent parts.* Consequently, it regards delinquency primarily as the result of some type of breakdown in the overall functioning of basic social institutions in society. The **conflict approach** *views society as being comprised of a variety of heterogeneous groups all competing for the highly valued resources society has to offer (such as wealth, power, and prestige).* Consequently, deviant behavior such as juvenile delinquency tends to be viewed as the result of conflicting values held by members of various social groups who must socially interact with one another. The **interactionist approach** *views society as being a product of the shared expectations held by individuals as they socially interact on a face-to-face daily basis.* Thus, juvenile delinquency is viewed as a matter of social definition that arises out of the course of social interaction. In Part I, and throughout this book, we have chosen *not* to tie our analysis of juvenile delinquency to any one of these major theoretical approaches. Rather, we place delinquency in its broadest sociological context, using concepts, theories, and explanations from the functionalist, conflict, and interactionist approaches as they apply.

Part I includes Chapters 1, 2, and 3, which set the stage and furnish direction to our unfolding study of juvenile delinquency. For example, the Chapter 1 discussion of society, rules of conduct, conformity, and deviance places juvenile delinquency in an overall social context. Thus, the sociological perspective supplies an appropriate foundation and ongoing framework for the careful consideration of juvenile delinquency as a significant social problem in American society.

Chapter 2 identifies and analyzes various approaches to defining juvenile delinquency. For example, the **legal definition** emphasizes a specific age as the dividing line between juvenile delinquency and adult crime. A different approach characterizes the **role definition,** which discounts the occasional youthful misbehavior and focuses instead on the individual who sustains a consistent pattern of delinquent behavior. Yet a third image of the delinquent and the nonconforming behavior is supplied by the **societal response definition,** which concentrates on the perceptual exchanges between the actor (the alleged delinquent) and the audience (society) that judges the behavior in question and can impute a delinquent identity. In actual practice, and in Chapter 2, all three of these definitions are combined to give us a complete and operational description of what constitutes "juvenile delinquency" in American society.

Chapter 3 is an extensive and basic discussion of the various sources of juvenile crime statistics and a catalog of the various kinds and incidences of juvenile offenses. The longitudinal national trends in juvenile delinquency are set forth, and some of the weaknesses of data on delinquency are discussed. Chapter 3 concludes with a composite profile of those demographic traits that most nearly characterize the "typical" juvenile delinquent. The reader is cautioned, however, that while such profiles may be helpful in summarizing and pointing out statistical trends in arrests and court referrals, they can also unfairly stereotype those groups identified by the composite profile unless we are acutely aware of certain weaknesses in official crime and delinquency statistics.

As you read Part I, and embark upon your study of juvenile delinquency, we encourage you to approach the subject and this book with an open mind. While common sense can and should play an important role in the attempt to understand any social issue, unfortunately, much of what passes for common sense about juvenile delinquency may, in fact, be nothing more than "common nonsense." The astute student involved in sociological inquiry will attempt to avoid some of the common misconceptions and pitfalls related to the study of delinquency by developing critical thinking skills and laying aside personal feelings about the subject.

Chapter 1

Social Norms: Conformity and Deviant Behavior

READING OBJECTIVES

The reading of this chapter will help you achieve the following objectives:

1. Understand how our human need for interaction and interdependence resulted in the development of human society.
2. Trace the origins and purposes of social norms—rules of conduct for members of social groups.
3. Define and give examples of mores and folkways as different kinds of social norms governing our behavior.
4. Explain the concepts of conformity and deviance as alternative responses to the behavioral expectations of society for its members.
5. Understand why societal response to the violation of norms (degree of punishment, reward, or ambivalence) may vary with the culture, time period, social status of the offender, and other factors.
6. Comprehend how some deviant behavior can be beneficial to society.
7. Understand why juvenile delinquency, as a form of deviant behavior, is considered a serious social problem.

INTRODUCTION

Most people, at some time in their experience—exasperated or disappointed over some human weakness or conflict—have probably fantasized about the possibilities of becoming a hermit or disengaging from the human race in some radical way. Each of us may have speculated, "If only I could find some hidden and solitary place—perhaps a secret cave or a deserted island—where I could get away from the problems and troubles of other people!" However, on second thought, nearly everyone realizes the impracticality of such a course of action. Not only is it virtually impossible to escape permanently from social contact with other humans, but, after reflecting on the loneliness and vulnerability of isolation, few people really desire to totally and irrevocably separate themselves from society. On the contrary, intrinsic to human nature, and resting upon each of us, is an irresistible social imperative that demands our participation in society.

THE SOCIAL IMPERATIVE

Most species of animals and insects are social creatures. They band together in social groups for companionship and mutual aid as well as in response to the biological urges to propagate their kind and nurture their young. Thus, the bird gravitates to the companionship and security of its flock; the honeybee orients its entire life-span to the hive and the swarm; the cow on the hillside lives in proximity to and association with her herd. Men and women are also social creatures, drawn and driven by powerful forces to communicate and cooperate with a social group in order to collectively enhance personal and species survival (Barash, 1982). However, the human social imperative is not solely a biological or genetically programmed response as in the lower forms of animal life. Mankind's compulsion toward sociality also is embedded in the cultural content of every society and consciously transmitted to each new generation as a learned response to our basic needs for social interaction and social interdependence. This vital concept and characteristic of humanity was the subject of John Donne's poetic metaphor regarding the death of a community member and the mournful tolling of the church bell:

> No man is an island entire of itself. Every man is a piece of the continent, a part of the main. If a clod be washed away by the sea, Europe is the less, as well as if a promontory were, as well as if a manor of thy friends or of thine own were. Any man's death diminishes me, because I am involved in mankind. Therefore never send to know for whom the bell tolls. It tolls for thee (Donne, 1623).

Our social interaction and social organization are overt manifestations of an intrinsic and vital social imperative that characterizes most species—including humans. We are drawn together for mutual aid and survival. We form friendships, groups, and societies.

Social Interaction

The human need for social interaction with our own kind is dramatically illustrated in the televised news account of a tired, tattered, and aged Japanese soldier who was discovered a few years ago on a remote Pacific island. Forty years earlier, during World War II, he was a young enlisted man in the Japanese garrison on the island. Near the end of the war, after most of the garrison had been killed or captured by invading American troops, this Japanese soldier and several comrades retreated into the jungle. They planned to hide until the tide of war turned again in their favor and Japanese military forces would return to the island. But they did not return. The handful of Japanese hid in caves, foraged for food at night, and carefully avoided detection by the local people and American soldiers. Thus, they were effectively cut off from communication with the outside world and did not know that the war had ended. The days stretched into weeks; the weeks into months; and the years passed. Their weapons rusted and their uniforms turned to rags. They were undernourished and sick. Finally, one by one, the Japanese soldiers died, leaving a lone survivor.

After his discovery and return to Japan, he told of his experiences during those years of self-imposed exile and isolation. He described the loneliness as worse than the swarms of insects, hunger, and sickness. He reported: "In despair I often carried on audible conversations with friends—long since dead. In the evenings I would creep to the edge of the village and secretly watch and listen to the people and vicariously interact with them." Thus, his social needs overruled even his fear of capture or death and ultimately led to his detection. He was finally defeated and captured by one of the greatest enemies of mankind—unrelenting and unnatural loneliness—which reduced him to a forlorn, desperate, shadowy figure, skulking on the periphery of human society.

Many social scientists have argued that our credentials as human beings rest on more than typical biological similarities. They conclude that the normal development of human nature and personality is largely dependent on prolonged and positive interaction with other people. For example, the early focus of Kingsley Davis (1940) and others on feral or "wild" children, who had been deprived of human companionship and socialization, sought to establish causal linkage between social interaction and "becoming human."

More recently, Eric Miller (1978) reported on the discovery of three small rural children, locked in a wire cage in their parents' backyard. County welfare officials described the children as unsocialized and uncivilized—naked, wild, covered with excrement, and unable to talk or feed themselves. In addition, a large number of contemporary researchers have gathered considerable evidence of an association between social isolation and psychological stress and maladjustment (e.g., Freeman and Giovannoni, 1969).

Social Interdependence

The desire and willingness to participate with other persons in an interdependent social relationship is to acknowledge the vulnerability of the individual in dealing with a difficult and often dangerous environment. From this perspective, the social imperative that moves us to join forces and collaborate with others immediately expands our intellectual and technological resources for personal and collective survival. More importantly, membership in society improves the accumulation and transmission of cultural knowledge to succeeding generations.

One of the earliest and most convincing statements supporting the necessity for social interdependence among humans came from the zoologist Peter Kropotkin (1914). After studying that phenomenon for a lifetime, this renowned scholar concluded that "the vast majority of species live in societies and they find in association the best arms for the struggle of life" (Kropotkin, 1914:57). Kropotkin's classic work on the subject is appropriately titled *Mutual Aid*.

Sociologists, too, have contributed major theoretical insights and empirical findings that support the idea of a social imperative as the compelling force in the formation of interdependent social relationships. Emile Durkheim ([1933] 1947) cited Charles Darwin's observation that two organisms having the same needs and seeking the same objects are in constant conflict. Durkheim saw a parallel in human behavior, and suggested that we find resolution to this conflict through social organization. For example, if there is a growing density of human population in an area, the struggle for space and other scarce resources is reduced through a complex division of labor or increased occupational specialization. In this way, Durkheim said, people can coexist and cooperate in a shared environment.

Robert Park (1936) perceived social interdependence as a kind of symbiotic or collaborative relationship between diverse individuals and segments of the population. The competition is balanced with a pragmatic cooperation for the mutual benefit of all parties and groups involved. Park's theory has had widespread application in explaining the development and social organization of human communities and cities.

A large number of more recent studies have verified that human society everywhere is characterized by a pervasive and persistent web of social relationships. For example, Arnold Green (1972) reported how preliterate societies have well-established patterns of communal and collective behavior in the procurement of sustenance, religious practices, government, and other dimensions of social life. William Foote Whyte (1943), in his well-known *Street Corner Society*, found extensive social organization, primary group relationships, and social control mechanisms in lower class urban slums that some earlier writers had suggested were lacking in such areas.

The informed consensus of these scholars is that human isolation is contrary to human nature and detrimental to the survival of the species. Consequently, we have gathered ourselves together to form families, tribes, villages, communities, cities, nations, and a wide variety of other social groupings. **Society** is the general term for *people living in social interaction and social interdependence*.

SOCIAL ORGANIZATION

Social interaction varies in intensity and complexity, depending on the size of the group, the relationship of the participants, the environment, and the objective or purpose of the interaction. In other words, social interaction ranges from the brief and superficial contact between strangers who wait on a street corner for a traffic light to change, to the secondary and instrumental relationship between store clerk and customer, to the more permanent and intimate interrelationships between marriage or business partners. It includes the relatively passive interaction of a theater audience or a class of students, as well as the dynamic collective behavior of a football team or an angry gang fight.

Seldom is social interaction as spontaneous and unstructured as it may seem on the surface. Nearly all of the social interaction between the members and groups that comprise a society is guided by an extensive and detailed network of social organization. Every social group and society organizes its members and their behavior into generally recognized and accepted patterns so as to ensure the smooth operation and continuity of its collective existence. Most people, though not all, are willing to standardize their behavior in many ways and to relinquish some individuality in order to function effectively as a social unit.

NORMS

We have already indicated that much of our human behavior is social in that it takes other people into account, their expected responses to one's actions, and the shared meanings that members of the group place upon these actions. It follows that an important dimension of social organization is the vast array of rules that serve as guidelines for socially acceptable behavior. All of these *rules, standards, laws, regulations, customs, and traditions—the "do's and don'ts" of human conduct and social interaction*—are referred to as **norms** by social scientists. *Behavior that conforms or is in harmony with this code of rules* is said to be **normative.**

Some societal norms are **prescriptive**—that is, *they "prescribe" certain kinds of behavior as acceptable or desirable*—such as the generally accepted practice in our society that men shake hands with each other when they are introduced, and the legal requirements that children must attend school until a certain age and that men must register with Selective Service for possible military conscription when they reach their eighteenth birthday. Another prescriptive norm is that we must wear clothing in public (although the style and amount of clothing may vary widely, for example, whether one is going to the beach or to the senior prom). Other norms are **proscriptive**—that is, *they prohibit certain kinds of behavior as unacceptable to society*—such as our laws forbidding assault and theft, and the less seriously enforced curfew ordinances in some cities that deny minors access to public places after a specific nighttime hour. Other examples of prohibitive norms that govern the behavior of American youths are age restrictions on marriage and voting in public elections.

SOURCES OF NORMS

Where did we get our system of norms? There are several contrasting and controversial theoretical viewpoints regarding the origin of norms that societies utilize to control the behavior of their members. The two most widely discussed and accepted viewpoints are the models of **Social Consensus** and **Social Conflict.**

Social Consensus

The political philosopher Thomas Hobbes ([1651] 1914:63) was convinced that the uncontrollable natural inclination of man is predatory, that is, "as a wolf to his fellow man." Hobbes believed that in the distant past, people had willingly surrendered much of their independence to a central and absolute government in order to protect themselves from one another and so created an ordered, workable society. This voluntary abdication of a measure of personal autonomy and submission to group norms in exchange for security supplied by a dominant power structure is known as a **Social Contract.**

The theoretical viewpoint that societal norms are founded upon longstanding consensus among the members of a society about how to best organize behavior was more fully developed by Max Weber (1925), William Graham Sumner (1906), Kingsley Davis (1948), and others during this century. These sociologists argued that the major rules of conduct are "traditional" in that they have deep roots in the historical cultural values of a people. Over time, and with continual usage in fulfilling basic needs of the society, these norms become well-established and institutionalized as "the right way to do things." As long as they work and do not become obsolete through advancing technology or other social change, these norms tend to remain in what Durkheim ([1933] 1947) called "the collective conscience of the people." Thus, they are successfully passed on from generation to generation through socialization.

Social Conflict

A contrary viewpoint on the origin of social norms has been offered by Karl Marx and Friedrich Engels ([1848] 1964), Marx ([1867] 1967), Ralf Dahrendorf (1959), and others who advanced the thesis that a great many norms are founded on the political and economic power of dominant owners of property who comprise a ruling class, rather than on the cultural consensus of the common people. Marx, with his orientation toward social class conflict, viewed the normative system of society as generated by the greed of the ruling capitalistic class in order to consolidate its ownership of the means of production and to control the working classes. This economic exploitation, according to Marx and Engels, would lead to an inevitable war of the classes and the overthrow of the dominant capitalistic system. Then, according to socialistic ideology, the norms of the new classless society would truly reflect the will of the people.

Class conflict as an original source of norms, especially laws, continues to have strong proponents (e.g., Dahrendorf, 1959; Chambliss, 1973; Quinney, 1970). Dahrendorf (1959) focused on the differential distribution of authority and coercive power in social organizations that represent the various social classes. He pointed to the legislative/political generation of law and the selective enforcement of the law as being exercises of the upper and middle classes to discriminate against the lower class. Dahrendorf (1959:165) hypothesized that "the patterns of domination and subjection that exist in social organizational arrangements lead to systematic social conflicts of a type that is germane to class conflicts in the traditional (Marxian) sense of this term." This theme has been further developed by Chambliss (1973) and by Quinney (1970), who have argued that criminal statutes are one of the ways that the powerful in American society can inflict their will upon the socially disadvantaged. Since statutes regulating the behavior of juveniles are passed by legislatures comprised of adults, and enforced and interpreted by adult police officers, district attorneys, and judges, the conflict model of the origin of norms has been utilized by some to help explain the phenomenon of juvenile delinquency.

Both theoretical explanations concerning the origin of norms—social consensus and social conflict—represent extreme **ideal types.** An **ideal type** is a term coined by Weber (1947:99–100) to describe *a kind of conceptual model, expressing in a pure, and therefore hypothetical, form, the core characteristics of a pattern of conduct.* The usefulness of the ideal type is that it offers a point of reference for comparing actual conditions and deviations. Thus, social consensus and social conflict models represent idealized, unrealistic norm-producing circumstances. More moderate theorists contend that, while there may be some historical instances in which social norms developed exclusively from one or the other of these two sources, most contemporary societies can trace their norms to a combination of these origins.

FOLKWAYS AND MORES

Sociologists classify norms into two categories on the basis of their importance to the social order and how seriously society regards their violation. William Graham Sumner (1906), by using the societal reaction to nonconformity to measure the value or importance of norms, helped us to distinguish between two types of social norms: **folkways** and **mores.**

Folkways

Folkways are *informal agreements or understandings about what is considered appropriate and inappropriate behavior.* Folkways may be very old and entrenched in the culture, such as our tradition of singing the National Anthem prior to sporting events, or they may be relatively new, and indicate normative conflict with older norms, as exemplified by the "streaking" custom on some college campuses whereby a few naked students celebrate the beginning of spring. Folkways may change or fluctuate periodically as do fads and fashions in clothing and hair styles. Some men have been embarrassed by their tardy discovery that the width in neckties and coat lapels of their outdated wardrobes were suddenly inappropriate attire. Similarly, the fashionably prescribed length for a woman's skirt seems to change almost annually. Folkways also include detailed rules of etiquette covering table manners, dating behavior, habits of grooming and cleanliness, language, and many other aspects of daily life.

Society does not consider the violation of a folkway as a serious offense, and severe penalties are seldom administered. However, the members of society show their displeasure in unofficial, informal ways. People whose eating habits are judged as uncouth and ill-mannered by society will not be arrested, though they may well find themselves avoided by others and dining alone. Someone who wears a sweatshirt and jeans to a formal church wedding will not be excommunicated, but will probably be the target of direct or indirect ridicule. The social group may be annoyed by such overt challenges to propriety but does not feel particularly threatened. This is precisely the difference, according to sociologists, between folkways and mores.

Mores

The most important and seriously enforced societal norms are called **mores.** **Mores** are *salient norms in that they are perceived as germane to the overall cohesion and survival of society.* Consequently, their violation is seen as threatening to crucial values. The mores are often reflected in our formal laws and are systematically written down in a legal code that defines their violation as criminal behavior and prescribes the method and degree of punishment. More specifically, the criminal law (and juvenile law) is a codified body of statutes generated by a political authority or government to standardize and regulate the behavior of societal members and to provide for punishment of the violators of the rules. Since these more important and serious rules are "regarded as a conserving force in the life of human beings, protecting what society stands for . . ." (Birenbaum and Sagarin, 1976:16), the formal law enforcement agencies of the state may be used in their enforcement. Examples of mores are laws forbidding theft and murder, reflected in the Ten Commandments as well as in the criminal codes of the various states.

The patience and permissiveness that often characterize the societal reaction to those who violate folkways are not extended to those who transgress important mores. Historically, society has shown little tolerance for anarchists, traitors, heretics, kidnappers, murderers, looters, terrorists, and others whose norm-violating behaviors were interpreted as a menace to the basic stability and security of society. This kind of extreme deviant behavior is still one of the surest ways for individuals to be declared "Public Enemies" and find their photographs and uncomplimentary descriptions of their conduct in the newspapers and perhaps on the local post office wall.

At the same time, it should be stated that the universal application of all the laws to all the people belonging to a national society like the United States, and the interpretation of all behavior as conforming or deviant in relation to these laws, are not as simple or clearcut as the aforementioned examples suggest. Most of the major social norms, or group-shared expectations, are designed to enhance, preserve, or accomplish something generally considered to be of great value in the culture of the larger society. When a cultural value does not undergird a social norm or law, it becomes very difficult (if not impossible) to enforce the law consistently or permanently. For example, due to the zeal and political influence of a minority group of social reformers, the prohibition of the manufacture and sale of alcoholic beverages became a national law through the Eighteenth Amendment to the Constitution in 1919. However, it soon became clear that law enforcement officers and agents could not control the illegal manufacture, transportation, and sale of alcoholic beverages. Too many Americans had values contrary to the intent of the prohibition law and finally, in 1933, the voters repealed the Eighteenth Amendment.

The general application of norms is sometimes made difficult by the population composition of a heterogeneous society. The United States contains many subgroups that are highly differentiated according to age, social class, occupation, religion, politics, and ethnic-cultural backgrounds. These groups often represent different circumstances and orientations and thus do not always share the same values and rules (Lemert, 1964). Becker (1963) cited the example of Italian immigrants who, by continuing to make wine for themselves and their friends during the prohibition era, were simultaneously conforming to the standards of the Italian subculture and breaking the law of their new country.

Robert Park (1928) was one of the influential scholars at the University of Chicago during the formative years of sociology in this country, and was one of the first to identify the plight of certain individuals and groups who experience only marginal and incomplete social assimilation. Stonequist's (1937) *The Marginal Man* pinpointed the second-generation immigrant as the classic example of this phenomenon. He traced this marginality to the abrasive cultural conflict experienced by the new ethnic minorities in America. The experience of divergent and often contradictory cultural norms has the potential for generating normative confusion, alienation, and, hence, deviant behavior in some individuals. Park, Stonequist, and others portrayed the **marginal** person as *being caught between two conflicting cultures*. The person's commitment is torn and fragmented between the two, and, consequently, the individual fails to fully identify with either of the groups in question. For example, many children of immigrants are exposed simultaneously to the language and traditions of the "old country" in their homes and ethnic neighborhoods, as well as to the intense socialization of their American school and youthful peer group. Thus, they become marginal in the sense that they lack complete integration into either the larger society or the subculture. The marginal person, with mixed and marginal status and identity, inhabits a frustrating social limbo between two societies and cultures (Arnold, 1970). This unfortunate situation has been considered a contributing factor in the cause of some juvenile delinquency, and as you will see in Chapter 6, the concept has been incorporated in some explanatory theories. While this cultural conflict between subgroups and the larger society may confound the definition of normative and deviant behavior, every society seriously endeavors to distinguish between behavior that conforms to prevailing norms of social life and behavior that deviates markedly from those norms.

NORMATIVE BEHAVIOR: CONFORMITY

Earlier in this chapter we discussed the origins and purposes of norms as they affect our personal and collective survival. This point can be further clarified by focusing on the definition of **norms** as *group-shared expectations* for behavior. Every social group operates under some set of fundamental regulations which each member starts learning from the day of birth. Charles Cooley (1922) perceived **conformity** as being *the attempt to maintain a normative standard established by a social group.* His early insight, that compliance and conformity with social expectations can be explained by the human tendency to adopt imitatively the prevailing patterns of behavior around oneself, has been expanded and refined into the contemporary viewpoint among sociologists that the individual internalizes the customs of his or her society through a process called socialization. **Socialization** is *the effective transmission and internalization of culture content* (Benedict, 1934). Thus, it includes learning to respond to social situations in socially acceptable ways. Every person, from earliest infancy, and through continual interaction with parents, siblings, peers, teachers, and many other members of the social group, is exposed to the values, attitudes, and behavioral practices that are expected and acceptable. The idealized objective of this socialization is the social control or conformity of the individual, although it is usually articulated as "getting educated," "being properly raised," or "brought up to be law-abiding." In this way, even the process whereby we "put society in man" (Berger, 1963) becomes an institutionalized norm. Social control is considered most effective when it is manifested as self-control in harmony with what is socially expected from others (Scott, 1971; Mantell, 1974).

Socialization, by analogy, is like a compulsory inoculation required by society of each member to ward off unacceptable nonconformity. The group-shared expectations are often imperceptibly "injected" into our human consciousness and we "react" by reflecting them in our personalities, characters, and behavior. Through successful socialization, most of us conform most of the time to most of the important norms of our society. This is not to say that *all* of our conformity is spontaneous and without complaint. Fear of punishment, penalties, and other negative sanctions can elicit a pragmatic conformity as an assist to internalization (for example, not all Americans pay their income taxes just because they are filled with an undeniable patriotic compulsion to do so).

When the socialization of group-shared expectations is ineffectual in producing the desired conformity, society has equipped itself with more direct and coercive techniques that may be applied to the nonconforming individual. These range from informal rebuke and ridicule at one extreme all the way to formal, state-imposed fines, imprisonment, and even capital punishment at the other. Obviously, we are never totally free or independent to determine our own course of action, for the society external to the individual continually monitors the behavior of each member.

In addition to eliciting our personal conformity, what we have learned about norms as group-shared expectations helps us to predict much of the behavior of other members of society. For example, the great majority of people learn while very young that the right to use the public streets and sidewalks is balanced with a personal responsibility to abide by certain social norms. We have learned to expect that under ordinary circumstances other individuals will respect us and our property. We may usually participate in public social life without fear of insult or physical assault. Those persons whom we meet also have learned to anticipate the same respect from us. We need not be personally acquainted with everyone who shares our community. Our group-shared social expectations—whether in the form of municipal ordinances, constitutional rights, religious dogma, federal or state laws, or simply tradition—usually function very well to preserve order on our streets and sidewalks, even among strangers.

The ability to control and predict human behavior, based on norms or group-shared expectations, pervades virtually every area of social life. This was the point made by a perceptive old man in the play *Fiddler on the Roof* who exclaimed: "It may seem foolish to those unacquainted with our ways, but without our traditions, we would be as unstable as a fiddler on a roof!" (Stein, 1964). And without doubt, our dominant cultural values—manifested in norms, traditions, customs, laws and group-shared expectations—are part of the "glue" that holds society together, contributing major support to its stability and social organization.

DEVIANT BEHAVIOR: NONCONFORMITY

Many persons find it disagreeable, inconvenient, or otherwise unsatisfactory to order their lives in harmony with all of the behavioral norms of their society, and are tempted to deviate. If their socialization experience or other forms of social control do not restrain them, some of these persons will not conform to all of the norms. Realistically, virtually everybody violates some social norm at some time. These nonconforming members of society and their deviant behavior are a major focus of study in sociology.

Deviant behavior is *conduct that is perceived by others as violating institutionalized expectations that are widely shared and recognized as legitimate within the* *society.* Simply put, deviance is the violation of norms. So, in sociological terms, deviant behavior involves a complex interplay between a social norm, a member of a social group whose actions are considered to be subject to that norm, and other members of the social group who observe the actor and define a particular behavior as nonconforming to a degree exceeding the tolerance limits of the majority (Cohen, 1966; DeFleur, 1976; Ritzer, et al., 1987).

Some people argue that our societal norms or standards of conduct are non-negotiable—that they should be treated as inflexible absolutes. Therefore, they have little patience or tolerance for deviant behavior. By taking the position that deviance is only disruptive and destructive to the social group, it becomes possible to classify everybody into one or the other of two opposing subgroups: the "Insiders" and the "Outsiders." Unfortunately, this kind of dichotomous thinking permits motivation and morality to be quickly and conveniently imputed to those on each side as they are adjudged "good" or "bad," "right" or "wrong," "friend" or "foe," "loyal and law-abiding," or "antisocial and criminal," a "good kid" or a "juvenile delinquent." While this approach is convenient and can be easily applied to almost any person or issue, it oversimplifies the realities of social life. Even though our society is surrounded with a scaffolding of behavioral norms, most of these norms are less rigid than they may seem at first glance. Sociologists have discovered that the members of society display a paradoxical and generous amount of tolerance for much deviant behavior, depending on several important variables.

First, the nature of the offense can determine the level of society's tolerance for norm violation. In many instances, our tolerance for minor norm-breaking requires only that the offender acknowledge the transgression. For example, a breach of etiquette such as a sneeze in a public place generally requires only the phrase "excuse me" from the offender to remedy the situation. Goffman (1965) called this "remedial work." Even some formal laws, such as traffic ordinances, or many of the statutes governing juveniles (such as curfews) can be occasionally violated and, if no accident results, or no harm is perceived, the transgressors can usually pay a fine or receive a warning, and gain the sympathetic understanding of society since such experiences have happened to most of us.

A second factor that determines the level of society's tolerance for deviant behavior is the social status of the offender. The seventeenth century political doctrine known as the Divine Right of Kings offers a classic illustration. James I of England and supporting royalists, in order to excuse and boost his shoddy reign, claimed that subjects are charged by God not to resist their monarch but passively to obey him, even if, in their view, he is wicked (Figgis, 1922). In this century, Edwin Sutherland (1961) pinpointed the reality of large-scale illegal acts committed by businessmen, corporation executives, and other middle- and upper-class professionals in the course of their occupation. He invented the term "white-collar crime" for such offenses as financial fraud, monopolistic practices, price fixing, and embezzlement, and contended that such professional malpractice enjoyed greater social tolerance. Offenders often go unpunished or

Deviant behavior may be different and even shocking. It may be troublesome and even irritating or intimidating. To many, it may be the opposite of conformity. But only a minor portion of deviant behavior is considered antisocial or criminal.

are treated leniently because they share the same social class as those with power and authority in society.

A third element affecting the level of tolerance manifested toward deviant behavior is the cultural context in which it occurs. In other words, there is a paradoxical kind of cultural relativity when it comes to tolerance toward many forms of deviance. An act that violates the norms of one particular society may represent approved conformity from the point of view of another social group. This principle of **cultural relativity** is especially helpful in understanding behavior and societal reactions to it in a heterogeneous society such as ours, made up of a number of subgroups with their own distinctive values and norms. Groups such as teenage gangs, homosexuals, drug addicts, and some urban slum dwellers support subcultures whose values, beliefs, normative practices, and shared attitudes run counter to those to which the larger society subscribes. Thus, a given act, and the level of tolerance it receives, must always be interpreted within the framework of the relevant cultural or subcultural system.

Fourth, tolerance for nonconforming behavior often has a temporal dimension. That is, types of behavior that are strongly disapproved of at one time may be tolerated and even encouraged at a later time in the same society. For example, in the 1950's hair extending below the ears on young men was considered deviant and even effeminate. Later, long hair on young men was thought of as stylish or inconsequential by a great many people. Similarly, in colonial America, youths in their early teens were allowed to carry guns and to marry, and were expected to engage in a variety of behaviors that would be considered deviant today.

In one sense, the entire country has become more tolerant of children and their behavior. Prior to the twentieth century, the violation of important laws by American children was considered to be criminal behavior, and children could be incarcerated with hardened adult felons. Today, in what most Americans consider to be a more enlightened society, there are special agencies, courts, and institutions to deal with juvenile delinquents. Our growing sensitivity and concern for the special problems of American youth is detailed in later chapters of this book.

NEGATIVE ASPECTS OF DEVIANCE

By the time most individuals reach college age, they are aware of many of the negative consequences of deviant behavior, especially for the person regarded as deviant. The socialization experience of children and adolescents includes enough penalties, punishments, threats, and warnings regarding misconduct that the unpleasant personal "payoff" for many forms of deviance becomes relatively clear. So pervasive is this message that our cultural folklore is replete with familiar proverbs and dire forecasts concerning the certain and ultimate doom for those who pursue a course of willful deviant behavior. The theme is apparent in such common expressions as: "Those who play with fire will get burned;" "Those who live by the sword will die by the sword;" "Chickens always come home to roost;" "You made your bed, now lie in it;" and "They enjoyed the dance, but now must pay the fiddler."

Deviant behavior such as juvenile delinquency also has a number of negative consequences for society. These negative consequences include, but would not necessarily be limited to:

1. **Personal Harm.** Deviance can hurt people. Violent acts such as murder, rape, assault, and robbery create obvious personal injury for their victims. Property crimes such as theft, auto theft, burglary, arson, and others also cause pain, suffering, and financial loss for those who are

victimized by them. While the majority of delinquent acts are non-violent, many of them create physical and emotional harm for the victims, the perpetrators, and their families.

2. **Threatens Norms.** Any act of deviance involves norm violation, and, hence, potentially calls into question the norm being violated. When social rules and guidelines are broken, if no discernible social harm is readily apparent, the norm may be judged to be unimportant. In some cases, when one rule is questioned, rules in general may be questioned. Juveniles, in particular, are likely to question rules that govern their behavior when they occasionally violate one of them and perceive no real harmful consequences. For example, the teenager who has been warned about the serious consequences of smoking marijuana may try it and feel that it caused no readily apparent harm. This may lead the youth to also question the potential harm of drugs such as cocaine and heroin against which similar warnings were received.

3. **Costs.** Deviance can be extremely expensive for society in both the literal and figurative senses. A tremendous amount of money, time, and energy is spent every year for law enforcement, courts, probation and parole, institutions, programs, and agencies whose sole purpose is to attempt to control, treat, and prevent social deviance. Juvenile delinquency, for example, costs Americans many millions of dollars each year. Beyond the monetary costs, deviance can take a tremendous psychological, emotional, and social toll on the members of a society. When people are afraid to go out at night, or to live in certain areas of a city, or in other ways feel threatened, deviance is costing a society far more than dollars and cents.

4. **Social Disruption.** Deviance also can be socially disruptive. When people do not know what to expect of their fellow human beings in a given social situation, social interaction can be severely disrupted. Norm violation can lead to fear, anxiety, mistrust, and confusion for the members of society.

5. **Social Order is Threatened.** Deviant behavior can threaten the stability and social order of a society. As indicated in the consensus model, societal members establish social norms in an effort to create and maintain a sense of social order. The violation of these norms, even in isolated cases, can temporarily threaten that order. Widespread norm violation can create havoc and threaten social stability, as in the cases of mobs, riots, and revolutions.

6. **Self-Perpetuation.** In some ways, deviance can create more deviance, and hence, be self-perpetuating. The old adage "Give 'em an inch, and they'll take a mile" reflects the widespread assumption that when one norm is broken, it is very likely to lead to other norms being broken. Part of the reason that there are so many norms regulating juvenile behavior stems from the view that youths must learn at an early age that

rules exist and that they must not be broken. Otherwise, many believe that the violation of one rule will encourage the violation of others. Similarly, the punitive view of our criminal justice system is based upon the idea that when caught, a law violator must be publicly punished in order to deter others from similar deviance.

Because of the negative consequences of social deviance, members of society attempt to prevent, limit, and control norm violation as much as possible. When a particular type of deviance, such as juvenile delinquency, is viewed as uncontrolled, or worse yet, uncontrollable, it is likely to be defined as a major social problem, and society is likely to mobilize in an effort to minimize its negative consequences.

POSITIVE ASPECTS OF DEVIANCE

It would be simplistic and unrealistic to terminate our discussion of deviant behavior with the assumption that *all* of the consequences of deviance are socially and personally destructive. On the contrary, some deviant acts may generate very positive results for the group or society in which they occur.

We can initiate the discussion of the importance of deviance to society by acknowledging that while all deviant behavior is nonconforming, not all deviant behavior is completely antisocial. In fact, sociologists have identified several forms of unorthodox and deviant behavior that, when generally recognized as beneficial to the social group or community, often elicit considerable tolerance. Emile Durkheim (1938) began this line of thought with his thesis of the "Functional Necessity of Crime." Later studies by Robert Dentler and Kai Erikson (1959) and by Lewis Coser (1954) further developed the concept. This discussion is indebted to all of those scholars for the following composite list of positive functions of deviance:

1. **Reaffirmation of Norms.** Often, the deviant is rejected and the group's norms are reaffirmed. In this way, the occasional violation may revitalize the collective conscience of the people. Just as we mentioned that norms may be threatened when norm violation occurs and no discernible harm is apparent, when deviance causes obvious social harm social norms are likely to be reaffirmed and strengthened. For example, the obvious harm caused by serious forms of juvenile crime lends support to prevailing social norms that regulate the less serious forms of juvenile misconduct.

2. **Social Solidarity.** In many cases, the deviant is rejected and the social group is united. Internal enemies, functioning as a built-in "out-group," can bring people together in a common defense of their community in much the same way as do external and hostile enemies. History is re-

plete with tragic examples of crucifixions, lynchings, and witch hunts that united the larger society and enabled people to blame their fear and frustration on selected scapegoats.

3. **Unity on Behalf of the Deviant.** The reaction of the social group is not always punitive toward the deviant. Juvenile delinquency, for example, provides a variety of instances in which various social groups, agencies, and society as a whole unite not against delinquents, but on their behalf. Many acts of delinquency are viewed as being the result of unfortunate social circumstances experienced by the youths committing them, and individuals and groups often unite in an attempt to alleviate those undesirable situations in order to help the delinquent.

4. **Contrast Effect.** The deviant offers a complementary contrast to those who conform. Sometimes the public exposure and chastisement of deviants is one of the means used to make conformity meritorious. Perhaps the unspoken message in some condemnations is: "Our indignation over deviant behavior is evidence of our virtue, and proof that we would never commit such offenses!" More overtly, parents often point their fingers at the youth in serious trouble with the law to warn their own children that if they don't behave themselves, they may face a similar fate some day.

5. **"Safety Valve."** Some forms of deviance may serve as a kind of safety valve for society. Some view human society as comparable to a boiler under pressure that might explode from inner social, political, and economic tensions unless some "steam" is periodically drained off. Many forms of nonserious juvenile misconduct are viewed as relatively harmless events of youths "letting off a little steam." Comments like "boys will be boys," or "kids have to sow a few wild oats" represent the view that minor deviance entered into periodically by youths is "normal" and far preferable to following all norms rigidly until the pressure builds and may ultimately lead to some serious type of deviant behavior.

6. **Leadership.** In some cases, deviant behavior can help to develop and promote new social leadership. Group dynamics, ranging from gang fights to social movements, often require and generate the development of leaders who excel in articulating group needs and organizing the efforts of the group to achieve their collective objectives. Occasionally someone on the order of Joan of Arc emerges, whose visionary and deviant behavior ultimately placed the 19-year-old at the head of the French Army! (Later, as Joan fell from favor, she was burned at the stake, thus also sadly fulfilling for her society the second positive aspect of deviance outlined in this list.)

7. **Social and Cultural Change.** Deviance and deviants may encourage meaningful social and cultural change. This may include the work of innovative administrators who cut through bureaucratic "red tape" to serve fellow workers, eccentric but brilliant inventors, and even revolution-

aries like Patrick Henry and George Washington, who helped bring about major social change. On a less dramatic scale, the first to try any hairstyle, dress style, or any other innovative fad or fashion is usually considered to be deviant.

8. **Warning Device.** Deviance may also serve as a warning signal. Rising poverty levels, divorce rates, levels of unemployment, and rates of juvenile delinquency—all in the same area of a city—may indicate defects in the social structure or organization of society. Astute political leaders, observing such indicators of impending social erosion, may then take preventive measures.

9. **Variety and Excitement.** Finally, some forms of social deviance merely reflect the wide variety of personalities, characters, cultural orientations, and behavior manifested by people who dare to be different. Imagine how incredibly dull human society would be if everyone was a total conformist, seemingly cut out by the same predictable, conforming "social cookie cutter."

The section of this chapter that dealt with conformity ended by stating that "norms . . . and group-shared expectations—are part of the glue that holds society together . . ." At the same time, and paradoxically, this discussion of nonconformity can be concluded with the statement that deviation from those norms is also part of the glue that holds society together.

JUVENILE DELINQUENCY

Deviant behavior can become a social problem when it is continuous, chronic, and widespread, and perceived by a substantial and significant part of the population as nonproductive and threatening to the general well-being of society. Juvenile delinquency is a form of deviant behavior because it involves the violation of norms by children and youths. However, this form of deviant behavior comes to national attention because many of the norms that are violated are deemed to be important enough that they have been codified into criminal and/or juvenile laws. It should be noted that many of the behaviors identified as juvenile delinquency are not criminal acts, but relatively trivial forms of deviance. The various criminal laws and juvenile statutes that are most frequently violated by American youths are detailed in Chapter 3. Nevertheless, juvenile delinquency involves enough of the nation's young people in serious, antisocial behavior that it is perceived by a large segment of our society to be a major social problem. Consequently, it receives a great deal of attention from scholars, civic leaders, law enforcement officers, and the mass media. News articles such as the following arouse citizen interest in the problem of juvenile delinquency:

"MORE KIDS ARE KILLING, ROBBING"

Orlando, Fla. (AP) Children increasingly are committing crimes ranging from armed robbery to murder, say sociologists and criminal justice experts.

"Ten years ago, it was a shock to see a 7, 8, or 9 year-old come into the system; now it's not," said Danny Dawson, chief of the Orange-Osceola County State Attorney's juvenile division. "It's a trend."

Nationally, records show, 1,311 youths under age 18 were charged with murder last year; in Florida during the past two years, children aged 5, 8, and 9 have been charged with killing younger playmates.

In one of the Florida cases, Jeffrey Bailey was described by Kissimmee detectives as "nonchalant" after drowning 3-year-old Ricardo Brown on May 31. Bailey, who turned 10 in October . . . told [police] he sat in a lawn chair and watched for about an hour until Ricardo sank to the bottom, and then he walked home . . .

Kathleen Heide, . . . at the University of South Florida . . . recently completed a two-year study of adolescent killers.

She characterized about 10 percent of them as "nihilistic"—those who derive pleasure from hurting others. Among six other categories were those who regard crime as a sport and homicide as an unavoidable aspect of robbery.

In another category were abused children, who might kill a parent but who tend more toward suicidal than homicidal behavior, she said.

"These are basically good kids," Ms. Heide said. "They go through life with an attitude that life is to endure" (From: *Manteca Bulletin,* Vol. 78, No. 363, Dec. 29, 1986).

One might attempt to rationalize that since juvenile delinquency has some positive consequences for society, such as reinforcing the validity of violated norms, mobilizing society for its control, and generating jobs for the army of law enforcement personnel, the resolution or serious reduction of juvenile delinquency could actually be dysfunctional to society. However, society is not inclined to make these theoretical "tradeoffs" for the sake of the status quo. Juvenile delinquency is perceived to jeopardize the basic social values regarding the safety and security of persons and property.

Richard Fuller and Richard Myers (1941) helped establish the linkage between deviant behavior such as juvenile delinquency and a national social problem:

Social problems are what people say they are. Two things must be present: (1) an *objective condition* (crime, poverty, racial tensions, and so forth) the presence and magnitude of which can be observed, verified, and measured by impartial social observers; and (2) a *subjective definition* by some members of the society that the objective condition is a "problem" and must be acted upon. Here is where values come into play, for when values are perceived as threatened by the existence of the objective condition a social problem is defined (Cited in McKee, 1974:496).

Paraphrasing David Dressler and Donald Carns (1973:532), juvenile delinquency is a social problem. It is social in that it has to do with human relationships within society. It involves people, their ethical values, and their relations with one another. Juvenile delinquency is a problem because it is "regarded as involving undesirable dislocations in social patterns and relationships within the society." It represents what is "wrong" or "improper," "dangerous" or "unfair." Society is committed to doing something about these discrepancies between social standards and the actual conduct of so many youthful citizens.

The sociological approach of this book capitalizes on sociologists' practical and demonstrated ability to clarify the underlying nature and etiology of social problems such as juvenile delinquency. As Broom and Selznick (1963:4) pointed out, this clarification includes the necessity "to estimate more exactly their dimensions, and to identify aspects that seem most amenable to remedy with the knowledge and skills at hand."

SUMMARY

Chapter 1 began by describing the social imperative experienced by human beings and the inherent need and desire for social interaction. This social imperative and need for interaction with other people create a network of social interdependence in any human society.

When people come together to form a society, generally acceptable forms of social interaction and patterns of behavior are recognized. This social organization is based upon the establishment of norms, both prescriptive and proscriptive, that serve as guidelines for behavior considered appropriate and/or inappropriate. The norms may arise out of general social consensus, or may emerge out of social conflict. Norms may take the form of folkways, which are informal yet very important guidelines for our everyday behavior. Or, they may be more seriously enforced mores, which are considered vital to the survival of society. When these norms are formally codified into legal statutes governing behavior, we refer to them as laws.

The establishment of norms immediately creates the concepts of conformity (adherence to social norms) and deviance (norm violation). Through the process of socialization, societal members are taught to internalize the norms of society as their own and to generally conform to the attitudes, beliefs, and behaviors considered appropriate.

When individuals violate society's norms they are considered deviant and their behavior is often socially sanctioned. Most people view extremely deviant behavior as serious, and perhaps antisocial; and we discussed several negative aspects of social deviance, such as personal harm, threat to norms, costs, disruption, threat to social order, and the perpetuation of other forms of deviance. On the other hand, there also are some socially positive aspects of deviance. These include the reaffirmation of norms, promotion of social solidarity, uniting on behalf of (or against) the deviant, contrasting deviance with conformity, providing a "safety valve," establishing leadership, bringing about social and cultural change, acting as a "warning device" to society, and providing variety and excitement. Therefore, just as conformity plays an important role in maintaining society, so does social deviance.

Juvenile delinquency is a specific form of social deviance and is regarded as a major social problem in the United States. Members of our society are concerned, and, in many cases, alarmed at the extent of law violation involving American youth. This book defines juvenile delinquency as a social problem, and contends that in order to be more clearly understood, it must be viewed in its broadest sociocultural context. The following chapters define and explore delinquency from this sociological perspective.

CONCEPT APPLICATION

ILLUSTRATIVE ANECDOTE

The many fundamental sociological concepts discussed in this chapter will be a useful foundation for the study of human behavior in general, and juvenile delinquency in particular. The following anecdote relates an experience of one of the authors and provides additional examples and a concrete application of some of these important concepts.

"DEVIANCE AND/OR DELINQUENCY?"

I grew up in an agricultural valley of Central California and attended a small-town high school. It was a quiet rural environment characterized by close-knit, informal relationships where nearly everyone knew a great deal about everyone else—including such details as family and marriage connections, religious and political persuasions, number of acres owned by each family, and any past scandals.

Nothing really exciting ever seemed to happen in our community. The business district of the town was just three blocks long and included a post office, grocery store, feed store, hardware store, and two gasoline service stations. Church, school, and Grange activities apparently satisfied the social needs of the community (the pool hall having been successfully closed by local ministers as a corrupting influence on the youth). My home town enjoyed a reputation as a very law-abiding place and the one elderly police officer had little difficulty in keeping the peace.

However, there was one night of every year when the high school boys of our town abruptly changed the usual pattern of their behavior, rampaged through the town, and broke a dozen laws. Everyone in the community knew when it was about to happen because considerable preparation always preceded this deviant behavior. During September and October of each year, the high school boys collected surplus and spoiled fruit, vegetables, and eggs. The activity came to a climax on Halloween night, when about 75 youths drove pickup trucks, loaded with their overripe "ammunition," onto the deserted Main Street of the town. Then and there, for several hours, bands of beer-saturated boys fought pitched battles with rotten produce. Other citizens seldom dared venture onto Main Street during this yearly melee. Even the old policeman was strangely absent. Any unwary motorists who did blunder into the area on Halloween night had their automobiles pelted and smeared with tomatoes and eggs.

The boys carried out many mischievous pranks. For example, one year they discovered a loaded manure spreader parked nearby and, after hooking it up to an old car, spread several inches of manure up and down the three blocks of Main Street. As usual, the following day two county sheriff's deputies arrived early at our high school with a truckload of rakes and shovels. All of the boys were dismissed from school for the day to clean up the town. Then our little community returned to its usual pattern of peaceful and predictable behavior—until the next Halloween.

*   *   *   *

In light of the chapter that you just read, were the high school boys violating any societal norms? List as many laws and regulations as you can that may have been violated. In your opinion, and in the judgment of their community, were the high school boys "juvenile delinquents?" Explain how their Halloween behavior was conforming to *another* group-shared expectation. Finally, point out how their "deviant behavior" may have had a positive function for the community.

CONCEPT INTEGRATION
QUESTIONS AND TOPICS FOR STUDY AND DISCUSSION

1. What evidence can you cite from your reading of this chapter or from your own experience to support the idea that humans need social interaction and social interdependence?

2. What is social organization? How are social institutions and norms related to social organization?
3. Identify and explain the differences between the two subcategories of social norms. Can you give at least one example from your own experience of each of the two kinds of norms?
4. Explain the theoretical origins of our social norms.
5. What are the purposes or functions of social norms? Try to think of a norm that you have encountered that seems to have no purpose or function for society.
6. What is the difference between conformity and deviance? In your judgment, is it fair for society to restrict some of our individual freedoms in order to achieve a general conformity to social norms?
7. Based on your reading of this chapter, and your own opinion, would it be possible and good for society to outlaw all deviant behavior? Briefly explain or justify your answer.
8. Why is juvenile delinquency considered deviant behavior? Is juvenile delinquency a social problem?

References

Arnold, D. O. (ed.) 1970. *The sociology of subcultures.* Berkeley: The Glendessary Press.

Barash, D. P. 1982. *Sociobiology and behavior* (2nd ed.). New York: Elsevier.

Becker, H. 1963. *The outsiders.* New York: The Free Press of Glencoe.

Benedict, R. 1934. *Patterns of culture.* Boston: Houghton-Mifflin.

Berger, P. 1963. *An invitation to sociology.* Garden City, NY: Doubleday.

Birenbaum, A. & Sagarin, E. 1976. *Norms and human behavior.* New York: Praeger.

Broom, L. & Selznick, P. 1963. *Sociology* (3rd ed.). New York: Harper & Row.

Chambliss, W. J. 1973. *Functional and conflict theories of crime.* New York: MSS Modular Publications.

Cohen, A. 1966. *Deviant behavior.* Englewood Cliffs, NJ: Prentice-Hall.

Cooley, C. H. 1922. *Human nature and the social order.* New York: Scribner's.

Coser, L. 1954. *The functions of social conflict.* New York: The Free Press.

Dahrendorf, R. 1959. *Class and class conflict in industrial society.* Palo Alto, CA: Stanford University Press.

Davis, K. 1940. Extreme isolation of a child. *American Journal of Sociology* 45:554–565. 1948. *Human Society.* New York: Macmillan.

DeFleur, M., D'Antonio, W. V. & DeFleur, L. B. 1976. *Sociology: Human society* (2nd ed.). Glenview, IL: Scott, Foresman and Co.

Dentler, R. & Erikson, K. 1959. The functions of deviance in groups. *Social Problems,* 7 (Fall):98–107.

Dresler, D. & Carns, D. 1973. *Sociology: The study of human interaction* (2nd ed.). New York: Alfred A. Knopf.

Durkheim, E. 1938. *The rules of sociological method.* Translated by Sarah A. Solvay & John H. Mueller. George E. G. Catlin (Ed.) New York: The Free Press of Glencoe. 1947. *Division of labor in society.* Translated by George Simpson. New York: The Free Press.

Donne, J. 1623. For whom the bell tolls. *Devotions upon emergent occasions XVII.* Cambridge, England: The University Press.

Figgis, J. N. 1922. *The divine right of kings.* London: Smith.

Freeman, H. E. & Giovannoni, J. M. 1969. Social psychology of mental health. Pp. 690–719. In Gardner Lindsey & Elliott Aronson (Eds.) *Handbook of social psychology* (2nd ed.). Reading, MA: Addison-Wesley.

Fuller, R. & Myers, R. 1941. Some aspects of a theory of social problems. *American sociological review* 6 (February):24–32.

Goffman, E. 1965. *Behavior in public places.* New York: The Free Press.

Green, A. 1972. *Sociology.* New York: McGraw-Hill.

Hobbes, T. 1914. *Leviathan* (Everyman's Library Edition). London: J. M. Dent.

Kropotkin, P. 1914. *Mutual aid: A factor in evolution.* Boston: Extending Horizons Books.

Lemert, E. M. 1964. Social structure, social control, and deviation. Pp. 957–971. In Marshall Clinard (Ed.) *Anomie and deviant behavior: A discussion and critique.* New York: The Free Press.

Manteca Bulletin. 1986. More kids are killing, robbing. AP Florida, *Manteca Bulletin,* Vol. 78, No. 363, Dec. 29.

Mantell, D. M. 1974. Doves and hawks: Guess who had the authoritarian parents? *Psychology Today* (September):56–62.

Marx, K. & Engels, F. [1848] 1964. *The communist manifesto.* Translated by Samuel Moore. Joseph Katz (Ed.). New York: Washington Square Press.

Marx, K. [1848]1967. *Capital.* Friedrich Engels (Ed.). New York: International Publishers.

McKee, J. B. 1974. *Introduction to sociology* (2nd ed.). New York: Holt, Rinehart and Winston.

Miller, E. 1978. We just put them in the cage so they won't get away. *The Dallas Morning News,* July 2, 1978:1.

Park, R. E. 1928. Human migration and the marginal man. *American Journal of Sociology* 33 (May):893. 1936. Human ecology. *American Journal of Sociology* 42 (July):1–15.

Quinney, R. 1970. *The social reality of crime.* Boston: Little, Brown & Co.

Ritzer, G., Kammeyer, K. C. & Yetman, N. R. 1987. *Sociology: Experiencing a changing society* (3rd ed.). Boston: Allyn and Bacon.

Scott, J. F. 1971. *Internalization of norms: A sociological theory of moral commitment.* Englewood Cliffs, NJ: Prentice-Hall.

Stein, J. 1964. *Fiddler on the roof.* New York: Crown Publishers.

Stonequist, E. H. 1937. *The marginal man.* New York: Charles Scribner's Sons.

Sumner, W. G. 1906. *Folkways.* Boston: Ginn.

Sutherland, E. 1961. *White collar crime.* New York: Holt, Rinehart and Winston.

Weber, M. [1925]1947. *The theory of social and economic organization.* Translated A. M. Henderson & T. Parsons. New York: The Free Press.

Whyte, W. F. 1943. *Street corner society.* Chicago: University of Chicago Press.

Chapter 2

Juvenile Delinquency: The Act, the Actor, and the Audience

The reading of this chapter will help you achieve the following objectives:

1. Comprehend the legal and social importance of carefully and accurately defined terms such as "juvenile" and "adult."
2. Understand the difference between criminal behavior and juvenile delinquency.
3. Understand the difference between criminal offenders and juvenile delinquents.
4. Conceptualize and compare the legal definition, role definition, and societal response (sociolegal) definition of juvenile delinquency.
5. Understand **status** and **role** and explain how they can be used to describe a youth's commitment to a delinquent career.
6. See how the identification of an individual or a behavior as delinquent is possible only in a social context, involving the interplay between the actor, a norm, an act, and audience perception of the act.

INTRODUCTION

In Chapter 1, we established a solid sociological foundation for the study of juvenile delinquency. We explored the social nature of humans and discussed the basic social processes involved in establishing norms and defining conformity and deviance. Juvenile delinquency was placed in the context of deviant behavior and identified as a social problem about which American society has become seriously concerned.

In this chapter, we emphasize the sociological nature of juvenile delinquency and how society defines delinquency by looking at the social dynamics of the act, the actor, and the audience. The terms "**act**," "**actor**," and "**audience**" conjure up images of the theatre, but can be used effectively as analogs to help us understand much of our behavior in everyday life. While Chapter 1 indicated the basic need for human social interaction, social organization, norms, and social control, Chapter 2 focuses these basic sociological principles upon how society defines juvenile delinquency.

Ever since the comedies and tragedies of life were adapted for the stage by early Greek actors, the theater has held fascinating appeal for performers and spectators alike:

> . . . the waiting audience filed slowly into [their] seats. . . . The cheerful conversation . . . spread from row to row and spilled into the foyer . . . The orchestra, emerging stooping, tuning its instruments; . . . Backstage—ropes, cables, hoisting gear being tried out . . . Lights being focused and shutters placed in readiness. In the dressing room each mirror framed a face being made up. Finally warning lights winked backstage. Silence—places—the overture had begun (Marshall, 1963:71).

This description of the English theater captures some of the infectious excitement connected with the "smell of the greasepaint" and the "roar of the crowd."

One reason for the powerful appeal of the stage, the actors, and the roles they play is that we humans are naturally imitative. We can readily identify with many parts and plots that reflect our own real or imaginary lives, in the past, present, or future. William Shakespeare (1623), the seventeenth century dramatist, was alluding to this trait in human nature when he generalized in Act II of *As You Like It* that all the world is a stage and we are the actors in the drama of life. Sociologist Erving Goffman (1959) artfully appropriated elements of the theatre to analyze social life as a carefully orchestrated drama. Similarly, we earlier referred to DeFleur and associates' (1976:175) observation that "deviance involves a complex interplay between a social norm, an actor, an act, and an audience that defines the act as nonconforming . . ." This dramaturgical analogy offers an excellent sociological framework within which to commence our study of juvenile delinquency.

WHAT IS JUVENILE DELINQUENCY?

In order for any communication to be successful, there must be common language or shared mutual understanding of key words, terms, and concepts. This applies to mass media communication, public stage performances, the classroom learning environment occupied by teachers and students, and even to an informal dialogue between two friends:

> When you tell a friend about a concert you have attended or a movie you have seen, you use a vocabulary that you know your friend will understand. You include all of the background information your friend needs in order to understand what you are talking about; you use an organizational plan that will make it easy for your friend to follow your explanation; and you use grammatical structures that make your meaning clear (Johnson, 1987:134).

The principle of effective communication is especially important in the academic and scientific communities, where the highly specialized and precise terminology of various disciplines must be used liberally to describe complex phenomena. Therefore, it is customary to begin a discussion or discourse with carefully structured definitions in order to promote clarity and comprehension (Johnson, 1987; Lastrucci, 1967).

To begin our study of the phenomenon of juvenile delinquency, two basic questions must be answered: First, what is a juvenile?; and second, what is delinquency? While the two terms of "juvenile" and "delinquency" are used frequently by Americans, it is interesting to note that they are relatively new concepts that do not necessarily connote the same meanings to all who use them.

What Is a Juvenile?

In early American society, essentially two lifestages existed: childhood and adulthood. In agrarian America, the normative expectations for children and for adults were clearly differentiated, and fairly well defined. Extremely young children were considered helpless and totally dependent upon other family members for survival. As soon as a child was physically capable of helping around the house or out in the fields, some routine chores were assigned. Children were expected to obey their parents, and the old adage "Children should be seen, but not heard" was widely practiced. The early American colonists, reflecting the sober and traditional child-rearing practices of their European and religious backgrounds, were strict disciplinarians. Normative conformity and "godliness" were almost synonymous; and parents, strongly supported by the clergy, considered the punishment and correction of children as largely a family responsibility.

While no American laws explicitly defined "childhood," the practice of exempting young children from legal responsibility for their deviant behavior was widely followed. British common law exempted children under the age of 7 from the criminal courts because they lacked **mens rea,** or *criminal intent,* required for criminal conviction. Since much of American criminal law is based upon British common law, the same practice was traditional in this country. Children over the age of 7 were considered old enough to know right from wrong and to understand the consequences of their actions, and were held legally responsible for their law violating behavior.

The child over the age of 7 was not viewed as an adult. Typically, adulthood was not reached until after the onset of puberty, when expectations of work, marriage, and other "adult" activities were assumed. An adult was perceived as a man or a woman who was physically grown and had reached mature size and strength.

As American society became urbanized and industrialized, child labor laws were ultimately passed to protect youths from being exploited by unscrupulous factory owners. No longer able to assume meaningful responsibilities on the farm, the urban youths experienced a longer period of dependency on the family and an extended delay before assuming the responsibilities of adulthood.

What developed in American society was the emergence of a new lifestage to identify the period in life in which a young person was no longer considered a child, but was not yet fully considered an adult. The concept of **adolescence** was socially created to describe *that period of life between childhood and adulthood.*

The creation of adolescence produced a legal dilemma in terms of dealing with the adolescent who violated the law. In response to society's desire to hold children over the age of 7 legally accountable for their behavior, but not as fully accountable as adults, new laws were enacted to deal with the special problem of law violation by youths. The term **juvenile** began to be used when states passed laws establishing the legal age for adulthood. **Juvenile** referred to *any person under the legal age of majority.* Hence, the term encompasses a broader age range than adolescence, which is generally considered to begin with the onset of puberty. However, most juvenile law violation that comes to the attention of juvenile courts occurs during the period of adolescence. Consequently, in relation to delinquency, the terms juvenile and adolescent are virtually interchangeable. The creation of the social concept of adolescence along with the legal concept of juvenile created a new social problem for American society: **juvenile delinquency.**

What Is Delinquency?

We may begin to answer this question by examining some newspaper headlines gathered from several states:

"TEEN GANG WAR ERUPTS IN CENTRAL CITY!"
"HIGH SCHOOL VANDALIZED AND BURNED BY STUDENTS!"
"SEVENTEEN-YEAR-OLD YOUTH HELD FOR MURDER OF PARENTS!"
"POLICE BATTLE PROFESSIONAL SHOPLIFTING RING OF JUVENILES!"

Many people at first glance might assume that these news reports announce unquestionable and typical cases of juvenile delinquency. However, consignment to a juvenile court is seldom that simple. The short, attention-grabbing headlines do not supply enough information upon which to base any conclusions. We know nothing about such important matters as guilt, motives, extenuating circumstances, or the age in each state at which people become legally responsible as adults for their behavior. Moreover, there is nothing typical about these publicized events. Most juvenile behavior conforms to the normative standards of the larger society, and conforming behavior is seldom considered newsworthy. Furthermore, most juvenile delinquency is less sensational, is treated routinely, and receives little public notice. Thus, at the beginning of this inquiry into the nature of juvenile delinquency, an operational definition is in order.

There are literally hundreds of definitions of juvenile delinquency already in existence. Their total number probably approximates the sum of the number of scholars, writers, and experts who have addressed the problem. The majority of the definitions contain only minor differences, that is, they use different words to describe the same idea. Many other definitions of juvenile delinquency vary only in emphasis or approach, according to the academic background, specialty, or interest of their originators. The sociological perspective and the dramaturgical analysis cited earlier suggest a summary of all these definitions into three categories:

1. **The legal definition.** Here the emphasis is almost entirely on *the act*, the norm-violating behavior that is legally classified as juvenile delinquency.
2. **The role definition.** In this case, the focus is primarily on *the actor*, the juvenile whose role performance is identified as delinquent.
3. **The societal response definition.** This approach concentrates more on *the audience*, the members of the social group or society that reacts to the actor and the act and finally determines whether an act of juvenile delinquency has actually been committed.

These definitional categories or approaches are not mutually exclusive. They cannot be completely separated or isolated from one another. Some overlap is inevitable and even desirable. They differ mainly in emphasis. Therefore, they are best understood as three vital dimensions of juvenile delinquency, and all must be considered together in order to formulate a

During the colonial period of American history, it was customary to publicly punish common criminals, religious nonbelievers, and disobedient children. (Illustration by Marilyn Thompson.)

complete definition of this complex social phenomenon. The thorough student of juvenile delinquency utilizes all three of these definitional approaches in determining whether the headlined incidents cited at the beginning of this section, or any other events, represent genuine cases of juvenile delinquency.

The Legal Definition

The oldest and most familiar description of juvenile nonconformity or misbehavior is the legal definition based upon formally codified laws, which specify offenses, sanctions, and age parameters. As previously mentioned, until the late nineteenth century, less serious deviance on the part of youths was considered to be a family matter. On the other hand, extreme or persistent cases of youthful nonconformity or obstinacy became a matter for community discipline. Public rebuke, whippings, and even capital punishment were administered to children (Reid, 1988).

As the American nation developed, major changes in social values and social organization took place. As the population grew and the power of the state was extended, the authority of the family and religious institutions was reduced. For example, stronger feelings emerged and prevailed that the prevention of juvenile crime and the treatment of offenders were community as well as familial responsibilities. The outcome was that more and more troublesome children and youths were subjected to confinement and community-based programs of correction (Schlossman, 1977). Finally, during the last quarter of the nineteenth century, as the concept of adolescence emerged, the nation experienced a growing humanitarian desire to deal differently with the delinquent juvenile than with the criminal adult. Further modification in juvenile corrections soon followed.

The historical development of a formal juvenile justice system in the United States began in 1899. The Illinois state legislature passed a revolutionary bill regarding "juvenile delinquency" and authorized the establishment of the first juvenile court in Cook County (Chicago). From that beginning, similar court legislation was successfully enacted in all the other states, creating special legal procedures apart from the older criminal court system, to deal with the cases of children and youths accused of violating a state law or municipal ordinance. The historical development of the juvenile court and subsequent developments in juvenile justice are more thoroughly discussed in Chapter 12, The Public Arena: The Juvenile Court.

Included within the various laws establishing juvenile courts is a formal, *legal definition* of juvenile delinquency. In general, **juvenile delinquency** is legally defined as *any act which, if committed by an adult, would be a crime.* For example, many states legally define delinquency as the behavior of children between specific ages (usually between the ages of 7 and 18) that violates state or local criminal statutes.

Many other youthful activities, while not criminal in the usual sense, may also come to the attention of a juvenile court if they appear to conflict with the best interests of a given community or the youth in question. Such acts as school truancy or the consumption of alcoholic beverages are not illegal when done by adults but are prohibited for juveniles. Thus, because the community forbids such behavior by minors, these acts are *illegal due only to the age status of the juvenile offenders* and are appropriately referred to as **status offenses.** This point is clearly reflected in a broad legal definition of juvenile delinquency supplied by The Children's Bureau, one of the federal agencies that compiles statistics on juvenile delinquency:

> Juvenile delinquency cases are those referred to courts for acts defined in the statutes of the State as the violation of a state law or municipal ordinance by children or youth of juvenile court age, or for conduct so seriously antisocial as to interfere with the rights of others or to menace the welfare of the delin-

quent himself or of the community. This broad definition of delinquency includes conduct which violates the law only when committed by children, e.g., truancy, ungovernable behavior, and running away (*Juvenile Court Statistics* 1974:11).

What has emerged is a two-fold legal definition of delinquency. This definition includes criminal acts by juveniles along with the acknowledgment of the juvenile court's ability to adjudicate children as delinquent if they have committed an act that, while not illegal when carried out by adults, is considered inappropriate for juveniles. Consequently, the **legal definition** of delinquency has become *any act which would be a crime if committed by an adult, or any act which the juvenile court may deem inappropriate and for which a juvenile can be adjudicated delinquent.*

Each state legislature has designated a specific age as the dividing line between juvenile and criminal offenders. This arbitrary boundary between childhood and adulthood reaffirms the historical position that most individuals below the "age of majority" or "adulthood" are presumed to lack the maturity and "criminal intent" necessary for full legal responsibility. Therefore, their cases are normally processed through the juvenile court where treatment and penalties are usually less severe. The legal concept of **mens rea** still prevails in United States jurisprudence and typically sets the minimum age for delinquency at 7 years, when it is assumed that the child is old enough to consciously demonstrate criminal intent. The upper chronological boundary line is demarcated by the laws of most states, which declare people to be adults on their eighteenth birthday, and juvenile court jurisdiction ends. In recent years, some states have lowered this maximum age for persons under juvenile court jurisdiction (*Children in Custody,* 1974). Cox and Conrad (1987:82) indicated that four states designated the age of 16 as the maximum age; eight states, 17; and the rest, 18. Persons older than the maximum age under juvenile court jurisdiction in their state are generally considered to be adults and their cases are adjudicated in the criminal court. There are important exceptions to these rules, however, which apply to juveniles remanded to the criminal court to face trial as adults. In 1978, for instance, "over a quarter of a million juveniles were arrested, detained, tried, and sentenced as adults" (Hamparian, 1981:25).

Most Americans are more or less familiar with the legal definition of juvenile delinquency, especially the chronological demarcation between juvenile delinquency and adult crime. This may be traced to the cultural importance many people place on the attainment of the legal age of 18, when citizens can vote, enlist in a branch of the military forces, marry without parental consent (in some states), and do many other things that are forbidden before adult status is achieved. The legal definition is also in harmony with the traditional view held by laymen regarding criminals and delinquents. According to Don Gibbons (1976:1), the man on the street tends to divide the world into "the good guys" and "the bad guys" . . . "The common view is that delinquents, criminals, and other deviants are alien persons among us." It follows that the arbitrary and apparently explicit codification of illegal behavior, and recommended procedures for dealing with it, are supported by the majority of people.

The establishment of a legal definition of juvenile delinquency that differentiated youthful offenders from adult criminals was generally viewed as a commendable development and step forward in the jurisprudence of this country. It reinforced the normative system of society and simultaneously offered a humane measure of differential treatment for children and youth who ran afoul of the law. A major strength of the legal definition is its practicality and utility for law enforcement officers, who often must make procedural decisions in the field based upon the age of suspects.

Problems with the Legal Definition A recurring complaint about this approach to classifying juvenile misbehavior is that the "explicit" guidelines are often extremely vague. The legal definitions of delinquency used by the various states adequately extend the adult criminal code forbidding such acts as murder and rape to children and youths. However, annual statistical summaries reveal that the largest proportion of juvenile offenses are status offenses and are included under such imprecise, catch-all phrases in the legal definitions as "ungovernable behavior" and "incorrigible." Rather than defining delinquent conduct with any uniform and objective consistency, these broad descriptions permit much more subjective interpretation by local police and juvenile authorities than is found in adult criminal cases.

As an example of how such wide latitude in interpretation of juvenile laws can lead to capricious adjudication, we note that children can be referred to juvenile courts for "knowingly associating with vicious and immoral persons." In such cases, someone in authority must resolve these ponderous issues: What is an "immoral person?" What are the criteria for immorality? Exactly what is meant by "associating" with such persons? Can guilt by association be imputed to a child? Does "associating with vicious and immoral persons" make one an accomplice to crime? Does "association" mean *any* contact or is association a matter of degree? It is little wonder that there is great inconsistency and variability in the adjudication of delinquency from state to state, court to court, and case to case. The problem is compounded when vague definitions of delinquency and subjective dispositions lead to questionable credibility of national delinquency statistics. For how can the incidence of various forms of youthful crime be compiled and compared adequately in the absence of a fairly uniform legal definition?

Many authorities believe that this weakness could be significantly reduced by the adoption of revised legal definitions that delimit the scope of juvenile delinquency to parallel the criminal code (Sellin and Wolfgang, 1964). This was the thrust of a resolution passed by the Second United Nations Congress for the Prevention of Crime and the Treatment of Offenders in 1960:

> The Congress considers that the scope of the problem of juvenile delinquency should not be unnecessarily inflated . . . it recommends that the meaning of

the term juvenile delinquency should be restricted as far as possible to violations of the criminal law (Report Prepared by the Secretariat, 1961:61).

Thorsten Sellin and Marvin Wolfgang (1964) strongly urged that such a modification in the legal definitions of delinquency would improve the quality of data. They believed that in order to obtain any useful measurement of the volume, character, and trends of juvenile delinquency, definitions of delinquency must be clearly delimited.

Another problem encountered with the legal definitions of juvenile delinquency is the common practice among young and professional criminals in big cities to use the juvenile court age limitation as a shelter to avoid criminal prosecution. A magazine article graphically reported how society's program for lenient and rehabilitative treatment of juvenile offenders has been misused in some places:

> When he is caught, the courts usually spew him out again. If he is under a certain age, 16 to 18 depending on the state, he is almost always taken to juvenile court, where he is treated as if he were still the child he is supposed to be. Even if he has murdered somebody, he may be put away for only a few months . . . Small wonder that hardened juveniles laugh, scratch, yawn, mug and even fall asleep while their crimes are revealed in court. A New York teenager explained in a WCBS radio interview how he started at the age of twelve to rob old women: 'I was young, and I knew I wasn't gonna get no big time. So, you know, what's to worry? If you're doin' wrong, do it while you're young, because you won't do that much time' (Time, 1977:19).

The Role Definition

The legal definition, if used as the sole criterion for determining delinquent behavior and juvenile status, would make it difficult for law enforcement officers to consider any relevant variables other than age and the specific offense brought to their attention. The role definition of juvenile delinquency, by focusing mainly on the actor rather than on the antisocial or nonconforming act, functions as an important corollary to the legal definition. This definitional approach expands the inquiry from "What is juvenile delinquency?" to include the question: "Who are the juvenile delinquents?"

The role definition partially repudiates the strictly legal definition by rejecting the notion that the casual or occasional experimenter with such behavior as truancy, vandalism, fighting, and running away is a true juvenile delinquent. According to the **role definition,** the juvenile delinquent is *the individual who sustains a pattern of delinquency over a long period of time, and whose life and identity are organized around a pattern of deviant behavior* (Hirschi, 1969).

With this definition in mind, the ordinarily conforming and law-abiding boys who, on Halloween night, disregarded laws concerning the drinking of alcoholic beverages by minors, disturbing the peace, malicious mischief, assault, and the curfew were not juvenile delinquents even though they violated those norms (see the **Concept Application** at the end of Chapter 1). In fact, the entire community seemed to anticipate and aid the annual Halloween "riot," which functioned as a "release valve," permitting bored and restrained teenagers to "blow off some steam." Thus, the role definition insists that the actor's behavior must reflect a commitment to a delinquent role and lifestyle before the actor can be realistically identified as a juvenile delinquent.

Two fundamental sociological concepts are inherent in this description of the delinquent: **status** and **role. Status** is defined as *the prestige position of a person in relation to other persons in the social group or society.* Any social group or society of people who are together for any length of time will develop a status hierarchy. Those at the top of the social stratification system nearly always have more wealth, power, prestige, and authority than those at the bottom. Most of us learn where we and others stand on the "ladder of social status" in our social group and community.

There are two ways by which we may acquire social status in our society. **Ascribed status** is *a status position and level of prestige that is granted some people by virtue of their birth.* For example, Queen Elizabeth the First of England was fortunate enough to have been born to parents who were members of the royal family, and thus passed this high status position on to the present queen. Similarly, some of the descendants of oil magnate John Rockefeller, automobile manufacturer Henry Ford, and other successful industrialists hold high status positions today because of inherited wealth. Ascribed status is also the category of status often imputed to those at the bottom of the stratification system who, because of the poor and lowly circumstances of their birth, may always be relegated to an inferior status as residents of the slums, ghettos, and migrant labor camps.

The second way to acquire social status is through the exercise of individual ability or effort or by undertaking certain status-changing experiences in life such as attending college. This is called **"achieved status,"** and in our society is *usually based upon educational level and occupation.* Sociologists have found that Americans have a well-defined hierarchy of occupations, each with a designated level of prestige or status attached (Hodge et al., 1964). As each person enters the work force, there is general consensus regarding the appropriate level of the individual's social status based upon occupation, together with concomitant levels of formal education and income (Bynum, 1973).

The juvenile status in our society is a rather precarious one. Neither adult nor child, the adolescent has a *marginal* social status. The juvenile is torn between the normative expectations and responsibilities associated with adulthood, and the freedom from accountability afforded children. The marginality experienced by juveniles is extremely important from a sociological perspective, and will be further explored throughout this book as a contributing factor to the problem of juvenile delinquency.

The marginal status of adolescents may lead them to experiment with legal adult behavior such as the consumption of alcoholic beverages. Such behavior is illegal for juveniles and constitutes a status offense. (Photo by Laimute Druskis, © 1981.)

Role is defined as *the behavioral performance expected of a person who holds a certain status in the social group or society.* A role assignment goes with every status and thus becomes an important part of the normative system that organizes society and controls the behavior of its members. Over time, certain statuses and their concomitant roles become infused with honored tradition, and little deviation is tolerated. For example, in our society, men are expected to be "masculine"—traditionally viewed as being competitive and aggressive, and to stoically refrain from weeping. Women are expected to be "feminine"—stereotypically viewed as being nonassertive, and eager for fulfillment as wives and mothers. Soldiers are expected to be brave and not cowardly. Ministers are expected to be devout and less susceptible to the temptations of "the world, the flesh, and the devil." The role expectations for juveniles are much less clear than they are for adult men and women. However, as was indicated in the legal definition of delinquency, certain behaviors by adults that are tolerated clearly violate the normative expectations for youth (e.g., drinking, smoking, and sexual activity). Consequently, society's perception of the juvenile status and its concomitant role expectations are major influences in the process of defining juvenile delinquency.

Like status, some roles are imputed to members of society and can be difficult to change. Generally, people can perform only the roles that are approved and assigned by social consensus. However, occasionally roles can be successfully manipulated or modified. For example, the feminist movement has made substantial gains in weakening the traditional and stereotyped role of women in the United States by promoting contemporary and alternative roles.

Some roles are considered permanently "off limits" to all the members of society. Theoretically, at least, the criminal and delinquent roles are not legal or legitimate alternatives. This is the heart of the role definition of juvenile delinquency. A persistent and consistent pattern of delinquent behavior may be perceived as a valid index of the desired and intended role and lifestyle of the youth in question. Although some role behavior is the result of unconscious socialization and the internalization of social expectations, at other times we consciously and purposely act out roles that afford a dramatized presentation of self-identity (Goffman, 1959, 1967).

Problems with the Role Definition Attempts have been made to integrate the legal definition with the role definition of juvenile delinquency. The legal definition, with its emphasis on the norm and the act of violation, theoretically merges very well with the role definition stressing the actor's patterned delinquent performance. However, the combined product is, in some instances at least, difficult to operationalize:

> For example, New Mexico rests its definition of delinquency on the word 'habitual': A delinquent child is one who, by habitually refusing to obey the reasonable and lawful commands of his parents or other persons of lawful authority, is deemed to be habitually uncontrolled, habitually disobedient, or habitually wayward; or who habitually is a truant from home or school; or who habitually so deports himself as to injure or endanger the morals, health, or welfare of himself or others (Cavan, 1961:243).

A problem with these laws is that there is no clear definition of what is meant by terms such as incorrigible, habitual, or indecent conduct. As Cavan (1961: 243) asked, "How often may a child perform an act before it is considered habitual?" Paradoxically, the search for a committed and consistent pattern of delinquency can sometimes frustrate the effort toward consistent judicial treatment of American youth.

Another criticism of the role definition is that it overlooks the fact that a deviant role seldom occupies all of a person's life, time, and behavior. Nearly everyone, even a child, has several different roles and is usually able to easily and quickly move from one to another. A juvenile delinquent may alternately be student, part-time employee, brother, son, and gang member, depending upon the circumstances and with whom he is interacting. He spends his time eating, sleeping, working, playing, stealing cars, and doing many other diversified activities. Only one of his roles and a very small portion of his time involves illegal behavior. David Matza (1964), with forceful logic, contended that juvenile delinquents are very much like everyone else; that only intermittently are the social bonds tying them to the mass of conforming society loosened enough to permit an occasional deviation. Obviously, this is a serious contradiction in the role definition, which describes the delinquent as an actor whose life and identity are wholly organized around deviant behavior.

The Societal Response Definition

The emphasis on a social norm, an individual actor, or a norm-violating act, either alone or in combination, does not equate to an adequate and complete definition of juvenile delinquency. While these factors are all relevant and vital to a definitive description and conceptualization of the process and condition of delinquency, something is still lacking.

According to the **societal response definition,** *in order for an act and/or an actor to be defined as deviant or delinquent, an audience must perceive and judge the behavior in question.* The **audience** is *the social group or society to which the actor belongs or aspires to belong.* It is not possible or necessary for all the members of the social group to personally view and evaluate the conforming or nonconforming quality of a person's behavior. In the case of juvenile delinquency, significant and representative members of the social group—parents, teachers, neighbors, police officers, or others—may perform the audience function by witnessing the act or acts and making the initial societal response. It is even possible for the juveniles committing law-violating behavior to identify their actions as delinquent, and, in a sense, to act as their own social audience. The social consequences of delinquency are not experienced, however, unless the deviant perception is shared by others.

You will recall from your reading of Chapter 1 that we began with an audience—the social group that formulated the rules or norms, and thereby prejudged the subsequent behavior of all the members of the group. In this sense, "social groups create deviance by making the rules whose infraction constitutes deviance . . ." (Becker, 1963:9). In other words, without society there would be no norms; without norms there would be no deviant behavior; without deviant behavior there would be no system of sanctions. Albert Cohen and James Short applied this idea to juvenile delinquency when they stated, "Just as crime is a creation of the criminal law, so juvenile delinquency is a creation of the statutes establishing the juvenile courts" (cited in Merton and Nisbet, 1971:91). Over time, the process of becoming delinquent develops sequentially from a socially derived norm, to the violation of that norm by an actor, to social definition and adjudication by an audience. A youth is finally and officially defined as a juvenile delinquent when that status is conferred upon the youth by a court. This process is thoroughly discussed in Chapter 12.

We may extend the dramaturgical analogy a bit further by perceiving society as being somewhat more involved than a passive audience of spectators. Society's active audience role is similar to that of the theater audience that scrutinizes each actor's performance. The audience communicates to the actors its estimation of the quality of the performance with appropriate sanctions— applause, hisses, or other expressions of judgment. Societal response to behavior—the official judgment regarding normative expectations and the actor's conforming or deviant act—is the last and determining dimension to be incorporated into a more complete *sociolegal* definition of juvenile delinquency.

Problems with the Societal Response Definition
This definition gives rise to the labeling approach to juvenile delinquency. The labeling perspective views delinquency as being a social "label" placed on juveniles and their actions when those viewing the acts (or who are later apprised of them) judge them to be deviant. The labeling perspective is more thoroughly explained in Chapter 6, Sociological Explanations of Delinquency.

In Chapter 1, human society was described as an association designed to improve the personal and collective welfare and survival chances of all of its members. A society is endowed with remarkable endurance and usually outlives its individual members. Over time, social norms, values, attitudes, and viewpoints are also manipulated, changed, discarded, or replaced, in harmony with the changing needs of the social group. So, while a society may prevail for a relatively long time, the component parts are not nearly as permanent and invariable. This adaptability and flexibility have greatly aided the survival of society. For example, every major world religion traces the norm "Thou shalt not kill" to both social and divine origins. Modern nations have institutionalized that canon, and compliance is required of their citizens. The norm is widely and thoroughly internalized so that people are generally shocked and indignant by the disregard for human life manifested in some criminal activities. However, when society perceives it as necessary, that norm can be quickly modified or reduced in importance or relevancy. Medals and public honors are bestowed on military men for their prowess in killing the national enemy. One of the most successful and popular dramatic plots involves a United States Marshal or other "good guys" heroically gunning down the "bad guys" in "winning the west." The point is that an **a priori** definition of the situation intervenes between the definitive norm and its application which influences the outcome of the application.

The societal response definition of juvenile delinquency, while incorporating some elements of other definitional approaches, is not without its problems. The sociolegal focus on the audience, comprised of direct and indirect witnesses, becomes the key variable in determining the delinquent or nondelinquent status of an act or actor. But witnesses do not always agree on what they are seeing. As an example, consider the case of a teenage girl who is caught shoplifting in a department store. Her parents may view this as a single isolated act, totally incompatible with their daughter's usual behavior. If the police are called, the responding officer may see the shoplifting activity as theft and feel obliged to arrest the youth. The perception and reaction of the store manager are also influenced by personal background and circumstances. If continually victimized by widespread shoplifting on the part of high school students, the store manager may decide to "make an example" of the girl, and prosecute her. On the other hand, if her parents are affluent or prominent in the community, the store manager may regard the incident as trivial rather than risk alienating the family and their friends. Audience evaluation of the act and the actor may be further diversified if the youth belongs to a peer group in her school or neighborhood that values such daring and nonconforming escapades and consequently rewards her with higher status. The conflict and varying dominance of these segments of the perceiving and reacting audience often result in differential treatment of many young offenders. This persistent definitional problem is heavily underscored in the discussion of juvenile delinquency statistics presented in Chapter 3.

A SYNTHESIZED DEFINITION OF DELINQUENCY

The conceptual definition of juvenile delinquency that will be utilized throughout this book combines aspects of all three of the major definitional categories. It includes criminal acts committed by juveniles and the status offenses deemed to be inappropriate behavior for youths. It includes the fulfillment of the delinquent role and also takes into account the complex social processes involved in the societal response to delinquency. Consequently, when we use the term **juvenile delinquency,** we are referring to *those actions that are illegal for juveniles, that place the juvenile in the delinquent role, and that result in society regarding the juvenile as deviant.* This synthesized definition, however, while operational for present consideration, also suggests a variety of problems, as lack of uniformity in laws, and lack of consistency in what is considered appropriate and inappropriate behavior, are a social reality in American society. Resolutions to these problems in defining juvenile delinquency are suggested in Chapter 15 as we rethink the delinquency problem.

SUMMARY

In this chapter, we explored the complex definitions of juvenile delinquency. The definitions of delinquency tend to fall into three broad categories: **legal, role,** and **societal response.**

The legal definition focuses upon the act committed by the youth. Every state has established statutes that define criminal behavior. The legal definition indicates that delinquency occurs when juveniles between a specified age range (usually 7 to 18 years) commit an act that would be considered a crime if committed by an adult. The legal definition goes beyond this, however, as states also have enacted statutes that make it illegal for juveniles to commit certain acts that would not be considered criminal if committed by an adult. These status offenses are legally defined as acts of delinquency because they violate the normative role expectations associated with the juvenile status in our society. Criminal statutes are norms that have been formally codified by society. These laws usually reflect the prevailing values of a society, and prohibit behaviors viewed as being dysfunctional to the overall stability of society. Murder, rape, robbery, theft, and other criminal offenses clearly threaten the established social order. Likewise, while the drinking of alcoholic beverages, smoking, and truancy are not crimes when done by adults, they are viewed as threatening the socialization process, which is considered vital to the internalization of society's cultural values and social norms by the young.

We also explored the role definition of delinquency. This definition shifts the focus of delinquency away from the specific act and onto the actor. The role definition tends to overlook the occasional transgression against social norms, and views delinquency as being a persistent pattern of law violating behavior by a youth. This definition focuses heavily upon the status accorded juveniles in our society and the social role expected to accompany that status. While there is little argument over the validity of the values reflected in laws against murder, rape, robbery, theft, and other violent and property offenses, the values reflected in the laws creating status offenses are not uniformly supported.

The third major definitional category focuses upon the societal response or sociolegal definition of delinquency. This definition views delinquency primarily as being a result of the reaction of a social audience to a particular actor and act. As the interplay unfolds between the act, the actor, and the audience, different interpretations of what has happened and what is happening confound the implementation of any definition of juvenile delinquency. Thus, efforts to make practical application of the definitions often appear ambiguous. The legal definition of juvenile delinquency is plagued by vague phraseology that permits subjective criteria as to what constitutes a delinquent act. The role definition is weakened by a lack of consensus about exactly how much nonconforming, antisocial behavior is necessary to indicate commitment to a delinquent role and identity. The societal response or sociolegal definition is dependent upon some type of consensus on the part of a social audience that deviance has been committed and that something should be done about it.

Finally, we constructed a synthesized definition to be used for our purposes in exploring the problem of juvenile delinquency. This definition encompasses the major elements of all three of the aforementioned definitions. While not without some problems and limitations, this synthesized definition provides a clear conceptual framework for our study of the delinquency problem.

CONCEPT APPLICATION
ILLUSTRATIVE ANECDOTE

The following anecdote shares an experience of one of the authors while he was an assistant principal at a public high school, and illustrates one of the important concepts discussed in this chapter.

"Child or Adult?"

Juvenile is a status in our society—a social position somewhere between "child" and "adult." Like any social status, it is accompanied by a set of role expectations. While the normative role expectations for adults and for children are fairly clearcut, those for juveniles are much more ambiguous. Told constantly by parents, "You're a young adult now, why don't you act like it?" only to be denied responsibilities and freedom with the phrase "You're too young," juveniles find themselves in a societal "Catch-22" where they are simultaneously "too old" and "too young" for the pleasures of life.

I recall an encounter with a ninth-grade student. He had been sent to my office for "acting childishly" in class. He had no doubt been involved in behavior that was disruptive, and the teacher had finally become exasperated and sent him to the office. In my typical assistant-principal-disciplinary tone, I asked, "What seems to be the problem?" With a genuinely confused look, the student replied, "I don't know what the teacher expects out of me . . . in fact . . . I don't know what anybody expects out of me!"

Without any coaxing on my part, the student went on to describe the predicament he had experienced in the classroom. He pointed out that since the first day of school, all the teachers had emphasized that he was in high school now; that he was a young adult and would be treated as such; and that he was expected to act like one. He said that even though one particular teacher constantly reminded her students that they were adults, she often treated them like small children. He cited some of the classroom rules that he considered petty and humiliating, including not being allowed to chew gum and having to ask permission to go to the bathroom. "Does that sound like the way to treat adults?" he asked. Before I could answer, he related a brief story about his parents constantly demanding that he "act his age" and show more responsibility and maturity. Yet, when he wanted to stay home one weekend when his parents had planned to be out of town, they flatly refused, reminding him that "he was only fourteen," and that if he insisted on staying home, they would have to hire a *babysitter*.

I tried to interrupt to respond (I probably would have offered some type of defense for both the teacher and his parents), but before I could speak, he recited some examples of contradictory expectations he had recently experienced:

After passing a required examination, he was legally licensed to operate a motorcycle, and was expected to obey all traffic laws like an adult—but he could not legally drive a car ... If he went to see a Disney movie rated G he was considered an adult and was required to pay adult admission; but if he tried to see an X-rated movie, he was told that it was for adults only, and he was a child.

These examples reflect some of the obviously inconsistent, confusing, and often contradictory normative expectations faced by juveniles in our society. Between the ages of 12 and 18 (and in some cases 21) the majority of American youth find themselves in a social "no man's land." They are no longer children and childish behavior is not tolerated, yet they are not adults and many adult behaviors are strictly prohibited.

*   *   *   *

Compare and contrast juveniles and adults with regard to legal and social rights and responsibilities. Have you experienced similar circumstances where you were expected to behave as an adult while still being treated like a child? What problems did you experience? What could be done to help reduce some of the problems associated with the ambiguity of the status of adolescence?

CONCEPT INTEGRATION

QUESTIONS AND TOPICS FOR STUDY AND DISCUSSION

1. Define and explain the following terms and concepts: juvenile, adult, mens rea, social role, social status, ascribed status, and achieved status.
2. What is juvenile delinquency?
   - from the perspective of the legal definition?
   - from the perspective of the role definition?
   - from the perspective of the societal response definition?
3. What is a juvenile delinquent? How does a delinquent differ from the adult criminal? How does the delinquent differ from the occasional experimenter with nonconforming or antisocial behavior?
4. Define *status offense*. Should status offenses be part of the legal definition of delinquency? Why? Why not?
5. Use the dramaturgical analogy to help explain the interplay and relationship between the social norm, the act, the actor, and the audience, and some common form of youthful misbehavior such as truancy from school, shoplifting, or something of your choice or from your experience.
6. Outline the problems associated with each definition of juvenile delin-

quency. In your judgment, can any of these problems be resolved? If so, how?

References

Becker, H. 1963. *The outsiders.* New York: The Free Press of Glencoe.

Bynum, J. 1973. Social status and rites of passage: The social context of death. *Omega* 4 (4):323–332.

Cavan, R. S. 1961. The concepts of tolerance and contraculture as applied to delinquency. *Sociological Quarterly* 2 (Fall):243–258.

Children in Custody. 1974. *A Report on the Juvenile Detention and Correctional Facility Census of 1971.* Washington, DC: National Criminal Justice Information and Statistics Service, LEAA.

Cohen, A. & Short, J. 1971. Crime and juvenile delinquency. In *Contemporary Social Problems* (3rd ed.) R. K. Merton & R. Nisbet (Eds.). New York: Harcourt, Brace, Jovanovich, pp. 89–146.

Cox, S. M. & Conrad, J. J. 1987. *Juvenile justice: A guide to practice and theory* (2nd ed.). Dubuque, IA: Wm. C. Brown.

DeFleur, M., D'Antonio, W. V. & DeFleur, L. B. 1976. *Sociology: Human society* (2nd ed.). Glenview, IL: Scott, Foresman and Co.

Gibbons, D. 1976. *Delinquent behavior* (2nd ed.). Englewood Cliffs, NJ: Prentice-Hall.

Goffman, E. 1959. *The presentation of self in everyday life.* Garden City, NY: Doubleday and Company (Anchor Books).
1967. *Where the action is.* Garden City, NY: Doubleday and Company.

Hamparian, D. 1981. Juveniles tried as adults. In *Issues in Juvenile Corrections,* Series 2, No. 2. College Park, MD: American Correctional Association, pp. 25–29.

Hirschi, T. 1969. *Causes of delinquency.* Berkeley: University of California Press.

Hodge, R., Siegel, P. M. & Rossi, P. H. 1964. Occupational prestige in the United States, 1925–1963. *American Journal of Sociology* 70 (November):290–292.

Johnson, J. 1987. *The Bedford guide to the research process.* New York: Bedford/St. Martin's Press.

Juvenile Court Statistics. 1974. DHEW Pub. No. (SRS) 73-03452. Washington, DC: U. S. Department of Health, Education, and Welfare.

Lastrucci, C. L. 1967. *The scientific approach.* Cambridge, MA: Schenkman.

Marshall, P. 1963. *John Doe, disciple.* New York: McGraw-Hill Book Co.

Matza, D. 1964. *Delinquency and drift.* New York: John Wiley.

Oates, S. B. 1977. *With malice toward none.* New York: Harper & Row.

Park, R. E. 1928. Human migration and the marginal man. *American Journal of Sociology* 33 (May):893.

Reid, S. T. 1988. *Crime and criminology* (5th ed.). New York: Holt, Rinehart and Winston.

Report Prepared by the Secretariat. 1961. New York: The United Nations, iv, 95 pp.

Schlossman, S. L. 1977. *Love and the American delinquent.* Chicago: University of Chicago Press.

Sellin, T. & Wolfgang, M. E. 1964. The measurement of delinquency. New York: John Wiley.

Shakespeare, W. 1623. *As You Like It* (Act II. sc. vii, l. 139).

Stonequist, E. H. 1937. *The marginal man: A study in personality and culture conflict.* Charles Scribner's Sons.

Time. 1977. The Youth Crime Plague. *Time* (July 11):18–28.

Chapter 3

The Dimensions of the Delinquency Problem

READING OBJECTIVES

The reading of this chapter will help you achieve the following objectives:

1. Define the various kinds of crime according to the common catalog and criteria used throughout the United States.
2. Identify the sources of the data and statistical information on juvenile delinquency in the United States.
3. Explain the various data-collecting techniques that are used and the strengths and weaknesses of each methodology.
4. Understand how unreliable and/or invalid data or data-gathering procedures can lead to questionable findings and conclusions regarding the magnitude of juvenile delinquency.
5. Trace the general dimensions of the delinquency problem with official FBI and juvenile court statistics on the incidence and trends of juvenile crime in the various offense categories.
6. Conceptualize the Delinquent Profile as a summary and descriptive statement of many characteristics of the "average" juvenile delinquent based on arrest statistics.
7. Analyze and critique the data supporting the various traits comprising the composite Delinquent Profile. Explain why the amount and kind of juvenile delinquency varies, or seems to vary, according to the sex, race, place of residence, and other characteristics of the offenders.

INTRODUCTION

In 1930, a voluntary national program of collection of crime statistics was initiated by the International Association of Chiefs of Police (IACP) and the United States Federal Bureau of Investigation (FBI). The resulting annual reports on criminal activity in the United States have revealed serious and consistently high rates of juvenile delinquency. The *First Annual Report of the National Institute of Law Enforcement and Criminal Justice* (1974:15) reported that "during the 1960's, the arrest rate for juveniles increased six times faster than for adults." By 1970, juveniles under the age of 18 accounted for one-fifth of all arrests for violent crime and for more than half of all arrests for burglary. In 1973, The National Advisory Commission on Criminal Justice Standards and Goals identified juvenile delinquency as a critical, high priority, national concern:

> The highest attention must be given to preventing juvenile delinquency, minimizing the involvement of young offenders in the juvenile and criminal justice system, and reintegrating them into the community (*Standards and Goals for Juvenile Justice*, 1974:3).

The news media also continually focus on the crimes committed by American youths, especially those crimes of a violent and sensational nature:

> Many youngsters appear to be robbing and raping, maiming and murdering as casually as they go to a movie or join a pickup baseball game. A new, remorseless, mutant juvenile seems to have been born, and there is no more terrifying figure in America today (Warner, 1977:18).
>
> . . . More than a million juveniles were arrested in 1984—yet police estimate that for every arrest five crimes are committed. Even so, the number of juveniles in correctional facilities is on the rise. The FBI reports that the rate of violent crime by juveniles is double what it was 20 years ago. In 1983 and 1984, offenders less than 18 years old were arrested in connection with nearly 2,000 murders, 7,000 rapes and 60,000 aggravated assaults (Santoli, 1986:16).

It is not surprising, therefore, that the national problem of juvenile delinquency continues to receive almost constant attention from an army of law enforcement personnel, criminologists, and other scholars in the social and behavioral sciences. Without minimizing the gravity of youthful crime, it should be pointed out that much of what we read or hear on the topic in the news media is selective reporting of those aspects of juvenile delinquency that will quickly capture public attention. Obviously, headline or feature stories of juvenile gang wars raging in the streets or of a maniacal teenager committing mayhem with an axe sells more newspapers than a report that the vast majority of juvenile arrests are for property crimes, vandalism, and juvenile status offenses such as the violation of liquor laws (*FBI Uniform Crime Reports*, 1980:180). Equally lacking in sensationalism are the data-based findings that only 7 percent to 10 percent of delinquents are chronic and violent offenders, and this hard-core group commits 60 percent to 70 percent of all serious juvenile crime (National Advisory Committee, 1984).

In this chapter, in order to more fully comprehend the magnitude of juvenile delinquency in the United States, we review the methods by which information on crime is acquired, the various kinds and incidence of criminal activity, current trends, and characteristics of offenders as indicated by available statistics.

JUVENILE DELINQUENCY DATA

Statistical data and quantitative information are regularly collected in order to provide fresh insights regarding juvenile delinquency in the United States. If this social problem is ever to be completely understood, prevented, or controlled, accurate up-to-date information must be available to answer such questions as: How many juvenile offenses and arrests occur each year? What kinds of juvenile misbehavior are most common from year to year? What trends can be extrapolated from the past and the present, and projected for the future? Is there a "typical" juvenile delinquent? If so, what are his or her social, economic, and demographic characteristics?

Validity and Reliability

The methods and procedures used to collect and analyze data determine their accuracy and, from that, the usefulness of the findings. For example, it is impossible to identify all the children and youths who have violated a juvenile statute or whose behavior could be interpreted by others as delinquent. Even if this prodigious task of identification could somehow be accomplished, administering a questionnaire or interviewing in every case would be too expensive and impractical. Consequently, most research efforts to measure the amount and kinds of delinquent behavior utilize information collected by law enforcement agencies about known offenders. Conversely, such data are severely limited in informing us about the offenses and traits of delinquent youths who are not apprehended.

Other investigators into juvenile delinquency have implemented sampling strategies in which a relatively small number of known delinquents or other subjects are selected and surveyed on the assumption that they are representative of a much larger population. However, if the respondents who comprise the "sample of representative delinquents," for example, are conveniently gathered from Chicago street gangs, the findings would not give an accurate picture of all of the juvenile delinquency in Chicago. **Validity** and **reliability** are two precise concepts that will help us understand these common problems and errors in research methodology.

Validity   A measure has **validity** when it *in fact measures whatever it is supposed to measure*. A finding or conclusion is valid if it accurately reflects factual evidence. As an example, suppose Professor Smith at University A decides to interview a sample of students about their possible participation in unreported or undetected delinquent activities. The professor may be extremely careful to randomly select subjects so that they are representative of all the students attending the college (this is a very difficult task since every student must have an equal chance of being included in the sample). However, during the interviews, if the professor directly or indirectly, consciously or unconsciously, indicates expectations or desired responses, there is an excellent chance that the students will tell the professor exactly what they think is the desired response. Consequently, the findings will be invalid. In addition, if the students feel intimidated by the investigator's attitude, questions, or presence, they may be inclined to misrepresent their responses. So, besides a random sample, other factors in the survey instrument, the subjects, and the lack of anonymity in the situation can affect the validity of the results.

Reliability   A measure has **reliability** when *it yields the same results upon repetition of the measuring procedure or replication by other investigators*. For example, suppose that another teacher at a different school—Professor Jones at University B—hears or reads about Professor Smith's research at University A on unreported and undetected delinquency. Professor Jones then decides to conduct a similar investigation to see how many students at her institution committed various kinds of unreported and undetected crime. Jones also wants to see if her findings agree or disagree with Smith's.

In order to make a fair comparison of the findings from the two studies, the survey conditions, methodology, and subjects must be as nearly identical as possible. Professor Jones therefore uses the same survey questionnaire used by Professor Smith at University A. She also carefully selects her subjects with the same random sampling procedures, and makes every effort to ensure that the sample of students at University B is as similar as possible in background to those surveyed by Smith at University A. It follows that if, after replicating Professor Smith's study, Professor Jones discovers that her findings are essentially the same, we may conclude that the survey instrument or measuring procedure is reliable—that is, it can be relied upon to yield similar results when used by different, independent researchers at different points in time.

In summary, validity and reliability clearly are related, and both are enhanced if survey questions are structured so that they can be readily understood by the subjects and elicit informative, straightforward answers. Additionally, validity and reliability are reinforced if subjects are systematically and consistently selected in the same way each time data are collected. Comparisons should be made only between the two or more samples, or of a single sample at different points in time, if variables such as age, race, sex, and social class have been **controlled,** or *held reasonably constant and similar,* from group to group, and from time to time.

These general principles of social science research methodology will be useful in our later evaluations of juvenile delinquency data and concomitant findings and conclusions. They are appropriate considerations with regard to truancy, homicide, unreported crimes, or any other statistical report on juvenile delinquency.

OFFICIAL SOURCES OF DELINQUENCY INFORMATION

Two agencies of the federal government, operating independently of each other, collect and summarize juvenile crime statistics on a national scale into annual reports. They are the Federal Bureau of Investigation (FBI) and the Office of Juvenile Justice and Delinquency Prevention.

FBI Uniform Crime Reports

Since 1930, the FBI has compiled data on crime and delinquency from a network of city, county, and state law enforcement agencies across the country. The numbers and kinds of reported offenses, the numbers and kinds of offenses resulting in arrest, and characteristics of offenders such as age, sex, race, and place of residence form the basis of the FBI compilations. Each year the FBI summarizes the data into statistical tables and issues a *Uniform Crime Report* for the information and use of law enforcement officers and others concerned with the national crime problem.

The FBI Uniform Crime Reporting Program is designed to attain three basic objectives:

1. To measure the extent, fluctuation, distribution, and nature of serious crime in the United States . . .
2. To measure the total volume of serious crime known to police.
3. To show the activity and coverage of law enforcement agencies through arrest counts and police employee strength data (FBI Uniform Crime Reports, 1975:2).

In addition, the division of arrest data into "ages under 18" and "ages 18 and over" categories is of tremendous help to law-enforcement personnel and researchers using FBI *Uniform Crime Report* data to separate juvenile delinquency from adult crime, according to the legal definition of delinquency presented in Chapter 2.

A major strength of the Uniform Crime Reporting Program is that *stan-*

dardized definitions of the main kinds of crime are utilized by *all law enforcement agencies* reporting from the various states. This is why the annual FBI compilations are called "*Uniform* Crime Reports." The definitions follow:

1. **Murder and Nonnegligent Manslaughter.** The willful (nonnegligent) killing of one human being by another.
2. **Forcible Rape.** The carnal knowledge of a female forcibly and against her will. Assaults or attempts to commit rape by force or threat of force are also included.
3. **Robbery.** The taking or attempting to take anything of value from the care, custody, or control of a person or persons by force or threat of force or violence and/or by putting the victim in fear.
4. **Aggravated Assault.** An unlawful attack by one person upon another for the purpose of inflicting severe or aggravated bodily injury.
5. **Burglary.** The unlawful entry of a structure to commit a felony or theft. (A felony is any offense punishable by death or imprisonment.)
6. **Larceny-theft.** The unlawful taking, carrying, leading, or riding away of property from the possession or constructive possession of another.
7. **Motor Vehicle Theft.** The theft or attempted theft of a motor vehicle.
8. **Arson.** Any willful or malicious burning or attempt to burn, with or without intent to defraud, a dwelling house, public building, motor vehicle or aircraft, personal property of another, etc. (FBI Uniform Crime Reports, 1986:7, 13, 16, 21, 24, 28, 33, 36).

Because of their seriousness, frequency of occurrence, and likelihood of being reported to the police, these eight crime categories were chosen as the basis for the Uniform Crime Report Index, and are referred to as **Index Offenses.** The Index is useful for charting and analyzing changes in the volume of crime in its various and most serious forms from year to year. Table 3–1 is a part of the 1986 *Uniform Crime Reports;* the first eight crime offense categories listed at the top comprise the *UCR* Index for that year.

Juvenile Arrests for Specific Offenses   The first four Index Offenses—murder, forcible rape, robbery, and aggravated assault—are often grouped together and referred to as "violent crimes." **Violent Crimes** are *those that are directed against a person.* During 1986, persons under 18 years of age accounted for 15.4 percent of the 465,391 violent crimes in the United States. The last four Index Offenses—burglary, larceny-theft, motor vehicle theft, and arson—are combined under the heading of "property crimes." **Property Crimes** are *non-violent crimes directed against property.* In 1986, persons under age 18 were credited with over a third (33.5 percent) of the property crimes. In other

TABLE 3-1

Total Arrests, Distribution by Age, 1986. (10,743 agencies; 1986 estimated population: 198,488,000)

Offense Charged	Total All Ages	Ages Under 15	Ages Under 18	Ages 18 and Over	Ages									
					Under 10	10-12	13-14	15	16	17	18	19	20	21
TOTAL	10,392,177	536,609	1,747,675	8,644,502	46,408	126,809	363,392	333,648	416,663	460,755	494,197	492,884	481,996	482,724
Percent distribution[a]	100.0	5.2	16.8	83.2	.4	1.2	3.5	3.2	4.0	4.4	4.8	4.7	4.6	4.6
Murder and nonnegligent manslaughter	16,066	156	1,396	14,670	7	15	134	245	443	552	729	790	802	771
Forcible rape	31,128	1,514	4,798	26,330	77	297	1,140	982	1,121	1,181	1,220	1,272	1,344	1,431
Robbery	124,245	6,615	27,987	96,258	199	1,244	5,172	5,792	7,334	8,246	8,227	7,791	7,163	7,103
Aggravated assault	293,952	10,816	37,528	256,424	781	2,517	7,518	6,934	9,251	10,527	10,884	11,268	12,078	12,989
Burglary	375,544	47,080	134,823	240,721	4,201	11,727	31,152	27,367	30,032	30,344	28,510	23,858	19,717	17,574
Larceny-theft	1,182,099	156,033	378,283	803,816	15,238	45,210	95,585	70,640	77,171	74,439	66,530	56,489	47,888	44,770
Motor vehicle theft	128,514	11,961	50,319	78,195	193	1,360	10,408	12,278	13,797	12,283	9,785	8,073	6,611	5,774
Arson	15,523	3,837	6,271	9,252	1,028	1,113	1,696	954	784	696	655	549	484	448
Violent crime[b]	465,391	19,101	71,709	393,682	1,064	4,073	13,964	13,953	18,149	20,506	21,060	21,121	21,387	22,294
Percent distribution[a]	100.0	4.1	15.4	84.6	.2	.9	3.0	3.0	3.9	4.4	4.5	4.5	4.6	4.8
Property crime[c]	1,701,680	218,911	569,696	1,131,984	20,660	59,410	138,841	111,239	121,784	117,762	105,480	88,969	74,700	68,566
Percent distribution[a]	100.0	12.9	33.5	66.5	1.2	3.5	8.2	6.5	7.2	6.9	6.2	5.2	4.4	4.0

Crime Index total[d]	2,167,071	238,012	641,405	1,525,666	21,724	63,483	152,805	125,192	139,933	138,268	126,540	110,090	96,087	90,860
Percent distribution[a]	100.0	11.0	29.6	70.4	1.0	2.9	7.1	5.8	6.5	6.4	5.8	5.1	4.4	4.2
Other assaults	593,902	30,411	85,905	507,997	2,642	8,040	19,729	16,107	18,678	20,709	20,608	22,521	24,562	26,904
Forgery and counterfeiting	76,546	1,101	7,234	69,312	39	206	856	1,204	1,937	2,992	3,695	4,202	4,210	4,257
Fraud	284,790	6,722	17,727	267,063	178	1,398	5,146	6,028	1,958	3,019	5,765	8,287	10,362	11,938
Embezzlement	10,500	52	696	9,804	1	9	42	61	205	378	494	563	515	504
Stolen property; buying, receiving, possessing...	114,105	7,613	28,739	85,366	327	1,412	5,874	5,915	7,191	8,020	8,528	7,340	6,447	5,859
Vandalism	223,231	45,247	95,479	127,752	7,156	13,872	24,219	16,654	17,145	16,433	13,266	10,853	9,436	8,859
Weapons; carrying, possessing, etc...	160,204	6,394	25,170	135,034	244	1,172	4,978	4,893	6,317	7,566	8,572	8,141	7,993	8,020
Prostitution and commercialized vice...	96,882	247	2,192	94,690	22	23	202	271	594	1,080	2,916	4,486	5,210	6,629
Sex offenses (except forcible rape and prostitution)...	83,934	6,110	13,753	70,181	558	1,551	4,001	2,611	2,514	2,518	2,517	2,591	2,764	2,870
Drug abuse violations...	691,882	9,374	68,351	623,531	187	959	8,228	12,181	20,008	26,788	34,664	37,041	37,808	39,792
Gambling...	25,839	105	610	25,229	5	13	87	128	142	235	366	376	507	618
Offenses against family and children	47,327	1,255	2,521	44,806	632	167	456	432	433	401	1,155	1,266	1,461	1,697

TABLE 3-1 *(cont.)*

Offense Charged	Total All Ages	Ages Under 15	Ages Under 18	Ages 18 and Over	Under 10	10-12	13-14	15	16	17	18	19	20	21
Driving under the influence	1,458,531	456	22,749	1,435,782	147	33	276	945	5,957	15,391	33,816	45,632	53,946	68,535
Liquor laws	490,436	10,163	132,335	358,101	430	615	9,118	19,264	40,669	62,239	73,733	58,559	45,566	19,965
Drunkenness . .	777,866	3,283	26,589	751,277	470	247	2,566	4,245	7,293	11,768	20,197	23,764	25,791	32,367
Disorderly conduct.	564,882	22,517	82,986	481,896	1,746	5,384	15,387	14,723	20,413	25,333	29,094	30,745	30,975	32,459
Vagrancy	32,992	539	2,550	30,442	32	79	428	520	664	827	1,552	1,597	1,401	1,350
All other offenses (except traffic)	2,272,589	70,918	276,876	1,995,713	6,906	15,289	48,723	46,318	72,400	87,240	106,256	114,469	116,652	118,944
Suspicion	7,455	846	2,595	4,860	98	172	576	617	600	532	463	361	303	292
Curfew and loitering law violations.	72,627	19,260	72,627	. . . .	654	3,199	15,407	16,781	20,333	16,253	. . . .	. . . .	. . . .	. . . .
Runaways	138,586	55,984	138,586	. . . .	2,210	9,486	44,288	38,558	31,279	12,765	. . . .	. . . .	. . . .	. . . .

a Because of rounding, the percentages may not add to total.
b Violent crimes are offenses of murder, forcible rape, robbery, and aggravated assault.
c Property crimes are offenses of burglary, larceny theft, motor vehicle theft, and arson.
d Includes arson.

Source: Federal Bureau of Investigation, *Uniform Crime Reports: Crime in the United States, 1986.* Washington, DC: U.S. Government Printing Office. 1987. Table 33, p. 174.

words, FBI arrest records show that youths under 18 are less likely than adults over age 18 to be arrested for violent crimes. At the same time, the probability is much higher that youths will be arrested for property crimes than will adults (see Table 3–1).

Of the eight specific offenses comprising the Crime Index, 8.7 percent of the 1986 arrests for murder were of youths under age 18. During the same year, 9 percent of the murder victims were also under 18 years of age. Of the total clearances by arrest for forcible rape in 1986, 10 percent involved persons under 18 years of age. Arrests of youths under age 18 for rape increased 14 percent during the 5-year period 1982 through 1986. Persons under the age of 18 were the offenders in 11 percent of all 1986 robbery clearances. Total juvenile arrests for robbery in 1986 were down 16 percent from the 1982 total, while the number of adult arrests for this offense showed little change over that time period. Only 8 percent of the national aggravated assault clearances by arrest involved persons under 18, while 21 percent of all burglary offenses led to the arrest of people under age 18. Larceny-theft and motor vehicle theft are common forms of juvenile crime, with persons under age 18 accounting for 32 percent and 39 percent respectively of all 1986 arrests for offenses falling in those two categories. Between 1985 and 1986, arrests of persons under 18 were up 19 percent for these two kinds of offenses.

Arson was added to the Crime Index in 1979 in response to national concern over rapidly rising arson rates. Of special significance to our study of juvenile delinquency is the fact that 1986 arrest statistics for arson demonstrated a higher percentage of juvenile involvement than any other Index crime. Arrestees under age 18 represented 40 percent of all arson cases cleared by arrest (FBI *Uniform Crime Reports, 1986*, 1987:1, 5, 8, 14, 15, 20, 23, 27, 32, 35, 38, and 39). Wayne Wooden (1985:23–24) warned of an "Arson Epidemic:"

> . . . Children are responsible for two out of every five cases of arson, a share that also appears to be increasing rapidly. And unlike other juvenile crimes, arson is disproportionately a white, middle-class activity . . . (Also see: Karchmer, 1984:78–83; and Schaaf, 1986:16–19).

Status Offenses   By far, the largest amount of law violating behavior by American youth falls into those vague areas collectively referred to as "status offenses." In contrast to crimes—specific and punishable offenses whether committed by adults or juveniles—status offenses are violations that are applicable only to juveniles. They cover such behavior as school truancy, the purchase and consumption of alcoholic beverages, knowingly associating with immoral persons, running away from home, being beyond parental control, and curfew violations. While status offenses may vary from place to place and in the consistency and seriousness of law enforcement, they are considered violations of the codified laws of a state or municipality as are traditional crimes such as

Every year hundreds of thousands of American youths are arrested for violating state laws, as well as municipal and county ordinances. These data are collected and published annually as a part of the FBI *Uniform Crime Reports.*

assault and robbery. The difference is that the conduct described as a "status offense" is illegal only if the offender happens to have the social and legal status of a "juvenile," defined in most jurisdictions as a person under 18 years of age. In New York state, a status offender is defined as a child under 16 who does not attend school or "who is incorrigible or ungovernable or habitually disobedient and beyond the lawful control of parents or other lawful authority" (Diegmueller, 1987:15). Critics argue that such legal definitions and codes of conduct are sufficiently numerous and vague as to result in great disparity in law enforcement and thereby attach undeserved criminal stigma to many thousands of young people. In 1971 more than half the referrals to juvenile court were status offenders (Manley, 1979:23).

Status offenses, as an appendage to criminal law especially designed for wayward youths, appeared very early in American jurisprudence, reflective of conservative and traditional concern with child rearing and character development. Such laws, while often appearing today as arbitrary and intrusive, were based on the state's generally accepted role as *parens patriae*. This Latin phrase imputes to the state the ultimate parental authority over citizens who demonstrate a need for protection and direction because of age, infirmity, immaturity, or some other condition that limits personal responsibility. Although idealistic in origin, the widespread application of juvenile status ordinances prior to 1965 resulted in the incarceration of a tremendous number of children and youths. For example,

> Wisconsin researchers found that nearly 41 percent of the state's detained youths were status offenders. Studies conducted in Arizona, California, Utah, and Delaware produced similar findings (Diegmueller, 1987:14).

Since the mid 1960s, through a series of landmark decisions from the United States Supreme Court (detailed in Chapter 12), society has become more aware of children as individuals and more sensitive to their legal rights. Reforms have been instituted that soften the treatment and adjudication of status offenders. For example, Wisconsin and California no longer send status offenders to correctional institutions. Seventeen other states have passed laws that separate status offenders from juvenile criminals under varying conditions. Under the Juvenile Justice and Delinquency Prevention Act of 1974, a state desiring federal funding for delinquency prevention must refrain from placing in detention or correctional facilities children who are charged with status offenses.

There is growing support for the idea that the large majority of status offenders should not be arrested and that their cases should be removed from the juvenile justice system. These advocates contend that the juvenile court should be reserved for youths who commit more serious offenses. Nevertheless, the 1986 *Uniform Crime Reports* reveal that many thousands of youngsters were arrested for status offenses. For example, Table 3–1 lists over 132,000 arrests of persons under age 18 for violation of liquor laws, 72,627 for curfew and loitering law violations, and 138,386 for running away from home. The differential treatment sought for the youngsters in these categories is epitomized in a sign on the office wall of Doug Gibson, Executive Director of a Youth Crisis Center in Oklahoma City (Manley, 1979:23). The sign is a simple reminder and appeal for understanding of the special and common problems of youth: "HUCK FINN WAS A STATUS OFFENDER." To those who recall Mark Twain's story, Huckleberry Finn as a truant and runaway was indeed a status offender (Manley, 1979:23). Moreover, as is shown in a later section of this chapter, most of us were probably status offenders at one time or another!

Male and Female Involvement in Juvenile Delinquency   Table 3–2 divides the number of arrests of persons under age 18 in 1986 into separate categories for male and female offenders. The *Uniform Crime Reports* consistently reveal that male juveniles are arrested, on average, nearly four times more often than females for most offenses. This male/female disparity continues in those cases that are processed by juvenile courts and among young people who are institutionalized as a consequence of their delinquent behavior. Exceptions to the pattern of higher arrest percentages for males is the incidence of arrests of females under 18 years of age for prostitution and the status offense of running away from home. For example, 1,442 females under age 18 were arrested for prostitution in 1986. However, we must keep in mind that these statistics reflect the traditional societal practice of exercising more rigorous sanctions on females than males for sexual offenses. Economically speaking, female prostitution would be negligible without a male "market," and "customers" are seldom arrested. Running away continues to be an especially common recourse of young females to situations that appear untenable to them, and rates and percentages for this offense are relatively stable from one year to the next.

TABLE 3–2
Juvenile Arrests According to Sex, 1986.

Offenses	Number of Arrests Under Age 18	Percent[a] Male	Percent[a] Female
All Offenses	1,747,675	78	22
Crime Index:			
Violent Crimes[b]	71,709	89	11
Property Crimes[c]	569,696	80	20
Other Selected Crime Categories:			
Vandalism	95,479	91	9
Prostitution and commercialized vice	2,192	34	66
Weapons (carrying, possessing, etc.)	25,170	94	6
Drug abuse violations	68,351	86	14
Liquor law violations	132,335	74	26
Curfew law violations	72,627	74	26
Running away	138,586	42	58

[a]Percentages are rounded to nearest whole number.

[b]Violent Crimes are offenses of murder, forcible rape, robbery, and aggravated assault.

[c]Property Crimes are offenses of burglary, larceny-theft, motor vehicle theft, and arson.

Source: Based on data derived from Federal Bureau of Investigation, *Uniform Crime Reports: Crime in the United States, 1986.* Washington, D.C.: U.S. Government Printing Office. 1987. Tables 34 and 35, pp. 176 and 178.

The percentages of male and female participation in the two general categories of the Crime Index (as summarized under that head in Table 3-2) have remained fairly constant in recent years. However, larceny-theft and motor vehicle theft showed significant increases in involvement by youthful females in 1986. Females were arrested for larceny-theft more than for any other offense, and 25 percent of all female arrestees for this crime were under 25 years of age. "From 1985, arrests for motor vehicle theft of persons under age 18 went up 19 percent, with arrests of males in this age group up 20 percent and those of females up 14 percent" (FBI *Uniform Crime Reports*, 1986:35).

Among the juvenile arrest data for "Selected Crime Categories" reported in Table 3-2, there have been significant increases in the proportion of female arrests for drug abuse, infractions of liquor laws, and curfew violations. For example, arrests of minor females for violating laws covering alcoholic beverages increased from 22 percent in 1982 to 26 percent of all juvenile arrests for that offense in 1986. While such increases are still moderate, they are interpreted by some observers as indicative of the slow but steady breakdown of the double standard for male/female behavior that for so long has dominated western culture.

The Racial and Ethnic Factor in Juvenile Delinquency   The term **"racial group"** applies to *"those minorities, and corresponding majorities, that are classified according to obvious physical differences"* (Schaefer, 1979:9). Among the obvious attributes used to differentiate and classify racial groups are skin color, facial features, and hair color and texture.

There are at least four races represented in the population of the United States. Whites, although a numerical majority, may be traced to over a score of different national origins in Europe. The black segment of our population traces its origins to a wide spectrum of ancient African nations. United States citizens of Asian or Pacific Islands backgrounds have roots reaching back to China, Japan, and many other diverse cultures and nationalities. American Indians and Alaskan Natives are descendants of the original and indigenous populations of the geographical areas now included in the United States. Blacks, Asians/Pacific Islanders, and American Indians/Alaskan Natives are numerically smaller groups than whites and are considered to be racial minorities.

The racial background of juvenile delinquents has received considerable attention from law enforcement agencies and criminologists, who seek to understand this antisocial form of behavior and the offenders. This focus was intensified by the discovery that racial minorities do not always manifest the same level of delinquency involvement as do members of the dominant racial group. For example, official FBI Crime Reports consistently show that young blacks are disproportionately overrepresented in juvenile arrest statistics (Table 3-3). While blacks comprise only about 12 percent of the total United States population, in 1986 they accounted for nearly 29 percent of Index Crime Arrests under 18 years of age.

TABLE 3-3

Number and Percent of Juvenile Arrests by Racial Groups, 1986.

	White		Black		American Indian/ Alaskan Native		Asian or Pacific Islander	
	Number	Percent	Number	Percent	Number	Percent	Number	Percent
Index Crimes	443,344	69.2	182,016	28.7	6,321	.9	7,747	1.2
Violent crimes[a]	33,344	46.4	37,230	52.2	407	.6	561	.8
Property crimes[b]	410,189	71.7	144,786	25.4	5,914	1.6	7,186	1.3
Non-Index Crimes	859,537	78.0	223,755	20.3	8,249	.7	11,331	1.0
TOTAL ARRESTS	1,302,881	74.8	405,771	23.3	14,570	.8	19,078	1.1

[a] Violent crimes are offenses of murder, forcible rape, robbery, and aggravated assault.

[b] Property crimes are offenses of burglary, larceny-theft, motor vehicle theft, and arson.

Source: Based on data derived from Federal Bureau of Investigation, *Uniform Crime Reports: Crime in the United States, 1986.* Washington, D.C.: United States Government Printing Office. 1987. Table 38, p. 183.

As indicated by the FBI data given in Table 3-3, white youths are much more likely than black youths to be arrested for property crimes, accounting for nearly 72 percent of all property crime arrests of persons under age 18. At the same time, the probability of young blacks being arrested for crimes of violence is higher than for young whites, accounting for nearly 52 percent of all arrests for crimes of that type by persons under 18 years of age. The great majority of violent assaults by blacks are committed against members of their own racial group.

According to Table 3-3, the official tabulation of participation in delinquency by young American Indian/Alaskan Natives and Asian/Pacific Islanders is proportionately insignificant. Their population size, as well as the number of arrests made among them, are very small compared to the much larger white and black populations and the delinquency involvement of youngsters from those two groups.

Minority groups that are designated by **ethnicity** are *differentiated from the dominant group on the basis of cultural rather than physical differences* (Schaefer, 1979:9). Many millions of people, representing every other nation on earth, have immigrated into this country. Over time, as they learned and accepted the language, norms, and beliefs of the dominant culture, most of these new citizens and their descendants were assimilated and "Americanized." However, some groups retained a residual of pride in their "old country" heritage, reflected in ethnic values, traditions, and practices that have been perpetuated to distinguish particular subcultures within the United States.

As in their studies of racial backgrounds, criminologists have found that official statistics on juvenile delinquency also vary with ethnicity. Of special importance in this regard is the large ethnic minority classified by government agencies as Hispanic or Chicano, which includes anyone of Spanish, Mexican, Puerto Rican, Cuban, or other Latin American background in the United States. Table 3–4, based on FBI *Uniform Crime Reports* for 1986, indicates that Hispanic young people account for a disproportionately large share of juvenile arrests.

In 1986, there were 1,563,204 arrests of persons under age in the United States. Although Hispanic youths comprise just 8.3 percent of our national population under age 18 (*United States Census, 1980*), they accounted for 11.8 percent of the total juvenile arrests in 1986 (FBI *Uniform Crime Reports*, 1987). In Table 3–4, comparisons of juvenile arrests for Hispanic and non-Hispanic youths indicate that Hispanics under age 18 are proportionally overrepresented in arrest statistics for both violent and property crime categories (14.5 percent and 11.8 percent respectively). These proportions of Hispanic participation in juvenile crime have remained consistent over the 5-year period 1982–1986 (*FBI Uniform Crime Reports*, 1983; 1987). The reader is cautioned to avoid racial and

TABLE 3–4
Juvenile Arrests: Hispanic and Non-Hispanic Comparisons, 1986.

| | Under 18 Years of Age | | | | | |
| | Number of Arrests | | | Percent Distribution | | |
	Total	Hispanic	Non-Hispanic	Total	Hispanic	Non-Hispanic
TOTAL	1,563,204	183,772	1,379,432	100.0	11.8	88.2
Violent crime[a]	61,906	8,972	52,934	100.0	14.5	85.5
Property crime[b]	497,783	58,769	439,014	100.0	11.8	88.2
Crime Index Total	559,689	67,741	491,948	100.0	12.1	87.9
Non-Crime Index Total	1,003,515	116,031	887,484	100.0	11.6	88.4

[a]Violent crimes include murder, forcible rape, robbery, and aggravated assault.

[b]Property crimes include burglary, larceny-theft, motor vehicle theft, and arson.

Source: Derived from Federal Bureau of Investigation, *Uniform Crime Reports: Crime in the United States, 1986.* Washington, D.C.: U.S. Government Printing Office. 1987. Table 39, p. 186.

ethnic stereotypes of criminal involvement based on statistical summaries; as Chapter 4 demonstrates, there is no valid biological explanation for high rates of juvenile delinquency for any group. The most plausible explanations point to social forces that impact upon many members of these minority groups which tend to generate delinquent behaviors.

Place of Residence and Arrest Statistics

For as long as arrest statistics have been compiled in the United States, numbers of arrests have been highest in the large cities, moderate in suburban communities, and lowest in rural areas. This numerical pattern partially reflects the fact that a larger part of the population has lived in urban areas for well over a century. However, the likelihood of an individual being arrested also has consistently varied with place of residence. For example, in 1982, cities with over 250,000 residents had an arrest rate of 7,856 per 100,000 inhabitants; in suburban areas the rate was 4,341 per 100,000 residents; and in rural counties, it was 3,501 per 100,000 persons. In addition to heavier population concentrations in cities, the more formal organization and strictly enforced norms associated with urban social life also contribute to the higher incidence and rates of arrest in those areas. While the number of offenses cleared by arrest reflects a heavily urban concentration, in 1982, for the first time in our history, the percentage of persons under age 18 arrested for violent and property crimes in suburban areas exceeded the percentage of persons under 18 arrested for those offenses in larger cities. Several studies have suggested that this modified geographical pattern of arrests reflects the centrifugal expansion of urban population and concomitant social problems into the smaller communities ringing the central cities (Cassidy, 1979; Palen, 1975; Harries, 1974). The tendency toward the equalization of arrest rates between large cities and the suburbs also may indicate a greater sensitivity of law enforcement agencies and the public to the incidence of crime and delinquency in middle class, suburban districts. Table 3–5 summarizes the 1986 arrest statistics for persons under 18 years of age according to urban, suburban, and rural areas.

Urban and suburban youngsters are very similar in the kinds of crimes for which they are arrested, with each group averaging about 20 percent of Index offenses. In contrast, rural youths are more likely to be involved in less serious crimes and status offenses than their urban and suburban counterparts (although the difference is not dramatic).

Juvenile Court Statistics

After a juvenile is arrested for an alleged delinquent act, a number of alternative courses may be followed before final settlement of the case. As detailed in Chapter 12, the seriousness of the alleged offense, the number and nature of prior contacts the suspect has had with police, the quality of the offender's relationships with family and school, and other factors determine whether the case is to be treated informally, dismissed or informal probation offered, or if the

---

TABLE 3-5

Offenses Cleared by Arrest of Persons Under 18 Years of Age by Urban, Suburban, and Rural Place of Residence, 1986.

Population Group	Crime Index Total	Violent Crime[a]	Property Crime[b]
TOTAL CITIES: 9,279 cities; populations 151,832,000:			
Total clearances	2,132,779	534,370	1,598,409
Percent under 18	19.5	9.1	23.0
SUBURBAN AREAS[c] population 90,510,000:			
Total clearances	829,354	173,656	655,698
Percent under 18	21.3	10.4	24.2
RURAL COUNTIES population 28,651,000:			
Total clearances	120,123	32,707	87,416
Percent under 18	15.8	6.3	19.3

[a]Violent crimes include murder, forcible rape, robbery, and aggravated assault.

[b]Property crimes include burglary, larceny-theft, and motor vehicle theft. Data are not included for the property crime of arson.

[c]Includes suburban city and county law enforcement agencies within metropolitan areas. Excludes central cities. Suburban cities are also included in other city groups.

Source: Derived from Federal Bureau of Investigation, *Uniform Crime Reports: Crime in the United States, 1986.* Washington, D.C.: U.S. Government Printing Office. 1987. Table 23, pp. 161–162.

---

youth will be formally charged in a juvenile court. Most alleged and actual cases of juvenile delinquency are filtered out and diverted away from the ultimate court confrontation that could lead to the youth being placed in a correctional institution. Only a small percentage of suspected juvenile delinquents are actually arrested; about half of those individuals arrested under the age of 18 are referred to juvenile courts (Nimick et al., 1987:3); and less than 10 percent of the cases disposed by juvenile courts result in commitment to custodial institutions. Although annual compilations of juvenile court data are a more reliable measure of the workloads of the nation's juvenile courts, the nationwide network of over 3,000 reporting juvenile courts also has provided a data-gathering system, giving another crude overview of the more serious dimensions of juvenile delinquency in the United States.

The National Juvenile Court Statistical Reporting System Program was initiated in 1926 by the Children's Bureau, a division of the United States Department of Labor which issued annual reports on cases of children processed through a sample of juvenile courts. These reports included juveniles who had violated a state law or municipal ordinance, as well as children who were dependent or neglected and who required special proceedings to determine custody or adoption, permission for medical treatment, and other miscellaneous conditions. In short, the Juvenile Court Statistics Reporting Program was intended to furnish an index of the general nature and extent of the kinds of problems being brought before the juvenile courts. For our purposes we will consider just those juvenile court proceedings focusing on delinquent behavior. In 1975, the Juvenile Court Statistical Reporting System was transferred to the National Center for Juvenile Justice and Delinquency Prevention in the United States Department of Justice. The practice of publishing annual summary reports has continued.

Methodology   Through the years, data collection from juvenile courts has become more extensive and systematic. In order to document the volume of delinquency, current practice attempts to collect data from every juvenile court in the nation. Reliability of reporting techniques is enhanced through the distribution of standardized forms, instructions, and definitions of key terms. Officers of each court are asked to submit an annual report to the National Center for Juvenile Justice containing limited but specific information about each case processed through the court during the preceding year.

In 1983, 2,754 of a possible 3,096 counties (reporting units) in the nation provided data on delinquent cases. This data set represented approximately 90 percent of the nation's delinquency child population. However, due to reporting irregularities, data from only 1,480 counties could be used to generate national estimates of petitioned cases, and similarly, 1,378 counties were used to produce estimates of nonpetitioned cases. (Nimick, et al., 1987:21.)

The 1983 data are summarized in Tables 3–6 A, 3–6 B, and 3–6 C.

TABLE 3-6A

Estimated Number of U.S. Juvenile Court Petitioned Delinquency Case Dispositions: 1983.

Size of County	ALL COUNTIES		SAMPLE COUNTIES			Reported Petitioned Cases Disposed	Estimated Petitioned Cases Disposed
	Total Number	1983[a] Child Population Served	Number in Sample	1983 Child Population Served	% of Child Population Served		
Over -999,999	26	5,354,000	22	4,699,000	87.8	103,473	117,900
500,000–999,999	63	5,159,000	37	3,127,000	60.6	89,205	147,200
250,000–499,999	98	4,205,000	46	1,843,000	43.8	34,506	78,700
100,000–249,999	228	4,282,000	111	2,014,000	47.0	41,573	88,400
50,000–99,999	368	3,247,000	154	1,330,000	41.0	22,120	54,000
25,000–49,999	610	2,728,000	245	1,087,000	39.9	18,585	46,600
10,000–24,999	955	1,985,000	447	923,000	46.5	14,160	30,500
Under -10,000	748	536,000	418	282,000	52.6	4,434	8,400
TOTAL	3,096	27,460,000	1,480	15,305,000	55.7	328,056	571,700

TABLE 3–6B

Estimated Number of U.S. Juvenile Court Nonpetitioned Delinquency Case Dispositions: 1983.

	ALL COUNTIES		SAMPLE COUNTIES			Reported	Estimated
Size of County	Total Number	1983a Child Population Served	Number in Sample	1983 Child Population Served	% of Child Population Served	Nonpetitioned Cases Disposed	Nonpetitioned Cases Disposed
Over –999,999	26	5,354,000	22	4,699,000	87.8	91,390	104,100
500,000–999,999	63	5,159,000	37	3,118,000	60.4	107,695	178,200
250,000–499,999	98	4,205,000	41	1,657,000	39.4	35,409	89,800
100,000–249,999	228	4,282,000	99	1,814,000	42.4	46,621	110,100
50,000–99,999	368	3,247,000	150	1,332,000	41.0	37,438	91,300
25,000–49,999	610	2,728,000	217	975,000	35.7	23,024	64,400
10,000–24,999	955	1,985,000	410	854,000	43.0	23,606	54,900
Under –10,000	748	536,000	402	270,000	50.4	5,579	11,100
TOTAL	3,096	27,497,000	1,378	14,719,000	53.5	370,762	703,900

TABLE 3–6C

Estimated Total U.S. Juvenile Court Delinquency Case Dispositions: 1983.

Size of County	Total Number	1983a Child Population Served	Estimated Petitioned Cases Disposed	Estimated Nonpetitioned Cases Disposed	Estimated Total Cases Disposed
Over –999,999	26	5,354,000	117,900	104,100	222,000
500,000–999,999	63	5,159,000	147,200	178,200	325,400
250,000–499,999	98	4,205,000	78,700	89,800	168,500
100,000–249,999	228	4,282,000	88,400	110,100	198,500
50,000 –99,999	368	3,247,000	54,000	91,300	145,300
25,000– 49,999	610	2,728,000	46,600	64,400	111,000
10,000– 24,999	955	1,985,000	30,500	54,900	85,400
Under – 10,000	748	536,000	8,400	11,100	19,500
TOTAL	3,096	27,497,000	571,700	703,900	1,275,600

a Child population figures were produced by the National Center for Juvenile Justice using population counts generated by the 1980 Decennial Census. The child population is defined as the number of children from age 10 to the upper age of jurisdiction.

Source: Nimick, E.H., Snyder, H.N., Sullivan, D.P., & Tierney, N.J. *Juvenile Court Statistics, 1983*. National Center for Juvenile Justice. Office of Juvenile Justice and Delinquency Prevention. U.S. Department of Justice. June 1987. Tables 10A–10C, p. 22.

From such collections of data, the National Center for Juvenile Justice estimates the total number of cases of delinquency disposed of by juvenile courts during a given year. For example, in 1983, the estimated total of juvenile court dispositions was 1,275,600. This figure was then broken down into estimated subtotals for cases disposed of in one of two ways: petitioned cases and nonpetitioned cases.

Petitioned cases are those that appear on the official court calendar for adjudication by the judge or referee through the filing of a petition, affidavit, or other legal instrument used to initiate court action. Nonpetitioned cases are those cases which duly authorized court personnel screen for adjustment short of filing a formal petition or affidavit . . . The 'nonpetition' category includes cases which probation officers handle and cases petitioned but dropped or withdrawn prior to scheduling a formal hearing (Nimick et al., 1987:5).

In 1983, an estimated total of 571,700 petitioned cases and an estimated total of 703,900 nonpetitioned cases were disposed of by juvenile courts. In addition, annual compilations and estimates are made of juvenile court cases by type of offense, sex, race, age, and other characteristics of the offenders. The cases also are compiled based on their occurrence in urban, suburban, and rural areas.

Findings

Official data collected from the juvenile courts and disseminated by the National Center for Juvenile Justice present the same general picture of delinquency and delinquents as do the FBI *Uniform Crime Reports*. The volume of delinquency cases processed through the juvenile courts steadily increased to a high of 1,445,400 cases in 1980 and slowly declined thereafter to about 1,275,600 cases in 1983. In 1983 the large majority (77 percent) of young people appearing before a juvenile court were males, about half of whom were referred for property crimes. In the same year, nearly one-fourth of the referrals were females, primarily referred for status offenses. Table 3–7 charts a gradual increase in female involvement in delinquency from 19 percent of the total cases in 1957 to a peak of 26 percent in 1972–1974, after which females consistently accounted for about 23 percent of cases each year. While these trends run contrary to arrest statistics compiled by the FBI *Uniform Crime Reports* which point to a slow but steady increase in female delinquency in recent years, the discrepancy may be accounted for by procedures that favor informal treatment of females outside the juvenile justice system. Thus we may have the paradox that the percentage of female arrests is increasing while, simultaneously, the percentage of female delinquents appearing before juvenile courts remains constant.

Although whites account for about three-fourths of all cases disposed of by juvenile courts in the United States, the number of blacks and Hispanics brought before juvenile courts is out of proportion to their share of the national population. Smith et al. (1980) reported that minority youths in juvenile courts are more likely to have had prior referrals, and more often are charged with crimes against people than are whites. These researchers presented evidence that racial minorities are less likely to receive lenient treatment such as probation and are more likely to be committed to correctional institutions by juvenile courts than are whites for the same offenses.

The National Center for Juvenile Justice and Delinquency Prevention,

TABLE 3-7

Estimated Number and Percentage of Juvenile Court Delinquency Cases by Gender: 1957-1983.

Year	Male		Female	
	Number	**Percent**	**Number**	**Percent**
1957	358,000	81	82,000	19
1958	383,000	81	87,000	19
1959	393,000	81	90,000	19
1960	415,000	81	99,000	19
1961	408,000	81	95,000	19
1962	450,000	81	104,500	19
1963	485,000	81	116,000	19
1964	555,000	81	131,000	19
1965	555,000	80	142,000	20
1966	593,000	80	152,000	20
1967	640,000	79	171,000	21
1968	708,000	79	191,000	21
1969	760,000	77	228,000	23
1970	799,500	76	252,000	24
1971	845,500	75	279,000	25
1972	827,500	74	285,000	26
1973	845,300	74	298,000	26
1974	927,000	74	325,700	26
1975	1,001,700	76	315,300	24
1976	1,092,700	76	339,000	24
1977	1,063,200	77	326,400	23
1978	1,055,000	78	303,800	22
1979	1,058,000	77	315,800	23
1980	1,121,200	78	324,200	22
1981	1,024,500	76	326,000	24
1982	989,900	77	302,600	23
1983	980,400	77	295,200	23

Source: Nimick, E.H., Snyder, H.N., Sullivan, D.P. & Tierney, N.J. *Juvenile Court Statistics, 1983.* National Center for Juvenile Justice. Office of Juvenile Justice and Delinquency Prevention. U.S. Department of Justice. June, 1987. Table 2, p. 12.

with the annual inflow of data on juvenile court case dispositions, continues to examine the geographical and residential patterns of delinquency. Table 3-8 depicts the urban, semi-urban, and rural distribution of juvenile court case dispositions over the 27-year-period, 1957-1983. It is clear that about two-thirds of the delinquency cases are consistently adjudicated in urban areas; about one-fourth are disposed of in semi-urban jurisdictions; and the remaining small proportion are handled by courts in rural areas. In other words, the larger and more congested the population and settlement pattern of an area, the greater the number of cases being processed through juvenile courts. These findings regarding racial/ethnic minority overrepresentation and the geographical/residential distribution of juvenile court case dispositions are in close harmony with findings based on arrest statistics in the FBI *Uniform Crime Reports*. There is agreement among most investigators that delinquent behavior

---

TABLE 3-8

Estimated Number and Percent of Juvenile Court Delinquency Case Dispositions by Type of Area: 1957-1983[a]

Year	Urban Number	Urban Percent	Semi-urban Number	Semi-urban Percent	Rural Number	Rural Percent
1957	280,000	63	113,000	26	47,000	11
1958	298,000	63	120,000	26	52,000	11
1959	295,000	61	127,000	26	61,000	13
1960	344,000	67	128,000	25	42,000	8
1961	350,000	69	119,000	24	34,000	7
1962	383,000	69	132,500	24	39,500	7
1963	414,000	69	146,000	24	41,000	7
1964	456,000	67	181,000	26	49,000	7
1965	470,000	68	183,000	26	43,000	6
1966	490,000	66	206,500	28	48,000	6
1967	525,000	65	235,300	29	50,700	6
1968	588,200	65	256,400	29	55,200	6
1969	646,600	66	280,800	28	61,100	6
1970	686,000	66	296,800	28	69,200	6
1971	717,000	64	331,000	29	77,000	7
1972	692,000	62	345,000	31	75,500	7
1973	694,700	61	362,000	31	87,000	8
1974	776,600	62	375,800	30	100,300	8
1975	753,600	57	464,400	35	98,900	8
1976	931,800	65	406,700	28	93,200	7
1977	875,100	63	406,900	29	107,600	8
1978	854,700	63	386,600	28	117,400	9
1979	875,300	64	390,800	28	108,400	8
1980	1,012,900	70	337,700	23	94,800	7
1981	928,900	69	318,100	23	103,500	8
1982	876,100	68	325,900	25	90,500	7
1983	876,200	69	306,700	24	92,700	7

[a] The classification of a county as being urban, semi-urban, or rural is based on information developed by the U.S. Bureau of the Census during an analysis of its decennial census data. Therefore, when a county is classified in 1970 based on the census description of the percent of its total population living in urban areas, the county maintains this classification until the next decennial census. Throughout the 1970s, the composition of the urban, semi-urban character of each county was reassessed. Paralleling the general increase in the urban character of the nation between 1970 and 1980, the reclassification resulted in an increase in the number of urban counties and a decrease in the number of semi-urban and rural counties. With this redistribution of counties, it is inappropriate to compare the number of cases handled within each type of area over time without considering the changing compositions of the "type of area" groupings.

Source: Nimick, E.H., Snyder, H.N., Sullivan, D.P., & Tierney, N.J. *Juvenile Court Statistics*, 1983. National Center for Juvenile Justice. Office of Juvenile Justice and Delinquency Prevention. U.S. Department of Justice. June, 1987. Table 3, p. 13.

by females, whites, and middle and upper classes is generally underestimated and underrepresented in official statistics.

THE COMPOSITE DELINQUENT PROFILE: TYPICAL OR STEREOTYPICAL?

By combining findings and conclusions based on the two national official sources of juvenile delinquency data, it is possible to construct a composite picture of the "typical" delinquent. According to annual arrest statistics compiled by the FBI and the records of case dispositions from juvenile courts, this composite juvenile delinquent is most likely to be male, between 15 and 18 years of age, a member of a racial or ethnic minority, and to have a prior record of both status and criminal offenses. In addition, Cantwell (1983) and numerous others have reported that juvenile offenders reflect a much higher incidence of unstable home life because of parental separation, divorce, desertion, or death. They are also characterized by chronic poverty, little motivation or success in school, and few occupational opportunities. The probability is also statistically high that officially defined juvenile delinquents reside in lower class slum neighborhoods. A strong linkage also appears between the violent behavior of some juveniles and their having been exposed to extreme abuse and violence within their own families (Cantwell, 1983:37).

Unfortunately, such composite summaries—based on the simple statistical majority and averages—of arrested and/or adjudicated youths—portray an over-simplified and distorted image of juvenile delinquents and the delinquency problem. The next section of this chapter demonstrates that the generalizations that comprise the "composite" or "typical" delinquent are based on data that have several serious deficiencies. A vast number of delinquents do not fit the statistical model. In addition, in recent years several studies have sparked a vigorous debate regarding the so-called "correlates of delinquency." While gender, social class, and race/ethnicity remain statistically significant in describing a great deal of juvenile delinquency, some investigators consider these characteristics as largely illusory as causal variables (Elliott and Huizinga, 1983: Hindelang et al., 1979; Tittle et al., 1978). Finally, such broad-stroked portrayals of the "typical" juvenile delinquent may be more stereotypical than typical. It has been repeatedly suggested that youth possessing certain easily identifiable traits and backgrounds may be socially prejudged and thereby encouraged to follow a course leading to delinquent behavior (Matza, 1964).

Limitations of Official Delinquency Data

Arrest Statistics
A decided advantage of the annual FBI crime reports is that juvenile arrest data are now available for almost all cities, and the *Uniform Crime Reports* cover more than 95 percent of the nation's population. However,

there are several intrinsic and probably insoluble problems associated with the use of data based on arrests. First, the number of arrests is a questionable index of crime and delinquency because law enforcement motives, techniques, and success vary widely from time to time and from place to place. For example, a low arrest rate may indicate little criminal or delinquent activity in a particular community. A low arrest rate can also mean that the police force is inactive or ineffective in that area. Conversely, a high arrest rate may mean that there is a high level of criminal and delinquent activity in a particular city. A high arrest rate also can mean that the police are making arrests on slight pretext or pursuing a highly publicized "war on crime and delinquency" for political purposes. In some places campaigns emanating from city halls to "make our streets safe" are not uncommon during election years. Police activity then may be intensified as large numbers of vagrants, prostitutes, gamblers, delinquents, and other "undesirables" are caught in the police dragnet. Much less publicized is the rapid release of most "suspects" and the inflation of local arrest statistics (Haskell and Yablonsky, 1978).

Similarly, researchers argue that conclusions based upon official statistics should be tempered by the observation that law enforcement is often more rigorous in lower-class neighborhoods inhabited largely by racial and ethnic minorities (Geis, 1972:65). Smith and Visher (1981) examined variations in police arrest practices. They found that the decision to take a suspect into custody is influenced by such extralegal factors as the dispositional preferences of victims, the race and demeanor of the suspect, and the presence of by-standers. "Specifically, members of socially disadvantaged groups such as blacks and youths are more likely to be taken into custody independent of the seriousness of their behavior" (Smith and Visher, 1981:167). The point here is that while the FBI has attempted to standardize definitions of various crimes for law enforcement personnel and agencies participating in the Uniform Crime Reporting Program, no way has yet been devised to standardize the subjective decision-making processes involved in making arrests which can statistically inflate or deflate the participation of some groups in crime and delinquency.

A second fundamental problem with the *UCR* arrest statistics is that they tell us nothing about juvenile crime that is undetected, unsolved, or unreported. According to popular belief, the police, astute television detectives, and federal agents, like the Royal Canadian Mounted Police, "always get their man." On the contrary, there is overwhelming evidence that numbers of arrests and court referrals reveal only the visible tip of the crime/delinquency iceberg.

Many violent crimes often go unreported. According to the Department of Justice (1983), many victims fail to report assaults and thefts because they feel that these are "private matters" or that the police can or will do nothing about them. Probably most of the status offenses and less serious instances of juvenile delinquency never become a matter of public record or concern. Many thousands of juveniles are confronted daily by parents, teachers, neighbors, and law enforcement officers who administer informal warnings, censures, punishments, or other controls over nonconforming youthful behavior. Such informal procedures are especially characteristic of small towns and rural areas, as illustrated by the youthful Halloween disturbance described at the end of Chapter 1.

Juvenile Court Dispositions   The most serious problem encountered with annual compilations of juvenile court cases is the lack of representation of several states. In 1983, Minnesota, Nevada, Oklahoma, and Rhode Island failed to submit reports; or, irregularities and errors in recording juvenile court dispositions made their data unacceptable. Such deficiencies in data collection represent a longstanding and apparently insoluble problem. As another example, in 1974, Florida, Illinois, and Maryland were not represented in the national summary of juvenile court case dispositions. Thus, while official surveys of juvenile court proceedings are helpful in measuring court caseloads at a given time and trends over time, the incomplete and estimated nature of the data invalidate their use for making comparisons between years and between some states and communities.

A second dilemma confounding the use of juvenile court statistics centers directly on the estimating procedures used by the National Center for Juvenile Justice in projecting from the sample of reporting courts the total court activity and populations served in given areas. Periodic changes in boundary lines, population size, and composition of many juvenile court jurisdictions make longitudinal comparisons of court activity tentative and often conjectural.

Over half a century of recording and reporting of juvenile court case dispositions passed before steps were taken to correct or reduce the effects of those basic methodological flaws. Consequently, a number of years of consistent data gathering and analysis will be needed before The National Juvenile Court Reporting System Program can achieve a high degree of longitudinal and comparative credibility, beyond very recent years.

The third limitation of juvenile court statistics is that these accumulated data and annual reports cannot serve as a viable indicator of the extent of juvenile delinquency that exists in any county, court jurisdiction, state, or the nation as a whole. While the point is clearly made by The National Center for Juvenile Justice that the juvenile court statistical reports are designed to measure annual court caseloads, researchers should be cautioned not to read any more than that into the data. Although the reporting counties in 1983 represented about 90 percent of the national delinquent population, the *usable* juvenile court data from 1,480 counties that was projected to estimate the total number of petitioned cases (based on police referrals) disposed or processed through juvenile courts could represent as little as 55.7 percent of those youngsters apprehended for juvenile crime (Table 3–6 A). Thus, the representativeness of the sample is highly questionable. At the same time, every referral of a juvenile to a court is regarded as a case. Therefore, a youth referred to a court three times during the course of a year is counted as three cases. While this procedure is appropriate for measuring court caseloads, it would contribute to inflation of the data if we were measuring the number of juvenile delinquents in a given area.

UNOFFICIAL SOURCES OF DELINQUENCY INFORMATION

Self-Report Studies

Some of the limitations of the FBI *Uniform Crime Reports* and the *Juvenile Court Statistics* as indices of the scope and nature of the national delinquency problem are overcome by self-report studies. A large number of researchers, rather than relying on official reports of arrests and court dispositions, have drawn samples of various populations and have directly inquired through survey questionnaires about their respondents' previous delinquent behavior. This approach, aimed at adolescents and young adults not identified by law enforcement agencies as juvenile offenders, is designed to reveal and measure undetected and unreported instances of juvenile delinquency. These self-report studies clearly show that delinquent behavior is far more common than is indicated by official data (e.g., Nye and Short, 1957; Akers, 1964; Jensen and Eve, 1976). Findings from repeated self-report studies led The President's Commission on Law Enforcement and Administration of Justice (1968:55) to conclude that "enormous numbers of young people appear to be involved in delinquent acts." This finding can be generalized to apply to the entire population:

> Evidence indicates that over 90% of all Americans have committed some crime for which they could be incarcerated. The observation does not deny that crime may be more concentrated in some groups, but only that it is unlikely to be absent in others (Bohm, 1986:197).

Self-report surveys can be expensive and time consuming, and the absence of a national unbiased sample presents a virtually insurmountable methodological problem. In spite of these limitations, such studies clearly support the contention that official statistics fail to completely measure the volume of delinquency and the incidence of many specific offenses.

Table 3–9 summarizes data from two self-report surveys, independently administered by the present authors to 555 undergraduate students attending two midwestern state universities in 1987. Nearly all of the subjects were white and they were about equally divided between males and females. Because they were not randomly selected, no assumption can be made that these 555 students accurately represent the total population of youth at risk of committing delinquent behavior, or even the overall student population at their schools. Nevertheless, even within these limitations, some remarkable findings emerged (Table 3–9).

While nearly one-third of the 555 subjects at the two universities had

Anonymous self-report surveys have revealed that virtually every young person has violated some legal statute or ordinance at some time. Juvenile misconduct involves all social classes, all races, and both sexes.

shoplifted, over one-fourth had damaged property and inflicted physical harm to others, four out of five had purchased and/or consumed alcoholic beverages, and about 14 percent had taken an automobile without the owner's permission—less than 4 percent of the subjects had ever been arrested for any reason while under the age of 18! This figure is fairly close to national arrest statistics. In 1986, there were 1,747,675 arrests of persons under age 18 for all offenses, which includes multiple arrests during the year for the same individuals. Even if we assume that this total number of arrests represents 1,747,675 separate individuals, that number still equals just 3.3 percent of the national population under age 18. Based on such information derived from self-report studies, we can conclude that juvenile delinquency is much more common and widespread than official statistics would lead us to believe. The similarity of findings from "State University A" and "State University B" and with those from other self-report studies confirms a reasonable degree of reliability for this measuring technique.

TABLE 3-9

Self-Reported Delinquency Among Students Attending Two Midwestern State Universities.

Type of Offense	State University A (N = 300)		State University B (N = 255)	
WHILE UNDER THE AGE OF 18, DID YOU EVER:	**YES**	**NO**	**YES**	**NO**
1. Get arrested?	3.4%	96.6%	3.8%	96.2%
2. Break into a place?	13.8%	86.2%	15.3%	84.7%
3. Shoplift?	32.3%	67.7%	28.2%	71.8%
4. Steal something worth less than $100? (Do not include shoplifting)	1.1%	98.9%	2.5%	97.5%
5. Steal something worth more than $100?	.5%	99.5%	1.4%	98.6%
6. Beat up or hurt someone on purpose?	26.%	74.%	24.8%	75.2%
7. Get into fist fights or brawls? (Do not include details you counted in item # 6)	33.8%	66.2%	30.4%	69.6%
8. Ruin, break, or damage someone else's property on purpose?	24.1%	75.9%	29.9%	70.1%
9. Take a car without the owner's permission?	13.8%	86.2%	15.%	85.%
10. Have sexual intercourse?	65.5%	34.5%	68.7%	31.3%
11. Violate curfew?	82.8%	17.2%	*	*
12. Skip school without parent's knowledge?	58.6%	43.3%	63.4%	36.6%
13. Defy parents? (Do not include skipping school and curfew violations.)	48.3%	51.7%	60.1%	39.9%
14. Purchase and/or consume alcoholic beverages or illegal drugs?	82.1%	17.9%	84.5%	15.4%

* Data not available

Source: Thompson, W. & Bynum, J. Unpublished data from self-report surveys conducted at two midwestern universities, 1987.

Research conducted by Maynard Erickson and Lamar Empey (1963) demonstrated how data generated from self-report studies can be combined with official statistics on arrests and court referrals to produce a more complete account of juvenile delinquency. They found that court records accurately revealed which juvenile offenders demonstrated persistent patterns of more serious misbehavior, thus facilitating societal identification of juveniles who may have incorporated the delinquent role more decisively into their lifestyles. At the same time, self-report studies help us to comprehend more precisely the magnitude of delinquency among young people.

Critics of self-reports have questioned the honesty of respondents who may falsify their answers to make themselves "look good" by denying that they committed delinquent acts when they actually have done so; and of respondents who may exaggerate their true delinquent acts. Such objections to self-reports are largely overcome by the use of anonymous questionnaires, which tend to frustrate subjects who may view the survey situation and their responses as a status-gaining opportunity. Also, it can be assumed that if respondents falsify information, as many are likely to exaggerate their delinquency as are likely to deny it. Hence, these falsifications will offset each other within a large enough sample.

Travis Hirschi (1969) effectively countered the suspicion about respondents' dishonesty with data derived from police records and his own self-report study of those same youths. He found a strong similarity between the numbers and kinds of self-reported offenses of incarcerated juvenile delinquents and those listed in their official records. While this finding supports arguments for the validity of both measures, Hirschi (1969:64) contended that police records are *less* valid than self-reports as a measure of delinquency:

> As defined, every delinquent act committed by a person is witnessed by him; he cannot commit delinquent acts without knowing it (otherwise, there is nothing to explain). Obviously, the police do not have such omnipresence . . . In short, the records of the police are, on a priori grounds, a weaker measure of the *commission* of delinquent acts than presumably honest self-reports [italics in original].

In addition to aiding researchers in ascertaining the actual dimensions of juvenile delinquency, self-report studies also have challenged the widely held view that since blacks and Hispanics are overrepresented in official statistics, they must have a stronger proclivity toward delinquent behavior. Summarizing a number of self-report studies (Voss, 1963; Winslow, 1967; Chambliss and Nagasawa, 1969; Donovan, 1977), Arnold and Brungardt (1983:152) concluded that:

> . . . analyses consistently indicate that whites' offenses are so similar in number and type to those of the minority groups that the official data appear to be highly distorted. . . . [The] differences revealed do not approach the magnitude of the differences in official data.

Thus, while we cannot claim the absence of empirical documentation (national arrest and juvenile court statistics), that lower-class and minority youths are more likely to be involved in delinquency than their white, middle-class counterparts, self-report studies have made the argument of the so-called "correlates of delinquency" more problematic and less emphatic.

Michael Hindelang and his associates (1979), in their insightful focus on the traditional correlates of delinquency, may have resolved the issue. They reviewed the research literature and found that studies of delinquency that use official records and those utilizing self-report surveys typically have measured different types of behaviors; official data tend to reflect more serious offenses, while self-report studies tend to measure much more common and less serious types of behavior. In other words, the notion that official and self-report methods produce discrepant results with respect to sex, race, and social class is largely illusory because the two methodologies tap different domains of behavior. They noted:

> . . . other evidence from victimization surveys, studies of the reliability and validity of self-reports, and studies of biases in criminal justice processing, suggest that both official data and self-reports provide valid indicators of the demographic characteristics of offenders, *within the domain of behavior effectively tapped by each method* [italics in original] (Hindelang et al., 1979:995).

Victimization Surveys

Another useful source of juvenile delinquency information is the victimization surveys conducted by the United States Department of Justice and a number of private researchers. These studies focus on victims and their recollections of the crimes, the circumstances, and the offenders. Some of the variables included are the age, sex, race, and other demographic characteristics of assailants and victims, the relationship between victim and offender, and the types of crime.

The most ambitious victimization surveys have been conducted by the Law Enforcement Assistance Administration of the Department of Justice, beginning in 1973. This agency, together with the Census Bureau, operationalized an ongoing National Crime Survey to measure the victimization of persons ages 12 and over, households, and commercial establishments. Twice each year data are obtained through interviews with a national sample of approximately 60,000 households (containing about 136,000 individuals) and 15,000 businesses, from which rates of victimization for persons, households, and businesses are generated.

Like self-report studies, victimization surveys have the advantage over arrest and juvenile court statistics in offering an avenue through which to explore and estimate the extent of unreported crimes, especially when victims are allowed to respond anonymously. Law enforcement officers and researchers are convinced that vast numbers of offenses are not brought to the attention of police. For example, forcible rape is grossly underreported. The actual number of forcible rapes is thought to be several times greater than is reflected in official statistics (Barlow, 1987). Many rape victims may understandably shrink from the embarrassment of reporting and detailing the experience to the police and in open court (The President's Commission on Law Enforcement, Task Force Report, 1968). Thus, like self-report studies, victimization surveys are also more likely to uncover information about more serious types of unreported crimes.

Table 3–10, listing the percentage of victimizations *not* reported to the police, clearly establishes the usefulness of such surveys as an adjunct to arrest statistics in achieving a more complete picture of crime and delinquency.

Although there is some variation from city to city in victimization rates, the surveys of both national and city samples have produced findings in agreement with self-report studies; that is, only about a third of all crimes are reported to the police (Klaus et al., 1983). Some types of crime are even more underreported. In addition to rape, all other forms of personal assault, as well as the various forms of larceny, are vastly underreported. Of 14,022,709 larcenies disclosed by victimization surveys in 1980, only 3,835,487 (27 percent) were reported to the police (Flanagan and Mcleod, 1982).

A statistical projection technique has been developed for use with the victimization data collected by the Law Enforcement Assistance Administration, whereby a more accurate picture of juvenile delinquency emerges:

> Victimization surveys provide a way of setting up a ratio of known to unknown crimes. With the information that the ratio of known to unknown larcenies is one to five (1:5), for example, if we know that 378 larcenies were reported to the police in a week, we can estimate that five times that number, or 1,890 larcenies, actually took place. Further, by estimating the proportion of juveniles typically involved in various crimes, we can come up with a more realistic idea of how many delinquent acts have been committed. Thus, if we estimate, on the basis of victimization survey ratios, that 1,890 larcenies were committed in a week and that 50 percent were delinquent acts, we have a more accurate figure—945 juvenile involvements in crime (Sanders, 1976:14).

The victimization studies also have supplied important and frightening facts regarding the victims of crime. Citing Bureau of Justice Statistics for 1982–1984, *Parade Magazine* (1987:15) announced that "it's downright dangerous to be a teenager in this country":

> . . . teens are more than twice as likely as adults to be the victims of rape, robbery, assault and crimes of violence. In the violent-crime category, for example, more than 60 of every 1,000 teens were victims during the 1982–84 period, compared to 27 of every 1,000 adults (Parade Magazine, 1987:15).

The major limitation of the victimization data collected by the National Crime Surveys is that the victims are the only source of information. Their perceptions and conclusions regarding such factors as the race and age of offenders generally must be made just after the crimes have been committed. It is understandable that judgment could be faulty and distorted by reason of the stress associated with the crime. In addition, victims have personal contact with offenders only in such crimes as rape, robbery, assault, and personal larceny, whereas the majority of crimes against persons and property are outside

TABLE 3-10
Percent of Victimizations Not Reported to Police, by Reason for Not Reporting.

	Not Important Enough	Private or Personal Matter	Reported to Someone Else	Lack of Proof	Police Would Not Want to Be Bothered	Police Would Be Inefficient, Ineffective, Insensitive	Fear of Reprisal	Too Inconvenient or Time-consuming	Other and Not Given
All personal crimes (15,153,080)	26.4	8.5	15.5	13.1	6.0	2.8	1.3	2.5	23.8
Crimes of violence (3,497,760)	19.4	25.2	11.2	6.4	6.3	4.0	4.7	2.9	19.5
Rape (75,340)	2.9	17.7	8.0	5.5	7.1	10.4	16.7	2.0	29.7
Robbery (554,590)	15.2	15.0	7.2	13.0	9.1	8.2	9.1	3.0	24.9
Aggravated assault (753,710)	15.9	29.6	6.3	4.7	5.9	4.7	5.6	1.6	22.5
Simple assault (2,114,110)	22.3	26.6	14.1	2.5	5.7	2.5	4.0	3.5	17.3
Personal larceny (11,655,320)	28.6	3.5	16.8	15.1	5.9	2.5	0.3	2.4	25.0
All household crimes (11,490,200)	28.6	7.1	3.5	16.4	8.2	3.6	0.5	2.2	29.8
Burglary (3,378,180)	21.0	8.1	5.6	16.4	6.9	4.1	0.5	1.9	35.5
Household larceny (7,683,710)	32.8	6.4	2.6	16.5	8.9	3.4	0.5	2.3	26.5
Motor vehicle theft (429,190)	12.9	11.7	2.9	15.0	6.6	2.9	0.0	3.0	45.0

Note: Detail may not add to total shown because of rounding. Number of reasons shown in parentheses. Some respondents may have cited more than one reason for not reporting victimizations to the police.

Source: Adapted from U.S. Department of Justice. *Criminal Victimization in the United States, 1985.* Washington, DC: U. S. Government Printing Office, 1987. Table 98, pp. 82–83.

these categories. Thus, while systematically gathered reports from victims help researchers to determine the magnitude and trends of some crimes by incorporating measurements and projections of the unreported dimension, there remain doubts about the complete accuracy and specificity of the victims' reports (McDermott and Hindelang, 1981).

THE MAGNITUDE AND TRENDS OF JUVENILE DELINQUENCY: A DEMOGRAPHIC ANALYSIS

In view of the acknowledged limitations of the data with which they must work, social scientists, criminologists, law enforcement officers, and others who seek to measure and control crime and delinquency may be tempted to agree with Disraeli, who exclaimed: "There are three kinds of lies—lies, damned lies, and statistics" (also attributed to Mark Twain) (Wheeler, 1976:7). Nevertheless, the conjunction of official and unofficial data, especially when gathered over a period of years, *does* present a fairly clear and rather consistent pattern of juvenile delinquency. In total, American young people account for a large and often disproportionate share of our national crime problem. Table 3–11 compiles arrest data on youth under age 18 for 1982, 1985, and 1986.

Reference to Table 3–11 makes possible longitudinal comparisons of juvenile arrests for each of the eight Index offenses included in the *Uniform Crime Reports* and demonstrates that short-term fluctuations over a few consecutive years cannot necessarily be interpreted as a "trend." For example, 21,012 juveniles were reported for committing murder in 1982, while in 1985 18,976 were reported for that offense. There was a similar decline in reported juvenile property offenses between 1982 and 1985. However, these figures were not valid indicators of a genuine downward trend. By 1986, the number of Reported Juvenile Offenses in both of those categories was again very close to the 1982 figures.

Another measurement of juvenile crime is shown in the arrest rate for 1982, 1985, and 1986. For example, 33.6 Americans under age 18 per 100,000 population were arrested for committing rape in 1982, compared to 36.7 in 1985 and 37.5 in 1986. Likewise, there were increases in aggravated assault and motor vehicle theft by persons under age 18. But, here again, such statistics cannot be interpreted as warning of a rising tidal wave of juvenile crime. Additional data from future FBI *Uniform Crime Reports* will need to be assessed before such a dire forecast could become reasonable. Even more importantly, both Reported Juvenile Offenses and Arrest Rates per 100,000 Population have meaning only in the overall context of the age composition of the larger population. It is conceivable that the changing proportion of our national population under 18 years of age at different points in time may account in part for the rising and falling rates of juvenile crime.

Perhaps the most insightful data in Table 3–11 are given in the third

TABLE 3–11

Comparison of Reported Juvenile Offenses, Arrest Rates, and Percentages of Arrests under Age 18 on UCR Crimes Index for 1982, 1985, and 1986.

FBI UCR CRIMES INDEX	1982			1985			1986		
	Reported Juvenile Offenses	Arrest Rate per 100,000 Population	Percent U.S. Arrests Under Age 18	Reported Juvenile Offenses	Arrest Rate per 100,000 Population	Percent U.S. Arrests Under Age 18	Reported Juvenile Offenses	Arrest Rate per 100,000 Population	Percent U.S. Arrests Under Age 18
Murder	21,012	9.1	4	18,976	7.9	5	20,613	8.6	5
Forcible rape	77,763	33.6	10	87,671	36.7	10	90,434	37.5	10
Robbery	536,888	231.9	26	497,874	208.5	12	542,775	225.1	11
Aggravated assault	650,042	280.8	9	723,246	302.9	9	834,322	346.1	9
Burglary	3,415,540	1,475.2	24	3,073,348	1,287.3	22	3,241,410	1,344.6	21
Larceny-Theft	7,107,663	3,069.8	32	6,926,380	2,901.2	24	7,257,153	3,010.3	32
Motor vehicle theft	1,048,310	452.8	36	1,102,862	462.0	19	1,224,137	507.8	39
Arson	106,501	57.3	36	103,420	50.3	41	110,732	52.9	35

Source: Federal Bureau of Investigation Uniform Crime Reports, 1986.

column under each year entitled, Percent U.S. Arrests Under Age 18, which lists the percentages of total arrests of juveniles for each of the eight Crime Index offenses. Again, the data are presented independently for 1982, 1985, and 1986, thus facilitating comparisons for those years. The first finding that emerges is that while American young people commit more than their proportional share of serious property crimes (i.e., burglary, larceny-theft, motor vehicle theft, and arson), they commit far less of the more serious crimes against persons (i.e., murder, forcible rape, and aggravated assault) than their proportion of the general population might suggest. Overall, it cannot be denied that youths contribute a very large share to our national crime problem.

The second conclusion that may be drawn from Table 3–11 is that the proportion of juvenile arrests of all arrests is remarkably stable in nearly all crime categories. For example, the percentage of arrests of those under age 18 for murder was relatively consistent for 1982, 1985, and 1986. Approximately 10 percent of all arrests made for forcible rape during each of those 3 years was of minors. Most of the other Index categories reveal only small or moderate fluctuations among 1982, 1985, and 1986 for Percent U.S. Arrests Under Age 18. Thus, the degree or proportion of youthful involvement in all crime has remained fairly constant over the three years. However, when trends are extended over a much longer period of time, some dramatic changes in juvenile involvement in crime can be identified.

Table 3–12 enables us to trace the longitudinal fluctuations and trends in Juvenile Court Case Dispositions for well over two decades: 1957 through 1983. Note the almost constant and often rapid increase in annual totals between 1957 and 1976.

The patterns in juvenile court case dispositions depicted in Table 3–12 can be at least partially explained by placing them in the larger context of major historical events and demographic changes in the composition of our national population over the past half century.

In brief, the severe economic depression of the 1930s, followed by the uncertainties and dislocations of World War II (over 16 million Americans served in the military forces between 1941 and 1945), combined to produce a long period of inhibited fertility. Consequently, the number of children entering adolescence during the decades of the 1940s and 1950s was small compared to later decades. Beginning in 1946, young American couples launched the now famous "baby boom" that would continue for nearly two decades. As a result of this greatly increased national fertility, it should come as no surprise that as the baby boomers became teenagers in the 1960s and 1970s, there would be significant increases in the number of juveniles arrested and processed through the courts. According to Department of Justice statistics (Report to the Nation, 1983:32), property crime arrests peak in persons aged 16, and those related to violent crime in persons aged 18. Demographically, in harmony with the reported increases in the number of youths arrested and appearing in juvenile courts between 1957 and 1976, there were 11,309,000 more children

| TABLE 3-12 |

Estimated Number and Rate of Delinquency Case Dispositions: 1957-1983

Year	Estimated Number of Delinquency Cases[a]	Child Population 10-17 Years of Age[b]	Rate[c]
1957	440,000	22,173,000	19.8
1958	470,000	23,433,000	20.0
1959	483,000	24,607,000	19.6
1960	510,000	25,368,000	20.1
1961	503,000	26,056,000	19.3
1962	555,000	26,989,000	20.6
1963	601,000	28,056,000	21.4
1964	686,000	29,244,000	23.5
1965	697,000	29,536,000	23.6
1966	745,000	30,124,000	24.7
1967	811,000	30,837,000	26.3
1968	900,000	31,566,000	28.5
1969	988,500	32,157,000	30.7
1970	1,052,000	33,141,000	31.7
1971	1,125,000	33,643,000	33.4
1972	1,112,500	33,954,000	32.8
1973	1,143,700	34,126,000	33.5
1974	1,252,700	34,195,000	36.6
1975	1,317,000	33,960,000	38.8
1976	1,432,000	33,482,000	42.3
1977	1,389,000	32,896,000	42.2
1978	1,359,000	32,276,000	42.1
1979	1,374,500	31,643,000	43.4
1980	1,445,400	31,171,000	46.4
1981	1,350,500	30,725,000	44.0
1982	1,292,500	29,914,000	43.2
1983	1,275,600	29,345,000	43.5

[a] Estimates for 1957-1969 are based on data from a national sample of juvenile courts. Estimates for 1970-1983 are based on data from all units reporting consistently for two consecutive years.

[b] Based on estimates from the Bureau of the Census, U.S. Department of Commerce Current Population Reports, Population Estimates and Projections, Series P-25, No. 965. Issued March, 1985 and the data file entitled "County Population Estimates (Provisional) by Age, Sex and Race: 1980-1982 prepared in 1985." Also included are population figures for Puerto Rico and the Virgin Islands.

[c] Rate is the number of delinquency cases per 1,000 children 10 through 17 years of age.

Source: Nimick, E.H., Snyder, H.N., Sullivan, D.P., & Tierney, N.J. *Juvenile Court Statistics,* 1983. National Center for Juvenile Justice. Office of Juvenile Justice and Delinquency Prevention. Pittsburgh, PA. June, 1987, p. 10.

and young people between 10 and 17 years of age in 1976 than there were in 1957 at risk of becoming delinquent—a 50 percent increase due to the earlier baby boom (Table 3-12)!

Ongoing research confirms that cohort size is significantly related to the extent of juvenile crime involvement (e.g., Smith, 1986). The only notable exception to this body of research is that of Darrell Steffensmeier and his associates (1987) who contended that cohort size had less influence than other contributing factors. No doubt, research in this area will continue, and somewhat conflicting conclusions may be drawn. As indicated, however, there are noticeable trends in the official data on delinquency which reflect the impact of changing demographics on juvenile arrest rates.

It is important to note that beginning about 1977, the upward surge in juvenile delinquency case dispositions leveled off. Then, between 1981 and 1983, a very gradual decline in the number of dispositions took place (Table 3–12). However, we must not conclude from these juvenile court statistics that delinquency has been brought under control or that the resolution of this complex social problem is imminent.

The general stabilization of juvenile arrest rates and court dispositions, or even a modest downward trend over a few years, should not be perceived as permanent. Again, let us note the fluctuating volume of delinquent behavior in relation to the overall demographic dynamics of the national population. Beginning in 1965, a sharp decline in fertility took place in response to changing values regarding family size, enhanced career opportunities for young women, and role alternatives available to them (Weller and Bouvier, 1981). And, the baby boom was over. It follows that the current statistical stabilization of youth involvement in delinquency activities can be traced, at least in part, to the smaller proportion of the national population that was between 10 and 17 years of age after 1974. As the Baby Boom generation matured out of the more delinquency-prone adolescent years, there were proportionately fewer young people at risk of becoming delinquent. Thus, reports of declining crime rates probably indicate a changing population composition rather than more effective law enforcement or increased conformity by the adolescent citizenry. Many criminologists believe that youth crime will again increase when children of the very large Baby Boom generation reach the delinquency-prone adolescent years. With those under age 18 presently accounting for 5 to 39 percent of each of the eight serious offenses listed in the Crime Report Index (FBI *Uniform Crime Reports*, 1987; see Table 3–11), juvenile delinquency persists as a challenge for improved understanding and social control.

SUMMARY

This chapter focused on the challenging task of measuring the magnitude of juvenile delinquency in the United States in response to such questions as:

1. Approximately how many people under age 18 are directly involved in crime each year?
2. What kinds of crime are most common among American young people?

3. How do such variables as gender, race, ethnicity, and place of residence affect the incidence and kinds of juvenile offenses that are committed?
4. What are the long-range trends in juvenile delinquency? Is it increasing or decreasing?

Evolving from these concerns, two continuous national, data-gathering programs were instituted. The Federal Bureau of Investigation collects, summarizes, analyzes, and reports arrest data from a network of city, county, and state law enforcement agencies and compiles this information in its annual *Uniform Crime Reports*. These FBI reports include the incidence of juvenile arrests for various crimes and tabulate for such variables as age, gender, race, and place of residence. The second official source is the National Center for Juvenile Justice and Delinquency Prevention of the Department of Justice which collects and summarizes data on case dispositions submitted from juvenile courts across the nation. The annual reports on *Juvenile Court Statistics* also identify and summarize those court dispositions characterized by a limited number of demographic variables such as gender and race.

Other sources of systematically collected data on juvenile delinquency include self-report studies and victimization surveys. Self-report studies are usually questionnaires directed at samples of the general population, in which subjects are asked about their participation in delinquent and/or criminal activities. The advantage of self-report studies is that they identify and measure some of the vast amount of undetected and unreported criminal and delinquent behavior. Victimization surveys are designed to accomplish the same objective. However, the subjects are asked to indicate crimes perpetrated against them and their property, and, if possible, to describe the offenders by age, sex, and race.

All of these data-gathering programs suffer from serious methodological limitations regarding validity and reliability. For example, arrest statistics are subject to distortion due to differences in law enforcement techniques. Some data are lost while being compiled, or are incorrectly tabulated and reported. In addition, arrest data present a picture only of offenders who were apprehended. Juvenile court data have been plagued by reporting irregularities and fluctuating court jurisdictions. Self-report studies and victimization surveys have been criticized for biased samples and inflated or deflated reports that severely limit generalizations to larger populations.

In spite of these shortcomings, the accumulation and combination of all these data on delinquent behavior over a long period of time present a clear and consistent conclusion that American young people generally account for a disproportionate amount of criminal activity. According to official statistics, lower-class, minority group males represent the most typical juvenile delinquents—a finding that has been moderated by unofficial statistics. While some juvenile delinquents have committed very serious crimes against persons, most juvenile delinquency is composed of status offenses and property crimes. At present, the trends in the magnitude of the delinquency problem are fairly stable, generally reflecting demographic changes in the composition of our national population.

CONCEPT APPLICATION

The following experience was related in a paper anonymously and voluntarily submitted to one of the authors by a female student enrolled in a Juvenile Delinquency course.

"Undetected and Unreported Delinquency: The Missing Statistics"

I was a juvenile delinquent. Juvenile delinquency to me is like a disease. It grows inside of you and becomes an obsession. It takes over everything you do. I can write about my experience now with some objectivity because it is over. But I still feel pangs of guilt and regret for some of the things I have done and tried to do.

It does not seem likely that a delinquent could come from a respectable, conservative, upper middle class family with every kind of advantage available to an adolescent. But it can happen and happen very easily, even to a girl like me from that kind of background.

I was a victim of the busing system in my state. Not that the idea of desegregation and busing is totally bad, but in many cases it can cause more harm than good—especially with younger kids who must be separated from their familiar neighborhoods and other family members that might restrain them from getting in trouble. I was forced to catch a bus at seven o'clock every morning to travel to a high school twelve miles away from my home while my older brothers attended a high school less than a mile away.

My delinquent phase started when I was in the eighth grade. First I was pressured by my peers to try smoking cigarettes. I haven't kicked that habit yet. Next came the pot smoking. "Oh, I'll try it just this once" I could hear myself saying. Some harder drugs came next. Speed, quaaludes, reds, yellow jackets, and black mollies were names I heard and used regularly. Soon I was up to a $35 to $75 weekly drug habit. All this by the time I was a sophomore in high school. And nobody knew, except for my few so-called "connections." Certainly not my parents who thought that I was a perfectly well-adjusted high school student. Both of them worked and they placed top priority on their careers and material success. They assumed that if they supplied a comfortable home, nice clothes, and a healthy allowance, that I had everything I needed—especially since I didn't complain about anything or tell them about my "private" life. Somewhere in the back of my mind, I was confident that I could get out of the new lifestyle I was following before I developed any serious habits.

My grades began to suffer, especially when my friends and I began to ditch regularly. And I soon learned how to do a reasonable forgery of my mother's name on notes excusing my absences from school for "illness" or other lies. A large group of us regularly took off from school together and hung around in theaters, pool halls, and alleys.

The vandalism, things we did for fun, came later. I was never really involved, but always around. But one too many times, I was there and we got caught, just for smashing some windows for kicks. One trip to the "pokey" was enough for me. No report to our parents was made, thank God. I was literally "scared straight."

Of course, there were always unusual happenings at school. For instance, I can remember a shooting in the cafeteria. One guy just pulled a gun on another and shot him in the hand. Many fights occurred. I was even subjected to one once. I was just banged up a bit. And to think it was all over a lousy cigarette. I lost. I didn't have a menthol one. After that, I carried a knife. And, in a desperate moment, I could or might have been forced to use that knife.

Needless to say, there was always the talk of prostitution and promiscuity. Talk of the "tricks" the night before always fascinated and horrified me at the same time. Luckily, I never contacted that realm of delinquency.

Not all of my experiences in high school were bad. Some teachers really cared. I grew out of my juvenile delinquency phase. In a way I'm glad of what I experienced but I wouldn't want anyone else to go through it. I learned some important lessons. I learned the value of constructiveness, and I will do something good in my life. I was a lucky delinquent. I'm no longer involved in drugs of any kind. Now my education is everything. Plus the fact, that I grew up. Now I'm aged nineteen going on thirty-five, a decent, conservative, well-adjusted, upper middle class college student.

* * * *

As a review of this chapter, what characteristics of the young woman in this account are contrary to those derived from official arrest statistics to typify the "average" juvenile delinquent? Do you agree that this self-reported, delinquent experience is evidence that much delinquent behavior goes undetected, unreported, and does not result in arrest? Did you ever participate in any illegal act prior to your eighteenth birthday that, if detected or reported, could have led to your arrest?

CONCEPT INTEGRATION

QUESTIONS AND TOPICS FOR FURTHER STUDY AND DISCUSSION

1. Define each of the first 8 crime categories of the FBI Uniform Crime Report. Why are they of major significance? Do you know anyone who

has committed any of these major offenses? Do you know a victim of any of these crimes? Was the offense reported and the offender arrested?

2. Explain how information on crime and delinquency is collected for the F.B.I. *Uniform Crime Reports*, the National Juvenile Court Statistical Reports, self-report studies, and victimization surveys. What are the advantages and limitations of each of these data-gathering techniques?

3. List and explain each of the variables that compose the composite profile of the "typical juvenile delinquent." Is this a completely reliable and valid portrayal of juvenile delinquents in the United States? Explain your answer.

4. Discuss the statistical evidence of delinquent behavior among racial minorities. How can we explain the high rates of juvenile delinquency among such minority groups by looking at their social environment and economic background?

5. Reported crime declined by about 5 percent in 1983. Does this mean that we have finally begun to resolve this serious social problem? What are the most recent trends in crime and delinquency as reported in this chapter?

References

Akers, R. 1964. Socio-economic status and delinquent behavior: A retest. *Journal of Research in Crime and Delinquency* 1:38–46.

Arnold, W. R. & Brungardt, T. M. 1983. *Juvenile misconduct and delinquency.* Boston: Houghton-Mifflin.

Barlow, H. D. 1987. *Introduction to Criminology* (4th ed.). Boston: Little Brown.

Bohm, R. M. 1986. Crime, criminal and crime control policy myths. *Justice Quarterly* 3 (June):193–214.

Cantwell, M. 1983. The Offender. In *Report to the nation on crime and justice: The data* (M. W. Zawitz, Ed.). Bureau of Juvenile Statistics, U.S. Department of Justice. NJC-87068. (October):29–40.

Cassidy, R. 1979. Fortress suburbia. In *Urban life and the struggle to be human* (A. J. Mayer & L. Gordon, Eds.). Dubuque, IO: Kendall/Hunt Publishing Co. p. 149.

Census of the Population: 1980. 1983. Vol. 1. *General social and economic characteristics of the population.* U.S. Department of Commerce, Bureau of the Census. Washington, DC: U.S. Government Printing Office, December.

Chambliss, W. J. & Nagasawa, R. H. 1969. On the validity of official statistics: A comparative study of white, black, and Japanese high school boys. *Journal of Research in Crime and Delinquency* VI (January):71–77.

Diegmueller, K. 1987. The forgotten juveniles: Crimeless criminals. *Parade* September 3:14–15.

Donovan, J. E. 1977. A typological study of self-reported deviance in a national sample of adolescents. Unpublished Ph.D. Dissertation. Boulder: University of Colorado.

Elliott, D. S. & Huizinga, D. 1983. Social class and delinquent behavior in a national youth panel, 1976–1980. *Criminology* 21 (May):149–177.

Erickson, M. L. & Empey, L. T. 1963. Court records, undetected delinquency and decision-making. *Journal of Criminal Law, Criminology and Police Science* 54, No. 4 (December):456–469.

Federal Bureau of Investigation. 1976. Crime in the United States: Uniform Crime Reports—1975. Washington, DC: U.S. Government Printing Office.

1980. Crime in the United States: Uniform Crime Reports—1979. Washington, DC: U.S. Government Printing Office.

1983. Crime in the United States: Uniform Crime Reports—1982. Washington, DC: U.S. Government Printing Office.

1987. Crime in the United States: Uniform Crime Reports—1986. Washington, DC: U.S. Government Printing Office.

Flanagan, T. J. & McLeod, M. (Eds.). 1982. *Sourcebook of criminal justice statistics—1980.* Washington, DC: U.S. Department of Justice, Bureau of Justice Statistics.

Geis, G. 1972. Statistics concerning race and crime. In *Race, Crime and Justice* (C. E. Reasons & J. L. Kuykendall, Eds.). Pacific Palisades, CA: Goodyear, pp. 61–69.

Harries, K. D. 1974. *The geography of crime and justice.* New York: McGraw-Hill Book Co.

Haskell, M. R. & Yablonsky, L. 1978. *Crime and delinquency* (3rd ed.). Chicago: Rand McNally.

Hindelang, M. J., Hirschi, T. and Weis, J. 1979. Correlates of delinquency: The illusion of discrepancy between self-report and official measures. *American Sociological Review* 44 (Dec.):995–1014.

Hirschi, T. 1969. *Causes of delinquency.* Berkeley: University of California Press.

Jensen, G. and Eve, R. 1976. Sex differences in delinquency: An examination of popular sociological explanation. *Criminology* 13:427–448.

Karchmer, C. L. 1984. Young arsonists. *Society* 22 (November/December):78–83.

Klaus, P. A., Rand, M. R. and Taylor, B. M. 1983. The Victim. In *Report to the Nation on Crime and Justice: The Data* (M. W. Zawitz, Ed.). Bureau of Justice Statistics, U.S. Department of Justice. NJC 87068. (October):17–27.

Manley, D. 1979. Status offenders—Helping them cope. *The Sunday Oklahoman* June 17, 1979:23.

Matza, D. 1964. *Delinquency and drift.* New York: John Wiley.

McDermott, M. J. & Hindelang, M. J. 1981. *Juvenile criminal behavior in the United States: Its trends and patterns.* National Institute for Juvenile Justice and Delinquency Prevention, LEAA, U.S. Department of Justice. Washington, DC: U.S. Government Printing Office.

National Advisory Committee for Juvenile Justice and Delinquency Prevention. 1984. *Serious juvenile crime: A redirected federal effort.* Washington, DC: U.S. Government Printing Office.

Nimick, E. H., Snyder, H. N., Sullivan, D. P., and Tierney, N. J. 1987. *Juvenile Court Statistics, 1983*. U.S. Department of Justice, Office of Juvenile Justice and Delinquency Prevention, National Center for Juvenile Justice. Pittsburgh, PA. June.

Nye, I. & Short, J. F., Jr. 1957. Scaling delinquent behavior. *American Sociological Review* 22 (June):326–331.

Palen, J. 1975. *The urban world*. New York: McGraw-Hill Book Co.

Parade Magazine. 1987. Tough for teenagers. March 22:15.

Sanders, W. B. 1976. *Juvenile delinquency*. New York: Praeger Publishers.

Santoli, A. 1986. How should we handle young offenders? *Parade Magazine*. (April 20):16–19.

Schaaf, D. 1986. The fire starters. *Friendly Exchange* (August):16–19.

Schaefer, R. T. 1979. *Racial and ethnic groups*. Boston: Little Brown.

Smith, D. A. & Visher, C. A. 1981. Street-level justice: Situational determinants of police arrest decisions. *Social Problems* 29 (December):167–177.

Smith, D. D., Finnegan, T., and Snyder, H. N. 1980. *Delinquency 1977: United States Estimates of Cases Processed by Courts with Juvenile Jurisdiction*. Pittsburgh, PA: National Center for Juvenile Justice.

Smith, M. 1986. The era of increased violence in the United States: Age, period, or cohort effect? *Sociological Quarterly* 27:239–251.

Steffensmeier, D., Streifel, C., and Harer, M. D. 1987. Relative cohort size and youth crime in the United States, 1953–1984. *American Sociological Review* 52 (October):702–710.

The President's Commission on Law Enforcement and Administration of Justice, Task Force Report. 1968. *The challenge of crime in a free society*. New York: Dutton.

Tittle, C., Villemez, W. & Smith, D. 1978. The myth of social class and criminality. *American Sociological Review* 63 (December):643–656.

United States Department of Justice. 1974. First Annual Report of the National Institute of Law Enforcement and Criminal Justice. LEAA. Washington, DC: U.S. Government Printing Office.

1974. *Standards and Goals for Juvenile Justice*. Washington, DC: U.S. Government Printing Office.

1983. *Report to the nation on crime and justice: The data* (M. W. Zawitz, Ed.). Bureau of Justice Statistics. NJC-87068. (October).

Voss, H. L. 1963. Ethnic differentials in delinquency in Honolulu. *Journal of Criminal Law, Criminology, and Police Science* LIV (September):322–327.

Warner, E. 1977. The youth crime plague. Chicago: Time, Inc. (July 11):18–28.

Weller, R. H. & Bouvier, L. F. 1981. *Population, Demography and Policy*. New York: St. Martin's Press.

Wheeler, M. 1976. *Lies, damn lies, and statistics: The manipulation of public opinion in America*. New York: Laurel Edition, Dell.

Winslow, R. W. 1967. Anomie and its alternatives: A self report study of delinquency. *Sociological Quarterly* VIII (Autumn):468–480.

Wooden, W. S. 1985. Arson is epidemic—and spreading like wildfire. *Psychology Today* 19 (January):23–28.

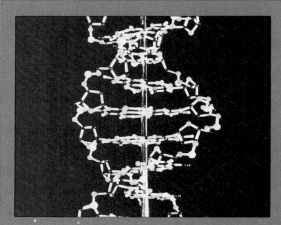

Part II
Causes of Juvenile Delinquency

Part II

INTRODUCTION: THEORY AND THE ETIOLOGY OF JUVENILE DELINQUENCY

In Part I, we defined juvenile delinquency as "those actions which are illegal for juveniles, which place the juvenile in the delinquent role, and result in society regarding the juvenile as deviant." Even though a very large proportion of juvenile delinquency is composed of such relatively trivial status offenses as running away from home, chronic school truancy, and curfew violation, a persistent trend of increasing youthful involvement in serious crimes against persons and property qualifies juvenile delinquency as a national social problem.

Now, after our discussion in Part I of "what is delinquency?" and "who are the delinquents?" we are ready to investigate the "why" of juvenile misconduct. In other words, how do we explain seriously deviant and antisocial behavior by young people. The study of **etiology**—*the cause(s) of an event, phenomenon, or behavior*—is a common inquiry and exercise in the scientific community and many academic disciplines. For example, the quest to explain biological variations in certain animal species prompted Charles Darwin to develop the theory of evolution. Similarly, Isaac Newton's observations of falling objects led him to conceptualize the law of gravity and other theoretical principles regarding cause and effect in the physical world. The application of the scientific method of investigation and theory building in the social sciences is somewhat more complicated than in the biological and physical sciences because of the incomparable complexity of human subjects and the ethical considerations involved in subjecting them to fully controlled laboratory test conditions. Nevertheless, within these limitations, sociologists and other students of human behavior are on the same etiological quest to explore, identify, understand, and explain the cause(s) of social phenomena. Serious efforts to establish valid and reliable findings and conclusions involve an objective, systematic approach to observation, data collection, and the testing of hypotheses. Finally, if findings and conclusions warrant, the ultimate result of the research enterprise may be the generation of explanatory theories.

In popular usage, the term "theory" means a "hunch" or a calculated guess that explains why some event occurs, or the possible relationship between cause and effect variables. To the lay person, a theory often suggests mere speculation, based on unfounded assumptions and little factual data, concerning an event or a form of behavior. For example, in hypothetically reconstructing events leading up to an automobile accident, an onlooker might speculate: "My theory of what happened is that the driver fell asleep and ran off the road." Or, as it was erroneously "theorized" in 1971, by extending voting rights to 18-year-olds, young Americans between 18 and 21 would generally and enthusiastically take advantage of the opportunity to participate in the political process.

To the scientist or researcher, the term "theory" means much more than an "off-the-cuff" guess or estimate. To these scholars, a **theory** is *a general statement that systematically and objectively relates concepts or variables together to explain events or behavior.* If a theory is valid, it correctly predicts that identical relationships, events, or behaviors will occur in the future if the conditions and circumstances are identical.

A large number of scholars from many disciplines, utilizing many approaches and methodologies, have attempted to develop causal theories explaining why some juveniles become delinquent. There has been considerable variation in the adequacy of these theories as they have been exposed to continual scrutiny and testing. In some cases, theories of delinquency have been modified, expanded, or discarded as inadequate explanations. Other theories have survived relatively intact as useful contributions to delinquency etiology. The three chapters comprising Part II present some of the more interesting, prominent, and useful theories of deviant behavior in general, and juvenile delinquency in particular.

Chapter 4 begins with an overview of eighteenth century philosophical speculations regarding the causal origins of criminal behavior. There follows a more detailed discussion of the nineteenth century biological determinism and the "born criminal" suggested by Cesare Lombroso, the twentieth century typology based upon body-types and the "mesomorphic delinquent" described by William Sheldon, and others who argued that criminal and delinquent behavior can be traced to genetic and physiological factors. The chapter concludes with a discussion of more current and methodologically sophisticated efforts to establish causal linkage between biology and juvenile delinquency, as well as some controversial insights offered by sociobiology.

Chapter 5 surveys the early and contemporary concepts and contributions of psychiatrists and psychologists in explaining juvenile delinquency. These psychogenic theories perceive the delinquent's misbehavior as symptomatic of underlying emotional and personality maladjustment.

Chapter 6 provides an extensive treatment of the major sociological theories of juvenile delinquency. These sociological explanations share and amplify in various ways the basic rule of faith of those who pursue sociological investigations and theory construction—that delinquency and most other human behaviors emerge as part and product of the context of human groups and relationships that comprise the individual's social environment. Each section of chapter 6 concludes with a synopsis of contributions and criticisms of the various sociological theories of juvenile delinquency.

Chapter 4

Biological Explanations of Juvenile Delinquency

The reading of this chapter will help you achieve the following objectives:

1. Explain the nineteenth century effort of Cesare Lombroso to link biological or physical characteristics with criminal behavior.
2. Compare and contrast the "rational individual responsibility for behavior" of the Classical School of Criminological Thought with the "biological determinism" of the Positive School of Criminology.
3. Become more aware of how society often casually and carelessly applies biological causes to human behavior in everyday life.
4. Describe the twentieth century research of William Sheldon and of Sheldon and Eleanor Glueck who tried to establish a causal relationship between body type and juvenile delinquency.
5. Discuss several recent areas of investigation that focus on abnormal chromosomal and electroencephalograph patterns, diet, physical appearance, and other biological variables as a possible background for some antisocial behavior.
6. Critique the weaknesses and limitations of theories of deviant and delinquent behavior that are based on biological and physiological variables.
7. Understand how the inclusion of social factors such as the attitudes and reactions of one's social group can reinforce the relationship between biological or physical characteristics and the tendency toward deviant and delinquent behavior.

INTRODUCTION

In Chapters 2 and 3, we examined the questions "What is juvenile delinquency?" and "Who are the delinquents?" Our understanding of the issues and answers raised by those initial questions form the foundation for the discussions in Part II of the theoretical causes of juvenile delinquency. In other words, there was a logical need to define the *What* and the *Who* of juvenile delinquency before we consider the *Why*.

Many explanations of misconduct have been suggested. From the dawn of recorded history, philosophers, theologians, and social thinkers have conjectured that deviance and antisocial behavior might be traceable to demons, original sin, or man's insatiable and self-serving lust for power, gratification, and material possessions. The development of the "age of science" offered a plethora of additional explanations based upon scientific reasoning.

THE LINK BETWEEN BIOLOGY AND BEHAVIOR: MYTHS AND FOLKLORE

The notion that there is an intrinsic relationship between human physical traits and behavior is also very old. For example, Franz Joseph Gall (1758–1828) speculated that mental faculties and traits of character—such as acquisitiveness, benevolence, destructiveness, spirituality, combativeness, and imitativeness— are manifested in separate portions of the brain. **Phrenology,** as Gall's system was called, noting that individuals vary in these traits of character and personality, further *contended that there is a positive relationship between these specific cerebral functions and the formation or shape of the human skull.* Although phrenology has been repeatedly and convincingly disproved anatomically and physiologically, the belief and fad was popularized by practitioners claiming to ascertain these mental characteristics and behavior propensities by measuring the shape, irregularities, and protuberances of the skull.

History also is replete with suggestions from many writers that geographic location is reflected in temperament and behavior. For example, the Greek historian Polybius (200–118 B.C.) wrote, "There is an inevitable tendency for society to yield to climatic influences and these influences cause personality and physical differences in them." The Roman Paulio expanded on this view:

> Southern European people are keen in intelligence due to the keen air. Northern peoples are sluggish, chilled by the air. People in warm climates have passionate natures; people in cold climates are stolid.

The Frenchman Jean Bodin (1530–1596) held a related view: "Northern climate causes people's life fluids to make them cruel . . . but loyal to the government." Mondescuer, in a callous expression of unwitting male chauvinism, wrote:

> In the South the women mature early due to the climate and marry early to older men. Since women are inferior in wisdom to their more experienced husbands, this affects the woman's social status.

Unfortunately, ethnic and racial biases and slurs have crept into modern times in some places where a disvalued ethnic background is equated with undesirable behavior. For example, there are still those who erroneously generalize that "all Irishmen drink too much"—perhaps traceable to the large quantities of Irish whiskey exported to the United States during the Prohibition era. Similarly, the Germans have been stereotyped as "militaristic" due to the political circumstances in their nation preceding World Wars I and II. And, American blacks have suffered for generations the degrading and simplistic assumption by some unenlightened whites that there is an affinity between being black and "a preference for fried chicken and watermelon."

Such allusions to a mystical linkage between biological inheritance or physical appearance and human behavior often appear as taken-for-granted truisms in the language and culture of a people and, alas, probably affect important relationships and decisions. The life chances, ranging all the way from marriage to employment, of many people can be negatively influenced by such unfair stereotypes and unfounded generalizations as "People with red hair are hot-tempered"; "Fat people are always jolly"; and "Tall men make the best leaders." Only in recent decades has objective and sympathetic attention been given to the universal and longstanding stigma imposed on left-handed people. Michael Barsley (1966) carefully documented the history of prejudice and even persecution experienced by a large and visible minority who favor the use of the left hand and, therefore, were falsely assumed to be sinister, deviant, or criminal in some way.

In the theater and motion picture industry, physical appearance consistently has been related to character and behavior. Actors generally portray transparent characters whose personalities, motives, and actions must be obvious to the audience and easily interpreted. Thus, on the stage or screen, each character is usually unidemensional—presented as either "good" or "bad." It was a common joke for many years that cinema "westerns" always portrayed the hero as physically attractive, well groomed, idealistic, God-fearing, wearing a white hat, and kind to women, children, and horses. On the other hand, the villain was quickly identified as ugly, slovenly, uncouth, ignorant, immoral, cruel, and (of course) wearing a black hat. Only in the movies are the "good guys" and the "bad guys" so easily and dichotomously sorted out. People and situations are much more complex in real life and defy immediate character evaluation. Unfortunately, however, in real life as in the cinema, physical appearance is often the basis for imputing character and judging behavior.

THE CLASSICAL SCHOOL OF CRIMINOLOGICAL THOUGHT

The first organized and logical inquiry and hypothesis regarding criminal deviance emerged in the eighteenth century. Charles Montesquieu (1689–1755), Cesare Beccaria (1738–1794), Jeremy Bentham (1748–1832), and other Enlightenment writers propounded a "naturalistic" approach to explaining criminal behavior by contending that the only acceptable explanations for human conduct were to be found in man himself. From that beginning, the

Classical School of Criminological Thought was developed. The Classical theorists were guided by the assumption that humans are rational, reasoning individuals who weigh and control their actions and destinies. The focus was upon the criminal as totally responsible for personal behavior. Thus, according to Graeme Newman's *The Punishment Response* (1978), appropriate punishment "to suit the crime" would not only encourage the reformation of offenders, but discourage criminality in the general populace. The idea was that a person would conform to the standards and behavioral expectations of society in order to avoid physical pain—like a bull with a ring in his nose. Punishment was thought to be appropriate under most circumstances and for most offenses because it was assumed that crimes were the result of free will based on conscious, reasoned decisions.

While the Classical position did not clearly differentiate between children who violated laws and adult offenders, the later **Neoclassical School** recognized that not all persons are equally rational and personally responsible for their behavior. Consequently, "judges were allowed some discretion in dealing with the young, the mentally disturbed, and those confronted with unusual circumstances that decreased responsibility" (McCaghy, 1985:6). Nevertheless, the Classical/Neoclassical approach has been severely criticized. Its fatal flaw lay in overlooking how society is a major force in shaping human behavior, including criminality. Even if the highly questionable assumption of equal rationality among humans is valid, social inequality is a pervasive reality. An individual's decision to engage in criminal activity is based on much more than the simple equation and anticipated balance of pleasure minus pain. Level of poverty, alienation, social status, and numerous other forces and factors also must be taken into account.

THE POSITIVE SCHOOL OF CRIMINOLOGY

The first efforts to apply scientific and systematic research methodology to establish the principle of biological determinism as the fundamental cause of criminal behavior occurred in the late nineteenth century. Implicit in the deterministic model is that a given thing cannot simply appear out of nothing or nowhere; it is determined or caused by some other thing, event, or phenomenon in the environment. Biological and physical scientists, in their study of plants, animals, and objects, already had found the deterministic explanation very useful in reasoning from cause to effect or, inversely, from effect to cause. This approach attracted a number of nineteenth century researchers and theorists, including some early criminologists, who enthusiastically tried to apply various forms of biological determinism to crime and juvenile delinquency.

Cesare Lombroso (1835–1909), an Italian army physician, who is often referred to as the "Father of Criminology," measured the jawbones, skulls, hands, and other physical traits of a group of prisoners and proposed that criminals are biological reversions to an earlier, more primitive stage of human development (Ferrero, 1911). The ideas of Lombroso and his followers formed the basis of the **Positive School** of criminology and constituted a reaction to the earlier Classical School. Whereas the Classical School theorists had assumed that humans are rational and endowed with free will, and thus able to calculate the advantages and costs associated with any course of action, the positivists denied the existence of free will and argued that each person is born with an innate propensity toward certain forms of behavior. In other words, just as people inherit specific physical traits, reflective of their genetic background, so, too, they contended, some people are motivated by an inborn tendency toward behavior that may be criminal according to the standards of a modern society. Lombroso viewed this antisocial human behavior as an almost genetically programmed response, much as lower animals are driven by instinct. This biological inheritance, Lombroso felt, when joined with conducive social circumstances and opportunities, irresistibly moves some individuals to act as they do.

From his late nineteenth century study, Lombroso concluded that there is a *born criminal type*, "bestial" in appearance, and characterized by "low cranial capacity; retreating forehead; highly developed frontal sinuses; . . . early closing of the cranial sutures; . . . tufted and crispy hair; and large ears . . . [and] relative insensibility to pain" (Lombroso, 1911:365). In short, Lombroso identi-fied the *born criminal* as one whose body structure and criminal behavior are dual manifestations of an underlying **atavism,** that is, *a biological throwback to the savage, lower phase of human evolution.* Such persons (*homo delinquens*), he reasoned, are biological and social misfits in a society of modern men (*homo sapiens*) whose civilization includes extensive behavioral restrictions.

Lombroso later refined and expanded his original thesis on the born criminal to include other types whose antisocial behavior he traced to biolog-ical or physiological traits. For example, the etiology of the *insane criminal,* according to Lombroso, may be linked to diseases or abnormalities of the mind. The *criminaloid* was different from the born criminal only in that his predatory conduct was less savage and more occasional. Lombroso described the *criminal by passion* as characterized by a romantic sensitivity and capacity for altruistic motives in the commission of crime—and thus contrasting sharply with the born criminal.

The premises, methodology, and conclusions of Lombroso and the Pos-itivistic School of Criminology have been subjected to intense scrutiny and criticism by subsequent investigators, who cite the weaknesses of descriptive data, broad generalizations from few cases, and the absence of comparative control groups of nonprisoners (Goring, [1913] 1972). At the same time, more charitable scholars have applauded Lombroso for at least implementing a rudimentary scientific approach to criminology and for ultimately acknowledg-ing the impact of sociological causes of crime interacting with inherited traits and tendencies to produce antisocial behavior (Wolfgang et al., 1972).

TWENTIETH-CENTURY CONSTITUTIONAL TYPOLOGIES

Biological explanations of crime and delinquency have continued to fascinate many investigators. For example, William Sheldon and associates (1949) equated personality and character with body type and contended that youths with a certain physical appearance have an inherited and enhanced potential for delinquent behavior. According to Sheldon, three distinct body types can be identified and characterized:

1. **Endomorph.** Physically characterized as having a rotund, soft, fleshy body. The endomorph tends to be easygoing, gregarious, and self-indulgent in temperament.
2. **Ectomorph.** A slender and fragile body, with small features and weak appearance. The ectomorph tends to be a loner, introspective, and emotionally high-strung.
3. **Mesomorph.** The body is generally muscular and firm, with a strong frame and resilient constitution. The mesomorph tends to be energetic, impetuous, and insensitive.

Sheldon compared 200 boys referred by social agencies and courts to a center for problem children in Boston with 4,000 college males and found the center's children to be more mesomorphic. He concluded that although mesomorphy does not predestine youths to delinquent behavior, it is the constitutional background most favorable to delinquency, since the mesomorph has the emotional makeup and physical resources to "translate impulse into action" and to become a predatory person (Cohen, 1966:51).

In 1950, Sheldon and Eleanor Glueck, a husband-wife team of researchers, reached conclusions similar to those presented by William Sheldon. The Gluecks compared 500 white male delinquents with 500 white male nondelinquents and agreed with Sheldon that mesomorphs apparently possess higher delinquency potential than youths having other body types. They stressed that while a mesomorphic body does not make delinquent behavior inevitable, the aggressive, muscular youth seems more likely to relieve his tensions and frustrations in ways that society defines as troublesome and delinquent.

Broad generalizations from the Sheldon and Glueck studies cannot be made since both suffer from serious methodological problems. These efforts to correlate physical characteristics with a delinquent propensity have been severely criticized by other scholars (e.g., Clinard, 1968; Cohen, 1966) for lack of objectivity and nonrepresentative samples. For example, black, middle class, female, and more intelligent delinquents are conspicuous by their absence. Furthermore, the studies based their findings on the small proportion of youngsters who had been caught and were under treatment. This is a sampling bias that badly distorts the findings. Those who have been apprehended represent

Endomorph   Ectomorph   Mesomorph

Sheldon's Body Types   (Illustration by Marilyn R. Thompson)

the unsuccessful delinquents. They tell us nothing about the successful ones! Finally, if mesomorphy represents a constitutional predisposition to delinquent behavior, what of the millions who fit this body type but are not delinquent?

While the limitations of the constitutional typologies are extremely formidable, Sheldon and Eleanor Glueck made their argument for the connection between biology and behavior more convincing when they extended a linkage to social variables. Their statement that "A physical characteristic may be socially defined and treated in ways which encourage criminal behavior" is a noteworthy contribution (Hartl et al., 1982:557–558). Observations and perusal of juvenile court procedures and records indeed reveal that those youths who are aggressive, socially assertive, nonsubmissive to authority, and essentially mesomorphic in physique, are those most likely to be arrested and committed to a correctional institution. This topic is expanded in Chapter 6 in a discussion of how society assigns the "delinquent label."

THE CONTINUING SEARCH FOR THE BIOLOGICAL CONNECTION

Many criminologists, researchers, and theorists are still searching for a direct link between human biology and human behavior. In view of the extensive societal commitment to alleviate the juvenile delinquency problem, such ongoing investigations are worthwhile. Although findings thus far are discredited or inconclusive, several research studies warrant our attention in the context of this chapter.

Sex

In Chapter 3, statistical evidence was presented showing that American males commit much more crime and delinquency than American females, except for prostitution and running away from home. Each year, more males than females have been arrested for each of the eight Index offenses. This sexual variation in crime rates is consistent in virtually all societies.

It generally has been believed that some part of the difference in crime rates between males and females in our country might be attributed to biological differences (such as hormones that predispose men to aggressive behavior). However, most of the difference is due to the contrasting gender roles that men and women are socialized to play. Traditionally, most boys and young men have been socially encouraged to be aggressive and competitive. Such attributes were generally considered useful in achieving occupational success and upward social mobility. On the other hand, girls and young women were expected to achieve only the family-oriented and home-based objectives of marriage and motherhood. These nurturing female roles were associated with a dependent, pliant, and nonaggressive disposition. Slowly at first, and at an accelerated pace in recent years, role restrictions have been lifted for many women and more options have become available. At the same time, female participation in crime and delinquency has dramatically increased. According to Freda Adler (1975:1) "The phenomenon of female criminality is but one wave in this rising tide of female assertiveness . . ."

Statistics compiled in the United States, Italy, France, West Germany, and Russia have recorded a marked rise in violent crimes committed by women in recent years. For example, of 52 alleged terrorists captured in West Germany, 22 were women; since 1970 murders by women have increased 87 percent and cases of assault and battery by 45 percent (Brothers, 1985). Several experts have related this increase in aggressive criminal behavior to the recent emancipation of many women from their traditional passive and subservient roles in male-dominated societies. Leon Salzman (1980), Clinical Professor of Psychiatry at the Albert Einstein College of Medicine, reported that there was no biological reason for females to be less aggressive, except that being aggressive had no meaning in a woman's life until she had the same possibilities as a man.

Race and Ethnicity

The national statistics on juvenile arrests are compared and contrasted in the last chapter for white, black, American Aborigine (Indians and Eskimos), Asian or Pacific Islander, and Hispanic subgroups. It is clear that there are statistically significant variations in crime rates in the United States when comparing racial and ethnic group. Parallel findings from other sources concur that the rates of delinquency for Chinese-Americans, Japanese-Americans, and Jews, for example, are lower than the rates for the rest of the population. On the other hand, the crime rates for blacks and Hispanics are higher than those of other groups (Voss, 1963; Wolfgang et al., 1972; FBI *Uniform Crime Reports,* 1987).

Similarly, Siegel and Senna (1981) summarized data from several authoritative sources (Klein, 1969; Miller, 1975; Short and Strodtbeck, 1965; Spergel, 1964; Thrasher, 1927) in identifying the racial and ethnic composition of urban youth gangs. They found that the racial and ethnic composition of gangs reflects that of the population in their urban environment; gang members are usually recruited from minority groups; and most gangs are racially/ethnically homogeneous and exclusive:

> . . . the various cities differ in the racial makeup of their gangs. For example, in Philadelphia and Detroit, the overwhelming number of gang members are black. In New York, Hispanic gangs predominate. San Francisco's small gang population is mostly oriental (Siegel and Senna, 1981:263).

Great caution must be exercised lest the reader assume that the aforementioned data prove that there is an inherent connection between racial or ethnic background and delinquent behavior. When a long-range analysis of criminal and delinquent rates and patterns in urban areas is utilized, the high incidence of such antisocial behavior appears related more to the poor socioeconomic circumstances of inner-city minority groups than to the biology of race or ethnicity. Clifford Shaw and Henry McKay (1969) followed a number of different ethnic groups such as the Irish, Polish, and Italians as, over time, they improved their general occupational, educational, and income levels, and moved from the grim, inner-city tenements and slums into better neighborhoods. In all instances, the crime and delinquency rates for each group fell as higher social status was achieved. The current occupants of inner-city, lower class areas are mostly black and Hispanic minorities, and these groups manifest the typical high crime and delinquency rates of previous area residents. It is expected that as the present minority group residents improve their socio-economic situations and move to better neighborhoods, they too will experience reduced rates of crime and delinquency.

Genetic Crime Causation: The XYY Hypothesis

Before we discuss chromosomal abnormalities as a possible cause of crime and delinquency, a brief review of basic genetics will prove useful. Each human cell has 46 chromosomes. Upon conception, each parent donates 23 gene-carrying chromosomes concerned with the transmission and development of hereditary characteristics. These chromosomes combine into 46 chromosomes in the offspring. Among the 46 chromosomes is a set which determines sex. The female has two X chromosomes, referred to as XX. The male has one X and one Y chromosome, referred to as XY. The X chromosome, because it is inherited from the mother, is believed by some to convey gentle and passive traits; the Y chromosome, inherited from the father, is thought to carry tough and aggressive traits. Normal males, then, described as 46XY, are those in whom gentle and tough characteristics supposedly balance each other.

Occasionally, a male will have an extra Y chromosome, indicated by the symbol 47XYY. Although males with this chromosomal abnormality comprise only about one-seventh of 1 percent of the male population, the existence of an extra Y chromosome has led to the XYY hypothesis: "Men cursed with this rare cellular structure are predisposed to violent, antisocial acts" (Rosenberg et al., 1982:6).

> The major characteristics of these people are that they are a little mentally retarded, have too much acne on their faces, stand taller than the average normal male (6 feet 3 inches versus 5 feet 10 inches), and—most importantly—have a strong tendency to be unusually aggressive. Thus it has been theorized that the extra Y chromosome can drive the XYY male into committing a dangerous, violent crime such as murder (Thio, 1988:124).

The XYY hypothesis has fueled considerable speculation and some research efforts to collect supporting data. Richard Fox (1971) studied inmates of prisons and mental institutions and found that as many as 3 percent displayed the 47XYY characteristics, compared to an estimated frequency for the abnormality of 0.13 percent among the population at large. In addition, several highly publicized, violent crimes between 1942 and 1968 were found to have been committed by individuals with an XYY constitution. Richard Speck, who in 1967 murdered eight nurses in Chicago, was alleged to have the 47XYY trait. The quality of such information is highly questionable as a basis for establishing a valid connection between human genetic background and antisocial behavior. Not to be overlooked is the fact that the vast majority of murderers apparently do not have an XYY chromosome pattern. Moreover, the sample of prisoners who have been tested is biased, since many criminals are not confined in institutions and therefore not subject to chromosomal analysis. Nor is the true prevalence of XYY in the general population known. Put differently, no one can tell how many XYY men are noncriminals and serve as model members of their communities.

Social scientists hasten to point out that the suspected connection between biology and behavior is more complex than it appears. Even though an extra Y chromosome may have the potential to lead its carrier to violent behavior, sociocultural factors supply the triggering mechanism and largely determine whether the potentiality will become an actuality. As one geneticist admits:

> A social mechanism is entirely possible. Large, possibly slightly retarded, males may be ridiculed . . . and may respond aggressively. In any case, it would appear that of the total amount of violence in our society only a very small part is contributed by XYY individuals (McClearn, 1969:1003).

Despite the absence of convincing empirical evidence supporting a possible chromosomal combination and criminal behavior, several premature and radical proposals have been made to incorporate the idea into correctional practices, even as a predictive tool for identifying potential delinquents. For example:

> [The most] frightening . . . is a suggestion made in 1971 by Arnold Hutschnecker, one of President Nixon's personal medical advisors. Hutschnecker, a physician, proposed a massive program of chromosomal screening for every six-year-old in the country. He suggested that 'hard core' six-year-olds showing evidence of criminal potential be sent to 'therapeutic' camps where they could learn to be 'good social animals.' This particular plan was sent to Elliot Richardson, Secretary of Health, Education, and Welfare, for consideration. Richardson turned down the plan 'because it was not feasible to implement on a national scale, at that time' (Hunt, 1973; Moran, 1978:347; cited in Thornton et al., 1987:95).

Diet and Deviant Behavior

One of the more plausible and promising areas of contemporary research into possible organic causes for misbehavior is the apparent association between dietary deficiencies and biochemical irregularities which cause some youngsters to become hyperactive, unruly, and delinquent. Students of nutrition as it relates to human behavior have amassed considerable and convincing evidence that children who develop poor nutritional habits can grow into disturbed adolescents and violent adults. "Because their bodies are smaller, . . . and because their minds and bodies are still developing, children are especially vulnerable to the dietary risks we all experience" (Reed et al., 1983:118).

Some recent researchers have contended that deviant and delinquent behavior can often be linked to the overconsumption of carbohydrates and other dietary deficiencies common among many adolescents.

The popular overconsumption of junk foods and refined carbohydrates by youths in the United States is increasingly suspected by researchers as a culprit in stimulating aggressive and antisocial behavior. Not only can such foods quickly raise blood sugar levels, but they may temporarily impair the brain's ability to perceive, process information, and regulate behavior. Lonsdale and Shamberger (1980) examined a group of children whose marginal malnutrition was traced to a junk food diet high in sugar. The devastating effects included reduced self-control and troublesome behavior. Lonsdale and Shamberger (1980:210) concluded:

> Scientifically, we have reason to believe that this approach to diet is changing the balance of neurological transmission which is the hallmark of the function of the brain and the central nervous system. It means that the quality and quantity of nutrition can change your behavior.

Criminologists Alexander Schauss and Clifford Simonsen, along with University of Puget Sound chemistry professor Jeffrey Bland, conducted an analysis of the diets of chronic juvenile offenders (Schauss et al., 1979). They found that on average the juveniles ingested 32 percent more sugar than a control group of children who were behaviorally disordered but had no criminal record (Reed et al., 1983). A remarkable experiment was conducted by Stephen Schoenthaler and Walter Doraz (1983) in which refined sugar was drastically reduced in the diets of 276 incarcerated youths. Honey and molasses were substituted for sugar, fruit juices took the place of beverages with high sugar content, and so forth. In a short while the dietary modifications apparently resulted in behavior modification among the subjects. Schoenthaler and Doraz (1983) reported that physical assaults, fighting, thefts, and various other forms of disobedience were reduced by nearly 45 percent.

Supporting evidence has continued to accumulate regarding the subtle but direct link between diet and deviant behavior. Food additives and preservatives—previously considered generally safe for human consumption—are now suspected of causing numerous allergic reactions including hyperactivity, learning disability, and aberrant behavior. For example, Schauss and his associates (1979) discovered that hundreds of chronic juvenile offenders drank on average 12 to 15 eight-ounce glasses of milk per day! The researchers theorized that preservatives in the milk caused the impaired behavior. While commercial food producers are likely to be dismayed and to challenge such findings, such promising research inquiries regarding causal linkages between diet and criminal or delinquent behavior should be encouraged.

Brain Malfunctions

Since 1959, the administration of the electroencephalograph (EEG) test to criminal and delinquent offenders has aroused considerable interest. The theory holds that a deviant's brain emits waves that are abnormal in frequency. While some fragmentary findings support this contention in a very general and tenuous way, much more refined and systematic research needs to be done in this area:

> In 143 cases . . . a high percentage of EEG changes was found among abnormal personalities . . . It was emphasized that the EEG may only answer the question as to the existence of a brain lesion which in turn is frequently causally associated with behavioral disturbances (Schulz and Mainusch, 1971).

Similarly, many studies searching for a connection between hyperactivity and delinquent behavior have produced inconsistent and controversial findings. For example, Lee Robins (1978) and James Satterfield (1978) found unusually high incidences of hyperactivity among the delinquent children in their studies. This hyperactivity, or *hyperkinesis*, is characterized not only by frenetic activity, but often by learning disabilities, extreme aggressiveness, and the inability or refusal to clearly distinguish between right and wrong. The conclusion that this deviant behavior has a biological connection is based on the hypothesis that some of these hyperkinetic children may be suffering minimal brain damage due to birth injury and/or heredity. Other researchers (Conrad, 1975; Broder et al., 1978) vigorously disagreed. The latter group not only challenged the basic premise of "minimal brain damage" as a valid diagnosis, but found no evidence supporting such a biological connection with deviant or delinquent behavior.

A more successful avenue of inquiry has focused on the association between learning disability and youth crime. A 1975 survey of all youngsters admitted to correctional institutions in Colorado found that an astonishing 90 percent had some form of learning disability (Poremba, 1975). The learning disability known as dyslexia has come under special scrutiny. **Dyslexia** is *a brain malfunction whereby visual signs are scrambled.* For example, the dyslexic child might see the letters and words on this page in reverse order or perhaps upside down. Consequently, average skills in reading, spelling, and arithmetic are impossible to attain if the malady remains undiagnosed. Until recent years, little was known about this type of cognitive abnormality, and teachers often misinterpreted the learning difficulties of apparently healthy children as laziness. Sometimes dyslexic children are assumed to be retarded; as their frustration and alienation deepens, they often become emotionally maladjusted, hostile, and delinquent. Ultimately, this learning disability can lead to their being expelled from school or dropping out entirely and never reaching full intellectual potential (Eitzen, 1986:398; Murray, 1976). A growing public awareness of dyslexia and its implications about learning and disciplinary problems for afflicted children has led to the creation of special intervention and educational programs in most states.

SOCIOBIOLOGICAL EXPLANATIONS

One of the most imaginative and controversial directions for scholarly inquiry on the biological basis for deviant behavior lies in the relatively new field of sociobiology, which combines elements of several biological subareas in explaining social behaviors among animals and humans. A major proponent is Edward O. Wilson (1975), a Harvard University zoologist specializing in the study of insect life. Wilson (1978:16) defines **sociobiology** as follows:

> The systematic study of the biological basis of all forms of social behavior, in all kinds of organisms, including man . . . [is a] hybrid discipline that incorporates knowledge from ethology (the naturalistic study of whole patterns of behavior), ecology (the study of the relationships of organisms to their environment), and genetics in order to derive general principles concerning the biological properties of entire societies.

Sociobiologists maintain that social behavior is a product of evolutionary history and genetics. Just as Charles Darwin traced the evolution of physical traits, sociobiologists attempt to do the same for social behaviors. It is generally accepted that some of the social behavior of monkeys and apes was adapted in the long course of evolution into their biological endowment. That is, behavior that promotes survival is passed on to the offspring of such species through inherited genes. This involves temperament and personality traits as well as physical characteristics. Thus, for male animals, physical traits that assist in the hunt, such as quickness and motor skills, are supplemented by an aggressive disposition. For females, the biological ability to become pregnant is supported by nesting and nurturing instincts. Sociobiologists claim that these and many other predispositions toward personal and species survival are genetically programmed into the organism.

Despite the fact that no one has yet isolated any of those genes in humans, some sociobiologists have enthusiastically made wholesale transfer of the conclusions regarding the assumed life-and-death genetic struggle of lower animals to human beings. For example, they explain kinship ties, social bonding, and the incest taboo as reflecting unconscious inborn needs to protect and perpetuate one's own genetic endowment. Similarly, according to some sociobiologists, several million years of human biological-genetic evolution have made us aggressive, acquisitive, and apparently amoral at times, since these characteristics and behaviors can enhance gene survival. Thus, through sociobiological reasoning, another deterministic explanation has been made for what ordinarily appears as deviant, criminal, and delinquent behavior.

The position that perceives human behavior as genetically programmed has elicited vigorous opposition from those espousing the view that human conduct is, in general, culturally relative. Austin Turk (1969:10–11) spoke for many social scientists by arguing that validation of biological-predisposition hypotheses would require us to agree that there are persons born to commit certain acts that will invariably be criminal—anywhere and everywhere:

> There is apparently no pattern of human behavior which has not been at least tolerated in some normative structure. While there do seem to be universal categories of norms (e.g., norms limiting the use of violence) no specific explicit or implicit rule has ever been shown to be present in all human societies . . . From the absence of universal norms it follows that research on the etiology of any specific form of 'criminal' behavior must inevitably be culture-specific and time-bound, because the phenomenon under study will change from culture to culture . . . [italics in original].

In addition to the criticism that sociobiology does not take culture into account, and that culture is dominant over most genetic, inherited, behavioral tendencies, other opponents contend that the application of animal instincts to human beings is nothing more than a grossly imperfect transfer by analogy. Thus, it is assumed: they are animals and we are animals; all species are the result of a long evolutionary process; therefore the same inherited survival needs and instincts that characterize other primates also may be invoked to explain human behavior. Critics of sociobiology argue that its tenets are simplistic in light of the sophistication and complexity of the human organism and human societies. Finally, critics point out that the essential principles and hypotheses of sociobiology are scientifically untestable and therefore remain nothing more than interesting speculations.

Nevertheless, numerous efforts are being made to utilize sociobiology in the study of deviant behavior. For example, Sarnoff A. Mednick (1977), in harmony with the sociobiological perspective, argued that law-abiding behavior must be learned; that it is not inherent in people to conform to the normative behavioral expectations that prevail in their social group. Mednick theorized that people learn to conform because they are afraid to deviate. He acknowledged that this learning process is an intrinsic part of the culture content of a people. Furthermore, he indicated that the vast majority of cases of deviant and criminal behavior can be traced to socioeconomic and situational factors that temporarily neutralize the socially learned avoidance of punishment. There remain a very small number of deviant individuals whose antisocial behavior falls into a consistent pattern and for which there is no apparent social cause. Mednick's research concentrated on that minority of offenders and suggested that their habitual misconduct is caused by an autonomic nervous system that is biologically unique to them. Their autonomic nervous system recovers very quickly from threats and fear of social punishment for misdeeds, thus reinforcing their ability to inhibit previously learned conformity responses:

> As Mednick points out, his is a learning theory. It is a *social* learning theory to the extent that people's behavior is influenced by previous reactions of others. It is a *biological* theory to the extent that biological factors (in this case, the ANS) regulate the efficiency of the learning process (McCaghy, 1985:38–39) [*italics in original*]

Thus far, the main thrust of sociobiology has been centered on animal behavior. However, as new findings accumulate and subsequently are extended to explain human behavior, we may expect renewed controversy and debate between extremists in both the biological and social science camps. As one scholar put it:

> Unfortunately, most of the debate concerning genetic aspects of human behavior has been highly emotional and, hence, extremist in each direction. On the one hand, many social scientists advocate that human beings are born as *tabula rasa*, blank slates with infinite potential to become anything at all, depending only on experience. On the other end of the spectrum is extreme genetic determinism, in which free will and the capacity for self-betterment are denied, and we are literally prisoners of our heredity. As usual in such outlandish debates, the truth doubtless lies somewhere in between (Dobzhansky, 1976:169) [*italics in original*]

Other leading scholars in sociobiology have taken a moderating and compromising position. Barash (1982:146) cautiously declared that sociobiologists are justified in assuming an influence of genetics in human behavior although not necessarily a controlling influence. On the other hand, most social scientists feel that any conclusions regarding the validity of sociobiology are very premature and must await the empirical testing and theoretical scrutiny to which all established theories are subjected.

SUMMARY AND CONCLUSION

We began this chapter by exploring some of the myths and folklore that attempted to directly link biology to behavior. We pointed out how many of these attempts led to racial and ethnic slurs and created some unfair stereotypes.

The eighteenth century gave rise to the Classical School of Criminological thought which assumed that crime/delinquency was the result of the exercise of free will and logical, rational thought. The Neoclassical School modified the assumptions of the classical theorists by allowing for extenuating circumstances, and recognized that not all people were equally rational. This allowed for some discretion and differential treatment for young offenders, or adults who were adjudged mentally disturbed.

In the late nineteenth century, the Positive School of criminology developed, and through the leadership of men like Cesare Lombroso attempted to scientifically link biological and physiological characteristics to criminal behavior. This biological determinism laid the foundation for twentieth century research, which attempted to attribute delinquency to the shape of one's body. As the search for a biological connection to delinquency has continued, research has been conducted on many biological variables such as sex, race, ethnicity, genetics, diet, and brain malfunctions.

In an attempt to link biological determinism with an understanding of the contributing influence of social and cultural determinants, sociobiological explanations for delinquency emerged. Sociobiologists insist that social behavior is a product of evolutionary history and genetics. Hence, delinquent behavior is viewed as being genetically programmed into certain individuals.

Social scientists, especially sociologists, have acknowledged that genetics, biology, and physiology may all play an important role in understanding juvenile delinquency. However, they insist that it is the manner in which these traits are dealt with in a social and cultural context that explains deviant behavior.

It is apparent that the Gluecks' insightful conclusion—that physical characteristics may be socially defined and treated in ways that encourage criminal or delinquent behavior—sheds light on the probable relationship between biology and sociology. C. R. Jeffery (1979) suggested that the interaction between biological traits and social factors represents a powerful force in producing deviant or delinquent behavior (Figure 4–1).

FIGURE 4–1

Relationships Between Biological and Social Factors in Producing Deviant and Delinquent Behavior

Personal biological factors and conditions ⟷ Social-environmental factors and situations ⟷ Deviant and delinquent behavior

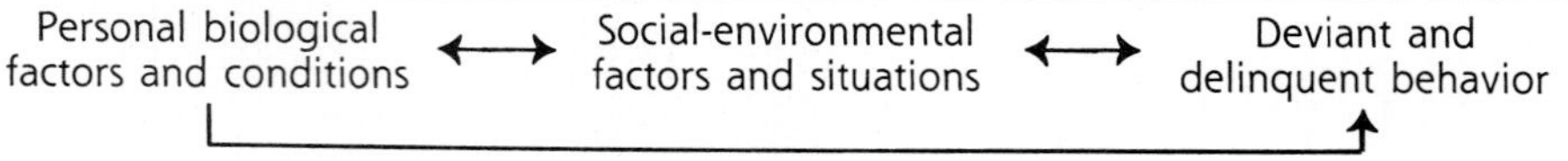

Source: Adapted from Shoemaker, D. *Theories of Delinquency.* New York: Oxford Press, 1984:14. Reprinted by permission.

Donald Shoemaker (1984:14) utilized the diagram shown in Figure 4–1 to illustrate and argue that there is more than one plausible connection between the biological makeup of a youth and the youth's delinquent behavior. For example, the long arrow represents the direct relationship between biological factors or medical conditions such as a brain tumor or a dietary problem that can lead to juvenile misconduct. This direct causation approach bypasses social and cultural factors that may combine with biological and/or physiological traits to produce delinquent behavior. The latter possibility is depicted by the shorter arrows in Figure 4–1 that link unfavorable biological factors with negative circumstances in the social environment such as an unhappy home life, inadequate parental role models, poor academic performance in school, and/or the presence of delinquent peers in the neighborhood. Together, these biological and social factors combine to produce or generate antisocial behavior in the youth.

CONCEPT APPLICATION

ILLUSTRATIVE ANECDOTE

The following anecdote describes an experience of one of the authors, who encountered a young woman who demonstrated how the negative social evaluation of physical characteristics can result in deviant behavior. As you read it, look for the synthesis of biological and social variables that may be causally related to deviance and delinquency.

"An Ugly Girl"

When I was fresh out of graduate school and relatively inexperienced in my new academic role, I found myself thrust into a traumatic conflict situation that

I will never forget. In addition to my teaching duties, I was asked to serve on "The Student Counseling Committee." That mild title belies the gut-level, arena-like confrontation I experienced at my first meeting with the committee.

My first sense of impending disaster occurred when I arrived and discovered that the committee functioned with a rotating chairmanship and—like a game of tag or Russian Roulette—I was "it" . . .

Immediately the door opened and the first student came in for "counsel." To my astonishment, a powerfully built and angry young woman was ushered into the committee room. It became quickly apparent that she had been there before and that she was unimpressed with the committee—especially the green young sociologist at the head of the table. She turned out to be an extremely formidable adversary.

The reason for her periodic visits with the Student Counseling Committee was her continuous and unprovoked verbal assaults upon her teachers and other students. Occasionally, she would punctuate her words with a slap or a kick. She was not only unpleasant and uncooperative, but loud and rude in all of her social contacts. She was a bully. As a consequence, she was feared, hated, and socially isolated. Other students rejected her; teachers were driven to exasperation, but agreed that she was a superior student. Her trademark was a sharp tongue with which she mercilessly belittled the physical shortcomings of others. Even during our interview, she scornfully referred to the baldness, fatness, crooked teeth, and other imperfections of the committee members. To every overture we made, she replied in the same insolent and insulting manner.

. . . I quickly leafed through her dossier on the table in front of me and discovered that she had scored exceptionally high on an intelligence test. She was not stupid; quite the contrary. "But why is she acting this way?" I kept asking myself. "If we can explain her strange behavior, perhaps we can help her . . ."

It was a grim and tension-filled situation as the young woman berated the school, teachers, students, the committee, and me. Finally, as I sought to blunt her attack and grope for some insight, I asked pointedly, "Young lady . . . what is wrong with you?" She recoiled momentarily before lashing out again. But her reaction led me to believe that she did have some conscious inkling of why she behaved as she did. A bit later, when she paused for breath in her tirade, I demanded of her: "Tell me what is wrong with you." She looked around the room and shuddered. And we were dumbfounded as she covered her face with her hands and cried out one of the most pitiful stories I have ever heard. "I'm so ugly!" she began.

The basis for her incorrigible and deviant behavior (often officially classified as "juvenile delinquency") had been laid in her early childhood. Her parents had openly compared her with more winsome sisters, and with grotesque humor referred to her as "the ugly duckling in the family." She felt rejected because of prominent facial features and a boyish, muscular build. Her dilemma deepened when she became the target of cruel nicknames and taunts in elementary school. Not only did she accept the negative and painful appraisal as valid, but acted as she surmised an "ugly person ought to act." As she talked, I was reminded of the classic commentary of W. I. Thomas on the social psychology of human behavior: "A thing is real as it is real in its consequences." Ultimately, that socially injured and stigmatized young woman transformed her hurt into hatred. She felt that her survival was at stake so she went on the offensive and struck back at society.

While her case was extreme, a negative evaluation of personal physical appearance is a common problem among adolescents. Many young people, already under the strains associated with moving into adulthood, become dismayed when they compare themselves with the illusory physical ideals of peer and reference groups (Erikson, 1956). Failing to meet group standards for physical appearance can result in great personal stress. Stolz and Stolz (1944) extensively interviewed ninety-three teen-age boys and eighty-three teen-age girls regarding their physical characteristics and their relative attitudes about their appearance. Nearly all of them were worried about something. Boys were distressed by lack of size, particularly height, eyeglasses, fatness, poor physique, lack of muscular strength, unusual facial features, skin blemishes, and lack of shoulder breadth. Girls were concerned about tallness, fatness, facial features, late development, skin blemishes, thinness, large limbs, and eyeglasses. There is some evidence that this adolescent anxiety over undesirable appearance can be transformed into antisocial behavior.

Source: Jack E. Bynum. "So You Think You Are Ugly?" Life and Health, December, 1975:9–11 (reprinted by permission).

*   *   *   *

Based upon the information available in the short story about the "ugly" girl, what evidence can you find to support the view that biological factors, when joined with social conditions, can cause or reinforce antisocial behavior, from the viewpoints of the Positivists, the sociobiologists, William Sheldon, and Freda Adler?

CONCEPT INTEGRATION

QUESTIONS AND TOPICS FOR STUDY AND DISCUSSION

1. Reexamine the research of Lombroso, Sheldon, and the Gluecks. Identify and critique their methodology, findings, and conclusions.
2. What are the main assumptions of the Classical School of Criminological Thought and the Positive School of Criminology? What are the differences between these two early approaches to explain criminal behavior?

3. Discuss and explain the hypothesized links between the following variables:
   (a) The XYY chromosome and criminal behavior.
   (b) Abnormal EEG patterns and deviant or criminal behavior.
   (c) Diet, biochemical irregularities, and misbehavior.
4. Crime statistics show that males commit more violent crimes than women. Based on your reading of this chapter, why might this be so? Is this pattern changing? If so, why?
5. Carefully define and explain "sociobiology." How does this field of study attempt to bridge the social and biological sciences? What contribution may sociobiology make toward an understanding of human behavior?
6. Why are rates of crime and delinquency highest in the inner city? How did Shaw and McKay explain the relationship between race/ethnicity, socioeconomic status, place of residence, and rates of crime and delinquency?
7 What did the Gluecks mean by their statement: "A physical characteristic may be socially defined and treated in ways which encourage criminal behavior?" Give several examples.
8. Define the following terms and concepts: biological determinism, atavism, constitutional typology, phrenology, endomorph, ectomorph, mesomorph, electroencephalograph, tabula rasa, chromosomal abnormality, dyslexia.

References

Adler, F. 1975. *Sisters in crime.* New York: McGraw-Hill Book Co.

Barash, D. P. 1982. *Sociobiology and behavior* (2nd ed.) New York: Elsevier.

Barsley, M. 1966. *Some of my best friends are left-handed people.* Hollywood, CA: Wilshire Book Company.

Broder, P. K., Peters, G. W., & Zimmerman, J. 1978. The relationship between self-reported juvenile delinquency and learning disabilities: A preliminary look at the data. Omaha, NE: Creighton University Institute for Business, Law, and Social Research.

Brothers, J. 1985. Women and violent crime. Fort Worth, TX: *Star Telegram.* June 15, 1985:D-3.

Bynum, J. E. 1975. So you think you are ugly? *Life and Health* 90, 12 (December):9–11.

Clinard, M. B. 1968. *Sociology of deviant behavior* (3rd ed.) New York: Holt, Rinehart and Winston.

Cohen, A. K. 1966. *Deviance and control.* Englewood Cliffs, NJ: Prentice-Hall.

Conrad, P. 1975. The discovery of hyperkinesis: Notes on the medicalization of deviant behavior. *Social Problems* XXIII, 2 (April:12–22).

Dobzhansky, T. 1976. The myths of genetic predestination and of tabula rasa. *Perspectives in Biology and Medicine* 19:156–170.

Eitzen, D. S. 1986. *Social Problems* (3rd ed.) Boston: Allyn and Bacon.

Erikson, E. 1956. The problem of identity. *Journal of the American Psychiatric Association* 4, 1 (January):56–121.

Federal Bureau of Investigation. 1987. *Crime in the United States: Uniform Crime Reports—1986*. Washington, DC: US Government Printing Office.

Ferrero, G. L. 1911. *Criminal man according to the classification of Cesare Lombroso*. New York: Putnam.

Fox, R. G. 1971. The XYY offender: A modern myth? *Journal of Criminal Law, Criminology and Police Science* 62, 1:63.

Glueck, S. & Glueck, E. 1950. *Unraveling juvenile delinquency*. Cambridge: Harvard University Press.

Goring, C.[1913] 1972. *The English convict: A statistical study*. Montclair, NJ: Patterson Smith.

Hartl, E. M., Monelly, E. P., & Elderkin, R. D. 1982. *Physique and delinquent behavior*. New York: Academic Press.

Hunt, J. 1973. Rapists have big ears: Genetic screening in Massachusetts. *The Real Paper*, July 4, 1973:4.

Jeffery, C. R. 1979. *Biology and crime*. Beverly Hills, CA: Sage.

Klein, M. 1969. Violence in American juvenile gangs. In D. Mulvihill, M. Tumin, with L. Curtis (Eds.) *Crimes of Violence*. National Commission on the Causes and Prevention of Violence, Vol. 13. Washington, DC: US Government Printing Office, p. 1429.

Lombroso, C. 1911. *Crime, its causes and remedies* (trans. H. P. Horton). Boston: Little, Brown.

Lonsdale, D. & Shamberger, R. J. 1980. Red cell transketolase as an indicator of nutritional deficiency. *American Journal of Clinical Nutrition* 33 (February):205–211.

McCaghy, C. 1985. *Deviant behavior: Crime, conflict, and interest groups* (2nd ed.) New York: Macmillan.

McClearn, G. E. 1969. Biological bases of social behavior with specific reference to violent behavior. In D. Mulvihill, M. Tumin, with L. Curtis (Eds.) *Crimes of Violence*. Staff Report to the National Commission on Causes and Prevention of Violence, Vol. 13. Washington, DC: US Government Printing Office, p. 1003.

Mednick, S. A. 1977. A biosocial theory of the learning of law-abiding behavior. In S. A. Mednick & K. O. Christionsen (Eds.) *Biosocial Bases of Criminal Behavior*. New York: Garden Press.

Miller, W. 1975. *Violence by youth gangs and youth groups as a crime problem in major American cities*. Washington, DC: US Government Printing Office.

Moran, R. 1978. Biomedical research and the politics of crime control: A historical perspective. *Contemporary Crises* 2:335–357.

Murray, C. A. 1976. *The link between learning disabilities and juvenile delinquency*. Washington, DC: US Department of Justice.

Newman, G. 1978. *The punishment response.* Philadelphia: JB Lippincott.

Poremba, C. D. 1975. Learning disabilities, youth and delinquency: Programs for intervention. In H. R. Myklebust (Ed.) *Progress in Learning Disabilities*, Vol. 3. New York: Grune and Stratton, pp. 123–149.

Reed, B., Knickelbine, S., & Knickelbine, M. 1983. *Food, teens, and behavior.* Manitowoc, WI: Natural Press.

Robins, L. N. 1978. Aetiological implications in studies of childhood histories relating to antisocial personality. In R. D. Hare & D. Schalling (Eds.) *Psychopathic behavior: Approaches to research.* New York: John Wiley, pp. 252–272.

Rosenberg, M. M., Stebbins, R. A., & Turowetz, A. (Eds.) 1982. *The sociology of deviance.* New York: St. Martin's Press.

Salzman, L. 1980. *Treatment of the obsessive personality.* New York: Jason Aronson, Inc.

Satterfield, J. H. 1978. The hyperactive child syndrome: A precursor of adult psychopathy? In R. D. Hare & D. Schalling (Eds.) *Psychopathic behavior: Approaches to research.* New York: John Wiley, pp. 329–346.

Schauss, A., Simonsen, C. & Bland, J. 1979. Critical analysis of the diets of chronic juvenile offenders, Part 1. *Journal of Orthomolecular Psychiatry*, 8, 3:149–157.

Schlapp, M. G. & Smith, E. H. 1928. *The new criminology.* New York: Boni and Liveright.

Schoenthaler, S. & Doraz, W. 1983. Type of offenses which can be reduced in an institutional setting using nutritional intervention. *International Journal of Biosocial Research* 4:74–84. And item, Diet and crime. In *International Journal of Biosocial Research* 4:29–39.

Schulz, H. & Mainusch, G. 1971. Contribution of clinical electroencephalography to forensic expert opinion. Summarized in *Abstracts on Criminology and Penology.* W. K. Nagel (Ed.) 11, 478:138–139. The Hague: A. E. Klewer, Deventer.

Shaw, C. R. & McKay, H. D. 1969. *Juvenile delinquency in urban areas.* Chicago: University of Chicago Press.

Sheldon, W., Hartl, E. M., & McDermott, E. 1949. *Varieties of delinquent youth.* New York: Harper & Row.

Shoemaker, D. J. 1984. *Theories of delinquency: An examination of explanations of delinquent behavior.* New York: Oxford University Press.

Short, J. F. & Strodtbeck, F. 1965. *Group process and gang delinquency.* Chicago: University of Chicago Press.

Siegel, L. J. & Senna, J. J. 1981. *Juvenile delinquency: Theory, practice, and law.* St. Paul, MN: West.

Spergel, I. 1964. *Racketville, slumtown, haulberg: An exploratory study of delinquent subcultures.* Chicago: University of Chicago Press.

Stolz, H. R. & Stolz, L. M. 1944. Adolescent problems related to somatic variations. Chapter V. *National Society for the Study of Education.* Adolescence, 43rd Yearbook.

Thio, A. 1988. *Deviant behavior* (3rd ed.) New York: Harper and Row.

Thornton, W. E., Jr., James, J. A., & Doerner, W. G. 1987. *Delinquency and justice* (2nd ed.). New York: Random House.

Thrasher, F. 1927. *The gang.* Chicago: University of Chicago Press.

Turk, A. T. 1969. *Criminality and legal order.* Chicago: Rand-McNally.

Voss, H. L. 1963. Ethnic differentials in delinquency in Honolulu. *Journal of Criminal Law, Criminology, and Police Science* 54 (September):322–327.

Wilson, E. O. 1975. *Sociobiology: The new synthesis.* Cambridge: Harvard University Press.

1978. *On human nature.* Cambridge: Harvard University Press.

Wolfgang, M. E., Figlio, R. M., & Sellin, T. 1972. *Delinquency in a birth cohort.* Chicago: University of Chicago Press.

Chapter 5

Psychogenic Explanations of Juvenile Delinquency

READING OBJECTIVES

The reading of this chapter will help you achieve the following objectives:

1. Explain the psychological concepts of the unconscious and personality as motivating sources of human behavior, including juvenile delinquency.
2. Describe some of the techniques and tools used by psychiatrists and psychologists, such as psychoanalysis and projective tests, to trace symptomatic conduct disorders to deeply hidden mental stress and conflict.
3. Outline and discuss some of the specific theories developed by psychiatrists and psychologists to explain the causes of juvenile delinquency.
4. Perceive psychologically based juvenile delinquency as organized into a typology of various causes and kinds of misbehavior.
5. Be aware of some major limitations and weaknesses of the psychogenic approaches to identifying and explaining the causes of juvenile delinquency.

INTRODUCTION

March 30, 1981 was a cool and rainy day in Washington, D. C. Ronald Reagan, the fortieth President of the United States, was concluding a speech to a labor union convention at the Washington Hilton Hotel. Outside, on the sidewalk near a doorway, a small crowd of people huddled under umbrellas and waited for a glimpse of the President as he exited from the hotel. As the President's entourage came into view, a murmur of friendly greeting came from the crowd, and President Reagan turned to wave and smile before entering the limousine that would carry him back to the White House.

Suddenly, a young man stepped forward on the sidewalk and simultaneously pulled a small automatic pistol from his pocket. Before anyone could react, he assumed a shooter's crouch and rapidly fired at the President. One bullet entered the brain of White House Press Secretary, James S. Brady. A Secret Service agent and a Washington policeman were also gunned down and lay sprawled on the sidewalk. Another bullet entered President Reagan's chest, broke a rib, punctured a lung, and lodged near his heart.

In that one frightening and chaotic moment, John W. Hinckley, Jr. became more than just the latest and youngest would-be assassin of an American President. In Hinckley's long trial that followed his assassination attempt, there would be a renewed and intense focus on insanity as an explanation for criminal behavior and as a valid legal defense (Camper et al., 1982). No effort was made to deny that Hinckley had attacked the President's party with murderous intent. After all, news reporters had captured the entire episode on videotape, from the firing of the gun by the expressionless John Hinckley, Jr., to the moment when he was disarmed, subdued, and arrested at the scene. The facts that he had purchased the gun and ammunition with assassination in mind, that he had previously stalked President Carter, that his March 30 attack on President Reagan had been carefully planned, and that he was caught with "the smoking gun in his hand," were readily acknowledged, but received much less attention than Hinckley's mental processes and state of mind leading up to the assassination attempt.

Legal scholars agree that criminal conduct is not enough to elicit sanctions from society. It must be demonstrated to the satisfaction of the court that a criminal offender has **mens rea**—*a guilty mind or evil intent,* in order to be punished. In other words, it must be conclusively established that the offender consciously intended to break the law (Halleck, 1966).

Thus, Hinckley's trial was a contest between the professional opinions of psychiatrists, those called as expert witnesses by federal prosecutors, and those who testified for the defense. The prosecution sought to establish that Hinckley was legally sane and therefore fully responsible for his criminal conduct. On the other hand, attorneys for the defense sought to convince the jurors that Hinckley's mental illness was so severe that he lacked substantial capacity to appreciate "the wrongfulness of his acts and could no longer control his own

John Hinkley, Jr. (center, between federal agents) the young man charged with the attempted murder of President Ronald Reagan, was finally institutionalized at St. Elizabeth's Mental Hospital in Washington, D.C.

conduct" (San Francisco Chronicle, 1981:24). When the long trial ended, John W. Hinckley, Jr. was declared to have "diminished mental capacity" at the time of the assassination attempt. He was sent to St. Elizabeth's Mental Hospital in Washington, D.C. where he received psychiatric evaluation and treatment.

The legal and moral controversy regarding mental illness as it affects human behavior and individual responsibility for one's behavior is not new, nor have we heard the last of it. And this issue has important implications for our study and understanding of the psychogenic explanations of juvenile delinquency.

THE PSYCHOGENIC APPROACH

In the nineteenth century, mankind began to accumulate new and important knowledge about human anatomy, physiology, neurology, chemistry, and general medicine. From that, there were many far-reaching implications and applications for the scientific study of human behavior, including some of the early and unsubstantiated biological theories of crime and delinquency discussed in the preceding chapter. More noteworthy, the discovery of an organic basis for many physical illnesses led to the further discovery of an organic basis for some mental illnesses (Reid, 1988). This latter finding lent impetus to the development of psychiatry and psychology as academic disciplines and serious areas of research and knowledge.

Psychiatry is *a medical specialty concerned with the diagnosis, treatment, and prevention of disordered or abnormal behavior.* After completion of their initial medical school education, some physicians take further specialized training in psychiatry in order to become professional psychiatrists. Because psychiatry is a subarea of medicine, psychiatrists tend to view and conceptualize aberrant behavior as caused by some form of mental illness or abnormality. An easy application of this medical model to deviant behavior by juveniles was widely popularized in the late nineteenth century when The Child Savers, an influential group of social reformers, began to use such terms as "disease," "illness," and "contagion" to describe adolescent crime. They promoted the ideas that criminals were the natural product of biological heritage and corrupt urban environments. The Child Savers, together with some prominent penologists of that time, "presupposed that crime was a symptom of 'pathology' and that criminals should be treated like irresponsible, sick patients" (Platt, 1969:45).

Psychology is *a behavioral science that investigates and associates mental processes with behavior.* Psychologists try to understand why people act the way they do by exploring how they grow up, how they react to and cope with stress and change, how their personalities form, and how they become disturbed or get into trouble:

> Unlike psychiatry, which is a medical specialty devoted to the understanding and cure of mental disease, psychology has a broader task, ranging from the laboratory study of simple behavior in animals . . . to the complicated behavior of human beings in social groups (Rehm, 1983:593).

Although psychiatry and psychology are independent fields of study, they have much in common. Both focus primarily on individuals and perceive human behavior as originating in the mind. Extreme deviance or delinquency is generally seen by psychiatrists and psychologists as overt symptoms or behavioral expressions arising from underlying personality or emotional maladjustments and as alternatives to mental illness (Halleck, 1971).

In addition, psychiatrists and clinical psychologists "devote much of their effort to helping disturbed, troubled, and mentally ill people" (Rehm, 1983:593) and share many similar diagnostic and treatment techniques. In view of the extensive common ground shared by professionals in these two disciplines, psychiatric and psychological contributions will be discussed together as the *psychogenic approach* to human behavior in general and juvenile delinquency in particular.

THE DISCOVERY OF THE UNCONSCIOUS

The pioneering work of Sigmund Freud (1856–1939) laid the foundation for the twentieth century psychogenic approach to understanding and explaining human behavior. Freud was originally trained in medicine and neurology but his interest in the aberrant behavior associated with mental illness led him to conclude that biological, physiological, and genetic attributes cannot completely or adequately account for human behavior. He demonstrated that much human conduct is not consciously motivated. Instead, Freud identified a deep, unconscious dimension of the human mind as the motivating source of many acts (Freud, 1961). The **unconscious** may be defined as *a subterranean mental reservoir of unfulfilled needs, desires, and feelings accumulated throughout life and not ordinarily available to conscious thought.* These unconscious drives may manifest their presence through dreams, mistakes, and symptoms (Ellenberger, 1970).

According to Freud, humans suffer mental conflict because of desires and needs that are repressed into the unconscious mind, often during childhood development of personality, identity, and acceptable social roles. Thus, while an individual's behavior may appear to observers as illogical and even abnormal, the troublesome conduct is actually a purposive expression of specific needs that are submerged in the subconscious mind of the subject.

THE FORMATION OF PERSONALITY

The concept of personality has been another intriguing focus for the study and explanation of human behavior by those employing the psychogenic approach. **Personality** refers to *the unique organization of relatively stable psychological traits possessed by an individual, as revealed by one's interaction with people, events, situations, and other components of the environment.* For example, "enthusiastic," "energetic," "fun-loving," and "idealistic" are some descriptive personality traits that seem to characterize many young people. But if a youth is cheerful and upbeat one day and sad or depressed the next day, we would have some difficulty in ascertaining a dominant personality. A psychologically healthy person maintains a certain consistency and identifiability of personality most of the time that is apparent in the day-to-day presentation of self.

Freud and his colleagues contended that the normal adult personality has three fully developed components: the *id*, the *ego*, and the *superego*. Each of these three dimensions of the human personality performs critical, complex, and interrelated psychic and social functions for the individual.

At birth, the infant's personality is largely unidimensional, dominated by the **id**—*a set of primitive, self-centered impulses and instincts.* The sensuous and hedonistic id seeks immediate gratification and has no sense of time or reality. The spontaneous id functions to enhance the survivability of the infant organism. During the first few years of life the individual develops an ego and a superego. We may conceive of the **superego** as *an antithetical or opposite force that restrains the impulsive id.* The superego is developed in the individual through socialization, and represents socially conditioned and culturally learned moral values and a sense of right and wrong. It includes the formation of conscience and an ego ideal. Whereas the id clamors for self-satisfaction, "The ego ideal represents what we should do and the conscience gives us guilt feelings when we do 'wrong' " (Haskell and Yablonsky, 1978:569).

The **ego,** in Freud's model, is *that part of the personality or self that arbitrates between the demands of the id and the socially sensitive and idealistic superego.* The more pragmatic ego is designed to unify extreme personality positions into balanced, behavioral responses to stimuli. If successful, it directs behavior toward satisfaction of urges consistent with a knowledge of social and physical reality. By living in harmony with the reality of the social situation through the ego, the individual may postpone immediate gratification but does not abandon those personal desires.

FREUDIAN THEORY AS AN EXPLANATION OF CRIME AND DELINQUENCY

Freud's theoretical contributions regarding the mental or psychic origins and motivations for human behavior have been adopted, adapted, expanded, and applied by numerous other psychiatrists and psychologists to the inner conflicts, personality maladjustments, emotional problems, and feelings of insecurity, inadequacy, and inferiority among their patients. In addition, Freud's insights have guided countless psychogenic efforts to identify and explain the mental cause or causes of such conduct disorders as sexual deviations, alcoholism, drug addiction, crime, and juvenile delinquency.

As a common example, Freud and many neo-Freudians have argued that crime is an outgrowth of the repressed, unconscious, emotional traumas of childhood (Sykes, 1980:8; Samenow, 1984). According to this view, most crime is a result of an imbalance in the ego between uncontrolled drives (the id) and society's expectations about behavior (the superego). Usually the problem is ascribed to an overly strict superego in which the offender, as a child, was socialized with a supercharged, unconscious sense of guilt. In such cases, as drives are repressed, pressures build up until the drives become manifest in abnormal and dangerous ways. Freud (1961) contended that children and adults often misbehave in order to be punished, which then temporarily relieves that guilt. On the other hand, much deviant and delinquent behavior has been credited to a deficient or underdeveloped superego, which fails to intervene or restrain the antisocial impulses of the id. These individuals were also inadequately conditioned to internalize "the socially adequate responses which society requires them to integrate into some form of 'conscience' " (Eysenck, 1979:13).

In both examples just cited, the psychiatrist or clinical psychologist would likely look to the subject's early childhood relationship with parents for explanatory causes of the disordered behavior. It is suggested that the socialization imposed by overly strict or overly permissive parents can create an ego insufficient to perform its assigned task of mediating between the id and the superego.

PSYCHOANALYSIS

In addition to substantiating the existence of the unconscious and introducing the concepts of the id, ego, and superego in personality formation, Freud and his followers also developed various techniques for probing and examining the unconscious forces and motives that energize human behavior:

> The most ambitious and intensive form of psychotherapy is represented by *Freudian psychoanalysis* . . . The intention is to afford the individual insight into the unconscious motivation of his behavior and to allow the development of a 'healthy' personality structure. Frequently, the aim is not the removal of the symptom, rather it is to solve the unconscious problems which have led, according to psychoanalytic theory, to the development of a particular symptom. The major technique is that of free association, in which the individual is asked to say everything which comes into his mind without any effort to select or repress. This material, together with the individual's reports on his dreams, is then explored and interpreted by the analyst (Feldman, 1978:234).

Free association, or *saying whatever comes to mind,* is still the basic tool of psychoanalysis. But psychiatrists and psychologists have continued to develop instruments designed to elicit the unconscious, subjective responses of their patients. Prominent among them is a wide variety of projective tests.

PROJECTIVE TESTS

Projective tests are founded on the principle that a patient undergoing psychoanalysis will reveal deep characteristics and unconscious feelings such as hatred, fear, frustration, and aggression, when expressions and responses are most unrestricted and unstructured. For instance, if the subject is asked to say something or respond to some external stimuli for which there are no previously well-learned conventional responses, it is assumed that hidden, sublimated emotions, motives, drives, and personality traits are likely to guide responses. Consequently, projective tests such as the Rorschach are specially designed to elicit these unconscious projections.

FIGURE 5-1

An Ink-Blot Pattern Similar to Those in the Rorschach Ink Blot Test.

The Rorschach Ink-blot Test

The Rorschach Test was created by Hermann Rorschach in 1921 and utilizes a series of ink-blots as undefined visual stimuli. Each ink-blot in the series is produced by placing drops of ink on a sheet of paper, which is then folded and opened to form an unfamiliar, random pattern (Figure 5–1).

It is assumed by the psychoanalyst administering the Rorschach Ink-blot Test that if an individual is asked to identify what is perceived in the vague and unstructured ink-blots, definitions and responses *must* come from the subjective, subconscious self and are *not* determined by any familiar, prelearned, objective definition of the stimuli. It is further assumed that the responses reflect important (though hidden) emotions, drives, and motives that originated early in the subject's life and experiences. The patient's responses to the series of ink blots are carefully examined and catalogued for evidence of consistent patterns and themes, and then interpreted by the psychoanalyst as an explanation of the subject's disorders.

Projective Tests and Homicidal Children

Enthusiastic advocates of projective tests have suggested a wide range of diagnostic applications, including the identification and explanation of paranoia, schizophrenia, phobic reactions, and other neurotic and psychotic conditions. One of the most controversial applications has been proposed by some zealous psychiatrists who believe that projective tests could help to identify, in advance, those children most likely to commit murder. The idea is based on the assumption that youths with delinquent propensities go through an early *predelinquent stage* before the delinquent personality and identity are fully developed (Hakeem, 1957–58). The position is taken that children afflicted with this condition of latent delinquency will become delinquent unless there is remedial intervention. For example, Dr. Edward Glover, a renowned British psychiatrist and psychoanalyst, submitted a memorandum to the Royal Commission on Capital Punishment, on behalf of the Institute for the Scientific Treatment of Delinquency, which contended that children liable to commit murder could be detected in early childhood, even in infancy, with projective tests such as the Rorschach. He called for adequate prediction of future homicidal children in order to prepare programs of prevention. Here is a small portion of the amazing dialog between the Chairman of the Commission and Dr. Glover:

[Dr. Glover]: . . . I have no hesitation in saying that the crux of the whole approach to the problem of murder and the problem of prevention or punishment lies in an adequate psychiatric attack at the right point. The right point is theoretically at any age, from birth upwards, but in practice between the ages of 2½ and 8. There should be an adequate service of child guidance, including the use of batteries of tests; and we feel fairly convinced that although you would not recognize all the potential murderers, . . . you would strike seriously to the root of the problem of murder and its prevention . . .

[The Chairman]: Can you at that stage identify those who have these potentialities in them?

[Dr. Glover]: That can be done quite rapidly. There are so-called projective techniques of examination which are valuable, because they eliminate subjective bias on the part of the examiner and of the case examined. They have now arrived at a state of, not perfection, but adequacy, so that it is possible to take a child who is to all appearances merely an inhibited child, without any history of bad behaviour, and discover that he is potentially violent . . . (Minutes of Evidence Taken from the Royal Commission on Capital Punishment, 1949:501; Reported in Hakeem, 1957:58).

Critics of projective tests, including many psychologists and psychiatrists, point out that these instruments are limited in their usefulness because their reliability and validity are still uncertain (Bell, 1948; Kuhlen, 1952; Vold, 1958). While they may be helpful in minimizing the subjective intrusion of the psychotherapist during the actual testing situation, there are inadequate safeguards against the subjective biases of the person who later synthesizes and interprets the subject's responses.

The most severe criticism of projective tests is aimed at their use in identifying and diagnosing innocent persons as potential criminals—before they are guilty of serious offenses. Sociologists see this psychoanalytical approach as grossly unfair to the subjects, leading to unavoidable social stigma as they are evaluated by professionals with such character-tainting labels as "predelinquent" or "potential murderer" (see the discussion on labeling theory in Chapter

6). In addition, the American criminal justice system prohibits arresting, punishing, and/or rehabilitating people *before* they have allegedly committed a criminal offense. However, because of the popularity and influence of psychology and the general acceptance of the predelinquent model by social workers and juvenile courts (Lubove, 1965; Mennel, 1973), the notion that very young children should be the diagnostic focus for latent criminality is still very common. For example, former Jackson County (Oregon) Circuit Judge L. L. Sawyer confidently stated:

> You can recognize future criminals back in the second grade . . . And because that's where it starts, the early grades of elementary school are the best battleground for attacking crime (Mitchell, 1972:2).

DELINQUENT ACTS AS SYMPTOMS

A basic tenet of the psychogenic approach to explaining and treating juvenile delinquency is that delinquent acts are symptoms—an obvious and natural application of the psychiatrist's medical training and jargon to the study of human behavior. Delinquency is not generally viewed by the psychiatrist and the clinical psychologist as behavior that is primarily learned from associates, or that springs from frustrating social circumstances, or that is the outcome of some social process such as labeling (as do sociologists). Rather, they view delinquent conduct as a manifested symptom of **psychopathology:** *some internal neurological disorder or deeply hidden personality disturbance.* Psychiatrists typically consider the delinquent act or symptom as "the sick or hurt child's cry for help." These clinicians generally would agree that such children do not consciously seek psychiatric treatment when they are disturbed enough to need it. The psychoanalytic literature contends that overt delinquency is an indirect appeal for help in resolving some internal conflict (Shoemaker, 1984).

Several psychogenic theorists and practitioners have looked with suspicion upon a number of other common childhood activities besides outright delinquent behavior which, if carried to excess, may be viewed as symptoms of some underlying emotional disturbance or personality maladjustment. William Healy and Augusta Bronner (1957), Raymond Kuhlen (1952), and others have variously associated bed-wetting, nail-biting, interest or activity in sports, nervousness, and movie attendance with personality deviations and possible delinquency. This medical model approach is discussed further in Chapter 12, and prevention and treatment strategies based upon these alleged predelinquency symptoms are discussed in Chapter 14. Critics of these suggestions contend that the preoccupation with so-called behavioral symptoms as indicators of predelinquency can not only blur the boundaries for socially tolerable behavior, but can also place virtually everyone under suspicious scrutiny. Furthermore, the psychoanalyst's reliance upon such symptoms is really evidence that the patient's inner mental life is not subject to direct observation and it is difficult to offer objective proof or empirical evidence supporting psychogenic assessments (Johnson, 1974).

OTHER PSYCHOGENIC EXPLANATIONS OF JUVENILE DELINQUENCY

Though Freudian and neo-Freudian theories probably have been the most influential, several other prominent psychogenic explanations of crime and delinquency merit discussion. It will become clear to the reader that there is considerable overlap among some of these theoretical constructs, and their difference is often a matter of emphasis. Moreover, underlying all of the psychogenic and biological approaches to etiology is a fundamental belief that criminals and delinquents are aberrant individuals, possessing some quirk of mind or body that is not present in the rest of the population.

Early Theories of Feeblemindedness

A bridge between the biological explanations discussed in the last chapter and the psychogenic theories accounting for crime and delinquency may be seen in the studies of feeblemindedness during the early decades of the twentieth century. Just as Lombroso (1911), Sheldon (1949), and other biological determinists argued that some individuals are constrained to antisocial behavior by a genetic or physiological predisposition, Goddard (1920), Healy and Bronner (1926), and other psychologists contended that mental deficiency is a primary cause of crime and delinquency. This interest was further stimulated by the popular studies of the Juke (Dugdale, 1910; Estrabrook, 1916) and Kallikak (Goddard, 1927) families that purported to trace inherited feeblemindedness and criminal tendencies through several generations. These assumptions have been subsequently declared invalid.

Those conclusions rested heavily upon the early application of measures of intelligence to institutionalized juvenile offenders. These were developed for the measurement of an individual's Intelligence Quotient (IQ), which is the ratio of a child's Mental Age (MA) to Chronological Age (CA). Thus, an IQ score of 100 means that one's MA and CA coincide at the national average. The higher the IQ, the brighter the individual; the lower the IQ, the more pronounced the retardation is assumed to be.

Many psychologists, with the popularized IQ tests, helped to replace the previously dominant idea that delinquents were somehow biologically defective with the newer notion that they were mentally defective. From this perspective, juvenile delinquents are viewed as retarded or lacking the mental capacity to know the difference between right and wrong; or cannot foresee serious consequences of misbehavior for themselves and for others; or cannot avoid being induced into crime by others.

In more recent decades, psychologists, educators, and other scholars have expanded their knowledge of how people learn, of how sociocultural variables and learning opportunities affect the accumulation of information by different individuals and groups, and of how test construction and administration procedures can affect responses to so-called Intelligence Tests. In addition, the ability of IQ tests to indicate or predict delinquent behavior has been widely challenged. IQ measurements of incarcerated or institutionalized offenders is a biased representation of the criminal and delinquent population since the subjects are those who were caught and convicted. Such scores tell us nothing about those who are successful in their deviance and avoid detection or apprehension. The preponderance of current, empirical evidence also fails to support the proposition that delinquents are inherently less intelligent than the general population (Samenow, 1984:19). Instead, it would be more accurate to say that low IQ scores are related to educational opportunities, and the likelihood of being officially identified as a delinquent is much greater in the most deprived socioeconomic groups whose educational opportunities are drastically circumscribed (Menard and Morse, 1984).

Neurological Abnormalities

It was a rather natural development for psychiatric research and theory as a medical specialty to advance the premise that some individual offenders may be suffering from a brain abnormality or some form of neurological damage. This psychogenic approach has variously linked criminal and delinquent behavior with congenital brain defects, a mental impairment induced by a tumor, or the residual neurological effects of an earlier injury.

Numerous cases have been documented in which atypical, deviant, and antisocial behavior can result from pressures, lesions, and other injuries to those vital areas of the cerebrospinal system that are closely associated with intellect, emotion, and inhibition. Not infrequently, the "problem child" with a conduct disorder is finally found to have suffered from a severe trauma to the brain at an earlier stage of development (Roth, 1968). Douglas (1960) found significant correlation between premature birth (associated with a greater incidence of minor brain damage than normal birth) and "bad behavior" of school children as rated by their teachers.

Richard Speck, who was convicted in 1967 of the slaying of eight student nurses in Chicago, is cited as a classic example of how neurological impairment from blows on the head may be a contributing factor in criminal behavior:

Before Speck's trial began, psychiatrist Ziporyn spent over 100 hours interviewing him. In a book written afterward he quoted Speck at length: 'When I was playing in a sandbox I hit myself on the head with a claw hammer. Accidentally, I knocked myself out. Then, a few years later—I must have been about 10—I was playing with some kids. They chased me and I climbed a tree. I . . . lost my hold. I fell on my head. My sister found me. She thought I was dead.' Speck's tale of head injuries continued: 'About five years after that, I did it again . . . I was running down a street and ran my head into a steel awning rod. I was knocked out again.' In Ziporyn's opinion 'Speck was a killer because his brain was damaged.' And he reached the conclusion that the 'lethal outburst was inevitable' (Adams, 1976:49).

In their ongoing search for empirical evidence linking mental processes and malfunctions with antisocial behavior, psychiatrists and neurologists have turned to highly sophisticated medical technology to measure and interpret brain activity. One method of studying nervous system functioning is to record the electrical activity of the brain. The summated electrical activity of the neurons in the brain is so great that it can be recorded through electrodes attached to the outer surface of the head. Such recordings are known as electroencephalograms (EEGs). One finding from this technique is that different patterns of electrical activity in the brain accompany different levels of alertness. For example, one kind of brain wave is recorded when a person is asleep and another pattern is recorded when the person is excited. Some researchers believe that EEG data suggest that the brains of many criminals and delinquents do not function normally. They point out that antisocial behavior may develop following the appearance of brain tumors, head injuries, or the onset of diseases like encephalitis and epilepsy; and that the incidence of abnormal EEG waves is greater among persons who chronically violate important social norms than among conformists (White, 1981). Thus far, however, the findings based on the use of electroencephalographic examinations are contradictory (Shah and Roth, 1974).

Considerably more research comparing larger groups of representative juvenile offenders with nonoffenders needs to be conducted in this important area before there can be general acceptance that neurological abnormalities offer a credible explanation of juvenile delinquency. Although there are some instances in which *violent* offenders suffer from some mental anomaly (Pincus, 1979), research has yet to demonstrate consistent correlations between neurological disorders and delinquency. Nor is there convincing evidence of a general association between mental retardation, epilepsy, or the constitutional aspects of personality to juvenile delinquency (Krisberg and Austin, 1978). A more balanced viewpoint accepts the fact that brain abnormalities are found in many cases of violent misbehavior, although this is rarely the single causal factor. Rather, neurological defect, damage, or malfunction, when joined with negative factors in the home and other segments of the social environment, contribute to the development of delinquent propensities in some individuals (Narramore, 1966).

The Flawed Personality

The theories and research findings of psychiatrists and psychologists have greatly increased our understanding of why people behave as they do. The development and dynamics of human personality have been their most fruitful areas of inquiry, as extensions or alternatives to Freud's early and basic conceptualizations.

In the common language of the lay person, the word "personality" usually refers to a person's social skills. We often use the term as a synonym for "charm," "pleasant disposition," or "verbal agility." The term also may refer to the most striking impression that an individual makes on other persons. Thus, we may say, "She has a shy personality" or "He has an aggressive personality" (Mischel, 1982:264). However, as pointed out earlier in this chapter, the professional psychologist uses the term **personality** in reference to *relatively stable psychological traits possessed by an individual*. In other words, each person maintains a certain consistency of character, an identifiability that endures through time, by which that person can be recognized.

The basic unit of personality organization and psychogenic analysis is the personality trait. A **personality trait** is *a distinguishing feature, quality, or disposition of mind or character*. Personality traits are virtually countless, and include such emotions and associated behaviors as anxiety, fear, anger, religiosity, cheerfulness, and so forth. Each individual's personality probably contains most personality traits to a greater or lesser degree. And each personality trait is regarded as a dimension that ranges from high to low:

> For example, anxiety is a trait that varies from the greatest anxiety to the least anxiety. Most people have some degree of anxiety along the scale between the two extremes. Psychologists have studied such personality dimensions as aggressiveness, dependency, and extroversion/introversion. People differ greatly in the degree to which they show such traits (Mischel, 1982:264).

Personality theorists maintain that an individual's relatively stable behavioral patterns reflect specific personality traits of measurable strength. Moreover, the particular combination and magnitude of personality traits within a given individual represent the perceptions, concepts, and tendencies that motivate actions in certain situations. Thus, the composition and functioning of human personality has been a rich field of study for those scholars seeking psychogenic explanations for deviant behavior, crime, and juvenile delinquency.

The Psychopath   Some of the important work in this area has focused on the identification, description, and causal explanation of the psychopathic personality. The **psychopath** (or sociopath) *has a "flawed personality" in the sense that he or she has failed to internalize some of the major values and norms of society*. As a result of this incomplete or unsuccessful socialization, the superego part of the personality that monitors the individual's deportment as "conscience" is partially defective and impotent. The psychopath lacks self-control or internal restraints in the face of temptation and shows little genuine guilt or remorse for crimes committed (Rabin, 1961). We may compare this unsuccessful socialization and the development of the "flawed personality" with an unsuccessful smallpox vaccination.

By law, virtually every child in the United States is required to receive a smallpox vaccination prior to commencing the first grade of school. Thanks to the medical technology that gave us the smallpox vaccine and the state laws requiring its general use, we have eradicated this dread epidemic disease. Most of us carry a small scar as evidence that we were successfully inoculated with smallpox vaccine and rendered immune to the disease. Occasionally, a child does not develop the usual, localized, and temporary reaction to the smallpox vaccine and we say that "the inoculation did not take."

Somewhat similarly, the transmission and learning of the basic values, norms, laws, beliefs, and attitudes of a shared culture is considered vital to societal survival. The transmission of culture content from older generations to succeeding generations is accomplished through the process of *socialization*. Through socialization—the shared experience and exposure to our cultural knowledge—each of us learns and internalizes a repertoire of generally accepted social norms, roles, and behavioral expectations. Most of us rather consistently demonstrate in our personalities and characters the learned cultural conformity of our society.

However, just as with the smallpox vaccination, occasionally someone does not experience successful socialization. Perhaps the socialization process was inconsistent or the culture content unclear and therefore the internalization of normative behavioral expectations "did not take." In such cases, the person may manifest extreme nonconformity and even antisocial, criminal deviance. That individual's personality and behavior tend to reflect a lack of concern or an inability to clearly distinguish the difference between right and wrong. Hervey Cleckley (1976), in his book, *The Mask of Sanity*, pointed out that whereas most people suffer from anguish and guilt for wrongdoing, true sociopaths (or psychopaths) are loose and easy. They have little sense of regret and cannot seem to learn from experience. Often they have superficial charm and above average intelligence. But they keep doing wrong. Starting out perhaps as truants and juvenile vandals, they may proceed along criminal paths through theft, robbery, rape, or murder to become the classic recidivists who are released only to be re-institutionalized. This emphasis on failed childhood socialization leading to aggressive and predatory adolescence has characterized the valuable contributions of developmental psychologists (Bandura and Walters, 1959).

Distinctive Patterns of Criminal Thinking   In addition to investigating psychoses and antisocial personality disorders, psychologists continue to search for traits that can be studied as potential sources of crime and delinquency. One approach is to give batteries of tests such as the Minnesota

Multiphasic Personality Inventory (MMPI) to both criminals and noncriminals. These tests contain questions about the beliefs, values, attitudes, feelings, and habits of the subjects. The purpose is to distinguish between criminal and noncriminal personality traits and profiles. As yet, no distinguishing criminal personality type has been isolated (Johnson et al., 1979:34–35).

A variation of the search by personality inventory for the etiology of antisocial behavior is based on a central premise common to most psychogenic explanations of behavior: we are seeing a person's reaction to a situation or issue as defined and interpreted by the individual, perhaps subconsciously. Therefore, observers must refrain from the rigid imposition of societal standards of good or bad, or a definition of the situation external to the individual under examination. Psychiatrists and psychologists believe that the individual's subjective and personal needs must be the focus for study and understanding. With this assumption in mind, Samuel Yochelson and Stanton Samenow (1976) and others have sought to identify the specific motives and thinking patterns of criminals.

This controversial approach is sometimes implemented through extensive interviews in an effort to determine exactly what the offender was thinking prior to and during the time when the crime was committed. It has been well documented, however, that when adult and juvenile "offenders discuss what they were thinking when they committed a crime, they often seek to slant what they reveal in a socially acceptable way" (Zastro and Bowker, 1984:44). Psychologist Samenow (1984:17) in *Inside the Criminal Mind,* underscored this shortcoming in acquiring reliable information from offenders:

> When they are interviewed after being apprehended, criminals invariably relate a tale of horrors about their early lives. They seize upon any hardships in their lives, real or made up, to justify their acts against society. By portraying themselves as victims, they seek sympathy and hope to absolve themselves of culpability.

Adolescent Identity Crisis

The final psychogenic explanation of juvenile delinquency to be reviewed here focuses on the role confusion and behavioral experimentation common among American youths as they make the awkward social adjustments associated with their transition from childhood to adulthood. The concept of an "adolescent identity crisis" not only builds on the earlier theoretical constructs of the subconscious and personality development, but incorporates a strong sociological element with its emphasis on adolescent role modeling as a response to external social forces (this aspect is further explored in Chapter 8, The Youth Subculture). Part of the popularity for this theory must be credited to Erik Erikson (1956; 1968), who presented a convincing picture of delinquent behavior as a reflection of the inadequacy felt by many young people as they seek to

Adolescents often experience an identity crisis which may lead to some forms of juvenile delinquency.

establish new self-identities and social acceptance to go along with their newly acquired biological maturity.

According to Erikson (1968:50), a psychologically healthy adult has successfully integrated the self and social aspects of identity. Such an individual has achieved an **ego-identity**—*a persistent "sameness and continuity" within oneself that coincides with a consistently shared fundamental character and meaning with others.* Ego-identity is acquired during the formative adolescent years as youths mature and experiment with various poses and roles until they "find themselves" and their new roles and statuses in society.

Erikson contended that it is normal for "gaps" to exist in the personalities of young people that can lead to an identity crisis for some. Until these gaps are "filled in" by experience, the youth's personality pattern and behavior may be unpredictable at times, reflecting a state of **ego-diffusion,** which is the opposite of ego-identity. This *personality presentation of diffusion or inconsistency in ethics, roles, loyalties, and behavior,* characteristic of many adolescents, often worries and irritates adults who have probably forgotten their own adolescent waverings.

Sometimes the significant adults in the youth's life (parents, teachers, and others) may misinterpret the young person's desire and need to experiment with trial roles and to disengage from adult control in a quest for self-identity and adulthood. When the adults who previously successfully controlled the youth's behavior are confronted with what they perceive as a vacillating, rebellious teenager, they may overreact with stern, corrective measures designed to reform and restructure the young person's life. Unfortunately, these authoritarian adults do not realize that the adolescent's "bad" behavior is often just a tentative and temporary experiment at role-playing while seeking to solidify autonomy and self-identity. Misinterpretation and overreaction to minor adolescent non-conformity by the important adults in the life of the youth may, according to Erikson, actually precipitate a serious alienation of the youth and reinforce the tendency to choose a genuinely negative and antisocial role.

In addition to the effect of negative feedback from parents and others who express dismay over youthful posturing with nonconforming roles, the ultimate choice of a delinquent role can be exacerbated by the availability of genuine antisocial role models in the youth's environment. Dorothy Rogers (1977), in *The Psychology of Adolescence*, pointed out that as youngsters experiment with different roles they often fantasize an ego-ideal. The **ego-ideal** is *a personality, character, or image to which the youth may aspire.* While youths are testing their independence from traditional authority figures, they may admire and seek to emulate persons whose behavior is the antithesis of parental expectations:

> . . . flamboyant crooks, lurid heroes and heroines lend glamour to erotic or vi-cious behaviors and afford a measure of catharsis for tendencies ordinarily re-pressed. Such figures . . . represent the romantic longings of almost everybody's adolescence.
>
> Even gangsters may serve as worthy ego-ideals. During the prohibition era, a certain notorious gangster was a hero-in-absentia for a good many adolescent boys. Their hero was portrayed as having certain desirable traits—courage, loy-alty, and kindness to the poor—which his teenage followers tried to emulate (Rogers, 1977:196).

A PSYCHOLOGICAL TYPOLOGY OF DELINQUENCY

A **typology** is *a classification system that organizes a diversity of information or objects into predetermined and orderly categories.* For example, a set of 26 manila folders, each labeled with one of the letters of the alphabet, and arranged sequentially in a file cabinet, is a simple typology, effective enough for sorting and categorizing office documents or correspondence.

In Chapter 3, we referred to two general kinds of crime: felonies and misdemeanors. That, too, is a simple but useful typology. The FBI *Uniform Crime Report* is an annual summary and very extensive typology of all the various types of criminal offenses committed in the United States during a given year. The typology is therefore an extremely helpful device for the logical organization and utilization of a great mass of diversified information.

Psychiatrists and the psychologists have been among the most productive in generating typologies of mental illness, personality types, and aberrant behavior. A large number of these psychogenic typologies have classified juvenile delinquency according to patterns of behavior, symptoms, personality disorders, and causes. (For examples, see Abrahamsen, 1960; Eysenck and Eysenck, 1968; Hewitt and Jenkins, 1947; Weinberg, 1952).

A comprehensive typological contribution toward classifying delinquency was developed by Theodore Ferdinand (1966), who synthesized many previously developed and often incomplete psychogenic typologies. Ferdinand's typology, phrased in terms of psychoanalytical theory, contains three general kinds of delinquent behavior under which are subsumed 9 specific delinquent types (Table 5–1). It suffers the shortcomings of most typologies in that it oversimplifies the division of complex material into broad and somewhat artificial categories. Nevertheless, Ferdinand's system offers a useful framework for a wide-ranging discussion of a number of specific forms of delinquent behavior that may be traced to psychological causes.

TABLE 5-1
Ferdinand's Typology of Delinquency

I. Impulsive Delinquency
  1. The Unsocialized Aggressive Child
  2. The Self-Centered Indulged Delinquent
  3. The Psychopath (or Sociopath)
  4. The Sexual Pervert

II. Neurotic Delinquency
  1. The Inadequate Delinquent
  2. The Crystallized Delinquent

III. Symptomatic Delinquency
  1. The Kleptomaniac
  2. The Pyromaniac
  3. The Sexual Delinquent

Source: Ferdinand, T.N., *Typologies of Delinquency*, New York: Random House, 1966:179–197. Reprinted by permission.

I. Impulsive Delinquency

This kind of misbehavior is acted out spontaneously, vigorously, and with little sense of guilt. The personalities of the individuals are basically antisocial— against or in opposition to society. According to Ferdinand (1966:177), "such adolescents become delinquent because their own imminent impulses throw them into direct conflict with the mores of their society." Among the subtypes within this general category, Ferdinand identified the Unsocialized Aggressive Child, the Self-Centered Indulged Child, the Psychopath, and the Sexual Pervert.

1. The Unsocialized Aggressive Child.

This type is characterized and dominated by feelings of frustration, hostility, and explosive aggression toward anyone unfortunate enough to encounter the child's rage. It is suggested that the genesis of this lack of self-control and sympathy may be traced to the family of origin wherein the mother subjected the child to unrelenting rejection (Hewitt and Jenkins, 1947).

2. The Self-Centered Indulged Delinquent.

The mood swings and alternating behavior of this youth resemble the "split personality" of the Dr. Jekyll/Mr. Hyde syndrome. This delinquent is able to make an easy and rapid transition from a friendly personable attitude to one of unreasonable dangerous fury. The source of the antisocial personality structure and behavior of the self-centered, indulgent delinquent also lies in the family of origin in which the mother is the main power figure and is overly attentive to the children (especially the male children) while the father plays only a marginal and insignificant role.

3. The Psychopath.

The psychopath, or sociopath as this type is more commonly referred to today, seeks immediate gratification of personal desires regardless of the consequences for others:

> The classic description of the psychopath states that he appears emotionally warm and charming but that he is incapable of close interpersonal relationships. If he becomes involved in crime, it is probably as an individual, not as part of the gang (McKeachie and Doyle, 1966:515).

While the exact cause(s) of psychopathic development is/are widely debated among psychiatrists and psychologists, some researchers point to organic brain disorders, such as tumors and head injuries (White, 1981). Others emphasize the lack of primary relationships with adults during infancy that can result later in a youth incapable of experiencing caring emotions for other people (Fenichel, 1945). In either case, the net result is an unsocialized individual who lacks the normal personality development that ordinarily restrains one from impulsive, aggressive, irresponsible, and immoral manipulation and exploitation of others.

4. The Sexual Pervert.

By this now outmoded term, Ferdinand referred to the juvenile who manifests deviant feelings and behaviors toward members of the same sex. Homosexuality may be either a permanent or a temporary practice. In an adult, homosexual tendencies are usually more persistent and fully developed; in a juvenile they are more likely to be impulsive, experimental, and transitory but are still considered as delinquent.

Although homosexual behavior is generally considered by the public as deviant from traditional societal expectations, law enforcement and public sanctions have become more inconsistent in recent times, possibly due to a slowly growing tolerance for those with alternative sexual preferences.

II. Neurotic Delinquency

With this term, Ferdinand was referring to psychoneuroses, which are disorders that are functional in origin, that is, there is no observable damage to nervous tissue or to any organic structure. The neurotic delinquent's personality is often stressful and confused, causing the youth to make faulty responses to ordinarily clear social norms and situations. Consequently, the juvenile's misbehavior is usually "an attempt to correct an imbalance or distortion in the inner dynamics of his personality" (Ferdinand, 1966:187–188). Ferdinand illustrated this general classification of psychogenic delinquency with two subtypes: The Inadequate Delinquent and The Crystallized Delinquent.

1. The Inadequate Delinquent.
Ferdinand's primary example of the neurotic delinquent was a youth whose personality is inadequate, that is, the youth is unable to cope with the increasingly complex and demanding social environment concomitant with approaching adulthood. To this delinquent, the role expectations and growing responsibilities are often overwhelming. "Eventually," Ferdinand (1966:189) said, "his ego, in effect, goes on strike" and he becomes vacillating, indecisive, and inadequate.

Erik Erikson (1956) contributed very useful insights regarding adolescent personality development and the psychogenic cause for the "inadequate delinquent." He viewed the emergence of delinquent behavior in such youths as related to their problems in establishing a personally and socially satisfying identity.

2. The Crystallized Delinquent.
The misbehavior of the crystallized delinquent is a means of temporary control or relief from the disrupting inner feelings of guilt and inferiority (Ferdinand, 1966).

Ferdinand utilized the metaphor of the colorless, transparent quartz crystal to describe a kind of delinquency in which misbehavior clearly and transparently functions as a convenient means of relief from a deep and pervasive sense of inner guilt and interpersonal tensions. The basis for this psychological explanation of juvenile delinquency can be traced to Sigmund Freud (1961), who observed how surprising it was to find that an increase in the unconscious sense of guilt could turn people into criminals. Freud reached this conclusion after examining many adults, ordinarily law abiding, who admitted to crimes when they were children. "His psychoanalysis of these patients indicated that they had committed the crimes precisely because they were forbidden and because doing them led to a sense of mental relief" (Adams, 1976:51). Of that type of offender, Freud (1961:48) said:

He suffered from an oppressive feeling of guilt of which he did not know the origin, and after he had committed a misdeed, the oppression was mitigated. The sense of guilt was at least in some way accounted for. Paradoxical as it may sound, I must maintain that the sense of guilt was present prior to the transgression, that it did not arise from this, but contrariwise—the transgression from the sense of guilt.

III. Symptomatic Delinquency

According to Freudian psychoanalytical theory, everyone is confronted with innate psychological demands to satisfy basic sexual and aggressive needs. Some persons, when denied legitimate gratification of these basic needs in conscious behavior, will repress them into the unconscious where—like the pent-up energy and pressure of a dormant volcano—these unfulfilled needs may burst forth as symptomatic, illegitimate, delinquent behavior. Thus, symptomatic delinquents are compelled to violate the laws of society by the pressures of unfulfilled needs suppressed in their unconscious. Ferdinand cited the kleptomaniac, the pyromaniac, and the sexual delinquent as examples and subtypes of the Symptomatic Delinquent.

1. The Kleptomaniac.
Early psychoanalytical theorists often traced an ungovernable desire to steal to sexual frustration, with the act of theft and the item stolen symbolically representing unconscious sexual needs and maladjustments. Other studies refined and expanded this thesis. For example, Grosser (1952) suggested a link between the sex of the juvenile offender and the kinds of things that are stolen. Among the youth he studied, Grosser found that boys were somewhat diversified in their choices of items to steal, apparently motivated more by the lure of illicit gain or the adventure entailed in the situation. Girls, on the other hand, appeared to be more selective, preferring to steal cosmetics, jewelry, or clothing. From this finding, Grosser hypothesized that the stolen items symbolically reflect the sexual orientation and/or objectives of the offenders. In other words, boys may hope to gain a measure of masculine status through money or through daring to risk being caught; and girls may aspire to gain in feminine status through grooming, beauty, and clothing. Several other researchers have challenged Grosser's thesis, contending that shoplifting and other forms of theft are motivated by many complex variables, such as the socioeconomic status of the offender and the opportunity for theft, which seriously confound any correlation between theft and the offender's sexual orientation. In Chapter 8, we point out that the peer pressure experienced in the youth subculture to acquire expensive material possessions, the lack of meaningful employment opportunities, and the sheer "thrill of the steal" may motivate some apparently compulsive adolescent shoplifting.

2. The Pyromaniac. The second example of Ferdinand's Symptomatic Delinquent has an obsessive fascination with fire setting and is an extremely serious threat to life and property. Psychogenic explanations of this form of deviance have varied through the years. Early theorists, following Freud, also associated arson with sexual drives and viewed it as a symbol of unfulfilled needs. They suggested that the excitement of the fire and subsequent efforts to extinguish it functioned as a form of sexual release.

"Today, most psychologists and psychiatrists intentionally avoid use of the word pyromaniac—an archaic term employed more as a catch-all category for those who set fires for no apparent reason other than to obtain sensual gratification" (Karchmer, 1984:79). More recent theorists have viewed the compulsive, habitual arsonist from a wider perspective.

While many fires set by youngsters are the consequences of immaturity or natural childhood curiosity with fire, which has an elemental warmth and beauty, other incendiary activities by children appear to be symbolic acts, expressing a wide variety of underlying emotional or physical needs:

> These juveniles set fires for a variety of reasons. Some are simply the kids whose cries for help went unanswered and whose firesetting behavior became a conditioned response to deal with stress. For others, firesetting is an act of vandalism, a cover for other crimes or a way of creating excitement. These kids are likely to torch objects and structures that appear safe to burn, such as an abandoned building; . . . (Wooden, 1985:24).

3. The Sexual Delinquent. A sexual deviation is generally perceived as an act that is contrary to the dominant sexual mores of the society in which it occurs. If the deviation is also seen as offensive or threatening to the society, it may be treated as illegal or criminal. In this final subtype of symptomatic delinquency, Ferdinand grouped together fetishism, exhibitionism, and voyeurism.

Fetishism is *the sensual gratification derived from touching a typically nonerotic part of the body of a person or a piece of clothing belonging to someone.* **Exhibitionism** is *the deliberate exposure of one's own genitalia,* thus affirming potency or sexuality through the shock registered by the viewer. **Voyeurism** is *the secretive watching of persons who are in private or intimate situations,* thus manifesting the subconscious needs and maladjustments of the spectator.

Compared to other forms of juvenile misbehavior, these psychologically based aberrations seem to have low incidence. Ferdinand (1966:197) agreed with Fenichel (1945) that such sexual deviations, usually found in males, "can be traced back to childish fears of castration." Some more contemporary studies contend that Fenichel's explanation is incomplete and cannot be generalized to all who demonstrate these unacceptable behaviors; for example, it does not take into account certain key social factors, such as the absence of sex education or legitimate opportunities for sexual gratification.

CRITICISMS AND LIMITATIONS OF THE PSYCHOGENIC APPROACH

Psychiatric and psychological theories of criminal and delinquent behavior have been helpful to our understanding and treatment of many conduct disorders and many individual delinquents. However, as with other causal explanations, they are not without their theoretical and methodological weaknesses.

Critique of Theoretical Assumptions and Concepts

Marshall Clinard and Robert Meier (1985:39) criticized psychogenic explanations of deviant behavior stating that they ". . . blur the line between 'sickness' and simple deviation from norms." In other words, the medical analogy comparing delinquent acts with physical ailments lacks generality and is unconvincing, since only a small proportion of juvenile misconduct can be traced to an organic cause, of either the mind or the body. The metaphor of the delinquent act as a symptom of underlying emotional maladjustment is seldom grounded in reality and, in fact, glosses over individual responsibility for behavior. In addition, Clinard and Meier (1985:40) disagreed with the assumption that ". . . adult behavior and personality are almost wholly determined by childhood experiences, most of them in the family, whereas evidence suggests that behavior varies according to situations and social roles and that personality continues to develop throughout life."

Sue Titus Reid (1988:129) contended that the psychogenic "terms are vague, so vague that they may be described as the unknown." No operational definitions for such concepts as *id, ego, superego,* or *unconscious* are given (Reid, 1988). Finally, there is no consensus or agreement among psychiatrists and psychologists concerning the objective criteria to be employed in assessing degrees of mental well-being or mental aberration.

Critique of Research Methodology

The research methodological problems associated with most studies applying the psychogenic approach to the analysis of criminal and delinquent behavior are succinctly summarized by Reid (1988). The research has been based on samples that are too small, that have usually been selected from among psychiatric patients and often from among institutionalized patients, and the use of control groups has not been adequate. The focus on the individual seldom generates group patterns of behavior and prevents generalization. And, as discussed earlier in this chapter, projective techniques are open to the subjective interpretation of the analyst:

> Although there is limited evidence that psychological disorders may cause some crime, there is little empirical support for the argument that they cause much crime. So far as studies of the topic have been able to tell, the mix of psychological types among criminals does not differ greatly from that among the general population. Lunde (1970), for example, argued that the incidence of psychosis is no higher among murderers than among the general public (Farley, 1987:152–153).

Critique of Psychogenic Applications to Crime and Delinquency

Theorists who contend that some psychological factor makes delinquents different from nondelinquents have difficulty in explaining the preponderance of conforming behavior in those who possess the suspected psychological trait. At the same time, self-report studies consistently show that most people have committed delinquent acts sometime during their lives. If these data-supported findings are valid, it is futile to try to find an explanation of widespread behavior based on an alleged psychological abnormality, for, by definition, *abnormal* means *unusual,* or *out of the ordinary.*

Gwynn Nettler (1974:28) reported how efforts to expand the legal defense of insanity to include all those personality and emotional weaknesses and defects that afflict human beings have encountered opposition from the legal and psychological professions:

> While 77 percent of the psychiatrists expressed confidence in their expert testimony in criminal trials, only 44.5 percent of the lawyers expressed confidence in psychiatric expertise . . . As might be expected, the two professions disagreed also on the relationship between serious criminal activity and mental illness . . . [While] *half* of the psychiatrists believed that 'anyone who commits a serious crime is mentally ill' or 'most people who commit serious crimes are mentally ill,' only a *third* of the lawyers agreed (Nettler, 1974:28).

To sociologists, the critical dilemma of the psychogenic approach is that it attempts to explain juvenile delinquency and many other forms of deviant behavior on the basis of individual characteristics, but the explanations it offers about how individuals developed those characteristics are often social. Thus, they take an unnecessarily circuitous and often erroneous route to the more viable causal variables. For example, psychoanalytic theory emphasizes inherent drives and emotional stress, but social interaction with parents and others during childhood and adolescence is what can produce an imbalance between those drives and learned social expectations about behavior. "Hence, the ultimate cause of the problem is to be found in the social experiences that led to the development of the personality pattern" (Farley, 1987:153). Though psychogenic explanations may help in the treatment of individual cases, increasingly, criminologists have turned to societal forces for explanations of behavior.

SUMMARY

This chapter began by defining and explaining the psychogenic approach to crime and delinquency. The fields of psychiatry and psychology were defined, pointing out their similarities, areas of overlap, and significant differences.

Sigmund Freud's work involving the discovery of the "unconscious" and personality formation was then reviewed. Freudian theory was applied to crime and delinquency, primarily attempting to explain these forms of deviant behavior as resulting from problems in personality development. We briefly summarized how psychoanalysis has been used in the treatment of criminals and delinquents.

Freudian theory and psychoanalysis led to the development of a variety of projective tests designed to identify maladjusted individuals likely to commit delinquent and criminal offenses. This medical model approach to delinquency contends that delinquency is a symptom of deeply embedded psychological problems. If identified early enough, and corrected, future delinquency and criminality can be avoided.

Other psychogenic explanations included feeblemindedness, neurological abnormalities, flawed personalities, and the adolescent identity crisis. In an attempt to categorize and explain a wide variety of delinquent behaviors, psychologists and psychiatrists constructed extensive typologies. For example, Theodore Ferdinand attempted to explain virtually all cases of juvenile delinquency as falling into one of three broad categories: impulsive, neurotic, and symptomatic.

There are a number of theoretical and methodological weaknesses in the psychogenic approach to juvenile delinquency. Suffering from questionable theoretical assumptions, and small and nonrepresentative samples, the psychogenic approach has failed to provide empirically tested and supported causal explanations for delinquency. While it does provide some useful insights, only a few delinquents seem to suffer from organic brain disorders, or seriously maladjusted personalities. The majority of juvenile delinquents are both physically and psychologically normal.

From a sociological perspective, the psychogenic theories fail to view delinquency in its broader social context, and to acknowledge the impact of the many social and cultural factors that influence and shape human behavior. In Chapter 6, and throughout the remainder of this book, we turn to these social and cultural variables in order to more fully understand the phenomenon of juvenile delinquency.

CONCEPT APPLICATION

"THE DEBATE OVER TELEVISION VIOLENCE AND CHILDHOOD PERSONALITY DEVELOPMENT"

WASHINGTON (AP). A teacher told a Senate panel Thursday that her young charges kick like "Kung Fu" and drive toy cars like the "Dukes of Hazzard" as she contended television is a triggering factor in children's aggressiveness (Daily O'Collegian, 1984:15). How television impacts upon a child's personality development, especially in regard to how television violence affects a child, is a hotly debated topic.

Howard Muson (1978) pointed out that millions of dollars have been spent on researching the impact of television violence on young people. In a major research project conducted by William Belson, involving 1,565 boys randomly selected in London, the researcher concluded, "The evidence was very strongly supportive of the hypothesis that long-term exposure to violence increases the degree to which boys engage in violence of a serious kind" (Muson, 1978:50). Other studies have arrived at essentially the same conclusion—the continued viewing of violence on television leads to increased aggressiveness and violence on the part of youth (e.g., Murray et al., 1972; Comstock and Rubinstein, 1972).

In a Senate subcommittee hearing seeking to determine the effects television violence may have on children, David Pearl, Chief of the Behavioral Sciences Research Branch at the National Institute of Mental Health, said there is "a plausible causal relationship between the viewing of televised violence and subsequent aggressive behaviors" (Daily O'Collegian, 1984:15). But Philip A. Harding, Vice-President of the Office of Social and Policy Research in the CBS Broadcast Group, said "the types of behavior measured in so much of the research on this question simply do not enable us to reach a scholarly conclusion as to whether violence on television leads to crime or violence in the real world" (Daily O'Collegian, 1984:15).

In an exchange before the Senate subcommittee, Pearl and Harding sharply disagreed over the effects of viewing television violence:

Pearl cited a study that began in 1960 of third grade pupils. "The best single prediction of aggressiveness at 19 years of age turned out to be the violence of the television programs the subjects preferred when they were 8 years old," he said.

However, CBS' Harding said most studies seek to measure aggression, not violence.

But Pearl said "we know that television presentations of various antisocial or violent acts have instigated imitations or what some have called 'copy-cat' behaviors."

Harding said copy-cat violence does exist, but television is not the only culprit (Daily O'Collegian, 1984:15).

The debate continues over the effects of television violence on the behavior of children and adolescents.

* * * *

What psychogenic concepts and theoretical explanations of juvenile behavior are illustrated in the testimony and behavior of witnesses who appeared before the Senate Subcommittee on Juvenile Justice? What position do you, your parents, your classmates, and the course instructor take on the issue of the possible relationship between television violence, childhood personality development, and delinquent behavior?

CONCEPT INTEGRATION

QUESTIONS AND TOPICS FOR DISCUSSION AND STUDY

1. Briefly define the psychogenic approach to explaining and interpreting human behavior and list its shortcomings and limitations.
2. What did Judge Sawyer mean when he said: "You can recognize future criminals back in the second grade"? Do you agree with him? Why or why not?
3. Based upon your reading of this chapter, briefly outline the contributions of Sigmund Freud, Hermann Rorschach, and Erik Erikson. Compare and contrast the ideas of Freud and Erikson regarding the development of human personality as they may relate to juvenile delinquency.
4. What do psychiatrists mean when they say "The delinquent act is the hurt child's cry for help"? Do you agree with them? Why or why not?
5. Outline the specific psychogenic explanations of juvenile delinquency discussed in this chapter. Which one makes the most sense to you? Which one seems least logical to you?
6. What is a psychopath (or sociopath)? Have you known or read of anyone who seemed to manifest this particular kind of personality? Could there be other explanations for his or her behavior besides personality maladjustment?
7. What is a typology and how is such a system useful in analyzing and understanding psychopathologically caused juvenile delinquency? Try to think of examples from your reading or your experience for each of the kinds of delinquent behavior and delinquents in Ferdinand's typology.

References

Adams, V. 1976. *Human behavior: Crime.* New York: Time-Life Books.

Abrahamsen, D. 1960. *Psychology of Crime.* New York: Columbia University Press.

Bandura, A. and Walters, R. A. 1959. *Adolescent aggression.* New York: The Ronald Press.

Bell, J. E. 1948. *Projective techniques.* Longmans.

Camper, D., Kasindorf, M., Clausen, P., Monroe, S., Shapiro, D., & Taylor, J. 1982. The insanity plea on trial. *Newsweek* (May 24, 1982:56–61). Produced by ARIC Press.

Cleckley, H. M. 1976. *The mask of sanity* (5th ed.). St. Louis: C. V. Mosby Co.

Clinard, M. B. & Meier, R. F. 1985. *Sociology of deviant behavior* (6th ed.). New York: Holt, Rinehart and Winston.

Comstock, G. A. & Rubinstein, E. A. (Eds.) 1972. Television and Social Behavior. Reports and Papers, Volume III: *Television and adolescent aggressiveness.* A Technical Report to the Surgeon General's Scientific Advisory Committee on Television and Social Behavior. Washington, DC: U.S. Government Printing Office.

Daily O'Collegian. 1984. Debate over television violence and childhood development. *The Daily O'Collegian,* October 26:15.

Douglas, J. W. B. 1960. Premature children at primary schools. *British Medical Journal* 1 (1960):1008.

Dugdale, R. 1910. *The Jukes.* New York: Putnam.

Ellenberger, H. 1970. *Discovery of the unconscious: The history and evolution of dynamic psychiatry.* New York: Basic Books.

Erikson, E. 1956. The problem of identity. *Journal of the American Psychiatric Association* 4:56–121.

    1968. *Identity: Youth and crisis.* New York: Norton.

Estrabrook, A. 1916. The Jukes in 1915. Washington, DC: The Carnegie Institute of Washington.

Eysenck, H. J. 1979. *Crime and personality.* London: Routledge and Kegan Paul.

Eysenck, H. J. & Eysenck, S. B. F. 1968. A factoral study of psychoticism as a dimension of personality. *Multivariate Behavioral Research* (special issue) 15 (1968).

Farley, J. E. 1987. *American social problems: An institutional analysis.* Englewood Cliffs, NJ: Prentice-Hall.

Feldman, M. P. 1978. *Criminal behavior: A psychological analysis.* New York: John Wiley.

Fenichel, O. 1945. *The psychoanalytic theory of neurosis.* New York: Norton.

Ferdinand, T. N. 1966. *Typologies of delinquency: A critical analysis.* New York: Random House.

Freud, S. 1961. The ego and the id. *The Complete Psychological Works of Sigmund Freud.* Vol. 19: 12–68. London: Hogarth.

1963. *An outline of psychoanalysis* (Trans. James Strachey). New York: Norton.

Goddard, H. 1920. *Efficiency and levels of intelligence.* Princeton, NJ: Princeton University Press.

1927. The Kallikak family: A study in the heredity of feeble-mindedness. New York: Macmillan.

Grosser, G. 1952. *Juvenile delinquency and contemporary American sex roles.* Ph.D. Dissertation. Cambridge: Harvard University.

Hakeem, M. 1957–1958. A critique of the psychiatric approach to the prevention of juvenile delinquency. *Social Problems* 5:194–206.

Halleck, S. 1966. Current psychiatric roles in the legal process. *Wisconsin Law Review* Spring:379–401.

1971. *Psychiatry and the dilemmas of crime.* Berkeley: University of California Press.

Haskell, M. R. & Yablonsky, L. 1978. *Crime and delinquency* (3rd ed.). Chicago: Rand McNally College Publishing Co.

Healy, W. & Bronner, A. J. 1926. *Delinquents and criminals—Their making and unmaking.* New York: Macmillan.

1957. *New light on delinquency and its treatment.* New Haven, CT: Yale University Press.

Hewitt, L. E. & Jenkins, R. L. 1947. *Fundamental patterns of maladjustment.* Springfield, IL: State Printer.

Johnson, E. 1974. *Corrections and society* (3rd ed.). Homewood, IL: Dorsey Press.

Johnson, G., Bird, T., & Little, J. W. 1979. *Delinquency prevention: Theories and strategies.*
Washington, DC: U.S. Department of Justice, LEAA.

Karchmer, C. L. 1984. Young arsonists. *Society* (Nov.–Dec.):78–83.

Krisberg, B. & Austim, J. 1978. *The children of Ishmael.* Palo Alto, CA: Mayfield Publishing Co.

Kuhlen, R. G. 1952. *The psychology of adolescent development.* New York: Harper & Brothers.

Lombroso, C. 1911. *Crime, its causes and remedies* (Trans. H. P. Horton). Boston: Little Brown.

Lubove, R. 1965. *The professional altruist.* Cambridge: Harvard University Press.

Lunde, D. T. 1970. *Murder and madness.* San Francisco: San Francisco Book Co.

McKeachie, W. J. & Doyle, C. L. 1966. *Psychology.* Reading, MA: Addison-Wesley.

Menard, S. & Morse, B. J. 1984. A structuralist critique of the IQ-delinquency hypothesis: Theory and evidence. *American Journal of Sociology* 89 (May):1347–1378.

Mennel, R. M. 1973. *Thorns and thistles.* Hanover, NH: University Press of New England.

Mischel, W. 1982. Personality. *The World Book Encyclopedia,* Vol. 15. Chicago: World Book, Inc., pp. 264–270.

Mitchell, L. 1972. Criminal beginnings in elementary schools. *Ashland Daily Tidings:* Ashland, OR, November 6:2.

Murray, J. P., Rubenstein, E. A., & Comstock, G. A. (Eds.). 1972. Television and Social Behavior. Reports and Papers, Vol. II: *Television and social learning.* A Technical Report to the Surgeon General's Scientific Advisory Committee on Television and Social Behavior. Washington, DC: U.S. Government Printing Office.

Muson, H. 1978. Teenage violence and the telly. *Psychology Today* (March):50–54.

Narramore, C. M. 1966. *Encyclopedia of psychological problems.* Grand Rapids, MI: Zondervan Publishing House.

Nettler, G. 1974. *Explaining crime.* New York: McGraw-Hill Book Co.

Pincus, J. H. 1979. Mental problems found in delinquents. *Tulsa World* April 30:10.

Platt, A. M. 1969. *The child savers: The invention of delinquency.* Chicago: University of Chicago Press.

Rabin, A. I. 1961. Psychopathic personalities. *Legal and Criminal Psychology* (H. Toch, Ed.). Hinsdale, IL: Holt, Rinehart and Winston.

Rehm, L. 1983. Psychology. *Academic American Encyclopedia,* Vol. 15. Danbury, CT: Grolier, Inc., pp. 593–598.

Reid, S. T. 1988. *Crime and criminology* (5th ed.). New York: Holt, Rinehart and Winston.

Rogers, D. 1977. *The psychology of adolescence* (3rd ed.). Englewood Cliffs, NJ: Prentice-Hall.

Roth, M. 1968. Cerebral disease and mental disorders of old age as causes of antisocial behavior. In *The mentally abnormal offender* (Rueck and Porter, Eds.). Boston: Little Brown, pp. 35–38.

Samenow, S. E. 1984. *Inside the criminal mind.* New York: Times Books.

San Francisco Chronicle. 1981. A report that Hinckley is sane. *San Francisco Chronicle,* July 23:24.

Shah, S. A. & Roth, L. H. 1974. Biological and psychophysiological factors in criminality. In *Handbook of criminology* (D. Glaser, Ed.). Chicago: Rand McNally, p. 120.

Sheldon, W. 1949. *Varieties of delinquent youth.* New York: Harper & Brothers.

Shoemaker, D. J. 1984. *Theories of delinquency: An examination of explanations of delinquent behavior.* New York: Oxford University Press.

Sykes, G. 1980. *The future of crime.* Washington, DC: Alcohol, Drug Abuse, and Mental Health Administration, National Institute of Mental Health.

Vold, G. 1958. *Theoretical criminology.* New York: Oxford University Press.

Weinberg, S. K. 1952. *Society and personality disorders*. Englewood Cliffs, NJ: Prentice-Hall.

White, R. W. 1981. *The abnormal personality* (5th ed.). New York: The Ronald Press.

Wooden, W. S. 1985. Arson is epidemic—and spreading like wildfire. *Psychology Today* January, 1985:23–28.

Yochelson, S. & Samenow, S. E. 1977. *The criminal personality*. Vol. I (1976) and Vol. II (1977). New York: Jason Aronson Co.

Zastrow, C. & Bowker, L. 1984. *Social problems: Issues and solutions*. Chicago: Nelson-Hall.

Chapter 6

Sociological Explanations of Juvenile Delinquency

READING OBJECTIVES

The reading of this chapter will help you achieve the following objectives:

1. Define and explain the sociological perspective or approach in explaining human behavior in general and juvenile delinquency in particular.
2. Understand the principles and purposes of theory building as this intellectual exercise applies to the explanation of delinquent behavior.
3. Define, explain, and give examples of various sociological concepts and theories of deviant and delinquent conduct, including Strain or Anomie Theory, Cultural Transmission Theory, Social Learning Theory, Social Control Theory, and Labeling Theory.
4. Apply sociological theories of human behavior to explaining juvenile delinquency.
5. Summarize the contributions and limitations of the various sociological theories of deviance and delinquency.

INTRODUCTION

Sociology is a comparatively young academic discipline, yet its influence upon modern criminology and contributions to theoretical explanations of deviant behavior have been more extensive and enduring than the preceding theories of biological determinism and psychological maladjustment. Despite some meaningful contributions to the understanding of deviance, the biological and psychological explanations tend to neglect a most prominent aspect of deviance, that is, like any other human activity, deviant behavior is inherently social in nature.

Sociologists, in explaining and interpreting human behavior, consistently have maintained that human behavior is intrinsically social and that "social facts should be explained by other social facts and not by psychological, biological, or any non-social facts" (Durkheim 1950:18–22). More specifically, sociological explanations stress that juvenile delinquency emerges from the complex network of social groups, institutions, and human interrelationships that exist in our society. Therefore, in order to better understand juvenile delinquency, we must examine it within the social context in which it occurs. While sociologists are not unanimous in pinpointing the exact causes of juvenile delinquency (or any other kind of nonconformity or deviance), the ubiquitous and inseparable social nature of human behavior is the common thread throughout all sociological attempts to explain delinquency.

Before we present the major sociological theories of juvenile delinquency it is important to briefly define theory and explain its purpose.

THEORY

The study of **etiology**—*the cause(s) of an event, phenomenon, or behavior*—is a common inquiry and exercise in the scientific community and many academic disciplines. Ideally, systematic and controlled observations, data collection, and the testing of hypotheses will result in valid and reliable findings that then can be stated in a theoretical explanation of what has occurred (Lastrucci, 1967). In other words, a **theory** is *a general statement that accurately relates cause and effect variables together so as to explain events or behavior.* Thus, sociologists, in their pursuit of theoretical explanations of delinquency, have linked youthful misconduct to the home, family, neighborhood, school, peer group, and a host of other variables, singly or in combination, found in the juvenile's social milieu.

Sociologists agree that causation is present if three conditions are met (Cole, 1980). First, causation can occur only if the independent variable exists before the dependent variable. That is to say, the "cause" must precede the "effect." For example, it has been theorized that young people exposed to dominant adult criminal elements in their neighborhoods have increased opportunity to learn and participate in delinquent behavior. In other words, the presence and availability of adult criminals as role models is the causal independent variable, and exists before the emergence of delinquent behavior, the affected or dependent variable, in this line of reasoning.

Second, if causation exists, then change in the independent variable also affects the dependent variable, but in a different way. Thus, if a youngster is removed from the old neighborhood and surrounded by a preponderance of neighborhood models and influences favorable to law abiding behavior, the youth would be less likely to commit delinquent acts.

Finally, causation cannot be established until researchers have ruled out the influence of other possible independent variables. The way to do this is to analyze the effect(s) of each possible independent variable, while keeping constant all other possible independent variables. Referring back to the previous example, perhaps the degree of stability and cohesiveness of the child's family and home environment is the true independent variable that determines whether the youth will actually participate in delinquent activities, and not the older established criminal elements that exist in neighborhoods. It is conceivable that a strong and secure family and home life may insulate many children from becoming juvenile delinquents, regardless of their neighborhood environment, whereas children from fragmented and divisive families and homes are those most likely to gravitate toward the available criminal models in their area.

It is much more difficult to identify and control for possible antecedent or intervening variables that can confound conclusions regarding causality in social science research than in the laboratory conditions of the chemist or physicist. It follows, then, that sociological theories explaining the cause(s) of juvenile delinquency (or other social phenomena) are more tentative and subject to continual scrutiny, verification, and possible modification. As Schur (1973:170–171) noted:

> In their interminable search for 'causes,' sociologists have produced no definitive 'solution' to delinquency problems. They have, however, alerted us to many misconceptions and blind alleys, and begun to show us the direction that policy might sensibly take.

In order to conceptually understand the various sociological explanations of juvenile delinquency, we have divided them into five major categories:

1. Social Strain theories;
2. Cultural Transmission theories;
3. Social Learning theories;
4. Social Control theories;
5. Labeling theories.

While categorical typologies are useful structures for organizing and presenting a mass of data or information, it must be acknowledged that the theoretical categories that supply the framework for this chapter are neither exhaustive nor mutually exclusive. Thus, they share the common weaknesses of virtually all typologies in the social and behavioral sciences. In attempting to group together major theoretical explanations of juvenile delinquency that share a major conceptual basis it becomes clear to the astute reader that the real world of cause and effect of human behavior cannot be so easily packaged in discrete categories. As demonstrated in all such endeavors, the etiological theories often merge, overlap, and build on each other. In addition, these sociological theories are presented in only approximate order of chronological development. In fact, the theories often were formulated simultaneously as the research and intellectual products of contemporary scholars.

SOCIAL STRAIN THEORIES

The theoretical explanations of deviance and delinquency that are grouped together in this category share the underlying assumption that nonconforming behavior arises out of social circumstances in which individuals or groups experience normative confusion or disruption. Confronted with a new, traumatic, or frustrating social situation, some people respond in a defiant and perhaps criminal manner.

Durkheim's Concept of Anomie

Emile Durkheim, in his landmark study of suicide ([1897] 1951), developed the concept of **anomie** to characterize *the condition of a society or group with a high degree of confusion and contradiction in its basic social norms.* Durkheim traced the unusually high suicide rates during periods of serious economic depression, severe political crises and upheavals, rapid societal change, and other unstable social conditions, to the absence or sharply reduced efficacy of normative regulation which prevails during such times. Under such conditions, Durkheim hypothesized, the usual rules that restrain us from committing socially unacceptable acts can become weakened or suspended for some members of society. In this state of anomie, sometimes referred to as "normlessness," it is difficult for some individuals to know exactly what is expected of them. In extreme cases, such persons may be "free" to take their own lives. Durkheim contended that unusually high suicide rates could be predicted from a careful study of prevailing social conditions.

Merton's Theory of Anomie

Suicide is just one form of deviant behavior. In 1938, Robert K. Merton modified and expanded Durkheim's concept of anomie into a general theory that would help to explain and account for many different kinds of deviant behavior (Merton, 1957). As a result of this conceptual connection with Durkheim's early work, Merton's more fully developed **Strain Theory** of deviant behavior is often referred to as **Anomie Theory.** There are very few sociological theories that are broad enough in basic concepts and assumptions to encompass a spectrum of forms of deviant behavior with any degree of specificity. A general theory is like an umbrella. Just as several different individuals may find shelter under a shared umbrella, so Merton's general theory of anomie offers an organized and helpful framework of logical explanations that can be applied to several kinds of deviant behavior including juvenile delinquency.

Merton perceived anomie as a state of dissatisfaction arising from a sense of discrepancy between the aspirations of an individual and the means that the person has available to realize these ambitions. In his essay on anomie as related to deviant behavior, Merton observed that Americans are exposed to powerful socialization processes that stress the success ethic. Consequently, nearly everyone has internalized the culturally approved goal of "getting ahead," that is, making money, accumulating material possessions, and achieving high social status based on money and occupation. At the same time, our society gives a clear message regarding the culturally approved means to achieve these lofty objectives. We are encouraged to strive for them as society says we should: attend school, work hard, save money, lead lives of virtue, thrift, patience, and deferred gratification, and ultimately we will realize our hopes and dreams of material success. However, Merton maintained that some people, particularly among the disadvantaged lower classes, unhappily realize that they will not be able to achieve those idealized goals through the legitimate means that society endorses. They may lack the academic background to attend college, and the only jobs available to them may be unskilled, low paying "dead end jobs" that lead to neither promotion nor financial security. Yet, the desire to fulfill the internalized objectives persists. This juxtaposition of idealized, socially approved goals, and the reality of reduced life chances and opportunities for achievement in the socially approved ways, places many individuals in a state of helpless and hopeless frustration or anomie. Denied legitimate opportunities, the rules of the game may come to have diminished importance. What really matters to such anomic individuals is not how one "plays the game" but whether one "wins." Under such circumstances, some persons will turn to illegitimate means to attain the culturally approved goals. However, Merton contended, not everyone who experiences the anomic frustration over blocked goals will resort to illegitimate means. Other avenues of adaptation are also open. Merton's Typology of Modes of Adaptive Behavior is an innovative contribution and is the heart of his general theory of deviance.

In his Typology of Modes of Adaptive Behavior, Merton schematically identified five logically possible behavioral patterns for individuals as they respond to the culturally approved goals that predominate in American society and the socially approved and institutionalized means for achieving those

FIGURE 6-1

Merton's Typology of Modes of Individual Adaptive Behavior

Individual Adaptations		Culturally Approved Goals	Institutionalized Means of Achievement
I.	Conformity	(+)	(+)
II.	Innovation	(+)	(−)
III.	Ritualism	(−)	(+)
IV.	Retreatism	(−)	(−)
V.	Rebellion	(−,+)	(−,+)

NOTE: (+) signifies "acceptance" by the individual.

　　　(−) signifies "rejection" by the individual.

　　　(−,+) signifies "rejection of existing goals and means and the substitution of new goals and means" by the individual.

Source: Merton, R.K. Social structure and anomie. *American Sociological Review* 3 (1938):676. Reprinted by permission of Macmillan Publishing Co.

idealized objectives (Figure 6–1). Merton stressed that these are role adaptations and *not* personality types. People may readily shift from one of these roles to another.

The first adaptation is *Conformity,* which encompasses most members of our society. These are individuals who accept both the culturally approved success goals and the institutionalized work ethic for achievement. Thus, their behavior generally conforms to societal expectations.

The other four possible adaptations in behavior represent deviant responses to one's recognition of the conflict between cultural goals and institutionalized means and the individual's related state of anomie. Adaptation Number II is *Innovation* and characterizes those individuals who subscribe to the typical cultural goals of monetary and material success but realize that they lack the socially approved and legitimate means to achieve those goals. They become dissatisfied, frustrated, and anomic, and resort to innovative, norm-violating behavior to achieve the coveted cultural goals. This adaptation to blocked goals is often a criminal or delinquent response.

Behavioral Adaptation Number III is *Ritualism* and involves a rigid adherence to the culturally approved methods for getting ahead and making progress. However, like a caged squirrel on a treadmill, the individual's overconformity isn't really going to "pay off." In time, perhaps the person will realize that the attained level of achievement will not equal the level of effort exerted. This person also experiences a feeling of despair and anomie, and may abandon the idealized cultural goals, but persists at a ritualized, unfulfilled line of work.

Adaptation Number IV is *Retreatism.* Here the individual, in anomic frustration, abandons both cultural goals and the institutionalized means for attaining them. In a sense, the person gives up in the struggle to reach the seemingly unreachable goals via unrewarding methods, and retreats from a social system and a culture that imposes such unreasonable "ends" and "means." This adaptation is reflected in the retreatist behavior of some runaways, drug users, and alcoholics who turn their backs on the struggle for material success and other socially approved values.

The fifth behavioral adaptation is *Rebellion.* In this case, the individual malcontent, angry over the anomic situation experienced, rejects both the culturally approved goals and the institutionalized means of achievement. In their place are substituted new goals and new means of achievement. The individual interprets the disjunction between prevailing cultural objectives and the approved means for their accomplishment as patently unfair, and the call for a new social order is a typical response of the social reformer or revolutionary.

Cohen's "Delinquent Boys"

Albert Cohen (1955) elaborated upon Merton's anomie theory with his theory that a large amount of delinquent behavior results from blocked goals and "status frustration." According to Cohen, lower class boys want to achieve success and higher social status, just like middle and upper class boys. Yet, due to their unpromising social circumstances, they find that they are blocked from achieving status (especially in school). Essentially, Cohen reported, lower class boys who aspire to increased social status in a dominant, middle class value system can respond in one of three ways:

1. The "college-boy" response;
2. The "corner-boy" response;
3. The "delinquent-boy" response.

The "college-boy" response roughly corresponds to Merton's Conformity mode of adaptation. In this case, the lower class youth accepts the challenge of the middle class value system and, through higher education and deferred gratification (foregoing small immediate rewards for larger longterm rewards), attempts to achieve social status by conforming to middle class expectations. This response is chosen by comparatively few lower class boys, according to Cohen, because their limited financial resources make chances for graduation and occupational success extremely low.

Probably the most common response in Cohen's scheme is the "corner-boy" response, which involves the youth's withdrawal into a subculture of working class boys who share a mutual set of values by which status can be gained within the group without having to compete with middle class society. This is analogous to Merton's Retreatism mode of adaptation to anomic conditions. While this group is not specifically delinquent in its purpose, the boys who choose this response are likely to become involved in delinquent activities (especially status offenses such as truancy, smoking, and alcohol consumption).

The final response in Cohen's typology is the "delinquent-boy." Similar to the boys of Merton's Rebellion adaptation, these boys become frustrated with their inability to gain status through conventional means. Consequently, they develop what Cohen referred to as a delinquent subculture, whose values and behavior are antithetical to those espoused by the middle class. Paradoxically, in acting out their subcultural values, these boys find themselves in harmony with the expectations of their group, but perceived as nonconforming delinquents by the larger society.

The similarities between the theories of Merton and Cohen are striking. However, some major differences do exist. Merton's approach tended to focus on individual responses to social situations, whereas Cohen's approach was much more oriented toward group responses. Also, Merton viewed criminal deviance as practical and utilitarian in nature, whereas (Cohen, 1955:25) saw delinquency as more "nonutilitarian, malicious, and negativistic."

Cloward and Ohlin's "Delinquency and Opportunity"

Richard Cloward and Lloyd Ohlin (1960) further added to the social strain approach to explaining delinquent behavior with their concept of "illegitimate opportunity." Like Cohen, they also accepted Merton's view that lower class juveniles generally internalize the standard success goals. They also agreed with Merton and Cohen that the blockage of these goals can lead to status frustration for some youths and place them in a position of untenable strain. This situation can then result in a sense of alienation and anomie in which those affected may turn to delinquent, illegitimate means to achieve an increment in status. It is at this point that Cloward and Ohlin moved their theoretical formulation beyond those suggested by both Merton and Cohen.

Cloward and Ohlin contended that while lower class juveniles have differential opportunities for achieving success through *legitimate* means, they also have differential opportunities for achieving it through *illegitimate* means. They pointed out that there are some areas in which illegitimate opportunities for youth to acquire success and status are not readily available. In such surroundings, some juveniles may be totally frustrated with their locked-in lowly status and lack of opportunity to achieve the idealized success goals but, lacking deviant or delinquent opportunities, their frustration is unrequited and their aspirations remain unfulfilled. In situations where there are illegitimate opportunities, Cloward and Ohlin saw response to anomic frustration as being group-oriented. However, the type of delinquent response depends upon the kind of illegitimate opportunity available to the youths. Thus, in contrast to Cohen who saw blocked goals leading to a rather standard delinquent gang response, Cloward and Ohlin delineated three possible delinquent subcultural responses. In other words, while anomic status frustration over blocked goals could well be a common denominator in groups of lower class boys scattered throughout a city, the form of collective, delinquent response any given group might make would depend on the kind of delinquent opportunity available to the group.

Cloward and Ohlin presented three types of juvenile gangs, each characterized by different kinds of delinquent activities:

1. The "crime-oriented gang";
2. The "conflict-oriented gang";
3. The "retreatist-oriented gang."

The kinds of gangs and delinquent responses that are generated depend, according to Cloward and Ohlin, upon the differential opportunities available in their environments.

The first response of lower class youths to their collective sense of unjust deprivation and alienation described by Cloward and Ohlin involves such criminal activities as theft, fraud, and extortion. The criminal orientation of this group of young people is elicited and orchestrated by adult criminal elements that operate in the neighborhood or district in which this group of disenchanted and anomic youths reside. In the perceived absence of a legitimate opportunity structure, they become vulnerable to the influence of adult criminals whose activities and prosperity have relatively high visibility in the area. The adult criminals are in a position to serve as viable role models and mentors for youths feeling the disappointment and frustration of blocked avenues to success. According to Cloward and Ohlin, the criminal alternative and the opportunity for enhanced social status lead these boys into instrumental delinquency, in which they serve as "apprentice criminals" under the direction and control of adult professionals.

The second anomic response of lower class youths described by Cloward and Ohlin is the formation of a conflict-oriented gang. Again, the emergence of this particular gang pattern of delinquency is contingent upon the kind of opportunity available to the gang members. Cloward and Ohlin suggested that youthful gangs that turn to fighting and violence as important means of securing status live in areas where both conventional and criminal opportunities are either absent or very weak. In other words, the conflict-oriented activities of these street gangs develop under conditions of relative detachment from all institutionalized systems of opportunity and social control, either legitimate or illegitimate. These are neighborhoods where opportunities for upward social mobility are essentially nonexistent and conventional law enforcement agencies are weak, and where opportunities to participate with adult criminals in their illegal but successful operations are also absent. In such areas frustrated and discontented youths often must generate their own status hierarchy and activities in physical combat with one another and with society.

Cloward and Ohlin termed the third kind of collective, delinquent response as the retreatist-oriented gang. While this response is a *group* reaction to

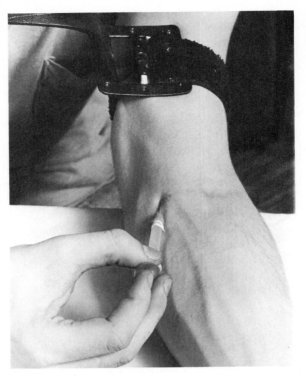

Cloward and Ohlin contended that some youth gangs, in "retreating" from their own sense of frustration over failure to achieve socially approved status and success, may develop a drug subculture in which the consumption and sale of illegal drugs becomes paramount in their lives.

social strain engendered by blocked success opportunities, it is similar to Merton's fourth Mode of Individual Adaptation, in which the actor disengages and retreats from the larger society. Cloward and Ohlin depicted the members of the retreatist gang as overwhelmed with feelings of failure, despair, and normlessness. These youths withdraw into the restricted world of their group and center their attention and activity upon the consumption of drugs in quest of physical or emotional "highs." In this way, they not only demonstrate their contempt for the normative standards of conforming society, but mask their sense of failure. As with the other two types of delinquent gang responses, the development of the retreatist group and its characteristic behavior depends upon the presence of certain opportunity structures in the members' environment. There must be easy access to sources of drugs and the lore of drug use in the area where the potential gang members live. The genesis of a drug subculture in lower class neighborhoods is often aided by "rapid geographical mobility, inadequate social controls, and other manifestations of social disorganization" (Cloward and Ohlin, 1960:178).

Contributions of Social Strain Theories to Delinquency Etiology

In summary of the social strain theories put forward by Merton, Cohen, and by Cloward and Ohlin, deviance and delinquency are viewed as being primarily a result of the social structure in which they occur. Juveniles who grow up in areas where access to culturally approved objectives by conventional means is denied, and where a large degree of social disorganization is present, are likely to find themselves in situations where the social norms governing behavior are not clearly defined. It follows, based on social strain theories, that these youngsters may find in delinquent activities the opportunities to achieve social identity and social status.

For many years, Social Strain Theory, with its fundamental implications of anomie and social disorganization, dominated sociological explanations of deviant and delinquent behavior. It is an inherently sociological approach; and, because official arrest statistics seem to support the idea that juvenile delinquency is primarily a lower class phenomenon, strain theory has offered a great deal of explanatory power.

The Strain Theories of delinquency have contributed to an understanding of the relationship between the status frustration experienced by lower class youths and poor performance in school. For example, Polk and Schafer (1972) indicated that poor school performance and the feelings of frustration due to blocked educational opportunities for lower class youths have been linked to juvenile delinquency (this phenomenon and its relationship to delinquency is further explored in Chapter 10).

Although Merton made no direct application of his anomie theory to juvenile delinquency, it is widely regarded as one of the most influential and useful formulations in describing and explaining the process behind many forms of deviant and delinquent behavior. A number of other social scientists were quick to recognize the potential of Merton's general theory of deviance in explaining why at least some juveniles become delinquent.

Perhaps the greatest contribution of the strain theories has been in its application to gang delinquency (discussed in detail in Chapter 9). Cohen, Cloward and Ohlin, and others effectively applied the basic assumptions of anomie and the strain theories to help explain the formation and activities of juvenile gangs. Irving Spergel (1964), for example, studied lower class gangs, and while his typology of gangs differed from the one constructed by Cloward and Ohlin, he documented that juvenile gangs indeed tend to specialize in certain types of delinquent activities.

While debate continues over whether lower class youths actually internalize middle class aspirations and goals as assumed by the proponents of strain theory, and while most juvenile delinquency does not involve juvenile gangs, the strain theories emphasized the importance of socioeconomic status, neighborhood environment, and adaptation to the social structure as being important variables in the understanding of delinquency. These contributions have provided insight into some types of juvenile delinquency, especially those related to the activities of lower class gangs.

Criticisms and Limitations of Social Strain Theories

A number of weaknesses in the explanatory argument of strain theory have been advanced. For example, the anomie theory of deviance, while useful in explaining some kinds of lower class nonconformity, makes some questionable assumptions about the situation of lower class people. It assumes, first, that people from the lower social classes develop about the same level of aspiration for themselves as do people from the more favored classes. Studies of lower class subjects show that this is not always the case, that lower class people tend to develop a fairly realistic assessment of their lowered life chances and adjust their expectations accordingly (e.g., Han, 1969).

Another apparent assumption of the anomie theory that may be faulty is the generalization that structural frustration causes delinquency. This being so, Sanders (1976:31) asked:

> . . . why is it that only a relatively few members of the lower socioeconomic strata commit delinquent acts frequently? Why are boys ten times more likely to engage in delinquent acts than girls in the same social position?

Travis Hirschi (1969) pointed out that most delinquent boys eventually become law abiding adults, which is a potential source of embarrassment to the strain theorist. Indeed, most delinquents do come to terms with society as they mature. They do *not* graduate into a life of adult crime. Typically, as they mature, they abandon juvenile crime and misbehavior. But their eventual reform cannot be explained by changes in the lower class conditions that purportedly forced them into their initial deviance.

In *Delinquent Boys* (1955), Cohen's main focus was on the nonutilitarian behavior of lower class juveniles. It was at this point that Sykes and Matza (1957) cast doubt upon Cohen's theory by contending that the delinquent gangs they studied stole in order to get money for entertainment—which may have been impractical, but merely demonstrated that they were adolescents, not that they were "nonutilitarian."

Cohen's point that lower class youths make a delinquent response as a frustrated attack upon middle class standards also has been targeted for criticism. Kitsuse and Dietrick (1959) argued that the initial motives of youths for joining gangs and participating in delinquent activities are many and varied, ranging from self-preservation in the neighborhood to the desire for friends.

Cloward and Ohlin's theory of Differential Opportunity also has been subjected to sharp criticism. The main complaint has been that the theory's emphasis on a set of delinquent subcultural reactions to perceived lack of economic opportunity ignores other major factors in delinquency causation. For example, Bordua (1962) charged that Cloward and Ohlin had a tendency to ignore the life histories of their delinquent subjects. The delinquents of Thrasher, Cohen, Miller, and other theorists were presented as having family, school, and other background experiences that affected their subsequent delinquent behavior. "On the other hand, Cloward and Ohlin's delinquents seem suddenly to appear on the scene sometime in adolescence, to look at the world, and to discover: 'There's no opportunity in my structure!' " (Bordua, 1962:255).

Cohen (1966) pointed out that Cloward and Ohlin suggested a false dichotomy between "legitimate opportunities" and "illegitimate opportunities." He argued:

> . . . the same things are typically, and perhaps always, both. [For] example, identical firearms can be used to kill deer in season; or deer, policemen, and estranged spouses out of season. It is one of the most fundamental and pervasive dilemmas of social life that all legitimate power, whether over things or people, can be used to implement or to violate social norms (Cohen, 1966:110).

Cloward and Ohlin's contention that youthful gangs specialized in criminality, fighting, or drug use also has been challenged. Numerous studies consistently have shown delinquent gangs to be engaged in a wide variety of illegal activities (Short et al., 1963; Kulik et al., 1968).

Another common complaint regarding the Theory of Differential Opportunity centers on the rather rigid typological structure (a criticism also shared by Merton's Anomie Theory and most other behavioral typologies). Lemert (1967), Short (1963), and Bordua (1962) all contended that the assignment of groups to one or another category is too mechanistic, that is, much gang delinquency in working class areas is more spontaneous and unstructured than Cloward and Ohlin would have us believe.

CULTURAL TRANSMISSION THEORIES

Another line of theory building was established in 1938 with a focus on the contradictory and often competitive cultural content of different social groups. The underlying assumption was that the heterogeneity of the population and the complex division of labor associated with twentieth-century industrialization and urbanization resulted in an inharmonious mosaic of ethnic, religious, political, and social class subcultures, each with its own distinctive beliefs, traditions, values, norms, and behavioral expectations. Moreover, it was assumed to be self-evident that the proximity of these diverse segments of the urban population would lead to unavoidable culture conflict as each group judged its own standards as moral and normal and those of other groups as deviant and delinquent.

Sellin's Theory of Culture Conflict

Thorsten Sellin, a criminologist, laid important groundwork for this theoretical approach to explaining criminal and delinquent behavior with the publication of *Culture Conflict and Crime* (1938). Sellin, in explaining fluctuating crime rates in different parts of urban society, noted that values, customs, and standards of conduct were not uniform throughout the population. On the contrary, many districts and neighborhoods of our large cities more truly represent the ethnic culture of foreign countries than the general culture of the United States. Additionally, the various social classes also occupy their own subcultural "islands" where their own distinctive beliefs, norms, and conduct prevail.

If these different groups were not in direct geographical and social contact with each other and with the larger society, their behavior would not be subject to comparison and evaluated so closely. However, because such diverse groups coexist in proximity to one another, chronic and abrasive culture conflict often ensues. Thus, Sellin concluded, culture conflict creates a great potential for misunderstanding and antagonism, especially among the subordinate, lower class groups regarding what is conforming and what is deviant behavior. Even the definitions of crime and delinquency can become culturally relative and subject to interpretation within the cultural context of particular groups and neighborhoods in which assimilation into the dominant society is incomplete.

Burgess' Concentric Zone Theory

Considerable evidence of the spatial patterns and concentrations of minority groups, social classes, and specialized land uses was amassed during the 1920s and 1930s by sociologists Robert Park, Ernest Burgess, R. D. McKenzie, and others in the forefront of human ecology, a newly emerging sociological subarea. For example, Burgess (1925), using Chicago as his model, demonstrated the variation in naturally formed urban areas, each occupied by a particular part of the population and reserved for a particular land use, such as commercial, lower class housing, middle class housing, and so forth. Burgess hypothesized that these population groupings and specialized land uses develop as a series of concentric zones spreading out from the dominant and dynamic city center and that this pattern characterized the industrial city of his time (Figure 6–2).

Burgess pinpointed Zone II as an urban environment especially conducive to a wide variety of individual maladjustments and social problems, including crime and delinquency. Zone II, The Zone of Transition, was so designated because it was the area most subject to rapid change. Population was ever-shifting as waves of new and generally impoverished immigrants settled first in the crowded tenements to begin their American experience. Many of the neighborhoods in Zone II reflected the culture and ethnic identity of groups of

FIGURE 6-2
Burgess' Concentric Zone Pattern of Urban Development

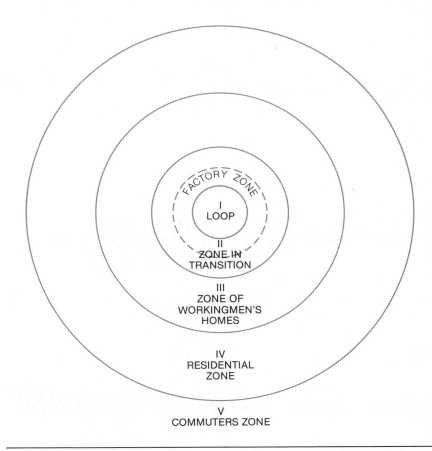

Source: Burgess, E. W. "The Growth of the City: An Introduction to a Research Project." In Park, Burgess, and McKenzie (Eds.), *The City.* University of Chicago Press (1925), pp. 47-62. Reprinted by permission.

inhabitants from Ireland, Poland, Italy, and other foreign countries (Figure 6-3).

Zone II was also called The Zone of Transition because it lay between the more prosperous and expanding commercial center of the city and the more established residential areas of blue-collar workers in Zone III. Thus, encroachments, invasions, and successions of new groups of people and new land uses, and other forms of social change, were most obvious and traumatic in Zone II.

FIGURE 6-3

Burgess' Ecological Depiction of Chicago Sub Areas

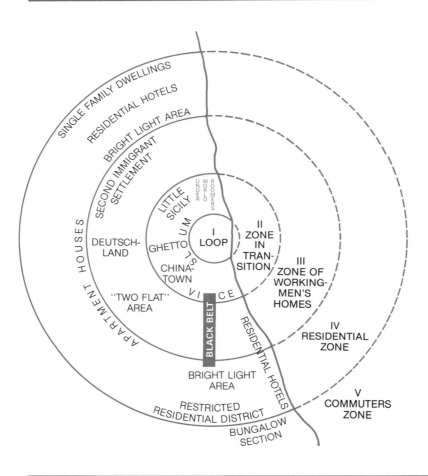

Source: Burgess, E. W. "The Growth of the City: An Introduction to a Research Project." In *The City*, Park, Burgess, and McKenzie (Eds.), University of Chicago Press (1925), pp. 47–62. Reprinted by permission.

To people living in such an area, nothing seems to be permanent, as society is in a continual cycle of disorganization and reorganization.

A number of researchers investigated these dynamics of social disorganization, industrialization, population movements, and changes in neighborhoods to determine their influence on crime and delinquency in cities. For example, W. I. Thomas and Florian Znaniecki, in their study *The Polish Peasant* (1918) examined social disorganization in a Polish neighborhood of Chicago. They noted the failure of existing social rules and norms to control behavior, and they documented the fact that the home, neighborhood, church, and friendship groups lost some of their influence to control behavior when rapid social change occurred.

Shaw and McKay's "High Delinquency Areas"

Clifford Shaw and Henry McKay (1942), influenced by the early ecological studies coming from the University of Chicago, began to chart the spatial distribution of crime and delinquency on maps of Chicago and other cities. They discovered that crime and delinquency and other social pathologies had definite patterns and areas of concentration in the urban community. They listed their findings as follows:

1. Juvenile delinquents are not distributed uniformly over the city of Chicago but tend to be concentrated in areas adjacent to the central business district and to heavy industrial areas;
2. There are wide variations in the rates of delinquents between areas in Chicago . . .
3. The rates of delinquents tend to vary inversely with distance from the center of the City (Shaw and McKay, 1931:383–385).

The areas identified by Shaw and McKay as characterized by high incidence of juvenile delinquency were called High Delinquency Areas. Their data pointed to the same central districts of the city identified by Burgess as the Zone of Transition whose substandard, slum housing was occupied by poor immigrants and ethnic minorities with problems of adjustment similar to those uncovered in the classic study by Thomas and Znaniecki (1918).

Shaw and McKay concluded that delinquency rates reflected the kinds of neighborhoods in which children were raised. They contended that deteriorated areas of cities tend to produce social disorganization which, in turn, produces delinquency. In their view, high delinquency areas are characterized by local values and norms that are contrary to the values, norms and best interests of the larger society. A local subculture develops that successfully transmits these antisocial values and norms to younger generations growing up in the area.

Miller's Focus on Lower Class Culture

Walter Miller (1958) offered a different explanation of adolescent misbehavior. Miller's theory disagreed with the reactive subculture theories of Cohen and of Cloward and Ohlin which portrayed groups of lower class delinquents responding in anomic frustration to their blocked access to idealized, middle class, success goals. Rather, Miller proposed that lower class culture is an effective

The lower class, inner city, slum environment—characterized by severe poverty and disorganization—has been linked with juvenile delinquency by many social theorists and reformers.

body of values, norms, and behavioral expectations in its own right. Moreover, children and youths from lower class families and neighborhoods internalize their culture content just as thoroughly as young people from the middle class learn their culture. It follows, Miller argued, that much of what Cohen, Cloward and Ohlin, and others interpreted as a lower class, delinquent reaction to the unfair imposition of middle class values was actually a rather "normal" reflection of their own lower class values.

Miller's theory rightly belongs in this section of cultural transmission theories because the motivation for the aggressive and often antisocial conduct is successful lower class socialization. According to Miller, the youth's delinquency results not from a lack of commitment to middle class values, but from a commitment to lower class values. Thus, lower class conformity does not harmonize with the behavioral expectations of the dominant middle class.

In circumventing the "delinquent subculture" as etiologically related to the objectionable conduct, Miller went directly to the lower class in general and identified six "focal concerns" or "values" that have high priority to young males:

1. **Trouble.** Chronic anxiety over possible confrontation with law enforcement personnel and the consequences of illegal behavior. Staying out of "trouble" is a major, practical concern of many lower class people.
2. **Toughness.** The exhibition of physical prowess; fearlessness; masculinity. Miller saw this kind of posturing as extremely important to lower class boys who come from female-based households (absent fathers) who are trying to establish a sexual identity. Thus, they equate femininity with weakness.
3. **Smartness.** Display of verbal agility; quick-witted; ability to outsmart.
4. **Excitement.** Thrill-seeking; taking a chance; fighting over women.
5. **Fate.** A tendency to trust in luck; to assume that what will be, will be.
6. **Autonomy.** The need to feel independent and free from external authority. Here again, the youth can publicly manifest his bravado by declaring: "I can take care of myself!"

Miller believed that such class-specific focal concerns or values develop because the social classes are continually being divided and segregated from each other spatially, economically, and socially. Hence, youths are likely to develop values and behaviors distinctive of their own class. The internalization of lower class values combined with a need to demonstrate their "manhood" can, according to Miller, cause some young males to defy authority and participate in fighting and other activities that, in turn, could be interpreted by middle class people as a predisposition to juvenile delinquency.

Contributions of Cultural Transmission Theories to Delinquency Etiology

The four formulations presented in this section offer significant contributions in data, concepts, and fresh insights that help explain juvenile delinquency. Each one is like a different lens on a microscope that reveals new and fascinating details regarding the content of culture and subculture as it relates to delinquent behavior.

Sellin's Culture Conflict Theory recognized the pluralistic nature of American society. Rather than viewing society as a homogeneous entity wherein unchallenged, universal norms prevail, Sellin emphasized the vast diversity of groups and subcultures within the larger society. Many of these ethnic and social class subcultures come into contact with one another in the urban environment—a contact made unpleasant and abrasive by conflicting codes of conduct. Crime and delinquency as a precipitate of culture conflict between dominant and subordinate social groups is convincingly detailed.

Burgess (1925) paid careful attention to ecological space relationships as human groups interact in a crowded, heterogeneous, urban environment. He pointed to the ethnic enclaves in Chicago and other large cities that generate and reinforce subcultures with territoriality, social identity, and solidarity. The more entrenched and resistant the subculture is to assimilation, the greater the likelihood of normative conflict, especially for younger generations of subordinate subcultures. This was the idea behind the concept of "the marginal man" suggested by Burgess' colleague, Robert Park (1928) who, followed by Everett Stonequist (1937), traced the alienation and delinquency of many children of immigrants to their marginal social status and identity as they are caught between two conflicting cultural systems. These second-generation residents of the ethnic area were exposed to the norms, traditions, and language of the "old country" in their homes and neighborhood and, at the same time, experienced the socialization of their American school and peer group. Thus, they became "marginal"—without complete commitment or integration into either of the conflicting cultures.

Shaw and McKay (1942) incorporated an ecological dimension from Burgess into their criminological scrutiny of Chicago. They identified distinctive spatial patterns of crime and delinquency that corresponded with specific ethnic and social class areas, particularly in the inner city. Perhaps Shaw and McKay's greatest contribution was the discovery that High Delinquency Areas of Chicago retained that statistical reputation in spite of major changes in the ethnic composition of the population in the areas. Repeated collection, examination, and comparison of population and crime data for those troubled areas revealed that they were inhabited by successive waves of poor immigrants from various European countries. Over time, older immigrant groups improved their economic standing with better jobs, experienced a measure of assimilation, and moved further out from the central city into better residential areas. Their places in the old, least desirable neighborhoods were taken by the most recently arrived immigrant groups. Associated with successful, economic escape from inner-city blight and poverty, each ethnic group manifested lower rates of juvenile delinquency, while rates remained extraordinarily high in the old areas adjacent to centers of commerce and heavy industry, irrespective of the ethnicity or national origin of the new residents. From this, Shaw and McKay (1969) concluded that the delinquency-producing factors are inherent in the socioeconomic conditions of the community, not in the racial or ethnic composition of the population.

Miller (1958) embarked in a different direction in making his contribution to Cultural Transmission Theory. His focus on lower class culture identified a fascinating set of basic values that can motivate lower class, adolescent behavior that, in turn, may be perceived as overly aggressive and delinquent by middle class people. Miller did not justify or rationalize lower class gang delinquency; rather, his analysis adds significantly to our understanding of why lower class youngsters become delinquent. While such behavior may reflect a culturally relevant quest for manhood, it is still often dangerous and undesirable.

Criticisms and Limitations of Cultural Transmission Theories

The studies of Burgess (1925), Thomas and Znaniecki (1918), Shaw and McKay (1942)—as well as the work of Cloward and Ohlin (1963), discussed under Strain Theories—all strongly suggest that social disorganization often characterizes individuals and groups living in high delinquency areas. This assumption has been seriously questioned. A number of more recent studies have concluded that lower class neighborhoods are not without social organization. Rather, their social organization is different from that found in middle class areas.

Shaw and McKay implied that social disorganization was most prevalent in areas whose local institutions were unable to control the behavior of local residents. Certainly, many of the families, schools, churches, and formal law enforcement agencies appear weakened and impotent in high delinquency areas. The strength of local organizations is to a large extent a function of local participation, and participation in such organizations is most likely among people who have positive feelings about their neighborhoods (Bursik, 1984:403). On the other hand, in areas of oppressive poverty, status deprivation, and urban blight that withers hope, local residents may give up on traditional institutions and develop a form of social organization more realistic to their prospects and satisfying to their needs. Certainly, William Whyte's *Street Corner Society* (1943) and other similar studies indicate that there is a high degree of social organization in slum neighborhoods. While the nature of that social organization is different from larger, middle class society, it is no less meaningful and viable to participants. Jane Jacobs, in *The Death and Life of Great American Cities* (1961:53, 57), insightfully described the more casual and less structured social organization of inner-city neighborhoods:

> Reformers have long observed city people loitering on busy corners, hanging around in candy stores and bars and drinking soda pop on stoops, and have passed a *judgement*, the gist of which is: "This is deplorable. If these people had decent homes and a more private . . . outdoor place, they wouldn't be on the street!"
>
> This judgement represents a profound misunderstanding of cities. It makes no more sense than to drop in at a testimonial banquet in a hotel and conclude that if these people had wives who could cook, they would give their parties at home.
>
> The point of both the testimonial banquet and the social life of city sidewalks is precisely that they are public . . .
>
> Formal types of local city organizations are frequently assumed by planners and even by some social workers to grow in direct, common sense fashion out of announcements of meetings, the presence of meeting-rooms, and the exis-

tence of problems of obvious public concern. Perhaps they grow so in suburbs and towns. They do not grow so in cities. Formal public organizations in cities require an informal public life underlying them, mediating between them and the privacy of the people of the city.

Delinquency area studies also have been criticized by other researchers on the ground that official statistics of arrests and court appearances, used to measure the amount of delinquency in an area, are probably biased because of more rigorous law enforcement in such areas compared to more affluent, middle and upper class suburbs.

Another complaint regarding the logic of the High Delinquency Area thesis is that such urban areas may be *collectors* of deviants rather than the *generators* of deviant behavior. In other words, the socioeconomic conditions and social disorganization of the local community may not be the primary causal variables of crime and delinquency in the area. This argument holds that the real antecedent variable is the pre-existing condition or propensity to illegal behavior in some persons prior to their movement into the high delinquency neighborhood. For example, the district of cheap bars and saloons commonly referred to as skidrow does not produce alcoholics. Rather, many people who already have a serious drinking problem gravitate to skidrow because they can merge without difficulty into an area subculture and lifestyle similar to their own. Similarly, "the red light district" does not produce prostitutes. Many prostitutes will move there to find a supportive subculture and other people who share their values and behavioral expectations. The same reasoning can be applied to some of the criminal and delinquent elements that inhabit high delinquency areas. It is conceivable that they brought with them certain character flaws or social circumstances in their families that were already conducive to juvenile delinquency as they settled in the area.

SOCIAL LEARNING THEORIES

The social learning approach to explaining crime and delinquency is dominated by the assumption that all human behavior is socially learned. Consequently, deviance, like conformity, must be learned through the complex process of socialization. **Socialization** refers to *"the process whereby individuals learn and internalize the attitudes, values, and behaviors appropriate to persons functioning as social beings and responsive, participating members of society"* (Encyclopedia of Sociology, 1974:272). In other words, socialization is learning to participate in group life through the acquisition of culture. Social learning theorists view juvenile delinquency as another pattern of learned behavior that some juveniles are taught through social interaction with the family, peer group, and other major agents of socialization.

Sutherland and Cressey's Theory of Differential Association

One of the most popular of the social learning theories is the Theory of Differential Association developed by Edwin Sutherland and Donald Cressey (1943). They stated that most criminal behavior is learned through contact with criminal elements and patterns which are present, acceptable, and rewarded in one's physical and social environment. Sutherland and Cressey argued that this is why juvenile delinquency rates vary among social groups and neighborhoods. In more stable and prosperous neighborhoods, the socialization of the young is largely dominated by values that stress conformity to middle class standards and respect for law enforcement agencies. On the other hand, in a High Delinquency Area, delinquent behavior may be an integral part of the area culture. In the presence of a "criminalistic tradition," youths have the opportunity to associate with those who can teach them alternative and illegal behaviors. Thus, Sutherland and Cressey called their explanation of juvenile delinquency the Theory of Differential Association. They summarized their theory with a set of nine propositions:

1. Criminal behavior is learned.
2. Criminal behavior is learned in interaction with other persons in a process of communication.
3. The principal part of the learning of criminal behavior occurs within intimate personal groups.
4. When criminal behavior is learned, the learning includes (a) techniques of committing the crime, which are sometimes complicated, sometimes very simple; and (b) the specific direction of motives, drives, rationalizations, and attitudes.
5. The specific direction of motives and drives is learned from definitions of the legal codes as favorable or unfavorable.
6. A person becomes delinquent because of an excess of definitions favorable to violation of law over definitions unfavorable to violation of law.
7. Differential associations may vary in frequency, duration, priority, and intensity.
8. The process of learning criminal behavior by association with criminal and anticriminal patterns involves all the mechanisms that are involved in any other learning.
9. While criminal behavior is an expression of general needs and values, it is not explained by those general needs and values, since noncriminal behavior is an expression of the same needs and values (Sutherland and Cressey, 1978:80–83).

The sixth proposition is at the heart of differential association theory: "A person becomes delinquent because of an excess of definitions favorable to violation of law over definitions unfavorable to violation of law." The picture is one of the youth subjected to a variety of influences; some endorse the rejection of the law and suggest deviant behavior; others uphold the normative standards of society and recommend conformity. By analogy, the youth is like a balance scale, as the two antagonistic forces of socialization strive for supremacy. On one side are placed the "definitions favorable to violation of law"—perhaps the negative influence of a street gang; on the other side are placed those "definitions unfavorable to violation of law"—perhaps the positive influence of parents. According to the reasoning of Sutherland and Cressey, if the definitions favorable to law violation outweigh the definitions unfavorable to law violation, the balanced scale is tipped and the youth slips into juvenile delinquency. However, the struggle for supremacy in directing the individual's behavior between the two accumulating and antithetical definitions is subject to several subtle and complex nuances. As Sutherland and Cressey stated in their seventh proposition: "Differential association may vary in frequency, duration, priority, and intensity." Thus, the actual point of commitment to either a conforming or a deviant career will vary widely among individuals.

Glaser's Concept of Differential Identification

Daniel Glaser (1956) supplemented Sutherland and Cressey's theory of differential association by adding the concept of Differential Identification. Viewing Sutherland and Cressey's theory as too mechanistic, Glaser emphasized the individual's ability to make choices and take on social roles. Glaser contended that it is not merely association with criminals or delinquents that is important, but the extent to which the individual *identifies* with those who are involved in criminal and delinquent patterns of conduct:

> During any period, prior identification and present circumstances dictate the selection of the persons with whom we identify ourselves. Prior identifications which have been pleasing tend to persist (Glaser, 1956:441).

According to Glaser, criminal or delinquent role models can be real or imaginary, nearby or far away—thus allowing for human ability to identify with certain individuals (and learn from their behavior) without direct association. For example, the mass media, notably television and motion pictures, have come under scrutiny and sharp attack as a powerful socializing agent that can influence some children to seek to replicate the violence they have seen on the screen. A 1971 report by the Surgeon General's Advisory Committee concluded that children whose parental attitudes on violence, prior socialization, and emotional makeup predispose them to imitate or to be incited by violent content on television were most likely to try to transfer the fictionalized aggression into real life (US Department of Health, Education, and Welfare, 1971:10). In this context, and from the perspective of Glaser's differential identification, the fantasized heroics of Rambo or Dirty Harry can become viable role models for some youngsters.

Akers' Theory of Differential Reinforcement

Ronald Akers is one of the principal theorists behind the view that deviant (and delinquent) behavior is learned and acted out in response to rewards and reinforcements that are available in the individual's environment. Burgess and Akers (1956) reported that Sutherland and Cressey failed to specify the learning process in their Theory of Differential Association and therefore sought to improve differential association theory by incorporating some basic concepts from B. F. Skinner's (1938) operant conditioning. In their synthesis of sociology and psychology, Burgess and Akers said that people are motivated to behave in certain ways if they have been rewarded for doing so. Likewise, they are discouraged from repeating behavior for which they have been punished or denied positive reinforcement. Akers collaborated with others in refining the Theory of Differential Reinforcement into seven propositions that detailed the process of learning and performing deviant behavior through interaction with individuals and groups who have the power to bestow gratification, social status, and other commensurable rewards (Akers et al., 1979; Lanza-Kaduce et al., 1982). Moreover, Akers recognized the impact of public acclaim and reward of selected individuals for certain kinds of behavior. These individuals may then serve as role models for many others who, in experiencing vicarious reinforcement, are also encouraged to imitate the rewarded behavior (Akers, 1985).

Contributions of Social Learning Theories to Delinquency Etiology

The social learning approach to explaining delinquency causation has enjoyed considerable support from many sociologists. Its emphasis on the socialization process as well as the influence of peer and reference groups clearly identifies the sources of delinquent behavior as social in nature. Numerous studies have supported the basic concepts of the social learning approach, especially as proposed by Sutherland and Cressey's Theory of Differential Association (e.g., Short, 1957; Reiss and Rhodes, 1964; Thompson et al., 1983). Going beyond scientific studies, the basic postulates of the social learning theories also appeal to many "common sense" assumptions about human behavior. The old axiom that "birds of a feather flock together" implies that individuals' behavior is greatly influenced by those with whom we associate and identify.

The social learning theories as propounded by Sutherland, Glaser, and Akers have had wide application to juvenile delinquency. For example, James Orcutt (1983:221) pointed out:

Social learning theories suggest that when delinquent behavior, such as fighting, is positively reinforced by peers, juveniles are likely to continue or repeat the deviant behavior.

Sutherland's development of the principle of differential association to account for the 'specific direction of motives and drives' has been particularly pertinent to the study of drug and alcohol use among adolescents. Primary group associations and favorable attitudinal definitions have emerged as the key causal factors.

In a study on marijuana use, Orcutt (1987:354) further supported differential association theory and concluded that the theory can be readily empirically tested, and ". . . perhaps no other theory of deviance can generate such exact conditional predictions about the initiation of any deviant act."

Schicor (1983) applauded the generality of theories that employ socialization as an explanatory factor in human behavior. He contended that socialization is an acceptable and meaningful approach to an understanding of delinquency whether one is looking at societies dominated by capitalistic or by socialistic political ideology.

Criticisms and Limitations of Social Learning Theories

Despite much support, the social learning approach to explaining illegal behavior by juveniles is not without weaknesses. Several of the criticisms are shared by other theoretical contributions discussed in this chapter, such as the questions raised by Gibbs (1966) and others that the relationship between delinquency and association with other delinquents may in fact be just the opposite of Sutherland and Cressey's view. It may well be that as delinquents are rejected by the conforming segments of society they are forced to seek association with each other. From this perspective, high delinquency areas and delinquent groups *do not generate* delinquency, but merely *collect* and concentrate it. Thus, the social learning theories of Sutherland, Glaser, and Akers may not explain the original causes of crime, but simply describe a process whereby crime is transmitted and perpetuated in some delinquents.

Critics also have questioned the generality of social learning theories (a charge that can be leveled at almost any sociological theory, since exceptions to explanatory schemes are legion!). In this instance, it has been argued that social learning theories do not cover crimes of impulse or passion, or delinquencies springing from emotional maladjustment.

Another flaw in social learning theories and other explanations involving delinquency areas is that even in areas with the highest crime and delinquency rates, there are many nondelinquents. It has been suggested that some children are insulated from primary contact and intimate association with neighborhood delinquents by their own unaggressive dispositions and/or careful parental supervision. In addition, other juveniles are only episodically or superficially involved in delinquent activities. In any case, the fact remains that deteriorated, poverty-stricken areas containing lower class minorities and criminal elements do not produce delinquency in *all* young people residing there.

Matza (1964) offered another interesting alternative to Sutherland and Cressey's Theory of Differential Association and other causal explanations of this kind. Contrary to these theorists, Matza contended that deviants do not consistently give moral support to one another by approving deviant acts. He pointed out that most delinquents share with nondelinquents the view that their antisocial behavior and that of their peers is wrong. Thus, the idea that the purposeful teaching and learning of delinquent values and techniques occur as more experienced delinquents intimately communicate with youthful novices is misleading. Even among adult criminals, there is a certain measure of respect and acknowledgment for the legitimacy of major social norms. We seldom hear of criminals, incarcerated or otherwise, endorsing and encouraging kidnapping, assassination, child molestation, and other serious offenses. In fact, many times, persons imprisoned for a particularly shocking or heinous crime must be isolated for their own protection from other inmates.

In spite of efforts to revise, clarify, and expand Sutherland's original thesis (Theory of Differential Association) by Glaser (Differential Identification), Akers (Differential Reinforcement), and others (DeFleur and Quinney, (1966), the most valid criticism remains. A large number of researchers have expressed difficulty in operationalizing the variables involved in order to empirically test social learning theory (Short, 1960; Stickland, 1982). For example, the reasoning behind the concept of Criminalistic Tradition is somewhat circular; that is, Criminalistic Tradition is viewed as creating high rates of crime and delinquency, yet the only way we can identify it is by identifying an area as having high rates of crime and delinquency. Crime and delinquency rates are measurable; Criminalistic Tradition is not (Reiss and Rhodes, 1964).

SOCIAL CONTROL THEORIES

Whereas the first three sociological approaches discussed (as well as the biological and psychological explanations of previous chapters) have attempted to answer the question "What causes delinquency?" the social control approach tends to ask "What causes conformity?" Albert Cohen (1966:1) succinctly stated the inseparable nature of deviance and conformity:

> Why do so many people insist on behaving in certain ways despite rules to the contrary? Or, to turn the question around: Why, despite the manifest convenience and utility of violating rules, do so many people insist on complying with them so much of the time? Our view is that these are two ways of putting the same question, because in order to explain why men behave, we would have to know those circumstances that make the difference between complying with rules and not complying, and in order to explain why men do *not* behave, we would have to know the same.

While the search for answers to these two questions may lead down similar paths (looking at environment, family, peers, social class, and the socialization process), the assumptions behind the theoretical approaches are vastly different. In the previously explored theories is the central idea that deviants are somehow inherently different from conformists. This leads to the assumption that juveniles can be neatly divided into two distinct categories: delinquents and nondelinquents. This division is seemingly supported by official data showing that of those young people arrested and processed through the courts for delinquent behavior, a disproportionate number of them are from lower class minority groups (Erickson and Empey, 1963). The delinquent/nondelinquent notion is again reinforced when we recall that much of the theory that we have studied thus far in explaining the presence and persistence of juvenile delinquency rests heavily on those statistical findings. Thus, while offering many valuable insights into anomie, culture conflict, subculture response, and the social learning of delinquent behavior, those theories consistently suggest that delinquency is largely a lower class phenomenon, and is clustered together with other social problems such as poverty, unstable family life, and central-city slum neighborhoods.

With increasing frequency, social scientists and criminologists are declaring that the delinquent/nondelinquent dichotomy is an oversimplification of juvenile behavior toward social norms. It has become apparent that young people cannot be easily classified into those two opposite types. As Cloward and Ohlin (1963) stated:

> Deviance and conformity generally result from the same kinds of social conditions. People are prone to assume that those things which we define as evil and those which we define as good have their origins in separate and distinct features of society. Evil flows from poisoned wells; good flows from pure and crystal fountains. The same sources cannot feed both. Our view of this phenomenon is different (Cloward and Ohlin, 1963:37–38).

This broader perspective on the origins of juvenile delinquency also is supported by unofficial data. Self-report and victimization studies show that a great deal of juvenile delinquency is undetected, unreported, or informally handled. In fact, there is considerable evidence that the majority of youths commit the same illegal acts for which only a small minority are officially categorized as delinquent.

The social control theories include a focus on conformity as an approach to identifying and explaining the causes of deviance and juvenile delinquency. The social control approach does not view deviance as abnormal. All of us, from this perspective, contain the inherent potential to commit deviant acts. The reason, then, that people tend not to commit deviant acts is seen as a result of effective restraint or social control.

Reckless' Containment Theory

Walter Reckless (1961) approached conforming and nonconforming behavior as two alternative responses to the control system that regulates human conduct. The control system was perceived by Reckless as a double line of defense that protects society against serious deviance. One protective barrier is socialized into each member of society and is comprised of such personal attributes as *self-control, self-identity, and internalization of social norms.* This defense barrier is called **Inner Containment** and represents *the ability of the person to resist temptations to deviate and to maintain normative loyalty.* The strength of inner containment varies from individual to individual.

The social group or society to which one belongs also supplies the other line of defense. But this barrier to serious deviance is external to the individual and is called Outer Containment. **Outer Containment** is *the formidable array of legal demands and prohibitions that keep most people within the behavioral bounds of their society.* The ability of the formal laws that comprise outer containment to control behavior also varies from person to person.

Together, this double defense line is called **Containment Theory** and, when functioning adequately, is designed to insulate the individual and protect the society from deviant or antisocial behavior. Applying this theory to delinquency, Reckless contended that the barriers of inner and outer containment are subjected to the onslaughts of powerful "push factors" within the individual and "pull factors" within the individual's social environment. **Push factors** are *such variables as mental conflict, anxiety, alienation, and frustration.* **Pull factors** are *such variables as membership in a street gang or participation in a criminal subculture.* If there is some weakness in this carefully balanced control system, conformity will give way to deviance, and even delinquent behavior.

Sykes and Matza's Techniques of Neutralization

Gresham Sykes and David Matza (1957) argued that much delinquent behavior occurs because many young persons, under simultaneous pressure from the larger society to conform and from a peer group or subculture with conflicting values and norms urging them to deviate, extend a set of psychological defense mechanisms to justify delinquent behavior. Thus, they are able to rationalize their actions with a set of sliding, situational ethics. Sykes and Matza appropriately called their construction of the delinquency process **Techniques of Neutralization.**

According to Sykes and Matza (1957) juvenile delinquents are not members of a deviant subculture which adheres to a totally different set of norms. Nor are they victims of anomie or norm confusion as a result of social disorganization. On the contrary, most juveniles who commit delinquent acts know what the norms are, and, for the most part, have respect for those norms. Sykes and Matza contended that most delinquents experience a sense of shame or guilt for their actions. Why then do some juveniles refrain from delinquency or commit only a few sporadic acts, while others repeatedly violate the laws? The answer, Sykes and Matza indicated, rests with the juveniles' ability to rationalize their actions in such a way as to neutralize their negative impact (from the point of view of the delinquent offender). As they stated:

> It is our argument that much delinquency is based on what is essentially unrecognized extension of defenses of crime, in the form of justifications for deviance that are seen as valid by the delinquent but not by the legal system of society at large (Sykes and Matza, 1957:667).

Specifically, Sykes and Matza cited five major techniques of neutralization:

1. **Denial of Responsibility.** The delinquent contends that delinquent acts are due to forces beyond one's control (e.g., environment, family situation, poverty). This leads to what Sykes and Matza described as a "billiard ball" conception of self in which some juveniles see themselves as "acted upon" rather than "acting."
2. **Denial of Injury.** The delinquent insists that although a law was violated, nobody was actually hurt. Acts of vandalism and theft become interpreted as mere pranks. Victims are usually insured, and thus

compensated for their losses. Since much juvenile misconduct is defined as harmless or normal, the youth can appeal for social support for this neutralization technique.

3. **Denial of the Victim.** Even if the delinquent must accept responsibility and admit that someone was hurt (such as in cases of willful assault), many times the delinquent reinterprets the wrongful act as some form of rightful retaliation. The victim may be depicted as one deserving of injury. The urban "sport" of "fag bashing" (assault on homosexuals) by juvenile gangs is often justified by participants on the basis that the victim was a "pervert" and therefore deserved punishment.

4. **Condemnation of the Condemners.** The delinquent may shift the attention away from personal actions to the motives or behaviors of those who show disapproval. This "turning of the tables" is used to put the accuser on the defense, and demonstrates the tactical stance that "the best defense is a good offense." For example, parents scolding a child for curfew violation may be reminded that they too on occasion come home late without notifying the family. Many parents are faced with this neutralization technique in regard to youthful behaviors such as drinking or smoking, in which the parents themselves may engage.

5. **Appeal to Higher Loyalties.** The delinquent argues that the social expectations and demands of smaller groups (friends, gangs, siblings, etc.) must take precedence over the social expectations of the larger society. Conformity to peer pressure or doing something "for the good of the group" neutralizes the negative aspects of the act committed.

Sykes and Matza, in their initial exposition of Techniques of Neutralization in 1957, did not fully develop the linkage between background factors and the repertoire of justifications so readily available to delinquents when confronted with their misdeeds. Consequently, the listed Techniques of Neutralization appeared to many readers as transparent excuses for criminal responsibility. In a subsequent paper, Matza and Sykes (1961) expanded and reinforced their argument by maintaining that juveniles subscribe to a "subterranean" adult value system,

> . . . which tacitly encourages the pursuit of thrills and irresponsibility among juveniles. This underground system of values . . . also contributes to adolescent justifications for delinquency by allowing one to charge that 'Everyone is doing it, so why can't I?' (cited in Shoemaker, 1984:145).

Matza's major work, *Delinquency and Drift*, was first published in 1964 and contains his fully developed version of Control Theory. He expanded on the neutralization concept and expressed the view that since most juvenile delinquents conform most of the time, they are evidently able to alternate loyalty between different sets of norms—between conformity and nonconformity. In other words, the juvenile delinquent experiences a kind of "episodic release" from normal moral restraints that permits him to intermittently act out the deviant role. Matza presented a picture of the delinquent as occasionally free to "drift" with ease between conformity and nonconformity.

From this perspective, delinquents are not propelled into their deviance by irresistible biological forces, psychological maladjustments, or even social circumstances, but instead rather casually "drift" into it through an ongoing social process of temporary negation of conventional normative expectations. Virtually every juvenile commits delinquent acts, just as every juvenile commits acts of conformity. According to Matza, the juveniles most likely to continually violate major norms are those who can most successfully rationalize their delinquent acts through the techniques of neutralization. Thus, conventional social restraints and mechanisms of social control are effectively overcome by the juveniles.

Hirschi's Social Bond Theory

One of the most tested theories of adolescent crime was presented by Travis Hirschi in his book *Causes of Delinquency* (1969). Unlike most earlier theorists, Hirschi (1969:34) did not set out to explain why some juveniles violate the law, but sought to explain why some do not. Hirschi attacked Strain theorists for depicting the delinquent as typically a lower class gang member, forced into delinquency by the frustrating realization of his own underachievement of common societal goals. Likewise, Hirschi rebuked the Cultural Transmission theorists for their standard picture of the "innocent foreigner" who, in his failed attempt to understand and obey what are perceived as the irrelevant rules of the larger society, turns to deviant but more satisfying norms of his subgroup.

The main building block of Hirschi's theoretical construction is the social bond that attaches a person to the basic values and expected behaviors of society. In general, the social bond is established early in childhood through a natural attachment to parents, peers, teachers, and others who manifest and model the expected conformity and respected sanctions. Quite simply, according to Hirschi, if the social bond is firmly intact for an individual, there will be no pattern of delinquent behavior. Conversely, if the social bond is weakened or absent, juvenile delinquency can be expected.

More specifically, Hirschi enumerated and detailed four elements of the social bond that, singly and in combination, tie the individual to conventional society and thus prevent juvenile delinquency.

1. **Attachment.** This emotional dimension of the social bond explains conformity as emanating from sensitive regard and respect for one's fellow human beings. It signifies how much one really cares about other people.
2. **Commitment.** This component of the social bond encompasses the indi-

vidual's pursuit of idealized and conventional objectives, such as the development of an occupational career and the establishment of a reputation for virtue. The ideological commitment to such enterprises functions as a buffer against nonconformity.

3. **Involvement.** The individual's preoccupation and heavy investment of time and effort in conventional pursuits serve to ensure conformity by reducing the availability for deviant activities.

4. **Belief.** This element of the social bond entails one's perception of the moral worth of societal norms. If the laws are perceived as right and proper, they will probably be respected; if the individual entertains doubts about the viability or validity of social norms, it is altogether likely that he or she will violate them.

Hirschi asserted that there is wide variation among people on the degree of their attachment, commitment, involvement, and belief in conventional behavior and thus variability in their individual ability to resist deviant and delinquent conduct. He said that delinquents tend to have relatively weak social bonds and consequently feel little remorse for violating generally accepted social standards.

Contributions of Social Control Theories to Delinquency Etiology

The Social Control Approach seems to be more eclectic than some of the other approaches to explaining delinquency. For example, Reckless's Containment Theory embodies some of the ideas of the Social Learning Approach in that inner containment would most logically be developed through the process of socialization in interaction with positive influences in one's social environment, as described by Sutherland (1943). Sandhu (1977:58), in an enthusiastic endorsement of Containment Theory, also referred to its eclectic quality:

> A most useful theory, the one that explains the largest amount of criminal and delinquent behavior, is the containment theory of Reckless. It not only combines both the sociological and psychological theories, but also fills in the gap between the two. It satisfactorily answers the persistent question: Who succumbs and who remains immune to crime when exposed to a crime-provoking situation? It takes into account both the macro and micro levels of explanation.

Reckless and various associates conducted several intensive longitudinal studies of boys in a high delinquency area who did not become delinquent (Dinitz et al., 1962; Reckless et al., 1956; Scarpitti et al., 1960). They were seeking to establish a relationship between the level of a child's self-concept and the development of successful inner control in resisting the temptation to become delinquent.

Reckless and Dinitz asked school teachers of 12-year-old white boys to nominate "good" and "bad" boys. In subsequent interviews with these boys, the researchers found that the "good boys" also perceived themselves as good boys, planned to complete high school, and looked upon their friends and families in a favorable light. In contrast, the "bad boys" had already developed an unfavorable self-image. They did not plan to graduate from high school. Moreover, they did not like their families and assumed that they and their friends would get into trouble.

Four years later, in a follow-up study of the same subjects, it was found that their previous self-concept assessments were significant predictors of future behavior and events:

> . . . nearly all of the good boys were still in school and had had little or no trouble with the law. On the other hand, 39 percent of the bad boys had been in a juvenile court an average of three times (Sandhu, 1977:49).

Regarding these findings, Dinitz et al. (1962:517) observed:

> We believe we have some tangible evidence that a good self-concept, undoubtedly a product of favorable socialization, veers slum boys away from delinquency, while a poor self-concept, a product of un-favorable socialization, give the slum boy no resistance to deviancy, delinquent companions, or delinquent sub-culture.

A more recent study by Thompson and Dodder (1986) reported successful operationalization of the inner and outer containment variables in a manner conducive to empirical investigation. Factor analysis of data collected from a varied sample of 677 subjects from public high schools and juvenile correctional institutions generally supported Reckless' theory. Control of delinquency potential was related to favorable self-image, goal orientation, frustration tolerance, retention of norms, internalization of norms, availability of meaningful roles, and reinforcement. A major finding was that Containment Theory provided valuable explanatory insights regarding delinquency across three of four race and sex categories (for white males, white females, and black males).

Sykes and Matza's *Techniques of Neutralization* (1957) and Matza's expanded construction in *Delinquency and Drift* (1964) have received mixed reviews and partial support from other theorists and researchers in the field. Nevertheless, Matza's assumption that juvenile delinquents casually and intermittently fluctuate in their loyalty and behavior between conformity and deviance seems reasonable and convincing (Goodman, 1962). In a study of institutionalized females, Regoli and Poole (1979) found support for the argument that delinquents drift into and out of delinquent behavior. Their findings offered evidence that the internalization of values proscribing delinquent involvement had taken place but that individuals are episodically released from moral constraint so they may engage in delinquency. They also found support for Matza's and Sykes' "subterranean value" idea that delinquent conduct reflects hidden and more permissive adult values (Regoli and Poole, 1979:53). Earlier research (Short and Strodtbeck, 1965; Krisberg, 1974) also found general acceptance of middle class, conventional values among juvenile gang members, which is consistent with Sykes and Matza.

Control or Containment Theories, more than the other explanations of delinquency presented earlier in this chapter, have provided points of departure for empirical testing. Hirschi (1969) offered a rigorous definition of delinquency suitable to quantitative research and then proceeded to conduct research to test his social bond theory. His research methodology was systematic and thorough as he surveyed a broad sample of youths from a California city and, with reference to rates and kinds of delinquency, examined the basic bonding elements that tie individuals to society. The empirical evidence was consistent with Hirschi's theory as he demonstrated how variation in the strength of these ties is associated with the commission of delinquent acts. More specifically, Hirschi found that juvenile delinquents were not as attached to parents, peers, and teachers as were nondelinquents. Delinquents were less involved in conventional behavior and were less conforming than nonoffenders. One of the most important conclusions emerging from Hirschi's study was that his social bond theory cuts across social classes. Hirschi found that the lower class child is no more likely to commit delinquent acts than the middle class child. Furthermore, Hirschi contended that the broken home and the working mother have very little significance for delinquency (Hirschi, 1969).

A number of subsequent researchers have generated support for Hirschi's theory. For example, Hindelang (1973) enhanced the predictability of Hirschi's theory by partially replicating the finding that variations in the strength of social bonding are linked to the likelihood of delinquent behavior. A revised model of Hirschi's social bond theory was operationalized in a research project conducted by Michael Wiatrowski et al. (1981), and indicated that large correlations do exist between Hirschi's basic four bond elements and participation in delinquent conduct. Linden (1978) questioned the view that separate theories are required to explain the delinquency of lower and middle class boys, and turned to Hirschi's theory which does not postulate class differences. He tested Hirschi's theory with data derived from a large sample of white boys attending public junior and senior high schools in Contra Costa County (California). The data combined information from school records, police records, and from a questionnaire administered to the subjects. Linden found that the nature and amount of self-reported delinquency did not vary greatly by social class, nor did the amount of official delinquency. He concluded that Hirschi's theory "explained both the self-reported and official delinquency of boys from different classes equally well suggesting that a general theory of delinquency involvement is possible" (Linden, 1978:428).

Criticisms and Limitations of Social Control Theories

The social control theorists' explanations of juvenile delinquency have drawn fire from proponents of other approaches. Cohen and Short (1958) indirectly struck at the heart of Reckless's Containment Theory by rejecting the notion that delinquency is an inherent potentiality in all human beings. In other words, the idea suggests greater biological determinism and freedom from deviant influences than is sociologically tenable for some. Matza, who prefaced his own version of control theory in *Delinquency and Drift* (1964) with a critique of hard biological, psychological, and sociological determinism causation, also rejected uncontrolled human nature as the sole source of delinquent behavior. Matza sought to resolve the motivational dilemma of Social Control Theory by perceiving the offending behavior not as a simple response to human nature, but as a response to the tempting nature of certain circumstances facing the adolescent. Matza utilized the concept of "will" which may be activated by the individual's realization that the deed can be accomplished without resulting in apprehension, or by the need to demonstrate daringness to others. Thus, temporarily free from conventional restraints and willfully motivated, the youth can "drift" into delinquency. Nevertheless, Matza's theory also has not been spared criticism. With his combination of will and drift, Matza may have constructed a contradiction in terms and a semantic quagmire that confounds more than clarifies. With the exercise of will, the casual drift into delinquency seems understated. If "drift" accurately describes the process, the concept of "will" is much too strong in conjunction. It is difficult to have it both ways.

Hirschi (1969:230) has been a forthright critic of his own social bond theory:

> The theory underestimated the importance of delinquent friends; it overestimated the significance of involvement in conventional activities. Both of these miscalculations appear to stem from the same source, the assumption of 'natural motivation' to delinquency. If such natural motivation could legitimately be assumed, delinquent friends would be unnecessary, and involvement in conventional activities would curtail the commission of delinquent acts.
>
> In other words, failure to incorporate some notions of what delinquency does *for* the adolescent probably accounts for the failure of the theory in these areas.

Marvin Krohn and James Massey (1980) examined the overall and relative effects of the elements of Hirschi's Social Bond Theory on four separate measures of deviance using data from a sample of 3,065 adolescents. While the magnitude and direction of the observed relationships moderately supported the theory, Krohn and Massey found that the elements of the bond were more predictive of the less serious forms of deviance than they were of the more serious forms. Their findings also suggested that commitment to academic pursuits and commitment to extracurricular activities had different effects on deviant behavior for males than for females. Overall, the variables used by Hirschi to measure attachment were slightly stronger in predicting male delinquency than they were for female delinquency. In conclusion, Krohn and Massey acknowledged sufficient support for the theory's major hypotheses but called for further research and evaluation.

LABELING THEORIES

One of the most popular sociological explanations of juvenile delinquency or any form of deviance is based on how society perceives, judges, and reacts to the behavior in question. It is appropriate to preface our explanation of Labeling Theory, as this formulation is commonly known, by briefly reviewing **social status** and **social roles,** and how we acquire these dimensions of personal identity (see Chapter 2 for a more thorough treatment).

Social status is *an individual's prestige position in relation to others in his or her social group or society.* Social status can also refer to the prestige position of a group in relation to other groups. The level of social status or prestige held by a person is determined by the social group as every member is ranked from high to low. Some status or prestige is automatically **ascribed** to a person as a consequence of biological characteristics such as sex or age. Individuals may also receive some unearned and vicarious status based upon the wealth and power of their parents. Some social status can be changed or **achieved** through personal effort, especially in an open class society that encourages its members to strive for upward social mobility. Considerable social status may be derived from one's level of education and occupation.

The level of social status assigned to an individual also may be modified by taking on new roles. Thus, not only is the prestige position held by a person founded on inheritance and personal achievement, but also on the social role(s) occupied. A **social role** is *the set of behavioral expectations that accompanies a particular status.* As people grow older and have new experiences, society often changes their social statuses, and assigns new roles to them. For example, your lifecourse will probably encompass the successive roles of child, sibling, adolescent, college student, spouse, parent, grandparent, and retiree, to name just a few. With each role assigned (and the related status position), society hands the individual a rather carefully structured "script" containing behavioral expectations to be fulfilled.

When each of us, as individual members of society, is made aware of the role assignment and the behavioral expectations associated with that role, we usually comply. To conform to the social expectations of our group or society is much easier than to digress from them. You will recall from your reading of Chapter 1 that "social expectations" is one of the definitions of social norms or rules. Societal judgments regarding a role assignment and the behavioral expectations regarded as appropriate for that role are very powerful forces and influences impacting upon the individual. Thus it becomes normative and virtually mandatory for the individual to comply with the role "label" that has been applied to him or her by manifesting the expected behavior.

"Dear, now would be a good time to tell him that this type of behavior may eventually lead to a clash with the criminal justice system and subsequent criminal labeling."

The fundamental sociological principles of social status, social roles, and social expectations comprise the foundation for the Labeling Theory of deviant and delinquent behavior. For even a deviant role can be assigned by society to some persons who, in the judgment of society, seem to warrant such a negative label. Labeling Theory concentrates less on the deviant acts themselves and instead focuses on the actor and the audience and their perceptions of each other (Gibbs, 1966). Howard Becker (1963:9) defined and described labeling as an interactive process:

> Social groups create deviance by making the rules whose infraction constitutes deviance. The deviant is one to whom that label has successfully been applied. Deviant behavior is behavior that people so label.

For example, if a person becomes known in society (community, school, neighborhood, etc.) as an alcoholic, prostitute, juvenile delinquent, or by any other negative label or reputation, the social status or prestige position of that individual is ranked accordingly. Moreover, with the label goes a new role and set of social expectations. The person is expected to behave in harmony with the social role assignment. In other words, labeling is a public declaration of one's social identity; of what society perceives and expects the individual to be. Thus, in one sense, societal labeling is being publicly "branded." It is extremely difficult to escape the label—whether rightly or wrongly applied—because it has led to a redefinition of the relationship and expectations between the person labeled and the conforming members of society (DeFleur, et al., 1971). Labeling

Theory strongly suggests that the causal explanation for much juvenile delinquency, as well as a large share of the responsibility, can be traced to society itself.

Early Contributions to Labeling Theory

The labeling approach has its theoretical roots in some of the early ideas of social psychologists such as Charles Horton Cooley and W. I. Thomas. Cooley ([1902] 1964), in his classic concept of the **Looking-Glass Self,** observed that *an individual's self-evaluation and self-identity are basically a reflection of one's perception of other people's reactions to his or her conduct.* Applied to juvenile behavior, juveniles use those with whom they interact like a mirror that reflects back an image (a social identity), which is then internalized as part of the youths' self-concepts. If juveniles perceive that others view them as delinquent, they are very likely to accept that label.

W. I. Thomas (1931) contributed the concept of **Definition of the Situation** which essentially means that *when people define a situation as real, it becomes real in its consequences.* This thought-provoking concept further illuminated the process whereby certain acts are socially defined as deviant or delinquent and the juvenile who commits an act so defined becomes labeled as "delinquent." This is similar to Robert Merton's idea of the **Self-fulfilling Prophecy** as a catalyst for eliciting future behavior of the prescribed kind. According to Merton (1968), when the members of a social group define a person or event in a certain way, they may in fact shape future circumstances and activities so that the anticipated and projected behavior comes to pass.

Tannenbaum's Concept of "Tagging"

In 1938, with the publication of *Crime and Community* by Frank Tannenbaum, an innovative application of the labeling perspective was made to criminology. Tannenbaum emphasized the treatment of the offender that makes a hardened criminal out of the accidental or occasional one. Thus, the greater evil lies in the societal treatment, not in the original act. Tannenbaum (1938:17–19) called this process tagging and pointed out:

> There is a gradual shift from the definition of the specific acts as evil to a definition of the individual as evil, so that all his acts come to be looked upon with suspicion. In the process of identification his companions, hangouts, play, speech, income, all his conduct, the personality itself, become subject to scrutiny and question. From the community's point of view, the individual who used to do bad and mischievous things has now become a bad and unredeemable human being . . . The young delinquent becomes bad because he is defined as bad and because he is not believed if he is good . . .
>
> The process of making the criminal, therefore, is a process of tagging, defin-

ing, segregating, describing, emphasizing, making conscious and self-conscious; it becomes a way of stimulating, suggesting, emphasizing, and evoking the very traits that are complained of . . .

The process of tagging led to Tannenbaum's (1938:8, 20) somber conclusion: "The adult criminal is usually the delinquent child grown up . . . The person becomes the thing he is described as being."

Lemert's Primary and Secondary Deviance

As we have unfolded the development of each theoretical explanation of deviance and delinquency, we have tried to demonstrate how successive theorists have added to the accumulating store of insights, concepts, and knowledge until the full theoretical formulation eventually takes shape and comes into view. Nowhere is this process of theory building more obvious than in the emergence of the labeling perspective of deviance and delinquency. While the modern labeling approach is often attributed to the work of Edwin Lemert (1951), it is obvious that he stood on the shoulders of numerous earlier theorists, as he synthesized and refined their work as foundation stones for his own contributions.

Lemert's expansion of Labeling Theory was in his concern for the consequences of an individual's being labeled on future behavior. Remember, Cooley indicated that an individual's evaluation of self is basically a reflection of other people's reactions. It follows that if the labeled person believes in the societal label, then the process of labeling can be a critical determinant of the subsequent deviant or conforming career of the individual.

In discussing the dynamics involved in becoming a juvenile delinquent, Tannenbaum implied that there is a progression between two types of criminal or delinquent acts. One is the *first* act, which the child considers as innocent but which adults define as delinquent. The second is the *final* behavior, which both the child and adults define as delinquent. Lemert went further than Tannenbaum, and made explicit the distinction between these two behavioral steps in deviance. He called the first one **primary deviation** and the second, **secondary deviation. Primary deviation** occurs when *an individual may commit a deviant act (or several deviant acts), but does not internalize the deviant self-concept and continues to occupy the role of conformist.* **Secondary deviation** occurs when *an individual's self-concept is altered and the deviant role is personally assumed.*

The labeling approach to explaining juvenile delinquency has the potential of going beyond the questions of how society defines, labels, and punishes the deviant, "or how group members alter their social expectations and behavior" in relation to the person. The theory poses the surprising question of how the revised self-concept of the socially labeled and stigmatized individual can possibly lead to the "emergence of stable patterns of deviance" (DeFleur, et al. 1971:385).

Becker's Developmental Career Model

Howard Becker is one of the leading practitioners of the labeling perspective. In his book, *The Outsiders* (1963), he propounded the view that deviance, like beauty, exists in the eye of the beholder. No act is intrinsically deviant, but must be defined as such. He emphasized that societal perception of an act as deviant automatically imputes a generalized deviant role to the individual. Everett Hughes (1945:357) described this process as taking on a **master status —** *a status which ". . . tends to overpower, in most crucial situations, any other characteristics which might run counter to it."* As Becker (1963:34) said:

> Treating a person as though he were generally rather than specifically deviant produces a self-fulfilling prophecy. It sets in motion several mechanisms which conspire to shape the person in the image people have of him.

Perhaps Becker's major contribution to Labeling Theory was his introduction of the notion of a developmental process that precedes the attainment of a deviant or delinquent identity and career. We are indebted to Becker's (1963) study of marijuana users which prompted him to outline an unfolding sequence of steps that could lead an individual to unreserved commitment and participation in a deviant career.

Becker argued that the identity and state of being a "confirmed marijuana user," or any other form of socially determined deviant, develops over time. It has history and longitudinal development. For example, Becker (1963:23) found that the developmental process for becoming a confirmed and consistent user of marijuana included the following sequence of related steps or stages: (1) the person must have access to the drug; (2) he or she must experiment with it; and (3) the individual must continue its use. Each of these steps toward the final condition involves subtle changes in the individual's attitudes and perspective, as well as behavior. Becker (1963:23) noted:

> Each step requires explanation . . . We need, for example, one kind of explanation of how a person comes to be in a situation where marijuana is readily available . . . , and another kind of explanation of why, given the fact of its availability, he is willing to experiment with it in the first place. And we need still another explanation of why, having experimented with it, he continues to use it . . . That is, no one could become a confirmed marijuana user without going through each step.

"The circumstances that determine movement along a particular path include properties of both the person and of the situation." The personal component involves the individual's susceptibility and vulnerability to the drug; the situational component in the developmental process consists largely of feedback from other actors, who witness it, and how they respond to the individual's use of marijuana (Cohen, 1966:104). It is within the social situation and context that the user of marijuana can encounter sanctions and a labeling experience that can stimulate further progress and development of a deviant career, according to Becker and other labeling theorists.

The developmental model or developmental process suggests considerable explanatory power for other forms of deviant and delinquent behavior besides the use of marijuana. In addition, Becker's formulation also helps to moderate the rigid delinquent/nondelinquent dichotomy by perceiving delinquent behavior at various stages of development and intensity.

Contributions of Labeling Theory to Delinquency Etiology

A significant contribution of the labeling approach to explaining the causes of juvenile delinquency is its analytical division of nonconforming behavior into primary and secondary deviance. Of equal importance is the focus on the societal perception and reaction to the initial deviant act and the subsequent revision in self-concept that enables the actor to continue into a more stable pattern of deviant behavior. Thus, as Matza (1969:89, 164, 196) pointed out:

> . . . we see how the effort of society to remedy or control deviance ironically becomes a factor in producing deviance. This paradoxical development runs against common-sense which usually sees social control efforts as an effective response rather than a cause of deviant behavior.

Wide application of the labeling perspective has been made in critiques of law enforcement procedures and the juvenile justice system. Piliavin and Briar (1964:214) contended that many dispositions made by police officers in cases of suspected juvenile offenders are based on intuitive character assessments which, in turn, are founded on the youth's group affiliations, age, sex, race, grooming, dress, and demeanor:

> . . . the official delinquent, as distinguished from the juvenile who simply commits a delinquent act, is the product of a social judgment, in this case a judgment made by the police. He is a delinquent because somebody in authority has defined him as one, often on the basis of the public face he has presented to officials rather than of the kind of offense he has committed.

The labeling process that occurs during police/juvenile encounters on the streets is further discussed in Chapter 11.

Similarly, Cicourel (1968) used a labeling approach to show differences between lower and middle class families in the administration of justice. He indicated that ad hoc interpretations of character, family life, and future possibilities—often retained in official and unofficial files by schools, police, departments, and courts—not only negatively and unfairly label some youths, but predetermine them toward future judicial litigation.

Regarding juvenile delinquency, Edwin Schur emerged as one of the more outspoken proponents of the labeling perspective. In his book *Radical Non-intervention* (1973) he asserted that we must rethink the delinquency problem. The label of delinquency has been so overused and so widely applied that it covers everything from talking back to parents and truancy, to forcible rape and first degree murder. As Schur pointed out, both the terms "juvenile" and "delinquent" are ascribed statuses. That is to say, they are labels assigned to youth by the society in which they live. Schur insisted that so-called delinquents are neither internally nor externally different from nondelinquents except for the fact that they have been officially processed by the justice system and so labeled.

A less radical labeling viewpoint of criminal and juvenile justice procedures has been set forth by Hugh Barlow (1987). He asserted that criminologists and legal authorities have long attempted to distinguish between those acts of **mala in se**—*considered inherently evil* (such as murder and rape) and **mala prohibita**—*those considered evil only because they are prohibited* (such as gambling and alcohol consumption by minors). The labeling approach provides valuable insights into the latter category, as a vast number of the acts committed by juveniles that come to be labeled as delinquent clearly fall under it. The wide variety of acts which become treated as status offenses for juveniles are not considered evil in and of themselves, but merely have been labeled as inappropriate behavior for juveniles.

Criticisms and Limitations of Labeling Theory

The reviews of Labeling Theory are mixed and contradictory. The weaknesses cited by critics are diametric opposites to the strengths referred to by proponents. For example, much has been made of Labeling Theory's focus on societal reaction as a key factor in producing deviance (e.g., Becker, 1963; Erikson, 1964). In response, Gibbs (1966) suggested that the approach is defective in that it tends to deny the existence of deviance as any reality apart from the process of social adjudication of deviance. Gibbs indicated that this approach cannot tell us why one person rather than another commits deviant acts. He believed that the usefulness of the approach was in its understanding of the societal response to deviance, while leaving the original or primary deviance unexplained.

Bordua (1967:48) challenged the depiction of societal reaction as a force totally external to the passive (and often innocent) actor, moving the actor to a secondary and more stable pattern of deviance. He pointed out that juvenile delinquents have often coveted, encouraged, and cultivated such labels as "tough" or "bad" for themselves as a matter of pride. Flaunting their presence and staging a confrontation with the police and their subsequent arrest are often sources of "rep" in delinquent gangs (Werthman and Piliavin, 1967).

As a counterbalance to Glassner's (1982:75) contention that "during the past few decades, more sociological research has derived from the labeling perspective than from any other model of deviance," a number of sociologists complain that "labeling theory lacks empirical verification and that therefore its pronouncements should be considered with caution" (Bordua, 1969:121). Moreover, Robins (1975) argued that it is unlikely that the proponents of the perspective will subject Labeling Theory to empirical study since they are the sociologists most suspicious of "hard" data. He contended:

> In short, labelling [sic] theorists believe that deviance in a society is largely the product of attempts to measure or record it. Like Archimedes, who realized he would have to stand outside the earth if he were to move it, the sociologist accepting labelling [sic] theory has nowhere to stand from which he or she can observe the 'natural' rates against which the size of the distortion in official rates and rates based on interviews can be measured, to estimate the impact of labelling [sic] (Robins, 1975:21).

Labeling Theory has been used to indict the juvenile justice system, charging that police, courts, and other agencies tend to negatively evaluate and label some suspected delinquents, thus increasing their likelihood of further involvement in secondary deviance. This contention was strongly disputed by Foster et al., (1972), who found that labeling by the juvenile justice system during an early stage of processing did not produce changes in self-concept nor increased delinquency by their subjects. Similarly, Thornberry (1979) found that the handling of delinquent youths in a stern manner did not generally result in greater criminality, as Labeling Theory suggests. Along the same line, Bordua (1967:154) and Gibbs (1966:50) charged that labeling theory does not take into account the positive aspects of societal reaction to deviant or delinquent behavior. Many children and youths are diverted from further misbehavior and delinquency by the serious and even threatening response of parents, teachers, and police officers to an initial offense. Even an uncomplimentary label and dire predictions about where a delinquent course can lead has deterrent value for many juveniles.

AN OVERVIEW OF THE SOCIOLOGICAL EXPLANATIONS

This chapter has provided an outline and analysis of the major theoretical constructs that comprise the sociological view of juvenile delinquency. The five categories we have created are not absolute, discrete, exhaustive, nor mutually exclusive. Instead, we have grouped together various sociological theories which generally share common assumptions and concepts. Rather than attempting to adhere to any single theoretical approach or perspective, such as social strain, cultural transmission, social learning, social control, or labeling, we have introduced each one as offering reasonable causal explanations for juvenile delinquency, together with appropriate summations of contributions and weaknesses.

We also have avoided the temptation to attempt the development of a single general theory to explain the entirety of all the acts defined as juvenile delinquency. Even without total synthesis, the various approaches and the specific theories and concepts presented here can, in combination, shed a great deal of light on the social problem we call juvenile delinquency. Going beyond the limitations of the biological and psychological explanations, the sociological explanations show delinquent behavior to be a very complex social phenomenon. Delinquency is a social act, from the very inception of the norms which govern juveniles, to the social institutions which affect juveniles, the environment in which the juveniles must live, the socialization process to which they are subjected, and the process whereby their actions are judged by others as conforming or deviant. Juvenile delinquency does not exist in a social vacuum. Each of the five categories of sociological approaches to the problem contributes a measure of understanding to some of the dynamic social factors involved in delinquency etiology.

THE QUEST FOR A GENERAL THEORY OF JUVENILE DELINQUENCY

The integration and unification of theoretical concepts and contributions from a broad spectrum of approaches into one overarching explanation of juvenile delinquency has been a tantalizing objective for many sociologists. The formulation of a general theory of etiology that encompasses racial, ethnic, environmental, gender, and socioeconomic status in delinquency participation is no small task. Thus far, it has been an impossible task. Nevertheless, a number of serious efforts have been made by sociologists to develop the ultimate and definitive theory explaining why some children become juvenile delinquents while others do not. Some have suggested expanded versions of their favorite theories as fulfilling this objective. Still others have sought to blend portions of some theories into an overall eclectic approach. In all cases, a commonly acceptable "grand theory" of juvenile delinquency has eluded formulation. There are still numerous unanswered questions regarding the validity and reliability of these theoretical suggestions. So far, empirical testing has been only partial, or in some cases, totally lacking. Consequently, predictability and generality remain tentative at best for such theoretical offerings.

Considerable interest in formulating a general theory of social deviance which encompasses juvenile delinquency was generated by a panel of scholars who gathered in Albany, New York in 1987. The participants included Ronald

Akers, Jack Gibbs, Travis Hirschi, James Short, Terrence Thornberry, and a number of other distinguished sociological theorists. The objective of the Albany Conference was to bring together leading scholars in the field of deviance to address some of the more important issues surrounding the integration of competing theories. For example, Short (1987:7) suggested that the considerable overlap among academic disciplines in their shared interest in delinquency and delinquents could offer a rationale and fertile common ground for the integration of theoretical explanations.

Not surprisingly, the Albany Conference did not produce consensus on such a general theory. In fact, many of the participants concluded that the search for such a theory was futile and misdirected. Nevertheless, if enough interest continues to be generated toward the integration of divergent theoretical explanations of social deviance, it may be possible that some day a general theory of juvenile delinquency causation may become a reality. As yet, it remains the task of sociologists to glean from existing theories the useful concepts, variables, and explanations which provide some measure of insight into the understanding of juvenile delinquency.

CONCEPT APPLICATION
ILLUSTRATIVE ANECDOTE

The following anecdote was related to one of the authors by a student enrolled in one of his off-campus courses.

"Going Into the 'Automobile Business' "

If I had not known otherwise, Mike could easily have been mistaken for one of the typical male college students who regularly sit in my classes at the state university. He was 23 years old; naturally gregarious with a disarming grin; wanted to get more education and ultimately a good job; and he liked football, girls, and automobiles—*especially automobiles.*

But we were not on the university campus, nor was Mike a typical 23-year-old student. I was teaching a university extension course at a federal reformatory and Mike was serving a 10-year sentence for "Grand Theft: Auto." He was assigned to assist me with the logistics of the classroom such as inmate attendance at my lectures, seating arrangements, distribution of books, paper, examinations, and other supplies, and so forth. Consequently, we had numerous opportunities to talk, both formally and informally, and an unusual degree of trust and rapport was established.

I soon learned that although Mike was a high school dropout, he was very bright and articulate. Moreover, he was streetwise and very cynical. During the last 11 years he had "graduated" from adolescent play group to youth gang to professional auto theft ring; from school yard to city streets to prison yard. He asserted proudly: "I can get into nearly any car without breaking a window and I can start over half of them without a key." At first, such declarations sounded like just so much bravado and bragging, but later when I had the opportunity to review Mike's official records, it became abundantly clear that he was a very professional automobile thief. His file record dated back to age 12 and was filled with documentation of confrontations with police and juvenile courts, and a multitude of suspected, alleged, and proven crimes against society.

Based on our series of discussions, I was able to reconstruct the course of events that finally brought Mike to the federal reformatory. He had grown up in the lower class slum neighborhoods of St. Louis and Chicago. The family was poor, characterized by his father's unemployment, with five people living in three small rooms and sharing a toilet and tub with two other families. They wore second-hand clothing that didn't fit; and they were often cold, hungry, frustrated, and angry. Mike played in the streets of his neighborhood with boys of similar backgrounds.

Mike reported that high school was a particularly trying ordeal for youths from the poorer neighborhoods:

> There were dudes there who had plenty of money, who wore nice clothes, and even drove cars to school. My ol' man didn't even own a car. We walked everywhere, or rode the bus if we had the fare. The teachers always gave us that bull about getting an education, working hard, and being successful. Man, it was unreal! I got out of there as soon as I could. Besides, I was flunking anyway.

On the streets of the city, Mike found other boys with similar experiences who shared his feelings of rejection, alienation, and hopelessness. Then, one day, he recalled:

> We spotted a parked, unlocked car with the keys just hanging there. It was like an invitation! We looked and laughed and someone dared me to get in. Well, I wouldn't have done it, but the guys were all watching me. So, I got in, and so did they. I was just fourteen, but I could drive it. We decided to borrow it for awhile, circle around the high school, and try to pick up some girls. However, something went wrong. The car swerved over a curb and got banged up a lot. Somebody saw us, and the cops picked me up. Later, a judge put a judgment against my father to pay for the damage. And he pulled out of the family after that.

There were other joyriding experiences for Mike and his friends. It was never hard to find a car in which some negligent driver had left the ignition key and the boys could not resist the temptation to "cruise the streets" and enhance an otherwise boring day or night.

At about age sixteen, Mike began associating with a street gang in his neighborhood. He described how the gang was inclined to "steal anything that wasn't nailed down." Sometimes they stole food from grocery stores "because they were hungry, or just for the hell of it." One would distract the clerk, while another filled his pockets and sneaked out the door. This same technique was used in clothing and hardware stores for merchandise they could sell or trade on the streets. Mike specialized in automobile parts—hubcaps, tires, and radios. A couple of older gang members showed Mike how to "hotwire" an automobile and thus start it by bypassing the ignition switch. The boys also discussed which types of cars were easiest to steal, and the older boys told Mike that the "high dollar" cars were best to steal, because "they were easy to wire, and the owners always had enough insurance" to cover their losses.

Mike complained bitterly about social conditions in his old urban neighborhood. There were no job opportunities and "the poor got no help and no respect," he said:

> Even though I had a few dollars and better clothes, even my own family and the neighbors called me a 'no good hood.' So, finally, I decided to have the game as well as the name, and got more involved in illegal activities. And, at least I had the guys in the gang who appreciated me.

As Mike grew older, however, many of those he knew best in the gang started dropping out. Some got married, several took jobs, some went to jail, and one or two even went back to school. Mike took a different course:

> As for me, I had made friends with some older men in the area who were into the rackets, you know, some were 'hustling prostitutes,' others were pushing drugs, or into gambling. But the ones that really appealed to me were in the 'used car business.' They made lots of money and drove big cars. I hung around their 'garage' and got acquainted.

As Mike described it to me, the "garage" was a basement with painted windows and a large automobile door that opened off a back alley. It was "open" only from midnight until dawn. When Mike was about 20, he was invited to "go into the automobile business" with the men at the garage. It was a professional auto theft ring comprised of eight men with a highly specialized division of labor: two of them were the "pickups" who cruised side streets and unattended parking lots near theaters and bars. They would locate automobiles they wanted, preferably large and expensive. With special tools and sets of keys they were usually able to open and drive off the automobile with minimal difficulty. Mike became one of these "pickup men."

Three other men were garage "mechanics." Their job was to change odometer readings, license plates, and even engine and body manufacturers' identification numbers. They could repaint an automobile and have it out of the door in 24 hours. Another man had the task of producing or procuring false registration documents. The other two men had the responsibility of transporting and selling the stolen and altered automobiles, often many hundreds of miles away in other states.

The scheme was successful for a long time until, as Mike summarized his career in the "automobile business," "one guy got caught, and in order to get a lighter sentence for himself, he led the cops to the garage, and we were all picked up."

* * * *

As you reflect on this case study, consider the various sociological explanations of deviant and delinquent behavior presented in this chapter. How do they fit as causal explanations for Mike's juvenile delinquency and ultimate criminal career? Which theories seem most applicable to Mike's case?

CONCEPT INTEGRATION

QUESTIONS AND TOPICS FOR STUDY AND DISCUSSION

1. Explain the sociological perspective regarding human behavior and social phenomena. How does it differ from the biological determinism and psychogenic explanations presented in previous chapters?
2. What is a theory as the term is used by the social scientist and the researcher?
3. List the major assumption(s) underlying the Social Strain Theories of delinquency etiology. Identify and discuss several prominent sociologists and their respective concepts and contributions to the social strain approach. What are some of the weaknesses and limitations of social strain explanations?
4. List the major assumption(s) underlying Cultural Transmission Theories of delinquency etiology. Identify and discuss several prominent sociologists and their respective concepts and contributions to the cultural transmission approach. What are some of the weaknesses and limitations of Cultural Transmission Theories?
5. List the major assumption(s) underlying Social Learning Theories of delinquency etiology. Identify and discuss several prominent sociologists and their respective concepts and contributions to the social learning approach. What are some of the weaknesses and limitations of social learning explanations?
6. List the major assumption(s) underlying the Social Control Theories of delinquency etiology. Identify and discuss several prominent sociologists and their respective concepts and contributions to the social control ap-

proach. What are some of the weaknesses and limitations of the social control explanations?

7. List the major assumption(s) underlying Social Labeling Theories of delinquency etiology. Identify and discuss several prominent sociologists and their concepts and contributions to the social labeling approach. What are some of the weaknesses and limitations of the social learning approach?

8. In your judgment, which of the various sociological theories explaining the cause(s) of delinquency makes the most sense? Why? Which one makes the least sense? Why?

References

Akers, R. L. 1985. *Deviant behavior: A social learning approach* (3rd ed.). Belmont, CA: Wadsworth.

Akers, R. L., Krohn, M. D., Lanza-Kaduce, L., & Radosevich, M. J. 1979. Social learning and deviant behavior: A specific test of a general theory. *American Sociological Review* 44 (August):635–655.

Barlow, H. 1987. *Introduction to criminology* (4th ed.). Boston: Little Brown.

Becker, H. 1963. *Outsiders: Studies in the sociology of deviance.* New York: Free Press.

Bordua, D. J. 1962. Some comments on theories of group delinquency. *Sociological Inquiry* 32 (Spring):245–260.

1967. Recent trends: Deviant behavior and social control. *Annals of the Academy of Political and Social Science* 369 (January):149–163.

1969. On deviance. *Annals of the Academy of Political and Social Science* 312:121–123.

Brown, B. B. 1982. The extent and effects of peer pressure among high school students. *Journal of Youth and Adolescence* 11 (April):121–133.

Burgess, E. W. 1925. The growth of the city. In R. E. Park, E. W. Burgess, & R. D. McKenzie (Eds.). *The city.* Chicago: University of Chicago Press, pp. 47–62.

Burgess, E. W. & Akers, R. L. 1956. A differential association reinforcement theory of criminal behavior. *Social Problems* 14 (Fall):128–147.

Bursik, R. J. 1984. Urban dynamics and ecological studies of delinquency. *Social Forces* 63 (December):393–413.

Cicourel, A. V. 1968. *The social organization of juvenile justice.* New York: John Wiley.

Cloward, R. A. & Ohlin, L. E. 1960. *Delinquency and opportunity.* New York: Free Press.

Cohen, A. K. 1955. *Delinquent boys: The culture of the gang.* New York: Free Press.

1966. *Deviance and control.* Englewood Cliffs, NJ: Prentice-Hall.

Cohen, A. K. & Short, J. F., Jr. 1958. Research in delinquent subcultures. *Journal of Social Issues* 14 (3):20–36.

Cole, S. 1980. *The sociological method: An introduction to the science of sociology* (3rd ed.). Chicago: Rand McNally.

Cooley, C. H. [1902] 1964. *Human nature and the social order*. New York: Schocken Books.

DeFleur, M. & Quinney, R. 1966. A reformulation of Sutherland's differential association theory and a strategy for empirical verification. *Journal of Research in Crime and Delinquency* 2 (January):1–22.

DeFleur, M., D'Antonio, W. and DeFleur, L. 1971. Sociology: Man in Society. Glenview, Illinois: Scott, Foresman and Company.

Dinitz, S., Scarpitti, F. R., & Reckless, W. C. 1962. Delinquent vulnerability: Across group and longitudinal analysis. *American Sociological Review* 27 (August):515–517.

Durkheim, E. [1895] 1950. *The rules of sociological method*. Glencoe, IL: Free Press. [1897] 1951. *Suicide: A study in sociology*. (Trans. J. A. Spaulding & G. Simpson) New York: The Free Press.

Encyclopedia of Sociology. 1974. *Encyclopedia of Sociology*. Guilford, Conn: Dushkin.

Erikson, K. 1964. Notes on the sociology of deviance. In H. Becker (Ed.). *The other side*. New York: Free Press, pp. 9–22.

Erikson, M. L. & Empey, L. T. 1963. Court records, undetected delinquency and decision-making. *Journal of Criminal Law, Criminology and Police Sciences* 64 (4):456–469.

Foster, J., Dinitz, S., & Reckless, W. 1972. Perceptions of stigma following public intervention for delinquent behavior. *Social Problems* 20:202–209.

Gibbs, J. P. 1966. Conceptions of deviant behavior: The old and the new. *Pacific Sociological Review* 9 (Spring):9–14.

Glaser, D. 1956. Criminality theories and behavioral images. *American Journal of Sociology* 61 (March):433–444.

Glassner, B. 1982. Labeling theory. In M. M. Rosenberg, R. A. Stebbins, & A. Turowetz (Eds.). *The sociology of deviance*. New York: St. Martin's Press, pp. 71–89.

Goodman, P. 1962. *Growing up absurd*. New York: Random House (Vintage).

Han, W. S. 1969. Two conflicting themes: Common values versus class differential values. *American Sociological Review* 34 (October):679–690.

Hindelang, M. J. 1973. Causes of delinquency: A partial replication and extension. *Social Problems* 20 (Spring):471–487.

Hirschi, T. 1969. *Causes of delinquency*. Berkeley: University of California Press.

Hughes, E. C. 1945. Dilemmas and contradictions of status. *American Journal of Sociology* 50 (March):353–359.

Jacobs, J. 1961. *The death and life of great American cities*. New York: Vintage Books.

Kitsuse, J. & Dietrick, D. 1959. Delinquent boys: A critique. *American Sociological Review* 24 (April):208–215.

Krisberg, B. 1974. Gang youth and hustling: The psychology of survival. *Issues in Criminology* 9:115–129.

Krohn, M. D. & Massey, J. L. 1980. Social control and delinquent behavior: An examination of the elements of social bond. *The Sociological Quarterly* 21 (Autumn):529–543.

Kulik, J. A., Stein, K. B., & Sarbin, T. R. 1968. Dimensions and patterns of adolescent antisocial behavior. *Journal of Consulting and Clinical Psychology* 32 (August):375–382.

Lanza-Kaduce, L., Akers, R. L., Krohn, M. D., & Radosevich, M. J. 1982. Conceptualization and analytical models in testing social learning theory. *American Sociological Review* 47 (February):169–173.

Lastrucci, C. L. 1967. *The scientific approach.* Cambridge, MA: Schenkman.

Lemert, E. 1951. *Social pathology.* New York: McGraw-Hill.

1967. *Human deviance, social problems, and social control.* Englewood Cliffs, NJ: Prentice-Hall.

Linden, R. 1978. Myths of middle class delinquency: A test of the generalizability of social control theory. *Youth and Society* 9 (June):407–432.

Matza, D. 1964. *Delinquency and drift.* New York: John Wiley.

1969. *Becoming deviant.* Englewood Cliffs, NJ: Prentice-Hall.

Matza, D. & Sykes, G. 1961. Juvenile delinquency and subterranean values. *American Sociological Review* 26 (October):712–719.

Merton, R. 1938. Social structure and anomie. *American Sociological Review* 3 (October):672–682.

1957. *Social theory and social structure* (2nd ed.). New York: Free Press.

1968. *Social theory and social structure* (enlarged ed.). New York: Free Press.

Miller, W. B. 1958. Lower class culture as a generating milieu of gang delinquency. *Journal of Social Issues* 14 (Summer):5–19.

Orcutt, J. D. 1983. *Analyzing deviance.* Homewood, IL: Dorsey Press.

1987. Differential association and marijuana use: A closer look at Sutherland (with a little help from Becker). *Criminology* 25 (2):341–358.

Park, R. E. 1928. Human migration and the marginal man. *American Journal of Sociology* 33 (May):893.

Park, R. E., Burgess, E., & McKenzie, R. D. 1924. *The city.* Chicago: University of Chicago Press.

Piliavin, I. & Briar, S. 1964. Police encounters with juveniles. *American Journal of Sociology* 70 (September):206–214.

Polk, K. & Schafer, W. B. (Eds.). 1972. *School and delinquency.* Englewood Cliffs, NJ: Prentice-Hall.

Reckless, W. 1961. A new theory of delinquency and crime. *Federal Probation* 25 (December):42–46.

Reckless, W., Dinitz, S., & Murray, E. 1956. Self concept as an insulator against delinquency. *American Sociological Review* 21 (December):744–746.

Regoli, R. M. & Poole, E. D. 1979. Assessing drift among institutionalized delinquents. *Journal of the American Criminal Justice Association* 42 (Winter/Spring):47–55.

Reiss, A. J., Jr. & Rhodes, A. L. 1964. An empirical test of differential association theory. *Journal of Research in Crime and Delinquency* 1 (January):5–18.

Robins, L. N. 1975. Alcoholism and labelling theory. In W. R. Gove (Ed.), *The Labelling of Deviance*. Beverly Hills: Sage, pp. 21–33.

Sanders, W. B. 1976. *Juvenile delinquency*. New York: Praeger.

Sandhu, H. 1977. *Juvenile delinquency: Causes, control, and prevention*. New York: McGraw-Hill.

Scarpitti, F., Murray, E., Dinitz, S., & Reckless, W. C. 1960. The "good" boy in a high delinquency area: Four years later. *American Sociological Review* 25 (August):555–558.

Schicor, D. 1983. Socialization: The political aspects of a delinquency explanation. *Sociological Spectrum* 3 (January–March):85–100.

Schur, E. 1973. *Radical non-intervention: Rethinking the delinquency problem*. Englewood Cliffs, NJ: Prentice-Hall.

Sellin, T. 1938. *Culture conflict and crime*. New York: Social Science Research Council.

Shaw, C. R. & McKay, H. D. 1931. *Social factors in juvenile delinquency: Report on the causes of crime*, Vol. II. Washington, DC: National Commission on Law Observance and Enforcement.

1942. *Juvenile delinquency and urban areas*. Chicago: University of Chicago Press.

1969. *Juvenile delinquency and urban areas* (revised ed.). Chicago: University of Chicago Press.

Shoemaker, D. J. 1984. *Theories of delinquency*. New York: Oxford University Press.

Short, J. F., Jr. 1957. Differential association and delinquency. *Social Problems* 4 (January):233–239.

1960. Differential association as a hypothesis: Problems of empirical testing. *Social Problems* 8 (Summer):14–25.

1987. Exploring integration of the theoretical levels of explanation: Notes on juvenile delinquency. In *Theoretical integration in the study of deviance and crime: Problems and prospects*. Albany, NY: Unpublished proceedings of the Albany Conference, May 7–8.

Short, J. R., Jr. & Strodtbeck, F. L. 1965. *Group process and gang delinquency*. Chicago: University of Chicago Press.

Short, J. F., Jr., Tennyson, R. A., & Howard, K. I. 1963. Behavior dimensions of gang delinquency. *American Sociological Review* 28 (June):411–428.

Skinner, B. F. 1938. *The behavior of organisms*. New York: Appleton-Century-Crofts.

Spergel, I. 1964. *Racketville, slumtown, and haulberg*. Chicago: University of Chicago Press.

Stonequist, E. H. 1937. *The marginal man*. New York: Charles Scribner's Sons.

Strickland, D. E. 1982. Social learning and deviant behavior: A comment and critique. *American Sociological Review* 47 (February):162–167.

Sutherland, E. H. & Cressey, D. R. 1943. *Principles of criminology*. Philadelphia: JB Lippincott.

1974. *Criminology* (9th ed.). Philadelphia: JB Lippincott.

1978. *Criminology* (10th ed.). Philadelphia: JB Lippincott.

Sykes, G. M. & Matza, D. 1957. Techniques of neutralization: A theory of delinquency. *American Sociological Review* 22 (December):664–670.

Tannenbaum, F. 1938. Point of view. *Crime and Community.* Boston: Ginn and Co., pp. 8–22.

Thio, A. 1983. *Deviant behavior* (2nd ed.). New York: Harper & Row.

Thomas, W. I. 1931. *The unadjusted girl.* Boston: Little Brown.

Thomas, W. I. & Znaniecki, F. 1918. *The Polish peasant in Europe and America.* Chicago: University of Chicago Press.

Thompson, W. E., Mitchell, J., & Dodder, R. A. 1983. An empirical test of Hirschi's control theory of delinquency. *Deviant Behavior* 5:11–22.

Thompson, W. E. & Dodder, R. A. 1986. Containment theory and juvenile delinquency: A reevaluation through factor analysis. *Adolescence* 21 (Summer):365–376.

Thornberry, T. P. 1979. Sentencing disparities in the juvenile justice system. *The Journal of Criminal Law and Criminology* 70 (Summer):

United States Department of Health, Education, and Welfare. 1971. Television and growing up: The impact of televised violence. Washington, DC: National Institute of Mental Health.

Vold, G. 1958. *Theoretical criminology.* New York: Oxford University Press.

Werthman, C. & Piliavin, I. 1967. Gang members and the police. In D. J. Bordua (Ed.). *The police.* New York: John Wiley.

Whyte, W. F. 1943. *Street corner society.* Chicago: University of Chicago Press.

Wiatrowski, M. D., Griswold, D. B., & Roberts, M. K. 1981. Social control theory and delinquency. *American Sociological Review* 46 (October):525–541.

Part III
Collective Behavior and Juvenile Delinquency

Part III

Introduction: Collective Behavior and Social Groupings

Part I of this book developed the sociological perspective and emphasized the inherently social nature of juvenile delinquency. In Part II we presented some of the major theoretical explanations for delinquency. Now, in Part III, we look at juvenile delinquency within the context of collective behavior. **Collective behavior** refers to *behavior motivated and influenced by an individual's membership in or identification with a social group.* There are a variety of different types of social groups which impact upon human behavior. Three of the most important and readily identifiable are primary groups, secondary groups, and reference groups. The **primary group** is *a relatively small intimate group characterized by face-to-face interaction.* **Secondary groups,** on the other hand, tend to be *somewhat larger groups characterized by more formal interaction which are usually organized for a specific purpose.* A **reference group** is *a group with which an individual has a strong sense of identification regardless of his/her actual membership in the group.* The three chapters in Part III look at examples of all three of these types of groups and explore their relationship to juvenile delinquency.

Chapter 7 looks at the family—a primary group which is typically the first social group that teaches an individual basic attitudes, values, beliefs, and appropriate behaviors. This chapter traces the historical development and changing role of the traditional American family. We emphasize the family's role in influencing juveniles' behavior and summarize the importance of social variables such as social class, family size, birth order, and the nature of family interaction in terms of their relationship to juvenile delinquency. The effect on children of mothers working outside the home is explored, and various techniques of parental discipline are reviewed in regard to their theoretical link to delinquency. Research on the assumed link between broken homes and delinquency is summarized and discussed, and the chapter ends with an overview of the family's role in delinquency prevention.

Chapter 8 explores the phenomenon of the youth subculture, which serves as an important reference group for adolescents, its widespread influence on American teenagers, and its possible link to juvenile delinquency. The important sociological concepts of **culture, subculture,** and **counterculture** are defined, and the creation, development, and perpetuation of a youth subculture is placed within a sociological context. Distinctive elements of the youth subculture such as values, dress, grooming, fads, and language are described

216

along with their possible relationship to juvenile delinquency. The influence of mass media on American youth is discussed and two serious social problems linked with the youth subculture—teenage drug usage and permissive sexual practices leading to increased numbers of teenage pregnancies—are explored.

Chapter 9 deals with one of the most misunderstood dimensions of juvenile delinquency—the gang. The youth gang is one of the more difficult types of social groups to categorize. As we discuss in Chapter 9, some contend it is a primary group, others view it as a more loosely constructed secondary group, and still others see it as more closely resembling a reference group for some inner-city youths. As we point out in the chapter on gangs, this has led some researchers to categorize it as a fourth type of social grouping, the **near group** resting on a continuum between the extremes of an unorganized mob at one end and the primary group at the other, and *characterized by diverse membership, loose organization, ambiguous leadership, and impermanence.* While most delinquency does *not* involve juvenile gangs, juvenile delinquency is much more likely to take place within a group context than to be the act of an isolated individual youth. In this chapter we look at the phenomenon of "predatory youth" and the subtle social processes which occur when the play groups of some children evolve into full-fledged juvenile gangs. The organization of gangs is viewed from a sociological perspective, and motivations for joining a gang are explored. The participation of females in gang delinquency is summarized, and some of the major sociological theories which focus on explaining the formation of juvenile gangs are reviewed.

As you read Part III, keep in mind the discussion of the basic social nature of juvenile delinquency presented in Part I, as well as the many theoretical explanations for the causes of delinquency presented in Part II. Apply them to the material presented in these three chapters. You should note that while none of the theories presented in Part II can adequately explain *all* of the types of delinquency discussed in Chapters 7, 8, and 9, they can provide valuable insight into the roles played by the family, the youth subculture, and the juvenile gang in relationship to juvenile delinquency.

Chapter 7

The Family and Juvenile Delinquency

The reading of this chapter will help you achieve the following objectives:

1. Understand the changing role of the family in American society.
2. Identify how the family acts as a primary agent of socialization for youth in our society.
3. Identify how family variables such as social class, family size, the nature of family interaction, and parental discipline relate to the study of delinquency.
4. Summarize the research relating broken homes to delinquency.
5. Understand the impact of parental discipline upon youths and how various techniques of discipline may relate to delinquency.
6. Explore how the family may serve as an insulator against juvenile delinquency.

INTRODUCTION

Part III of this book explores how membership in social groups and collective behavior impact upon human behavior. This chapter discusses one of the most important social groups in which juveniles participate—the family. For most juveniles, the first social group to which they belong is their **family of origin.** The **family of origin** *is the family in which the child grows up,* and today, in western nations like the United States, it *usually consists of only the parents and children.* This concept of family need not be limited to biological relatives, and would include adoptive parents and their children. In other words, we are referring to the first family setting to which the child is exposed, and which serves as the primary socializing agent for the youth. This family might more accurately be referred to as the **family of orientation.**

THE CHANGING ROLE OF THE AMERICAN FAMILY

The shift in American society from being predominantly rural prior to the Industrial Revolution to predominantly urban after the turn of the century had tremendous impact upon the institution of the family. As Marcia and Thomas Lasswell (1982:10) pointed out, "Although the dramatic move away from the farm was not the result of changing ideas about love, marriage, and the family, it certainly had a profound effect on all of these."

Agrarian America often is depicted as being characterized by the **extended family** *in which several generations (which may include parents and their children, grandparents and other close relatives) living under one roof, sharing and cooperating in the economic, social, and psychological support of the family.* There is some question whether the extended family was actually the predominant type of family or not. Research indicates a lack of evidence that early American families typically followed the extended family pattern. According to Rudy Seward (1978:44), "The extended family was the exception rather than the rule." Whether it was extended or not, there is virtually unanimous agreement that the family was much larger in agrarian America. Children typically grew up in the same household as their parents. Families were usually large, hence, family rules had to be negotiated among several generations. Quite often, the oldest male assumed the role of head of the household, and was viewed as the ultimate source of power and discipline. While children were growing up, they rarely found themselves lacking supervision from adults or older siblings. There almost always was a parent, grandparent, or some other adult around to set limits on a child's behavior, or to mete out punishment should those limits be exceeded.

Often steeped in misinformed nostalgia, this earlier version of family life was not idyllic, as is sometimes portrayed in novels and movies, or in the minds of those who lament the downfall of the American family as they perceive it. Life was tough in preindustrial America and families faced a variety of problems on a daily basis, not the least of which was their very survival. However, there were aspects of family life in preindustrial America which tended to limit the likelihood that youths would get into trouble with law enforcement officials. One already mentioned is the amount of adult supervision to which the juvenile was exposed. Another important factor was the cultural attitudes toward childhood and adulthood which existed during that time. In agrarian America the role expectations for children and adults were fairly explicit. Children were assigned chores and expected to help around the house and farm (or store if they happened to live in town), but were exempted from responsibilities associated with adulthood. When children reached an age when they were physically and mentally capable of assuming the work responsibilities of adults (usually somewhere after the onset of puberty), they began to be treated as adults by family, friends, and the community. This clear transition from child to adult resulted in changing role expectations for youths who began to make plans for marrying and starting families of their own. The marriage ceremony symbolically marked the *rite of passage* into adulthood. The concept of adolescence had not been developed (Rogers, 1985), hence, much of the marginality experienced by juveniles today did not exist.

That is not to say that young people did not violate norms in preindustrial American society. They certainly did. However, most norm violations were handled by the family through parental discipline. If fairly minor violations occurred outside the home, they were usually handled informally, as local constables typically knew everybody in the community and either disciplined the youngsters themselves, or reported the behavior to their parents. When serious violations occurred, one of two things was likely to happen. Either the child's parents were held legally accountable for their child's actions, or the child was held directly responsible and treated as an adult (Reid, 1988). This evolution in the handling of criminal acts committed by youths is more thoroughly discussed in Chapter 12, The Juvenile Court.

INCREASING IMPORTANCE OF THE NUCLEAR FAMILY

The shift from an agricultural to an industrial society, and the concomitant transition from rural to urban residence for the majority of our citizens, had lasting impact upon family size and structure. Urban life put new demands on the family, many of which were not compatible with the traditionally larger or extended family pattern. Families needed to be located near industry, and if necessary be mobile enough to move should the father's place of employment change. A result was that families became smaller. As Dorothy Rogers (1985:228) noted:

At one time adults considered adolescents as an economic asset, useful in performing numerous household chores or in earning their keep. However, household appliances, urbanization, and labor laws have taken away most of the tasks that children used to perform, and some parents find children an economic burden.

As economic and social constraints acted upon the family, the large nuclear or extended family pattern gave way to the smaller **nuclear family** as the norm. The **nuclear family** was *limited to the husband and wife and their children, and was characterized by smaller size, greater independence for its members, and more geographical and social mobility.* Along with this transition to smaller nuclear families the characteristics previously mentioned in regard to extended and larger nuclear families were dramatically altered. The number of adults and older siblings available in the nuclear family to supervise the behavior of children was diminished. As the small nuclear family emerged, typically one parent (the father) went off to work, leaving only one adult (the mother) to supervise the children.

Further complicating the situation was the emergence of the concept of adolescence. No longer were role expectations clearly delineated for adults and children. The enactment of child labor laws prohibited children from working in the factories, and with the emergence of the concept of adolescence, routine chores and responsibilities were no longer assigned to physically capable youth. Instead, for a period of one's life (roughly from about 10 to 16 years of age) youths found themselves in a social "no man's land" where they were not allowed the tolerance of behavior granted children, or afforded the rights and responsibilities associated with adulthood. "Appropriate" behavior for teenagers became somewhat ambiguous, leading to the marginality of the juvenile status. As the normative expectations for youth became less clearcut, the void gave rise to what many refer to as the youth subculture, discussed in Chapter 8. Adolescents struggled for a sense of identity and a set of attitudes, values, and beliefs to which they could adhere.

Contemporary society presents the family with an everchanging set of circumstances causing the family to be redefined, restructured, and realigned in a variety of ways. Researchers disagree as to what relationship these changes may have to juvenile delinquency. Divorce, changing sex roles, working mothers, increased leisure time, economic pressures, and the increasing expectation for upward social mobility have all exerted numerous pressures on the family and the individuals within it.

Of the aforementioned changes, the effects of mothers working outside the home and divorce have been the most researched regarding their possible connections to juvenile delinquency. These two variables have received so much attention from researchers that they will be discussed later in separate sections of the chapter.

THE FAMILY AS AN AGENT OF SOCIALIZATION

As explained in Chapter 6, **socialization** refers to the *process whereby individuals learn and internalize the appropriate attitudes, values, beliefs, and behaviors of a particular culture.* This complex social learning process has appropriately been referred to as "people-making" by family therapist Virginia Satir (1972).

Socialization is a lifelong process. Virtually everybody with whom an individual comes in contact can influence the socialization process, but for the most part, sociologists contend that the major agents of socialization consist of the family, school, church, peer group, and mass media. Debate rises over which of these agents of socialization exerts the most influence; however, in almost all cases, the family is the first agent of socialization with which a child comes in contact. As Robert Bell (1983:437) pointed out, "In most cases the important agency for transmitting the culture is the immediate family . . . it gets him first, keeps him longest and is his major source of cultural imperatives." Larry Bumpass (1984:621–622) concluded it is "the 'family of orientation' that serves as the reference point for the transmission of social values." Thus, the family has the first opportunity to socialize the individual to the particular set of ideas, values, beliefs, and behaviors that family members deem appropriate.

Further, while the family cannot totally control outside influences upon its members, it can have significant impact in shaping the extent to which the child will be exposed to the other major agents of socialization. Whether a child attends church, and if so, what kind, is usually determined by parents early in the child's life. Likewise, the decision to own a television and how much and what type of viewing will be allowed, is at least initially a prerogative of the family. The child's first peer group is usually not chosen freely, but is often determined by the parents' choice of friends. Quite often, the first play group of most children consists of the children of their parents' adult friends and neighbors. Once children venture outside the home their initial peer group is largely determined by the geographic boundaries of the immediate neighborhood. Thus, parents' choice of residence (or socioeconomic circumstances which dictate place of residence) largely determine the initial peer group for most children (Colvin and Pauly, 1983). While school attendance is required by law, the choice of private versus public, church-related versus secular, or in which school district a child lives, is largely determined by the parents.

One of the most important ways in which a family socializes its young members is through the process of *role modeling.* Social learning theorists contend that an important part of the process of learning social role expectations occurs through the observation and subsequent identification with and imitation of those who already fill those roles (e.g., Bandura and Walters, 1963). Consequently, a significant part of the socialization of children consists of their observing their parents and older siblings in everyday social interaction. While parents verbally instruct their children in regard to the "do's" and "don'ts" of social behavior, the children also learn simply by watching their parents and older siblings. A substantial amount of the delinquency literature indicates that juveniles whose parents and/or older siblings had trouble with the law or committed other forms of deviance are more likely to become involved in law violating and deviant behavior (e.g., Hogan and Kitagawa, 1985; Barnes et al., 1986). While the biological theorists might use these studies as verification that criminality is inherited, from a sociological perspective the studies simply emphasize the importance of social environment, social learning, socialization, and role modeling.

There is considerable evidence that juveniles learn their attitudes toward the law, law enforcement officials, and law violation from those with whom they associate (e.g., Sutherland and Cressey, 1978). The social group from which children are likely to learn their first attitudes toward the law is the family. Thus, the early childhood socialization process cannot be overestimated in its importance in developing the foundation of attitudes, values, and behaviors likely to lead to law violating behavior in adolescence and young adulthood. Evidently, the family influence and its importance in early socialization are significant in virtually all societies. David Schicor (1983) in discussing the political aspects of delinquency, contended that socialization is a meaningful approach to understanding delinquency whether looking at capitalist or socialist societies.

WORKING MOTHERS AND JUVENILE DELINQUENCY

The phenomenon of women working outside the home is a fairly recent one, which has undoubtedly impacted upon the American family, but researchers cannot seem to agree on what the specific nature of that impact has been upon the children in the family. When "Rosie the Riveter" stepped into the factory to take the place of her husband, who had marched off to war, the event was viewed as temporary. The results, on the other hand, were long lasting. Women proved that they were capable of working in American factories alongside men, or in place of them. During that time, however, they were also expected to return home to perform all of their "wifely" and "motherly" duties, such as cleaning, cooking, and childrearing, which were not expected of their male counterparts. To a large extent, this expectation remains today. As Lasswell and Lasswell (1982) pointed out, if women with young children are employed outside the home, their family responsibilities are often considered paramount and the job, while important, comes second.

Over the decades since World War II, women increasingly assumed their place in the employment market and have gone to work outside the home in record numbers. Many researchers on the family view this phenomenon as being one of the greatest changes that has occurred in the traditional view of marriage. According to the 1980 census, 62 percent of all married women with school-aged children were employed outside the home (Bureau of the Census, 1981:29). In 1900 only one out of five women was employed outside the home, and most of them were single; however, by 1970, more than half (54%) of all women between the ages of 45 and 54 were in the labor force, and the number of working married women with children under the age of 6 more than doubled between 1960 and 1975 (Bell, 1983:265–267). Claire Brindis (1986:6) reported that over 50 percent of all mothers are now in the labor force, including women with children under the age of 6 who are the most likely to be considered full-time homemakers, and projected that "by the end of the 1980s, more than 38 million women will be in the job market."

One of the problems faced by working mothers is finding adequate child care for their children. The number of working women with children is large, but there is little organized child care to help them. Bell (1983:267) estimated that "organized day-care centers, cooperative programs, nurseries, and pre-schools together take care of no more than 10 percent of the children of working mothers." The changing structure and size of the American family means that in many cases there are no other family members available to care for the children in the home. Some mothers make arrangements with nonworking mothers to watch their preschoolers or to watch their school-aged children for a brief period of time before or after school. However, in many cases, the children must fend for themselves. A large number of school-aged children return from school to an empty house. A new phrase, **latchkey children,** has arisen to describe the numerous *school-aged children who return home after school to an empty house* (see Concept Application at the end of this chapter). Estimates indicate that there are anywhere from 2.1 million to 15 million of these latchkey children left unsupervised after school (Chollar, 1987:12). Susan Byrne (1977) contended that the latchkey children are much more likely to get into trouble than children who return home to a parent.

Despite the rhetoric associated with the detrimental effects on children of working mothers, there has been little research actually linking higher rates of delinquency to the children of mothers working outside the home. In fact, Sheldon and Eleanor Glueck (1950), Travis Hirschi (1969), and Mary Reige (1972) all found insignificant differences in rates of delinquency when comparing children of working mothers to those whose mothers did not work outside the home. In one study (Hill and Stafford, 1979) it was indicated that working mothers often make a point of spending more time with their children when they are home in order to compensate for the time away from them.

There also is the notion that the quantity of time spent between parents and children may be less important than the quality of the time spent. Parents who consciously make up for lost time with children because of work may attempt to enhance the quality of interaction during what limited time they do have with their children. Bell (1983:272–273) indicated that as a result of time constraints on working women:

. . . a great deal of stress may be placed on the quality of time spent with children rather than the quantity. Many working mothers devote their undivided individual attention to their children in the relatively short time they have with them.

As suggested by Hirschi (1983), this may be more effective in reducing the likelihood of delinquency than merely the mother's presence in the home. A 5-year study conducted by John Guidubaldi and his associates indicated that children of working mothers tended to do better in school, were absent fewer days, and had better communication skills than children whose mothers did not work outside the home (AP Washington, 1986:15). Their study indicated that mothers who stayed home expressed more confidence that they were good parents than did working mothers, but because mothers who worked outside the home were more worried about their parenting they seemed "to make an effort to spend 'quality time' with their offspring" (AP Washington, 1986:15).

There is also some evidence of detrimental effects when the mother works outside the home. Adam Booth and his associates (1984) found that any change in a wife's employment status can contribute to marital instability. They found that a wife's employment weakens marital stability, especially if she works more than 40 hours per week. Their research primarily examined the impact that working outside the home by the wife had on the husband-wife relationship, however, and did not examine its effects on the children in the family. The Lasswells (1982:361) reported that "having both parents employed outside the home is usually stressful to children only if the parents are suffering from stress about it." More research needs to be conducted on working mothers, latchkey children, and their possible relationships to juvenile delinquency.

OTHER FAMILY VARIABLES AND JUVENILE DELINQUENCY

The importance of the family in socializing its young members is without question. What is much less clear is which variables within the family are related to the problem of juvenile delinquency. While the possibilities are almost infinite, at least four variables have emerged in delinquency research which provide the basis for various theories of delinquency causation: social class, family size (and birth order), the nature of family interaction, and parental discipline.

Social Class

The first social status of a child is that of the family. To be born into an impoverished family, a blue-collar working class family, a middle class professional family, or a wealthy family is totally beyond the control of a child, yet has profound impact upon the child's life. This *ascribed status* affects choice of neighborhood, attitudes and values, parental discipline, education, career choices, and even life expectancy (Hollingshead, 1961; Silverman and Dinitz, 1974; Colvin and Pauly, 1983; Hogan and Kitagawa, 1985).

As indicated in Chapter 3, lower class juveniles are more likely to be arrested than middle or upper class youths, hence, they comprise more than their proportionate amount of the official data on delinquency. In Chapter 6, we discussed several sociological theories of delinquency causation which attempt to explain why lower class youths might be more prone to commit delinquency than their middle and upper class counterparts. We also discussed the unofficial data on delinquency (Chapter 3) in which self-report studies indicate that delinquency exists among all social classes, but that lower class youths are more likely to be officially processed. Lower class youths are more likely to come into contact with the police (Piliavin and Briar, 1964). They are also more likely to be arrested and petitioned to juvenile court (Goldman, 1963; Smith and Visher, 1981; Fagan et al., 1987); if petitioned, they are more likely to be adjudicated delinquent (Axelrod, 1952; Arnold, 1971; Fagan et al., 1987); and, if adjudicated delinquent, more likely to receive a severe disposition by the court (Axelrod, 1952; Arnold, 1971; Thornberry, 1973; Fagan et al., 1987). Whether the lower class commit more delinquency, or are merely more likely to be caught and processed, the family's social class emerges as an important variable. Likewise, whether upper class youths actually commit less delinquency (Empey and Erickson, 1966), or are just less likely to be apprehended and adjudicated, the importance of their social status cannot be denied.

The family's social class is also likely to affect the socialization experienced within the family. As indicated in Chapter 6, Walter Miller (1958) argued that lower class values were distinctively different from those of the middle and upper class. He viewed the focal concerns of the lower class as involving *trouble, toughness, smartness, excitement, fate,* and *autonomy,* all of which he contended led to gang delinquency. While Miller's assertions are highly questionable in that these same focal concerns may be emphasized by juveniles in general, regardless of social class, few would argue that social class does not impact upon one's set of values. Bell (1983:448) summarized some of the values he believes vary by social class:

> There are social class differences in values that are passed on to the children. The middle class are more apt to stress values dealing with self-direction, such as freedom, individualism, initiative, and creativity. Working class parents are more apt to stress values of conformity to external standards such as orderliness, neatness, and obedience.

Other researchers have linked social class to different types of parental discipline and other aspects of family interaction (Strong and Devault, 1986). The extent to which social class is directly related to delinquency remains open to debate, but from a sociological perspective, socioeconomic status is an important determinant of social behavior. Chapter 9 explores some of the ways in which social class may impact upon the nature and type of delinquency in which youths might participate, particularly in groups.

Family Size and Birth Order

Research indicates that overall family size and position in the family (birth order) impact upon a child's behavior (e.g., Pfouts, 1980; Steelman and Mercy, 1980; Kidwell, 1981). Psychologists and sociologists long have emphasized the importance of parents in personality development, but research indicates that the number of siblings and the child's place in the birth order are also important.

Hirschi (1969, 1983), the Gluecks (1968), Nye (1958, 1974), and McCord et al. (1959) all related family size and/or birth ordinal position to delinquency. Hirschi (1969) indicated that large families tend to lack financial resources, discipline, and adequate socialization. Walter Toman (1970:45) also saw family size as an important variable indicating, "After all, as families get larger, children turn to each other for what they cannot get from parents." Michael Rutter (1980) attempted to more directly relate family size to problems which might lead to delinquency. He indicated:

> First, large family size is quite strongly associated with overcrowding and socio-economic disadvantage. Secondly, there is probably less intensive interaction and less communication between the parents and the children in large families if only because parental time has to be distributed more widely. Thirdly, parental discipline and supervision may be more difficult when there are a lot of children to look after. Fourthly, some of the children may have been unwanted. Fifthly, in some cases the lack of family limitations may reflect general parental qualities of inadequate foresight and planning (Rutter, 1980:155).

Numerous arguments could be raised regarding Rutter's assertions. For example, although rural families tend to be larger than urban, place of residence is evidently an intervening variable. As indicated in Chapter 3, urban delinquency rates tend to be much higher than rural. However, family size appears to be a relevant variable for further research as to its possible relationship to juvenile delinquency.

The Gluecks (1968), Nye (1974), and McCord et al. (1959) saw ordinal position as an important variable related to the likelihood of delinquency. Their research suggested that the first child tends to relate well to adults and experiences the undivided attention of parents for a period of time. First-born children apparently accept their parents' ways of doing things much more readily than do later-born children. Bell (1983:456) even contended that ". . . parents attach greater importance to first-born than to later-born children." Loretta Blerer (1980) also concluded that first-born children were less likely to become involved in delinquency because they tend to relate well to adults and internalize rules and regulations established by parents. The first-born also may act as a "third parent" to younger siblings, thus identifying more strongly with adult roles than subsequent children. The later child, however, tends to be intensely competitive and feel a strong "need *not* to conform" in order to contrast with the "conservative older sibling" (Blerer, 1980:52).

The youngest child also seems somewhat more insulated against delinquency. The youngest child benefits from the experience parents have gained in childrearing while also gaining from the experience of having older siblings as role models. Bell (1983:456) pointed out that the older sibling "who is further along in the socialization process but still relatively close in age actions to the younger sibling, may be a more effective agent of socialization than the much older adult parents." The "baby" of the family typically receives a great deal of attention from parents and older brothers and sisters, which may make the youngest child less likely to become involved in delinquency.

Middle children may tend to get "lost" in the childrearing process. They are not usually given the responsibility and meaningful roles assigned to the oldest child, but also are not granted the tolerance and freedom from responsibilities afforded the baby of the family. Hirschi (1969, 1983), Nye (1958, 1974), and McCord et al. (1959) all found middle children to be more likely to be delinquent. It may be that middle children feel relatively deprived of parental attention as compared to the oldest and youngest children, and perceive getting in trouble as one method of gaining attention from adults.

Family size and position in the birth order impact upon the socialization process and are relevant variables to be considered in the study of delinquency. In the ongoing argument of heredity versus environment, it is often ignored that different children in the same family experience different *social* environments. When answering questions about why children of the same parents (and hence, same environment) have such different personalities, Blerer (1980:52) stated, "The fact is that it is *not* the same environment: each child, depending upon his birth order position is born into an environment that is entirely different from that into which any of his siblings is born." Lasswell and Lasswell (1982:323) confirmed "that the addition of each child changes the family structure . . . not only does each sibling change the parents' relationship . . . but also the children's relationships." The extent to which family size and birth order are related to delinquency poses interesting prospects for future sociological research.

Family Interaction

The dynamics of family interaction include infinite possibilities, and undoubtedly vary from family to family and within families, depending upon which family members are involved and what circumstances surround the given situation. Consequently, it would be difficult to predict what specific types of family interaction might be most likely to lead to juvenile delinquency. However, there are certain types of family interaction between parents and children which tend to appear on a fairly consistent basis throughout much of the research on the family and delinquency.

One type of family interaction which seems most consistently related to problematic youth is that of family violence. Murray Straus and his associates (1980) indicated that violence ranging from spanking and shoving to shooting and stabbing has become a common element of social dynamics in an increasing number of American families. It has been estimated that annually over 50 million Americans are victims of physical violence at the hands of family members (US News and World Report, 1979:60–61). In 1981, the California Commission on Crime Control and Violence Prevention indicated that millions of American children are violently abused, molested, or seriously neglected by their parents each year (cited in Strong and DeVault, 1986:459). Family violence does not only involve parents abusing children; it is estimated that "138,000 children use a gun or knife on a sibling each year" (Lasswell and Lasswell, 1982:382).

Numerous studies have linked violence within the family (especially abuse by one or both parents) to juvenile misbehavior and delinquency (e.g., Gil, 1970; Steinmetz and Straus, 1973; Gelles and Straus, 1979; Straus et al., 1980; Kratcoski, 1982). The violence-begets-violence theme suggests that children who are socialized in a family environment in which violence is the norm are much more likely to commit violent behavior and to perceive violence as a viable solution to problems (Straus et al., 1980; Hamner and Turner, 1985).

Besides the issue of physical violence, the overall relationship between parents and children appears relevant to understanding delinquency and its relationship to home environment. David Abrahamsen (1960:43) pointed out that "homes racked with a great deal of tension . . . may produce a great deal of hostility and arguing which threatens family cohesiveness and could lead to delinquency." McCord et al. (1959:83) contended, "Quarrelsome, neglecting families actually had a higher crime rate than homes in which permanent separation disrupted the family" and suggested that homes characterized by neglect and conflict were more likely to produce delinquents than those broken by divorce. August Aichorn (1969:164) indicated that in homes where youths are confronted with constant bickering and quarreling, they often leave the home and take "refuge in the streets." As Chapter 11 indicates, when juveniles take to the streets, their likelihood of involvement in delinquency and with the police is great. Stephen Cernkovich and Peggy Giordano (1987) concluded that patterns of interaction within the family are more important in explaining delinquency than structural factors such as family size and broken or intact home. As discussed in Chapter 6, social control theorists contend that attachment to parents is a significant element of the "social bond" and extremely important in insulating a child against delinquency. Hirschi (1969:88) indi-

Studies suggest that children who experience family violence, abuse, or neglect are more likely to become delinquent during their adolescent years. (Comstock Photos)

cated that children who had developed a strong social bond with their parents were more likely to feel the "psychological presence" of their family when out in the social world. He viewed "affectional identification, love, and respect" as important delinquency inhibitors (Hirschi, 1969:91). Later research (e.g., Jensen, 1972; Gove and Crutchfield, 1982; Rosen, 1985; Cernkovich and Giordano, 1987) confirmed that the social bond with parents was an important variable in family interaction for reducing the likelihood of delinquency.

Parental Discipline

One of the acknowledged role expectations in American society is that parents will discipline their children. The nature, type, and extent of the discipline varies a great deal, as do attitudes about what constitutes appropriate disciplinary measures. In general, as American society has progressed, acceptable methods of discipline have tended to become less severe.

In colonial America, children generally were viewed as the property of their parents (especially the father), and virtually any disciplinary method deemed appropriate by the parent was permitted. Corporal punishment was used fairly regularly, as the "spare the rod and spoil the child" school of childrearing tended to dominate. In fact, some colonies actually had what were called "stubborn child laws," which allowed parents to kill their children for serious or continuous misconduct (Straus et al., 1980). Arthur Calhoun (1960:42) documented the severity of discipline legally sanctioned in colonial America by citing a law from one of the colonies which read:

> If any child or children above 16 years old of competent understanding, shall curse or smite their natural father or mother, he or they shall be put to death unless it can be sufficiently testified that the parents have been very unchristianly negligent of the education of such child . . . if any man have a rebellious or stubborne [sic] son of sufficient years and understanding, that is to say, 16 years of age or upwards, which shall not obey the voice of his father or the voice of his mother, yet when they have chastened him will not harken unto them . . . such son shall be put to death, or otherwise severely punished.

While such extreme measures were probably rare if not virtually nonexistent, general attitudes toward parental discipline focused on the unquestioned authority of the parent. As time passed, attitudes toward children changed, and laws were passed to protect the rights of children. Corporal punishment was still used, but laws prohibited excessive physical abuse. Today, attitudes toward parental discipline are varied, but every state has laws designed to protect children from parental abuse. Discipline in the American family ranges from corporal punishment to no punishment at all, with virtually everything in between. In general, parental attitudes have tended to become more tolerant with less severe methods of punishment being used. Strong and DeVault (1986:375–377) summarized contemporary childrearing strategies into the following categories:

1. **Authoritarian.** Typically require absolute obedience; parents maintaining control seems most important; "Because I said so" is typical response to child's questioning of authority. More typical of lower class and working class families.

2. **Permissive.** Child's freedom of expression and autonomy are valued; parents are sometimes manipulative using such terminology as "do what we want you to do because you want to do it"; typical of middle class families.
3. **Authoritative.** Relies on positive reinforcement and infrequent punishment; encourages autonomy within reasonable limits; more typical of upper middle and upper class families.

Parental discipline is involved in the concept of delinquency in a variety of ways. If nothing else, in virtually every state parents can petition their own children to juvenile court for refusing to obey them. Usually handled under the umbrella of "incorrigibility," this type of misbehavior is treated as a status offense.

Beyond the possibility of parents bringing the court's attention to their own child's misbehavior, parental discipline influences the development of the juvenile in a multitude of other ways which might lead to delinquency. As previously mentioned, studies have indicated that children who have been subjected to parental violence are more likely to become delinquent than children from nonviolent homes. Also, as previously discussed, research shows that the quality of the relationship between parent and child is significantly related to delinquency.

While parental violence is linked to delinquency, strict discipline by parents is not. The McCords and Zola (1959) found that the consistency of discipline was more important in insulating against delinquency than the method used. Similarly, Tommie Hamner and Pauline Turner (1985) concurred that harsh treatment was less damaging to children's self-esteem than were lack of interest and lack of consistency in interaction with children. They suggested that parents adhere to the following guidelines if punishment is to be successful:

1. Before punishment is administered, the child should know clearly what the expectations for his behavior are and what consequences will occur if these expectations are not met;
2. Punishment should follow the act immediately;
3. Punishment needs to be deserved and understood;
4. Punishment needs to be related to the act;
5. Punishment should be administered within a context of love and respect (Hamner and Turner, 1985:45).

As discussed in Chapter 6, the social learning and social control theories emphasize parental influence in helping a child to internalize norms and values, develop a sense of social attachment, and to refrain from committing delinquent acts. Hirschi (1983:15) further emphasized the importance of parental discipline:

The parent who cares for the child will watch his behavior, see him doing things he should not do, and correct him. Presto! A socialized decent human being.

Admittedly, Hirschi may have oversimplified the complex art of disciplining children, but his point may be valid. Paying attention to their children's behavior, and then doing something about misbehavior, represents a basic element of the socialization process and the internalization of conforming behavior. He pointed out some potential problems that might enter into the socialization process and thwart the prevention of delinquency:

1. The parents may not care;
2. The parents may care, but may not have the time or energy to monitor the child's behavior;
3. The parents may care, may monitor the behavior, but may not see anything wrong with it;
4. The parents may care, may monitor the behavior, may view it as wrong, but might not have the inclination nor the means to impose punishment (Hirschi, 1983:15).

Any of these factors might interrupt the socialization process and lead to delinquency. The first factor would be a situation wherein the parents deserve "blame" for not properly socializing their child to internalize social norms and refrain from law violation. However, the second example implies that if both parents work, or a child is raised in a one-parent family, the parent may not be able to monitor the child's behavior. Scenario three alludes to a situation wherein the parent knows that the child has violated a norm, but sees nothing wrong with the child doing so. In a pluralistic society, if certain norms have no meaning for parents, they are not likely to enforce them within the family setting. Finally, the last situation addresses the problem faced by many parents in attempting to discipline their children. Sometimes, in an attempt to get along with their children, parents tolerate behavior that they know is wrong simply to avoid confrontation. Or, in other cases the inability to handle the youth or actual fear of the child (if the parent is physically smaller and/or weaker than the child) might prohibit intervention and punishment even though the parent(s) clearly feel(s) the situation warrants it. One study estimated that "8 million children—18 out of every 100, most of them teenagers— assault their parents" (US News and World Report, 1979:60–61). Regardless of the reasons, when parents fail to discipline their children, the burden is likely to shift to other agents of social control such as school, police, and the courts. The elements of social control ranging from voluntary through formal agencies are further discussed in Chapter 13.

BROKEN HOMES AND DELINQUENCY

Debate long has been waged over the relationship between broken homes and juvenile delinquency. **Broken home** usually *refers to any family situation in which both parents are not present on a permanent basis.* **Intact home** *is used to describe a family situation in which both parents are physically present.*

A common theme in much of the earlier literature on juvenile delinquency involved the idea that broken homes contributed to delinquency causation (e.g., Shideler, 1918; Gilling, 1933; Parsons, 1947; Glueck and Glueck, 1950; Monahan, 1957). As discussed in Chapter 6, many sociological explanations for delinquency focus upon the socialization process and its importance in the development of attitudes, values, and beliefs likely to encourage or discourage delinquency. Since the family as a social institution usually serves as the primary agent of socialization, a logical assumption was that any disruption in the family institution, especially something as significant as divorce, was likely to have negative impact upon the socialization process. Thus, social learning theories and social control theories tended to link broken homes to delinquency.

The number of marriages in the United States ending in divorce has increased dramatically during the twentieth century. The number of divorces per 1,000 population was 1.6 in 1920; 3.5 in 1970; and 5.3 in 1979 (National Center for Health Statistics, 1980). Only about 5 percent of all marriages in the 1860s ended in divorce (Preston and McDonald, 1979) while about 50 percent of marriages of the 1970s were estimated to terminate through divorce (Weed, 1980). Andrew Cherlin (1981) pointed out that the divorce rate doubled during the decades of the 1960s and 1970s. As the divorce rate increased, so did speculation about the impact of divorce upon juveniles and its assumed relationship to juvenile delinquency.

Empirical research on the relationship between broken homes and delinquency provided mixed results and led to a variety of interpretations and conclusions. Ivan Nye (1958) contended that the broken home had a stronger relationship to status offenses (especially truancy and running away) than to serious delinquency. John Johnstone's (1978) and Joseph Rankin's (1983) research, some 20 and 25 years later, essentially came to the same conclusion. Nye (1958) concluded that the broken home was related to delinquency among girls more than for boys. Susan Datesman and Frank Scarpitti (1975) also viewed the broken home as having differential impact on boys and girls, with the relationship to delinquency being stronger for girls. Rachelle Canter (1982), on the other hand, contended that boys were as affected as girls by the breakup of their parents.

Talcott Parsons (1947) promoted the idea that divorce was particularly dysfunctional for the development of young males because it created anxiety about their masculine identity. He viewed that anxiety as leading to **compul-**

sive masculinity, or *an overemphasis on what were considered "manly" characteristics,* which was likely to result in antisocial behavior. Jackson Toby (1966) amplified this theme 20 years later, and contended that compulsive masculinity was likely to develop in families where the father was absent. Compulsive masculinity, he claimed, was linked to delinquency, especially violent behavior. Ira Silverman and Simon Dinitz (1974) generally agreed that the absence of a male role model led to exaggerated masculinity and in an attempt to assert their masculinity, many young males commit delinquency. Barbara Cashion (1982) refuted these assumptions, however, indicating that her research findings on female-headed families showed that delinquency was not higher among juveniles in homes where the father was absent when the variable of socioeconomic status was controlled.

Other research on delinquency has questioned the relationship between broken homes and delinquency, especially the assumption that broken homes *cause* delinquency. Philip Smith (1955) suggested that juveniles from broken homes were treated differently by juvenile courts. Thus, studies linking broken homes to delinquency which used youths who had been adjudicated delinquent, and especially studies which used institutionalized sample, were called into question. Monahan (1957) confirmed that youths from broken homes were much more likely to be referred to juvenile court, while those from intact homes were more likely to be dismissed during intake. Further, he found that those juveniles from broken homes were more likely to be institutionalized than placed on probation (Monahan, 1957). A study of Massachusetts youth found that while prior record, nature of offense, and other legal variables were important factors in disposition, many social caseworkers viewed single-parent families as less capable of handling delinquents, and, consequently, were more likely to recommend that they be placed in some type of juvenile facility (Isralowitz, 1981).

In an excellent overview of the research conducted on broken homes and delinquency, Karen Wilkinson (1974) indicated that the variable of broken home has fluctuated in its importance to sociological research on delinquency. She suggested that perhaps the reason that sociologists have emphasized the broken home in delinquency causation more at some times than at others is because the relationship between broken home and delinquency has indeed been different over different periods of time. She went on to say that if the concept of broken home is going to be utilized in sociological theory it must be refined. She suggested that it is likely to have a different impact upon a juvenile if the home is broken as a result of the death of one of the parents as opposed to divorce or desertion. Richard Hardy and John Cull (1973) found that the loss of a parent through death was not nearly as likely to lead to delinquency as the loss of a parent through divorce or separation. Wilkinson (1974) pointed out that if the broken home factor in delinquency is going to be meaningful, it must be incorporated into a broader theory of delinquency causation such as Hirschi's (1969) control theory.

The relationship between broken homes and delinquency is, at best, ambiguous. Divorce is a much more common phenomenon in American society today than ever before. Data indicate that approximately 50 percent of all marriages end in divorce (NEA Today, 1986:31), and since 1970, there has been a 40 percent increase in the number of children living in single parent families (US Bureau of the Census, 1982). With divorce rates so high, it might even be argued that broken homes have become the norm. If not the norm, at least the negative attitudes and stigma associated with divorce have been reduced greatly and divorce has become much more socially accepted (Thornton, 1985). Whether the increased number of homes split by divorce has caused increased delinquency is debatable. If social agencies such as Big Brothers/Big Sisters and day care centers can help fill the void in a child's life caused by the absence of one of the parents, the juvenile may be no more likely to engage in delinquency than would a child from an intact home. Further, it might even be argued that the juvenile who has experienced a broken home eventually receives more adult supervision and more adult role models in the socialization process. Statistics indicate that most of those who divorce soon remarry, and it is estimated that 15 million minor children now live in step-families with an increase of nearly a million every year (Lasswell and Lasswell, 1982:430). Children of divorced parents are likely to have two families, not one, and four adults involved in the socialization process as opposed to two.

As mentioned earlier in this chapter, some research emphasizes the nature of the relationship between parents and children as being more importantly related to delinquency than whether the home is broken or intact (e.g., Cernkovich and Giordano, 1987). Lawrence Rosen and Kathleen Neilson (1982:134) concluded that "the concept of broken home no matter how it is defined or measured, has little explanatory power in terms of delinquency." A study by Margaret Farnworth (1984) came to essentially the same conclusion. Homes characterized by tension, even in intact families, may produce situations which could lead to delinquency (Abrahamsen, 1960:43). McCord et al. (1959) suggested that homes characterized by neglect and conflict were more likely to produce delinquents than those broken by divorce. Suzanne Steinmetz and Murray Straus (1973) reaffirmed that idea in a study indicating that children who experienced family violence were more likely to commit violence than those who had not. With increasing divorce rates, it is likely that the possible relationship between broken homes and delinquency will continue to capture the interest of researchers.

THE FAMILY AND DELINQUENCY PREVENTION

The specific nature of the relationship between the family and juvenile delinquency remains unclear. Variables such as the family's socioeconomic status, neighborhood, family size, birth order, quality of family interaction, parental discipline, working mothers, and family structure (broken or intact) all have been explored. Various studies have come up with different conclusions as to how these family variables relate to delinquency. About the only general consensus evolving from research on the family and delinquency is that the family unquestionably impacts upon its individual members. Perhaps the most meaningful way to view the relationship between the family and juvenile delinquency is in its broadest sociological context.

The family is a basic social institution regardless of its size, structure, and particular dynamics. As a primary social group, family members influence each other in a variety of ways. Individuals' roles in their families become a basic part of their personal and social identities. As an agent of socialization, attitudes, values, beliefs, and norms are transmitted from one generation to the next and within generations in the family setting.

How one perceives the role of the family in delinquency prevention is

Youth-parent conflicts are a normal part of adolescence. Evidence suggests that the relationship between parents and youths during this critical stage of development is one of the most influential variables related to juvenile delinquency. (H. Armstrong Roberts)

inherently linked to one's view of the role of the family in delinquency causation. The disparate findings of sociological research in this area suggest that a multicausal approach needs to be taken which assesses the variety of ways in which the family impacts upon its individual members.

Many of the problems of juvenile delinquency appear related to the marginal status accorded adolescents in American society. One of the ways in which the family might effectively attempt to prevent delinquency is to create clearly defined and meaningful social roles for its younger members. Societal and parental expectations should be consistent, well defined, and clearly articulated to children. Whether both parents are present in the home or not appears less important than the quality of the relationship established between the child and the parent(s) who is/are present.

Parental supervision and consistency in discipline also appear to be important insulators against delinquency. Much of the controversy over the relationship between broken homes and delinquency causation may be mediated by looking at the variable of extent of parental supervision. Donald Fischer (1983) concluded that high parental supervision is a significant variable in lower delinquency rates even under other adverse social conditions. One parent who is intimately involved in the supervision of the child's behavior may be more effective in preventing delinquency than two parents who show little or no interest in their children's behavior or who are distracted from their parental responsibilities by marital stress. While studies linking broken homes, physical and emotional abuse, and other family problems to delinquency causation create much controversy, there is almost irrefutable evidence that a stable family life characterized by love, concern, consistency in discipline, and adequate parental supervision is related to less likelihood of delinquency. Allen Liska and Mark Reed (1985:558) concluded that parents "are the major institutional sources of delinquency control."

The family serves as the first social group to which a juvenile belongs. While church, school, mass media, and peers greatly influence the values and behavior of youths, the family usually has the first opportunity in the socialization process. No doubt, the changing role of the American family has altered its preeminence in socializing its young members. Many of the functions formerly fulfilled by the family have been abdicated to other social groups and agencies. Yet, the family still plays a fundamental role in shaping the attitudes, values, beliefs, and behaviors that may promote or prevent future law violation.

The social bond between juveniles and their families appears to be one of the most effective insulators against delinquency. As American society has become more highly industrialized, urbanized, and bureaucratized, the juvenile's attachment to the family has become somewhat more difficult to maintain. William Arnold and Terrance Brungardt (1983) agreed that commitment to family is a conformity-producing process and represents a basic American value. But, as they pointed out, family commitment may also be somewhat contradictory to another basic value: individual freedom in interpersonal relations. They hypothesize that "forces detracting from commitment to family demands free persons to interact with others who lack commitments to conformity producing values" (Arnold and Brungardt, 1983:128). In today's urban environment, a multitude of sociocultural influences exist which potentially weaken a juvenile's commitment to family. In Chapter 8, The Youth Subculture, we discuss some of the competing values experienced by juveniles in the social and cultural milieu in which they interact.

Finally, the changing role of the family must be acknowledged. As was indicated at the beginning of this chapter, the American family has undergone and continues to experience dramatic changes. There is no *the* American family. Rather, the institution of the family is in a continuous process of transition. Bumpass (1984:621) reported:

> In 1980, only three-fifths of all children lived in the simple family composed of once-married parents, less than half will live out their childhood in this status. In this context, we must rethink our conceptualization of the family in sociological research.

In order to more thoroughly assess the family's impact upon juvenile delinquency, the changing role of the family will have to be more fully understood within its broadest sociological context.

SUMMARY

The role of the family in American society has changed a great deal over the past 200 years. The extended or large nuclear family that pragmatically fulfilled the necessary familial functions for individuals in a predominantly agrarian society gave way to the smaller more mobile nuclear family as America became more urbanized and industrialized.

The family serves as one of the most important agents of socialization in our society, and the first to which most people are exposed. A child's initial attitudes, values, and beliefs typically are those socially learned from family members. Additionally, a child's first play group, place of residence, exposure to religion, and a variety of other experiences primarily are determined by the family of orientation.

There has been tremendous interest in and much disagreement about the impact on children of having mothers who work outside the home. Each year, more women with children of preschool and school age join the American work force. A major problem associated with the increased number of working mothers is the lack of adequate child care facilities available in the United States. This situation has given rise to the phenomenon of "latchkey children" who must spend some time in the afternoons left unsupervised until one or both parents return home from work. Much speculation has occurred regarding the potentially increased likelihood of delinquency among these unsupervised youths. Research indicates, however, that if working parents are aware of the potentially negative impact of both parents working outside the home and spend "quality time" with their children when possible, that adequate socialization can overcome the negative aspects of temporary lack of supervision.

Some important family variables have been shown to be related to delinquency. Social class, family size, birth order, family interaction, and parental discipline all impact upon a juvenile's likelihood of becoming delinquent.

For many years a causal link was believed to exist between broken homes and delinquency. Data indicated that children of single parent homes were apparently more likely to commit delinquent offenses. However, subsequent research has indicated that the apparent relationship between broken homes and delinquency may be spurious, and better explained by other variables such as lack of supervision and differential treatment by members of the juvenile justice system.

Because of the significant impact the family has upon children, it potentially can play a vital role in delinquency prevention. Adequate socialization and the development of a strong social bond are important dimensions of the family's delinquency prevention role. The family also can reduce the marginality experienced by adolescents by providing meaningful familial roles and responsibilities. In short, the family's impact upon juveniles cannot be overestimated, and consequently, should remain a major research focus for sociological inquiry into the social problem of juvenile delinquency.

CONCEPT APPLICATION

ILLUSTRATIVE ANECDOTE

"Latchkey Children: Independence or Neglect?"

Brandon and Mica step off the school bus at approximately 4:00 p.m. every day. They wave goodbye to their bus driver and all their friends on the bus. Then they walk the two blocks to their home. When they reach their house, Brandon, who is the older of the two at age 12, reaches into his shoe to retrieve his housekey, unlocks the door for his 8-year-old sister, and they go inside. After relocking the door, Brandon and Mica proceed through their daily ritual. Brandon pours each of them a glass of milk while Mica unwraps the cookies, brownies, donuts, or similar snack that was covered in cellophane and left for them on the kitchen counter earlier that morning. They retire to the family room where Mica watches her favorite cartoon show and Brandon begins working on his homework.

Brandon and Mica are not orphans; nor are they victims of a broken home, severe neglect, or any other form of child abuse. Rather, they are part of the legions of "latchkey" children who return home from school each day to an empty house to await the arrival of their parents, both of whom work outside the home. In their case, they are not home alone for an extended period of time. Their mother teaches at the high school, and arrives home around 4:30 p.m. each day, approximately 30 minutes after the two children. If their mother must attend a meeting, run an errand, or is otherwise delayed, the two children are sometimes in the home alone until approximately 5:30 p.m. when their father, who teaches at the local university, usually arrives.

Brandon and Mica have been carefully schooled in their role of latchkey children. Their mother and father have established some basic house rules regarding their activities while in the home alone. They are not allowed to play outside or have house guests, are strictly forbidden from cooking, and do not answer the door under any circumstances. If the phone rings, they take a message, informing the caller that their mother is "in the shower" and cannot come to the phone at the moment. Their mother's and father's work phone numbers are posted near each of the telephones right below the emergency 911 number, and right above the phone number of their next-door neighbor, who is usually at home in the afternoon.

Brandon and Mica's parents are concerned about their children's welfare, and greatly fear the possibilities of harm coming to their children while home alone. Their mother's greatest fear is that of fire, and despite the presence of smoke alarms in every room, the practiced fire drills, and other precautions taken, she worries that if a fire should break out, the children would panic. Their father's major concern is related more to the possibility of personal harm which might come to the children from walking in on an intruder, or from someone noticing that the children walk home alone from the bus stop every day at the same time and following them to their home.

On the positive side, Brandon and Mica's parents have noticed a growing sense of independence and responsibility on the part of the two children over the past 2 years in which they have been coming home to an empty house. Brandon is remarkably mature for his age, and takes the responsibilities associated with his role as the older sibling quite seriously. He is very confident of his ability to take care of himself and his younger sister for the brief period that they are alone each afternoon. He has begged his parents not to hire a babysitter, although his parents continue their search for somebody to stay with the children during that period of time. Mica also has shown increased confidence in her own abilities, and no longer relies on her mother or father to perform minor tasks for her when she is physically capable of doing them for herself. Mica's mother remarked that when she was home waiting for the children when they came home from school, "they couldn't even get themselves a glass of water—or at least, they wouldn't—now they take the initiative to help themselves when they can."

Brandon and Mica are far from unique. They happen to be from a middle class background with well-educated parents, both of whom are pursuing professional careers. Many other children are in the same type of situation. Others come from lower class backgrounds where their parents are employed in unskilled or semiskilled occupations. There are as many possible scenarios as there are social situations for families, but one common element seems to permeate today's American family: more and more of them rely upon two paychecks. Either by choice or by necessity, many American families are characterized by the dual-income phenomenon and, consequently, the number of children who must spend a portion of the day in the home alone without adult supervision is growing.

* * * *

As noted in this chapter, some researchers lament the phenomenon of the "latchkey children" as being a form of child neglect, and predict that children left alone in the home even for a brief period of time are more likely to get into trouble and possibly become juvenile delinquents. On the other hand, some research has indicated that the children of working mothers tend to be well adjusted and no more likely to become delinquent than children whose mothers stay at home. What do you think? Should children be left alone in the home without adult supervision? If so, at what age should parents allow their children to be in the home unsupervised? In your opinion, are "latchkey children" more or less likely to become involved in delinquency? How do you feel about the case of Brandon and Mica? Are they being neglected, or are they becoming independent and learning to assume responsibility? If you were their parent, what would you do?

CONCEPT INTEGRATION

QUESTIONS FOR STUDY AND DISCUSSION

1. In what ways does the type of family a juvenile experiences (extended or nuclear) affect the likelihood of his or her becoming delinquent?
2. How does the socialization process in the family impact upon the likelihood of a youth becoming delinquent?
3. An increasing number of mothers work outside the home today. In your opinion, are the children of working mothers *more* or *less* likely to become delinquent? Why?
4. How do family variables such as social class, family size, birth order, family interaction, and parental discipline relate to juvenile delinquency?
5. Define the following terms: extended family, nuclear family, family of orientation, role modeling, latchkey children, broken home, and intact

home. How does the understanding of these terms and concepts help us in understanding juvenile delinquency?

6. In what ways can the family become more involved in delinquency prevention?

7. Think of your own family situation when you were growing up. What type of family did you live in (extended or nuclear)? In what ways did your family help prevent you from becoming delinquent? What family situations did you experience which potentially could have promoted delinquency on your part? As a parent, how would you go about trying to prevent your children from becoming delinquent?

References

Abrahamsen, D. 1960. *The psychology of crime.* New York: Columbia University Press.

Aichorn, A. 1969. *Delinquency and child guidance.* New York: International Universities Press.

AP Washington. 1986. Study says children of working mothers do better in school. *Emporia Gazette* August 25, 1986:15.

Arnold, W. R. 1971. Race and ethnicity relative to other factors in juvenile court dispositions. *American Journal of Sociology* 77 (2):211–227.

Arnold, W. R. & Brungardt, T. M. 1983. *Juvenile misconduct and delinquency.* Boston: Houghton-Mifflin.

Axelrod, S. 1952. Negro and white institutionalized delinquents. *American Journal of Sociology* 57 (May):569–574.

Bandura, A. & Walters, R. 1963. *Social learning and personality development.* New York: Holt, Rinehart & Winston.

Barnes, G. M., Farrell, M. P., & Cairns, A. 1986. Parental socialization factors and adolescent drinking behaviors. *Journal of Marriage and the Family* 48 (February):27–36.

Bell, R. R. 1983. *Marriage and family interaction* (6th ed.). Homewood, Ill: Dorsey Press.

Blerer, L. M. 1980. The meaning of birth order: First born, last born. *Parents* (March):52–55.

Booth, A., Johnson, D. R., & White, L. 1984. Women, outside employment, and marital instability. *American Journal of Sociology* 90 (November):567–583.

Brindis, C. 1986. The nation's changing demographic profile: Implications for the family life educator. *Family Life Educator* 5 (Fall):4–9.

Bumpass, L. 1984. Some characteristics of children's second families. *American Journal of Sociology* 90 (November):608–623.

Byrne, S. 1977. Nobody home: The erosion of the American family. *Psychology Today* 10 (May):40–47.

Calhoun, A. W. 1960. *A social history of the American family: Colonial period.* Vol. 1. New York: Barnes and Noble.

Canter, R. J. 1982. Family correlates of male and female delinquency. *Criminology* 20 (August):149–167.

Cashion, B. G. 1982. Female-headed families: Effects on children and clinical implications. *Journal of Marital and Family Therapy* 8 (April):77–85.

Cernkovich, S. A. & Giordano, P. C. 1987. Family relationships and delinquency. *Criminology* 25:295–321.

Cherlin, A. J. 1981. *Marriage, divorce, and remarriage.* Cambridge, MA: Harvard University Press.

Chollar, S. 1987. Latchkey kids: Who are they? *Psychology Today* 21 (December):12.

Colvin, M. & Pauly, J. 1983. A critique of criminology: Toward an integrated structural-Marxist theory of delinquency prevention. *American Journal of Sociology* 89 (November): 513–545.

Datesman, S. & Scarpitti, F. 1975. Female delinquency and broken homes. *Criminology* 13 (May):35–56.

Empey, L. T. & Erickson, M. L. 1966. Hidden delinquency and social status. *Social Forces* 44 (June):546–554.

Fagan, J., Slaughter, E., & Hartstone, E. 1987. Blind justice? The impact of race on the juvenile justice process. *Crime and Delinquency* 33 (April):224–258.

Farnworth, M. 1984. Family structure, family attributes, and delinquency in a sample of low-income, minority males and females. *Journal of Youth and Adolescence* 13 (August):349–364.

Fischer, D. G. 1983. Parental supervision and delinquency. *Perceptual Motor Skills* 56 (April):635–640.

Gelles, R. & Straus, M. 1979. Violence in the American family. *Journal of Social Issues* 35 (Spring):15–19.

Gil, D. 1970. *Violence against children.* Cambridge, MA: Harvard University Press.

Gilling, J. 1933. *Social pathology.* New York: Appleton-Century-Crofts.

Glueck, S. & Glueck, E. 1950. *Unraveling juvenile delinquency.* Cambridge, MA: Harvard University Press.

———. 1968. *Delinquents and nondelinquents in perspective.* Cambridge, MA: Harvard University Press.

Goldman, N. 1963. *The differential selection of juvenile offenders for court appearance.* New York: National Council on Crime and Delinquency.

Gove, W. R. & Crutchfield, R. D. 1982. The family and juvenile delinquency. *The Sociological Quarterly* 23 (Summer):301–319.

Hamner, T. J. & Turner, P. H. 1985. *Parenting in contemporary society.* Englewood Cliffs, NJ: Prentice-Hall.

Hardy, R. E. & Cull, J. G. 1973. *Climbing Ghetto Walls.* Springfield, IL: Charles C. Thomas.

Hill, C. R. & Stafford, F. P. 1979. Parental care of children. *Journal of Human Resources* 15 (Spring):219–239.

Hirschi, T. 1969. *Causes of delinquency.* Berkeley: University of Calif. Press.

———. 1983. Families and crime. *Current* 254 (July–Aug.):14–19.

Hogan, D. P. & Kitagawa, E. M. 1985. The impact of social status, family structure, and neighborhood on the fertility of black adolescents. *American Journal of Sociology* 90 (January):825–855.

Hollingshead, A. B. 1961. Elmstown's youth: The impact of social classes on adolescents. New York: John Wiley.

Isralowitz, R. E. 1981. Youth service caseworkers: Social and legal factors affecting their recommendations to place youths in secure care facilities. *Children and Youth Services Review* 3 (3):233–246.

Jensen, G. 1972. Parents, peers and delinquent action: A test of differential association perspective. *American Journal of Sociology* 78 (November):562–575.

Johnstone, J. W. C. 1978. Juvenile delinquency and the family: A contextual interpretation. *Youth and Society* 9 (March):299–313.

Kidwell, J. S. 1981. Number of siblings, sibling spacing, sex, and birth order: Their effects on perceived parent-adolescent relationships. *Journal of Marriage and the Family* 43 (May):315–332.

Kratcoski, P. C. 1982. Child abuse and violence against the family. *Child Welfare* 61 (Sept.–Oct.):435–444.

Lasswell, M. & Lasswell, T. E. 1982. *Marriage and the family.* Lexington, MA: DC Heath.

Liska, A. E. & Reed, M. D. 1985. Ties to conventional institutions and delinquency: Estimating reciprocal effects. *American Sociological Review* 50 (August):547–560.

McCord, W., McCord, J., & Zola, I. 1959. *Origins of crime.* New York: Columbia University Press.

Miller, W. B. 1958. Lower class culture as a generating milieu of gang delinquency. *Journal of Social Issues* 14 (3):5–19.

Monahan, T. P. 1957. Family status and the delinquent child: A reappraisal and some new findings. *Social Forces* (March):250–258.

National Center for Health Statistics. 1980. Births, marriages, divorces, and deaths for 1979. Monthly Vital Statistics Report 28, no. 12, Washington, DC: US Department of Health, Education, and Welfare.

NEA Today. 1986. Families. *Today's Education, NEA Today* 5 (1):30–41.

Nye, F. I. 1958. *Family relationships and delinquent behavior.* New York: John Wiley.

———. 1974. Emerging and declining family roles. *Journal of Marriage and the Family* 36 (May):238–245.

Parsons, T. 1947. Certain primary sources and patterns of aggression in the social structure of the western world. *Psychiatry* 10 (May):167–181.

Pfouts, J. H. 1980. Birth order, age spacing, IQ differences, and family relations. *Journal of Marriage and the Family* 42 (August):517–530.

Piliavin, I. & Briar, S. 1964. Police encounters with juveniles. *American Journal of Sociology* 70 (September):206–214.

Preston, S. H. & MacDonald, J. 1979. The incidence of divorce within cohorts of American marriages contracted since the Civil War. *Demography* 16:1–25.

Rankin, J. H. 1983. The family context of delinquency. *Social Problems* 30 (April):466–479.

Reid, S. T. 1988. *Crime and criminology* (5th ed.). New York: Holt, Rinehart and Winston.

Reige, M. G. 1972. Parental affection and juvenile delinquency in girls. *British Journal of Criminology* 12 (January):55–73.

Rogers, D. 1985. *Adolescence and youth* (5th ed.). Englewood Cliffs, NJ: Prentice-Hall.

Rosen, L. 1985. Family and delinquency: Structure or function? *Criminology* 23:553–573.

Rosen, L. & Neilson, K. 1982. Broken homes. In L. D. Savitz & N. Johnson (Eds.). *Contemporary criminology*. New York: John Wiley, pp. 126–135.

Rutter, M. 1980. *Changing youth in a changing society: Patterns of adolescent development and disorder*. Cambridge, MA: Harvard University Press.

Satir, V. 1972. *Peoplemaking*. Palo Alto, CA: Science and Behavior Books.

Schicor, D. 1983. Socialization: The political aspects of a delinquency explanation. *Sociological Spectrum* 3 (Jan–Mar):85–100.

Seward, R. R. 1978. *The American family: A democratic history*. Beverly Hills, CA: Sage.

Shideler, E. H. 1918. Family disintegration and the delinquent boy in the United States. *Journal of Criminal Law and Criminology* 8 (January):709–732.

Silverman, E. J. & Dinitz, S. 1974. Compulsive masculinity and delinquency: An empirical investigation. *Criminology* 11 (February):498–515.

Smith, D. A. & Visher, C. A. 1981. Street-level justice: Situational determinants of police arrest decisions. *Social Problems* 29 (December):167–177.

Smith, P. M. 1955. Broken homes and juvenile delinquency. *Sociology and Social Research* 39 (May–June):307–311.

Steelman, L. C. & Mercy, J. A. 1980. Unconfounding the confluence model: A test of sibling size and birth order on intelligence. *American Sociological Review* 45 (August):571–582.

Steinmetz, S. K. & Straus, M. A. 1973. The family as cradle of violence. *Society* 10 (Sept.–Oct.):50–56.

Straus, M., Gelles, R., & Steinmetz, S. 1980. *Behind closed doors: Violence in the American family*. New York: Anchor.

Strong, B. & DeVault, C. 1986. *The marriage and family experience* (3rd ed.). St. Paul, MN: West.

Sutherland, E. H. & Cressey, D. R. 1978. *Criminology* (10th ed.). Philadelphia: JB Lippincott.

Thornberry, T. P. 1973. Race, socioeconomic status, and sentencing in the juvenile justice system. *Journal of Criminal Law and Criminology* 64 (1):90–98.

Thornton, A. 1985. Changing attitudes toward separation and divorces: Causes and consequences. *American Journal of Sociology* 90 (January):856–872.

Toby, J. 1966. Violence and the masculine ideal: Some qualitative data. *Annals of the American Society of Political and Social Sciences* 364 (March):19–27.

Toman, W. 1970. Birth order rules all. *Psychology Today* (December):45–49, 68–69.

US Bureau of the Census. 1981. *Current Population Reports,* ser. P-20, No. 373. Washington, DC: US Government Printing Office.

1982. Marital status and living arrangements: March, 1981. *Current Population Reports,* ser. P-20, No. 372. Washington, DC: US Government Printing Office.

US News and World Report. 1979. Battered families: A growing nightmare. *US News and World Report* (January 15):60–61.

Weed, J. A. 1980. *National estimates of marriage dissolution and survivorship: United States. Vital Health and Statistics,* ser. 3 no. 19. Hyattsville, MD: National Center for Health Statistics.

Wilkinson, K. 1974. The broken family and juvenile delinquency: Scientific explanation or ideology? *Social Problems* 21 (June):726–739.

Chapter 8

The Youth Subculture

The reading of this chapter will help you achieve the following objectives:

1. Define subculture and explain what is meant by the concept of youth subculture.
2. Identify aspects of American culture which may lead to the creation and perpetuation of a youth subculture.
3. Identify specific attitudes, values, beliefs, behaviors, and norms characterizing the youth subculture.
4. Understand how participation in a youth subculture may result in committing delinquent acts.
5. Explore ways in which the youth subculture might be utilized to help control and prevent delinquency.

INTRODUCTION

It seems that virtually every generation of adults worries about the future of society being turned over to its children. History is replete with the theme of elders believing that the younger generation has abandoned the most important attitudes, values, and beliefs of their parents, and that each succeeding group of youngsters almost ensures that society's ruin is imminent. Likewise, as children begin to grow into young adults they marvel at the "old fogeyness" of their parents, teachers, and other older members of society. They often wonder how adults survived so long while being so ignorant, out-of-touch, and old-fashioned. These disparate views have led to the sense of a generation gap between adults and juveniles that has spawned both social speculation and scientific research into the phenomenon often referred to as the **youth subculture.**

In Chapter 7, we looked at the family as one of the most important primary groups to which people belong. We discussed the prominent role that the family plays in socializing its members to internalize the culture of society. We indicated, however, that as children grow up, they also become exposed to a variety of other socializing agents including church, school, peers, and mass media. In this chapter, we explore the ways in which the youth's movement outside the immediate family into a larger social world may lead to the development of a sense of social ties to other youths embarking upon the same process. This sense of identity along with a variety of other social factors may contribute to the formation of a youth subculture, some elements of which may contribute to the youth's likelihood of committing acts regarded as deviant by adults.

CULTURE, SUBCULTURES, AND COUNTERCULTURES

Culture is *the entire body of shared and learned beliefs, values, attitudes, traditions, normative expectations, and other forms of knowledge that is passed on from one generation to the next within a society.* Within the dominant culture of larger society, there exists a variety of **subcultures,** *which basically share most of the attitudes, values, and beliefs of the overall culture; however, they also adhere to certain attitudes, values, beliefs, and norms unique to them, somewhat setting them apart from larger society.* Hans Sebald (1968:205) referred to **culture** as *"a blueprint for behavior of a total society"* and **subculture** as *"the blueprint for behavior of a smaller group within the society."* He illustrated the concept by saying, "there are subcultures for narcotic addicts, longshoremen, inmates in prison, Texas oil men, those in the world of fashion, jazz musicians—and adolescents" (Sebald, 1968:205).

As long as the smaller group accepts and conforms to most of the norms of larger society while maintaining its uniqueness, it is usually considered to be a subculture. However, *when the subculture differs to the point that it rejects the overall attitudes, values, beliefs, and norms of larger society, and offers a substitute normative system,* it becomes a **counterculture.**

A great deal of debate has been waged as to whether America's youths constitute a subculture. A number of social and behavioral scientists contend that there is a youth subculture and that in order to understand juvenile behavior (including delinquency) it is necessary to put it in its subcultural context (e.g., Coleman, 1960; Smith, 1962; Schwendinger and Schwendinger, 1985). Some even contend that not only is there a youth subculture, but that the youth subculture is in direct conflict with the larger culture created and maintained by adults, and hence, constitutes a youth counterculture (Roszak, 1969; Yinger, 1982). Chapter 9 explains the concepts of deviant and delinquent subcultures and focuses upon gang membership as one form of a counterculture that pits juveniles against the mainstream of adult society. In the remainder of this chapter, we discuss the concept of a youth subculture in America in its broadest sense and explore its possible relationship to certain types of juvenile delinquency.

AMERICAN SOCIETY AND THE CREATION OF A YOUTH SUBCULTURE

Throughout this book, we have struck upon the recurrent theme of the marginal status accorded American youths. Ralph England (1967) contended that the beginnings of the youth subculture can be traced to the rapid urbanization and industrialization which occurred during the nineteenth century. He indicated that the status of youth became marginal—neither adult nor child. He saw the twentieth century as reinforcing the development of the youth subculture in a variety of ways. After World War II, England (1967) contended, the United States experienced the creation of a distinct youth culture separated from adults and children. He viewed this youth subculture as based on the values of hedonism and materialism, and supported by enough money to express those values socially. When those values lead to behavior disapproved by adults, delinquency can be the result (England, 1967).

David Gottlieb et al. (1966) agreed that industrialization and the marginal status of youths led to the formation of a youth subculture. They contended that "there is general agreement among many students of adolescent behavior that the emergence of distinct youth cultures is related to the emergence of industrialization" (Gottlieb et al., 1966:ix). According to Gottlieb and his associates, in a modern industrial society there is a prolonged period of adolescence which lacks a clearly defined rite of passage into adulthood. This helps to create an adolescent subculture with distinctive attitudes, values, and behaviors.

Ernest Smith (1962) also linked the marginal status of adolescence to the formation of a youth subculture. He indicated that "the absence of transitional rituals and the prolongation of dependence of American youth lead to parent-youth conflict" (Smith 1962:21). Robert Bell (1983) indicated that there probably always has been some type of conflict between the young and their parents in American society. However, as was pointed out in Chapter 7 (The Family and Juvenile Delinquency), the concept of adolescence and the marginal status of juveniles was not traditional in American society. Rather, as America experienced the shifts from rural to urban and agrarian to industrial, the role expectations for youths became much less clear. According to Dorothy Rogers (1985:8):

> . . . various factors have conspired collectively to designate adolescence as a discrete age stage. First, children inevitably became more separated from adults as society moved from a rural to an urban environment. Second, as cultures became more complex, the stages became increasingly refined, with a definite step-like transition from infancy to adulthood. While some societies ritualize the shift from youth to maturity, those lacking such rites have instead a *youth culture,* or institutionalized adolescence.

It appears that a youth subculture is not unique to American society, but certain characteristics of our culture seem to be particularly linked to the formation and perpetuation of such a subculture. James VanderZanden (1986) used the youth subculture as one of his examples of what is meant by the sociological concept of subculture. He indicated that western societies have "postponed the entrance of their adolescents into adulthood . . ." and ". . . have spawned conditions favorable to the development of unique cultural patterns among their youth" (VanderZanden, 1986:38). James Coleman (1960:337) suggested this same analysis in his description of the formation of youth subcultures:

> Industrial society has spawned a peculiar phenomenon, most evident in America but emerging also in other Western societies: adolescent subcultures, with values and activities quite distinct from those of the adult society—subcultures whose members have most of their important associations within and few with adult society.

ROLE OF THE YOUTH SUBCULTURE

It should be pointed out that social and behavioral scientists who support the idea that a distinctive youth subculture exists in America are *not* suggesting that American youth in general constitute any kind of delinquent subculture. Rather, they argue that American youths, especially teenagers, experience social conditions that tend to alienate many of them from the parental generation and many of their parents' traditional social values. This feeling of alienation can be manifested in a variety of ways, most of which would not be considered delinquent. We will look at some of the specific elements of the youth subculture which might contribute to some forms of delinquency. Chapter 9 deals with delinquent subcultures and juvenile gangs. At this point, we turn our attention to the social situation of American youths and why they tend to experience alienation from the adult world, and why that sense of alienation leads to the formation of a strong sense of identity with the youth subculture.

Erich Goode (1984:181) described a subculture as a group whose members:

1. interact with one another more frequently and more intimately than they do with members of other social categories;
2. [have a] way of life, and . . . beliefs, [that] are somewhat different from members of other social categories; and
3. think of themselves as belonging to a specific group, and they are so defined by those who do not share this trait.

American youths tend to fit this description of subculture fairly well. It should be pointed out, however, that a subculture is not a primary group. Unlike the family, discussed in Chapter 7, the youth subculture is not characterized by intimate face-to-face interaction. Although many ethnic, religious, social class, and other subcultures often profit from spatial proximity and direct interaction, the existence of a youth subculture indicates that value sharing does not necessarily require direct contact nor primary social interaction. Unlike some of the smaller street gangs and other juvenile groups (clubs, fraternities, sororities, etc.) which depend upon the interpersonal contact among members for transmission of values, norms, and social support, a subculture may be widely distributed geographically and without interpersonal contact. However, if a subculture is to perpetuate itself, there must be mechanisms for transmitting its values from one generation to another. Our massive and technologically sophisticated communications network contributes the necessary cohesiveness among youths through affording instant awareness of news and issues relevant to young people, innovations in dress and language, and the rapid sharing of values and norms across the country.

Perhaps one of the most thorough sociological analyses of youth subculture participation in America is that of Hans Sebald (1968, 1984). He pointed out that there is not a uniform adolescent subculture, but a very diverse one. He acknowledged that important differences exist in youth peer cultures based upon socioeconomic status, age, race, ethnicity, and rural or urban residence (Sebald, 1968:201–202). Despite these differences, however, he contended that there is a sense of unity among virtually all teenagers. "They know they belong together and observe norms and values not necessarily consistent with the adult world's folkways and mores" (Sebald, 1968:203).

Why do subcultures form? What purposes do a youth subculture serve for American adolescents? Sebald approached these questions from a structural functionalist perspective and identified eight commonly agreed upon functions provided by subcultures in general, and showed how these functions are specifically fulfilled by the youth subculture. According to Sebald (1968:206; 1984:207–208), subcultures provide:

1. **Common Values and Norms.** Typically, youth subcultural values are different from those of children and those of adults;
2. **A Unique "Lingo."** Youths speak an *argot* that is often only partially understood and approved by adults (the illustrative anecdote at the end of this chapter addresses this aspect of the youth subculture);
3. **Distinct Forms of Mass Media.** For example, certain movies, magazines, television programs, and music appeal primarily to the youth subculture;
4. **Common Styles and Fads.** This is especially evident in styles of dress, grooming, and make-up;
5. **A Sense of Belonging.** Thinking of and referring to one's peer group in terms of "we" instead of "they";
6. **Unique or Distinctive Status Criteria.** Adolescents tend to choose different standards for selecting leaders or earning prestige;
7. **Social Support.** Teenagers provide one another with a sense of understanding and support for behavior that may violate adult norms;
8. **Gratification of Specific Needs.** There are some basic needs of teenagers which larger society prohibits (e.g., sexual activity) and which are provided for in the youth subculture.

An analysis of the utility of the youth subculture need not be limited to the functionalist perspective. Many of the reasons that a youth subculture exists are also compatible with the conflict and interactionist approaches in sociology. Identifying with a youth subculture alleviates some of the frustrations experienced by juveniles as a result of their marginal status in society. It also provides group support for norms and values that run counter to those of their parents, teachers, and other adults. Membership in the youth subculture also provides a sense of identity and belonging for juveniles. The sense that other people are in the same situation as they and understand their problems serves as an important symbolic expression of a sense of belonging for American teenagers. Researchers who most strongly contend that there is a youth subculture tend to focus on three assumptions:

1. Adolescents suffer a certain amount of turmoil and stress due to their uncertain position in the social structure,
2. A teenage subculture develops as a social reaction to this uncertainty and it has a widespread and powerful pattern among American adolescents,
3. The adolescent subculture provides a sense of security during the period of adolescent discontinuity (Sebald, 1968:198–200).

Consequently, the formation of a youth subculture is viewed as serving as an important frame of reference for teenagers to enhance personal and social identity and give meaning to their lives. Again, the marginal status of juveniles in American society plays an important role in assigning importance to the youth subculture. Very few meaningful social roles are provided for adolescents in the adult world. Smith (1962:26) pointed out, "Contemporary American society provides no clearly defined status-roles for youth, except perhaps the dependent-subordinate ones of children and students." The roles of child and student often alienate youths as they begin to view themselves as young adults. Herman and Julia Schwendinger (1985:34–35) pointed to the marginality of adolescents in the family and school as leading to the formation of youth subcultures.

DISTINCTIVE ELEMENTS OF THE YOUTH SUBCULTURE

The persistent conflict between adult and juvenile values appears to contribute to the ongoing phenomenon of the youth subculture. Theodore Roszak (1969:1) proclaimed, "The struggle of the generations is one of the obvious constants of human affairs." This struggle apparently takes place in a variety of arenas. Part Four of this book looks at three specific public arenas in which the confrontation between adults and youths is manifested (the schools, streets, and courts). Here, we identify some of the elements of the youth subculture which distinguish it from the larger society and set the stage for potential confrontation with adults. Juveniles differentiate themselves from adults in a multitude of ways, but that differentiation is probably most clearcut in regard to values.

Youth Values

Values *are beliefs and ideas that are held in high esteem by a particular group.* It would be virtually impossible to make a comprehensive list of the values of young people across America, and any list would necessarily be stereotypical. As previously indicated, there is great diversity within the juvenile subculture reflective of the pluralism found in the larger society. Variables such as race, age, sex, socioeconomic status, and even geographical location impact upon youth values as they do upon those of adults (Sebald, 1968; Schwendinger and Schwendinger, 1985). There are, however, some rather consistent areas in which adults and juveniles tend to differ in their value judgments. Two of the most notable are in regard to attitudes toward sex and drugs.

A large amount of research has been conducted on teenagers' attitudes and behaviors related to premarital sex and the use of drugs. Since both of those activities are illegal for juveniles, they are explored in some detail in the next section of this chapter which directly relates the juvenile subculture to the problem of juvenile delinquency. In this section we confine our treatment of youth values to a brief discussion of some of the values of young people which differ from those of adults and which may contribute to the cleavage between the generations.

The contention that American youths adhere to a particular set of social values that are different from those of most adults is not to imply that there are no similarities in the value systems of youth and their parents. After all, as discussed in Chapter 7, children are first socialized within the context of their family, and, hence, learn their first values from their parents and older siblings. Consequently, most American youths, especially those with middle class parents, are socialized to the dominant values of society. Cultural pluralism notwithstanding, most teenagers understand the norms of larger society and feel a sense of guilt when they violate them (Sykes and Matza, 1957). How, then, do the values of the youth subculture come into conflict with those of their parents and other adults? It has been suggested that the differentiation of youth values is largely symbolic, and resides not so much in conflicting ideology, as in conflicting lifestyle.

You may remember that in Chapter 6 we discussed sociological theories which speculated that a great deal of delinquency can be attributed to the existence of delinquent subcultures (e.g., Miller, 1958; Cohen, 1955). These theorists contended that delinquent subcultures tend to be comprised of lower class youths who take dominant middle class norms and turn them "upside down" (Cohen, 1955). While there is much debate over the validity of these subcultural theories, they may provide insight into the basic value system of American teenagers. Gary Schwartz and Don Merten (1967) suggested that the major subcultural elements of adolescent social life are in the symbolic aspects of their values, beliefs, and standards. "The distinctiveness of the youth subculture is not necessarily that their norms and values are fundamentally at odds with the adult world, but that their evaluative system which provides cultural meaning for their life is vastly different" (Schwartz and Merten, 1967:453).

In other words, many of the distinctive values of the youth subculture are not all that different from the values they were taught by their parents. Rather, the difference resides in the ways that teenagers express those values in their behavior. For instance, Talcott Parsons (1942) used the automobile as an example in which youths take basic American social values and reinterpret them in a way that is socially meaningful to them, but leads to behavior that is at odds with the norms prescribed by adults. By the 1930s, the automobile had become a basic part of American culture. Virtually every family owned one and adults highly valued the automobile for its utilitarian purpose—transportation. American youths also highly valued the automobile, but for very different purposes. The automobile, approved and sanctioned by adults for transportation, was used by juveniles for entertainment, drag racing, and other activities frowned upon by adults (Parsons, 1942). By the 1960s, the automobile had taken on even more importance for teenagers, becoming, perhaps, the most important symbol of the youth subculture providing prestige, a place for dating and sexual activities, and a hobby for many teenage boys (Sebald, 1968:257–258).

There are several other basic social values that parents tend to teach their children that the youth subculture internalizes, but expresses in ways that may lead to conflicts with parents, teachers, law enforcement officials, and other adults. For example, independence is a basic value in American society. Liberty, freedom, and independence are concepts taught to children from birth. Reciting the Pledge of Allegiance, celebrating Independence Day, and donating coins to restore the Statue of Liberty are acceptable behaviors. However, when teenagers begin to assert their own independence, it often meets with disapproval from adults. Adults usually conceive of independence, freedom, and liberty in a more nationalistic and abstract sense. When juveniles speak of independence, freedom, and liberty, they typically mean freedom from parents, school, and other adult rules and regulations. Hence, it is not the value which

Many common activities of the youth subculture involve harmless activities such as simply "hanging out" together. Often the automobile becomes the focal point of such activities. When police officers or other adults show their disapproval of such activities, confrontations between youths and adults often occur. Some may result in arrests. (H. Armstrong Roberts)

conflicts with adult society, but the ways chosen for expressing it which lead to being viewed as deviant.

Another basic middle class American value is conformity. While parents encourage individuality, they insist that it be tempered with the ability to get along with others, to be part of an accepted group, and to conform to normative expectations. Evidence suggests that juveniles value conformity as much as their parents, and perhaps even more. Again, the problem does not lie in internalizing the value, but in exhibiting it in behavior. In fact, if the youth subculture indeed exists, it is probably a result of the strong desire on the part of young people to conform with one another.

A multitude of studies indicate that one of the strongest motivations for behavior among juveniles is their desire to gain and maintain acceptance with their peers (e.g., Smith, 1962; Sebald, 1968; Clasen and Brown, 1985; Schwendinger and Schwendinger, 1985). Gerald Pearson (1958:88) stated, "A fundamental evidence of the existence of youth culture is the compulsive conformity required of its members." Smith (1962:9) explored the phenomenon of the **clique,** *a small primary group within the youth subculture,* and indicated that the clique "sets norms that are often the highest authority for its members and may take precedence over both family and other adult norms." Schwendinger and Schwendinger (1985:106–107) described various youth cliques such as "greasers," "jocks," "surfers," "squares," "intellectuals," and "nerds," and pointed out that whatever the particular clique membership, all were characterized by extreme peer pressure from within to conform to a particular set of attitudes, values, beliefs, and behaviors. They went on to explain that these various social groups begin to form during the elementary school years, but become most pronounced during early adolescence in junior high school. Despite the differences between these various cliques, all groups share values placed on peer acceptance (Schwendinger and Schwendinger, 1985).

It is apparent that the peer pressure to conform provides a strong sense of identity for juveniles. Thomas Cosner and Gerald Larson (1980) contended that the youth subculture is a reaction to the increased demands of the larger society for juveniles to conform while mediating much of the tension and rebellion experienced as a result of their status. This need to conform to and identify with the youth subculture hinges on adherence to its values. Bennett Berger (1963) contended that there *is* a youth subculture, but it is not merely a function of one's chronological age. Rather, it is a distinctive set of attitudes, values, beliefs, and behaviors which focus on hedonism, irresponsibility, and expressiveness. Support for the notion that the youth subculture is not totally based on age may be seen in a quote from 1960s "Yippie" leader Jerry Rubin, who, in his forties, declared, "We ain't never, never gonna grow up . . . we're gonna be adolescents forever!" (Time, 1986:24). The hedonism and irresponsibility on the part of middle class American youths has received widespread attention in the sociological literature on the youth subculture. Lamar Empey (1982:202) summarized some of the research on youth subcultures by pointing out that while there are questions as to the "uniqueness of adolescent subculture, most theorists suggest that it helps to produce an adolescent world of hedonism and irresponsibility, and the more adolescents are involved in it, the more likely they are to be delinquent."

In summary of youth subculture values, Sebald (1968) proposed that American young people are socialized to some basic cultural values which contradict each other. He described some of the "dichotomous values with which juveniles must come to grips" as including: competition versus cooperation; work versus leisure; piety versus freethinking; individualism versus conformity; and sexuality versus chastity (Sebald, 1968:145–150). It may well be that identity with a youth subculture provides a temporary social frame of reference for teenagers within which to handle these value discrepancies. Hence, a feeling of group support allows juveniles to validate their behaviors based upon their interpretation of appropriate values and behaviors.

Dress, Grooming, and Fads

Some of the ways in which teenagers express their identity and give credence to the existence of a youth subculture can be found in their norms regarding dress, grooming, and widespread acceptance of various fads. VanderZanden (1986:38) indicated that the "unique cultural patterns among youth . . . find expression in fads having to do with musical recordings, entertainment idols, and dance steps, personal adornment and hair styles . . . ." The distinctive and often faddish dress of teenagers clearly operates to set them apart from their adult counterparts. It simultaneously unifies members of the youth subculture while distinguishing them from the larger culture (Richards, 1988). Smith (1962) indicated that one of the ways that the youth subculture reinforces conformity among its members is by setting them apart in appearance and behavior. Dress, grooming, and personal appearance become the most important vehicles by which juveniles can symbolize their status. Bell (1983) indicated that distinct styles and tastes, especially in regard to personal appearance, develop within the youth subculture. He indicated, "The youth subculture has become highly subject to the dynamics of fashion . . . the youth culture has produced its own version of the game of keeping up with the Joneses" (Bell, 1983:477). The so-called preppies of the mid-1980s exemplify this.

England (1967) indicated that after World War II, a large market of goods emerged aimed primarily at the youth culture in America. Adherence to the normative expectations of youths regarding dress and other material possessions (cars, athletic equipment, stereos, cosmetics, etc.) demands access to a certain amount of money. Sebald (1968:112) indicated that in the mid-1960s, teenagers spent over 1.5 billion dollars annually on entertainment; 700 million dollars annually on records; 450 million on cosmetics and toiletries; and 3.6 million on women's clothing. The cost of albums, stereo equipment, cosmetics, and clothing has increased significantly. For example, 1984 retail record sales totaled approximately 1.5 billion dollars (Information Please, 1986:653). While not all of those records were purchased by teenagers, a very large portion was. Nancy Needham (1986:16) estimated that Americans under the age of 18 spend more than 70 billion dollars annually on everything from breakfast cereal to name brand clothing. The importance to conform to peer expectations regarding these items has not diminished. Consequently, virtually every parent has been confronted with a teenager demanding the purchase of a particular brand of athletic shoe, or some similar item, when a much less expensive brand would have been equally functional. Teenagers are constantly bewildered by their parents' failure to understand that one shoe style is "in" and another is definitely "out." This failure to recognize such a widely known and accepted "fact" only serves to underscore the so-called generation gap.

Juvenile hairstyles also accentuate the existence of a youth subculture and broaden the gap between parents and teenagers in regard to acceptable taste. It seems almost axiomatic that when adults are wearing their hair short, teens will be wearing theirs long, and vice-versa. In the mid-1960s the Beatles launched a revolution in hairstyles for teenage boys. Crewcuts rapidly disappeared, and the "Beatle cut" swept across America much to the chagrin of parents, teachers, and other adults. Many schools passed dress and hair codes (it was at about the same time that the miniskirt became the style for teenaged girls) and the battle of generational values once again surfaced. Eventually, adults became more tolerant of the longer hair; ultimately, not only were teen rock stars wearing their hair longer, but so were middle-aged crooners, country and western singers, and talk show hosts. When lawyers, doctors, teachers, and "good ol' dad" followed suit, it was inevitable that the teenagers of America would make the move back to shorter hair. By 1986 "flat tops," "buzzes," "spikes," and other shorter (but deviant) hairstyles dominated the youth culture. Athletes like Jim McMahon of the Super Bowl champion Chicago Bears and Brian "the Boz" Bosworth of the 1985 national champion Oklahoma Sooners, and later the Seattle Seahawks, set the trend in "radical" hairstyles for the teenagers of America.

While various styles of dress, grooming, and cosmetics vary somewhat by race, social class, ethnicity, and other social and demographic factors, juveniles seem to have much more in common with each other than they do with their parents or other adults (Smith, 1962; Sebald, 1968; Wein, 1970; Bell, 1983). As mentioned earlier, the youth subculture is not a small primary group within which all members interact directly with one another. Consequently, the youth subculture becomes very dependent upon the mass media to carry the message of current trends in style to teenagers across the country. This necessitates a communication network primarily aimed at adolescents to express and reinforce their particular values and norms. Those youths who feel the most committed to the youth subculture are most likely to express conformity to its norms.

Mass Media

A perusal of any magazine rack quickly indicates that this mass medium acknowledges the existence of a large youth subculture and makes every effort to cater to its tastes and styles. England (1967) asserted that after World War II, a large number of magazines, books, records, movies, and television shows were aimed at the huge youth market. Today, magazines such as *Teen, Teen Beat, Spin,* and *Rolling Stone* are clearly aimed at a youthful audience and seem almost to simultaneously dictate and reflect teenagers' preference in music. Likewise, *16, Seventeen, Glamour, Teen,* and other magazines cater to a juvenile audience, setting the pace for teen dress and hair styles. *Mad* magazine still satirizes adult life and appeals directly to the sense of humor of junior high and high school students. All of those magazines, and a variety of others, influence and rein-force values of American youth. When a 1986 *Sports Illustrated* issue featured Brian Bosworth with his multicolored, striped flat top, accentuated by 14 karat gold earrings in the shape of his jersey number (44), even some Boy Scouts quickly imitated the style (Reilly, 1986).

Television producers, writers, directors, and commercial advertisers also have recognized the large teen market and have routinely catered to its particular tastes and values. In 1984, approximately 978 million dollars was spent on advertising cosmetics and toiletries on television (Statistical Abstract, 1986:553). Much of that advertising was aimed directly at teens, using popular teenaged stars and models. Frances Lawrence et al. (1986:434) found that adolescents on average watched 147 minutes of television daily—approximately 17 ¼ hours every week. Lawrence discovered that many of the attitudes, values, and beliefs of adolescents, especially regarding standards of dress and personal conduct, were formed by television. In the 1980s, cable television offered 24 hours every day of "rock videos" and music programming aimed specifically at the American youth market.

Writers, producers, and directors of movies also have acknowledged the existence of a youth subculture and have attempted to capitalize on movies geared toward its values. Richard Corliss (1986) described some of the trends in youth-oriented movies over the past few decades. During the 1950s, the movies starring James Dean and Marlon Brando exemplified the rebellion of youth; the 1960s were dominated by Beach Party movies, and later by social protest films; the 1970s gave rise to teen "sexploitation" films such as the Porky series; and the 1980s witnessed what Corliss described as a revamp of the Andy Hardy movies—films characterized by kids struggling with values, drugs, sex, parents, and school (Corliss, 1986). Corliss (1986) discussed the youthful stars such as Molly Ringwald, Anthony Michael Hall, Emilio Esteves, Judd Nelson, Andrew McCarthy, and Ally Sheedy, who affectionately became known as the "Brat Pack" by their young fans.

Language

One of the most important ways that any subculture can symbolically distinguish itself from the larger culture is by adopting a unique language or jargon. American Old Order Amish speak German, Orthodox Jews speak Yiddish, and various ethnic groups adhere to the language of their homeland in urban subcultural enclaves like Chinatown and Little Italy.

Language also appears to be a vehicle with which America's young people, especially teenagers, differentiate themselves from adults. According to some researchers, the most important symbolic element of the youth subculture is its distinctive language (Schwartz and Merten, 1967). Smith (1962), Sebald (1968), Rogers (1985), and VanderZanden (1986), to name a few, all pointed to the distinctive jargon of youths as being one of the significant aspects of the youth subculture. Smith (1962:14) saw language as a means for teenagers to "exclude outsiders" and "intensify group identity." Yinger (1982:152–171) pointed out ways in which juveniles reverse language by using words to mean their exact opposite, such as using the word "bad" as a compliment to actually mean "good." For example, when one teenaged male tells another that his car is "really bad," he is paying him a high compliment.

One of the most thorough treatments of the distinctive language of the youth subculture can be found in Sebald's (1968) sociological analysis of adolescence. He contended that teens have created a unique **argot** *(specialized slang, or jargon)* to promote group cohesiveness and provide boundary maintenance. He contended that many of the terms and idioms used in teen argot provide a form of verbal shorthand, summarizing very complex ideas and meanings into only one or two words (Sebald, 1968:249–251). The illustrative anecdote at the end of this chapter pursues the phenomenon of a distinctive language among American youths.

THE YOUTH SUBCULTURE AND JUVENILE DELINQUENCY

The focus of this chapter up to this point has been to lay a conceptual foundation for understanding a particular basis for potential juvenile delinquency. When people think of delinquents, listen to television news reports, or read newspaper headlines about delinquency, they are most likely to hear or read about rapes, robberies, murders, and other violent offenses committed by youths. Youth crime is a major problem, and much of this textbook has focused on the typical street crime types of delinquency. Yet, as indicated in Chapter 3, the vast majority of youthful offenses are not serious violent crimes. Rather, a much larger proportion of juveniles who get in trouble with the law commit what would be considered misdemeanors if they were adults, or not crimes at all (status offenses). Consequently, exploring the existence of a youth subculture which promotes values, attitudes, beliefs, and norms that violate adult normative expectations may provide valuable insight for understanding status offenses and nonviolent crimes committed by youths. In this chapter we are referring not to the crimes committed in a delinquent subculture (see Chapter 9), but to law violations which may result from involvement in the youth subculture.

Research dealing with the existence of a youth subculture consistently has linked it to middle class delinquency, especially status offenses and nonviolent crimes (Shoemaker, 1984; Empey, 1982). It is highly unlikely that theoretical frameworks attempting to explain rape or murder are also going to explain the motivations for truancy, drug use, or premarital sex. The issue of truancy is addressed in Chapter 10, but in this chapter we provide a brief sociological analysis of juvenile drug use and premarital sexual behavior in relation to the youth subculture.

Juveniles and Drugs

In September of 1986, President Ronald Reagan, with wife Nancy alongside, appeared on national network television to "declare war" on drug use in the United States. A series of drug-related deaths of famous athletes and other celebrities, together with network news coverage of widespread drug smuggling and dealing in the United States, clearly had stirred public sentiment to be ready to "take up arms" in that war.

Of course, drug use is not new in the United States. James Inciardi (1986) traced opium use back to the eighteenth century. Later, opium, morphine, and even heroin were openly used for their medicinal values (Inciardi, 1986). The Harrison Act of 1914 regulated most addictive narcotics, and, taken together with the Supreme Court Decisions of *Webb v U.S.*, *U.S. v Behrman*, and *Lindner v U.S.* it became almost impossible for the estimated 200,000 narcotics users to legally obtain their drugs (Inciardi, 1986:15). Illegal drug markets and dealers emerged, and the nation had a drug problem.

For the most part, drug use was perceived as being associated with lower class urban ghettos and adult derelicts. By the 1950s, it became linked with juveniles, but was mostly viewed as an aspect of youthful rebellion, and was thought to be most clearly associated with lower class ghetto youths and juvenile gangs (Inciardi, 1986).

In the 1960s and early 1970s drug use within the youth subculture came to national attention. Harvard professor Timothy Leary openly advocated LSD use, and the so-called hippie movement preached free love, sex, and drugs as mind-expanding experiences. Smith (1962), Sebald (1968), Roszak (1969), Wein (1980), and others all linked drugs to the youth subculture as one of the means by which juveniles could express their rebellion against the adult world. Marijuana appeared to be the drug of choice of the youth subculture, and popular motion pictures such as *Easy Rider* depicted youth cult heroes using drugs the way children might nibble on cookies.

The decade of the 1970s saw the drug-related deaths of rock and roll stars

The widespread use of drugs among many members of the youth subculture indicates that it is a serious problem for youths from all social classes and backgrounds. (© Eric Kroll/Taurus Photos)

Jimi Hendrix and Janis Joplin. Their music was considered fairly wild by most parents and even some teens. Later, during that same decade, however, Elvis Presley, The King of Rock 'n' Roll, died, and a subsequent investigation looked into possible drug involvement. The 1980s saw numerous drug-related deaths of famous celebrities, many of whom had mass appeal among America's teenagers. John Belushi of *Saturday Night Live* and movie fame died of an overdose, as did the Cleveland Browns star Don Rogers. Two very celebrated cases involved the airplane crash of Ricky Nelson (could the son of *Ozzie and Harriet* have been on drugs as news accounts alleged?) and the cocaine overdose of University of Maryland's All-American basketball star Lynn Bias just 2 days after he signed a lucrative contract with the Boston Celtics. Public awareness of a drug problem mushroomed; virtually everybody wondered just how widespread the problem was, especially among the nation's young people.

Coryl Jones and Catherine Bell-Bolek (1986:5) cited a 1985 study indicating that 61 percent of students surveyed reported trying an illegal drug at some time, and 40 percent had used a drug other than marijuana. Evan Thomas (1986:64) cited a 1985 study indicating that at the time the survey was taken, 25.7 percent of the high school seniors surveyed had used marijuana within the preceding 30 days. Cocaine had been tried by 17 percent of those students surveyed in 1985 as compared to 10 percent in 1976 (Jones and Bell-Bolek,

1986:6). In their analysis of the widespread drug use among juveniles, Jones and Bell-Bolek (1986) contended that it was a social event in most cases. They suggested that drug abuse was "a function of the adolescent's social interaction and experimentation with life-style" (Jones and Bell-Bolek, 1986:7). Similarly, Glassner and Laughlin (1987) pointed out that adolescent drug use almost always occurs in a social context, and while "peer pressure" may be too strong a term, certainly "peer interaction" is one of the most important influences. Denise Kandel (1985) also found drug use among juveniles to be social in nature and cited peer influence as the most important factor. Delbert Elliott et al. (1985) further underscored the influence of peers. They integrated Strain, Social Control, and Social Learning theories (see Chapter 6) into a synthesized perspective to account for delinquency and drug use. They postulated that "involvement with and commitment to delinquent peers is the most proximate cause of delinquency and drug use and mediates the influence of weak bonding to parents, school, and conventional norms" (Elliott et al., 1985:85).

Part of the allure of drugs for youths may be tied to their parents' abhorrence of them. Glassner and Loughlin (1987:1) succinctly pointed out that adolescent drug use scares adults. Evan Thomas (1986:65) indicated that "In the age of youth rebellion, the fact that parents were shocked by drugs was all the more reason for children to take them." Recent studies indicate that drug use appears to be more widespread and socially accepted among juveniles (Beschner and Friedman, 1986). The existence of a youth subculture in which value is placed on breaking away from parents may be influential in drug acceptance. Jones and Bell-Bolek. (1986:7) stated:

> Even the identification of drug taking as a severe risk provides a fascination for the risk-taking adolescent. For some adolescents, risk is not a deterrent, but a challenge.

Juvenile drug use is illegal, hence it constitutes delinquency. Even the use of drugs that are socially acceptable for adults, such as alcohol, nicotine (cigarettes), and caffeine (coffee) are deemed inappropriate for youth. A juvenile subculture which encourages and/or promotes violation of parental norms is likely to accentuate drug taking among its members.

Juveniles and Sex

Perhaps no subject sparks more interest among juveniles and provokes more fear among parents than premarital sexual activity. Smith (1962:5) suggested, "Probably the most important area within which adult norms attempt to dominate youth behavior is that of sex . . ." On the other hand, he contended that the youth culture often dominates adolescent behavior "particularly in relation to sex activities" (Smith, 1962:7). In a treatise on the youth subculture of the 1920s, Paula Fass (1977) discussed sex mores of the period, and indicated that peer influence and conformity to peer culture were the most important guidelines youths considered in regard to sexual behavior. In her book *Barriers Between Women*, Caplan (1981) found that it was in the area of sexuality that mother-daughter relationships were most conflictual.

Not only do parents typically socialize their children to premarital sexual taboos; virtually all sexual activities are illegal for juveniles. Juvenile statutes prohibit premarital sexual behavior for both males and females. One of the status offenses for which juveniles can be adjudicated delinquent is that of promiscuity. Official data indicate that females are more likely to be brought to court for committing sex offenses than males (Chesney-Lind, 1977) but either sex can be petitioned to court for being sexually active. Adolescents must somehow balance the biological and physiological changes which are turning them into sexually potent young men and women against the traditional values of their parents which discourage adolescent sexuality and the laws of the state which make it illegal. Research suggests that the scales are not very well balanced.

A 1986 article in *Ladies Home Journal* estimated that 12 million adolescents (40 percent of all teenagers) were sexually active (Sherman, 1986:199). Researcher Su Yates commented, "For many kids, you're considered out of it if you're not having sex—it's a rite of passage" (Sherman, 1986:199). Clearly, the values of many youths toward premarital sexual activity differ from what most parental norms allow. Wein (1970:11) interviewed street kids in New York City and Los Angeles and concluded "Most kids seem to find the *idea* of premarital intercourse quite acceptable" [italics in the original]. Other studies suggest that the youth culture approves of more than just the idea. Elizabeth Stark (1986:28) found that in 1986 among 15 to 17-year-olds, "almost half of the boys and a third of the girls were sexually active." In a study of college students, Carol Darling and J. Kenneth Davidson (1986) found that 84 percent of the females and 99 percent of the males had experienced sexual intercourse before marriage. They indicated that there was a "major increase over the past 15 years in the numbers of adolescent males and females engaging in heterosexual intercourse" (Darling and Davidson, 1986:403). Stark (1986:28) stated that "teenagers are becoming sexually active at younger ages."

Invariably, increased sexual activity among juveniles has led to another youth social problem: teenage pregnancies. Stark (1986:28) pointed out that "one out of ten teenage girls in the U.S. becomes pregnant every year and almost half of those pregnancies result in births—30,000 of them to girls under the age of 15." Eric Sherman (1986:202) pointed to popular "television shows, music videos, and movies with names like *Losing It* and *The Last American Virgin* as leading adolescents "to believe that *everyone* fools around." Yinger (1982:120) pointed out that when youths "misperceive that 'everyone else' is participating in a particular activity, they may be tempted to join the fictitious 'everyone else.'" Joyce Ladner, a professor of sociology at Harvard, indicated that teenage pregnancy "knows no color . . . it is not a black problem or a white problem," she stated. "It is an American problem" (Sherman, 1986:202).

When teenagers become pregnant, a host of other problems arise such as whether to keep the baby, get married, have an abortion, drop out of school, and how to handle the situation. Sherman (1986:202) indicated that teens account for 30 percent of all abortions in the United States, with about 450,000 abortions each year. Numerous studies have shown that youths are consistently becoming more liberal in their attitudes toward sex (e.g., Sherwin and Corbett, 1985), and more unmarried teens are opting to keep their babies (Stark, 1986). Stark (1986) pointed out that some teens (both male and female) *want* pregnancy, feeling that it asserts their entrance into adulthood. A reflection of the changing attitudes of many teens toward sex and pregnancy in the 1980s can be found in the lyrics of a popular song by rock superstar Madonna in 1986. In a song entitled "Papa Don't Preach," she declared "I'm gonna keep my baby" (written by Brian Elliot © Elliot/Jacobsen Pub. Co.—quoted by permission).

THE YOUTH SUBCULTURE AND DELINQUENCY PREVENTION

It should be pointed out that the youth subculture has not thrown out all adult values. Consequently, the same subculture which may promote some forms of juvenile delinquency may also serve as a potential preventive. For example, Robert Sherwin and Sherry Corbett (1985) found that while college students had indeed become more liberal in sexual attitudes compared to their counterparts of 1963 and 1971, they had not developed an attitude of "anything goes." Rather, while more sexually active, students also held a stronger belief that sexual intimacy should occur in relationships in which there was a feeling of commitment on the part of the couple. John Roche (1986) contended that in some ways, youths were actually becoming more conservative. When he analyzed premarital sex on the basis of dating stages, he found that both males and females were much more permissive in their attitudes toward sex than in their actual behavior. One of his findings was that teens tend to think that everybody else is much more sexually active than they are. He indicated that sexual mores tend first to be generated by parents and early religious training; later, they are influenced more by peers and the media (Roche, 1986). He also suggested that a greater social awareness of sexually transmitted diseases such as herpes II (and AIDS) might make many young people "think twice about engaging in premarital sex" (Roche, 1986:107).

We have discussed the influence of mass media on juveniles. While movies, television programs, and other media aimed at youths might promote rebellious or delinquent behavior, they also can be used to present delinquency prevention messages. For example, rock and roll music has both influenced and reflected the values of the youth subculture. By the mid-1980s, while the themes of many popular rock songs encouraged engaging in sex, drug use, and rebellion against parents, some entertainers used that same forum to encourage young girls to "just say no" to sex. Although these songs were urging girls to limit their sexual behavior, they nevertheless reflected the overall tone of the youth subculture, and did not put parents' minds completely at ease.

During the 1980s, organizations such as Students Against Drunk Driving (SADD) were filling the airwaves with messages against drinking and driving. Likewise, young celebrities made public service announcements on television urging teenagers to enter into contracts with their parents in which they agreed not to use alcohol and drugs. Perhaps one of the most influential media campaigns aimed at the youth subculture focused on encouraging youths not to start smoking. Again, teenaged celebrities warned youths of the dangers of smoking. More importantly, the campaign not only pointed out the dangers associated with smoking, but also emphasized that it simply was not "cool" to smoke.

The youth subculture and its heavy emphasis upon conforming to certain distinctive values, attitudes, beliefs, and norms undoubtedly contributes to certain forms of delinquency. This seems to be especially the case for middle class delinquency such as status offenses and other nonviolent law violations. Thus, that same youth subculture may hold tremendous potential for delinquency prevention. Peer pressure to conform to the law can be just as strong and influential as peer pressure to violate it.

SUMMARY

We have reviewed a substantial amount of sociological literature documenting the existence of a youth subculture in American society which perpetuates distinctive attitudes, values, beliefs, and norms, and that they may lead to delinquent behavior. The subculture apparently developed during the latter part of the nineteenth century primarily as a result of industrialization, urbanization, and the increasingly marginal status of adolescents.

Youth values reflect early socialization by family, school, and church, but clearly become more influenced by peers and mass media during late adolescence. The values are fairly consistent with the values of the adult culture, but are manifested in many distinctive ways. Fashion, grooming, dress, music, fads, and language are a few of the easily observable vehicles by which youths strive to symbolically differentiate themselves from their parents, teachers, and other adults.

While the youth subculture does not necessarily constitute a deviant subculture, some aspects of it can be directly linked to delinquent behavior, especially in the areas of drug use and premarital sexual behavior. Research tends to associate the youth subculture with middle class delinquency, primarily involving nonviolent crimes and status offenses.

The existence of a distinctive youth subculture is open to debate, but it seems clear that the marginal status of adolescents and the lack of any clearcut rites of passage into adulthood in American society have created a social situation which tends to bond youths in spirit if not in ideology. As a result, much of the youthful behavior reflects values supported by their peers and not by their parents or other adults. Friedenberg (1963:4, 9) asserted, "the young disturb and anger their elders, and are themselves angered and disturbed . . . the plight of the adolescent is basically similar to that of the emigrant in that he can neither stay what he was nor become what he started out to be." While questioning the existence of a distinctive youth subculture, William Arnold and Terrance Brungardt (1983) acknowledged that youths are uncommitted to the normative system of adults.

Howard Becker (1963) surmised that rules about youthful behavior are made without regard to the problems of adolescence; hence, juveniles are "outsiders" who are often labeled deviant as a result of violating rules which have little or no meaning for them. This relative powerlessness in rulemaking may lead to social alienation, which could result in delinquency. The lyrics to a hit song of the mid-1980s seem to summarize the attitudes of many American youths, as the rock group Twisted Sister chants:

We're not gonna take it,
No, we're not gonna take it,
We're not gonna take it anymore.
(Quoted with permission from "We're Not Gonna Take It" sung by Twisted Sister. From the album "Stay Hungry" produced by Tom Worman. Atlantic Recording Company, New York, 1984.)

While all youths are certainly not rebellious in attitude, they can undoubtedly relate to the sentiment. Wein (1970:223) described an interview with a 16-year-old "chemistry whiz" on his way to a Rotary Club meeting. It may reflect the strong sense of unity among American teens:

Youth: "Being a part of the subculture I'm in, I don't believe what's going on."

[Wein]: "What subculture?"

Youth: "Oh, teenagers. Our little subculture."

Wein: "Is there anyone your age whom you would exclude from that?"

Youth: "Oh, probably not . . . you can't help but be in it."

Acknowledging the existence of a youth subculture and its powerful influence upon adolescent behavior is not the same as identifying all American teenagers as belonging to a delinquent subculture. Rather, the much broader context of a youth subculture provides a meaningful sense of social identity for American youths. It also provides a social context in which adolescent nonconformity to both adult and child normative expectations can be viewed as acceptable. We have demonstrated ways in which that acceptance can promote certain types of juvenile delinquency. Given that fact, it is reasonable to assume that the youth subculture also can provide a significant influence for discouraging and preventing juvenile delinquency.

CONCEPT APPLICATION

ILLUSTRATIVE ANECDOTE

"Neat-o, Peachy Keen—The Specialized Language of Youth"

One of the most significant ways in which teenagers differentiate themselves from adults is through their distinctive use of language. The particular **argot** of the youth subculture serves as a form of boundary maintenance and reinforces a sense of unity among all of those who share the meaning of their specialized language.

Almost every generation of young people develops a specialized jargon that they can use as a code to communicate with each other in front of parents and other adults while hiding the true meaning of their words. A few of these codes are even recurring. For example, almost every elementary school child learns to speak pig Latin, in which the first consonant of each word is dropped and the sound of the consonant is added at the end of the word followed by the sound "ay." Most kids think that their particular group invented the pig Latin code, and are befuddled when their parents and/or teachers figure out "at-whay ey-thay aid-say." Often children use their special code in order to curse in front of parents and teachers, and are amazed to find that their parents are able to "break the code."

Each generation also seems to create a whole new vocabulary, however, which is often unique to them. As Sebald (1968) indicated, much of the distinctive language of adolescence serves as a type of linguistic shorthand to express highly complex ideas in only one or two words. When teens of the 1950s described somebody as "hip," or those of the 1960s as "neat," those of the 1970s as "cool," and those of the 1980s as "awse" (short for awesome), they were using one word to describe a set of highly regarded personal characteristics that included looks, dress, demeanor, personality, and behavior. While virtually no teenager could give a concise definition of those terms, every teenager of those particular times knew exactly what they meant.

Many of the terms used in the teen culture are harmless, and while adults may not understand the connotation of the word, they are not particularly upset by their child's using it. Other terms, however, are not so inconsequential. For example, in the 1960s "bitchin'" was a slang term used to describe something as being highly valued, as in "Hey Jim, I like your wheels [car]; it's really bitchin'." During the 1970s the notorious "F" word became a part of many youths' vocabulary, being used as an adjective, and sometimes even being inserted between two syllables of a word, as in "Listen to that f***in' stereo, it sounds fan-f***in'-tastic!" Needless to say, that type of youthful language attracted a great deal of adult attention.

An entire book could be written on the specialized argot of youths and endless examples could be given. The point is, teenagers do feel a sense of identity and camaraderie, especially within their particular cliques or primary groups. One of the ways in which they express those feelings is through their unique language. While using the argot of teens certainly does not constitute delinquency, it reflects many attitudes, values, and beliefs that adults view as deviant. Deviant attitudes and values are sometimes translated into deviant behavior. When that happens with juveniles, delinquency may be the end product.

* * * *

Based upon the reading of this chapter, in what ways do you think the distinctive language of youths may contribute to the formation and perpetuation of a youth subculture? In your opinion, does the language of youths contribute to their potential involvement in delinquency? If so, in what ways? What examples can you cite from your own experience that reflect a specialized language among youths?

CONCEPT INTEGRATION

QUESTIONS AND TOPICS FOR STUDY AND DISCUSSION

1. Define culture, subculture, and counterculture. What is meant by the concept of youth subculture?
2. Is there a youth subculture in America? If so, what are some of the distinctive elements of it? If not, why does there seem to be a sense of unity among juveniles? Are there other explanations? If so, discuss them.
3. In what ways do youth values differ from those to which they were socialized by adults? In what ways are they similar? How do these similarities and differences create conflict between juveniles and adults?
4. How do the mass media contribute to the formation and perpetuation of a youth subculture? How do they possibly contribute to juvenile delinquency?
5. In what ways does participation in a youth subculture potentially lead to juvenile delinquency? Are there ways in which a youth subculture might be utilized for delinquency prevention? Discuss some of these.

References

Arnold, W. R. & Brungardt, T. M. 1983. *Juvenile misconduct and delinquency.* Boston: Houghton Mifflin.

Becker, H. 1963. *Outsiders: Studies in the sociology of deviance.* New York: Free Press.

Bell, R. R. 1966. Parent-child conflict in sexual values. *Journal of Social Issues* 22 (2):34–44.

———. 1983. *Marriage and family interaction* (6th ed.). Homewood, IL: Dorsey Press.

Berger, B. M. 1963. On the youthfulness of youth cultures. *Social Research* 30 (Autumn):319–342.

———. 1981. *The survival of a counterculture.* Berkeley: University of California Press.

Beschner, G. & Friedman, A. S. (Eds.) 1986. *Teen drug use.* Lexington, MA: Lexington Books.

Caplan, P. J. 1981. *Barriers between women.* New York: Spectrum.

Chesney-Lind, M. 1977. Judicial paternalism and the female status offender. *Crime and Delinquency* 23 (April):121–130.

Clasen, D. R. & Brown, B. B. 1985. The multidimensionality of peer pressure in adolescence. *Journal of Youth and Adolescence* 14 (December):451–468.

Cohen, A. K. 1955. *Delinquent boys.* New York: Free Press.

Coleman, J. S. 1960. The adolescent subculture and academic achievement. *American Journal of Sociology* 65 (January):337–347.

Corliss, R. 1986. Well, hello Molly! *Time* 127 (May 26):66–71.

Cosner, T. L. & Larson, G. L. 1980. Social fabric theory and the youth culture. *Adolescence* 15 (Spring):99–104.

Darling, C. A. & Davidson, J. K. 1986. Coitally active university students: Sexual behaviors, concerns, and challenges. *Adolescence* 21 (Summer):403–419.

Elliott, D. S., Huizinga, D., & Ageton, S. 1985. *Explaining delinquency and drug use.* Beverly Hills, CA: Sage.

Empey, L. T. 1982. *American delinquency: Its meaning and construction* (Rev. ed.). Homewood, IL: Dorsey Press.

England, R. W., Jr. 1967. A theory of middle class juvenile delinquency. In E. W. Vaz (Ed.). *Middle class juvenile delinquency.* New York: Harper & Row, pp. 242–251.

Fass, P. S. 1977. The damned and the beautiful: American youth in the 1920s. New York: Oxford University Press.

Friedenberg, E. Z. 1963. *Coming of age in America.* New York: Random House.

Glassner, B. & Loughlin, J. 1987. *Drugs in adolescent worlds: Burnouts to straights.* New York: St. Martin's Press.

Goode, E. 1984. *Deviant behavior* (2nd ed.). Englewood Cliffs, NJ: Prentice-Hall.

Gottlieb, D., Reeves, J., & Tenhouten, W. D. 1966. *The emergence of youth societies: A cross-cultural approach.* New York: Free Press.

Inciardi, J. A. 1986. *The war on drugs: Heroin, cocaine, crime, and public policy.* Palo Alto, CA: Maysfield.

Information Please. 1986. *Information Please Almanac and Yearbook* 1986 (39th ed.). Boston: Houghton-Mifflin.

Jones, C. L. & Bell-Bolek, C. S. 1986. Kids and drugs: Why, when and what can we do about it? *Children Today* 15 (May–June):5–10.

Kandel, D. B. 1985. On processes of peer influence in adolescent drug use: A developmental perspective. *Advances in Alcohol and Substance Abuse* 4 (Spring–Summer):139–163.

Lawrence, F. C., Tasker, G. E., Daly, C. T., Orhill, A. L., & Wozniak, P. H. 1986. Adolescents' time spent viewing television. *Adolescence* 21 (Summer):431–436.

Miller, W. B. 1958. Lower class culture as a generating milieu of gang delinquency. *Journal of Social Issues* 14 (Summer):5–19.

Needham, N. R. 1986. Big bucks in little hands. *NEA Today* 5 (November):16–17.

Parsons, T. 1942. Age and sex in the social structure of the United States. *American Sociological Review* 7 (October):604–616.

Pearson, G. H. J. 1958. *Adolescence and the conflict of generations.* New York: W. W. Norton.

Reilly, R. 1986. The Boz. *Sports Illustrated* 65 (September 3):18–28.

Richards, L. 1988. The appearance of youth subculture: A theoretical perspective on deviance. *Clothing and Textiles Research Journal* 6 (Spring):56–64.

Roche, J. P. 1986. Premarital sex: Attitudes and behavior by dating stage. *Adolescence* 21 (Spring):107–121.

Rogers, D. 1985. *Adolescents and youth* (5th ed.). Englewood Cliffs, NJ: Prentice-Hall.

Roszak, T. 1969. *The making of a counterculture: Reflections on the technocratic society and its youthful opposition.* Garden City, NY: Anchor Books.

Schwartz, G. & Merten, D. 1967. The language of adolescents: An anthropological approach to the youth culture. *American Journal of Sociology* 72 (March):453–468.

Schwendinger, H. & Schwendinger, J. S. 1985. *Adolescent subcultures and delinquency.* New York: Praeger.

Sebald, H. 1968. *Adolescence: A sociological analysis.* New York: Appleton-Century-Crofts.

Sherman, E. 1986. Teenage sex: A special report. *Ladies' Home Journal* 103 (October):138,199.202–206.

Sherwin, R. & Corbett, S. 1985. Campus sexual norms and dating relationships: A trend analysis. *Journal of Sex Research* 21 (August):258–274.

Shoemaker, D. J. 1984. *Theories of delinquency: An examination of explanations of delinquent behavior.* New York: Oxford University Press.

Smith E. A. 1962. *American Youth Culture.* Glencoe, IL: Free Press.

Stark, E. 1986. Young, innocent and pregnant. *Psychology Today* 20 (October):28–35.

Statistical Abstract. 1985. *Statistical Abstract of the United States* 1986 (106th ed.). Washington, DC: US Bureau of the Census.

Sykes, G. M. & Matza, D. 1957. Techniques of neutralization: A theory of delinquency. *American Sociological Review* 22 (December):664–670.

Thomas, E. 1986. America's crusade: What is behind the latest war on drugs. *Time* 128 (September 15):60–68.

Time. 1986. Growing pains at 40. *Time* 127 (May 19):22–41.

VanderZanden, J. 1986. *Core sociology.* New York: Alfred A. Knopf.

Wein, B. 1970. *The runaway generation.* New York: David McKay Co.

Yinger, J. 1960. Contraculture and subculture. *American Sociological Review* 25 (October):625–635.

   1982. *Countercultures: The promise and peril of a world turned upside down.* New York: Free Press.

Juvenile Gangs and Delinquent Behavior

READING OBJECTIVES

The reading of this chapter will help you achieve the following objectives:

1. Extend the sociological perspective to help you understand and explain group dynamics, that is, in what ways human behavior is social in origin, social in content, and social in consequences.
2. Understand how neighborhood play groups of juveniles can evolve into delinquent youth gangs.
3. Define and understand the concept of "gang."
4. Comprehend the magnitude of the juvenile gang problem, that is, the number of gangs, number of gang members, and gang involvement in delinquent behavior.
5. List the common motives of members for joining gangs and outline the general organization, officers, and roles within fighting gangs.
6. Explore the compositional factors of gangs—social class, race, and gender—and link these factors to reasons why gangs are formed and the illegal behavior of gang members.
7. Trace gang formation and behavior back to the theoretical causes and explanations developed by sociologists.

INTRODUCTION

The theoretical explanations of deviance and delinquency discussed in Part II included the important perspective that human behavior is social in origin. In general, our conduct reflects the powerful socializing influences of our families, neighborhoods, communities, subcultures, and other social groups and aggregates in which we share membership and with whom we interact. More specifically, we looked at the etiological or causal linkages between a broad spectrum of social variables and delinquent behavior.

In earlier chapters of Part III, we have already focused directly on the family and the youth subculture as potential, contextual generators of alienated and delinquent youths. In this chapter we turn our attention to juvenile gangs, whose delinquent behavior is not only social in origin but social in content, that is, they act out their misconduct within supportive and cooperative groups.

PREDATORY YOUTHS: A NATIONAL ALARM

MICHIGAN: Three teen-agers have been charged with murder because they allegedly burst into the home of a 94-year-old man who died of fright after he was robbed of 80 cents, authorities said. Eighteen-year-old Alvin W. was charged with the death and jailed on $50,000 bond. Two younger youths, aged 13 and 14, were ordered held at the County Youth Home, where they await prosecution as juveniles on the same charges (*The Daily Oklahoman*, 1984:32).

OREGON: Two teenage boys were arrested Tuesday night and charged with attempting to use a dangerous weapon in connection with the placement of Vietnam-style booby traps in a suburban Portland park. The traps included sharp "punji sticks" and a long pole with sharp spikes fastened across it. The police were called by neighbors who saw two boys wearing camouflage shirts and carrying sharpened stakes in the park. Police reported that the traps they found hidden in the park had every potential to kill somebody. Included were covered pits with sharp sticks pointing up in them and a log suspended above a path rigged with a trip wire (*The Daily Tidings*, 1985:5).

NEW YORK: Four teen-agers, who giggled when their videotaped confessions were played at a preliminary hearing, were indicted Thursday on charges of killing a 60-year-old woman during a $3 robbery. Each youth admitted following the elderly woman into the elevator in her apartment building.

The woman was shot in the head and died immediately. Her purse yielded $3, which the youths said they used to buy soda and cake. "She just fell to the floor," Robert J., 14, said in the taped interview. Robert admitted he held the pistol that killed the woman, but said it went off accidentally. Another youth, Darryl S., claimed that 13-year-old Terry W. had urged Robert: "Shoot her, Robert, shoot her." He added, "Robert pulled the hammer back and bang, she fell . . . She was dead before she hit the floor." Terry claimed he said nothing on the elevator. "She just looked at us and smiled like it was a joke," Terry said. "Just then, he shot her."

The fourth youth, Tyrone Q., age 15, said that the robbery was done on impulse. According to Tyrone, the youths were standing outside the building when the woman walked by "and one of my friends said, 'Let's rob that lady' " (*New York Times*, 1984:15).

CALIFORNIA: In what is similar to a war zone, ghetto residents often must eat and sleep on the floor to avoid the stray bullets whizzing through their windows. One former gang member confessed that he was always stalking a rival gang member or a potential robbery victim. "Whenever I was shootin' (had a gun), I had someone in mind. If I couldn't get him, I'd get his partner or a substitute" (*Time*, 1977:20).

Although only a small proportion of juvenile crime in the United States is as violent as reported in these news excerpts, or impacts so tragically on individual victims or society, such scenarios are repeated often enough to warrant our serious concern and study.

THE SOLITARY DELINQUENT

As with many other forms of deviant behavior, some juvenile crime is committed by solitary individuals acting alone, and this phenomenon must be acknowledged. Opportunities arise for youngsters to make delinquent responses that do not require encouragement from peers or other influential persons. For example, malicious mischief, petty theft, and status offenses such as school truancy appeal to many juveniles because they can be carried out alone and privately, without an accomplice or even a tolerant witness. Such solitary operatives seek to protect and maintain respectable ties and status within the nondeviant society (Goffman, 1963). Solitary delinquents may also be emotionally or socially maladjusted in some way. They avoid companionship and group interaction and express their frustration or anger in a delinquent, loner role:

> The solitary delinquent may be a social isolate, who is unable to make friends or who prefers to work or play alone. Throughout society there are people who do not make close affiliations with groups. If such a person is motivated toward delinquency, he would tend to carry out his delinquency alone, just as he prefers to study alone, read instead of play with others, or have a hobby that does not require cooperation. It is normal for him to act as an individual and not as a member of a clique or gang (Cavan and Ferdinand, 1981:225).

Although nearly a third of the boys who come before the juvenile court have, for one reason or another, committed their delinquencies alone (Cavan and Ferdinand, 1981), little research has focused on the solitary delinquent. As a result, causal explanations are largely speculative.

Many sociologists, while acknowledging the statistical reality of solitary individuals, counter that the popularized picture of "the lone gunman," "the secretive alcoholic," "the closet homosexual," or "the solitary delinquent"—acting out deviant behavior with little or no connection with other members of society—is an oversimplification. Theoretically, it is virtually impossible to conceive of any human behavior as occurring in a complete social vacuum, without an interlocking web of human interaction and totally devoid of social causes, social support, and/or social consequences. Applying this sociological principle to deviant or delinquent behavior, no act can be judged as conforming or nonconforming without the societal audience.

Sociologists often conceptualize each individual and his or her behavior as being at the hub or vortex of a social network. For example, consider the shoplifter. Although there are professional shoplifting gangs that prey upon retail merchants, much shoplifting involves single individuals, operating alone. However, many observers are oblivious to the social linkages between a solitary delinquent shoplifter and numerous other members of society who, while usually not responsible for the illegal behavior, are nevertheless related to it in some way. Figure 9–1 outlines the shoplifter's social network.

FIGURE 9–1
The Shoplifter's Social Network

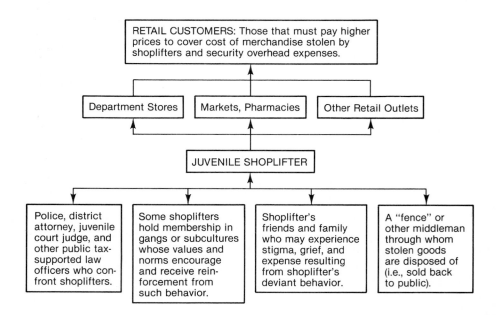

The model of the shoplifter's social network (Figure 9–1) contains only some of the linkages and associations between the individual offender and other people. If we look at the apparently solitary actor closely, we can discern an abstract, dynamic, and complex societal web that connects the individual and the behavior in question to a wide array of other persons and groups that in some way support, influence, or are affected by the behavior. These often inescapable connections and relationships may be voluntary or involuntary, formal or informal, primary or secondary, but the impact of deviant or delinquent behavior on other persons sharing a social network can be extremely negative and traumatic.

GROUP DELINQUENCY

In addition to the sociological argument regarding the social causes and consequences of human behavior, there is considerable documentation that most juvenile delinquency is committed by social groupings of varying size, purpose, and organization.

One of the most extensive studies along this line of inquiry was conducted by Maynard Erickson and Gary Jensen (1977) who administered self-report questionnaires to 1,700 high school students from three small towns and three urban schools in Arizona. The subjects were asked how many times during the past year they had committed each of 18 delinquent acts, and in how many of those times they had been in the company of others. The findings suggested that the youths generally engaged in delinquent behavior when they were with their friends. However, the tendency varied with the type of offense. Group violations were more common with drug offenses and least common with status offenses other than drinking alcoholic beverages and smoking tobacco. The study also found that females were even more likely than males to commit delinquent acts in groups.

The findings of Erickson and Jensen generally agreed with those of similar investigations carried out in other countries. For example, Brunner (1974) found that group membership and processes played a central role in three major types of juvenile crime in West Germany; that between 80 and 90 percent of illegal behavior by juveniles involved groups of youths, particularly gang crime, violent crime, and drug abuse.

The group context of juvenile misbehavior should come as no surprise when we recall from Chapter 1 that we human beings share with most other species a strong social imperative that constrains us toward social interaction with others of our kind. Thus, most nonconforming, delinquent behavior, like most conforming, law-abiding behavior, has been widely observed and documented in social groupings. LaMar Empey (1982:121, 146) concluded that "the gregarious and companionate character of law-violating behavior" is clearly reflected in self-report studies of juvenile delinquency:

. . . the preponderant majority of all delinquent acts are committed in groups—whether male or female, black or white, middle- or lower-class.

Paradoxically, the initial social stimulant for potentially serious delinquent behavior by some children has been traced to innocent neighborhood play groups.

THE PLAY GROUP

The natural, spontaneous, and initially innocuous emergence of neighborhood play groups among urban youngsters was well described in Frederick Thrasher's (1927:26) early study of gangs:

On a warm summer evening children literally swarm over areaways and sidewalks, vacant lots and rubbish dumps, streets and alleys . . . This endless activity has a tremendous fascination, . . . and it would be a marvel indeed if any healthy boy could hold himself aloof from it . . .

The play groups engage in all sorts of childhood games including "hide-and-go-seek," "cowboys and Indians," "pick-up softball," and crap-shooting. These are natural groupings of participants who live in the same area and know each other as well as brothers. In time, as the boys grow older, more adventuresome, and more mischievous, such childhood games may become less satisfying. Building on the loosely organized alliances and innocent activities of the play group, some youths begin to experiment with more aggressive and predatory group behavior, directed toward youths outside the group and against society in general. Thus, the "game" is extended over time and territory to include higher stakes and involuntary victim-participants.

Fifty years after Thrasher's landmark study, in a *Time* magazine report (1977), a youth who attended a school for problem youngsters said: "Mugging is like playing a game; kids do it for the fun of it."

Clifford Shaw and Henry McKay (1931:251) also reported on the playful, game-like approach of juveniles at the beginning of their delinquent careers:

When we were shoplifting we always made a game of it. For example, we might gamble on who could steal the most caps in a day, or who could steal caps from the largest number of stores in a day, or who could steal in the presence of a detective and then get away. We were always daring each other that way and thinking up new schemes. This was the best part of the game . . . It was the fun I wanted, not the hat. I kept this up for months and then began to sell the things to a man on the west side. It was at this time that I began to steal for gain.

Sociologists have noted that spontaneous and informal neighborhood play groups sometimes evolve over time into more formally organized and predatory street gangs. (H. Armstrong Roberts)

Since the family usually offers the first social setting for childhood play activities, siblings sometimes move on to engage in delinquent behavior together. Seattle, Washington even had a one-family gang: seven brothers, aged 11 to 20, were arrested 192 times during a 9-year period 1968 through 1976. Enough of the boys were always at liberty to keep up the family tradition (*Time*, 1977).

THE JUVENILE GANG

Some studies, done in the United States and elsewhere, have concluded that much juvenile delinquency consists of gangs committing crimes as social activities. For instance, Sarnecki (1983) suggested that committing crimes together satisfy juveniles' needs for togetherness and excitement. Notwithstanding, society shows little tolerance for serious misconduct by youth groups, even if interpreted as "social activities" fulfilling juvenile needs for "togetherness" and "excitement." For while gang members may view their predatory behavior as "fun and games," their victims see it as violent and frightening crime. From the viewpoint of the larger society, there is a great difference between the neighborhood play group and the intimidating street gang. Despite the play group basis for the early association among some gang members, once they advance beyond the occasional and spontaneous prank to a conscious and deliberate pattern of illegal conduct, they become a threat to society.

James R. Davis (1978) contended that street gangs have increased and that the misconception that street gangs are play groups has in the past led to the underestimation of the extent of street gang crime by the media and its dismissal by police officials.

What is a Gang?

In its broadest sense, the term **gang** means *a group of persons assembled and acting or working together.* In time, common usage applied the term to places and things utilized by some organized groups of workers. For example, sailors have traditionally referred to the movable bridge used in boarding or leaving a ship at a pier as a "gangplank." Similarly, the opening by which a ship is boarded is the "gangway." Additional applications of the term were made to describe "a set of similar instruments arranged so that they function together." For example, a "gang cultivator" or a "gang plow" is built to turn multiple and parallel furrows. Most fishermen are acquainted with the concept of the "gang hook," which is actually a cluster of several fishhooks with their shanks joined together (Funk and Wagnalls, 1975).

The term "gang" has often been used to signify a group of close associates or friends with no criminal or antisocial intentions or connotations. For example, a generation or so ago "the gang" could have signified a familiar and collegial name encompassing members of an informal male group whose activities center on social drinking, cardplaying, and sporting events. In the early part of the twentieth century, several popular songs romanticized the notion with such lyrics as: "Those wedding bells are breaking up that old gang of mine" (Miller, 1981; Lotz et al., 1985:131).

In the late-nineteenth century, large sections of the American West were terrorized by gangs of adult criminals. The collective cruelty, robbery, and violence of those outlaw bands reinforced the definition of the gang as a group of persons united in working to unlawful and antisocial ends. While the word "gang" is still occasionally used in law enforcement, the news media, and by the public in reference to organized groups of adult criminals engaged in extortion, racketeering, theft, and prostitution, the most recent and prominent application has been to hostile groups of urban youths who are reputed to terrorize neighborhoods, victimize innocent people, and fight each other over territory and status. This image of urban gangs involved in crime and delinquency was popularized in recent decades by such motion pictures as *West Side Story, The Wild Ones, The Lords of Flatbush, Rumblefish, The Outsiders,* and *Colors.*

Although several decades of serious attention have been given to juvenile gangs by criminologists, sociologists, and law enforcement personnel and agencies, the great variability among these gangs and the many dimensions of their behavior have confounded the development of an all-encompassing answer to the question "What is a gang?" However, Walter Miller (1975:1), after interviewing law enforcement and social service professionals who dealt with youth gangs in six large American cities, brought together some of the major variables into one of the better working definitions of the term *"gang"*:

> A gang is a group of recurrently associating individuals with identifiable leadership and internal organization, identifying with or claiming control over territory in a community, and engaging either individually or collectively in violent or other forms of illegal behavior.

In later sections of this chapter we address the multiple variations in gang objectives, orientation, and organization, and offer theoretical explanations for their formation and behavior.

James Short (1987:16–17) extrapolated a useful set of definitional criteria from the gangs he studied with Fred Strodtbeck, contending gangs manifest these characteristics:

1. recurrent congregation outside the home;
2. self-defined inclusion/exclusion criteria and continuity of affiliation;
3. a territorial basis consisting of customary hanging and ranging areas, including self-defined use-and-occupancy rights;
4. a versatile activity repertoire; and
5. organizational differentiation, e.g., by authority, roles, prestige, friendship, or special interest cliques.

History of Youth Gangs

Antisocial and criminal conduct by members of juvenile gangs is not a new phenomenon. Nor does history exempt any western nation from this form of deviant behavior. Cyril Burt (1925) reported that many troublesome and even dangerous delinquent gangs were present in England during the first quarter of this century. Thrasher (1936:40) noted in 1936 that tens of thousands of poverty-stricken Russian youths were gravitating to gangs for survival:

> Russia's 100,000 neglected children are said to travel in gangs, winning a precarious living by stealing and finding shelter in deserted buildings and in Moscow and other cities in the sewers and catacombs.

James Inciardi (1978:34–36) documented the presence of youth gangs engaged in criminal activity in American cities during the nineteenth century:

> The earliest gangs consisted almost entirely of Irishmen. The Irish, emigrating to this country in vast numbers and lacking funds, education, and skills, were met with contempt by native New Yorkers and were forced into the city's worst slum—the Five Points district . . . and lacking other means of earning a living, many developed criminal careers.
>
> . . . The Plug Uglies were formed in the mid-1820's and took their name from the giant plug hats which each member filled with rags and straw to protect their heads during gang battles. The Shirt Tails were so called because they wore their shirts on the outside of their trousers, like Chinamen . . . These gangs of the Five Points, Bowery, and Hell's Kitchen, which often included hundreds of men and boys, consisted of many small gangs grouped together and led by a supreme chieftain who commanded absolute loyalty . . .
>
> The gangs of youthful and young adult criminals who made war on one another and terrorized the streets of New York were also evident in other cities. Philadelphia had its 'Buffaloes,' 'Blood Tubs,' 'Rugs,' and 'Copper Heads'; Baltimore had its 'Stringers'; and a group known as the 'Crawfish Boys' plagued the streets of Cincinnati.

CONTEMPORARY YOUTH GANGS IN THE UNITED STATES

The first scholarly investigation of youth gangs in the United States was Frederick Thrasher's (1927) work in Chicago. Although Thrasher verified that a great many of the gangs were primarily organized for conventional participation in athletic, dancing, and other socially acceptable activities, many gang members were routinely involved in collective or individual delinquency.

Locale

Robert Park, in the Editor's Preface to Thrasher's study, reminded readers that:

> Gangs are not confined to cities, nor to the slums of cities . . . Every village has at least its boy gang . . . composed of those same foot-loose, prowling, and predacious adolescents who herd and hang together, after the manner of the undomesticated male everywhere . . . (Thrasher, 1927:ix).

However, Park's important generalization has been largely overshadowed by Thrasher's forceful portrayal of the inner city as the normal and natural habitat of the street gang. The image of the leather-jacketed, streetwise, and dangerous gangs roaming the inner city streets has prevailed, not only because of their high visibility, but also because of recurring news reports of their criminal activities and the public outcry for protection.

Criminologists and social scientists, supported by the official data on crime and delinquency, have often contributed to the stereotype of the youthful street gang as an inner city phenomenon with their conclusion that urban areas of blighted slum neighborhoods are the focal points of numerous social ills, including juvenile delinquency. The research of Shaw and McKay (1969) supported the belief that delinquency is especially associated with the normative confusion and corruption manifested in the high delinquency areas of large American cities. These writers and numerous others argued that criminal and delinquent behavior is concentrated, encouraged, and reinforced by the prevailing customs and norms of such deteriorated areas (see Chapter 6 for a detailed discussion).

In the lower socioeconomic slum districts of the city, gang behavior can take on a spatial, ecological dimension as members relate and interact with each other and their mutual environment. It has been well documented that urban gang members generally demonstrate a territorial imperative in which they consistently identify and defend boundaries around their "turf"—the geographical area they intend to dominate. The gang territory may be the immediate neighborhood in which members reside or the area around a recreational center, store, school, park, or pool hall. The familiar range and sense of possession lends social and psychological security and much needed status and identity to gang members. Similar to the citizens of formally organized nations, gang boys will defend their established boundaries against competing gangs from another area, and other outsiders who are perceived as threatening. Ronald Halvorsen, a former gang member, described this territorial behavior and the careful demarcation of boundary lines:

> If you were to visit the Coney Island beaches, you would find they are divided into sections by rock walls that run out into the water. These sections are called 'bays,' and each is claimed by a different gang. The Avenue X gang held Bay 13, and the Swords had Bay 17, up to the Steeplechase Pier. We Beachcombers staked out our claim on Bay 11, just down from the big Cyclone roller coaster. We practically camped there during the summer months. At last, I was really living! (Halvorsen and Hawley, 1973:56).

Contrary to official arrest statistics and the media emphasis on inner city gangs, considerable evidence now shows that delinquent gang activity also exists in suburban communities that ring large cities, small towns, and even rural areas (Muehlbauer and Dodder, 1983). John Johnstone (1981) found intense gang activity in several suburban communities near Chicago. These suburban gangs also lived in rundown tenements whose black majority experienced high levels of unemployment and poverty similar to those found in central city ghettoes.

Harrison Salisbury (1958) painted a grim picture of marauding bands of middle class teenagers, living in fashionable suburbs of Boston and New York, and committing gang rapes and malicious vandalism on schools:

> A typical outbreak occurred at Maplewood, New Jersey, a fine community of middle-class families, proud of a low juvenile delinquency rate. A gang of boys broke into the Maplewood Junior High School and sacked it. They destroyed the principal's office, wrecked classrooms, carried kerosene and alcohol from the art department into the library, toppled books from the shelves, poured inflammables over them and set fire to the place. School authorities estimated the damage at $300,000 (Salisbury, cited in Vaz, 1967:196).

James Coleman (1970) charted and described the development of a youth gang in a middle class suburb. Boys frequenting an area near the community library formed a friendship group that evolved over time into a delinquent gang. Their delinquent activities included vandalism, the theft of guns and automobiles, and the illegal use of alcohol and drugs.

Number of Gangs and Members

Thus far it has been very difficult to measure the full and exact magnitude of the youth gang problem. Nevertheless, the available data have led several researchers to conclude that the number of gangs and gang members are increasing, though most individual gangs consist of fewer than 20 active members (Davis, 1978). During the 1970s, Walter Miller (1975) studied youth gangs and their criminal activities in 12 American cities, including the six large metropolitan areas where such groups were thought to be the most troublesome. Some of Miller's estimates are summarized in Table 9-1.

Miller found that gang-related crime and delinquency in New York City, Chicago, Detroit, Los Angeles, Philadelphia, and San Francisco involved at least 760 gangs and 28,500 members up to a maximum possible of 2,700 gangs with 81,500 members. Over 90 percent of the gang members were male and more than 80 percent were black or Hispanic. Nearly all of the gangs were located in corresponding racial or ethnic neighborhoods where slum conditions prevailed. Between 1972 and 1974, there were 525 gang-related murders in the six cities.

Gang membership continues to grow dramatically as youths in larger cities have joined gangs in increasing numbers. Los Angeles alone had over 30,000 gang members in 1981, and gangs were perceived by police as a menace in over 300 cities (Bradley, 1981). In 1985, Chicago police arrested over 17,000 gang members (CNN Broadcast, 1986). By 1987, there were up to 80,000 members in 600 Los Angeles gangs (The Sunday Oklahoman, 1988).

TABLE 9-1

Numbers of Gangs and Gang Members in Six Gang-Problem Cities, 1973–75

City	Estimated No. Gangs		Source of Information	Date	Estimated No. Gang Members	Source of Information	Date
New York	high	473	P.D.	11/73	40,000	Juvenile Cts.	6/74
	low	315	P.D.	3/74	8,000–19,500	P.D.	3/74
Chicago	high	700	U.S. Sen., J.D. Comm.	4/75	10,000	P.E.L.[a]	6/74
	low	150–220	P.D.	4/75	3,000–5,000	P.D.	4/75
Los Angeles	high	1,000+	P.D.	3/75	15,000	P.D.	1/75
	low	160	Juvenile Ct.	1/75	12,000	P.D.	3/75
Philadelphia	high	400	P.E.L.[a]	6/74	15,000	P.E.L.[a]	6/74
	low	88	P.D.	1/74	4,700	P.D.	1/74
Detroit	high	110	P.D.	4/75	1,250	P.D.	4/75
	low	30	Soc. Agency, Bd. of Ed.	4/75	500	P.D., Soc. Agency	4/75
San Francisco		20	P.D., Prob'n.	2/75	250	P.D., Prob'n.	2/75
Six Cities	high	2,700			81,500		
	low	760			28,450		

[a]P.E.L. = Pennsylvania Economy League. "The Gang Problem in Philadelphia." Report #375. June 1974.

Source: Walter B. Miller, *Violence by Youth Gangs and Youth Groups as a Crime Problem in Major American Cities* (Washington, D.C.: U.S. Government Printing Office, 1975), p. 17.

THE MOTIVES FOR GANG MEMBERSHIP

Although a large number of gang members collectively commit deviant and delinquent acts, they rarely cite that as a reason for becoming a gang member. Many gang members contend that they joined a gang out of fear of being alone and vulnerable in a tough neighborhood. Others expressed much the same rationale—that the gang offered an opportunity to develop and maintain a peer group, or friendship network. Certainly this is a natural human desire, made particularly urgent for youngsters who see former associates from their play group and school affiliating with the neighborhood gang. Other reasons given by gang members for joining the gang include boredom, defiance of authority figures, loyalty to one's own racial or ethnic group, and poor relationships with parents and teachers. Thus, in a sense, the gang can represent a surrogate or substitute family for some youths who perceive a lack of rapport and positive interaction with their own biological families.

Other gang boys have suggested that gang membership was the only available avenue open to them to achieve some measure of recognition and identity. This unfulfilled need can be especially pressing in lower class neighborhoods where residents who lack status and recognition on the basis of occupations, material possessions, and educational achievements can find social support, security, and a sense of power within a gang of similarly situated persons. According to Short and Strodtbeck (1965), members of delinquent gangs tend to be characterized by a general social disability, lacking skill in interpersonal relations, social assurance, knowledge of the job market, and sophistication in their relations with girls. By displays of toughness and by committing crimes, these unskilled, unemployed school dropouts can assert their masculinity and feel successful in the eyes of friends in the gang (Zastrow and Bowker, 1984). Short (1987:31), in citing earlier research on gangs, observed that "The greater social skills possessed by gang leaders . . . and their supportive and nurturant style of leadership . . . confirm the value of group membership to gang members."

Lewis Yablonsky (1970) contended that motivation for gang affiliation is also related to the primary purpose of the specific gang in question. Gangs that focus on social activities such as athletic competition with other groups, dancing, and group discussions (or "bull sessions") attract youths who crave camaraderie and fellowship by engaging in generally innocent activities, and seldom resort to serious crime.

On the other hand, Yablonsky noted, juvenile gangs whose major pursuit is the procurement of money and material possessions through theft and other illegal activities recruit members who are not only interested in such endeavors but have those skills of organization and guile that will be useful to the gang.

Yablonsky's final type of gang was the violent-prone gang whose main function and activity centers on the planning and implementation of intragroup confrontation and conflict in defense of territory or status. New members are attracted into alliances and associations with the gang by the prospects of excitement and violence (Yablonsky, 1970:250).

Initiation Rituals

Most gangs, whose members are informally organized and have only vague objectives, have no initiation ceremonies or rituals. Youths may become members by virtue of their living in proximity to other gang members or their hangout, or casually interacting with gang members in a play group, at school, or on the streets. Thus, the role and status change from nonmember to member is likely to be a taken-for-granted, natural transition. However, researchers have discovered that some of the more aggressive gangs, in keeping with their ominous names and hostile posturing, do have formal and often violent initiation ceremonies for new members. An older study by Herbert Block and Arthur Niederhoffer (1958) cited a wide assortment of rituals and symbols, including leather motorcycle jackets decorated with the gang's name and logo, distinctive and sometimes radical hairstyles, and scarification and tattooing sessions resulting in the permanent display of gang affiliation.

A longstanding practice among many lower class gangs is to initiate new members with an ordeal of hazing, which often takes the form of physical punishment called "cramping" or "the pink belly." The new applicant for membership is held by two of the older boys while the rest of the gang take turns striking him in the stomach. If he "chickens out" of the ordeal, he is rejected for gang membership.

In Los Angeles one gang is called the Cripplers (with a special auxiliary for girls known as the Crippettes), because a youth can be initiated into membership only after proving that he had physically injured someone (*Time,* 1977:20). While such initiation rituals appear cruel, bizarre, and senseless to the outside observer, they represent highly coveted badges of honor, courage, and membership to new gang inductees.

GANG ORGANIZATION

Frederick Thrasher's (1927) observation that "No two gangs are just alike" is still valid. He indicated:

> Wide divergency in the character of its personnel combined with differences of physical social environment, or experience and tradition, give to every gang its own peculiar character. It may vary as to membership, type of leaders, mode of organization, interests and activities, and finally as to its status in the community (Thrasher, 1927:45).

While this complex variability among delinquent gangs confounds the formation of discrete, categorical types, there are some overarching patterns of social organization that can be identified.

In smaller, less goal-oriented youth gangs, one or two older, tougher, more articulate boys with forceful personalities may be the informally acknowledged leaders, who set the pace and determine the nature of the groups's activities. On the other hand, larger and more instrumental gangs have a functional organization, generally reflecting the nature of their orientation and activities. For example, the leadership of such well-known fighting gangs as the Egyptian Kings and Dragons, the Mau Maus, and the Jesters includes the president, vice-president, treasurer, a "light-up man" or "armorer" who maintains the gang's arsenal, and the "war counselor" who serves to identify enemy gangs and arrange for "rumbles" or fights.

Formal and informal alliances may be worked out between gangs that find some practical advantage or benefit in such alliances. Malcolm Klein (1964) identified such affiliations among several traditional gangs in Los Angeles. Typically, a "gang cluster" consists of three or four age-graded male subgroups plus a female auxiliary. Each subgroup maintains its own identity yet clearly affiliates with the overall cluster and its "generic name." In this way, several small and relatively weak gangs can muster a more formidable appearance through their alliance network, in confrontations with rival gangs. A few crime-oriented youth gangs have contacts and working agreements with adult criminals in their areas.

Meetings and meeting places may be loosely defined by most smaller gangs and their members as "anytime" or "all the time," "anywhere" or "everywhere," and a centrally located street corner, pool hall, or convenience store may serve as gang headquarters. At the other extreme, a few large gangs have become virtually institutionalized in some cities. The Vice Lords in Chicago, for example, created an administrative Board of Directors comprised of representatives from subgroups within the "Vice Lord Nation." Regular weekly meetings were instituted, along with membership fees, and membership cards featuring the Vice Lords' logo—a top hat, cane, and white gloves (Keiser, 1969).

The Near Group

Lewis Yablonsky (1959) complained that most efforts to explain gang organization begin with the imprecise assumption that gangs fit the pattern of the traditionally defined sociological group. His research on delinquent gangs concluded that the delinquent gang is organizationally midway between the stability of the established group and the instability of the mob. Thus, the gang is a kind of social collectivity in its own right, with characteristics especially suited to meet the varied needs of its members.

> One way of viewing human collectivities is on a continuum of organization characteristics. At one extreme, we have a highly organized, cohesive, functioning collection of individuals as members of a sociological group. At the other extreme, we have a mob of individuals characterized by anonymity, disturbed leadership, motivated by emotion, and in some cases representing a destructive collectivity within the inclusive social system (Yablonsky, 1959:109).

Yablonsky maintained that most delinquent gangs are midway on the group-mob continuum and thus are structurally neither groups nor mobs. He described the gang as a "near group" characterized by "diffuse role definitions, limited cohesion, impermanence, minimal consensus of norms, shifting membership, disturbed leadership, and limited definition of membership expectations" (Yablonsky, 1959:109).

Several other researchers have challenged parts of Yablonsky's generalization. Cohen (1958) and other proponents of the gang subculture concept (see Chapter 6) argued that many gang members share a remarkable consensus regarding norms and roles. Klein (1971) contended that the large majority of gang leaders are *not* sociopathic nor do they otherwise suffer serious emotional maladjustment.

COMPOSITION OF GANG MEMBERSHIP

The composition of a group or population of people refers to those common demographic traits that best describe or typify the group. For example, if we were studying the behavior of a group of college students, information about their sex, race, marital status, social class, and other variables would probably be very helpful in understanding their behavior. The same kind of population data are useful in our analysis of gangs and their behavior. Three population characteristics of gang members are discussed here that will contribute to our overall understanding regarding the formation and delinquent behavior of youthful gangs: social class, racial and ethnic composition, and female participation in delinquent gangs.

Social Class

Official crime reports indicate that juvenile delinquency is statistically concentrated in lower socioeconomic urban neighborhoods. While this conclusion is somewhat tempered by the class bias of law enforcement as reflected in arrest statistics, there is considerable evidence from other studies of the strong relationship between lower class unemployment, poverty, and a high incidence of property crime (Gillespie, 1978). Similar to juvenile delinquents in general, gang members are nearly always characterized as being from poor neighborhoods with substandard housing in which the residents have little hope for educational or occupational achievements.

A broader picture of social class and juvenile gang membership has emerged from several important studies that found definite groupings of young people in more affluent social classes who participate in delinquent activities. For example, Howard and Barbara Myerhoff (1964), in their observations of middle class gangs, found youngsters informally and loosely organized for many socially acceptable activities. However, drag racing, drinking of alcoholic beverages, sexual activity, and other forms of deviant and illegal behavior often emerged. The middle class subjects of the Myerhoffs' study generally lacked the disturbed leadership and violent behavior often attributed to lower class gangs. In addition, and again in contrast to the lower class subjects targeted by most research on gangs, the middle class youngsters did not demonstrate well-developed delinquent values, nor did they define themselves as delinquents or troublemakers. Rather, they fully expected to ultimately abandon their temporary deviant behavior and take respectable and law-abiding places in society. These optimistic feelings about the future were shared by the adults in their environment, thus eliciting more tolerance for middle class juveniles than for lower class youngsters.

The existence of middle class gangs performing very serious acts of delinquency in fashionable suburban communities also was documented in studies by Muehlbauer and Dodder (1983) and by Salisbury (1958) and discussed earlier in this chapter. A number of such reports have been brought together in a significant work, *Middle-Class Juvenile Delinquency*, edited by Edmund Vaz (1967).

Racial and Ethnic Composition of Gangs

The United States is composed of a variety of different racial and ethnic groups including blacks, Hispanics, Native Americans, Orientals, and whites. From the very beginning of the American experience as a developing nation, tens of millions of immigrants added to our national population.

Many of these racial and ethnic groups initially settled in their own urban enclaves, where they often preserved distinctive subcultural values, beliefs, and behaviors with which they were familiar, in spite of an intense social pressure to assimilate or Americanize. Many of the racial and ethnic neighborhoods and districts of our cities still retain place names reflecting the traditional background of the residents such as Little Italy, Chinatown, Harlem, and so forth. It follows that many of the youthful street gangs that emerged in these particular urban neighborhoods are racially homogeneous as a natural consequence of families of similar racial and ethnic backgrounds living near one another.

Race and ethnicity are, of themselves, powerful forces that can draw people together into cohesive groups. Birds of a feather do indeed flock together! Moreover, if the race or ethnicity of a group is associated in the minds of group members with social, economic, or political injustices they feel they have suffered, additional solidarity and commitment to group objectives can result. With this in mind, Davis (1978) argued that gang ethnicity should always be considered when the modalities and motivations of gangs are examined. Thus, race or ethnicity can serve as a unifying and sacred cause for some gangs—more symbolic and preeminent than their leather jackets and intimidating names (Moore, 1985). Howard Erlanger's study (1979) of the relationships between the subcultural values of the Chicano barrios in East Los Angeles, estrangement from the dominant white society, and gang violence offers a classic example of this phenomenon:

> . . . while subcultural values of the barrio may be different from those of the Anglo society and may exist independently of Anglo society, they do not directly require or condone violence . . . [However], under situations of estrangement or alienation from the Anglo society brought about by discrimination or negative images of Chicano culture, young Chicanos may become collectively

violent as they respond to the strong Chicano cultural emphasis on values such as courage and dignity for males (Erlanger, 1979:235).

Erlanger described the deep resentment Chicanos felt about the educational situation in East Los Angeles, in which their children were punished for speaking Spanish, even among themselves in the schoolyard. Chicano youth interpreted this as rejection by the Anglo society, and this scenario elicited a readiness to fight among some youthful barrio gangs.

Juvenile gangs continue to develop in every racial category. One of the most recent racial gang groupings is the Vietnamese, emerging from the relatively new, closeknit Vietnamese communities of California (Morganthau, 1982; Senate Subcommittee on Juvenile Justice, 1983). These gangs are particularly violent, utilizing robbery, bombing, extortion, and murder as terror tactics.

Although the large majority of gangs of racial and ethnic minority origin are homogeneous in composition, some demonstrate a degree of racial and ethnic integration in their membership, especially in neighborhoods where

Los Angeles police search suspected members of the Rolling 60's gang for weapons and drugs during a sweep in south Los Angeles. This one urban area accounts for the largest number of street gangs in the nation—about 150 groups of mostly black and hispanic youths. (UPI/Bettmaun Newsphotos)

housing has previously been well integrated. However, Kobrin and Peluso (1968) in their "Criteria of Status among Street Groups" observed strikingly different levels of social status within the gangs for members of various races. The numerically dominant race carefully retained positions of highest prestige and power within the group.

Female Participation in Delinquent Gangs

Chapter 3 underscored the statistical evidence that juvenile delinquents are predominantly male. The same generality applies to gang membership. Traditionally, female involvement in gang delinquency has been more passive than active, with girls and young women functioning as support personnel to male members rather than as equal participants. James Short (1968:4) and numerous other writers have aptly depicted these females and their secondary roles and statuses as a branch organization or female auxiliary:

> The gang world is dominated largely by males . . . But girls are important, too, for many reasons: as sex objects, hustles to be exploited, sources of prestige among the boys with whom they are associated, and in their own right. 'Female auxiliary' groups are not uncommon, and when they exist they perform many functions for boys' gangs and enjoy a degree of autonomy among themselves. Their names characteristically suggest their association with boy's gangs, e.g., Vice Queens (associated with the Vice Kings), Egyptian Cobrettes (associated with the Egyptian Cobras), and Lady Racketeers (associated with the Racketeers).

It has been reported that before and after gang fights, the girlfriends of gang members sometimes concealed the weapons, since the police have been more hesitant to pursue, search, and arrest females not directly involved in the melee. For the same reasons, and in order to avoid the situation of suspicion and the prospects of interrogation, gang boys congregated on the same street corner will break up into subunits of two or three, or pair off with their girlfriends, when a squad car appears in the area. "Similarly, unmarried, older boys will occasionally wear wedding rings in order to bolster their moral status in the eyes of the police" (Werthman and Piliavin, 1967:86).

While auxiliary status has been the most common form of gang participation available to females, there is some evidence that a small minority of gangs permit sexually integrated membership (Hardman, 1969). This phenomenon is more likely in middle class, suburban gangs, whose youthful members have not been seriously alienated from middle class norms and values and still aspire to middle class educational and occupational objectives. This does not mean that females may not be members of lower class urban street gangs, however. Anne Campbell (1984:5) estimated that there were anywhere from 8,000 to 40,000 gang members in New York City, approximately 10 percent of whom were females ranging in age from 14 to 30.

There is considerable debate among scholars and researchers in the field concerning the statistical increase in female delinquency in general and female participation in gangs. Some writers like Freda Adler (1975) have pointed to the revitalization of the feminist movement since 1960, and the greater assertiveness, freedom from traditional restraints, and the more equitable status and opportunity now enjoyed by women, as opening the door for more female involvement in criminal activities formerly dominated by males. On the other hand, Rachelle Canter (1982) flatly denies that girls are catching up with boys in juvenile delinquency. Still others, while acknowledging that girls may have increased their involvement in damaging property and theft of items worth less than 10 dollars more rapidly than boys, insist that girls are *not* catching up with boys in "fist fighting, gang fighting, carrying a weapon, strongarm theft, and major theft" (Steffensmeier and Steffensmeier, 1980).

Interviews with gang boys seem to support that last position. Data on female participation in gang and nongang delinquency, collected from black male delinquents in the Los Angeles County Juvenile Hall, reveal a systematic exclusion of females from the planning and action stages of delinquent activities. The research, reported by Lee Bowker and his associates (1980), indicated that female presence at a delinquent activity site tended to have a suppressive effect on the activity.

The most recent reports have again modified previous findings and reversed conclusions regarding female involvement in gang delinquency. While researchers all the way back to Thrasher (1927) have identified isolated instances of all-female gangs, it now appears that a rapidly growing number of highly organized, crime-oriented gangs of this type are creating a major problem for law enforcement. A CBS News Report (1986) estimated that approximately 1,000 girls are involved in over 100 female gangs in Chicago alone. It was emphasized that these are not sister organizations or auxiliaries to male gangs, but independent female gangs. Similar to their male counterparts, these female gangs stake out their own "turf" or territory, adopt distinctive colors and insignia, and have physical confrontations and fights with rival gangs. The CBS Report documented one case in which a nonmember was badly beaten because she wore a yellow article of clothing and yellow happened to be the official color of a nearby female gang. Another juvenile, a 13-year-old girl, was shot in the head and assassinated by other gang members because they thought she was a police informant.

A very large portion of the research carried out to date on juvenile delinquency and gang behavior has concentrated on male delinquents. Many explanations of female motivation and participation have been only partial and often supported by inadequate data. However, an empirical study by Bowker and Klein (1983) on "The Etiology of Female Delinquency and Gang Membership" has weakened the previously accepted, psychological and social-psychological reasoning that females commit delinquent acts or join delinquent gangs because they are socially maladjusted, come from broken and unhappy homes, and do not relate well to the opposite sex. A fuller explanation of the emergence and delinquent behavior of the new, all-female gangs awaits further research investigations.

GANG VIOLENCE

Law enforcement agencies, criminologists, and others who specialize in the study of juvenile crime generally agree that gang membership increases the likelihood of delinquent behavior. The reason, according to Klein and Crawford (1968), lies in the cohesiveness generated in the group, as tough talk, "macho" posturing, and alienation are shared and reinforced. It follows that the individual youth who might ordinarily be intimidated by law enforcement officers and reluctant to violate major social norms can become emotionally involved and committed to acts of bravado and delinquency in the context of the gang. But, here again, we must take into account the great variation among gangs in purpose, social class, level of perceived estrangement from the dominant society, and subcultural values.

Most gangs do not have crime as their dominant activity; offenses are committed spontaneously; and most members have temporary gang memberships and short criminal careers (Sarnecki, 1982).

Walter Miller (1966) sought to counter the popular media reports that urban gangs are massively, consistently, and continually involved in violent behavior. His research revealed that while theft and vandalism were common among gang members, violence was not a major activity of urban street gangs, nor a central reason for their existence. Only a small minority of gang members participated in violent crime. When violence did occur, it most frequently involved unarmed physical encounters between male antagonists, usually motivated to defend honor or prestige. More often than not, the fight was between two males:

> Generally, it was not 'ganging up' by malicious sadists on the weak, the innocent, the solitary. It did not victimize adult females. With few exceptions, violent crimes fell into the 'less serious' category, with the extreme or shocking crimes rare (Miller, 1966:111).

During the years since Miller's research, the level and scope of gang violence has dramatically increased. Toplin's (1975) gripping *Unchallenged Violence: An American Ordeal* supported the view that today's gangs engage in violence of greater severity than did gangs of past years:

> During the 1950's, gangs fought with bottles, clubs, chains, knives, and fists. Now they fight with handguns, revolvers, and shotguns (Toplin, 1975:81).

In a later study, Miller (1975) reversed his former position with new data showing that in the mid-1970s the rate of murder by youth gangs with firearms or other weapons was higher than ever before:

> The five cities that had the most serious gang problems averaged at least 175 gang-related killings a year between 1972 and 1974. Forays by small bands, armed and often motorized, seemed to have replaced the classic 'rumble' (cited in Bartollas, 1985:370).

Ed Bradley (1981), in a special CBS documentary on violence among youths, observed that:

> there are nearly 200 million guns in this country and American teenagers have obtained access to these in large numbers . . . Many of today's schools and city streets have the appearance of war zones.

Violence touches and terminates the lives of a large and growing portion of American young people, over and above the conspicuous and aggressive street gangs. This alarming point was underscored by Robert Blum (1987), Director of the Adolescent Health Program at the University of Minnesota, and published in the *Journal of the American Medical Association*. Blum's (1987) statistical analysis revealed that three of four 15- to 24-year-old Americans who die are victims of violence. Accidents, primarily auto accidents, account for 53.5 percent of the fatalities and remain by far the leading cause of death in that age group. But homicide deaths among young people have climbed 300 percent in three decades to become the number two killer:

> The homicide rate in the general population in 1980 was 10.8 per 100,000 population, a 100 percent increase from 1950. But among 15- to 24-year-olds, homicide was the cause of 15.6 deaths per 100,000 people per year. The number rose to 72.5 deaths per 100,000 among black males, largely because more blacks fall below the poverty line (Blum, 1987:3394).

Blum credited these grim statistics on homicide and other forms of violence to the increasing "juvenilization of poverty." He projected that in the next 5 years, one of every five adolescents will live at or below the poverty level. Blum agreed with numerous social scientists that impoverished and hopeless youth are subject to more substance abuse, more adolescent pregnancy, higher school dropout rates, more crime, and higher death rates due to violence.

Drug Franchises and Gang Warfare

As discouraging and somewhat frightening as these reports of persistent and collective violence by young people may be, they have proved to be but a mild prologue for the escalating and bloody urban gang wars that erupted in 1987:

LOS ANGELES (AP)

Gang violence has disrupted the easygoing life of this sunny city, where the gang related killings last year claimed more than four times the 1987 death toll in Northern Ireland's sectarian bloodshed . . .

Many residents of the nation's second largest city live in fear of gunmen who often are not men at all but rather children with guns. The 'good old days of tire irons and chains are over,' laments Ira Reiner, district attorney for Los Angeles County.

Today's young thugs prefer weapons such as Uzi submachine guns and Chinese copies of the Soviet AK-47 assault rifle.

Police and Community service experts estimate between 70,000 to 80,000 young people belong to about 600 gangs across Los Angeles. Last year, 387 people were slain by this city's baby gangsters who battle each other over drug profits, or kill on a dare or over taunts that become battle cries . . .

The gang killers are children of poverty and come from the city's toughest streets in the mostly black neighborhoods south of downtown or the largely Hispanic districts on the city's east side (The *Sunday Oklahoman*, 1988:A7).

This rapid proliferation of street gangs and violence is driven by the economics of drug trafficking. Urban districts and perhaps entire cities are being literally franchised for the marketing of "crack" cocaine. Thus, the gangs have become the pushers and enforcers for the international drug trade (*Nightline*, 1988).

Each gang has its own jargon and graffiti, spray-painted on walls and fences to mark its 'territory.' These gang alliances are proclaimed by the colors they wear: Gangs affiliated with the Crips wear blue, and the Bloods prefer red . . .

'Gangs like the Crips are highly mobile, very sophisticated, . . . Just like businessmen. They've acquired a lot of money through selling drugs. I've seen them operate as far north as Anchorage, Alaska, into Las Vegas, the Southwest, and as far east as New Jersey' [says Gerald Ivory, L.A. county probation officer].

'Kids (gang members) are . . . now flying to other cities, seeking fertile ground to sell their drugs. Being a gang member, I've said, is better than being a Harvard MBA. They never operate in the red' (Davis, 1988:A18).

As these new drug oriented gang wars expanded in 1988, and as casualties mounted (often of innocent bystanders caught in the crossfire), thousands of heavily armed lawmen fought to regain control of those Los Angeles streets dominated by the gangs.

Gang Rape

Gang rape is another form of violent crime that involves surprisingly large numbers of American youths. Multiple rape or group rape is almost as common as single rape. Menachem Amir's (1971) study of a large number of rape cases revealed that 43 percent were multiple rapes. The most significant fact about multiple rape, as shown by Amir's data, is that its perpetrators were largely adolescents from 10 to 19 years of age.

Some psychiatrists interpret gang rape as an expression of latent homosexuality, arguing that the co-rapists have an unconscious wish to have sex with each other. Such an interpretation, according to Alex Thio (1983:133), makes as much sense as the suggestion that several men who rob a store together unconsciously want to rob each other. Actually, participation in a gang rape fulfills a social need rather than a sexual desire, particularly for youngsters who feel peer pressure to prove that they are not "chicken" (Groth and Birnbaum, 1979:115).

One of the startling byproducts of such acts of violence is the failure of many bystanders to heed calls for help from the victim. A vivid example was the 1983 gang rape of a young woman in a bar in New Bedford, Massachusetts. She entered the building to make a telephone call and was promptly assaulted by a group of young men:

> Despite the presence of numerous patrons other than the several rapists, none intervened. Only after the victim ran naked into the street did a passing motorist provide assistance and summon the police (Ritzer, 1986:461).

Although such widely publicized events are relatively infrequent, and are not limited to occurrence in large cities, they reflect an apparent pattern of reduced social involvement among many urban residents.

In order to sensitize the public to the growing threat of gang violence and to marshal resources for intervention by both government and private citizens, the Subcommittee on Juvenile Justice of the Judiciary Committee, United States Senate, held hearings in 1983 in Los Angeles and San Francisco which centered on judicial and law enforcement options (Subcommittee on Juvenile Justice, 1983).

DYADS AND TRIADS

A **dyad** is *a social group comprised of just two persons;* a **triad** is *a social group of three persons in social interaction.* These sociological descriptors for small groups are the focal point of a comparatively recent finding that has weakened the common stereotype of large groups or gangs of youths participating together in collective delinquency.

Beginning with the work of Paul Lerman (1967), who used self-report techniques, the fact emerged that the large group context of juvenile delinquency needed revision. Lerman's research dealt with 700 boys, aged 10 through 19, living in New York City. He determined that until the age of 14 or 15, most of the boys committed delinquent acts together with one or two close friends. At ages 16 through 19, more of the youths could be classified as loners, but pair and triad participation in illegal conduct continued to be the most dominant grouping. While the gang fight—in which squads of youths from opposing neighborhoods meet in armed and angry conflict—still occasionally occurs, most delinquent acts usually involve just two or three close friends, operating together in a less sensational manner. As Michael Hindelang (1986) emphasized in his "With a Little Help from Their Friends," our revised concept of collective delinquency more accurately focuses on a small network of two or three trusted pals and peers. They may well be members of a larger gang, whose values, norms, and behavioral expectations are far from altruistic, but most delinquency is acted out in much smaller social units than the gang.

EXPLANATORY THEORIES OF GANG FORMATION AND BEHAVIOR: A SUMMARY

Part II of this book containing Chapters 4, 5, and 6, is totally devoted to causal theories of juvenile delinquency. Chapter 6 contains an extensive discussion and critique of theories related to the etiology of juvenile gangs. However, in the context of this chapter a brief review and summary of the most prominent explanatory theories of gang formation and behavior is appropriate.

The sociological examination and application of the related concepts of culture and subculture formed the foundation for the major theoretical explications of juvenile gang delinquency. As indicated in Chapter 8, **culture** is *the entire body of shared and learned beliefs, values, attitudes, traditions, normative expectations, and other forms of knowledge that is passed on from one generation to the next within a society.* **Subculture** refers to *the beliefs, values, attitudes, norms, behavior patterns, and accumulated knowledge that characterize subgroups and uniquely set them apart in some ways from the larger society.* These subcultures may be based on social class, occupation, religion, racial or ethnic background, ideology, or any number of other variables that can characterize specific subgroups.

Once they had carefully defined culture and subculture, it was a short step for sociological theorists to turn their attention to deviant subcultures and criminal and delinquent subcultures as explanatory social contexts for nonconforming and/or antisocial behavior.

Deviant subculture is *a term applied to any subgroup that deviates markedly* *from the generally accepted values, norms, and behavioral expectations of the dominant society.* Such nonconformists as "punk rockers," homosexuals, and religious snake handlers may be classified as members of deviant subcultures because they share with others some beliefs, practices, and life-styles that significantly set them apart. However, they are not ordinarily perceived by the larger society as major threats to the social order.

On the other hand, a **criminal** or **delinquent subculture** *manifests such extreme and negative nonconformity to the normative prescriptions of the larger society that its members are generally viewed as antisocial—against society.* Sutherland (1939), Shaw and McKay (1942), and other early sociologists/criminologists pinpointed the locus of many of these subcultures in high delinquency areas of central cities, where criminal behavior is supported by the cultural values and prevailing practices of those particular districts. Thus, juvenile delinquents gain identification and encouragement from other delinquents and from criminal elements in their area with whom they associate. In that environment, such behavior is socially learned, expected, and rewarded. Such youngsters, with strong loyalties and deep emotional attachment to peers, have also learned to distrust established institutions, and expect little from them. They clash with society because the values of their subculture are in conflict with the laws of the land. Once these youths have become involved in lawlessness, their problems snowball, making it more and more difficult for them to stay out of trouble.

After World War II, the most important advances in understanding the causes of delinquency emerged from studies of urban youth gangs. Collectively, these theoretical formulations are sometimes referred to as "Theory of the Reactive Subculture," though actually this is a group of theoretical constructs. They have in common the idea that misconduct is elicited in lower class boys who have internalized the middle class cultural values and objectives of educational, occupational, and materialistic success and are frustrated in their achievement. For example, Cohen (1958) advanced the theory that gangs develop a delinquent subculture, which represents solutions to the problems of some lower class males. A gang gives them a chance to belong, to amount to something, to develop their masculinity, and to fight middle class society. In particular, the delinquent subculture, according to Cohen, is an anomic response toward resolution of the status problems of working class boys.

The theoretical contribution of Richard Cloward and Lloyd Ohlin (1960), like Cohen's, is also a spinoff from Robert Merton's (1957) general theory of anomie as an explanation for deviant behavior. As was discussed in Chapter 6, Cloward and Ohlin, while agreeing with Merton and Cohen that the disunion between cultural goals and the inadequate means available for their achievement can create strain for lower class youths, argued that they still need to have the opportunity to break away from the dominant, middle class values and turn to illegitimate means to achieve status and self-esteem. In other words, Cloward and Ohlin's "Theory of Delinquency and Opportunity" postulated that every youth who feels deprived and disadvantaged does not turn to the same alterna-tive illegitimate avenues to success. Even delinquent opportunities may not be readily available in the frustrated youth's social environment. Moreover, not only does the quantity of delinquent opportunity vary from area to area and from neighborhood to neighborhood, but there is a quality differential as well. In recognition of that fact, Cloward and Ohlin suggested that there are three kinds of gang subcultures that can develop: the crime-oriented, the conflict-oriented, and the retreatist/drug-oriented. The type that emerges to satisfy the needs for group support and status among lower class youth depends upon the available opportunity for them in their local communities.

Walter Miller (1958) disagreed with Cohen and with Cloward and Ohlin that the gang is a reactive subculture whose delinquent behavior is a compensa-tion for lower class failure to reach middle class goals. Rather, Miller scrutinized lower class culture for values that could reflect in behavior identified as delinquent by the dominant, middle class society. Miller's study concluded that lower class culture is characterized by six "focal concerns" or values that could easily be interpreted as troublesome opposition to middle class values or a predisposition to delinquency. These lower class cultural values are **trouble, toughness, excitement, fate, smartness,** and **autonomy,** which, according to Miller, represent highly prized masculinity to lower class boys. Paradoxically, the youth's socialized allegiance to those values can produce delinquent behav-ior.

These sociological theories of gang delinquency offer many valuable in-sights into social class differences, culture conflict, and subcultural response, and suggest that gang delinquency is largely a lower class phenomenon and is clustered together with other social pathologies such as poverty, unstable family life, and inner-city slum neighborhoods.

As detailed in Chapter 6, the subcultural theories of juvenile delinquency are not without their critics. Some have contended that the entire concept of a subculture of juvenile delinquency is meaningless when compared with more powerful and permanent familial, ethnic/racial, and social class value systems impacting upon young people. David Matza (1964) argued that juvenile delin-quents, like all young people, spend only a limited amount of time with each other. They still go to their own homes, many attend school, some have jobs. There are prior and offsetting influences in place to counter the shared aliena-tion that is assumed to lead to the procriminal values of the gang. If juvenile delinquents did belong to a viable delinquent subculture, Matza argued, then those who are caught would not be embarrassed or remorseful, as they so often are. Do these youngsters really have a set of values of their own, or do they actually believe in those of their parents, teachers, and other more conforming authority figures with whom they are still in contact?

Travis Hirschi (1969) also has challenged the delinquent subculture theo-ries by pointing out that while frightening and highly publicized gang crimes do occasionally occur, most delinquency is committed with one or two companions. Hence, the small dyadic or triadic relationship and interaction is an inadequate base for the development of a subculture or a set of delinquent values. Hirschi further concluded that there is no evidence that delinquent companions and gang membership precede delinquency. Rather, an attitude and interest favorably inclined toward nonconformity will lead a youth to experimentation with delinquent behavior and association with like-minded peers.

Such criticisms as those have not undermined the popularity of the subcultural theories of gang delinquency. The works of Cohen, Cloward and Ohlin, Miller, and others, while imperfect, are still viewed as having considerable explanatory power regarding lower class juvenile gang delinquency. However, the failure of these subcultural theories to account for middle class group delinquency has led to new research and theoretical explanations within the past 15 years. In seeking the reasons why youths who have zealous role models, thorough socialization, and abundant opportunities—all conducive to achieving middle class values—become nonconforming and delinquent, attention has been focused on the youth culture argument. As we indicated in Chapter 8, youth itself can be perceived as an age-graded subculture, complete with its own shared attitudes, values, language, symbols, tastes in music, and styles of dress, sharpened and focused by marginal social status and separation from meaningful participation in the larger society. Thus, the youth subculture, functioning as a catalyst for the expression of collective alienation, is the dominant explanation of illegal behavior among the affluent and promising children of the middle class. In Chapter 8, we presented an in-depth discussion of the youth subculture as it relates to juvenile delinquency.

CONCEPT APPLICATION

"The Weapon of Choice"

During the summer of 1987, an outbreak of apparently unprovoked attacks by pit bull terriers across the United States received widespread coverage from news media. In Tampa, Florida, a 3-year-old girl required plastic surgery after being suddenly mauled by a pit bull in her neighborhood. A 2-year-old boy was killed by a pit bull in Santa Clara County (California). In Zachary, Louisiana, a woman was hospitalized in serious condition, her arm mangled by a pit bull. She had known the dog since it was a pup. And millions of American television viewers looked on in horror as they watched an animal control officer in Los Angeles being attacked by a pit bull she had been ordered to pick up because of an alleged attack the day before on a man and his daughter. One of the local news stations that was doing a story on pit bulls had sent a camera crew along with the animal control officer and captured the attack live on film. According to Paul Clancy (1987), since 1983 pit bull terriers have been blamed for 21 of 28 dog-attack deaths. During the first half of 1987, pit bulls were responsible for all six recorded deaths by dog attack.

The dissemination of information about the history, traditional use, physical endowments, and personality potential of the breed did little to alleviate public apprehension:

> 'These dogs can and do make good pets, but they also can be extremely dangerous,' says Sheyl Blair of the Tufts Center for Animals. 'They fight to the end and beyond.'
>
> A cross between bulldog and terrier, the pit bull goes back to early 19th century England where it was bred to fight in the ring (Clancy, 1987:2A).

As the storm of fear and anger toward the pit bull mounted, city council members in a score of communities moved to enact strict new ordinances to control potentially vicious dogs in general, and pit bull terriers in particular. Paradoxically, the negative publicity for the pit bull proved to be attractive to some people who admired the dog's tenacity, courage, and viciousness. In May of 1987, a man in Lawrence, Massachusetts, after being chased by a pit bull, collapsed and died of a heart attack. While the dog was locked up by the Society for the Prevention of Cruelty to Animals, six telephone calls were received from people who wanted to adopt the dog:

> 'That's frightening,' says shelter director Carter Luke. 'There are a lot of people out there who want the biggest gun, the sharpest knife, and baddest dog they can find. They're turned on by it' (Clancy, 1987:1A).

Much to the chagrin of responsible kennel operators and owners, who contend that the pit bull terrier can be a reliable family pet, some unprincipled breeders have chosen to capitalize on the aberrant demand for vicious pit bulls and have concentrated on those known bloodlines that produce the more aggressive and antisocial types. In the hands of an owner who derives some sense of gratification, importance, or power from owning such an animal, these particular dogs can be literally transformed into killers. ABC News (1987) has documented the appearance of pit bull dogs in the arsenals of inner-city street gangs. The gang members strut the dogs as status symbols, and also use them to intimidate crime victims:

> 'It's the macho thing to do,' says Elaine Newton of Philadelphia's SPCA . . .
> 'The kids are using them as potential weapons. If you can't get a handgun, get a pit bull. It [is] the one thing that makes them feel superior' (Clancy, 1987:1B).

The *Daily Oklahoman* (1987), an Oklahoma City newspaper, detailed the role of the pit bull terrier as a popular "weapon of choice" in many recent battles between rival gangs. Rather than directly attacking one another with knives and zip guns, opposing gangs set their dogs against each other in staged combats to the death. These pit bulls, bearing such names as Switchblade and Rambo, are well conditioned and ferocious. Just as in the traditional fights between rival gangs, the stakes can be high. Status and territory ("turf") can be won or lost by the gangs and their members, depending upon whose dogs emerge victorious. Unfortunately, losers may not live to fight again. Reports persist that those vanquished canine warriors that survive the crushing jaws of their opponents are often executed by being strangled by their disappointed owners.

* * * *

As a review of this chapter, what characteristics, motives, behaviors, and social/psychological needs of youthful gang members are exemplified in this short report on the "weapon of choice?"

CONCEPT INTEGRATION
QUESTIONS AND TOPICS FOR STUDY AND DISCUSSION

1. Imagine yourself as a youth living in a neighborhood contested by two rival street gangs. Would you join one of the gangs? Why or why not?
2. Although gangs are often thought of as having little redeeming value or positive function, can you think of any contributions that even a delinquent subculture can make to the social and psychological well-being of its members?
3. Diagram your own cultural and subcultural memberships and involvements. Be sure to include your social class, occupation (or major field of study in college), church affiliation, and racial/ethnic group (if appropriate). Next, discuss how membership in any of these subcultures can influence a person's values, attitudes, perceptions of what is right and wrong, and behavior.
4. Compare and contrast the locale, racial/ethnic composition, and delinquent behavior of lower and middle class youth gangs. How are gangs organized?
5. Based on your reading of this chapter, how do you explain the fact that even though there are serious violations of the law, middle class youths do not generally consider themselves as delinquent or in trouble with society? Why is this view shared by the adults in their environment?

6. Define and give examples of the following terms and concepts: Theory of Reactive Subculture, Theory of Differential Opportunity, lower class culture and focal concerns, the play group, gang, near group, dyad and triad, female auxiliary, high delinquency area, gang composition, deviant subculture, delinquent subculture, social network, and gang rape.

References

ABC News. 1987. The pit bull. *ABC News Report,* August 6.

Adler, F. 1975. *Sisters in crime.* New York: McGraw Hill Book Co.

Amir, M. 1971. *Patterns in forcible rape.* Chicago: University of Chicago Press.

Bartollas, C. 1985. *Juvenile delinquency.* New York: John Wiley.

Bernard, J. 1967. Teen-age culture: An overview. In E. W. Vaz (Ed.). *Middle-class juvenile delinquency.* New York: Harper & Row, pp. 23–38.

Block, H. & Niederhoffer, A. 1958. *The gang: A study in adolescent behavior.* New York: Philosophical Library.

Bowker, L. H., Gross, H.S., & Klein, M. W. 1980. Female participation in delinquent gang activities. *Adolescence* 15, 59 (Fall):509–519.

Bowker, L. H. & Klein, M. W. 1983. The etiology of female juvenile delinquency and gang membership: A test of psychological and social structural explanations. *Adolescence* 18, 72 (Winter):739–751.

Blum, R. 1987. Contemporary threats to adolescent health in the United States. *Journal of the American Medical Association* 257 (June):3390–3395.

Bradley, E. 1981. CBS reports: Murder, teenage style. Sept. 4, 1981.

Brunner, R. 1974. Focal points of juvenile crime: Typology and conditions. *Juvenile crime and resocialization.* Congress Report, 1974. Stuttgart, W. Germany: New York: Springer Verlag.

Burt, C. 1925. *The young delinquent.* New York: Appleton.

Campbell, A. 1984. *The girls in the gang.* New York: Basil Blackwell.

Canter, R. J. 1982. Sex differentials in self-reported delinquency. *Criminology* 20 (November):373–393.

Cavan, R. S. & Ferdinand, T. N. 1981. *Juvenile delinquency* (4th ed.). New York: Harper & Row.

CBS News Report. 1986. *CBS News Report,* September 11, 1986.

Clancy, P. 1987. Pit bulls—Best friend or time bomb? *USA Today* August 10:1A;2A.

Cloward, R. A. & Ohlin, L. 1960. *Delinquency and opportunity.* New York: Free Press.

Cohen, A. 1958. *Delinquent boys: The culture of the gang.* New York: Free Press.

Coleman, J. S. 1970. *The circle.* Ludlow, MA: Pro Litho.

CNN News. 1986. *CNN News Broadcast,* September 18, 1986.

Daily Oklahoman, 1984. Oklahoma City, OK, September 15, 1984:32.

Daily Oklahoman, 1987. Gangs using pit bulls. September 6:2.

Daily Tidings, Ashland, OR, June 5, 1985:5.

Davis, C. 1988. Probation officer says gangs operate nationwide. *The Sunday Oklahoman.* Section A, page 18—May 1, 1988.

Davis, J. R. 1978. Neighborhood nonsense: The street war. *Terrorists—Youth, biker and prison violence.* San Diego, CA: Grossmont Press.

Empey, L. T. 1982. *American delinquency: Its meaning and construction* (rev. ed.). Homewood, IL: Dorsey Press.

Erickson, M. & Jensen, G. 1977. Delinquency is still group behavior: Toward revitalizing the group premise in the sociology of deviance. *Journal of Criminal Law and Criminology* 68, 2 (June):262–263.

Erlanger, H. S. 1979. Estrangement, machismo, and gang violence. *Social Science Quarterly* 60 (September):235–248.

Funk and Wagnalls New Standard Dictionary of the English Language. 1975. New York: Funk and Wagnalls Company.

Gillespie, R. 1978. Economic factors in crime and delinquency: A critical review of the empirical evidence. Hearings, Subcommittee on Crime of the Committee of the Judiciary, House of Representatives, 95th Congress, Serial 47. Washington, DC: U.S. Government Printing Office, pp. 601–625.

Goffman, E. 1963. *Stigma: Notes on the management of spoiled identity.* Englewood Cliffs, NJ: Prentice-Hall.

Groth, A. & Birnbaum, H. J. 1979. *Men who rape: The psychology of the offender.* New York: Plenum.

Halvorsen, R. & Hawley, D. 1973. *From gangs to God.* Washington, DC: Review and Herald Publishing.

Hardman, D. G. 1969. Small town gangs. *Journal of Criminal Law, Criminology and Police Science* 60, 2 (June):173–181.

Hindelang, M. J. 1976. With a little help from their friends. *British Journal of Criminology* 11, 2 (April):109–125.

Hirschi, T. 1969. *Causes of delinquency.* Berkeley, CA: University of California Press.

Inciardi, J. 1978. *Reflections on crime: An introduction to criminology and criminal justice.* New York: Holt, Rinehart and Winston.

Johnstone, J. W. C. 1981. Youth gangs and black suburbs. *Pacific Sociological Review* 24 (July):355–375.

Keiser, R. 1969. *The vice lords.* New York: Holt, Rinehart and Winston.

Klein, M. 1964. Internal structures and age distributions in four delinquent Negro gangs. Paper presented at the annual meeting of the California State Psychological Association, Los Angeles. Youth Studies Center, University of Southern California (mimeo).

1971. *Street gangs and street workers.* Englewood Cliffs, NJ: Prentice-Hall.

Klein, M. & Crawford, L. 1968. Groups, gangs, and cohesiveness. In J. F. Short (Ed.). *Gang Delinquency and Delinquent Subcultures.* New York: Harper & Row, pp. 256–272.

Kobrin, J. P. & Peluso, E. 1968. Criteria of status among street gangs. In J. F. Short (Ed.). *Gang Delinquency and Delinquent Subcultures.* New York: Harper & Row, 178–208.

Lerman, P. 1967. Gangs, networks, and subcultural delinquency. *American Journal of Sociology* 63:63–71.

Lotz, R., Poole, E. D., & Regoli, R. M. 1985. *Juvenile delinquency and juvenile justice.* New York: Random House.

Matza, D. 1964. *Delinquency and drift.* New York: John Wiley.

Merton, R. K. 1957. *Social theory and social structure* (2nd ed.). New York: Free Press.

Miller, W. B. 1958. Lower class culture as a generating milieu of gang delinquency. *Journal of Social Issues* 14 (Summer):5–19.

1966. Violent crimes in city gangs. *Annals of the American Academy of Political and Social Science* 64 (March):97–112.

1975. *Violence by youth gangs and youth groups as a crime problem in major American cities.* Washington, DC: U.S. Government Printing Office.

1981. American youth gangs. In A. S. Blumbert (Ed.). *Current perspectives on criminal behavior.* New York: Knopf, pp. 291–320.

Moore, J. W. 1985. Isolation and stigmatization in the development of an underclass: The case of Chicano gangs in East Los Angeles. *Social Problems* 33, 1 (October):1–12.

Morganthau, T. 1982. Vietnamese gangs in California. *Newsweek* 100 (August 2):22.

Muehlbauer, G. & Dodder, L. 1983. *The losers: Gang delinquency in an American suburb.* New York: Praeger.

Myerhoff, H., & Myerhoff, B. 1964. Field observations of middle-class gangs. *Social Forces* 42 (March):328–336.

New York Times. 1984. *New York Times* June 6:15.

Nightline—American Broadcasting Company. 1988. April 15, 1988.

Park, R. 1927. Preface to Frederick Thrasher's *The gang.* Chicago: University of Chicago Press.

Ritzer, G. 1986. *Social problems* (2nd ed.). (Originally published as *Social Problems* by Rodney Stark in 1975). New York: Random House.

Sagarin, E. 1975. *Deviants and deviance: An introduction to the study of disvalued people and behavior.* New York: Praeger.

Salisbury, H. 1958. The suburbs. *The shook-up generation.* New York: Harper & Row.

Sarnecki, J. 1982. *Criminality and peer relations: Study of juvenile delinquency in a Swedish commune.* Stockholm, Sweden: Brottsforebyggande Radet.

1983. *Criminal juvenile gangs.* Stockholm, Sweden: Brottsforebyggande Radet.

Shaw, C. & McKay, H. 1931. Social factors in juvenile delinquency. In *Report on the Causes of Crime*. National Commission on Law Observance and Enforcement, Report No. 13. Washington, DC: U.S. Government Printing Office.

1942. *Juvenile delinquency in urban areas*. Chicago: University of Chicago Press.

1969. *Juvenile delinquency and urban areas* (rev. ed.). Chicago: University of Chicago Press.

Short, J. F. (Ed.). 1968. *Gang delinquency and delinquent subculture*. New York: Harper & Row.

1987. Exploring integration of the theoretical levels of explanation: Notes on juvenile delinquency. In *Theoretical integration in the study of deviance and crime: Problems and prospects*. Albany, NY: Unpublished proceedings of the Albany Conference, May 7–8.

Short, J. F. & Strodtbeck, F. L. 1965. *Group process and gang delinquency*. Chicago: University of Chicago Press.

Steffensmeier, D. J. & Steffensmeier, R. 1980. Trends in female delinquency: An examination of arrest, juvenile court, self-report, and field data. *Criminology* 18, 1 (May):62–85.

Subcommittee on Juvenile Justice. 1983. *Gang violence and control*. Hearings before the Subcommittee on Juvenile Justice of the Committee on the Judiciary. United States Senate, Ninety-Eighth Congress, First Session on Gang Violence and Control in the Los Angeles and San Francisco Areas with a View to What Might be Done by the Federal Government (Westwood, California, February 7, 1983 and San Francisco, CA, February 9, 1983).

Sunday Oklahoman. Police prepare weekend assault on gangs. 1988. Section A, page 1. April 17, 1988.

Sutherland, E. 1939. *Principles of criminology*. Philadelphia: JB Lippincott.

Thio, A. 1983. *Deviant behavior* (2nd ed.). New York: Harper & Row.

Thrasher, F. M. 1927. *The gang*. Chicago: University of Chicago Press.

1936. *The gang* (2nd ed.). Chicago: University of Chicago Press.

Time. 1977. The youth crime plague. *Time* 110, 2 (July 11, 1977):18–28.

Toplin, R. B. 1975. *Unchallenged violence: An American ordeal*. Westport, CT: Greenhaven Press.

Vaz, E. W. (Ed.). 1967. *Middle-class juvenile delinquency*. New York: Harper & Row.

Werthman, C. & Piliavin, I. 1967. Gang members and the police. In D. J. Bordua (Ed.). *The police*. New York: John Wiley, pp. 56–98.

Yablonsky, L. 1959. The delinquent gang as a near group. *Social Problems* 7, 2 (Fall):108–117.

1970. *The violent gang (Revised Edition)*. Baltimore: Penguin Books, Inc.

Zastrow, C. & Bowker, L. 1984. *Social problems: Issues and solutions*. Chicago: Nelson-Hall.

Part IV
Confrontation: Society and the Juvenile Delinquent

Introduction: The Concept of Social Arena

In Part III we explored juvenile delinquency within the context of collective behavior and focused our analysis upon specific types of social groupings in which juveniles participate. In Part IV we move beyond the social group to a much larger **social arena** in which juveniles find themselves. Within the context of the family, the youth subculture, and the juvenile gang, while delinquents may face minor confrontations, they are likely to be surrounded by other individuals who share very similar values, attitudes, beliefs, and normative expectations. Since those social groupings are informal social structures, sanctions for nonconformity are also likely to be informal. Further, as discussed in Chapters 8 and 9, it may be a youth's nonconformity to some of society's norms which enhances status within the youth subculture and/or the juvenile gang.

When youths venture beyond the social domain of friends, family, and other juveniles into the larger social world of school, streets and sidewalks, and, potentially, the juvenile court, they confront a more complex set of social institutions in which their nonconformity to social norms is quite likely to be formally sanctioned. We have chosen the concept of **social arena** carefully in order to illustrate the confrontation experienced when juvenile delinquents "collide" head-on with the larger social world which surrounds them. An **arena** is *a public place where individuals or groups are pitted against each other in struggles to determine dominance and often survival.* The schools, streets, and sidewalks represent the social arenas in which juveniles are most likely to come into direct confrontation with adult authority figures who represent and enforce values, attitudes, beliefs, and norms which may conflict with those experienced in the informal settings of family and juvenile peers. As youths struggle for meaningful statuses and roles and a sense of identity in the larger society, adversarial relationships may develop with teachers, school officials, merchants, police, and other adults which may result in the violation of a variety of formal social norms ranging all the way from truancy to murder. These encounters in school and on the streets may lead to youths ultimately coming into direct confrontation with the judicial system in the arena of the juvenile court.

In Part IV we explore these social arenas in order to provide a sociological analysis of the processes which occur within them, and their contributions to the understanding of juvenile delinquency. In Chapter 10, we develop the concept of the school as a social arena, and emphasize its role as a major agent of socialization transmitting the dominant attitudes, values, and beliefs of society to American youths. We explore how the school acts as a "screening device" in distributing academic credentials, and how, in some situations, it becomes a "combat zone" for those who socially interact there. We look at the relationships between schooling and delinquency, and conclude the chapter by exploring ways in which schools might become more actively involved in delinquency prevention.

Chapter 11 focuses upon juveniles' activities in the social arena of the streets and sidewalks. This chapter looks at youths' encounters with merchants, street people, police, and other adults, and how these encounters relate to juvenile delinquency. The social problems of runaways and juvenile prostitution as specific forms of delinquency are addressed from a sociological perspective.

In Chapter 12 we examine the juvenile court. The historical background which set the stage for development of the juvenile court is described with emphasis upon the Child Savers movement which dominated social philosophy toward juveniles in the late 1800s. Juvenile court procedures are described with a focus on the issue of due process in the juvenile justice system. Some of the major criticisms leveled at the juvenile court are summarized, with suggestions for reforming the juvenile court of the future.

As you read these chapters, we urge you to keep in mind the sociological framework, concepts, terms, and knowledge which have been developed through your reading of the first nine chapters.

Chapter 10

The Public Arena:
The Schools

The reading of this chapter will help you achieve the following objectives:

1. Describe and explain the role of the school as an agent of socialization in our society.
2. Identify ways in which the schools act as a "screening device" helping to channel students into future failure or success.
3. List ways in which the schools have become a "combat zone" or arena of confrontation between many students and their teachers and school administrators.
4. Describe how the bureaucratic structure of our schools has helped create and perpetuate juvenile delinquency.
5. Identify specific ways in which the schools can become actively involved in delinquency prevention.

INTRODUCTION

Education is one of the basic social institutions and is largely responsible for the transmission of culture, including values and norms, to the members of society. Because of this important socialization function, our society requires that every child attend school for a specified period of time. It follows that virtually every American has an early experience in elementary and secondary school. However, the quality and extent of that educational experience varies among our young people.

Most American children make a relatively quick and easy transition and adjustment as they move from home to school if the significant adults in these social environments share common values and norms. However, a large and significant number of young people arrive at school painfully aware of the differences between their socioeconomic status and that of their classmates and teachers. They soon learn that teachers and administrators have the authority and responsibility to teach and enforce standards of conduct that are difficult for them to understand and accept. Thus, the school may become an arena of conflict and confrontation for many youths as they develop delinquent patterns of behavior.

THE SCHOOL AS AN ARENA

As mentioned in the introduction to Part IV, an **arena** is *a public place where individuals or groups are pitted against each other in struggles to determine dominance and often survival.* According to ethologist Robert Ardrey (1966), **arena behavior** is a *struggle for both status and for territory* and is common in most animal species, including humans. Thus, examples of arena behavior include the battles between male elk during the mating season, ancient gladiator contests, many of our athletic events, and such collective violence as fights between rival street gangs and wars between nations. In the context of our study of juvenile delinquency, the public schools often become the arena where delinquent youths first encounter a society that opposes and resists their behavior.

SCHOOLS AND THE SOCIALIZATION PROCESS

The school is usually the first social institution beyond the family to be entrusted as a major agent of socialization. Basically, the school's responsibilities in regard to socialization are twofold: the transmission of cognitive skills, and the transmission of normative culture.

In contemporary America, the teaching of basic cognitive skills has become almost the exclusive domain of the schools. While a great deal of controversy may surround *how* the cognitive skills should be taught, there is virtually unanimous agreement that they *should* be taught. The teaching of the 3 Rs (readin', 'ritin', and 'rithmetic) as well as other basic skills is clearly the primary responsibility of the schools.

The role of the school in the transmission of normative culture is not nearly so clearcut, however. The teaching of normative culture involves the transmission of values, norms, attitudes, and beliefs. According to Emile Durkheim ([1906] 1956:71–72):

> [Education] consists of a methodological socialization of the younger generation . . . It is the influence exercised by adult generations on those that are not ready for social life. Its object is to arouse and to develop in the child a certain number of physical, intellectual, and moral states that are demanded of him by the political society as a whole and for the special milieu for which he is specifically destined . . . From the egoistic and asocial being that has just been born, [society] must, as rapidly as possible, add another, capable of leading a moral and social life.

Two basic questions arise in regard to the school's attempt to promote the internalization of cultural attitudes, values, and beliefs. First, which specific attitudes, values, and beliefs will be taught? Second, how does the school go about teaching them?

America is an extremely diverse, culturally pluralistic society composed of many ethnic, religious, economic, and social class subgroups. These various subcultural groups in our society view life from a wide spectrum of value perspectives. Since compulsory attendance laws require that virtually every child attend school for a specified period of time, the widest possible range of cultural values is represented among the student population as they enter school. On the other hand, the school officials who are charged with the socialization task are typically a much less culturally diverse group. For example, teachers tend to come from white, middle class, Protestant backgrounds. Numerous studies have indicated a strong bias favoring middle class values in our public schools (e.g., Cicourel, 1968; Jencks et al., 1972). The vastly divergent backgrounds of students in contrast to the predominantly middle class experience of their teachers can lay the groundwork for unfortunate social confrontations and nonproductive learning situations.

In a study of Chicago public schools, Howard Becker (1952) documented teachers' preferences for white middle class children. In a much more shocking exposé, in his book *Death at an Early Age* (1967), Jonathan Kozol described the cynicism, prejudice, and outright racism he saw lower class black students subjected to by white, middle class teachers in the Boston public schools. Aaron Cicourel (1968) argued that misbehavior, especially delinquent acts, from lower class youths elicited more severe responses from teachers and school administrators than the same behavior from middle and upper class youths. He indicated that school officials tended to view delinquency on the part of students of middle and higher socioeconomic status as out of character and only situational.

Later studies noted similar findings that students from middle class family backgrounds were more likely to have internalized the values of competitiveness, politeness, and deferred gratification which are more likely to lead to success in the public school experience (e.g. Jencks et al., 1971; Braun, 1976). Carl Braun (1976), for example, found that teachers' expectations were importantly influenced by noncognitive variables such as physical attractiveness, socioeconomic status, race, gender, name, and older siblings. His research indicated that teachers expected lower achievement from students who belonged to minority groups, came from economically disadvantaged homes, were physically unattractive, had unusual or unattractive names, or had older brothers or sisters who had been unsuccessful in their school experience. Undeniably, a student's family background (especially socioeconomic status) has been linked to educational aspirations (Jencks, 1971; Hurn, 1978), and educational aspirations appear highly related to educational achievement and success in school (Hurn, 1978).

As mentioned in Chapter 7, family background provides an important

Research indicates that teachers and administrators are likely to reward the conformity to middle class norms and values expressed by these class officers in a California junior high school and overlook minor rule violations without labeling them as delinquent.

prelude for a successful or unsuccessful school experience. Duane Alwin and Arland Thornton (1984) found that a family's socioeconomic status was significantly related to academic success during both early childhood and late adolescence.

JUVENILE DELINQUENCY AND THE SCHOOL EXPERIENCE

Thus far, our discussion has focused on the attempt to socialize students to the dominant value system in America and how that relates to a successful school experience. This takes on additional meaning for understanding delinquency when we further view the relationship between the school experience and the process of becoming a juvenile delinquent. In this regard, the value conflict and interactionist approaches in sociology may provide valuable insight. As pointed out in the Societal Response definition of delinquency (Chapter 2), in order for juvenile delinquency to take place, a social audience must react to an actor and an act, and make an evaluation of them in regard to social appropriateness. As further developed by the Labeling Approach, some group must react to the juvenile's behavior and apply the negative label of "delinquent" to it if the juvenile is going to be considered a juvenile delinquent by society. As pointed out by the value-conflict approach, the variable of social power becomes relevant if there is disagreement over the appropriateness of the act. Individuals, groups, and/or social agencies with the power and authority to label juvenile behavior as wrong and place the label "delinquent" on juveniles in such a way that it becomes a part of their identity are critical in creating the "juvenile delinquent." The schools have that power in our society.

Harry Gracey (1977) described how from their first day of school, children are subjected to authoritarian adults who arbitrarily judge students' behavior as "right" or "wrong" and label students as "good" or "bad" based on those judgments. Referring to kindergarten as "academic boot camp," Gracey contended that the primary purpose of kindergarten is not so much the preparation for the academic experience to come in future grades (as contended by most teachers and administrators), as it is to dramatically socialize children into fitting into the bureaucratic structure of the school system. Gracey (1977:217) stated:

> The unique job of the kindergarten in the education division of labor seems rather to be teaching children the student role. The student role is the repertoire of behavior and attitudes regarded by educators as appropriate to children in school.

Gracey found that learning classroom routines and submitting to rules and authority are the main elements of the student role. To a large extent, successfully fulfilling the student role means "doing what you're told and never mind why" (Gracey, 1977:225). Hence, those students who are most obedient, whose personal values either agree with the teacher's or have been successfully subjugated to the teacher's, are most likely to be labeled "good students" and have a successful school experience.

In his book *Creating School Failure, Youth Crime and Deviance*, Delos Kelly (1982) further developed this idea and specifically illustrated how the school's initial labeling has lasting impact on the child's entire educational career. Those students who disobey, question authority, refuse to suppress their own values (values gained from early childhood socialization in the family) are more likely to be labeled "bad students" and be unsuccessful in school. Ironically, this early application of the label "delinquent" (or "predelinquent" as it is often used for younger children) may encompass the students who are at both ends of the intellectual continuum. In other words, the students with the least academic potential, along with the most intellectually curious and innovative students, may be the most likely to violate normative expectations of teachers, and end up labeled as "problem students." According to the Labeling Approach (Chapter 6), this negative label tends to impact upon the juvenile's self-concept and may very well influence future behavior which culminates in the **self-fulfilling prophecy.** Students who are labeled early in their educational career as "dumb," "slow," "mean," or "troublemaker," may very well engage in the types of behavior which are expected to accompany those student roles. Conversely, students labeled as "bright," "advanced," "polite," and "obedient" are likely to conform to the positive expectations entailed in those roles. A possible example of this may be revealed in the findings that participation in school athletics serves as an insulator against delinquency for some students (e.g., Hastad et al., 1984; Segrave and Hastad, 1984).

Of course, not all negative labels are initiated at school. Parents, neighbors, police, and juvenile courts may also judge certain children to be more problematic than others. Consequently, negative labels and poor self-concepts can be brought from outside the school. In fact, Allen Liska and Mark Reed (1985) contended that their studies suggested that parents, not the schools, were the major institutional sources of delinquency control. They found that ". . . for most adolescents in high school, the good opinion of teachers and school administrators may be considerably less important than that of their parents" (Liska and Reed, 1985:558). The extent to which these factors affect the educational process is not clearly understood, but there is some evidence that they may negatively impact upon the school experience. For example, Kelly (1977) showed that juvenile delinquents, or at least those who had been officially identified by the legal system, were at a significant disadvantage in the classroom.

SCHOOLS AS A "SCREENING DEVICE"

One of the important functions of the educational institution in our society is to acknowledge academic performance and intellectual development through the awarding of academic credentials. In this sense, the school is designed to serve as a "screening device." Ideally, everybody in our society is supposed to be provided an equal opportunity in terms of access to our educational system. This supposition is, of course, highly questionable, since we know that individuals have been denied equal access to education on the basis of race, ethnic background, and other social variables. Nevertheless, it has become widely acclaimed in our society that the opportunity for education is a right, and not a privilege. Though everybody is supposedly given equal access to the academic credentials offered by our educational system, it never has been expected that everybody would attain them equally. As Peter and Brigitte Berger (1975:188) indicated, "Since the educational system contains an endless series of hurdles, it is important that not all should succeed in it; it is predetermined that some (indeed, many) should fail to reach the top." Those who have the most potential, work the hardest, and learn the most, are viewed as having legitimately earned higher academic recognition than the rest. We logically conclude that our high school graduates are smarter and more diligent than those who dropped out, but not as smart and diligent as those who have earned college degrees. Likewise, Bachelor's degrees signify something different from Master's degrees, and Master's degrees something different from Doctoral degrees. The assumption is that virtually everybody aspires to the highest level of academic certification (a highly questionable assumption), but the schools effectively "screen out" those who are not qualified, so that only the most "deserving" attain the highest credentials (an even more questionable assumption). These academic credentials, in turn, are then used in a variety of ways which affect occupation, income, housing, and virtually all components of lifestyle and social status.

As discussed in the previous section, however, the basis for this "screening device" very well may be variables other than intelligence, diligence, and academic performance. Edgar Friedenberg (1959) made a strong case that academic credentials do not certify ability, but the acceptance of larger society's dominant values and norms. Friedenberg contended that academic credentials, more than intelligence and academic performance, serve to signify an individual's willingness to endure the rules. In this sense, he argued that schools tend to preserve the status quo by guaranteeing that those who fail in school also fail in society. From this perspective, it is no wonder that failure in school and juvenile delinquency are closely related.

Mark Colvin and John Pauly (1983) elaborated upon the relationship between family background, school failure, and juvenile delinquency. They pointed out that a child's family's socioeconomic status has been linked to school "tracking," which to a large extent determines a student's immediate peer group. **Tracking** refers to *an educational strategy in which students considered to be roughly equivalent in intelligence, based upon standardized tests, previous academic performance, and other criteria, are placed in the same classroom*. Students in a particular "track" often also resemble each other in a variety of ways other than academic abilities. Sometimes, students who have reputations as "behavioral problems" may be placed in the same class, and placed under the supervisign of a teacher with the reputation of being a strict disciplinarian. Colvin and Pauly indicated that the initial bond to the school is developed at home by the family, but may be reinforced or weakened by the immediate peer group at school. If placed in a social setting in the school where a student is surrounded by delinquent peers, "this type of association continues the pattern of reinforcement toward more sustained delinquent behavior" (Colvin and Pauly, 1983:543).

As we discussed in Chapter 8, "The Youth Subculture," a variety of social cliques tend to form in the school environment. J. Milton Yinger (1982:274) pointed out that the "standard high school subcultures, with their emphasis on sports, fun, and a modicum of learning, are quite different in sociological meaning from groups oriented to truancy, petty theft, masculine hyperaggressiveness, and gang combat." To a large extent, Yinger attributed the youth's fear of failure as part of the motivation to join deviant groups.

In large part, a youth's status and social identity are directly connected to school performance. Carl Werthman (1976) compared the identity needs and materials available to adults and to youths. In our society, adult status and identity are typically gained through occupations and affluence. Young males (especially from lower classes), without access to the materials with which to build male identity and social status, will use whatever materials are available in their environment. They may assert their autonomy by fighting with other students or rejecting the rules and authority of the school. The adult authority figures and the normative structure of the school offer a situation of confrontation and risk in which the youth can gain a measure of identity and status from peers. On the other hand, the aggressive, rebellious stance is interpreted by school officials as a predisposition to delinquency and the stage is set for a confrontation and struggle.

Walter Schafer and Kenneth Polk (1976) reported another possible dimension of the school's role in projecting youth into delinquent behavior. They pointed out that educators often perceive a correlation between educational deficiencies and behavior problems and therefore categorically define some youngsters as "stupid" or "bad." As these children become aware of this negative evaluation, their alienation is deepened and they increase their truancy and other forms of delinquency. The possible link between low intelligence and/or learning disabilities and juvenile delinquency is unclear. The hypothesis that "academic competence is linked to delinquency by way of success in and attachment to the school" (Hirschi, 1969:115) has been very popular. Travis Hirschi and Michael Hindelang (1977) contended that IQ is an important but frequently ignored variable in juvenile delinquency. Margaret Farnworth and her associates (1985) indeed found that intervention prior to school entry that improves academic potential and future school performance for children categorized as "high risk" for school failure, may in fact reduce the likelihood of delinquency. However, they contended that the impact of the preschool intervention was independent of IQ scores.

Joel Zaba, an optometrist in Norfolk, Virginia, contended that numerous studies over the past 25 years have linked learning disabilities and juvenile delinquency (UPI Washington, 1979). Zaba indicated that a child who experiences problems in the classroom develops a negative self-concept, and "a very possible consequence of the situation is anti-social behavior, leading to juvenile delinquency" (UPI Washington, 1979). Zaba went further to contend that many of the learning problems could actually be attributed to poor vision, and, if they were corrected early, delinquency could be prevented.

Much of the apparent link between low IQ, learning disabilities, poor school performance, and juvenile delinquency has been seriously challenged. For instance, Bruce Lane (1980) reviewed the research examining the connection between juvenile delinquency and learning disabilities, and explained that no clear relationship has been established between the two. A study of 12 to 15-year-old boys, separated into groups of learning disabled and nonlearning disabled, indicated no more delinquency on the part of the learning disabled than the others (Broder et al., 1981). Interestingly, however, Paul Broder and his associates (1981) found that the learning disabled group members were more likely to be adjudicated delinquent by juvenile courts. Scott Menard and Barbara Morse (1984) reported similar findings. They argued that the IQ-delinquency hypothesis lacks empirical support and adds nothing to delinquency theory. They indicated that the correlation of IQ with delinquency is not because IQ exerts a causal influence on delinquent behavior, but because, in the schools, it may be selected as the criterion for differential treatment. Another study found that while learning disabled and nonlearning disabled students engage in essentially the same behaviors, learning disabled children are treated differently and are more likely to be considered delinquent (Keilitz et al., 1979).

Delbert Elliott (1966) expanded on the problems experienced by some youngsters at school and the alternative responses open to them. Elliott presented some interesting data and hypotheses regarding the variable rates of delinquency for boys from different socioeconomic neighborhoods who dropped out of school. His study showed that while in school, lower class boys had higher rates of delinquency. Interestingly, however, after lower class boys dropped out of school and took a job, their delinquency rates dropped dramatically. Later, in a very influential study, empirical evidence indicated that—consistent with Strain theories—when lower class boys dropped out of school, their delinquency rates decreased (Elliott and Voss, 1974). Colvin and Pauly (1983) provided additional insight into why this may occur. While in school, these boys experienced a great deal of failure. Failure in school may have made these boys "more receptive to the influence of delinquent groups in which they learn specific attitudes, motives, and skills to produce patterned delinquent behavior" (Colvin and Pauly, 1983:524). Out of school, these lower class boys moved into a setting where they could experience some success. Terence Thornberry and his associates (1985) questioned the methodology of these studies, however, and by using longitudinal data from a Philadelphia sample they determined that dropping out of school was positively related to delinquency and later crime over both the short and the long term. Their study indicated more support for the Social Control Theory approach, in that the severing of the social bond with the school apparently resulted in increased delinquency.

J. David Hawkins and Denise Lishner (1987) developed a theoretical model which illustrates how the aforementioned school experiences may be related to juvenile delinquency (see Figure 10-1).

The series of arrows in Figure 10-1 show how each of the school-related risk factors is directly and indirectly linked to juvenile delinquency among males. The figure also illustrates both direct and indirect interrelationships among the variables. Finally, the model depicts how these risk factors are also related to dropping out of school. It is important to note that there is no direct relationship indicated between dropping out of school and increased juvenile delinquency among males. Rather, consistent with the research of Elliott (1966) and Elliott and Voss (1974), the model suggests that both delinquency and dropping out are the result of similar negative school experiences. This supports

---

FIGURE 10-1

School-Related Risk Factors for Individual Delinquency Among Males

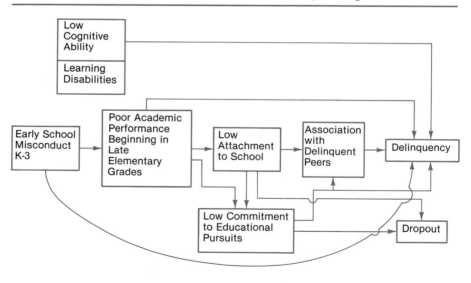

Source: J. David Hawkins and Denise M. Lishner. "Schooling and Delinquency." Pp. 179–221 in Elmer H. Johnson (Ed.), *Handbook on Crime and Delinquency Prevention*. Westport, Connecticut: Greenwood Press, 1987:185. Reprinted with permission.

the ". . . contention that school experiences themselves are factors in delinquent behavior, which, when removed, no longer contribute to [delinquency]" (Hawkins and Lishner, 1987:186).

One form of delinquency which grows directly from problems in school is that of truancy. Students who are having difficulty in school are most likely to be truant. As Jacob Getzels (1977:74) put it:

> What can be more tormenting than to be confronted day after day with a situation in which the language, and value codes seem different in inexplicable ways from those to which you are accustomed—and more a situation in which you cannot succeed and from which you are not permitted to escape without threat of severe punishment?

Truancy has become such a problem in some districts that administrators are actually willing to pay students to attend school. For example, at Memorial Junior High in San Diego, the school truancy rate was so high that the school began to pay students 25 cents a day to attend school (Tedrick, 1980:7). The special problem of truancy and what some school districts are doing to deal with it is further explored in the Concept Application at the end of this chapter.

One of the ways that schools act as a "screening device" is to (perhaps unintentionally) drive away those students who cannot succeed there. As these students grow more frustrated they are much more likely to skip school. Gayle Zieman and Gerald Benson (1980) interviewed junior high school boys who had histories of truancy, and found that they perceived the school as a place of discomfort associated with confrontations and lack of success. Most states have a compulsory attendance law up to a certain age (usually 16) and students below the legal age for dropping out are delinquent by virtue of their truancy.

Beyond the simple act of truancy making the juvenile a delinquent, the juvenile is also likely to get into other kinds of trouble while wandering the streets when school is in session (this subject is further pursued in Chapter 11). While this may not necessarily be the case when older students drop out to take fulltime jobs, as Elliott (1966) indicated, it is highly probable that younger students who skip school periodically, to frequent pool halls, video arcades, or simply roam the streets, are very likely to get involved in other forms of delinquency beyond their truancy. By virtue of being on the streets during school hours, the juvenile is highly visible to police and may very likely be routinely picked up, questioned, and possibly searched. In these cases, the general behavior of the youth which earned a reputation or label of being "smart aleck," "out of control," and "bad" at school is also likely to compound potential problems with the police. As Irving Piliavin and Scott Briar (1964) pointed out, the overall demeanor of juveniles as perceived by the police becomes one of the most significant variables in determining how the police handle the case.

SCHOOLS AS A "COMBAT ZONE"

Failing, truancy, and dropping out are only some of the responses available to students who cannot succeed in the school system. Another way they can respond to the value conflict, frustration, and damage to self-concept that they experience is to fight back. As William Glasser (1978) pointed out, students who cannot cope with an unsuccessful school experience feel faced with essentially two options: drop out, or go to school and cause trouble. Compulsory attendance laws can limit those options to the latter.

One of the prominent psychological explanations of human violence which was developed in the 1930's is the Frustration-Aggression Hypothesis. According to John Dollard and his colleagues (1939), frustration arises when an individual is unable to reach some desired goal. This frustration is then vented in the form of aggressive behavior. While there is much disagreement over the causal link between frustration and aggression today (especially over the early assumption that frustration *must* lead to aggression), it is generally agreed that frustration certainly *can* lead to aggression. Likewise, as presented in Chapter 6, Merton's Anomie Theory contends that juveniles who cannot pursue culturally prescribed goals through socially approved means become frustrated and often pursue a deviant adaptation strategy to the situation. Given this, it is not totally unexpected that when students find themselves at odds with the school system, are negatively labeled, and cannot achieve success through the approved standards, they will become frustrated. That frustration may be relieved by dropping out (if they are allowed to), or it may be vented through wreaking havoc on the school, teachers, and other students.

Juveniles sometimes strike back at the schools with violence and destruction. William Sanders (1976) reported that schools are the most common target of juvenile vandalism. He called this **malevolent vandalism**—*"activity in which property is destroyed out of malevolent motives on the part of the perpetrators"* (Sanders, 1976:101). The school becomes the target of violence because of the juveniles' contempt for the institution. Paul Chance (1984) indicated that vandalism is primarily a result of not liking school and feeling disliked by teachers and administrators. Estimates of the total annual costs of school vandalism in the United States range between $100 million to $600 million (cited in Neill, 1978:305). Vandalism is a property offense and generally not considered to be a violent act. But in this situation we are not referring to the petty types of vandalism which routinely occur at most schools, such as seniors spray painting the year of their graduating class on the sign in front of the building. Although even those types of acts can be costly, they are primarily engaged in for fun and mischief. Rather, we are referring to outright attacks on school property. Ruth Cavan (1962:147) provided an example of this type of vandalism:

Over the Memorial Day weekend, 1960, 25 Chicago schools received an estimated $50,000 worth of damage. Classrooms and offices were ransacked, a fire was set in the principal's office, windows were broken, and ink was splashed on walls and used to make crude drawings or write obscene phrases; . . . Many schools not entered had windows broken from the outside.

Vandalism is apparently one of the ways in which youths who are angry at the schools manifest their contempt for the system. James Truckenmiller (1982) identified students' perceived lack of access to educational success as one of the variables most predictive of vandalism. School districts are acutely aware of the problems associated with school vandalism, and many have taken steps to create programs in an effort to reduce it. G. Ray Mayer et al. (1983) reported the results of a 3-year study of 20 schools from 12 school districts which had tested strategies for reducing vandalism. The results showed that educators could take positive steps to reduce vandalism and other forms of inappropriate student behavior. Patricia Stagliano and Irwin Hyman (1983) also studied the efforts of school districts to reduce school vandalism and found that techniques

The school often becomes the target of both petty and malevolent vandalism as disenchanted and alienated youths strike out at a symbol of adult society.

such as implementing student conduct codes, student-teacher-community task forces, community training, and legislation requiring the monitoring of school vandalism had all met with at least some success.

Vandalism is not the only form that violence takes in the schools. Sometimes the frustration and anger felt toward the educational system are more openly directed against the teachers and administrators who represent it. Ron Halvorsen and Donald Hawley (1973:56) described the "combat conditions" of teaching in some of the poorer sections of Brooklyn:

> The school tool shed had a telephone in it, and if things got too difficult an instructor could make a run for it, lock himself in, and then telephone for help. In one classroom the students suspended the teacher out of a fifth-floor window, threatening him, 'Teach, if you assign any homework today, we're going to drop you.'

A study of 253 classroom teachers in the Los Angeles public school system in the 1970s indicated that 28 percent of those teachers had actually suffered physical assault (Bloch, 1978). It went on to describe how the reactions to long-term stress among these 253 teachers were extremely similar to combat neurosis.

In a 1975 Senate subcommittee report on juvenile delinquency, it was concluded that school violence in the form of vandalism and attacks on people was definitely on the increase (Bayh, 1975). A similar subcommittee report published in 1977 found that the types of crimes found in the public schools encompassed virtually every type of crime found on the streets, including fatal beatings, stabbings, and even rapes of both students and teachers (U.S. Senate Subcommittee on Delinquency, 1977:7–10). The same report found that an alarming number of students were arming themselves with knives and guns for personal protection.

Even grade schoolers are susceptible to the violence of other students, and often live in fear of the school bullies who torment and sometimes assault them. Studies estimate that one in seven school-aged children is either a bully or a victim, and that this problem directly affects almost five million elementary and junior high school students in this country (Roberts, 1988:52). Referring to the phenomenon as *peer terrorism,* school authorities from across the United States met at Harvard University in 1987 for a "Schoolyard Bully Practicum" (Bergmann, 1987:A–8). The event, sponsored by the National School Safety Center, emphasized the need for awareness of the widespread problem of violent assaults on the school playgrounds. One school official indicated that these are not just "kids being kids," but are violent attacks against young people (Bergmann, 1987:A–8). Consequently, many students who are the victims of such violence approach their school day with fear and trepidation.

Joan McDermott (1983) examined research on crime and the fear of crime and victimization in the school and community. She suggested that crime and the fear of crime should be viewed in a community context since schools which experienced high rates of crime tended to be located in high-crime neighborhoods. A longitudinal study of 532 young black males and their parents in Philadelphia seems to substantiate McDermott's assumption. In that study, it was found that both the juveniles and their parents had extremely high rates of fear about the boys being victims of crime in the school environment (Savitz et al., 1978). Over one-half of the boys indicated that they had personally been the victims of robbery, assault, or extortion. Even those who had not been personally victimized expressed a great deal of fear. These youths indicated that they greatly feared being mugged, robbed, and even murdered in school rooms, school hallways, school yards, streets, playgrounds, recreation centers, movie theatres, dance halls, and on modes of public transportation. The study found that attempts to reduce parental and juvenile fear of school-based crime included truancy, joining gangs for protection, and even relocation to safer schools in safer neighborhoods (Savitz et al., 1978).

Whether high crime neighborhoods lead to crime in the schools, or crime in the schools leads to high crime neighborhoods, has developed as an interesting sociological question. One study found that geographic proximity to a high school increased the likelihood of crime in neighborhoods in San Diego (Roncek and LoBosco, 1983). In fact, that study indicated that residential areas adjacent to public high schools experienced more crime than areas that were more than a block away from those same schools. Dennis Roncek and Donald Faggiani (1985) replicated that study in the city of Cleveland, and discovered similar findings. These studies suggest that crime and violence in the schools, like any other social problem, must be viewed within their broader sociological context, as opposed to being viewed as isolated acts.

Overgeneralizations are dangerous, and it would be a gross exaggeration to conclude that very many of today's youths are violent sociopaths ransacking the schools and terrorizing administrators, teachers, and fellow students. Nevertheless, the increasing rates of truancy, vandalism, and student violence (Rubel, 1977; US Dept. of HEW, 1978) indicate a significant problem for our schools in regard to juvenile delinquency. (For an excellent selected bibliography on this subject, see Rubel, 1979.) While certainly not all students are rebelling against the school, a refrain from a popular Pink Floyd song of the late 1970s might sum up the attitudes of a large number of American youths:

> We don't need no education
> We don't need no thought control
> No dark sarcasm in the classroom
> Teacher! Leave them kids alone!
> ("Another Brick in the Wall" © 1979 Pink Floyd Music Publishers, Inc. Reprinted with permission)

SCHOOL AS BUREAUCRACY

Beyond the outright hostility some students express toward the school as a result of their failure, or their inability to relate to the dominant values being expressed there, is the more subtle problem experienced by students in regard to dealing with the bureaucratic structure of the school. Max Weber ([1922]1968) indicated that **bureaucracy** as an *ideal type* is typified by: *a clearcut division of labor; a hierarchy of authority; an elaborate system of rules and regulations; people treated as "cases," not as "individuals"; and a clearcut career pattern for those working within the bureaucracy.* Clearly, the public schools meet the criteria for bureaucracy.

The bureaucratic elements which may create the most significant problems for students are those regarding the elaborate system of rules and regulations and the fact that people are often treated as cases rather than individuals. Certainly, no school could operate without a set of rules and regulations by which those working in and attending the schools must abide. However, in some situations, the schools, at least as perceived by many of the students, have adopted so many rules and regulations that it becomes virtually impossible to abide by all of them. Further, it seems that in some cases, the rules take precedence over the people who must enforce and abide by them. Rules for the sake of rules are likely to be broken for the sake of breaking them.

Ralph Hummel (1977) discussed the lack of purpose and frustration people experience in a bureaucratic structure. Students who feel they are being treated like numbers, rather than people, are likely to develop a sense of alienation in the school environment. The assembly line model of education which has tended to dominate our educational philosophy since the industrial revolution (e.g. Callahan, 1962) has led to viewing schools as analogous to factories. Thus, incoming students are seen as raw materials to be shaped, molded, and transformed into finished products (i.e., productive citizens) by those trained and skilled to do so (the teachers). Students' views of teachers and teachers' views of students are affected by the roles they are forced to fulfill within the bureaucratic structure. Students are often amazed to discover that their teachers have a life outside the bureaucratic structure of the school.

The depersonalization, and, in some cases, the dehumanization of the educational process in contemporary American society, have certainly taken their toll on America's young people. Standardized testing, tracking, technological teaching devices, and a variety of other developments in education undoubtedly have made positive contributions to the educational endeavor. However, on the negative side, it must be noted that these developments also have led to increased bureaucratization of the schools. The students, forced to survive in this bureaucratic structure, may find themselves unable or unwilling to cope with it, and hence become involved in a variety of nonconforming activities leading to delinquency (Polk and Schafer, 1972; Polk, 1975).

SCHOOLS AND DELINQUENCY PREVENTION

Because of the school's significant role in the socialization of American youth, a large part of the responsibility for preventing delinquency seems to fall upon the school system. Unfortunately, to a large extent, educators and administrators have interpreted this responsibility as meaning they should be on the lookout for those youths most likely to cause trouble, commit delinquent acts, and become adult criminals. This emphasis on individual pathology as an explanation for deviance has been nonproductive and extremely unsuccessful. Despite the widespread use of standardized personality inventories, aptitude tests, achievement tests, and tracking, the problem of delinquency has increased rather than diminished. As pointed out in the earlier discussion on the labeling processes in the schools, these developments in education have, if anything, compounded the problems of delinquency rather than alleviated them. As more potential delinquents are identified, labeled, and acted upon—more actual delinquents are produced.

Perhaps one of the most enlightened discussions of this problem and suggestions for modification is provided by Delos Kelly (1982:122):

> If change is to come about, then I believe that it must begin with the educational system. Not only is this one of our basic social institutions but most children spend at least ten years or more within the system; they also spend many hours each day in school. The same does not exist with many families or the community.

He goes on to point out that the problems of stereotyping, labeling, degrading, tracking, and programming failure into certain students must be stopped. Kelly (1982:123–124) calls for an all out resocialization of parents, teachers, educators, and students in regard to the success-fail philosophy of the schools.

The teacher plays a tremendously significant role in any strategy of changing the orientation of schools in such a way as to eliminate some of the problems of delinquency. As suggested by Glasser (1978), eliminating failure and making students feel accepted and cared for are viable approaches to solving many of the discipline problems in the public schools. According to Carl Werthman (1976), when faced with situations in the classroom which threaten serious disruption, the teacher can respond in one of three ways. The teacher can simply overlook any activities other than learning which take place in the classroom, and essentially attempt to teach those who are apparently willing to learn. Rarely do serious problems erupt, because the teacher fails to acknowledge the activities of those who are trying to disrupt the educational process. A second strategy is for the teacher actually to briefly participate in the disruption. Minor disruptions, such as jumping to the window to see a passing firetruck or discussing last night's homecoming game, do not have to be elevated into teacher-student confrontations if the teacher is flexible enough to allow the students these minor distractions for a brief period and then direct them back to the desired classroom activity. The third optional response is for the teacher to react to and confront any activities which do not directly relate to the learning planned for the class. This confrontational approach indicates that the teacher sees extraneous activities not only as disruptive, but as direct challenges to adult authority in the classroom. When the teacher responds in this fashion, an adversarial situation is created in which, if the teacher is to maintain control of the classroom, he/she must win each and every encounter. While some situations may not allow for the first two options (such as fights and other situations which threaten others), the tendency for a teacher to consistently choose the third response is likely to be viewed by the students as overreaction, and may in fact lead to problems in the classroom rather than reduce them. Thus, the personal reactions of teachers to potentially disruptive situations in the classroom cannot be overestimated as potential ways of reducing delinquency in the schools.

Kenneth Polk (1984) viewed the schools as one of the most important elements in delinquency prevention and control. He contended that the number of marginal youths is growing, not only because less successful students have an unpleasant school experience, but also because their future occupational aspirations are severely limited. He proposed that to counter the alienation experienced by these youths, they must be engaged in useful work and be more thoroughly integrated into the school community. William Pink (1984) concurred, viewing effective schools as the most cost-efficient delinquency prevention program. He contended that the current educational system perpetuates a two-trajectory system where the low-trajectory youth (less successful students) are not only ill prepared academically, but also meet with failure in the out-of-school world, creating social situations which generate delinquency and other forms of deviance.

J. David Hawkins and Joseph Weis (1980) acknowledged the school's importance in delinquency prevention also, and viewed the school's role as going beyond academic and intellectual development. They suggested that the school must provide more alternative educational options, such as enhanced skill training. They also suggested that the school take a more active role in the social development process, including education in civil and criminal law. Emphasizing the social context in which the schools operate, Hawkins and Weis (1980) argued for more student input into the educational process and urged schools to draw upon student leaders to exert peer influence in delinquency prevention. They pointed out that the student leaders should not be merely the academic leaders, but also the informal leaders of various social groups and cliques.

Barry Krisberg and James Austin (1978) further emphasized the social nature of the educational process and outlined some ways in which schools might meaningfully change in an effort to reduce delinquency. They suggested that schools might enter into agreements with local communities to enhance their role in serving the entire community. Their suggestions included utilizing local artisans, craftspersons, and other professionals in the community as guest lecturers. They also suggested revising the curriculum to include local internship programs and viewing the local community as a learning resource. Local museums, libraries, universities, scientific establishments, businesses, and industries should all be viewed as places of learning and instruction. Krisberg and Austin (1978) concluded that the enhanced school-community relations would better integrate school and community in the educational process and reduce the view that schools are socially set apart from the rest of the world.

SUMMARY

The educational system did *not* create youthful misbehavior and juvenile delinquency. As McPartland and McDill (1977) indicated, the main sources of delinquency reside in the features of broad society; however, schools can either aggravate or reduce the problem according to the way they dispense rewards and punishments to students, provide access to opportunities for success, and react to the problems of students. In this chapter, we illustrated some of the ways in which the schools as public arenas are interwoven into the phenomenon of juvenile delinquency. The schools usually represent the first social institution (outside the family) with which the child must contend.

The major role of the school is that of socialization. For the schools, this process involves not only teaching the necessary cognitive skills expected of all citizens, but also the teaching of what are considered to be appropriate attitudes, values, beliefs, and behaviors. The child's ability to conform to normative expectations of teachers and administrators and adapt to the student role is critical in helping to determine success within that institution.

Success within the educational system has become inherently linked to success in the larger society. Those who fail, create problems, cause trouble, and cannot achieve success in school are those who are most likely to be labeled "delinquent," and also to subsequently fail in life. The success/fail orientation of the educational system often acts as a "screening device" which may alienate the unsuccessful students to the point of truancy or dropping out. Those alienated students who choose to remain in school may do so at great costs to the schools, administrators, teachers, and other students, who become the victims of their violence and vandalism.

While schools cannot be blamed for causing juvenile delinquency, they may be able to play an important role in reducing and/or preventing it. Schools are an integral part of society and the single social institution in which juveniles spend the largest portion of their time. From a sociological perspective, if members of society want to make a serious effort to reduce many of the problems associated with juvenile delinquency, the schools must play a major role.

CONCEPT APPLICATION

"Creative Approaches to the Problem of Truancy"

Most children read of the exploits of Tom Sawyer and Huckleberry Finn with a great deal of excitement, enjoyment, and envy. Those two characters prowled the banks of the Mississippi River, having more fun and excitement in a day than most kids can anticipate in a lifetime. They fished, rafted, chewed tobacco, fought, explored, cussed, and created mischief in a way that Mark Twain portrayed as humorous, enjoyable, and downright lovable. A great many of their exploits occurred while they were in the process of "playing hookey" from school.

Truancy, or "skipping school," is a major problem for families, school districts, and communities across the nation. It is a problem for families, because children are not in school where their parents assume them to be, and they are not receiving the education for which their parents are paying (in the form of taxes, and, in some cases, tuition and other costs). It poses numerous problems for the school. One is that like the parents, school officials do not know where the child is—only where the child is not. Questions of legal responsibility arise if a student is injured while truant. Parents assume the child to be in school, while school officials assume the child stayed home. In such cases, the question of liability is sometimes one that must be determined by the court.

If the student is not hurt, the school still may be. In many states, local school districts are funded on the basis of their ADA (Average Daily Attendance). This means that school funding is based upon some type of formula which pays a specific amount of money per student per day of attendance. Thus, when students are absent, money is lost to the school district. In a large district, truancy can reduce the operating budget by several thousand dollars per year.

Truancy also poses a variety of problems for the community, not the least of which is the crime and mischief youths are likely to engage in while wandering the streets (Chapter 11). Vandalism, theft, and other property crimes, along with problems of policing youths who are supposed to be in school, make truancy a nuisance in some communities and a major problem in others.

As a result of these problems and others, numerous attempts have been made to reduce truancy. Many of these attempts have focused upon more closely policing juveniles in an effort to apprehend truants and return them to school. Ironically, in some school districts, the punishment for truancy is some type of formal suspension from school! Hence, a juvenile who hates school, skips it, and then gets caught, may find that for the next 3 to 5 days, it is not necessary to be truant to escape the agony of school. Now, the district won't allow that student to attend school. (This type of school policy defies the logic of all but the most astute of local school board members!) Nevertheless, that is the extent of the efforts of some districts at reducing the problem of truancy.

On the other hand, some districts have been more creative in their efforts to keep students in school. For instance, one school district in Chula Vista, California adopted a program called "Operation Stay in School" (Superintendent's Communicator, 1982). While it also involves "rounding up" truant students from the streets, it focuses the combined efforts of parents, police, probation officers, and school district staff on preventing truancy. In this program, "spot sweeps" are made of various locations in the area and students who are truant are apprehended and taken to a receiving center to be returned to their parents or guardians. Immediate follow-up action involves counseling whereby everyone is made aware of the legal, social, and personal problems associated with truancy. Results of this program have included improved attendance, reduced vandalism, and a reduction in daytime burglaries.

Other districts have been much more innovative in their battles against truancy. Memorial Junior High School had the highest truancy rate in San Diego, California in 1979, and consequently, lost approximately $132,000 in state attendance funds (Tedrick, 1980). In an effort to reduce the truancy problem, the school began the "cash-for-class" program. For each day of school attendance, the student receives a card stamped "25 cents." Perfect attendance is worth $5 per month. According to the principal, students aren't really being paid to go to school, but are being rewarded for their attendance. The "pay can be spent only for school-related items such as paper, notebooks, library fines, concerts, and gym clothes and for wholesome foods such as apples and milk" (Tedrick, 1980:7).

The Spring Valley Schools in California developed a lottery of sorts in an effort to reduce their truancy rates (CNN News, September 22, 1986). The school decided to give away 73 $1,000 U.S. Savings Bonds at the end of the academic year. All seventh and eighth graders with two or fewer absences were eligible to enter the contest.

Another possible solution to the truancy problem might be to eliminate compulsory attendance laws, or at least reduce the age limit for mandatory attendance. When juveniles in their midteens feel totally alienated from school, it is unlikely that any creative endeavor to thwart truancy will lure them into regular school attendance. While Gary, Indiana did not totally eliminate its compulsory attendance law, it developed an experimental program to alleviate truancy among some of its most chronic habitual truants. These students attended a special school that met for only half a day. Reading and writing were emphasized, but so were free time, drawing, and other activities. Lessons were designed to ensure that students experienced some type of success each day. Interestingly, although attendance was not compulsory, truancy was no longer a problem (Robison, 1960:482–483).

* * * *

Based upon the reading of this chapter, how serious a problem is truancy? Should truancy be considered a form of juvenile delinquency? What is your opinion of some of the strategies presented in this illustrative anecdote? What ideas do you have for reducing the problem of truancy?

CONCEPT INTEGRATION
QUESTIONS FOR STUDY AND DISCUSSION

1. Explain how the school acts as a major agent of socialization in our society. Should the school attempt to socialize students in regard to normative aspects as well as cognitive aspects of culture? If so, how can it best do that? If not, why not?
2. Academic credentials have become extremely important in our society. Discuss some ways in which schools determine what level of credentials a student should receive. Should a student's willingness to conform to school rules be a factor in determining academic success? Why? Why not?
3. What is meant by referring to the school as a "combat zone?" What might be done to alleviate some of the conflict in the schools?
4. Schools have become increasingly bureaucratized in recent years. What positive outcomes has bureaucratization had on the schools? What has been the negative impact?
5. What can school teachers and administrators do to help reduce and prevent delinquency in the schools?
6. Discussion topic: Should states require compulsory school attendance? If so, why? If not, why not?

References

Alwin, D. F. & Thornton, A. 1984. Family origins and the schooling process: Early versus late influence of parental characteristics. *American Sociological Review* 49 (December):784–802.

Ardrey, R. 1966. *The territorial imperative.* New York: Atheneum.

Bayh, B. 1975. Our nation's schools—A report card: 'A' in school violence and vandalism. *Preliminary Report of the Subcommittee to Investigate Juvenile Delinquency.* Washington, DC: US Government Printing Office.

Becker, H. 1952. The career of the Chicago public school teacher. *American Journal of Sociology* 57 (March):470–477.

Berger, P. & Berger, B. 1975. *Sociology: A biographical approach* (2nd ed.). New York: Basic Books.

Bergmann, R. 1987. Purdy: Few bullies in Manteca. *The Manteca Bulletin,* June 9:A–8.

Bloch, A. M. 1978. Combat neurosis in inner-city schools. *American Journal of Psychiatry* 135 (October):1189–1192.

Braun, C. 1976. Teacher expectations: Sociopsychological dynamics. *Review of Educational Research* 46 (Spring):185–213.

Broder, P. K., Dunivant, N., Smith, E. C., & Sutton, L. P. 1981. Further observations on the link between learning disabilities and juvenile delinquency. *Journal of Educational Psychology* 73 (December):838–850.

Callahan, R. E. 1962. *Education and the cult of efficiency.* Chicago: University of Chicago Press.

Cavan, R. S. 1962. *Juvenile delinquency.* Philadelphia: JB Lippincott.

Chance, P. 1984. Save our schools: Love a vandal. *Psychology Today* 18 (May):17–18.

Cicourel, A. V. 1968. *The social organization of juvenile justice.* New York: John Wiley.

CNN News. 1986. Schools attempt to cut truancy. *CNN News* September 22, 1986.

Colvin, M. & Pauly, J. 1983. A critique of criminology: Toward an integrated structural-Marxist theory of delinquency production. *American Journal of Sociology* 89 (November):513–545.

Dollard, J., Miller, N., Doob, L., Mowizer, O. H., & Sears, R. R. 1939. *Frustration and aggression.* New Haven: Yale University Press.

Durkheim, E. [1906] 1956. *Sociology and education.* (Trans. S. D. Fox) New York: Free Press.

Elliott, D. S. 1966. Delinquency, school attendance and dropout. *Social Problems* 13 (Winter):307–314.

Elliott, D. S. & Voss, H. 1974. *Delinquency and dropout.* Lexington, MA: Lexington Press.

Farnworth, M., Schweinhart, L., & Berrueta-Clement, J. R. 1985. Preschool intervention, school success and delinquency in a high-risk sample of youth. *American Educational Research Journal* 22 (Fall):445–464.

Friedenberg, E. Z. 1959. *The Vanishing Adolescent.* New York: Dell.

    1971. The high school as a focus of student unrest. *Annals of American Academy of Political and Social Science* 395 (May):117–126.

Getzels, J. W. 1977. Why some children do poorly in school. In H. Ehlers (Ed.). *Crucial Issues in Education* (6th ed.). New York: Holt, Rinehart and Winston, pp. 73–76.

Glasser, W. 1978. Disorder in our schools: Causes and remedies. *Phi Delta Kappan* 59 (January):331–333.

Gracey, H. L. 1977. Learning the student role: Kindergarten as academic boot camp. In D. H. Wrong & H. L. Gracey (Eds.). *Readings in Introductory Sociology* (3rd ed.) New York: Macmillan, pp. 215–226.

Halvorsen, R. & Hawley, D. 1973. *From gangs to God.* Washington, DC: Review and Herald Publishing Association.

Hastad, D. N., Segrave, J. O., Pangrazi, R., & Peterson, G. 1984. Youth sport participation and deviant behavior. *Sociology of Sport Journal* 1 (December):366–373.

Hawkins, J. D. & Weis, J. G. 1980. The social developmental model: An integrated approach to delinquency prevention. Seattle: University of Washington Center for Law and Justice.

Hawkins, J. D. & Lishner, D. M. 1987. Schooling and delinquency. In Elmer H. Johnson (Ed.). *Handbook on crime and delinquency prevention.* Westport, CN: Greenwood Press, pp. 179–221.

Hirschi, T. 1969. *Causes of delinquency.* Berkeley: University of California Press.

Hirschi, T. & Hindelang, M. J. 1977. Intelligence and delinquency: A revisionist review. *American Sociological Review* 42 (August):571–587.

Hummel, R. P. 1977. *The bureaucratic experience.* New York: St. Martin's Press.

Hurn, C. J. 1978. *The limits and possibilities of schooling.* Boston: Allyn and Bacon.

Jencks, C., Smith, M., Acland, H., Bane, M. J., Cohen, D., Gintis, H., Heyns, B., & Michelson, S. 1972. *Inequality: A reassessment of the effect of family and schooling in America.* New York: Basic Books.

Keilitz, I., Zaremba, A., & Broder, P. K. 1979. The link between learning disabilities and juvenile delinquency: Some issues and answers. *Learning Disability Quarterly* 2 (Spring):2–11.

Kelly, D. H. 1977. Labeling and the consequences of wearing a delinquent label in a school setting. *Education* 97 (Summer):371–380.

———— 1982. *Creating school failure, youth crime, and deviance.* Los Angeles: Trident Shop.

Kozol, J. 1967. *Death at an early age.* New York: Bantam Books.

Krisberg, B. & Austin, J. 1978. *The children of Ishmael: Critical perspectives on juvenile justice.* Palo Alto, CA: Mayfield.

Lane, B. A. 1980. The relationship of learning disabilities to juvenile delinquency: Current status. *Journal of Learning Disabilities* 13 (October):425–434.

Liska, A. E. & Reed, M. D. 1985. Ties to conventional institutions and delinquency: Estimating reciprocal effects. *American Sociological Review* 50 (August):547–560.

Mayer, G. R., Butterworth, T., Nafpaktitis, M., & Sulzer-Azaroff, B. 1983. Preventing school vandalism and improving discipline: A three year study. *Journal of Applied Behavior Analysis* 16 (Winter):355–369.

McDermott, J. 1983. Crime in the school and in the community: Offenders, victims, and fearful youths. *Crime and Delinquency* 29 (April):270–282.

McPartland, J. M. & McDill, E. L. (Eds.). 1977. *Violence in schools: Perspectives, programs and positions.* Lexington, MA: DC Heath.

Menard, S. & Morse, B. J. 1984. A structuralist critique of the IQ-delinquency hypothesis: Theory and evidence. *American Journal of Sociology* 89 (May):1347–1378.

Neill, S. B. 1978. Violence and vandalism: Dimensions and correctives. *Phi Delta Kappan* 59 (January): 302–307.

Piliavin, I. & Briar, S. 1964. Police encounters with juveniles. *American Journal of Sociology* 70 (September):206–214.

Pink, W. T. 1984. Schools, youth and justice. *Crime and Delinquency* 30 (July):439–461.

Polk, K. 1975. Schools and the delinquency experience. *Criminal Justice and Behavior* 2 (December):315–338.

1984. The new marginal youth. *Crime and Delinquency* 30 (July):462–480.

Polk, K. & Schafer, W. E. (Eds.). 1972. *Schools and delinquency.* Englewood Cliffs, NJ: Prentice-Hall.

Roberts, J. 1988. School yard menace. *Psychology Today* 22 (February):52–56.

Robison, S. M. 1960. *Juvenile delinquency: Its nature and control.* New York: Holt, Rinehart and Winston.

Roncek, D. W. & LoBosco, A. 1983. The effect of high schools on crime in their neighborhood. *Social Science Quarterly* 64 (September):598–613.

Roncek, D. W. & Faggiani, D. 1985. High schools and crime: A replication. *Sociological Quarterly* 26 (Winter):491–505.

Rubel, R. J. 1977. *Unruly school: Disorders, disruptions, and crimes.* Lexington, MA: DC Heath.

1979. *Crime and disruption in schools: A selected bibliography.* Washington, DC: National Institute of Law Enforcement and Criminal Justice, U.S. Department of Justice (January).

Sanders, W. B. 1976. *Juvenile delinquency.* New York: Holt, Rinehart and Winston.

Savitz, L. D., Lallix, M., & Rosen, L. 1978. Fear of school-based crimes and rational responses. From *Theoretical Perspectives on Poverty and School Crimes*, Vol. 2. New York: National Council on Crime and Delinquency.

Schafer, W. E. & Polk, K. 1976. Delinquency and the schools. In *Task force report: Juvenile delinquency and youth crime.* The President's Commission on Law Enforcement and the Administration of Justice. Washington, DC: U.S. Government Printing Office, pp. 228–234.

Segrave, J. O. & Hastad, D. N. 1984. Interscholastic athletic participation and delinquent behavior: An empirical assessment of relevant variables. *Sociology of Sport Journal* 1 (June):117–137.

Stagliano, P. A. & Hyman, I. A. 1983. State department of education activities to reduce school violence and vandalism. *Phi Delta Kappan* 65 (September):67–68.

Superintendent's Communicator. 1982. Operation stay in school. *Superintendent's Communicator* 3 (Sept. 30):2.

Tedrick, D. 1980. School will pay students to cut rate of truancy. AP, San Diego, *Emporia Gazette* November 1, 1980:7.

Thornberry, T. P., Moore, M. & Christenson, R. L. 1985. The effects of dropping out of high school on subsequent criminal behavior. *Criminology* 23 (1):3–18.

Truckenmiller, J. L. 1982. Predicting vandalism in a general youth sample via the HEW youth development model's community program impact scales, age, and sex. Unpublished paper presented at the 90th Annual Convention of the American Psychological Association, Washington, DC, August 23–27, 1982.

UPI Washington. 1979. Delinquency tied to learning problems. *Tulsa Daily World* January 2, 1979.

U.S. Department of Health, Education, and Welfare. 1978. *Violent schools—safe schools: The safe school study report to the congress*. Vols. I, II, & III. Washington, DC: U.S. Government Printing Office.

U.S. Senate Subcommittee on Delinquency. 1977. *Challenge for the third century: Education in a violent environment*. Washington, DC: U.S. Government Printing Office.

Weber, M. [1922] 1968. Bureaucracy. In G. Roth & C. Wittich (Eds.). *Economy and society: An outline of interpretive sociology* (3 Vols.) (Trans. E. Fischoff et al.). New York: Bedminster Press, pp. 956–1005.

Werthman, C. 1976. The function of social definitions in the development of the gang boy's career. In R. Giallombardo (Ed.). *Juvenile Delinquency* (3rd ed.). New York: John Wiley, pp. 327–347.

Yinger, J. 1982. *Countercultures: The promise and the peril of a world turned upside down*. New York: Free Press.

Zieman, G. L. & Benson, G. P. 1980. School perceptions of truant adolescent boys. *Behavioral Disorders, Programs, Trends and Concerns of Children with Behavioral Problems* 5 (August):212–222.

Chapter 11

The Public Arena: Streets and Sidewalks

The reading of this chapter will help you achieve the following objectives:

1. Understand how the public streets and sidewalks are social arenas in which juveniles come in contact with those who may come to define them as delinquent.
2. Identify ways in which juveniles' encounters with merchants are likely to result in the delinquent identification being placed on some youths.
3. Understand how interaction with various "street people" is likely to result in increased juvenile delinquency.
4. Identify important variables which influence police interaction with juveniles.
5. Understand the problem of youthful runaways and the associated problems of teenage prostitution, child pornography, and life on the streets.
6. Summarize some of the research on the problems of juvenile shoplifting and juvenile auto theft.

INTRODUCTION

Chapter 10 began with a definition and discussion of the concept of **arena,** and then went on to discuss the public schools as an arena in which juveniles come in contact with others who disapprove of their behavior and who may perceive them as delinquent. The largest social arena in which juveniles interact is the streets. As indicated in Chapter 8, "The Youth Subculture," a large portion of juveniles' activities are oriented to the public streets and sidewalks. "Cruising," "dragging the strip," and simply "hanging out" often bring juveniles by the tens of thousands out to America's streets. These activities bring juveniles together with a variety of other society members, which includes not only other juveniles, but also a multitude of adults.

Besides encountering adults who are on their way to and from work, shopping, and running errands, the arena of the streets brings the juvenile together with a variety of adults who may have direct impact upon the juvenile's likelihood of being unofficially and officially identified as a delinquent. Some of the more important adults, in regard to acquiring the delinquent identity, with whom the juvenile is likely to come in contact in the street arena, include local merchants, "street people," adults who often commit various street crimes (e.g., prostitutes, pimps, drug dealers, muggers, and vagrants), and, of course, the police.

In this chapter, we explore the nature of these social encounters of youths on the streets from a sociological perspective. Additionally, we explore some of the specific problems related to juveniles' social interaction on the streets, including juvenile shoplifting, juvenile prostitution, and juvenile auto theft.

JUVENILE ENCOUNTERS WITH MERCHANTS

Merchants depend upon the general public for their livelihood. They want and need as many people as possible to frequent their stores. The slogan "the customer is always right" epitomizes the merchant's awareness of the need to please shoppers. However, it is paying customers that merchants need to attract to their stores, not loitering juveniles. Local merchants whose shops are located in areas where teenagers congregate sometimes develop a relationship of mutual hostility with juveniles. The merchants usually fear that having groups of teenagers hanging around their stores will discourage adult customers and increase shoplifting and damage to property and merchandise. In this regard, the shopkeepers find themselves in a "catch-22" situation. If they refuse to serve the juveniles or frequently call the police, they may have to suffer vandalism and other forms of harassment from the teenagers as retaliation. Further, while the juveniles may not be true customers (it should be noted that many of them may well be; see Chapter 8 for a discussion of juveniles as mass consumers), their parents are. Thus, to alienate the juveniles may also mean alienating their parents. On the other hand, if the shopkeepers allow large numbers of juveniles to "hang out" in their stores, they will probably find that even though their store is "full of customers" very few purchases are actually being made and those made are usually of small dollar value.

It is not at all uncommon for store owners and managers whose shops are located near middle schools, junior high schools, and high schools to actually post signs on doors and windows stating that only a limited number of students will be allowed inside at any one time. This policy, of course, leads to inevitable conflicts with youths who feel (and rightfully so) that they are being singled out for discrimination. These conflicts often lead to calls to the police and juveniles receiving occasional "unofficial" and "official" warnings. Occasionally, an officer may even have to take juveniles to the station to call their parents. These contacts with police, if frequent, may lead to a juvenile becoming known to law enforcement officials, and eventually being considered delinquent.

Juvenile Shoplifting

Juvenile shoplifting can be a major problem for storeowners. Mary Owen Cameron (1964) pointed out in her research that women and children tend to account for most amateur shoplifting. Juveniles in their early teens tend to want make-up, records, tapes, jewelry, special clothing, and other expensive items. Because they are too young to work at most jobs, they must rely on their allowance, small amounts of money from odd jobs, or their parents' generosity if they are going to buy these items. The strong desire for those items, lack of cash, and relative ease with which these items can be concealed sometimes provide the incentive for shoplifting. Cameron (1964:102) found that juveniles tended to shoplift smaller inexpensive items, with boys most likely to steal gadgets such as cigarette lighters, flashlights, and cheap cameras, while girls were more likely to shoplift jewelry, make-up, small leather goods, and dress accessories.

In addition to the strong desire for goods and lack of funds for purchasing them, for some youths shoplifting simply constitutes another form of entertainment. The challenge of stealing without getting caught and the peer pressure to "prove" one's courage can serve as motivation to participate in shoplifting. Numerous studies have indicated that juvenile shoplifting tends to be a group activity (e.g., Robin, 1963; Cameron, 1964; Rosenberg and Silverstein, 1969; Cobb, 1982). The peer group seems to provide social support for shoplifting. Bernard Rosenberg and Harry Silverstein (1969) found that as a group activity, there tended to be a great deal of peer support for shoplifting. They discovered that a large number of juveniles believed that everyone their age steals. Data from research on juvenile shoplifting indicate that while not all juveniles actually shoplift, the prevalent attitude that *all* youths are doing it is not too far from correct. Ruth Cavan and Theodore Ferdinand (1981) concluded that shoplifting became a common pattern among members of the youth counterculture movement of the 1960s, but today is much more widespread among juveniles in general. They reported that more than half of all white males (52 percent) admitted to shoplifting at least once (Cavan and Ferdinand, 1981:141). Gerald Robin's (1963:167) study found that juveniles were disproportionately represented among shoplifters, with approximately 60 percent of the shoplifters apprehended being juvenile girls. Much of the increase in girls' property offenses can be attributed to their participation in shoplifting (Steffensmeier and Steffensmeier, 1980). Cameron (1964:102) also found that juveniles were the most frequently arrested for shoplifting in both actual numbers and in proportion to their numbers in the population in the city she studied. Sanders (1981:135) concluded, "With little to lose, and with support of their peers, shoplifting for juveniles is much easier socially than it is for adults."

Beyond providing normative support for shoplifting, the peer group also may provide the "courage" for some youths to participate in the activity. Rosenberg and Silverstein (1969:130) found that juveniles were much more likely to shoplift with other juveniles, and one boy frankly confessed, "When I go stealing, I got to be with somebody because I get scared being by myself." William Cobb (1982) described a juvenile shoplifting incident which exemplified the brazen nature which sometimes occurs when groups of youths shoplift. He described a scenario in which nine male juveniles, several of whom were known to the store security as previous shoplifters, gathered around a table in the clothing department and obscured the view of security personnel while they shoplifted. In an attempt to catch them, all of the store security personnel (seven people) approached the boys to make clear to them that they were being watched. Meanwhile, on another floor of the store, a group of youths helped themselves to merchandise "secure in their belief that their nine confederates were keeping the store detectives busy" (Cobb, 1982:374).

Shoplifting also may represent an attempt on the part of some youths to symbolically declare their independence from their parents. Sanders (1981) suggested that because juveniles are so economically dependent upon their parents, shoplifting may be one of the ways in which they can acquire necessary and/or desired items without having to rely upon their parents to purchase them. As we have suggested throughout this book (and most emphatically in Chapter 8), the marginal status of adolescence may provide a social milieu in which juveniles may act in a way which simultaneously reinforces and violates the values and norms of their parents. Materialism is a basic value in American society. Youths have been socialized to want nice things, to dress in style, and to want to acquire material possessions. On the other hand, most youths have been taught that stealing is wrong. Thus, shoplifting can represent both acceptance and rejection of dominant adult values. Sanders (1981) pointed out that shoplifting, like a number of other juvenile crimes, tends to stop as youths approach adulthood. The motivation for shoplifting among juveniles is further explored in the Concept Application: Illustrative Anecdote at the end of this chapter.

Regardless of the motivation, when theft, or the threat of theft arises, merchants and juveniles are likely to have very negative encounters. It may even be that estimates of the number of juveniles who participate in shoplifting are exaggerated, and that the proportion of juveniles to adults who are arrested for shoplifting is somewhat distorted. For example, Robin (1963) found that merchants and store security personnel were much more likely to approach and accuse juveniles of shoplifting than they were adults. He speculated that the consequences for falsely accusing a juvenile of shoplifting were minimal when compared to wrongly confronting an adult who might bring legal action against the store and/or the individual. Cameron (1964) also indicated that juveniles were treated differently from adults by store personnel. She indicated that youths who were suspected of shoplifting, or who were actually caught, were much more likely to be approached directly than were adults. When apprehended, they were usually "scolded, their names recorded, and their parents notified" (Cameron, 1964:20). John DeMott (1984) concluded that juveniles do their share of shoplifting, but not as much as previously thought.

The actual extent of juvenile shoplifting, like many other forms of social deviance that occur in our society, may never be known. As pointed out in Chapter 3, the official data from *Uniform Crime Reports* and other sources often do not coincide with data collected from unofficial sources such as self-report or victimization studies. When juveniles are caught shoplifting, merchants and security personnel essentially have three alternatives at their disposal: (1) release them (usually to their parents); (2) turn them over to juvenile authorities or the police for issuing a warning; (3) turn them over to juvenile authorities or the police for official action (Robin, 1963:167). Different merchants may use various methods to help them decide how to handle any particular shoplifting situation. Consequently, the extent of juvenile shoplifting can only be estimated. However, available data from arrest records and self-report studies indicate that juvenile shoplifting is a significant problem, and that many of the encounters between merchants and juveniles are predicated on the assumption that the juvenile is a potential threat to the merchant's profits.

JUVENILE ENCOUNTERS WITH "STREET PEOPLE"

The streets of our major cities, and even a surprising number of smaller towns, are "home" for an amazingly large number of people. Recent articles and television documentaries have uncovered a subterranean social world on the streets that most Americans never knew existed. Bag ladies, vagrants, and the chronically unemployed inhabit the street arena along with prostitutes, pimps, drug dealers, and other criminals who have been more highly visible in the past. Studies reveal that a large number of homeless youth also inhabit the streets (Senate Subcommittee Report, 1980).

Juveniles who spend much time on the streets are likely to encounter a wide variety of people, many of whom society views as deviant. Simply being on the streets with some of these people exposes the juvenile to a multitude of attitudes, values, and behaviors which violate a number of both informal and formal societal norms.

Beyond the eccentricities of many of these street people, the juveniles are also exposed to actual criminal behavior, and may either intentionally or inadvertently become involved in law violating behavior. Because adult criminals know that juveniles are treated more leniently by the law, they sometimes recruit them in various ways to participate in particular crimes. For example, drug dealers can pay innocent-looking juveniles to deliver merchandise to buyers on the street. The juveniles may or may not even know that they are participating in a crime. Even teenagers who don't take drugs or rarely break the law might agree to take a brown paper sack from one location to another for a quick $25 without asking many questions. Thus, the dealer can successfully have thousands of dollars' worth of drugs delivered with very little personal risk. If stopped by the police, the juvenile will not even be able to identify the actual drug dealer. If they have no prior arrests, and cannot be linked to any other crimes, the juveniles are likely to be placed on probation and released to their parents. In this manner, teenagers can be used as "numbers runners" for illegal gambling rackets, "mules" or "drops" for drug dealers, and "spotters" for auto thieves.

The large number of runaway and "throwaway" youths living on the streets and their interaction with other street people has led to increasing rates of delinquency involving theft, drug usage, prostitution, and other street crimes.

Of course, many juveniles who are involved in drug trafficking on the streets are far from being innocent dupes. Kids hustling a living on the streets are likely to get involved in a variety of illegal activities in an effort to support themselves (Wein, 1970; Weisberg, 1985). Dealing drugs, selling sex, stealing, or fencing stolen goods are means of survival for juveniles on the streets. Carl Klockars (1974) described the early life of a professional fence who began his trade on the streets hustling money, fencing goods, and conning adults in order to survive. All of these activities are illegal, and set up potential confrontations between juveniles and police.

Professional auto theft rings sometimes use juveniles in various stages of auto theft. Teenagers "cruising" the streets can be used to "spot" automobiles for theft. Their sole job may be to drive around looking for high-dollar cars left unattended and to radio their locations, on citizen's band radios, to people they have never met. At the end of each week these youths report to a predetermined location to pick up an envelope containing cash which might range from $10 to $100 for each "spot." Another role in which a juvenile may be used in the auto theft ring is to actually make the theft. The teenagers (usually 16- to 18-year-old boys who have drivers' licenses) are used to "hotwire" ignitions, steal the cars, and "drop" them at some street in a business area. The juvenile simply leaves the car, and, like the "spotters," probably collects cash periodically. The thief may receive anywhere from $100 to $500 for each "drop." If caught, the teenager can simply claim to be "joyriding," a common juvenile offense, and again, with no prior record, may escape any serious consequences. Even if charged by the police, the juvenile car thieves are not likely to know for whom they work, and thus cannot implicate any of the professional thieves in the ring. The juvenile will acquire a "delinquent" label, however, and if very many encounters with the police result, may even be treated as an adult and earn a criminal record.

Again, it should be noted that most juveniles involved in auto theft are not innocent dupes being used and manipulated by unscrupulous adults. A U.S. Senate subcommittee (1968) found that some juveniles specialize in stealing automobiles and found that there were even juvenile auto theft rings operating in some cities. Juvenile auto theft is such a common offense that it deserves special attention.

JUVENILE AUTO THEFT

Each year, more than half of all cars stolen in the United States are taken by persons under the age of 18 (Hughes, 1970:18). In 1982, there were 39,141 arrests of people under age 18 for automobile theft (FBI *Uniform Crime Reports*, 1983:176). In 1986, the number rose to 50,319, or 39 percent of the total arrests for car theft that year (FBI *Uniform Crime Reports*, 1987:174,35). The automobile has had a special fascination for American society since its invention.

This fascination seems to peak during the teenage years. William Wattenberg and James Balistrieri (1952) and Erwin Schepses (1961) found that most juvenile auto theft was initiated for fun and not for profit. Wattenberg and Balistrieri (1952) discovered that white middle class and upper class boys were likely to be involved in auto theft for the purpose of "joyriding." Similarly, Schepses (1961) found that many of the boys involved in stealing cars were not involved in any other type of delinquent behavior.

Not all car theft by youths is solely motivated by a desire for fun, however. A U.S. Senate subcommittee (1968) investigating juvenile auto theft found that some youths entered into auto theft for profit. Charles McCaghy and his associates (1977) also found data that seriously questioned the earlier studies which contended that juvenile auto theft was primarily done by middle class whites who were "joyriding." Their data indicated that urban lower class black youths were most responsible for auto thefts. These youths stole cars for their own use, but also stole them so they could be stripped and the parts sold, or could be sold on the "black market" (for example, see the Concept Application at the end of Chapter 6).

JUVENILE RUNAWAYS

Juvenile girls and boys on the streets (especially runaways) become easy targets for prostitution (Morgan, 1975; Hersch, 1988) and child pornography (O'Brien, 1983). Virtually every major metropolitan newspaper and the major television networks have run special features on the problems of teenage runaways and their being exploited for homosexual, prostitution, or pornographic purposes. In *America's Runaways*, Christine Chapman (1976) discussed the problems that runaway youths are likely to face on the streets of major cities. These almost invariably include being taken advantage of by more "streetwise" kids and adults. Alone, penniless, and often desperate, the runaways are very likely to become involved in behaviors which constitute delinquency (Mackey, 1983).

Running away from home is a delinquent act in and of itself. In 1982, 115,214 juveniles were arrested as runaways (FBI *Uniform Crime Reports*, 1983:176). In 1986, the number climbed to 138,586 (FBI *Uniform Crime Reports*, 1987:174). Of course, not all runaways are arrested. Johnson and Carter (1980) estimated that in 1975, over 600,000 children ran away from their homes. The F.B.I. estimated that there were one million juvenile runaways in 1980 (Wells and Sandhu, 1986:147), and O'Brien (1983) put the estimate at one million runaways per year in the U.S., while Hersch (1988) estimated the runaway figure to be 1.2 million. Running away from home seems to increase during certain social, political, and economic conditions. Mona Wells and Harjit Sandhu (1986) pointed out that throughout American history, periods of war and social upheaval have been accompanied by increased rates of running away. Lipschutz (1977) also documented specific periods in history when there was an increased incidence of running away. In the twentieth century, the periods of the Great Depression (1930s), World War II (1940s), and the "Flower Child Era" (1960s) saw large waves of runaways in this country.

Wells and Sandhu (1986) concluded that the phenomenon of running away from home seems to result from a combination of "push-pull" factors such as problems at home and pressures of school combined with the allure of perceived freedom and independence. A counselor for runaways in Los Angeles summarized:

> Kids are not really running away . . . they are running to something they think is there which isn't there. They think it's just a groovy street scene . . . which of course, isn't true. There's nothing more revolting than the street scene, but they really don't know it. They think it's really an exciting thing. It's complete freedom, but they don't realize it's kind of hard to have freedom if you're out pan-handling for food . . . (Wein, 1970:201).

Jennifer James (1982) confirmed that many runaways are lured to the streets by the anticipation of excitement to be found there, but often become disillusioned with the life they find. As mentioned, the act of running away is a delinquent act in itself, but it is only one aspect of the problem which links running away from home to delinquency. As D. Kelly Weisberg (1985) indicated, many juvenile runaways wind up in jail or prison because they get involved in a variety of street crimes such as prostitution, drugs, theft, and violence.

Runaways are extremely vulnerable prey for pederasts, pimps, and others who spot them on the streets, show them some attention and apparent affection, and offer them a warm meal and a place to sleep. In most American cities, the streets take on a much different social atmosphere after dark, when the seamier side of life seems to swing into action. Runaways are most likely to be out on the streets at night, as they try to stay off the streets during school hours because they "stand out as an open target for routine police questioning during the hours when school is in session" (Wein, 1970:189). Homeless youths are especially susceptible, and must either surrender to or become tougher than those who want to exploit them. Either way is likely to involve the juvenile in delinquent activities.

Life on the streets is extremely tough for juveniles who have run away from home with little or no money, no friends, and no legitimate means of making a living available. Tom Cox, of the Diggers Creative Society in Los Angeles (a group formed to help street kids), noted:

> A kid of fourteen can't cope with the streets. Even if they wanted to fool with the illegal part of it, they just can't manage it, they just can't make it. They are going to get busted, or they are going to get into some very bad situations where the people who are sheltering them have nothing to lose. In one case,

there's a guy who collects fourteen-year-old boys and sends them out to earn money for him (cited in Wein, 1970:196).

Juvenile Prostitution

For many juveniles on the streets, especially runaways, prostitution may become one of the few available routes to survival. Weisberg (1985:4) noted:

Since runaway episodes begin impulsively, the runaways seldom brought much money with them, and they frequently found themselves without resources for food and shelter. They might find shelter with strangers, but such aid might well be conditioned on an exchange of services involving drug dealing or prostitution.

Frances Newman and Paula Caplan (1981) verified that a significant number of teenage prostitutes were runaways. Similarly, Patricia Hersch (1988:31) pointed out that "wherever we turn, teenagers are being used for sexual recreation by men—lots of men . . ." In 1986, 2,192 people under age 18 were arrested for prostitution (FBI *Uniform Crime Reports,* 1987:174), and certainly that figure represents only the "tip of the iceberg."

When young girls run away from home, they make easy victims for pimps who prey on their vulnerability. Lisa Austin (1985), a staff writer for a Wichita newspaper, along with three other reporters, investigated a runaway network which operated in Kansas and Oklahoma as a juvenile prostitution ring. According to their report, girls between the ages of 15 and 18, who were having trouble at home or who had run away, were shuttled to truck stops and rest areas along the interstate highways of Oklahoma and Kansas for the purposes of prostitution. Calls transmitted via the CB radio, asking the drivers if they were interested in "a coin-operated meter," alerted the truckers to the location of the girls (Austin, 1985:7A).

Some of the juvenile prostitutes on the streets appear to have voluntarily entered into prostitution. James (1978) found that some female juvenile prostitutes were from affluent backgrounds but were attracted to street prostitution for the thrill and adventure of it. Many runaway youths conclude that prostitution means "easy money," even if not desirable. Many of Weisberg's (1985:57) subjects stressed that prostitution meant easy money, "with 'easy' referring to the short duration of the sexual encounter as well as the lack of difficulty in performing such employment." Some of the juvenile prostitutes actually indicated that they liked "the absence of fixed working hours, leaving them to 'do their own thing' " (Weisberg, 1985:57).

The so-called voluntary nature of such prostitution might be questioned, as it may be nothing more than rationalization for the norm violating behavior in which the youth is participating. For as Shirley O'Brien (1983:69) pointed out, "It is easy for children desperately in need to turn to pornography and prostitu-

Juvenile prostitutes work the streets of most American cities.

tion to support themselves." And Weisberg (1985:78–79) concluded that runaways were most likely to fit into the category of "situational" prostitutes (entering into prostitution temporarily due to specific social circumstances) as opposed to "vocational prostitutes" (entering into prostitution as a career). As O'Brien (1983:69) summarized, "Runaways who have been neglected and abused to a point that their home situation was more troublesome than whatever might be 'out there,' rationalize that food and shelter provided in exchange for sexual favors is better than living in an impossible home environment."

Juvenile prostitution (like adult prostitution) is not solely a form of deviance for females. Robin Lloyd (1976:211) estimated that there were approximately 300,000 male prostitutes under the age of 16 in the United States. Prostitution becomes an integral part of life on the streets for juvenile males (Weisberg, 1985; Hersch, 1988). Young males who have run away from home also find life on the streets extremely difficult and may find themselves exploited by adults for purposes of child pornography (O'Brien, 1983) and prostitution (Wein, 1970; James, 1982; Weisberg, 1985). The tenderloin district of San

Francisco attracts numerous runaways, and many young males congregate in that area as prostitutes. The area along Market Street from Mason to Tyler streets has become so well known for having male juvenile prostitutes that it is referred to as the Meat Rack (Weisberg, 1985:20).

Young male prostitutes, like females, may enter into prostitution for a variety of reasons. James (1982) found that the largest percentage of adolescent male prostitutes entered the trade out of economic necessity. Hersch (1988) estimated that male juvenile prostitutes often made $75 to $100 per night. On the other hand, an earlier study by Albert J. Reiss (1961) revealed that some male juvenile prostitution was primarily a form of "street hustle" highly supported among delinquent peers. Reiss described a situation in which delinquent males would hang around on the streets posing as prostitutes. When approached by older males they would agree to engage in fellatio for a price. The boys viewed what the older male was doing as homosexual, while rationalizing that their own participation in the act was simply a form of sexual release for which they were paid. Sometimes, after the act, they would even beat the older male to signify their own revulsion at homosexuality. This type of behavior was viewed as very "macho" by the delinquent boys, and never viewed as being homosexual (Reiss, 1961). Similar activities occur in urban areas where "tough" local teenagers cruise the gay areas, participating in "fag bashing" or "rolling queers" for money. Sometimes these juveniles sell sexual favors to the homosexuals before beating them.

Programs for Runaways

A vast literature has accumulated on the runaway phenomenon in the United States, and numerous theories have been postulated on why youths leave home and what can and should be done about it. Much of the research on running away focuses upon home and family problems which place unusual stress upon the juvenile who finally decides to flee the home environment (e.g., Gullotta, 1979; Roberts, 1981; Morgan, 1982). Some studies have specifically focused upon running away as being a result of child abuse (e.g., Guiterres and Reich, 1981), while others have examined the difference between **runaways**—*those who leave their home*—and **throwaways**—*those who are pushed out of their homes* (e.g., Gullotta, 1979; Adams et al., 1985).

In an effort to resolve some of the problems associated with running away, numerous programs have been established to deal with runaway youths and their families. Studies which have evaluated some of the programs show mixed results, and conclude that running away is a very complex social phenomenon which must be addressed in a broader social context than simply attempting to treat the problems of individual runaways (e.g., Libertoff, 1978; Mann, 1980; Libertoff, 1980; Spillance-Grieco, 1982). Even if the problem of runaways was significantly reduced, it would not eliminate the problem of delinquency generated by youths interacting in the public arena of the streets and sidewalks.

STREET KIDS

All the juveniles living in the streets are not runaways. Larry Cole's (1970) book *Street Kids* portrays life on the streets for youngsters who live in major cities and essentially fend for themselves. These children and youths hang around the streets and sidewalks hustling a living, and almost invariably come in contact with the police and acquire the "delinquent" label. As one street youth described:

> You are in constant sight of the law. Since you have no place to go you stand out in the open. You and the law always looking each other square in the face. When something happens near you, man, you're in it. Like it or not. You are part of the scene. You will get busted for just being (Cole, 1970:11).

City planners and urban reformers often have viewed children playing on the streets and sidewalks as a function of the lack of adequate yard and playground space. They further assumed that if adequate parks and playgrounds were available, the children would not be forced to linger on streets and sidewalks where their safety may be jeopardized and where, as they grow older, they are very likely to get in trouble. Jane Jacobs (1961) seriously questioned these assumptions. She concluded:

> Why do children so frequently find that roaming the lively city sidewalks is more interesting than backyards or playgrounds? Because the sidewalks are more interesting (Jacobs, 1961:85).

Unfortunately, part of the fascination of the inner-city streets and sidewalks resides in the norm-violating behavior which occurs there. O'Brien (1983) pointed out that the problem of youth pornography and prostitution was not solely related to the problem of runaways. She indicated that "city-bred street kids" become "models" for child pornographers and prostitutes as a way to get money (O'Brien, 1983:74).

Unsupervised juveniles on the streets and sidewalks are likely to become involved in activities which will bring them to the attention of the police. When juveniles encounter the police in the public arena, the potential for conflict is ever-present.

JUVENILE ENCOUNTERS WITH POLICE

If juveniles spend much time on the streets, it is inevitable that they eventually will have some encounters with the police. Younger children seem to be fascinated by police officers and often wave to the police as they drive by in their patrol cars, or stop and talk to them as they are walking their beats. In

some areas, this positive relationship between youngsters and police is consci-
entiously sought; for instance, police officers who encounter youths give them
football cards or baseball cards about area professional teams that list helpful
safety hints on the back side of the cards (Shown, 1986). However, many
juveniles, as they become older, tend to develop a different attitude toward
police officers; even though they may never have been in trouble with the law,
they often exhibit negative attitudes toward the police. Perhaps juveniles resent
the authority which the officers represent, or they may merely be conforming to
peer pressure to "not like cops." Similarly, police officers who are usually very
friendly to young children, are more likely to be a bit suspicious of teenagers on
the street. One gang member summarized the juvenile-police dilemma:

> They don't want us in the recreation centers, they don't want us on the
> streets, they don't want us hanging around the soda fountains. Where the hell
> do they want us? Home watching TV? We're too old for TV and too young for
> the bars. We get tired of just hanging around and we have to let off steam—
> even if it means fighting, stealing cars, breaking windows. They think we're all
> bad, some kind of punks (Tunley, 1962:40).

Because of the somewhat negative attitudes held by the police and juveniles toward each other, it is understandable that their encounters are often
punctuated with expressions of bad feelings.

The police are the most socially visible symbol of the juvenile justice
system. Thus, police become a central part of the processing of delinquents.
There is some disagreement as to what role the police should assume in dealing
with juveniles. Samuel Walker (1983) described two schools of thought on the
role the officer should fulfill. First is the strict **law enforcement role** which
contends that the police should *concentrate on arresting juveniles who violate
criminal laws* (Walker, 1983). In this approach, juveniles would be viewed and
treated by the police in essentially the same way as are adults. The other school
of thought maintains that police should take a **crime prevention role.** This role
calls for police officers to *act as social workers, helping juveniles to stay out of
situations which might lead to delinquency* (Walker, 1983). In many cases, police
officers attempt to fulfill both of these role expectations simultaneously, being
both crime fighter and friend as the situation dictates. Many officers believe,
however, that these roles are not complementary, and fear that "if they adopt a
friendly and helpful attitude in one situation, they will not be taken seriously
when the situation calls for a stricter law enforcement position" (Walker,
1983:131).

The dilemma which develops involves the question of how juveniles
should be treated by the police and in what ways that treatment should be
similar to and different from the treatment of adults. It seems that juveniles are
often likely to be treated in a stricter fashion than adults. There is frequently a

conflict between ideology and practice when it comes to policing juveniles. Barry Krisberg and James Austin (1978:78) pointed out:

> Assuming the overriding *parens patriae* ideology, one might expect the police to have developed an especially sensitive approach for dealing with children. On the contrary, evidence suggests that youths are treated as harshly as their adult counterparts, with less respect for their constitutional rights.

The issues of **parens patriae**—from British common law, meaning that *the king was the ultimate parent of every child,* was translated into American juvenile law *to allow the state to intervene on behalf of children,* and **due process**—*the constitutional safeguards designed to protect those accused of criminal acts,* are more thoroughly discussed in Chapter 12 dealing with the juvenile court. However, these issues are significant (especially the issue of due process) in arriving at an understanding of how the police deal with juveniles.

The Police and Due Process

As a result of the popularity of televised stories about the police, virtually everybody is familiar with the Miranda decision and the procedures it mandated. We all have viewed shows in which, at the moment of arrest, the arresting officer immediately informs the suspect: "You have the right to remain silent; you have the right to an attorney; if you cannot afford an attorney, the court will appoint you one; you have the right to remain silent; if you choose to waive that right anything you say can and will be used against you in a court of law." However, juveniles are not necessarily afforded all of those rights. As Krisberg and Austin (1978:80) indicated, "because the rights of due process and restrictions on evidence are not rigidly adhered to in juvenile courts, police can take advantage of the situation and use search, seizure, and interrogation procedures that would clearly be illegal if used with adult offenders."[1] Technically, in most states, juveniles are *detained* and *not arrested.* Although the difference is primarily one of semantics, it allows the due process afforded adult criminals to be circumvented. In an attempt to protect the rights of juveniles who have been taken into custody by the police, the National Advisory Commission on Criminal Justice Standards and Goals recommended:

1. Police should warn juveniles of their right to counsel and the right to remain silent during questioning;
2. Upon apprehension of a minor, police should notify the parents;

[1]For an excellent overview of due process, the police, and juvenile offenders, see Samuel Davis, Justice for the juvenile: The decision to arrest and due process. In the 1971 *Duke Law Journal,* pp. 913–920; also Samuel Davis, *Rights of juveniles: The juvenile justice system* (2nd ed.). New York: Clark Boardman, 1983.

3. Any statements made to police or court officers not in the presence of parents or counsel should be inadmissible in court;
4. Juveniles should not be fingerprinted, photographed, or otherwise put through the usual adult booking process;
5. Juvenile records should be maintained physically separate from adult case records (National Advisory Commission, 1973:764).

These are only guidelines, however, and not requirements. The police still exercise a great deal of discretionary power in dealing with juveniles.

Police Discretion in Handling Juveniles

Studies of police encounters with juveniles have found that police have wide latitude in the handling of most cases (e.g., Piliavin and Briar, 1964; Black and Reiss, 1970; Lundman et al., 1978; Smith and Visher, 1981; Morash, 1984). Krisberg and Austin (1978:83) pointed out that police have five options in deciding what course of action to pursue with juveniles:

1. Release, accompanied by a warning to the juvenile.
2. Release, accompanied by an official report describing the encounter with the juvenile.
3. Station adjustment, which may consist of:
   (a) release to parent or guardian accompanied by an official reprimand;
   (b) release accompanied by referral to a community youth services agency for rehabilitation; or
   (c) release accompanied by referral to a public or private social welfare or mental health agency.
4. Referral to juvenile court intake unit, without detention.
5. Referral to juvenile court intake unit, with detention.

Whether all of those alternatives are actually available to the police might depend upon individual community resources. In times of economic hardship, budget cutting at state and local levels, and other monetary restrictions, social service agencies are often the first targeted to be cut back or closed. Many communities do not sponsor youth centers or other agencies, and may actually limit police options to two: either release the juvenile, or petition the juvenile to court. On the other hand, some states and local communities provide many diversionary alternatives to police who deal with juveniles. Occasionally, political situations and current public policy play an important role in police discretion (Aaronson et al., 1984). "Get tough" philosophies of local public officials might preclude some of the alternatives usually left to the police.

Because police can exercise discretion in deciding who does and does not officially become identified as delinquent, they act as a "filter" in the creation of delinquency. Police "filter out" many youths who could potentially be arrested and adjudicated delinquent. As in a huge net, initially a large number of youths come in contact with the police. For example, in 1985, the police took more than one million juveniles into custody (U.S. Department of Justice, 1987:323). However, the "holes" in the net allow many of those juveniles to be "filtered out" and escape the official adjudication process. Of the more than one million youths processed by the police in 1985, almost 31 percent were released (U.S. Department of Justice, 1987:323). Later, as discussed in Chapter 12, we see that the juvenile court acts as a further element in the "filtering process" by which juveniles are finally adjudicated delinquent.

The question immediately arises about the criteria the police follow in this process. The criteria become extremely important in the process of determining whether the youth will be "officially processed" and identified as "delinquent," or "officially ignored" and, despite the commission of a law violating act, escape the official delinquency statistics.

Factors often identified as influencing police decision-making in regard to how to best handle a juvenile in a particular circumstance include:

1. The nature of the offense committed (serious or not serious).
2. The number of previous contacts the youth has had with police.
3. The age, sex, race, and socioeconomic status of the offender.
4. The appearance, attitude, and overall demeanor of the juvenile.
5. The apparent willingness of parents to cooperate with the police in preventing further offenses.
6. Social service agencies and other options available to the police in the local community.

Common sense would seem to dictate that the nature of the offense committed by the youth would greatly influence the disposition chosen by the police. Several studies have indicated that juveniles who have committed acts that would be classified as felonies if done by adults (e.g., murder, rape, robbery) and serious misdemeanors are much more likely to be arrested and confined than those who have committed status offenses such as running away or truancy (e.g., Piliavin and Briar, 1964; Krisberg and Austin, 1978; Lundman et al., 1978). However, the seriousness of the offense is only one variable which emerges as being significant in influencing police discretion in handling juveniles. Numerous other legal and extralegal factors influence police decisions in a particular case.

The number of previous police contacts also plays an important role in police discretion in handling juvenile offenders. These contacts may have represented nothing more than stopping the juvenile on the street and asking a few questions, or taking the youth to the police station for more extensive interrogation before releasing him or her. In the former instance, some officers will simply write the name of the juvenile in a small notebook—it is unofficial and probably won't even be shared with fellow officers. However, if the officer later encounters that same youth and sees that a prior contact had already been made, the officer might decide to handle the subsequent contact more formally. If taken to the station, it is likely that the youth's name will be recorded on a "rap sheet" and filed for future reference. Thus, even if the youth is released, a record of the encounter exists, and any future contacts with police might be regarded more seriously. Because of this, even a perfectly innocent youth who happened to be in the vicinity of a crime might fall victim to becoming "known" to the police, and this could influence police decisions should any future police encounters occur. A simply entry in the file such as "was questioned about school vandalism" could begin the labeling process discussed in Chapter 6, which might lead to the youth being officially defined as "delinquent."

The extralegal factors such as age, sex, race, and socioeconomic status (SES) have been heavily researched, and their impact upon police and judicial discretion is well documented in the literature (e.g., Piliavin and Briar, 1964; Black and Reiss, 1970; Cavan and Ferdinand, 1981; Smith and Visher, 1981; 1983; Morash, 1984; Sampson, 1986; Huizinga and Elliott, 1987). In general, older juveniles, males, members of racial and ethnic minorities, and members of the lower class are likely to be dealt with more severely (hence, more likely to be officially labeled as "delinquent") than are younger juveniles, females, and whites. Some controversy exists over whether the police are biased in favor of or against girls.[2] Virtually all studies indicate that minority youths, especially blacks, are more likely to be officially processed than whites. Whether this is primarily due to different cultural backgrounds between white police and black youths, as suggested by Ferdinand and Luchterhand (1970), differences in type of offenses committed by blacks and whites (Black and Reiss, 1970; Wilbanks, 1987), or by more overt racism as suggested by Piliavin and Briar (1964) and by Fagan et al. (1987), remains an issue for debate. Either way, data indicate that when all other variables are controlled (such as seriousness of offense, demeanor) minority youths are clearly more likely to be officially processed by police than their white counterparts (Smith and Visher, 1981; Huizinga and Elliott, 1987). The effect of the youth's socioeconomic status on police discretion is also controversial. Lawrence Cohen and James Kluegel (1978) argued that the seriousness of the offense and prior record were the most important determinants of police reaction, not race and social class. On the other hand, Robert Sampson (1986) pointed out that if police are in fact biased by the race and social class of the juvenile, and are more likely to arrest lower class youths and blacks, this helps create the record of "prior offenses" that affect subsequent police decisions. Overall, Sampson (1986:881) found that the factors of social class, race, and delinquent peers accounted for approximately one-third of the

---

[2]For an excellent discussion of this issue, see Gail Armstrong, Females under the law— 'Protected' but unequal. *Crime and Delinquency* 23 (April):109–120.

explained variation in official police reaction, as regards both males and females. In fact, Sampson (1986) found that neighborhood SES (the general social class level of the area in which the youth lives) was one of the most significant variables influencing the reaction of police. He concluded: "Apparently, the influence of SES on police contacts is contextual in nature, and stems from an ecological bias with regard to police control, as opposed to a single individual-level bias against the poor" (Sampson, 1986:884). In other words, juveniles who live in lower SES neighborhoods which have been identified by police as typically "high crime areas" are more likely to come into contact with police on the streets and sidewalks, and hence are more likely to be detained, arrested, and petitioned to juvenile court.

The appearance, attitude, and overall demeanor of the juvenile when confronted by the police seem to emerge as very important variables in influencing police discretion. Piliavin and Briar (1964) found that demeanor was the most important factor in police determination of the handling of apprehended juveniles. Similarly, Merry Morash (1984) found that juveniles who most closely fit the common image of delinquents held by police were most likely to be arrested. Neatly dressed, cooperative, and mannerly youths are much less likely to be viewed as suspect, and if they come into contact with police are probably more likely to be released. Robert Winslow (1973:116–117) quoted police officers as saying that an "antagonistic attitude" is very likely to lead to a juvenile's being arrested. Similarly, Douglas Smith and Christy Visher (1981:172) concluded that regardless of other factors, "failure to display deference toward an officer significantly increases the probability of arrest . . ." Aaron Cicourel (1968) and William Hohenstein (1969) both found that the police officer's perception of the juvenile's attitudes toward the police and law were the most important factors in the decision to release or officially process the offender. Donald Black and Albert J. Reiss (1970) discovered an interesting finding regarding the demeanor of the youth and likelihood of arrest. Like other studies, theirs confirmed that unusually disrespectful youths were more likely to be arrested than reasonably respectful youths, but found that juveniles at the other end of the continuum (those who were unusually respectful to the officers) also had a greater likelihood of arrest. Apparently, officers tend to become suspicious of teenagers who seem "overly respectful" during interaction. Thus, a youth's demeanor apparently plays an important role in the discretionary process.

When parents show an active interest in their children and a willingness to cooperate with the police, the likelihood is much greater (especially when the violation is minor) that the juvenile will be warned, and released in their custody. In the *Task Force Report: Juvenile Delinquency and Youth Crime* (1967:419), family situation and attitude and conduct of a youth's parents were listed (along with prior record, age, and attitude) as important criteria affecting police decisions on disposition of juvenile cases.

The number and types of social service agencies and other options available in a community help influence police decisions. In some communities there are youth centers, sheltered homes, and other facilities where juveniles can be detained or placed in a constructive program for short periods of time. If police officers view their role as being primarily that of *crime prevention*, they are likely to pursue one of those diversion programs on behalf of the juvenile. **Diversion** simply refers to *diverting the youth from the official juvenile justice system* (this is further discussed in Chapter 14).[3] On the other hand, in some communities, police may have only two options: release, or confinement in jail. If that is the case, police are likely to be reluctant to arrest juveniles or recommend their detention unless they have committed fairly serious offenses.

Two other factors which apparently affect police decisions on how to handle juveniles are whether there is an audience during the police/juvenile encounter, and whether the complainant has a strong preference for a particular alternative. Smith and Visher (1981:172–173) found that police were much more likely to arrest a juvenile when there was an audience to the encounter. Black and Reiss (1970) noted that most police encounters with juveniles were the result of direct response to a citizen complaint. If the adult registering the complaint insisted on arrest, the police were quite likely to accommodate their request. On the other hand, if the complainant suggested releasing the juvenile, this greatly influenced the officer.

SUMMARY

The streets and sidewalks serve as a major social arena in which juveniles come in contact with adults who might be influential in encouraging the juvenile to become delinquent. Teenagers and local merchants seem to develop what might be referred to as a mutually hostile, yet mutually dependent relationship. The shopkeepers need to make sales, and if they are in an area where juveniles "hang out" they may become somewhat dependent on the youth trade. On the other hand, this may result in driving away potential adult customers. Further, since many of the youths are simply there for social reasons, they may not make many purchases. If shoplifting occurs, as it often does, an even more antagonistic relationship is likely to develop, and the police are likely to become involved.

Because juveniles spend a great deal of time on the streets they often come in contact with a variety of "street people." Simply associating with these vagrants, vagabonds, drunks, pimps, prostitutes, and street criminals may earn the juvenile the "delinquent" label. By becoming involved in any of the street

---

[3]For a very thorough treatment of this topic, see Shepherd and Rothenberger, *Police-juvenile diversions: An alternative to prosecution* (2nd ed.), 1980. Also, *Diversion of youth from the juvenile justice system*, US Department of Justice, 1980.

people's criminal activities—either knowingly or inadvertently—the juvenile is likely to be arrested and become officially labeled as delinquent.

Life on the streets is extremely difficult for juveniles. Many youths who run away from home find that street survival may necessitate their involvement in crimes such as drug trafficking (and use), prostitution, pornography, theft, and violence. Runaways are not the only youths who make the streets and sidewalks their home. In large urban areas, numerous youths take to the streets to "hustle" a living by illegal means.

Juveniles are highly visible on the street, and therefore attract police attention. Police often stop "suspicious-looking" juveniles who may be alone or in groups, to question them about possible involvement in delinquent activities. Evidence suggests that the age, race, sex, and social class of the juvenile are variables which are likely to influence police-juvenile encounters. The police are allowed to exercise considerable discretion in handling juveniles, and play one of the most significant roles initially in determining whether a youth will be treated as delinquent. The youth's overall demeanor seems to emerge as one of the most dominant factors in determining the outcome of police-juvenile contacts. Juveniles who are polite and attentive, and who seem to be genuinely impressed (perhaps intimidated or even scared) are most likely to be released without being officially processed. However, juveniles who swagger and swear, and seem unimpressed by the police or show contempt for them, or who assume an overly respectful air are most likely to be taken to the station and acquire the official status of delinquent.

The streets and sidewalks serve as a public arena in which juveniles interact with other societal members. Juveniles who spend much of their time on the streets and sidewalks of their communities are quite likely to violate some of the normative expectations for behavior. If this violation is brought to the attention of the police, the juvenile is subject to being officially processed and identified as "delinquent."

CONCEPT APPLICATION
ILLUSTRATIVE ANECDOTE

In the following illustrative anecdote, one of the authors shares an experience of his adolescence which illustrates some of the concepts contained in this chapter.

"The 'Thrill of the Steal': Juvenile Shoplifting"

Studies indicate that a large amount of all amateur shoplifting is committed by juveniles (Robin, 1963; Cameron, 1964; Rosenberg and Silverstein, 1969; Cobb, 1982). Those same studies indicate that much of what juveniles steal is totally unrelated to their need for those items. Why, then, do so many juveniles participate in shoplifting? No doubt, the motivations are many and varied.

I never shoplifted as a youth. I would like to think that my reasons for not shoplifting were rooted in my great respect for the law, my unwavering integrity, and a deep sense of moral revulsion at the thought of stealing. No doubt, the values instilled by my parents which emphasized the importance of honesty and the sanctity of respecting other people's property were significantly influential. On the other hand, another strong deterrent was my fear of getting caught, and the humiliation and degradation (not to mention punishment) which would accompany such an event.

Interestingly, that same fear of getting caught which helped deter me from shoplifting, apparently acts as a strong motivating force for some youths to shoplift. While I didn't shoplift myself, I knew several kids who did. In fact, on at least one occasion, I actually accompanied an acquaintance on a shoplifting excursion, waiting outside the store, heart pounding, torn between the feelings of guilt about what I knew was taking place inside, and the sense of excitement in being involved (if only peripherally) in such a risk-taking adventure.

Many youthful shoplifters appear motivated by that risk taking. Acquiring the item stolen often plays a very minor role in instigating the theft. In fact, some juveniles enter stores to shoplift with no predetermined item even in mind. It is not the stolen article, but the "thrill of the steal" which often motivates the act. Many youths view shoplifting as a personal challenge. They want to pit their "skills" against those of the store employees, to experience the excitement and sense of daring associated with the risk being taken, and to test their luck.

I remember a particular situation in which I was with a friend in a grocery store where we each purchased a candy bar. When we left the store, mounted our bicycles and rode away, my friend began laughing. When I inquired as to his obvious good humor, he reached inside his shirt and proudly produced a pack of cigarettes. "Where'd you get those?" I demanded. "I stole 'em" he responded. "But you don't even smoke!" I shouted. Without missing a beat, he answered, "I know," and tossed the pack of cigarettes back over his head. He obviously was exhilarated by the escapade. I was simultaneously angry (because he had put me at risk without my knowledge), perplexed (why steal cigarettes when you don't even smoke?), and yet, at least a bit impressed (he had stood right next to me in the checkout line and stolen a pack of cigarettes without being noticed by the cashier or myself).

Juvenile shoplifting is often a group activity. Shoplifters often gain status within their peer group for such daring accomplishments. Likewise, some of the fear may be mitigated through "safety in numbers." Sometimes, the more brazen the act of shoplifting, the more the perpetrator feels there is to be gained in the eyes of peers. I recall one other incident in which I was an accomplice to shoplifting, but this time I had full prior knowledge of the act. I had a friend who kept a stack of *Playboy* magazines in his parents' garage underneath some old clothing stored there. By today's standards, the magazine was pretty bland, revealing little more than magazines such as *Time, Newsweek,* and the swimsuit issue of *Sports Illustrated* do today. Yet, in the early 1960s, these magazines were quite risqué and certainly prohibited for 12-year-old boys. I always wondered where my friend acquired the magazines, and after several queries, he finally confessed that he stole them. He said he went to a local drug store each month when a new issue arrived, and simply walked in, went to the magazine rack, and "got" one. I quickly challenged his story, and he subsequently invited me along for the next caper the following month.

A few weeks later, my friend informed me that "it was time." He had visited the drug store the previous day, and the new issue was on the shelf. We would go to the store that very afternoon after school, and he would show me how easy it was to "get" the magazine (interestingly, he never used the word "steal" or "shoplift").

For the remainder of the school day I was a "nervous wreck." I tried to think of excuses as to why I could not accompany him on this venture. At lunch, I casually mentioned that I wasn't sure that I could go that afternoon because of baseball practice. He reminded me that the school day ended at 3:00 pm and practice did not begin until 5 o'clock. He questioned aloud if I had "lost my nerve" and "chickened out." Bingo! He had said the magic words! I assured him that I was ready, and even implied that this was "no big deal" for me. That afternoon, we rode our bikes to the drugstore. My friend walked in while I sat on my bicycle outside, near the door, and holding the handlebars of his bike in my trembling hand. To my amazement, he walked through the door, proceeded to the magazine rack which was located only 10 to 15 feet from the cash register where the clerk stood, picked up the magazine, and calmly walked out. He didn't hide it, didn't fold it, and didn't run. I took off on my bike as fast as I could, amazed that he lingered behind, casually pedalling along. After we had traveled a few blocks we stopped. "You're nuts!" I yelled. "I can't believe you didn't get caught . . . that was the stupidest thing I ever saw!" "Works every time" he said. He then proceeded to tell me that he thought the reason a lot of people got caught was because they acted suspiciously and dawdled, looking to see whether somebody was watching. His technique was simply to walk in, take what he wanted, and leave. Needless to say, I was amazed. He also said that he never felt more excited than during the interval between picking up the item and exiting the store. I confessed that during that same time I had experienced such intense fear that I thought my heart was going to jump out of my body, and I vowed never to accompany him again.

Why do juveniles shoplift? It's an easy crime to rationalize, and actually requires little or no skill. What the offending youths view as their "courage" is actually little more than the manifestation of their stupidity. Yet, the "thrill of the steal" seems to be a major part of their motivation.

* * * *

Based upon your reading of this chapter and this illustrative anecdote, why do juveniles shoplift? In the anecdote, was the author also guilty of shoplifting? If not, why not? If so, should he be considered a juvenile delinquent? Have you had a similar experience in which you were aware that a friend or an acquaintance was committing a delinquent act but you did nothing to stop it? Should this also be considered a form of delinquency?

CONCEPT INTEGRATION
QUESTIONS AND TOPICS FOR STUDY AND DISCUSSION

1. What types of encounters with local merchants are likely to result in juveniles being identified as delinquent? In what ways might the mutually hostile relations between juveniles and merchants be resolved?
2. Discuss some of the ways in which juveniles' encounters with various "street people" might lead to delinquency. Are there some positive aspects to life on the streets for juveniles? If so, what are they?
3. What social problems and crimes are linked to the large numbers of runaways and urban street kids who attempt to survive on the streets of many cities? What might be done to reduce some of these problems?
4. Juvenile auto theft is one of the more common offenses committed on the streets. How does juvenile auto theft tend to differ from adult auto theft? What might be done to reduce juvenile auto theft?
5. Why are juveniles on the street so frequently accosted by the police? What factors are likely to influence police discretion? Should the police be given *more* or *less* discretion in handling juveniles?
6. If you were an urban planner in a major city what steps would you take to try to reduce some of the problems of delinquency on the streets and sidewalks?

References

Aaronson, D., Deines, C. T., & Musheno, M. 1984. *Public policy and police discretion.* New York: Clark Boardman, Ltd.

Adams, G. R., Gullotta, T., & Clancy, M. A. 1985. Homeless adolescents: A descriptive study of similarities and differences between runaways and throwaways. *Adolescence* 20 (Fall):715–724.

Armstrong, G. 1977. Females under the law—'Protected' but unequal. *Crime and Delinquency* 23 (April:108–120.

Austin, L. 1985. Troubled girls prey for runaway network. *Wichita Eagle Beacon* March:17:, 1A, 6A, 7A.

Black, D. J. & Reiss, A. J., Jr. 1970. Police control of juveniles. *American Sociological Review* 35 (February):63–77.

Cameron, M. O. 1964. *The booster and the snitch: Department store shoplifting.* New York: Free Press.

Cavan, R. S. & Ferdinand, T. N. 1981. *Juvenile delinquency* (4th ed.). New York: Harper & Row.

Chapman, C. 1976. *America's runaways.* New York: William Morrow.

Cicourel, A. 1968. *The social organization of juvenile justice.* New York: John Wiley.

Cobb, W. E. 1982. Shoplifting. In L. D. Savitz & N. Johnston (Eds.). *Contemporary Criminology.* New York: John Wiley, pp. 369–376.

Cohen, L. & Kluegel, J. 1978. Determinants of juvenile court dispositions: Ascriptive and achieved factors in two metropolitan courts. *American Sociological Review* 43:162–176.

Cole, L. 1970. *Street kids.* New York: Grossman.

Davis, S. 1971. Justice for the juvenile: The decision to arrest and due process. *Duke Law Journal:*913–920.

Davis, S. M. 1983. *Rights of juveniles: The juvenile justice system* (2nd ed.). New York: Clark Boardman.

DeMott, J. S. 1984. Light fingers: Thieves within and without. *Time* 124 (December 31):51.

Eldefonso, E. 1983. *Law enforcement and the youthful offender: Delinquency and juvenile justice* (4th ed.). New York: John Wiley.

Fagan, J., Slaughter, E., & Hartstone, E. 1987. Blind justice? The impact of race on the juvenile justice process. *Crime and Delinquency* 33 (April):224–258.

Federal Bureau of Investigation. 1983. *Uniform Crime Reports: Crime in the United States—1982.* Washington, DC: U.S. Government Printing Office.

1987. *Uniform Crime Reports: Crime in the United States—1986.* Washington, DC: U.S. Government Printing Office.

Ferdinand, T. N. & Luchterhand, E. G. 1970. Inner-city youth, the police, the juvenile court, and justice. *Social Problems* 17 (Spring):510–527.

Guiterres, S. E. & Reich, J. W. 1981. A developmental perspective on runaway behavior: Its relationship to child abuse. *Child Welfare* 60 (February):89–94.

Gullotta, T. P. 1979. Leaving home—Family relationships of the runaway child. *Social Casework* 60 (February):111–114.

Hersch, P. 1988. Coming of age on city streets. *Psychology Today* 22 (January):28–37.

Hohenstein, W. F. 1969. Factors influencing the police disposition of juvenile offenders. In T. Sellin & M. E. Wolfgang (Eds.). *Delinquency: Selected studies.* New York: John Wiley, pp. 138–149.

Hughes, H. M. 1970. *Delinquents and criminals: Their social world.* Boston: Holbrook Press.

Huizinga, D. & Elliott, D. S. 1987. Juvenile offenders: Prevalence, offender incidence, and arrest rates by race. *Crime and Delinquency* 33 (April):206–223.

Jacobs, J. 1961. *The death and life of great American cities.* New York: Vintage Books.

James, J. 1978. Entrance into juvenile prostitution: Progress report, June 1978. Washington, DC: National Institute of Mental Health.

1982. Entrance into juvenile prostitution. Washington, DC: National Institute of Mental Health.

Johnson, R. & Carter, M. M. 1980. Flight of the young—Why children run away from their homes. *Adolescence* 15 (Summer):483–489.

Klockars, C. B. 1974. *The professional fence.* New York: Free Press.

Krisberg, G. & Austin, J. 1978. *The children of Ishmael: Critical perspectives on juvenile justice.* Palo Alto, CA: Mayfield.

Libertoff, K. 1978. Runaway youth and social network interaction. Unpublished Doctoral Dissertation. Cambridge, MA: Harvard University.

1980. The runaway child in America: A social history. *Journal of Family Issues* 1 (June):151–164.

Lipschutz, M. R. 1977. Runaways in history. *Crime and Delinquency* 23 (July):321–332.

Lloyd, R. 1976. *For money or love: Boy prostitution in America.* New York: Vanguard.

Lundman, R. L., Sykes, R. E., & Clark, J. P. 1978. Police control of juveniles: A replication. *Journal of Research in Crime and Delinquency* 15 (January):74–91.

Mackey, A. 1983. Runaway teens: Trouble on the run. *Teen* 27 (January):5.

Mann, C. R. 1980. Legal and judicial battles affecting runaways. *Journal of Family Issues* 1 (June):229–248.

McCaghy, C. H., Giordano, P. C., & Henson, T. K. 1977. Auto theft: Offender and offense characteristics. *Criminology* 15 (3):367–385.

Morash, M. 1984. Establishment of a juvenile police record: The influence of individual and peer group characteristics. *Criminology* 22 (February):97–111.

Morgan, O. J. 1982. Runaways—Jurisdiction, dynamics, and treatment. *Journal of Marital and Family Therapy* 8 (January):121–127.

Morgan, T. 1975. Little ladies of the night: Runaways in New York. *New York Times* November 16:34–38.

National Advisory Commission. 1973. *Corrections.* Washington, DC: U.S. Government Printing Office.

Newman, F. & Caplan, P. J. 1981. Juvenile female prostitution as a gender constant response to early deprivation. *International Journal of Women's Studies* 5 (2):128–137.

O'Brien, S. 1983. *Child pornography.* Dubuque, IA: Kendall-Hunt.

Piliavin, I. & Briar, S. 1964. Police encounters with juveniles. *American Journal of Sociology* 70 (September):206–214.

Reiss, A. J., Jr. 1961. The social integration of queers and peers. *Social Problems* 9 (Fall):102–120.

Roberts, A. R. 1981. *Runaways and non-runaways in an American suburb—An exploratory study of adolescent and parent coping.* New York: John Jay Press.

Robin, G. 1963. Patterns of department store shoplifting. *Crime and Delinquency* 9 (April):163–172.

Rosenberg, B. & Silverstein, H. 1969. *The varieties of delinquent experience.* Waltham, MA: Blaisdell.

Sampson, R. J. 1986. Effects of socioeconomic context on official reaction to juvenile delinquency. *American Sociological Review* 51 (December):876–885.

Sanders, W. B. 1981. *Juvenile delinquency: Causes, patterns, and reactions.* New York: Holt, Rinehart and Winston.

Schepses, E. 1961. Boys who steal cars. *Federal Probation* 25 (March):56–62.

Senate Subcommittee Report. 1980. Homeless youth—The saga of 'pushouts' and 'throwaways' in America. Report of the Senate Subcommittee on the Constitution, December, 1980. Washington, DC: U.S. Government Printing Office.

Shepherd, J. R. & Rothenberger, D. M. 1980. *Police-juvenile diversion: An alternative to prosecution* (2nd ed.). Michigan Department of State Police.

Shown, C. Z. 1986. Police distributing chiefs cards again. *Emporia Gazette* September 4, 1986:1.

Smith, D. A. & Visher, C. A. 1981. Street-level justice: Situational determinants of police arrest decisions. *Social Problems* 29 (December):167–177.

Spillance-Grieco, E. 1982. Increasing effectiveness in counseling runaways and their families. *Juvenile and Family Court Journal* 33 (August):31–37.

Steffensmeier, D. J. & Steffensmeier, R. H. 1980. Trends in female delinquency: An examination of arrest, juvenile court, self-report, and field data. *Criminology* 18 (May):62–85.

Task Force Report. 1967. *Task force report: Juvenile delinquency and youth crime.* Washington, DC: U.S. Government Printing Office.

Thornberry, T. 1973. Race, socioeconomic status, and sentencing in the juvenile justice system. *Journal of Criminal Law and Criminology* 64 (March):90–98.

Trojanowicz, R. C. & Morash, M. 1983. *Juvenile delinquency: Concepts and control* (3rd ed.). Englewood Cliffs, NJ: Prentice-Hall.

Tunley, R. 1962. *Kids, crime and chaos: A world report on juvenile delinquency.* New York: Harper Press.

US Department of Justice. 1980. *Diversion of youth from the juvenile justice system.* Project Orientation Resource Handbook. Washington, DC: U.S. Government Printing Office.

1987. *Sourcebook of criminal justice statistics—1986.* Washington, DC: U.S. Government Printing Office.

US Senate Subcommittee. 1968. *Hearings before the subcommittee to investigate juvenile delinquency, Part 18, Auto theft and juvenile delinquency.* Washington, DC: U.S. Government Printing Office.

Walker, S. 1983. *The police in America: An introduction.* New York: McGraw-Hill.

Wattenberg, W. W. & Balistrieri, J. 1952. Automobile theft: A 'favored group' delinquency. *American Journal of Sociology* 57 (May):575–583.

Wein, B. 1970. *The runaway generation.* New York: David McKay.

Weisberg, D. K. 1985. *Children of the night: A study of adolescent prostitution.* Lexington, MA: Lexington Books.

Wells, M. & Sandhu, J. 1986. The juvenile runaway: A historical perspective. *Free Inquiry in Creative Sociology* 14 (November):143–147.

Wilbanks, W. 1987. *The myth of a racist criminal justice system.* Beaumont, CA: Wadsworth.

Winslow, R. W. 1973. *Juvenile delinquency in a free society* (2nd ed.). Encino, CA: Dickenson.

Chapter 12

The Public Arena:
The Juvenile Court

READING OBJECTIVES

The reading of this chapter will help you achieve the following objectives:

1. Understand the concept of "due process" as expressed in the United States Constitution and Bill of Rights.
2. Explain the motives and ideology of the Child Savers together with their positive and negative impacts upon the juvenile justice process.
3. Understand the historical development of the juvenile court.
4. Provide an overview of the implications of the Gault Decision and other major decisions by the United States Supreme Court and their impact upon the legal processing of cases involving juveniles.
5. Describe and explain the procedures of the contemporary juvenile court.
6. Identify some of the major criticisms and limitations of the contemporary juvenile court.

INTRODUCTION

In Chapter 10, we introduced the concept of **arena** and illustrated how the schools serve as a social arena in which juveniles strive for social acceptance, a sense of social identity, and a measure of success in an adult-dominated society. In Chapter 11, we further explored this struggle for identity and the confrontations encountered by juveniles in the social arena of the streets. The juvenile court also fits our concept of public arena in much the same way as the schools and the streets. Although it conducts private hearings, the juvenile court symbolically represents society's public disapproval of a youth's behavior and the public's official response to delinquency.

The United States was founded on the principles and ideals of democracy that all men are created equal under the law and entitled to certain inalienable human and civil rights. So dynamic and compelling was this "American Dream" that the nation's founders successfully revolted and separated from England. A later generation suffered a bloody civil war in order to extend these rights to an enslaved minority.

These fundamental rights were codified in the United States Constitution and the Bill of Rights. For example, the Fourth, Fifth, Sixth, Eighth, and Fourteenth Amendments to the Constitution combine to guarantee *due process of law*. The Fourth Amendment prohibits unwarranted and unreasonable arrest; the Fifth protects against self-incrimination; the Sixth guarantees the right to counsel and a jury trial, as well as the right to be informed of specific charges and the right to confront witnesses; the Eight Amendment prohibits excessive bail and fines and cruel and unusual punishment; while the Fourteenth ensures that no state will be allowed to deprive any citizen of right to life, liberty, or property without **due process of Law.** *Black's Law Dictionary* defined and described the essential elements of "due process of law" as:

> . . . notice and opportunity to be heard and to defend in orderly proceeding adapted to nature of case, and the guarantee of due process required that every man have protection of day in court and benefit of general law . . . Daniel Webster defined this phrase to mean a law which hears before condemns, which proceeds on inquiry and renders judgement only after trial (Black, 1968:590).

In light of these basic legal rights, it is one of the greatest paradoxes that American children and youths have been denied many of their constitutional rights in the juvenile justice system until very recent years. In order to fully understand the evolving legal status and adjudication of young people in this country, we first need to explore the historical background out of which the contemporary juvenile court developed.

HISTORICAL BACKGROUND OF THE JUVENILE COURT

Much of American law is founded on British common law which exempted children under the age of 7 from legal responsibility because they were considered incapable of **mens rea**—which means *"evil intent" or "guilty mind," and refers to one's ability to understand right from wrong, to understand the consequences of one's actions, and then willfully commit a wrongful act.* Above the age of 7, children were considered capable of *mens rea* and were held responsible for their actions in the same ways as adults.

The *chancery courts* arose in England in the fifteenth century. Part of the reason for their development was to deal with children's problems. The chancery courts required parents to provide support, supervision, and care for their children. The King of England was established as **parens patriae**—*"the father of his country"*—*which made the King the "ultimate parent" and gave him the right to care for the children of the state if their parents would not or could not do so.* Although the chancery courts were established primarily to deal with problems such as neglect and abuse rather than behavior problems on the part of youths, their existence set an important legal precedent that would have dramatic impact on juvenile courts some four centuries later. The concept or *parens patriae* established the principle that the state could intervene on behalf of a child even if this involved taking the child from the parents.

Much of eighteenth and nineteenth century criminology, both in theory and in practice, was structured on the traditional assumption that punishment is the best and most appropriate deterrent of crime. Thus, in the absence of definitive laws and a specialized court system for the legal processing of children, juvenile offenders were often treated and tried as adult criminals. As recently as the latter part of the nineteenth century, children were tried in criminal courts in both England and the United States; they were detained in the same jails, tried in the same courts, sent to the same correctional facilities, and sometimes even executed (Sanders, 1970). While the nature of the offense and the age of the offender generally determined the kind and degree of punishment to be exacted, there were enough cases of children who were executed by society to underscore the prevailing notion that people would avoid behavior they have identified with evil and pain.

Prior to the establishment of the juvenile court, at least three developments occurred during the nineteenth century which altered the way youthful offenders were treated:

1. In 1825, in New York City, the **House of Refuge** was established. This provided separate correctional facilities for children (usually between the ages of 7 and 14) after they had been convicted in criminal court.
2. In 1841, the city of Boston first tried **probation,** or *supervised release,* a

method of treating juveniles outside of a correctional institution, but still under the supervision of the criminal court.

3. In 1869, the state of Massachusetts officially established probation with supervision for juvenile law violators (Haskell and Yablonsky, 1978:26).

These developments were linked to the changing attitudes toward childhood and the creation of the concept of adolescence discussed earlier (Chapters 2, 7, and 8). They represented a desire to hold young law violators accountable for their actions, but also reflected a movement toward handling juveniles differently from adult criminal offenders.

THE CHILD SAVERS' MOVEMENT

Steps to provide specialized correctional treatment to children and youths were initiated by a group of influential social reformers in the late nineteenth century. The Child Savers, as they were called, were convinced that urban slum life exerted a corrupting influence on idle youths. "However," the Child Savers insisted, "because of their tender age, delinquent youth[s] could be reclaimed from a criminal life if proper steps were taken" (Platt, 1969:45). They were instrumental in shifting the focus away from the criminal nature of delinquency to what was generally considered to be a more humanistic approach built around the medical model and the rehabilitative ideal.

The **medical model** used by the Child Savers diagnosed nonconforming behavior with such analogous terms as "disease," "illness," and "contagion." In other words, within the **medical model** *crime was viewed as a kind of social pathology, and young people manifested the antisocial behavioral symptoms of criminality as a result of being exposed to it in their environment.* The older the criminal, the more chronic the "sickness," and chances of recovery were considered to be less than those for a young person.

The **rehabilitative ideal** *emphasized the temporary and reversible nature of adolescent crime, if remedial measures were strenuously applied at an early age.* Support for the Child Savers' ideology was forthcoming from the noted penologist Enoch Wines who wrote in 1880: "These delinquent children are born to it; brought up for it; and they must be saved" (cited in Platt, 1969:45).

The Child Savers had their greatest impact in changing the reformatory system. The **reformatory** was well established throughout the United States during the middle of the nineteenth century as *a special form of institutionalized discipline for teenagers and young adults.* However, the reformatory was recognized as little more than a school for a later career in crime since youngsters were often indiscriminately thrown together with toughened adult criminals and there was little opportunity for education or resocialization that might prepare a young person for a more constructive life (Platt, 1969:46–54).

By the end of the nineteenth century, the Child Savers had exerted enough political pressure to have laws passed that restructured the reformatory system. According to Anthony Platt (1969:54) the reformatory plan developed by the Child Savers included the following principles:

1. Young offenders must be segregated from the corrupting influences of adult criminals.
2. 'Delinquents' should be removed from their environment and imprisoned for their own good and protection. Reformatories should be guarded sanctuaries, combining love and guidance with firmness and restraint.
3. 'Delinquents' should be assigned to reformatories without trial and with minimal legal requirements. Due process is not required because reformatories are intended to reform and not to punish.
4. Sentences should be indeterminate, so that inmates are encouraged to cooperate in their own reform and recalcitrant 'delinquents' are not allowed to resume their criminal careers . . .

In summary of the Child Savers' movement, these reformers seem to have equated juvenile independence with delinquency and sought to exercise extensive and rigid control over most youthful activities. While the principles that guided the restructuring of the reformatory system for handling delinquent youths were motivated by idealistic and humanistic values, their arbitrary implementation denied multitudes of young people their basic constitutional right to due process.

THE JUVENILE COURT

The mounting pressure for a judicial system that incorporated specialized processing of juvenile delinquents culminated in 1899 when the Illinois legislature passed the *Juvenile Court Act,* creating the first statewide court especially for children. Today there is a juvenile court in virtually every American jurisdiction, with about 2,800 courts hearing juvenile cases.[1] **Juvenile courts** are *judicial tribunals that deal in special ways with the cases of young people.* The juvenile court is not a criminal court; it is a statutory court whose powers and limitations are defined by the laws of the state in which it exists.

Most state statutes regarding juvenile courts do not necessarily create a *separate, independent* juvenile court. Consequently, the role of juvenile judge is only "a part-time assignment" for many judges (Cox and Conrad, 1987:153). Martin Haskell and Lewis Yablonsky (1978:27) reported that in 40 states

---

[1]This figure is based on estimates from several other sources. It is extremely difficult to determine precisely how many juvenile courts exist, since juvenile cases are sometimes handled in separate courts; sometimes in municipal, county, or district courts; and sometimes in family and/or divorce courts.

juveniles were handled in courts whose primary purpose was some other function (either family or criminal courts). In those states a judge who sits on another court (usually criminal) sets aside a day to hear juvenile cases. On that day, the court becomes a juvenile court and follows the procedures that are prescribed for juvenile courts in that state.

To distinguish the proceedings of the juvenile court from those of the criminal court to which adults are brought to trial, a new vocabulary emerged. Rather than a criminal complaint, a juvenile court "petition" is issued ordering the accused offender to appear in court. Similarly, arraignments have come to be called "initial hearings," and convictions have been renamed "findings of involvements." Finally, sentences have been replaced by the more informal and less threatening term "disposition" (Coffey, 1974:37).

The establishment of juvenile courts in 1899 did *not* mean that children were automatically granted the constitutional right to due process. On the contrary, the Child Savers' well-intentioned but discriminatory philosophy and practices became officially institutionalized in the juvenile court system:

> The goals were to investigate, diagnose, and prescribe treatment, not to adjudicate guilt or fix blame. The individual's background was more important than the facts of a given incident; specific conduct relevant more as symptomatic of a need for the court to bring its helping powers to bear than as prerequisite to exercise of jurisdiction. Lawyers were unnecessary—adversary tactics were out of place, for the mutual aim of all was not to contest or object but to determine the treatment plan best for the child (Winslow, 1973:134).

In 1920, the U.S. Children's Bureau recommended the following as essential characteristics of the juvenile court:

1. Separate hearings;
2. Informal procedures;
3. Regular probation services;
4. Separate detention;
5. Special court and probation records; and
6. Provision for mental and physical examinations (cited in Belden, 1920:7–10).

While the Children's Bureau had no authority to make policy or enforce its guidelines, its suggestions for the operation of juvenile courts had tremendous influence on juvenile court proceedings. Juvenile hearings were almost always private, usually involving only the juvenile, his or her parents, the judge, and a social worker. Juries were not used, as the issue of innocence or guilt was much less the focus of the hearing than was the question "Why is this juvenile present in court?" and the judge's primary responsibility was to decide how best to handle the situation. The proceedings were conducted informally with very little attention to the ritualistic legal traditions which dominated adult criminal court proceedings. The judge generally addressed the juvenile by first name and asked a number of questions of the juvenile and parents; and the strict rules regarding testimony and evidence in criminal cases were not always applied. Thus, the juvenile hearing in the early juvenile court often resembled an informal conference more than a formal trial.

The traditionally informal and nonlegalistic nature of the juvenile court has changed a great deal in recent years. Today, more juveniles and their families secure legal counsel and more attorneys are involved in juvenile court proceedings (the impact of attorney involvement in juvenile court is addressed in the Concept Application at the end of this chapter). Several significant U.S. Supreme Court cases have impacted upon the legal rights extended to juveniles who appear before the juvenile court. One of the results has been that hearings have begun to take on a more formal atmosphere, and judges tend to handle them similarly to criminal proceedings (Coxe, 1967).

One of the most direct official confrontations with adult society an adolescent may have is to appear before a judge in juvenile court.

THE JUVENILE COURT AND DUE PROCESS

Juvenile courts were established for the protection of children, and initially ignored the concept of due process as outlined earlier in this chapter. When a youth was petitioned to the juvenile court, the court was philosophically and legally acting on behalf of the child. Therefore, the adversary relationship which exists in criminal courts (state vs. John Doe) was considered to be nonexistent in the juvenile court. For that reason, the rigid ritual, rules of evidence, and other formal procedures of the criminal court were not established as part of the juvenile court. Consequently, the basic constitutional rights (especially those of due process) traditionally were not accorded juveniles in their hearings.

In 1954, in the *Holmes Case,* the U.S. Supreme Court ruled that since juvenile courts were not criminal courts, the constitutional rights which are guaranteed to persons accused of crimes did not apply to juveniles (In re Holmes, 1954). Holmes was an 18-year-old boy who was arrested while riding in a stolen car. As a result of his juvenile court disposition, he was sent to a state training school. Holmes' lawyer appealed the case on the basis that Holmes had not been represented by counsel; had not been properly informed of the charges against him; had not been advised of his rights (especially the right not to testify against himself); that much of the testimony against Holmes should have been deemed inadmissible; and that Holmes had not actually committed an illegal act. In response to the appeal, the Supreme Court reaffirmed the position that an adversary relationship did not exist in juvenile court. Chief Justice Horace Stern asserted that the court was not trying to punish a criminal, but rather to salvage a boy who might become one (In re Holmes, 1954). In other words, due process was not necessary since the court was attempting to help and reform rather than punish the youth.

Due process, even in a limited form, was not to become a part of juvenile court procedure until 1967, and then it developed through some rather interesting events. In June of 1964, Gerald Gault, along with another boy, was taken into custody in Gila County, Arizona for allegedly making an obscene phone call to a neighbor woman. Both of Gault's parents were away from home and were not notified of his detention. On the following day, Gault was petitioned to the juvenile court (although his parents did not see the petition). Gault's mother attended the hearing. The judge informally questioned Gault about the phone calls. The disposition of the case resulted in Gault being adjudicated delinquent and committed to the Arizona State Industrial School for the remainder of his minority (6 years). The same charge against an adult would have resulted in a fine of $5 to $50, or imprisonment for not more than 2 months (Neigher, 1967). The case was appealed based on the issues that Gault had not been advised of his rights (especially against self-incrimination); and was not allowed to deny the charges or cross-examine the only witness against him (Neigher, 1967). The final appeal went before the U.S. Supreme Court, and in what is viewed as a landmark decision in juvenile justice, the Supreme Court in 1967, under Chief Justice Earl Warren, handed down the *Gault Decision* (In re Gault, 1967) which resulted in:

1. Right to notice of charges against the juvenile.
2. Right to counsel.
3. Right to face and cross-examine witnesses.
4. Right to refuse to answer self-incriminating questions.
5. Right to a transcript of the proceedings.
6. Right to appeal.

While the Gault decision was a major development in officially providing a measure of due process in juvenile hearings, care must be taken not to overestimate the impact of the case. The decision did *not* provide to juveniles all the constitutional rights afforded adult criminal suspects. A limitation of the decision is that because of the wording, it is not entirely clear whether the rights outlined therein must be accorded the juvenile or whether those rights can be waived by the juvenile's parents. In many cases that might be a moot point, but in cases where the parents originate a petition against their own child, the difference could be extremely important. Regardless, the Gault decision had tremendous impact on the juvenile justice system. More juveniles began seeking counsel, being represented in their hearing, and appealing their cases (Coxe, 1967). Perhaps the most significant impact of the Gault decision is the recognition by the U.S. Supreme Court that even in juvenile cases an adversary relationship exists, and in order to protect the best interests of the juvenile, at least limited due process must prevail.[2]

Several other important U.S. Supreme Court decisions have impacted upon the issue of due process in the juvenile justice system. For instance, in 1966, the famous *Miranda* decision was issued which ruled that when adults are arrested, they must be informed of their right to remain silent, that any statements made by them can be used against them in court, that they have the right to legal counsel, and that if they cannot afford legal counsel, the court will appoint them an attorney (*Miranda v. Arizona*, 1966). The Gault decision implied that these rights also must be afforded a juvenile when taken in custody, although it did not expressly state this. In subsequent U.S. Supreme Court decisions, the Court has contended that juveniles are entitled to the rights against self-incrimination outlined in the *Miranda* decision. There is some question, however, whether juveniles can waive those rights without their parents or attorney being present.

Another important U.S. Supreme Court decision was that of *Kent v. United States* in 1966 (cited in Cox and Conrad, 1987:295–311). Morris A. Kent was a

---

[2]For an excellent overview of juveniles' rights in court, see Samuel M. Davis, *Rights of juveniles: The juvenile justice system* (2nd ed.). New York: Clark Boardman, 1983.

14-year-old boy who had been arrested in 1959 for several housebreakings and attempted purse snatchings. Kent appeared before the juvenile court in the District of Columbia, and was placed on probation. Two years later, while investigating a housebreaking, robbery, and rape case, police found fingerprints at the scene which matched those of Morris Kent. Kent (then 16 years old) was taken into custody and interrogated over a period of 2 days, during which he admitted his involvement in the crime under investigation, and offered information about several other similar offenses he had committed. No record exists to establish when Kent's mother was notified that he was in custody, but after 4 days of his detention, she secured an attorney's services. The attorney filed several motions with the juvenile court including one asking for psychiatric and psychological examination of Kent. After approximately 1 week of detention of Kent, the juvenile judge waived jurisdiction (because he was 16, the juvenile court had exclusive jurisdiction in the case) and recommended that he be held over for trial in the District Court of the District of Columbia. No hearing was held in juvenile court, and there was no response to any of the motions filed by Kent's attorney (including a request that the juvenile court not waive its jurisdiction). Further, the juvenile judge issued no statement of reasons for waiving jurisdiction. A grand jury was convened and indicted Kent on three charges of housebreaking, three counts of robbery, and two counts of rape. Despite protests by Kent's attorney that Kent was mentally incompetent to stand trial, a trial was held. Interestingly, Kent was found not guilty by reason of insanity on the two rape charges, but was found guilty on the charges of housebreaking and robbery. He was sentenced to serve 5 to 15 years on each count, or a total of 30 to 90 years. The case was appealed to the U.S. Court of Appeals on the grounds that Kent was unlawfully detained and interrogated and was deprived of counsel, and his parents were not notified. Kent's attorney contended that young Kent had been deprived of the basic constitutional rights that would have been granted an adult facing the same charges, yet Kent was tried as an adult in criminal court. The Appellate Court upheld the conviction, and the case eventually came before the U.S. Supreme Court. The Supreme Court ruled that in order for a juvenile court to waive its exclusive jurisdiction, a hearing must be held (*Kent v. United States*, 1966). In its opinion, the Court stated, "We do not mean by this to indicate that the hearing must conform with all of the requirements of a criminal trial, or even of the usual administrative hearing; but we do hold that the hearing must measure up to essentials of due process and fair treatment" (cited in Cox and Conrad, 1987:309). Justice Fortas expressed some of the problems associated with the juvenile court, lamenting, "There is evidence, in fact, that there may be grounds for concern that the child receives the worst of both worlds: that he gets neither the protections accorded to adults nor the solicitous care and regenerative treatment postulated for children" (Cox and Conrad, 1987:305).

At least four other Supreme Court rulings had significant impact upon due process in juvenile courts: *In re Winship* (1970), *McKiever v. Pennsylvania* (1971), *Breed v. Jones* (1975), and *Schall v. Martin* (1984). Two of these cases extended the rights of due process in juvenile court (*In re Winship*, 1970; *Breed v. Jones*, 1975), and two of them denied specific elements of due process for juveniles (*McKiever v. Pennsylvania*, 1971; *Schall v. Martin*, 1984). *In re Winship* (1970) addressed the question whether "proof beyond a reasonable doubt" is required during the adjudication stage of a juvenile court hearing when the youth is charged with an act that would be a crime if committed by an adult (cited in Cox and Conrad, 1987:312–321). The case involved a 12-year-old boy who allegedly broke into a locker and stole $112 from a woman's purse. While the judge was convinced that Winship had committed the act, he acknowledged that there was not proof beyond a reasonable doubt. Winship was adjudicated delinquent and ordered to be placed in a state training school for a period of 18 months subject to yearly extensions until he reached the age of majority (potentially for 6 years). When he was brought before the U.S. Supreme Court, the Court ruled that proof beyond a reasonable doubt was necessary in a juvenile court hearing where a crime had been committed. The Court concluded, "civil labels and good intentions do not themselves obviate the need for criminal due process safeguards in juvenile courts" (Cox and Conrad, 1987:314). Further due process rights were guaranteed to juveniles when the Supreme Court ruled that juveniles, like adults, were protected against **double jeopardy,** or *being tried twice for the same offense* (*Breed v. Jones*, 1975). In that case, the court ruled that a youth cannot be tried in a criminal court for the same offense for which he/she has been tried as a delinquent in juvenile court.

The Supreme Court sent out mixed signals in regard to its commitment to extending the rights of due process to the juvenile court. In the case of *McKiever v. Pennsylvania* (1971), the court ruled that juveniles were not guaranteed the right to a trial by jury. Approximately three-fourths of the states follow that ruling and do not provide jury trials for juveniles (Mahoney, 1985:553). Later, in the case of *Schall v. Martin* (1984), the Court held that youths could be held without bail if they were being held for their own protection or the protection of society. In these two cases the court reflected a shift back toward the rehabilitative and protective philosophy of the earlier juvenile court. Consequently, there is some ambiguity as to precisely what rights are guaranteed juveniles when they are petitioned to juvenile court. It appears that in some areas, the extent of due process granted juveniles must be determined virtually on a case-by-case basis. However, based upon the legal precedence set in the aforementioned juvenile cases, in most states, juveniles are advised of their legal rights when detained, parents are notified as soon as possible, and juveniles are allowed legal counsel during all phases of the justice process.

JUVENILE COURT PROCEDURES

The juvenile court is characterized by three main operational procedures: *intake, adjudication,* and *disposition.*

Intake

The intake procedure typically begins when the juvenile court receives a **referral** on a particular youth. In most states, **referral** *simply means that the juvenile's name has been given to the court.* Referrals can come from a variety of sources including police, parents, schools, and others. Typically, the largest number of referrals come from the police (Table 12–1).

Upon receiving the referral, one of the officers of the court (usually a probation officer) is assigned to investigate the case to determine how the case can best be handled. A decision must be made on whether to hold or release the child while the case is being investigated. The nature of the referral is the main criterion at that point. When possible, juveniles being referred for minor offenses are likely to be released into the custody of their parents. If the intake officer views it as appropriate, an intake interview with the youth and the youth's parents or legal guardian may be requested (Miller et al., 1985). More serious offenders, or those who for some reason cannot or should not be released to parents, are usually detained. The district attorney has primary responsibility for this decision. Ideally, the probation officer conducts a thorough investigation into the youth's social background by interviewing teachers, neighbors, and others who might provide insight into the situation. The probation officer may then recommend that the case be dismissed entirely, be referred to some other agency, or may move that a petition be filed with the juvenile court for a hearing. A **petition** is *an official statement which contains the important facts of the case* such as the action which prompted the petition, along with relevant information about the juvenile and the youth's parents or guardians (Caldwell, 1961).

TABLE 12-1

Juvenile Court Referrals by Source (1982)

Source of Referral	Number of Referrals	Percent
Law enforcement	1,095,300	83.8
Parents, relatives	43,900	3.4
School	38,400	2.9
Probation officer	31,700	2.4
Social agency	13,800	1.1
Other courts	28,600	2.2
Other	55,000	4.2
Total	1,306,700	100

Source: *Sourcebook of Criminal Justice Statistics–1982.* Edited by T.J. Flanagan and M. McLeod. U.S. Department of Justice, Bureau of Justice Statistics (NCJ-86483) Washington, DC: U.S. Government Printing Office, 1983:437.

During the intake procedure in some states, the judge also has the option of declaring the juvenile to be an "adult" and ordering that the case be referred to an adult criminal court. There is some argument as to whether a youth is more likely to be certified as an adult based upon the seriousness of the offense and age (Fagan et al., 1987b) or upon extralegal factors such as the race and ethnicity of the offender (Osbun and Rode, 1984). As pointed out earlier, as a result of *Kent v. United States* (1966), a hearing must be held and justification given for waiving jurisdiction by the juvenile court. Some states have revised their juvenile codes to provide for automatic waiver of juvenile court jurisdiction. For example, in some states a juvenile over the age of 16 who commits an act that would be considered a felony if committed by an adult, is automatically certified as an adult, and handled by adult criminal court. In those states, for a juvenile to be handled in juvenile court instead of the adult criminal court, a **reverse certification** hearing must be held to *declare the youth a juvenile.*

The length of time for intake procedures varies. The court attempts to work as expeditiously as possible while taking the necessary time to thoroughly evaluate a youth's background and social circumstances. According to established juvenile justice standards, the intake process should not exceed 30 days (Miller et al., 1985:242).

Adjudication

If a petition is filed and the youth has a hearing, the adjudication process takes place. **Adjudication** refers to *making a judgement or ruling.* This phase of the juvenile court proceeding is analogous to the trial phase of adult judicial proceedings. The judge (usually with assistance from the probation officer and the district attorney) must decide whether to adjudicate the juvenile as *neglected, dependent,* or *delinquent.* During this stage evidence will be heard, and the judge will attempt to determine if the reason for which the juvenile was petitioned is valid, and if so, what should be done about it. If the child is adjudicated as neglected or dependent, the court identifies the youth as **INS** *(in need of supervision).* Youths sent to the court as a result of having been neglected, abused, wayward, truant, or runaways are most likely to be adjudicated INS.

A **delinquent** adjudication usually means that *the juvenile has committed a wrongful act for which the judge feels the youth must be held accountable.* Juveniles who have committed acts which would be a crime if committed by an adult are most likely to be adjudicated delinquent.

The adjudication hearing for a juvenile accused of committing a criminal act is very likely to take on many of the characteristics of an adult criminal trial. Attorneys are likely to be used, and in a few states, juveniles are even granted the right to a trial by jury (Mahoney, 1985). There are some notable distinctions, however, most prominent of which is that the juvenile hearing remains closed to the public, whereas adult criminal trials are open. There has been increased pressure exerted to attempt to open juvenile hearings to public scrutiny, particularly in light of recent events which have resulted in allowing media coverage (including cameras in the courtrooms) of adult trials (Day, 1984). The protective philosophy of the juvenile court has been reemphasized, however, as juvenile courts have steadfastly refused to hold open hearings for fear of public stigmatization of the youths involved. Louis Day (1984) contended that the increased public interest in juvenile delinquency will heighten the demand for public access to juvenile court hearings and records and ultimately will force the Supreme Court to determine two issues: (1) whether juvenile proceedings are criminal cases, subject to the same constitutional requirements as adult cases; and (2) the degree of access the media and public should have to juvenile hearings.

During the adjudication phase, children brought before the court may have their parents, guardian, and/or legal counsel present. As previously mentioned, while initially established as an informal hearing, the adjudication phase has become increasingly formalized and legalistic. More juveniles and their parents are seeking legal advice and securing counsel for juvenile cases. The juvenile's right against self-incrimination is acknowledged, and juveniles are allowed to present a defense to the charges filed against them. As one Supreme Court Justice noted, "This court believes that although the juvenile court was initially created as a social experiment, it has not ceased to be part of the justice system" (Miller et al., 1985:554).

Disposition

Disposition is *the stage of the hearing most analogous to sentencing in a criminal court.* Occurring after adjudication, it is the process by which the judge must decide the best way to handle the juvenile's case. The judge must attempt to do what is best for the child while also protecting the community and preserving the integrity of the law. At least in philosophy, the disposition is supposed to be oriented toward treatment which will benefit the youth, rather than toward punishment.

During disposition, the judge has several alternatives from which to choose. The district attorney plays an important part in making recommendations to the judge, but the judge has extensive discretionary power in determining the disposition of the case. The judge can choose to dismiss the case and release the juvenile to parents or guardians. Estimates vary, but roughly 50 percent of all juvenile cases are simply dismissed. If the juvenile is adjudicated as INS, the judge can declare the youth a "ward of the court" and order placement in foster care. Because of the insufficient number of adequate foster homes, however, this disposition may be ruled less often than others. If the juvenile's problem is thought to be a result of some type of emotional disturbance, the judge will probably order a psychiatric report and the youth may be sent to a residential treatment center.

The contemporary juvenile court has become more formal with many of its proceedings resembling adult criminal court.

If the youth is adjudicated delinquent, the judge has three basic alternatives. Probably the one most widely used is to place the juvenile on formal probation. While on probation, the juvenile must adhere to a specific set of guidelines and meet periodically with an assigned probation officer (see Chapter 13). If probation is deemed inappropriate, the judge can send the juvenile to a minimum security correctional institution. If the offense is of a serious nature, or the juvenile has appeared before the court several times, the judge may decide to send the offender to a maximum security correctional facility for youths. These institutions are often called "state training schools" and to a large extent operate as prisons for offenders under the age of majority (for further discussion see Chapter 13).

Several factors influence the outcome of the dispositional phase of juvenile hearings. As already mentioned, one factor is the extent and variety of alternatives available to the judge. As Mahoney (1985:555) pointed out, "a problem related to plea negotiating for juveniles is that in many juvenile courts there is essentially a small range of disposition alternatives."

Variables such as seriousness of the offense, prior record, age, race, and sex of the offender all enter into the discretionary decision of the juvenile court judge (e.g., Arnold, 1971; Chesney-Lind, 1977; Cohen, 1975; Perry, 1985; Fagan et al., 1987a,b). Just as the police are influenced by a variety of extralegal factors such as race, age, and sex of the offender in deciding how to handle juveniles on the street (Chapter 11), so are the courts. For example, William Arnold (1971), Terry Thornberry (1973), Robert Perry (1985), and Jeffrey Fagan et al., (1987a) all found that blacks and youths from lower socioeconomic backgrounds typically received harsher dispositions in juvenile court. Similarly, while it has been generally acknowledged that paternalistic attitudes of police and court officials may lead to lower arrest rates and fewer petitions to juvenile court for females, Meda Chesney-Lind (1977) found that once detained and petitioned to court, females are likely to be treated more harshly than their male counterparts regardless of seriousness of the offense.

Other variables related to dispositional decisions include the extent of demonstrated parental interest in the child and the case (O'Quin et al., 1985), known membership in a juvenile gang (Zatz, 1985) and prior dispositions (Thornberry and Christenson, 1984). Interestingly, through a longitudinal study, Thornberry and Christenson (1984) found that the single most important determinant of the type and severity of disposition levied against a particular youth was the type and severity of previous dispositions. They found that rather than dispositions becoming increasingly severe with each repeat offense by an individual, the same disposition was very likely to be imposed over and over again.

THE ROLE OF ATTORNEYS IN JUVENILE COURT

The role of attorneys in juvenile court is not nearly as clearcut as it is in adult criminal court. It has been only since the Gault Decision of 1967 that they have been formally introduced into the juvenile court proceeding; since then, attorneys have played an increasingly important role in the contemporary juvenile court.

The District Attorney

For purposes of law enforcement, each state is divided into judicial districts. Periodically, a public election is held in each district in which a prosecuting attorney is elected to represent the state in criminal cases within the district (Black, 1968). Thus, when the police or a citizen signs a petition alleging misconduct by a child or young person, the office of the district attorney comes in contact with the youngster. Before this petition is filed with the court and a hearing is scheduled, the district attorney may investigate the case and exercise one of three basic options:

1. Refuse to prosecute for lack of evidence and release the child.
2. Defer prosecution and place the child on informal probation. In many such cases the district attorney may make an arrangement with the child's parents not to prosecute if they will keep the child under close supervision.
3. Expedite the filing of the petition and prosecute the child in the juvenile court for the alleged offense.

Former juvenile judge Ted Rubin (1980) concluded that as a result of the Gault Decision (which provides the right to counsel for juveniles), prosecuting attorneys have taken a much more active role in the juvenile court, especially during the intake phase. We can view the district attorney as the law-enforcing officer in the median position between the policeman and the juvenile court judge. Here, the **filtering process** discussed in Chapter 11 is continued, as many cases are treated informally and not sent on to court. In this way, many young people avoid an official record of delinquency and the state avoids much expensive litigation. If the petition is formally filed with the court, the court procedures described in the previous section officially begin.

The district attorney can be involved in all three stages of the juvenile court proceedings. This officer may make recommendations to the judge regarding whether the case should be handled in juvenile court or transferred to adult criminal court. Along with a court services officer, the district attorney also advises the judge on adjudication and dispositional alternatives.

The Defense Attorney

The role of the defense attorney is the most ambiguous in the juvenile court. Since due process has been introduced into the juvenile justice system, more juveniles and their parents are seeking legal representation when appearing in juvenile court. The attorney for the juvenile performs many of the same functions as a defense attorney in criminal court. However, because of the less formal atmosphere of the juvenile court, and the more relaxed rules on testimony and evidence, the youth's attorney may not be able to protect the youth in some of the same ways a criminal lawyer can defend an adult in criminal court. While a juvenile may plead the Fifth Amendment (right not to testify against oneself), this behavior may be more likely to antagonize the judge than to help the juvenile's case. Similarly, Anne Mahoney (1985:556) discovered that in states where juveniles were entitled to jury trials, it was quite possible that such a request might actually produce negative results for the youth because the court could penalize those youths who asked for jury trials. While the criminal judge's decision hinges upon the legal and technical ramifications of the case, it must be remembered that the juvenile court judge's decision rests primarily upon what the judge considers best for the juvenile. Thus, even though an attorney may provide counsel which helps to legally protect the youth, it may in fact not favorably alter the adjudication and disposition decisions.

CRITICISMS OF THE JUVENILE COURT

Since 1899, when the first juvenile court was established, it has undergone a great deal of scrutiny and criticism from different sectors in society. One of the most prevalent criticisms has been that the juvenile courts are "too easy" on juveniles and have a tendency to coddle and protect what are basically just young criminals. As a juvenile officer in the Los Angeles Police Department put it, ". . . Some of these hoodlums are back on the street before I finish the paper work!" (Carter, 1976:124).

From its inception, the juvenile court has been viewed almost as a parent, charged with protecting those who are sent to it. The juvenile court was founded upon the philosophies of protection and rehabilitation. In a society where people are reading about teenaged rapists, murderers, and muggers, many citizens question the legitimacy of "protecting" juvenile offenders. Many critics of the court are shocked by its lenient dispositions and believe its philosophy should not be applied to youths who commit serious criminal offenses (Krisberg and Austin, 1978). Police often feel helpless in attempting to control the problem, knowing that many of their efforts at law enforcement will be negated by benevolent, well-meaning, or politically sensitive juvenile judges. Victims of juvenile offenders are often reluctant to file complaints or press charges because previous experience has shown that very little will be done to the juveniles; and often they are back on the streets the very same day, seeking revenge. In some states, the most severe penalty for a juvenile is to be adjudicated "delinquent" and institutionalized for a brief period of time. For example, a case in New York which received much media attention focused on a 15-year-old boy who committed a premeditated and particularly vicious murder. He was merely sent to a juvenile institution for 18 months (AP, New York, 1978).[3] On the basis of such cases, some members of society perceive the juvenile court as more helpless and impotent than benevolent and protecting.

Conversely, another criticism of the juvenile court has been that it is "too hard" on juveniles and tends to overreact to relatively minor offenses. Because a major goal of the juvenile court is to prevent juvenile offenders from becoming

---

[3]For an excellent bibliography on this problem see *The serious offender: A selected bibliography* compiled by Thomas Schrivel and edited by Marjorie Krautiz, Washington, DC: US Department of Justice, January 1982.

adult criminals, there may be a tendency on the part of some juvenile judges to treat relatively minor offenses very seriously in an effort to impress upon the juvenile that any further law violation will not be tolerated. As previously discussed in the Gault case, the punishment for an adult who made an obscene phone call would have been a minor fine or brief incarceration. Instead, Gault was ordered institutionalized for a period of 6 years! This type of disposition seems extreme in proportion to the severity of the alleged offense. Similarly, in some cases, much of what might be viewed as merely "adolescent mischief" is treated as if it were a major crime in order to "teach the youth a lesson." Unfortunately, the lesson taught may not be the one desired. When petty offenses are treated as major ones, at least in the mind of the juvenile, the difference between the two may become blurred. For example, in a state where murder and truancy might both result in 18 months of institutionalization, the vastly significant difference between the two acts becomes symbolically reduced. Several researchers have linked the widespread procedure of indeterminate sentencing (no specified length of sentence) by juvenile courts to terms of incarceration for juveniles often being longer than those for adults who commit the same offense (e.g., Lightholder, 1978; Sleeth, 1978; ACLU, 1978). Consequently, the question of discrimination against juveniles arises as a legal issue to be addressed (the issues of indeterminate and disproportionate sentencing are more thoroughly discussed in Chapter 15). Recent trends in juvenile justice indicate that this issue may be dissipated, as juvenile courts appear to be focusing their attention much more on the smaller number of serious juvenile offenders as opposed to the nonserious status offenders which have traditionally monopolized juvenile court dockets (Regnery, 1986).

The lack of total due process continues as another point of criticism of the juvenile court. As a result of the Supreme Court decisions discussed earlier in this chapter, and the increased utilization of legal counsel in juvenile hearings, this criticism has been somewhat reduced. Much of the concern now focuses upon preserving the rights of youths charged with status offenses. Since these youths have not violated criminal laws and are more likely to be adjudicated "in need of supervision" as opposed to "delinquent," their hearings are often much more informal. Consequently, the legal rights of these juveniles may not be protected as much as if they had been arrested for a criminal act. For example, Jan Costello and Nancy Worthington (1981) expressed concern that many states were circumventing the Juvenile Justice and Prevention Act which prohibits the incarceration of status offenders.

Perhaps the most persistent criticism leveled at the juvenile court has been that its jurisdiction is too broad. As former judge of the Denver Juvenile Court Ted Rubin (1976:66) expressed:

> This court is a far more complex instrument than outsiders imagine. It is law, and it is social work; it is control and it is help; it is the good parent, and, also, the stern parent; it is both formal and informal. It is concerned not only

with the delinquent, but also with the battered child, the runaway, and many others . . . The juvenile court has been all things to all people.

The criticism is that the juvenile court has tried to be too many different things to too many different people. Rubin (1977) said that the juvenile court must establish an identity which clearly outlines the court's responsibility. In broadening its jurisdiction to attempt to cover virtually any of the problems which involve juveniles, the court may have inadvertently diluted its ability to successfully handle any of them. This "jack-of-all-trades, master of none" image has plagued the contemporary juvenile court.

Francis Allen (1976:417) discussed several of the problems involved in juvenile justice, and pointed out that many of the court's ". . . difficulties arise from an insufficient conception of the court's role and the court's capabilities." Rubin (1979) further discussed some of the problems encountered by the juvenile court in attempting to handle too broad a range of cases. He contended that there is a definite need for a juvenile court, but it should not be expected to handle all types of cases. For example, he suggested that neglected and abused children should probably be handled by divorce and family courts.

THE MULTIFACETED JUVENILE COURT

One of the difficulties faced by the juvenile court resides in the fact that there really is no such thing as *the* juvenile court. Rather, juvenile courts vary from state to state in their size, nature, jurisdiction, and procedures. In short, there are a variety of juvenile courts. As previously mentioned, part of the criticism leveled at juvenile courts results from their attempt to be all things to all people. Throughout this chapter we have compared and contrasted the juvenile court to adult criminal court. In the process, we have discovered that while there are increasingly notable similarities between the two, there remain distinctive differences.

It has been suggested that the contemporary juvenile court no longer resembles the earlier chancery court out of which it developed, but is also unlike adult criminal court. In an attempt to analyze the juvenile court as a "people-processing organization," Yeheskel Hasenfeld and Paul Cheung (1985) pointed to the multidimensional personality of juvenile courts. They indicated that juvenile courts are faced with a "dual and contradictory mandate" of projecting a "social service orientation," while responding to the more legalistic orientation of preserving "law and order" (Hasenfeld and Cheung, 1985:806). In an effort to explain how the court attempts to fulfill this dual mandate, Hasenfeld and Cheung (1985:819–820) created the following typology of juvenile courts based upon the proportion of cases handled judicially (formally brought before a judge), and the rate of commitment (proportion of juveniles committed to juvenile institutions):

1. **Interventionist Court:** characterized by a *high* proportion of its cases being handled judicially, and by a *high* commitment rate; this is the traditional juvenile court that emerged from the childsaving movement.
2. **Paternalistic Court:** characterized by a *low* proportion of cases handled judicially and a *high* commitment rate; this is the most commonly found juvenile court which tries to combine social rehabilitation with community protection.
3. **Ritualistic Court:** characterized by a *high* proportion of its cases being handled judicially and a *low* rate of commitment; this court exercises its formal judicial authority, but feels less pressure to protect the community.
4. **Minimalistic Court:** characterized by both a *low* proportion of cases handled judicially and a *low* commitment rate; this court represents an attempt to legally reform juvenile courts by elevating their legal status and removing the judge from the political arena.

This typology addresses the multidimensional nature of juvenile courts and demonstrates that different courts handle cases in different ways.

David Aday (1986) created a simpler typology of juvenile courts based on important variations in court structure and procedure. He identified two different types of juvenile courts: the **traditional court** and the **due process court.** According to Aday (1986:111) the two courts were distinguishable by the following characteristics:

Traditional Court
1. **Low task differentiation:** decisions about cases are made by court staff; *the prosecutor does not participate in decisions to file formal petitions* [Italics in the original];
2. **Centralized authority:** the judge administers probation and other court services;
3. **Low discretion for court services staff:** probation staff cannot assign juveniles to informal probation;
4. **Status offender jurisdiction:** the court routinely handles cases alleging status offenses;
5. **Low formalization:** adjudication and disposition hearings are not bifurcated.

Due Process Court
1. **High task differentiation:** court services staff participate separately in decisions; *the prosecutor participates in decisions to file formal complaints.* [Italics in original];
2. **Decentralized authority:** the judge does not administer probation or other court services; these services are administered within the State Department of Social Services;
3. **High discretion for court services staff:** probation staff assign juveniles to informal probation; the court does not handle such cases;
4. **Status offender jurisdiction:** the court routinely handles cases alleging status offenses;

5. **Low formalization:** there is no requirement to bifurcate adjudication and dispositional hearings.

In the *traditional court* the role of the judge is to enact the philosophy of *parens patriae*; consequently, the roles of attorneys, staff, parents, and others in the court are minimized. The traditional court attempts to perpetuate a social service orientation. According to Aday (1986:115), "particularistic characteristics of juveniles and/or offenses influence decisions" and "attorney use represents token compliance with due-process requirements and has no effect on decision making." On the other hand, the *due process court* is dominated by legal factors (especially nature of offenses) in its decision making, and attorneys play a prominent role in determining the outcome of cases (Aday, 1986). In the two types of courts studied by Aday, some interesting data emerged regarding rates of detention, probation, and commitment. We have constructed Table 12–2 to illustrate his findings.

As can be seen in Table 12–2, the traditional court was more likely to detain juveniles before their hearing, but once juveniles appeared before the judge, the largest percentage were likely to be formally placed on probation. The due process court detained far fewer juveniles, electing to simply warn and release almost three-fourths (73 percent) of those with whom it came in contact. The traditional court and due process court differed in severity of dispositions, with almost twice the proportion of juveniles appearing before the traditional court being committed to a juvenile institution as compared to those from the due process court.

THE FUTURE OF THE JUVENILE COURT

Given the historical development of the juvenile court and the many criticisms directed toward it in recent years, the future of the juvenile court is somewhat unclear. Conservatives, moderates, liberals, and radicals all have different views

TABLE 12–2

Dispositions in Traditional and Due Process Courts

	Traditional Court	Due Process Court
Detained juveniles	50%	16.1%
Unofficially warn and release	24.3%	73%
Placed on probation	63.6%	20.2%
Committed	12.1%	6.9%

Source: Created from data in D.P. Aday, Jr. Court structure, defense attorney use, and juvenile court decisions. *Sociological Quarterly* 27 (1), 1986:p. 112.

on what the future should hold for the juvenile court, but almost all agree that some changes must and will occur.

We would like to offer some suggestions for the direction of the juvenile court in the future. Most of these have been advocated by some faction at some time, so we cannot claim originality about the source of these ideas. In our view, the juvenile court of the future should:

1. Limit its jurisdiction;
2. Operate under the provisions of due process;
3. Be administered by competent judges;
4. Have adequate court personnel; and
5. Have adequate availability of alternatives for disposition.

It is much easier to list these items than it is to actually implement them. But we would like to briefly suggest some pragmatic possibilities for reforming the juvenile court of the future. (We further explore these suggestions along with others for juvenile court reform in Chapter 15, Rethinking the Delinquency Problem.)

Limited Jurisdiction

In our view, the juvenile court should not attempt to be all things to all people. By spreading itself so thinly, the court is proving itself woefully inadequate much of the time. Much of what is brought to the attention of the juvenile court could probably be better handled through other courts, nonlegal channels, other agencies, or, possibly, even be ignored. Child abuse and neglect are serious problems and cannot be ignored. But should the same court which handles youthful murderers, rapists, robbers, and burglars attempt to deal with these? We think not. Likewise, while status offenses such as truancy, smoking, and drinking may need attention, it is not necessary to deal with them in the same way (or even in the same court) as serious criminal offenses. In our opinion, the juvenile court should handle only those juveniles who have committed an act that would be a crime if committed by an adult, but are considered too young to stand trial in adult criminal court.

It should be noted, however, that despite the arguments for the elimination of status offenses from juvenile court jurisdiction, there still are people who strongly believe they should be retained as a function of the juvenile court. These arguments tend to focus on the lack of alternatives for handling such problems, and the belief that families, schools, and other social agencies need the official support of the legal system to effectively deal with the types of problems identified as status offenses (Myren, 1988). While acknowledging that the behaviors associated with status offenses are problematic, we believe that the streamlining of the juvenile court's jurisdiction is necessary. Consequently, we contend that status offenses should be removed from the juvenile courts, and problems associated with those behaviors be addressed by other social agencies and institutions such as the family, school, church, welfare departments, counseling services, and others. This issue is further explored in Chapter 15.

Eliminating status offenses from the juvenile court has been a hotly debated issue for quite some time. The arguments for elimination have tended to focus on the issues of ". . . fairness, effectiveness, and efficiency" (Myren, 1988:92). The handling of status offenses by the juvenile court often is seen as unfair because many of the status offenses (such as "incorrigibility") are vague and only selectively enforced.

In order to facilitate these types of changes in the juvenile courts, a number of juvenile statutes, criminal statutes, social attitudes, and values would have to be significantly revised. Two very important changes which would help streamline the juvenile court in limiting its jurisdiction would involve the standardization of juvenile laws within each state and across the nation, and developing a standard age limit which legally distinguishes juveniles from adults in all 50 states.

Due Process

We have already discussed the concept of due process and its development. If the court's jurisdiction were limited to criminal law violations as we suggest that it should be, due process would be an important aspect of each juvenile case. Since only juveniles who have allegedly committed criminal acts would appear before the court, a judicial adversary relationship would clearly exist. The youth would be charged with violating a criminal statute. Though the case would be handled in a special court designed for such a purpose, all the basic rights of due process accorded the suspected adult criminal should also be available to the youthful offender. The right to know the charges, have counsel present during questioning and at the hearing, and the presumption of innocence until proven otherwise should be necessary components of the revised juvenile court. The right not to testify against oneself, to trial by jury, and to open access to records should also be included. Naturally, the right to appeal decisions would exist. The specific details of implementation would have to be worked out in each state (e.g., would the jury consist of adults; or of the literal peers of the accused—other juveniles?), but the complete application of due process should be an intrinsic part of the court proceeding.

Professional Judges and Court Personnel

The role of the juvenile judge is critical, and, if the juvenile court is to be successful, this role must be filled by the most competent people available. Yet, in most states, juvenile judges are either elected by the people or appointed by governmental officials. This is not to imply that they are incompetent, but that the criteria for selection have less to do with legal and professional training, than to political activity and party loyalty. In a report by the President's Commission on Law Enforcement and Administration of Justice (1967:6–7), a quoted survey indicated that one-half of all juvenile judges did not have a college degree; one-fifth had received no college education at all; and one-fifth were not members of the bar. Steven Cox and John Conrad (1987:153) lamented, "While many [juvenile judges] clearly have the best interests of juveniles at heart, far too many show . . . unfamiliarity with juvenile codes . . ."

The judge in a juvenile court should at least have a degree in law, be a member of the bar, be knowledgeable about juvenile statutes, and have some experience in legal proceedings. Further, some training in or at least familiarity with the areas of early childhood development, sociology, and adolescent psychology would be beneficial.

In addition to the judge, other well-trained court personnel and consultants should be available in order to effectively carry out the mission of the juvenile court (i.e., protect the juvenile while also protecting society). The specific types of professionals might vary in different courts, but would probably include social workers, psychologists, and paralegal professionals who would be responsible for background checks, social investigations, and prehearing screening. Regardless of the specific make-up of the court personnel, the judge should have all the necessary professionals to call upon in order to best decide a case. This would require total community support in addition to the hiring of persons for that specific purpose.

Dispositional Alternatives

The availability of wider dispositional alternatives also would necessitate large-scale community support. Often juvenile judges have no choices other than the extremes of incarceration in a maximum security institution, or outright release. Other alternatives should be available such as placement in foster homes, treatment centers, community youth projects, youth shelters, and hospitals. In most states, these options exist in theory, but in some states, not in practice. The lack of availability of qualified foster parents, lack of proper diagnostic and treatment centers, and the insufficient funding common in most states have severely limited dispositional alternatives available to the juvenile judge. Most communities could be offering many more placements than are now being offered. In Chapter 14 we describe some of the treatment and prevention programs that have been followed and offer suggestions for other strategies.

SUMMARY

The juvenile court is a relatively young institution in the United States, officially established in Chicago in 1899. Yet, the historical and legal traditions of the court are much older and can be traced to the chancery courts of fifteenth century England. During its short history in this country, the juvenile court has greatly extended its jurisdiction and has had dramatic influence on the lives of those with whom it has come in contact.

The establishment of the American juvenile court roughly corresponded to changing attitudes about childhood and represented a major development in separating youthful offenders from hardened criminals. With its protective philosophy, and overall goal of deterring troubled youths from becoming adult criminals, the juvenile court has made numerous contributions in the handling of juveniles. Perhaps one of its most significant contributions has been its symbolic representation of the notion that the state is genuinely concerned about its youths. It has been there to intervene on the behalf of abused, neglected, and misdirected youths.

Despite its laudable philosophy and numerous accomplishments, the juvenile court also has been the target of widespread criticism from a variety of sources. Too lenient, too harsh, too broad in its scope, too narrow in its power, the juvenile court in the view of many has become an ineffective mockery of what it was meant to be. Partly in response to some of these criticisms, and partly as a result of Supreme Court intervention, the juvenile court has undergone numerous changes since it first came into operation. Probably one of the most prominent changes has been in its shift toward a more formal legalistic approach to juvenile criminal offenses. The introduction of elements of due process and increased involvement of attorneys has altered its once informal omnipotent procedures.

We have suggested several additional changes which might better streamline the juvenile court, clarify its mission, and help it become more effective in dealing with the problem of delinquency. Some of the changes are merely procedural, and could probably be implemented with relative ease. Other suggested changes are philosophical and structural in nature and would demand more time, effort, money, and cooperation from various segments of society. Whether such changes can and will be realistically implemented depends upon numerous factors.

In Chapters 14 and 15, we more thoroughly address the inherently social nature of juvenile justice and the issue of modifying the social structure in an effort to mobilize the total community toward delinquency prevention, treatment, and control.

CONCEPT APPLICATION

"The Use of Attorneys in the Juvenile Court"

The Gault Decision of 1967 by the U.S. Supreme Court brought some major changes into the juvenile court process. Lauded as a landmark decision, one of its important effects upon juvenile justice was the determination that juveniles and/or their parents have the right to legal counsel when petitioned to the juvenile court. Since that ruling, more juveniles and their parents have opted to have legal counsel present for their hearings before the juvenile court.

While the role of attorneys in adult criminal court is well established, it remains somewhat ambiguous in juvenile court hearings. The role of the district attorney in the prosecution of juvenile delinquency has become very similar to that in a criminal case. Since the Gault Decision, prosecutors have taken a much more active role in juvenile court procedures. In fact, Rubin (1980) contended that the intake process of the court is dominated by the prosecutor.

The defense attorney, on the other hand, has a much less clearcut role in the juvenile court. The Institute of Judicial Administration and the American Bar Association (IJA/ABA) suggested in their *Juvenile Justice Standards Project* (1977) that there are three roles that the attorney can fulfill in the juvenile court: (1) officer of the court; (2) guardian; (3) advocate. In the first role, the attorney becomes an aide to the juvenile judge in attempting to help the judge determine what is best for the youth. This role seems most appropriate in cases of neglect, abuse, and other situations in which the juvenile appears before the court more as a "victim" than as an "offender." The guardian role involves a situation in which the attorney takes control of all of the juvenile's interests in the hearing, and, to be effective, requires that the juvenile and the juvenile's parents passively follow all advice given by the attorney. This role seems most appropriate when the juvenile is very young, mentally incompetent, or not accompanied by parents or legal guardian when appearing before the court. The advocate role is the traditional role assumed by attorneys when representing a client in adult criminal court. In this role, the attorney attempts to represent the client's best legal interests, and defends the juvenile against the charges outlined in the court petition. It is the third role which is most likely to be adopted by attorneys secured to represent juveniles who have committed offenses that would be a crime if committed by an adult.

The role assumed by the attorney in juvenile court may be controlled to some degree by the type of juvenile court in which he/she appears, and may be greatly limited by the type of juvenile judge presiding over the hearing. In the due process type of court discussed in this chapter, the attorney probably will have every opportunity to assume the advocate role on behalf of the juvenile. On the other hand, in the traditional court, where the judge assumes almost total control of the hearing, and in which the due process rights of the juvenile are severely limited, the attorney may be severely restricted in choice of role in the proceeding.

The impact of increased involvement of attorneys in the juvenile court is unclear. It is generally agreed that their presence in the juvenile court has tended to increase the formality of court proceedings and to make the judge more aware of the due process rights of the juvenile. However, research on attorneys' influence on the actual adjudication and disposition rulings by juvenile courts indicates that the presence of attorneys has made very little difference (e.g., Sosin and Sarri, 1976). In a collection of research articles, Sarri and Hasenfeld (1976) found that attorneys' impact upon the juvenile court is minimal, and that virtually all others involved in the court procedures exert more influence over the outcome of the hearing (e.g., judge, social workers, court officers, parents, and juvenile).

Perhaps it is the peculiar nature of the juvenile court (as discussed throughout this chapter) which limits the impact that attorneys have had on its proceedings. Based upon the philosophies of protection, treatment, and rehabilitation, while simultaneously charged with acting in the best interests of the juvenile and protecting society, the juvenile court has emerged as a truly unique institution in our society.

It might be argued that attorney involvement in juvenile courts has had a more significant impact upon their proceedings than is readily discernible from the types of research which have been conducted. In other words, although adjudication rates and types of disposition do not appear to have been significantly affected, perhaps more subtle changes have occurred owing to attorney representation in juvenile court. While the juvenile court hearing is technically informal, and the judge enjoys wide latitude in terms of discretion, no doubt the presence of legal counsel on behalf of a youth indicates a recognition that the juvenile court is still a legal proceeding and that regardless of the subjective nature of adjudication and dispositional decisions, the rights of the juvenile will be preserved to the fullest extent possible. While the juvenile court was established to act in the best interests of the juveniles brought before it, representation by legal counsel may underscore that effort.

* * * *

Based upon your reading of this chapter and this Concept Application, what do you think the role of attorneys should be in the juvenile court? Should every juvenile be represented by legal counsel? If so, why? If not, why not? In your opinion, has the impact of attorneys on the juvenile court primarily been positive? or negative?

CONCEPT INTEGRATION
QUESTIONS AND TOPICS FOR STUDY AND DISCUSSION

1. Explain "due process" and discuss how its introduction into the juvenile court has influenced the philosophy and operation of the court.
2. List some of the positive and negative influences the Child Savers movement exerted on the juvenile justice process.
3. Describe the historical development of the juvenile court.
4. Describe and explain the procedures of the contemporary juvenile court. In what ways are they different from those of the adult criminal court?

5. Identify some of the limitations and major criticisms of the juvenile court. What changes might be made in the juvenile court to overcome the limitations and address the criticisms?
6. Discuss some of the pros and cons of retaining status offenses as part of the juvenile court's jurisdiction.

References

ACLU. 1978. *Children's Rights Report* Vol. 2, No. 9 (May):8–11.

Aday, D. P., Jr. 1986. Court structure, defense attorney use, and juvenile court decisions. *Sociological Quarterly* 27 (1):107–119.

Allen, F. A. 1976. The juvenile court and the limits of juvenile justice. In R. Giallombardo (Ed.). *Juvenile Delinquency* (3rd ed.). New York: John Wiley, pp. 411–419.

Arnold, W. R. 1971. Race and ethnicity relative to other factors in juvenile court dispositions. *American Journal of Sociology* 77 (September):211–227.

AP New York. 1978. Cold blooded killer is given 18-month sentence. *Tulsa Daily World* June 30, 1978.

Belden, E. 1920. *Courts in the US hearing children's cases.* US Bureau Publication No. 65. Washington, DC: U.S. Government Printing Office.

Black, H. C. 1968. *Black's law dictionary* (4th ed.). St. Paul: West.

Caldwell, R. G. 1961. The juvenile court: Its development and some major problems. *Journal of Criminal Law, Criminology and Police Science* 51 (Jan.–Feb.):493–507.

Carter, R. M. 1976. The police view of the justice system. In M. W. Klein (Ed.). *The Juvenile Justice System.* Beverly Hills: Sage, pp. 121–132.

Chesney-Lind, M. 1977. Judicial paternalism and the female status offender. *Crime and Delinquency* 23 (April):121–130.

Coffey, A. R. 1974. *Juvenile justice as a system: Law enforcement to rehabilitation.* Englewood Cliffs, NJ: Prentice-Hall.

Cohen, L. E. 1975. *Juvenile dispositions: Social and legal factors related to the processing of Denver delinquency cases.* Washington, DC: LEAA, U.S. Government Printing Office.

Costello, J. C. & Worthington, N. 1981. Incarcerating status offenders: Attempts to circumvent the Juvenile Justice Delinquency Prevention Act. *Harvard Civil Rights–Civil Liberties Law Review* 16 (Summer):41–81.

Cox, S. M. & Conrad, J. J. 1987. *Juvenile justice: A guide to practice and theory* (2nd ed.). Dubuque, IA: Wm. C. Brown.

Coxe, S. 1967. Lawyers in juvenile court. *Crime and Delinquency* 13 (October):488–493.

Day, L. A. 1984. Media access to juvenile courts. *Journalism Quarterly* 61 (Winter):751–756, 700.

Fagan, J., Slaughter, E., & Hartstone, E. 1987a. Blind justice? The impact of race on the juvenile justice process. *Crime and Delinquency* 33 (April):224–258.

Fagan, J., Forst, M., & Vivona, T. S. 1987b. Racial determinants of the judicial transfer decision: Prosecuting violent youth in criminal court. *Crime and Delinquency* 33 (April):259–286.

Flanagan, T. J. & McLeod, M. (Eds.). 1983. *Sourcebook of Criminal Justice Statistics – 1982.* U.S. Department of Justice, Bureau of Justice Statistics. NCJ-86483. Washington, DC: U.S. Government Printing Office.

Hasenfeld, Y. & Cheung, P. P. L. 1985. The juvenile court as a people-processing organization: A political economy perspective. *American Journal of Sociology* 90 (January) 801–824.

Haskell, M. R. & Yablonsky, L. 1978. *Juvenile delinquency* (2nd ed.). Chicago: Rand-McNally.

Institute of Judicial Administration and American Bar Association. 1977. *Juvenile Justice Standards Project: Standards Relating to Counsel for Private Parties.* Cambridge, MA: Ballinger.

Krisberg, B. & Austin, J. 1978. *The children of Ishmael: Critical perspectives on juvenile justice.* Palo Alto, CA: Mayfield.

Lightholder, S. O. 1978. Stay no longer—California juvenile court sentencing practices. *Pepperdine Law Review* 5 (3):769–794.

Mahoney, A. R. 1985. Jury trial for juveniles: Right or ritual? *Justice Quarterly* 2 (December):553–565.

Miller, F. W., Dawson, R. O., Dix, G. E., & Parnas, R. I. 1985. *The juvenile justice process* (3rd ed.). Mineola, NY: University Casebook Series, Foundation Press.

Myren, R. A. 1988. *Law and justice: An introduction.* Belmont, CA: Wadsworth.

Neigher, A. 1967. The Gault Decision: Due process and the juvenile courts. *Federal Probation* 31 (December):8–18.

O'Quin, K., Vogler, C. C., & Weinberg, T. S. 1985. Parental interest, juvenile misbehavior and disposition recommendations. Paper presented at the 1985 meeting of the Society for the Study of Social Problems.

Osbun, L. A. & Rode, P. A. 1984. Prosecuting juveniles as adults: The quest for 'objective' decisions. *Criminology* 22 (May):187–202.

Perry, R. L. 1985. Differential dispositions of black and white juveniles: A critical assessment of methodology. *Western Journal of Black Studies* 9 (Winter):189–197.

Platt, A. 1969. *The Child Savers.* Chicago: University of Chicago Press.

President's Commission on Law Enforcement and Administration of Justice. 1967. *Juvenile Delinquency and Youth Crime.* Washington, DC: U.S. Government Printing Office.

Regnery, A. S. 1986. A federal perspective on juvenile justice reform. *Crime and Delinquency* 32 (January):39–51.

Rubin, H. T. 1976. *The courts: Fulcrum of the justice system.* Pacific Palisades: Goodyear.

1977. The juvenile court's search for identity and responsibility. *Crime and Delinquency* 23 (January):1–13.

1979. Retain the juvenile court? *Crime and Delinquency* (July):281–298.

1980. The emerging prosecutor dominance of the juvenile court intake process. *Crime and Delinquency* 26 (July):299–318.

Sanders, W. B. 1970. *Juvenile offenders for a thousand years.* Chapel Hill: University of North Carolina Press.

Sarri, R. & Hasenfeld, Y. (Eds.). 1976. *Brought to justice?: Juveniles, the courts and the law.* Ann Arbor: University of Michigan, National Assessment of Juvenile Corrections.

Sleeth, V. 1978. Child is a child, except when he's not—California's new approach to disposition of youthful offenders. *California Western Law Review* 14 (1):124–152.

Sosin, M. & Sarri, R. 1976. Due process—Reality or myth? In R. Sarri & Y. Hasenfeld (Eds.). *Brought to justice?: Juveniles, the courts, and the law.* Ann Arbor, MI: University of Michigan Press, pp. 176–206.

Thornberry, T. P. 1973. Race, socioeconomic status, and sentencing in the juvenile justice system. *Journal of Criminal Law and Criminology* 64 (March):90–98.

Thornberry, T. P. & Christenson, R. L. 1984. Juvenile justice decision-making as a longitudinal process. *Social Forces* 63 (December):433–444.

Winslow, R. W. 1973. *Juvenile delinquency in a free society* (2nd ed.). Encino, CA: Dickenson.

Zatz, M. S. 1985. Los Cholos: Legal processing of Chicano gang members. *Social Problems* 33 (October):13–30.

Supreme Court Rulings Cited*

Breed v. Jones (1975). 421 US 519, 95 S. Ct. 1779, 44 L. Ed. 2d 346 (1975)

In re Gault (1967). 387 US 1, 87 S. Ct. 142, 18 L. Ed. 2d 527 (1967).

In re Holmes (1954). 379 Pa. 599, 109A 2d. 523 (1954).

In re Winship (1970). 397 US 358, 90 S. Ct. 1068, 25 L. Ed. 2d 368 (1970).

Kent v. United States (1966). 383 US 541, 86 S. Ct. 1045, 16 L. Ed. 2d 84 (1966).

McKiever v. Pennsylvania (1971). 403 US 528, 91 S. Ct. 1976, L. Ed. 2d 647 (1971).

Miranda v. Arizona (1966). 384 US 436, 86 S. Ct. 1602, 1620, 16 L. Ed. 2d 694 (1966).

Schall v. Martin (1984). _____ US _____ 104 S. Ct. 2403, 81 L. Ed. 2d 207 (1984).

*All legal citations taken from: Miller, F. W., Dawson, R. O., Dix, G. E., & Parnas, R. I. 1985. *The juvenile justice process* (3rd ed.). Mineola, NY: University Casebook Series, Foundation Press.

Part V
Control: Strategies for Dealing with Juvenile Delinquency

Part V

Introduction: Elements of Social Control

In this book we are studying the social problem of juvenile delinquency from a sociological perspective. In this concluding section, we examine the social processes involved in attempting to control, reduce, treat, and prevent juvenile delinquency.

Sociologists seldom assume that any form of crime or juvenile delinquency can be totally eliminated. As indicated in Chapter 1, normative violation occurs in every society, and, in fact, deviance can be both socially functional and dysfunctional in its consequences. In this section, our sociological approach to juvenile delinquency focuses upon the many processes involved in societal elements to control juvenile delinquency. **Social control** refers to *the ways in which society members attempt to regulate the actions of their fellow human beings and reduce the negative impact of behavior which violates social norms.*

In Chapter 13, we discuss the sociological concept of social control and summarize the methods and efforts applied by society in an attempt to regulate the behavior of juveniles. Our discussion includes elements of **voluntary, informal,** and **formal** measures of social control and how they are applied to the problem of delinquency. We also explore the historical concept of vigilantism, and how modern-day neovigilantism has arisen as some private citizens seek to protect themselves and their property from juvenile delinquents. Finally, we look at the controversial issue of capital punishment for juveniles, the ultimate measure of social control that can be exerted by a society.

Chapter 14 deals with treatment and prevention strategies for juvenile delinquency. The chapter begins with a discussion of the treatment **ideology**—*a set of ideas or beliefs on which some established practice is based*—and outlines some of the most prevalent treatment strategies used in dealing with juvenile delinquents. The prevention ideology is also summarized and some of the more prominent delinquency prevention programs that have been used in this country are discussed. The current trend toward **diversion,** which attempts to *reduce juveniles' contact with the juvenile justice system,* and **deinstitutionalization,** *the avoidance of placing them in juvenile institutions,* are also discussed.

Chapter 15 concludes the book with suggestions for rethinking the problem of juvenile delinquency. It reiterates the inherently social nature of delinquency, and makes some specific recommendations for meaningful social change in the way that we view juvenile delinquency and its associated problems. Specific suggestions are made for reducing the marginal status of adolescence, decriminalizing status offenses, standardizing juvenile codes, revising the juvenile court, and modifying juvenile corrections. The chapter, and hence, the book concludes with a proposal for **redefining** juvenile delinquency.

We do not consider Part 5 or Chapter 15 as "the end." Rather, we hope that the information and discussion presented in these last three chapters stimulate your thinking and elicit your participation in the societal quest to better understand and control juvenile delinquency.

Chapter 13

Social Control and Juvenile Delinquency

The reading of this chapter will help you achieve the following objectives:

1. Understand the sociological concept of social control and explain how it relates to juvenile delinquency.
2. Distinguish between voluntary, informal, and formal methods of social control.
3. Define the concepts of juvenile probation, detention, incarceration, and aftercare.
4. Distinguish between different types of juvenile facilities such as detention facilities, training schools, and group homes.
5. Summarize the use of capital punishment for juveniles who have been convicted of capital offenses in adult criminal courts.
6. Define and explain vigilantism and neovigilantism and how they have been used in an attempt to control delinquent behavior.

INTRODUCTION

We repeatedly have emphasized the social nature of juvenile delinquency. Just as we look to human society and culture for understanding the processes involved in defining delinquency, and for providing insight into causal explanations of delinquency, we now must turn to those same sources for controlling juvenile delinquency.

This chapter focuses upon controlling juvenile delinquency, *not* eliminating it. Most social problems are never fully eliminated. Despite multimillion dollar programs and armies of professionals committed to the eradication of problems such as crime, suicide, mental illness, and juvenile delinquency, the problems persist. Even a constitutional amendment resulting in a national prohibition from 1920 to 1933 against the manufacture, sale, and possession of alcoholic beverages failed to resolve the problem of alcoholism. Ironically, some of our most strenuous efforts to eliminate a social problem may, in fact, only help perpetuate it, and in some cases, create others. For example, attempts to eliminate heroin addiction in this country have led to increased illegal drug trafficking, and in some cases the conversion of heroin addicts to methadone addicts. Some of our efforts to prevent delinquency have led to a preoccupation with identifying and treating "predelinquents." This attempt at identifying delinquents before they have actually committed delinquent acts involves identifying the "symptoms" in early childhood.

While this approach may be laudable from the medical model approach, viewing delinquency as an illness with readily identifiable symptoms is highly questionable. As researchers such as Michael Hakeem (1957–1958) and Jackson Toby (1965) pointed out, just about any type of behavior can be interpreted as a symptom of "predelinquency" including acts such as thumb sucking and bedwetting (this medical model approach is further described in Chapter 14). From the labeling perspective, identifying and then treating a child as a "predelinquent" may in fact later create the very phenomenon that one is trying to prevent.

This should not discourage us from seeking programs aimed at controlling social problems like delinquency, but should serve to caution us against anticipating the discovery of some type of panacea leading to utopian solutions. The distinction involves the attempt to develop realistic social mechanisms for reducing and controlling delinquency, not to attempt to eliminate it. By **social control** we are referring to *those aspects of society and culture which are designed to reduce the incidence of juvenile delinquency and to minimize its negative impact upon the members of society.*

Every society establishes social norms to regulate human behavior and provide guidelines for social interaction. Similarly, societies have established numerous ways of dealing with those individuals who violate the norms (folkway, mores, and laws) of their society. These *methods of enforcing norms* are referred to as **sanctions,** and can be either positive or negative. When people conform to normative expectations they receive positive sanctions in the form of respect, honors, awards, and social acceptance. When they violate norms their behavior is negatively sanctioned, or punished, in an attempt to exert control over their behavior. These methods of social control of deviant behavior can be divided into three general categories: voluntary, informal, and formal.

VOLUNTARY SOCIAL CONTROL

The most fundamental and effective method of social control is **voluntary control,** which most members of society *impose upon themselves*. Voluntary social control is dependent upon effective socialization of societal members so that they internalize the shared values and norms of their society. A stable and effectively functioning society depends upon most of its members sharing expectations and agreed-upon standards of social conduct. These shared expectations and standards are important aspects of culture and must be transmitted from one generation to the next through the process of socialization. Effective socialization goes beyond individuals obeying rules because they fear the consequences of violating them. Rather, it involves people conforming to social norms because they have been effectively socialized from childhood and have internalized the norms as their own personal behavioral guidelines. The socialization process involves not only teaching social norms to societal members, but causing individuals to believe in the moral and ethical validity of those norms. Thus, the teaching of social **values,** *attitudes about the rightness and wrongness of acts*, is just as important as teaching people the appropriateness of acts, if not more important. For example, most of us have refrained from committing forcible rape, murder, or armed robbery not only because such acts violate formal norms and are defined as criminal, but also because we believe it is wrong to commit such actions against our fellow human beings. We voluntarily obey many of our criminal laws not because we fear the consequences of violating them, but because most of us believe in the validity of such laws and would never consider violating them. On the other hand, in the aftermath of natural disasters such as floods, earthquakes, hurricanes, and tornadoes, we often see how quickly the restraints learned through socialization can be overcome as the police and National Guard must be called out to keep some people from looting the remains of the damaged property of their fellow citizens.

Some sociological theories of juvenile delinquency focus upon improper socialization as leading to delinquency. For example, the Social Learning theories contended that delinquency, as well as conformity, must be socially learned through socialization (see Chapter 6). Hence, the major agents of socialization—family, religion, school, peers, and mass media—all play an important role in helping a juvenile internalize society's norms.

Walter Reckless (1961) emphasized social control as being the primary distinguishing element between those who commit and those who refrain from committing delinquent acts. The first layer of insulation against delinquency in Reckless' Control Theory was that of **inner containment.** As we discussed in Chapter 6, this inner containment is primarily a result of effective socialization. When juveniles internalize society's values and norms as their own, they are much less likely to violate those values and norms. This element of voluntary social control relies upon the individual's set of values to act as a sufficient barrier to committing delinquent acts. What many of us refer to as conscience is in fact the manifestation of voluntary social control.

Another aspect of voluntary social control developed through effective socialization is the process whereby individuals recognize their membership in society and simultaneously acknowledge society as being part of them. Often referred to as a **social bond** (Hirschi, 1969), this acknowledgment promotes the conformity to social norms, and helps prevent involvement in delinquent acts. Because voluntary control is dependent upon the socialization process, the role of the family cannot be overemphasized. Primary responsibility for teaching appropriate values and behaviors rests with the family. The family's choice of neighborhood, schools, and church attendance all impact upon the socialization process. Perhaps most important is the role models provided in a family by parents and older siblings.

In a society such as ours, where there are infinitely more potential deviants than there are formal agents of social control, the importance of voluntary social control cannot be overestimated. If juveniles are going to conform to society's rules most of the time it is more dependent upon their willingness to do so, than upon the ability of adult society members to try to prevent them from committing delinquent acts. Through effective socialization and the juvenile's developing a sense of attachment to society, most juveniles usually refrain from committing delinquent acts.

INFORMAL SOCIAL CONTROL

When the internalization of social norms is insufficient for an individual to maintain behavioral control, it may be necessary for the social group to implement a second line of defense against deviance. One of the most effective methods members of a society can use in order to discourage deviance and encourage conformity is to implement various techniques of informal social control. **Informal social control** mechanisms are *applied by other societal members and include such tactics as gossip, ridicule, humor, ostracism, and peer pressure.* Despite their informality, the impact of these methods of social constraints should not be underestimated. They are especially powerful when exercised by groups characterized by close, informal, face-to-face, interdependent relationships (see the Concept Application at the end of this chapter for a good example). Hence, the family, peer groups, and members of the immediate neighborhood or other primary social groups can act as extremely important agents of social control in regard to discouraging nonconforming behavior.

Ferdinand Toennies ([1887] 1961) developed a theoretical continuum in an attempt to better understand the nature of social interaction and network of social relationships within different types of social structures. At one end of the continuum was the **gemeinschaft** type of community. The **gemeinschaft** community *is characterized by a smaller population, less complex division of labor, and is dominated by primary face-to-face social interaction.* In this type of community informal mechanisms tend to dominate social control strategies because they are so effective in this type of social structure.

While contemporary America, in general, has moved away from the gemeinschaft end of the continuum, there are many smaller communities and even sections of larger cities which closely resemble this type of social organization. For example, in rural America, informal social control mechanisms are probably still more predominantly utilized than formal types of social control. When a juvenile commits a delinquent act such as getting drunk over the weekend and driving a car through somebody's front yard, it is very likely that the entire community will know about it by Monday morning. Rather than placing the juvenile under formal arrest and levying a fine, it is highly likely that the local sheriff will simply pay a visit to the juvenile's parents. The parents may pay for the damage through some type of informal agreement with the injured party and simply promise the sheriff not to let such an incident happen again. Not only will the parents play a key role in attempting to control the juvenile's behavior through some type of disciplinary action, but the entire community probably will become involved in the social control process. Through whispering, finger-pointing, looks of disgust, and various degrees of ostracism, the community can clearly express its lack of tolerance for the delinquent act and issue a clearcut warning that similar acts should not be committed in the future.

Ostracism, *the experience of being expelled from a social group,* may serve as one of the most powerful and effective informal social control mechanisms available to a community or social group. Human beings are social by nature, and the inability to interact with others can be extremely punitive. Through real or threatened ostracism, a juvenile's peer group can exert extreme pressure upon individual members to conform to the group's expectations for behavior.

On the negative side, if the group is encouraging delinquency, an otherwise conforming youngster may feel compelled to break the law in order to gain or perpetuate acceptance by friends. As discussed in Chapter 6, the Social Learning Theories, especially Differential Association, point out the significance of the peer group in influencing a juvenile into delinquent or nondelinquent activities.

On the positive side, if the peer group demands conformity to the law, the juvenile whose own inner containment is not strong enough to prevent delinquency may be sufficiently constrained by the group. This **outer containment,** as Reckless (1961) called it, serves as another layer of insulation against delinquency for those who have not sufficiently internalized the norms. As Ronald Farrell and Victoria Swigert (1982) indicated, rejection from the group may serve as a significant deterrent for the deviant.

Some of the informal strategies for dealing with less serious juvenile offenders have included trying to involve them in what are considered to be positive activities with more desirable peers and role models. Problem juveniles are often encouraged to join Little League baseball, soccer, Boy Scouts, YMCA, and a variety of other youth organizations in the hope that by becoming involved in acceptable group behavior, these juveniles will be less inclined to become involved in delinquency. In the past, as juvenile boys in trouble approached the age of 18, they were often encouraged to join the military service. It was thought that the discipline, rigor, and positive aspects of military life would prevent the young man from further law violating behavior. Unfortunately, as a cadre officer at the United States Disciplinary Barracks at Fort Leavenworth mentioned to one of the authors, many of society's "misfits" later became the military's trouble makers, had to be more formally controlled, and were often released with dishonorable discharges back into the larger society.

FORMAL SOCIAL CONTROL

In large, complex, predominantly urban societies with heterogeneous populations such as prevail in much of the United States, social relations are likely to be secondary as opposed to primary in nature. This represents the other end of Toennies' ([1887] 1961) theoretical continuum, the **gesellschaft** society *characterized by larger population, a complex division of labor, secondary relationships, and formal social control.* In these social circumstances citizens, legislators, police, and court officials are likely to respond more formally to norm violations by juveniles. Laws are formal codified norms, and their violation is likely to bring about a formal response. As previously mentioned, occasional drinking, fighting, minor vandalism, and various forms of malicious mischief might be tolerated in a small rural community. But the same behavior in larger towns and cities is likely to be perceived as juvenile crime and a threat to the social order. Therefore, delinquent behavior is likely to evoke outcries for public protection and dictate that formal methods of social control be brought into action.

The schools, police, and courts as agents of social control were discussed in Chapters 10, 11, and 12. In school, juveniles are likely to experience both informal and formal sanctions for their deviant behavior. All the informal social control mechanisms discussed in the previous section can be imposed by other students, teachers, and administrators. However, as a major social institution, the school and its staff and administrators can also implement a variety of more formal social control procedures. Varying degrees of formal punishment, suspension, and expulsion are ways in which the school can negatively sanction a student's undesirable behavior. In addition, school officials can petition the student to juvenile court, and initiate formal delinquency proceedings against the youth for serious offenses.

Similarly, the police also can utilize both informal and formal techniques of control. When police officers choose the options of issuing warnings, or questioning juveniles and then releasing them, they are in fact exercising informal social control over the youths' behavior. When neighbors see a teenager being delivered home to the parents in a squad car, many of the informal social control mechanisms such as gossip and ridicule are initiated. Because they are employed as formal agents of social control, however, police are most likely to be associated with the formal sanctions at their disposal. Police can arrest, detain, create an official record, and petition a juvenile to court for law violating behavior. Thus, the police emerge as one of the most significant elements of formal social control of juvenile delinquency.

The juvenile court was discussed in Chapter 12, and the formal dispositional alternatives available to it were cited. Once a juvenile appears before the juvenile court, even if released outright, a formal control mechanism has been implemented. Despite its attempt to conduct informal hearings, the court represents an official governmental institution and, hence, is by its very nature a formal agent of social control.

Juvenile Probation

One of the most widely used methods of formal social control for juveniles in the United States is juvenile probation. Juvenile probation officers are usually involved in the juvenile court's intake procedure, and can be very influential in making recommendations to the juvenile judge. Probation also is one of the dispositional alternatives to incarceration for juveniles. **Probation** is *a form of supervised release in which a juvenile adjudicated as delinquent is allowed to remain free from institutionalization, but must adhere to a strict set of guidelines imposed by the court.* Additionally, the youth is required to report to a probation officer on a regular schedule. Probation is thought to have been used first by John Augustus in Boston in 1841 (Culbertson and Ellsworth, 1985). Augustus bailed out offenders and "in addition to providing them with emotional support, he made efforts to find his probationers jobs" (Culbertson and Ellsworth, 1985:127). When a juvenile lacks the necessary degree of voluntary control and does not respond to informal pressures to conform, probation can be used to implement some formal restraints. Theoretically, probation is assumed to provide outer containment (or external restraint and control) for a juvenile while simultaneously helping to resocialize the youth to a new set of values which it is hoped will provide sufficient inner containment (or self control). Thus, probation rules generally serve not only to prohibit law violations and establish curfews and other restrictions upon behavior, but they also often are likely to include guidelines such as requiring school attendance beyond the compulsory attendance age, church attendance, charity work, and enforced savings (Imlay and Flasheen, 1971).

Ideally, probation is supposed to combine the punitive and rehabilitative aspects of juvenile corrections by negatively sanctioning a juvenile's delinquent behavior and reinforcing dominant social norms. Realistically, because of very heavy caseloads, juvenile probation officers often cannot maintain close contacts with their charges. Further, Carl Imlay and Charles Flasheen (1971) pointed out that many of the requirements of probation are petty and violate the basic constitutional rights of juveniles (such as dress and haircut requirements and mandatory church attendance), and may paradoxically produce a general disrespect for the law as opposed to the desired effect.

There is mixed opinion regarding the effectiveness of juvenile probation. As William Sanders (1981:258) reported:

> Some children are affected by probation in ways that will either help them or harm them. A probation officer who helps a child overcome a problem that led the juvenile to delinquency can be said to "cure" the child. If the probation disposition serves to stigmatize a juvenile, it can be said to harm the youth.

Further, if the juvenile placed on probation refrains from committing subsequent delinquency, we have no way of knowing if this success is *because of* or *despite* the probation experience. In fact, Sanders (1981:259) contended "there seems to be little evidence that probation is any more successful in changing delinquents than doing nothing at all."

Most of the public criticism leveled at juvenile probation has centered on the perception that it is too lenient and allows juvenile offenders to escape punishment for their criminal actions. Gennaro Vito (1985), however, contended that probation, especially if linked with some form of victim restitution, is punitive, and can be an effective way of diverting juveniles from incarceration while holding them accountable for their law violating behavior. **Restitution** involves *the offender being required to compensate the victim (either the actual victim or the state) either in monetary payments or in labor for losses related to the offense.* It is most often used in property offenses such as burglary, larceny-theft, and vandalism in which an actual dollar figure can be placed upon the victim's losses. Calvin Remington (1982) positively evaluated the Ventura Restitution Project, which attempts to make juvenile offenders understand the ramifications of their delinquent behavior and make them take responsibility for their actions, as being a viable social control mechanism. Robert Evans and Gary Koederitz (1983) summarized the concept of restitution coupled with probation as being a promising, logical, and effective means of achieving the dual goals of deterrence and punishment for law violating juveniles.

Juvenile Incarceration

A prominent form of formal social control of juvenile delinquents is incarceration in an institution. There is a variety of types of institutions whose primary purpose is the incarceration of juvenile offenders. In order to simplify categorization of these institutions, James Carey and Patrick McAnany (1984:291) divided them into three basic types: detention facilities, training schools, and group homes.

Detention facilities *serve as places to detain, or hold, juveniles who are awaiting a hearing in juvenile court.* Communities provide various types of detention facilities for youths. In cities where there are large numbers of juvenile offenders, distinct facilities for juveniles which separate them from adult offenders are more likely to exist. "Juvenile halls" as these centers are often called, are usually located near the juvenile court, and might even be operated in conjunction with the court, thereby housing juvenile probation and parole officers and other juvenile court personnel. In smaller communities, where delinquency is less prevalent, juveniles are more likely to be detained in adult jails.

Dae Chang's (1979) study revealed that there were approximately 100,000 children being housed in jails and jail-like institutions in America. Rosemary Sarri (1974) conducted a thorough study of juvenile detention facilities, and found that they varied greatly from state to state, and from city to city within states. In some cases, the juvenile detention center is simply a jail cell (Sarri, 1974). In 1983, 1,736 juveniles were held in adult jails (U.S. Department of Justice, 1987:393). It seems logical that juvenile detention generally would be reserved for the more serious offenders, and in many instances that may be the case. However, we should be reminded that the police often make the decision as to whether to detain a youth, and a variety of factors beyond the seriousness of offense are taken into consideration. The problems associated with placing juvenile offenders in adult jails have been well documented (e.g., McGee, 1971) and all too frequently a sensational incident involving a juvenile detained in jail arises. For example, national attention was focused upon the problem of jailing juveniles in June of 1982, when an Idaho teenager who was put in jail for $60 worth of traffic violations in order to teach him "he should take responsibility for his actions" was tortured and murdered in his jail cell by his five cellmates (AP, Boise, 1982).

Juvenile **training schools** are *long-term facilities for housing juveniles, and serve a function analogous to adult prisons.* Virtually every state has at least one of these facilities (sometimes one for boys and one for girls). They may operate under various names such as "state industrial schools," "reformatories," or others, but basically share the common characteristic of being a place where the juvenile court can send a youthful offender for an extended period of time. As in adult prisons, security is generally a prominent concern, and custody tends to be of primary importance. However, in keeping with the general philosophy of the juvenile court, there is usually an attempt to integrate treatment and rehabilitation into the custody procedures. Charles Tittle (1974) argued that the widespread belief in the failure of prisons to rehabilitate is not justified by the empirical evidence, and suggested that there might well be rehabilitative benefits from incarceration.

These long-term incarceration facilities conform to Erving Goffman's (1961: xiii) concept of a **total institution** — *"a place of residence and work where a large number of like-situated individuals, cut off from the wider society for an appreciable period of time, together lead an enclosed, formally administered round of life."* In other words, juveniles eat, sleep, work, go to school, and play within the confines of the institution. Goffman (1961) discussed the social worlds which are constructed in total institutions in which virtually all spheres of one's life take place within the confines of one social setting, and pointed out that there is often a subterranean social world constructed by the inmates which may run counter to the official social structure of the institution.

The corrections literature is replete with studies analyzing the advantages and problems, successes and failures associated with this type of incarceration. Sanders (1981) pointed out that regardless of the treatment or rehabilitation efforts introduced into long-term incarceration facilities for juveniles, the staffs

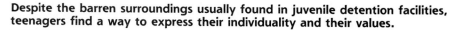

Despite the barren surroundings usually found in juvenile detention facilities, teenagers find a way to express their individuality and their values.

of these types of institutions tend to be increasingly concerned with basic custodial control.

Michael Sherraden and Susan Downs (1984) conducted an empirical historical study of the institutionalization of juvenile delinquents from 1820 to 1970, and pointed out that institutionalization rates were highest during the second half of the nineteenth century and again during the most recent decades of the twentieth century. The resurgence in the institutionalization of juveniles refocused public attention on many of the problems associated with incarcerating juveniles.

Zvi Eisikovits and Michael Baizerman (1982) interviewed 43 violent youthful offenders in one midwestern state who had been incarcerated in either maximum security youth facilities or adult prisons. In assessing how these youngsters "did time," they found that youths in both types of institutions lost sight of getting out, and instead learned to adapt to the institutional life imposed upon them. They learned quickly that violence was the norm in the institution, and that treatment language and jargon could be used to manipulate correctional officials into shortening their sentences. In short, they concluded that the young offenders learned to be "con artists" who did not benefit from the institutionalization, but merely adapted to it. Many officials who deal with delinquency contend that the state training schools are a costly disaster (costing anywhere from $20,000 to $45,000 per youth per year) where young law violators are warehoused and hardened into a "lifetime of lawlessness and . . . become permanent and costly liabilities of society" (Ryan, 1980:21).

The third category of juvenile institutions revolves around the **group home** concept. These types of facilities are relatively new to the juvenile correctional process. In 1975, it was estimated that there were some 195 public and 851 private facilities of this type in the United States (Carey and McAnany, 1984:293). These facilities can include halfway houses, drug and alcohol rehabilitation homes, and various types of youth shelters. Juveniles can be placed there either by the courts or parents who feel that a change in home environment will be beneficial for the juvenile. **Group homes** *usually resemble a dormitory type of living facility with juveniles being supervised during parts of the day and at night, while being allowed limited participation in the larger community either to attend school or work at part-time jobs.*

One of the forerunners of this type of juvenile institution was the so-called Provo Experiment begun in 1956 in Provo, Utah (Empey and Rabow, 1961). This program involved a group home type of setting and allowed a limited number of juveniles to live together under staff supervision while working and attending school in the larger community (for further discussion, see Chapter 14). The program was considered highly successful and has been followed in other areas of the country. Other community-based treatment programs for juveniles have been developed as an alternative to incarceration. They are discussed in Chapter 14, which deals with various treatment strategies and prevention efforts for juvenile delinquency.

Juvenile Aftercare

Another method of formal social control is aftercare. Essentially, aftercare for juveniles is the equivalent of parole for adults. In fact, in some states, the term "juvenile parole" is still used. **Aftercare** refers to *release of a juvenile who has been incarcerated in some type of institutional setting under the supervision of an officer of the court for a prescribed period of time.* In most states the officer of the court involved is a juvenile probation/parole officer who also may have been actively involved in the initial intake process for the youth (see Chapter 12). Upon release, the juvenile meets with an aftercare supervisor and agrees to a specific set of restrictions. These conditions are usually similar to those of probation and include requirements such as school attendance, curfew, notification of where-abouts, and often a list of specific individuals with whom the juvenile is forbidden to associate. Violation of any of the terms may result in the juvenile being returned to some type of facility. Pragmatically, juvenile aftercare and probation are virtually identical, with the distinction being that probation is used *instead of* incarceration, while parole or aftercare is used *after* incarceration. Both are forms of conditional release under the supervision of an officer of the court.

Unfortunately, one of the problems with this form of social control is that because of the large numbers of juveniles on probation and parole at any one time, caseloads for the court officers can be extremely high. Consequently, it is often difficult for probation and aftercare officers to meet regularly with all their charges, and some juveniles may be able to violate some of the conditions for their release without it coming to the attention of their supervisors. As a mechanism of formal social control, when supervised release becomes unsuper-vised, its effectiveness is significantly reduced.

CAPITAL PUNISHMENT FOR JUVENILES

The ultimate form of social control is capital punishment. The execution of criminal offenders is one of the most controversial elements of the American criminal justice system, and that controversy is compounded when it involves the execution of juveniles or of adults who committed their capital offenses while still under the age of majority. The United States has executed a total of 281 juveniles, and contemporary opponents point out that "America may be alone in the world in executing its young" (Seligson, 1986:5). The first suffi-ciently documented juvenile execution occurred in Roxbury, Massachusetts in 1642 when 16-year-old Thomas Graunger was executed for committing bestial-ity (Streib, 1987:55).

In 1972, the U.S. Supreme Court ruled in the case of *Furman v. Georgia* that capital punishment was discriminatory and constituted "cruel and unusual punishment," which is prohibited by the Eighth Amendment to the Constitution. The Court ordered its discontinuance. Inmates on death row awaiting execution had their sentences commuted to life imprisonment. However, in 1976, the Supreme Court ruled that three states (Florida, Texas, and Georgia) had rewritten their capital punishment statutes in such a way as to conform to the Constitution. Several states wrote new capital punishment statutes in compliance with the Supreme Court's guidelines, and in some states, these new statutes included the right to execute juveniles who committed capital offenses. In fact, among the 36 states which reenacted the death penalty, nine set no minimum age for execution (Arizona, Delaware, Florida, Maryland, Oklahoma, South Carolina, South Dakota, Washington, and Wyoming) (Seligson, 1986:5). Twenty-seven states enacted capital punishment statutes that specified a minimum age at the time the crime was committed, and several of those set the minimum age below the age of majority (see Table 13–1).

The constitutionality of executing juveniles has been legally challenged, but the Supreme Court has never clearly resolved the issue. The Supreme Court finally agreed to decide the issue of constitutionality in the 1982 case of *Eddings v. Oklahoma*. However, in a 5 to 4 vote, the court once again avoided deciding the constitutionality issue and simply sent the case back for resentencing urging

TABLE 13-1
Minimum Age for Death Penalty by State

State	Age	State	Age
Alabama	14	Nebraska	18
Arkansas	14	Nevada	16
Arizona	*	New Hampshire	17
California	18	New Jersey	18
Colorado	18	New Mexico	18
Connecticut	18	North Carolina	14
Delaware	**	Ohio	18
Florida	*	Oklahoma	**
Georgia	17	Oregon	18
Idaho	14	Pennsylvania	14
Illinois	18	South Carolina	*
Indiana	10	South Dakota	**
Kentucky	14	Tennessee	18
Louisiana	15	Texas	17
Maryland	*	Utah	14
Mississippi	13	Virginia	15
Missouri	14	Washington	*
Montana	12	Wyoming	*

*No minimum age, but age is a mitigating factor

**No minimum age and age is not a mitigating factor

Source: Adapted from Tom Seligson, "Are They Too Young to Die?" *Parade,* October 19, 1986:5. Reprinted by permission.

A youth on death row awaits execution for a crime he committed while legally classified as a juvenile.

the lower court to consider age as a mitigating factor (Streib, 1987). The Supreme Court has been asked numerous times to rule on the constitutionality of the death penalty for juveniles since the Eddings case, but thus far, has rejected those requests (Streib, 1987).

The use of the death penalty is extremely controversial, to say the least. Public opinion polls indicate that since 1933, over one-half of Americans surveyed indicated they supported capital punishment, and that figure was as high as 73 percent in 1977 (Allen and Simonsen, 1981:249). A 1986 Gallup poll indicated that 70 percent favored the death penalty (Seligson, 1986:5). Those public opinion polls did not survey Americans' attitudes toward the execution of juveniles, however. In late 1986, *Parade*, in an article on capital punishment for juveniles, conducted such a poll. It found that nearly 80 percent of respondents believed that there should be capital punishment in general, but of those who supported capital punishment, 46 percent said they believed there should be a minimum age for the death penalty (*Parade,* 1987:10). Interestingly, however, of those who indicated that a minimum age should be set for execution, only 11 percent said that the minimum age should be 21 and 23 percent said it should be 18. The rest indicated acceptable minimum ages below the age of majority in most states (*Parade,* 1987:10). Almost 55 percent indicated that there should be *no* minimum age for the death penalty (*Parade,* 1987:10). While this reader poll did not involve carefully and scientifically selected sampling procedures, it nevertheless reflected a sentiment among many Americans that the state should execute juveniles who have committed particularly heinous offenses.

At least two other more scientific polls on the execution of juvenile offenders have been taken. In 1936, 61 percent of the respondents favored the death penalty in general, and 46 percent approved of it for criminals under the age of 21 (Streib, 1987:33). In 1965, public sentiment toward the death penalty had shifted, and only 45 percent favored capital punishment in general with only 23 percent viewing it as acceptable for offenders under 21 years of age (Streib, 1987:33).

It should be noted that while all of those currently on death row awaiting execution for crimes committed as juveniles were convicted of homicide, capital punishment has not been reserved only for youths who were hardened killers. The most common offense in juvenile capital punishment cases has been homicide, but juveniles also have been executed for the crimes of arson, assault and battery, attempted rape, bestiality, and robbery (Streib, 1987:62). As Streib (1987:71) noted:

> [his data] . . . refute the commonly held belief that the penalty has always been reserved for our most hardened criminals, the middle-aged three-time losers. While they are often the ones executed, offenders of more tender years, down even to prepubescence, also have been killed lawfully, hanging from our gallows, restrained in our gas chambers, sitting in our electric chairs, and lying on our hospital gurneys.

Indeed, two juveniles as young as 10 years old have been legally executed in the United States (Streib, 1987:57).

The sentencing of a juvenile to die poses a particularly disturbing question to American citizens. Wayne Thompson, one of the juveniles awaiting execution on Oklahoma's death row, focused attention upon the marginality of adolescence, and the dilemma faced by the criminal justice system, when he pointed out that at the time of his offense (and conviction and death sentence) he was only 15 years old, considered too young to be able to legally drive an automobile, and "even now, at 19, if I went to buy a beer, they wouldn't sell it to me" (Seligson, 1986:5). Ironically, Thompson may never be able to legally purchase beer in Oklahoma as his execution is set to occur before his twenty-first birthday.

VIGILANTISM AS A MEANS OF SOCIAL CONTROL

When criminologists and sociologists discuss social control they generally refer to the three types that we have discussed in this chapter (voluntary, informal, and formal). However, there is another form of social control that does not fit neatly into any of these three categories. Although primarily informal in nature, **vigilantism** goes far beyond the usual methods of informal control. It attempts to formally control deviance when there is a feeling that the official agents of control are remiss in their ability to control it.

Webster's *New World Dictionary* (1979:666) defines the **vigilante** as *"one of an unauthorized group organized professedly to keep order and punish crime."* There probably have been vigilantes as long as there have been laws. In earlier societies the only way to redress a wrong was for a victim or the victim's family to "settle the score" with the wrongdoer by whatever means were at their disposal. "Blood feuds" often erupted, and norm enforcement was as much an act of anarchy as it was social control. However, as most societies developed, a social contract emerged between citizens and their government which encompassed a mutual promise. In exchange for taxes, relinquished authority, loyalty, and support, the government promised to protect its citizens from damage to their property and their persons. In exchange for this protection, citizens promised to obey the law and to allow the government to intervene on their behalf when their property or lives were damaged or threatened. An elaborate criminal justice system emerged to fulfill the government's promise and insure the safety and protection of both offenders and victims of law violation.

Citizens in some parts of the country were more reluctant than others to relinquish responsibility to the government for capture and punishment of law violators. Instead, vigilantes arose to enforce the law and "protect" law-abiding citizens. In some cases this vigilantism was primarily a response from citizens when they believed that duly elected or appointed legal officials were either unable or unwilling to "protect the innocent" and "catch and punish" the guilty. Wild west gunslingers, southern lynch mobs, the Ku Klux Klan, and a variety of other "upstanding citizens" took it upon themselves to enforce the laws (as they interpreted them), punish the "guilty" and "protect" the innocent. Law enforcement by these early vigilantes was in many cases merely another form of law violation. As federal, state, and local governments developed and grew in authority, and people began to place more trust in the criminal justice system, vigilantism greatly diminished.

Recent decades in America have seen the development of large, modern police forces, government agencies, and an extensive court system. Thus, it would seem logical that vigilantism would have completely disappeared in a society such as ours. However, those same recent decades have also witnessed a revival of vigilantism. This **neovigilantism** has emerged to correct what some view as the total inadequacy of our criminal justice system to protect law abiding citizens and punish criminals.

NEOVIGILANTISM

Neovigilantism may represent what anthropologists refer to as **private law.** Richards (1972), for example, discussed early frontier law in America and the transition from *private* to *public* law in frontier communities. Private citizens often believed they had authority to enforce norms and were reluctant to relinquish their perceived authority to others. Neovigilantism represents a somewhat different version of that same attitude, and presents some unique problems in contemporary urban industrial America. Hugh Graham and Ted Guerr (1969:103) pointed out some important differences between early vigilantism and neovigilantism:

> 'Neo-vigilantism' may be distinguished from the older frontier model not only by its urban environment but also, revealingly, by its victims. Whereas the old vigilantism sought to chastise mainly horse thieves, counterfeiters, outlaws, and bad men, the victims of neovigilantism have characteristically been ethnic, racial, and religious minorities, union organizations, and political radicals. Modern vigilance groups have frequently been supported by prestigious community leaders, often with tacit support of the police.

Various forms of neovigilantism have arisen in recent years and some that have been directed against delinquency and street crimes have captured national attention. Law enforcement officials tend to view vigilantism negatively (at least officially) while occasionally unofficially sanctioning it in its milder forms. The reaction of the general public is harder to assess, but at least in some cases, those reactions are quite positive, with groups and individuals being publicly applauded for their actions against alleged criminals.

Neighborhood Watch

The Neighborhood Watch program has been developed in virtually every community of any size. These programs are approved by the police and involve citizens joining together to reduce crime in their neighborhoods. These programs are primarily aimed at reducing burglary, vandalism, and other property offenses, many of which involve juvenile offenders. In most cases, the programs simply involve more awareness on the part of neighbors who call the police when anything of a suspicious nature occurs. Representatives from the police department usually meet with interested members of the neighborhood and conduct a brief training session on how to reduce property crimes by better protecting their homes with various locks and alarms, and more importantly, how to be more observant. Residents are encouraged to help watch each other's homes and to call the police if they notice any unusual or suspicious behavior in the neighborhood. Signs are usually posted in the neighborhood declaring that the neighborhood participates in the watch program and that residents call the police. However, in some cases, local communities have actually formed neighborhood patrols armed with walkie-talkies, and occasionally guns, who sometimes attempt to apprehend suspected offenders and make citizens' arrests. In the latter case, a certain amount of neovigilantism is clearly involved.

Guardian Angels

One of the better known examples of neovigilantism in recent years is the Guardian Angels. Founded in New York City in 1979 by Curtis Sliwa, this group of young adults and teenagers operates as self-appointed organized patrols of the streets, alleys, and subways of many of America's larger cities. What began as a group with just 13 members by 1982 claimed to have over 2,000 members in 41 cities (*Time*, 1982:21). In 1987 the Guardian Angels claimed to have a membership of "over 5,000 in 67 American, Canadian, and Mexican cities." Curtis Sliwa and his wife, Lisa, a fashion model and Black Belt in karate who serves as the Executive Director, organize groups throughout the country. Lisa also serves a public relations function by touring the country speaking on college campuses and on television and radio talk shows. Outfitted in their distinctive red berets, the Angels go out on patrol to reduce many of the street crimes in which juveniles are likely to participate. Members of the Guardian Angels contend they are merely exercising their rights as private citizens and acting within the law as civilian extensions of the police force. In a pamphlet they publish, the Guardian Angels assert:

> We are effective as visual deterrents to crime because we will not hesitate to make a citizen's arrest when we see a crime being committed. In our red berets and t-shirts, we have become familiar sights on mass transit systems, in shopping mall parking lots, at rock concerts, and in drug-infested public parks and streets.

Many law enforcement officials view the Guardian Angels in a different light, seeing them as vigilantes who hamper official law enforcement and could be potentially dangerous. When speaking on college campuses, the Sliwas vehemently deny that the Guardian Angels are vigilantes, preferring to refer to them as simply "concerned citizens." However, in their own literature they describe their efforts in their "war against drugs" in the following way:

> Increasingly, we are being called upon by frustrated residents and small business owners to assist them in reclaiming their streets from the drug dealers. We

Members of the Guardian Angels patrol the subways in an effort to reduce crime and delinquency.

have mounted major anti-drug and crackdown on crack campaigns in Los Angeles, West Palm Beach, Florida and 42nd Street/Times Square in New York.

In the same pamphlet, they estimated that their patrols had made over 800 citizens' arrests and that their presence had deterred countless other crimes. Thus, their actions clearly fit the definition of vigilantism. Where the Guardian Angels differ from most other forms of vigilantism and neovigilantism is that while they patrol, apprehend, and arrest, they do not routinely mete out punishment to their captives. Instead, they detain the offenders until legal authorities arrive to take them into custody.

Juvenile Vigilantism

Interestingly, many juvenile gangs often interpret much of their violent behavior, especially when directed against other gangs, as being a method of justified social control. As discussed in Chapter 9, juvenile gangs tend to be territorial, and an invasion of their "turf" is viewed as a violation that cannot go unpunished. Since official channels of law enforcement are unavailable, gang members enforce their own laws in neovigilante form. When one gang infringes on another's turf or in some other way violates its established "laws," some form of retaliation is inevitable. Also, within gangs, there is often a "code" which, if violated, requires some type of punitive action. Should the offending gang member refuse to submit to the gang's established ritual for handling such situations, he/she is likely to be hunted down by vigilantes bound to bring the offender to "justice."

The phenomenon of juvenile vigilantism is not limited to that of street gangs. Teenagers, especially in urban areas, are beginning to take law enforcement into their own hands in high schools where they believe the school administration is unable to successfully thwart the theft, vandalism, and drug use of other students. For example, in Fort Worth, Texas, a group calling themselves the "Legend of Doom," comprised of athletes and honor students, formed to protect themselves and their property, and to "terrorize" their high school's "troublemakers" (AP Fort Worth, 1985a). The police attributed over 30 incidents, including the exploding of a pipe bomb in a car, to this group's vigilante activities. Nine members of the vigilante group were arrested and charged with 35 separate offenses (AP Fort Worth, 1985b). Detective Ken Henry described the youths as "kids with good intentions who went outside the law" (AP Fort Worth, TX, 1985b).

Individual Vigilantism

Another form of neovigilantism capturing a great deal of public attention is that of "ordinary citizens" arming themselves to protect their person and property against criminals. In December, 1984, a young man named Bernhard Goetz shot four teenagers who he said attempted to rob him on a New York City subway. Goetz became an instant celebrity and became known as the "Subway Vigilante" (Lokeman, 1985:4K). Once again national attention focused upon vigilantism as a controversial method of social control. While public officials contended that Goetz's actions could not be condoned, a tremendous amount of public support for Goetz was forthcoming. Money from all over the country poured in for his defense fund, and many declared Goetz a "hero." When the New York City police set up a hotline for information about the incident, they were deluged with phone calls praising Goetz's actions, and New York City Mayor Ed Koch received calls and letters in support of the gunman in a ratio of 80 to 1 (Tucker, 1985:19). Even a song entitled *The Saga of Bernhard Goetz* was recorded in 1985 and a board game called "Subway Vigilante" was developed in which players start in Brooklyn with a gun and six bullets and attempt to progress around the board and reach home safely without having to use all their bullets (CNN News, 1986).

The district attorney initially decided not to file charges against Goetz for the shootings, and even the charge of carrying a concealed weapon was dropped. Goetz's supporters celebrated the decision as a reaffirmation of the right of American citizens to protect themselves. Others were shocked by the fact that the charges against Goetz were dropped. One of the boys who survived the shooting contended that he and his friends had simply approached Goetz on the subway and asked him for five dollars when he suddenly pulled a gun on them and began firing. The situation became more volatile when civil rights leaders pointed out that they suspected that part of the leniency toward Goetz could be explained by the fact that he was white while his four alleged assailants were black. They suggested that had the situation been reversed (a black had shot four whites), that there was no question but what charges would have been filed. Eventually, criminal charges were filed, and Goetz was ordered to stand trial on counts of carrying a concealed weapon and aggravated assault. During the trial, the public remained highly divided over the incident. A CBS/*New York Times* poll (1987) found that 46 percent of the respondents indicated that they would have done the same thing as Goetz, while 38 percent said they would not. In the trial little similarity could be found between the stories of Goetz and those of the surviving youths and witnesses. Goetz further complicated the case by publicly declaring to reporters that he had overreacted in gunning down the youths and deserved to be punished. On June 16, 1987, Bernhard Goetz was acquitted on the charge of attempted murder and was found guilty only on the much less serious charge of illegally possessing a weapon (AP New York, 1987). Public response to the verdict was mixed as it had been throughout the case, and prominent politicians such as Mayor Koch and Governor Cuomo were quite guarded in their comments about the verdict. Many of Goetz's supporters were ecstatic about the court's decision, and the district attorney and others lamented that the decision may be interpreted as encouraging vigilantism.

Only a few weeks after the Goetz incident occurred, and long before the Goetz trial, in a much less celebrated incident, a 68-year-old Chicago plumber was released without any charges being filed after he shot and killed one 18-year-old attacker and wounded another (AP Chicago, 1985).

In a 1983 incident in Buffalo, New York, a 35-year-old truck driver along with a group of men beat and stabbed a man who had kidnapped and sexually molested his 10-year-old daughter. He was arrested, but police officers reportedly congratulated him in his cell and a Buffalo city councilman led the campaign to raise funds for his bail; when he returned to his old neighborhood, he received a "hero's welcome" (Tucker, 1985:25).

These and other incidents of civilian vigilantism touched off public debate on the issue of one's right to self-defense, and how far an individual should be allowed to go in "enforcing the law." Syndicated columnist William Safire in his column "On Language" asked the question if calling someone a *vigilante* was an insult or a compliment (Safire, 1985), and other columnists stimulated public debate about the public's right and desire to "fight back" (e.g., Royko, 1985; Goodman, 1985). A major newspaper in Oklahoma City, *The Sunday Oklahoman,* ran a front page story on the rise of vigilantism in Oklahoma, citing numerous instances in which armed robbers had gotten a "dose of 'frontier justice'" (Casteel, 1985:A–1). In the same article, pictures of stickers being printed and sold for display in business and residence windows were shown, one of which depicted a skull and crossbones with the message "Criminals Beware We Shoot Back!" and another with a picture of a hand pointing a gun and the assertion "Never Mind the Dog, Beware of Owner!" (Casteel, 1985:A–2).

Public reaction to various forms of neovigilantism is greatly mixed. The retaliation and vigilantism of juvenile gangs are almost uniformly scorned. On the other hand, community efforts toward crime and delinquency prevention such as Neighborhood Watch are met with almost universal approval. The efforts of groups such as the Guardian Angels create responses ranging from condemnation to high praise. In cases of individual vigilantism, such as that of Bernhard Goetz, controversy is inevitable and most pronounced. While some celebrate the right of citizens to protect themselves, others point out that taking the law into one's own hands breeds anarchy, and is in fact merely fighting one type of criminal offense by committing another. In summarizing the renewed movement toward vigilantism in America, Tucker (1985:26–27) indicated:

> The social contract that says we will forswear private vengeance and allow the state to defend us in criminal matters is only that—a social contract. If there is widespread feeling that the state is no longer holding up its end of the bargain, then people will start 'taking the law back into their own hands'—which is where it was in the first place.

While "returning the law back into the hands of the people" might sound attractive to some, Tucker (1985:29) also cautioned, "Vigilantes may win widespread support, but they are inherently self-selective . . . [and] are almost inevitably that portion of the community that has already made up its mind."

Pseudovigilantism

Another form of social control which has many of the elements of neovigilantism involves the Crimestoppers, Crime Hot-Lines, and various other community programs that encourage citizens to call a particular phone number through which they can provide anonymous tips about various crimes in the area. If the information provided leads to the arrest and/or conviction of persons involved in a particular crime, some type of monetary reward is usually offered. These programs have become extremely popular, and virtually every large community, and many small ones, sponsor such a program. Local newspapers and radio stations often participate in advertising the program and helping to fund the rewards, and local television stations often provide "reenactments" of crimes while urging viewers to call the "hot-line" if they have any information relating to the crimes.

These programs are somewhat similar to the Neighborhood Watch programs discussed earlier, except that they do not involve citizens becoming actively involved in crime prevention, or being involved in neighborhood patrols. Rather, the programs rely upon *private citizens informing upon one another.* Hence, we have coined the term **pseudovigilantism** to describe this phenomenon. Vigilantism involves citizens actively taking the law into their own hands because they feel the state to be unable or unwilling to enforce the law. Crimestoppers, on the other hand, involves private citizens aiding the state in its law enforcement efforts. This is also the intent of the Neighborhood Watch programs, hence they operate from the same philosophical stance. On the other hand, the Neighborhood Watch programs demand actual community involvement in the law enforcement process, and in some cases, as we have pointed out, some citizens become far too involved to suit the police. The "hot-line" programs merely involve the sharing of information. A 1986 study of the success of the Crimestoppers and similar programs indicated that community participation in these types of programs is minimal. Two groups seem most likely to participate: the business community, and criminals themselves who may provide information about crimes committed by their associates (Rosenbaum, 1986:3). Nevertheless Rosenbaum et al. (1986) found that Crimestoppers was a very cost-effective method of social control in that the anonymous tips leading to the solution of previously unsolved crimes (usually property offenses) generally led to the recovery of goods which far exceeded the cost of the monetary awards for the information.

SUMMARY

In this chapter we have pointed out that every society attempts to encourage conformity to its norms and to control deviant behavior. The three general categories of social control involve *voluntary, informal,* and *formal* mechanisms. Voluntary social control relies upon successful socialization and the internalization of social norms and values. An individual's self-concept, personality, and overall socialization experience help determine the extent to which he/she will voluntarily refrain from committing delinquency. The development of a *social bond* or positive attachment to society seems to create a stronger likelihood of conformity among juveniles.

If a juvenile's internal voluntary control is not strong enough to prohibit law violation, a variety of informal social control mechanisms can be implemented. Gossip, ridicule, humor, ostracism, and peer pressure all can help control a juvenile's behavior. The nature of the offense as well as the type of society or community in which the juvenile resides help influence the type of informal social control that may be utilized and its probable effectiveness.

The third type of societal defense against delinquency is formal social control. The schools, police, courts, and various social agencies all play an important role in implementing formal social control measures against juveniles. Formal techniques of social control, such as juvenile probation, incarceration in juvenile institutions, and various community programs are all utilized in an attempt to prevent and control delinquency. In extreme cases, capital punishment exists as the ultimate form of social control for juveniles who have committed such heinous crimes that society has deemed execution to be the appropriate social sanction.

In addition to the three major categories of social control, individuals and groups sometimes take on the role of vigilantes and attempt to enforce the law, apprehend violators, and implement punishments for delinquent and criminal behavior. When voluntary, informal, and formal social control mechanisms seem ineffective, some believe it is their "right" and "duty" to protect themselves and others. As American citizens have become increasingly frustrated with the incidence of crime and juvenile delinquency in American cities, we have seen a resurgence in the attitudes and actions of vigilantism. Ironically, this form of social control which we have called neovigilantism threatens the very social order upon which a society is established and may threaten to break down all forms of social control.

Juvenile delinquency, like other forms of social deviance, is not likely to be eliminated. However, members of society must attempt to alleviate the problems associated with it by minimizing its negative consequences.

CONCEPT APPLICATION

"The Old Order Amish and Social Control"

The Old Order Amish illustrate Toennies' ([1887] 1961) concept of a gemeinschaft society. Rejecting most of the technological trappings of modern American society, the Old Order Amish strive to maintain a simple, agrarian society based upon their strong religious beliefs. Their communities are typically small (20 to 30 families) and are characterized by primary relationships based upon face-to-face interaction.

The Old Order Amish rely heavily upon voluntary social control. Members of the community are expected to adhere to the norms because they *want* to. From birth, Amish parents socialize their children to internalize the attitudes, values, and beliefs of their faith. They believe that by teaching their children the proper values and by setting the proper example by their own actions, their children will conform to the dictates of their religion, and hence the norms of the community.

When minor infractions of norms occur, the Old Order Amish usually implement informal methods of social control to sanction the behavior. Parents discipline their children as deemed necessary. When older children, juveniles, or adults in the community violate norms in some minor fashion, they are likely to become the victims of gossip and social avoidance. This is usually sufficient to inform the norm violator that the behavior in question has been deemed inappropriate and should not be repeated in the future.

If informal control mechanisms prove insufficient, the Old Order Amish may implement formal social control. Just as ostracism can be informally utilized, it also provides the Amish with their most severe form of social control. If a transgression is viewed as serious, or if the offender has repeatedly broken social mores, the bishop may issue an edict of *Meidung*. *Meidung* is a complete ban from the community and results in total *shunning* of the offender (Kephart, 1982). Reserved for the most serious norm violators, shunning virtually constitutes *social death*, in that the shunned individual is no longer recognized socially and other church members refuse to acknowledge the person's existence. There are some exemptions to the Meidung, however, and most acts of delinquency would be among these. Persons cannot be shunned until they have officially joined the church. For males, this does not occur until they marry, which occurs in their early twenties. Thus, most of what would constitute delinquency is handled informally, through the less severe sanctions of gossip, ridicule, and parental punishment. Regardless of which form it takes, the Old Order Amish firmly believe in social control and utilize all three methods (voluntary, informal, and formal) very effectively.

* * * *

Based upon your reading of this chapter, how do you think the Old Order Amish differ from the larger society in controlling the deviant behavior of their adolescents? Could the larger society successfully implement the same control strategies as the Amish? Why? Why not?

CONCEPT INTEGRATION
QUESTIONS AND TOPICS FOR STUDY AND DISCUSSION

1. Explain what is meant by the term "social control" and how this concept differs from the attempt to eliminate delinquency.
2. Explain what is meant by "voluntary social control." How is voluntary social control achieved? In what ways can voluntary control of delinquency be made more effective?
3. List and describe several techniques of informal social control that can be utilized against delinquency. In what type of community or society is informal social control likely to be most effective?
4. Give several examples of formal social control of juvenile delinquents. How do these methods differ from voluntary and informal techniques of social control? In your opinion is formal control *more* or *less* effective than voluntary and informal social control? Why?

5. With the return of capital punishment, individuals in many states are housed on death row awaiting execution for crimes they committed while still legally defined as juveniles. In your opinion, should capital punishment be meted out to juvenile offenders? Why? Why not?
6. Define vigilantism. How has neovigilantism been used to combat delinquency? Can a society like ours tolerate vigilantes? If so, how? If not, why not?

References

Allen, H. E. & Simonsen, C. E. 1981. *Corrections in America: An introduction.* New York: MacMillan.

AP, Boise. 1982. Teen tortured, murdered in jail. Boise, Idaho: *Emporia Gazette* June 2, 1982.

AP, Chicago. 1985. Police decide against charging man who shot, killed attacker. *Emporia Gazette* January 22:8.

AP, Fort Worth. 1985. 'Legion of Doom' terrorizes high school troublemakers. *Emporia Gazette* March 28, 1985.

AP, Fort Worth. 1985. 9 students targeted in vigilante probe. *Wichita Eagle Beacon* April 21, 1985.

AP, New York. 1987. Gunman is cleared by New York jury. *Emporia Gazette* June 17:1.

Carey, J. T. & McAnany, P. D. 1984. *Introduction to juvenile delinquency: Youth and the law.* Englewood Cliffs, NJ: Prentice-Hall.

Casteel, C. 1985. Some Sooners shooting back at gunmen. *Sunday Oklahoman* January 27:A-1;A-2.

CBS/New York Times. 1987. CBS/New York Times Poll, *CBS News* June 10, 1987.

CNN News. 1986. *CNN Headline News* December 21, 1986.

Chang, D. H. 1979. *Introduction to criminal justice: Theory and application.* Dubuque, IA: Kendall-Hunt.

Culbertson, R. G. & Ellsworth, T. 1985. Treatment innovations in probation and parole. In L. F. Travis III (Ed.). *Probation, parole, and community corrections.* Prospect Heights, IL: Waveland Press, pp. 127–147.

Eisikovits, Z. & Baizerman, M. 1982. 'Doin' time': Violent youth in a juvenile facility and in an adult prison. *Journal of Offender Counseling, Services and Rehabilitation* 6 (Spring):5–20.

Empey, L. T. & Rabow, J. 1961. The Provo experiment in delinquency rehabilitation. *American Sociological Review* 26 (October):679–695.

Evans, R. C. & Koederitz, G. D. 1983. The requirement of restitution for juvenile offenders: An alternative disposition. *Journal of Offender Counseling, Services and Rehabilitation* 7 (Spring–Summer):1–20.

Farrell, R. A. & Swigert, V. L. 1982. *Deviance and social control.* Glennview, IL: Scott, Foresman.

Furman vs. Georgia 1972. 408 U.S. 238, 371, 1972.

Goodman, E. 1985. Bernhard Goetz hits a public nerve. *Wichita Eagle Beacon* January 20:3B.

Goffman, E. 1961. *Asylums.* Garden City, NY: Anchor Books.

Graham, H. & Guerr, T. 1969. *The history of violence in America: A report to the National Commission on the Causes and Prevention of Violence.* New York: Bantam Books.

Hakeem, M. 1957–1958. A critique of the psychiatric approach to the prevention of juvenile delinquency. *Social Problems* 5 (Winter): 194–206.

Haskell, M. R. & Yablonsky, L. 1978. *Juvenile delinquency* (2nd ed.). Chicago: Rand McNally.

Hirschi, T. 1969. *Causes of delinquency.* Berkeley: University of California Press.

Imlay, C. H. & Flasheen, C. R. 1971. See what condition your conditions are in. *Federal Probation* 35 (June):3–11.

Kephart, W. M. 1982. *Extraordinary groups: The sociology of unconventional lifestyles* (2nd ed.). New York: St. Martin's Press.

Lokeman, R. C. 1985. Just why is Goetz a hero? *Kansas City Star* Sunday Edition (January 27):1K,4K.

McGee, R. A. 1971. Our sick jails. *Federal Probation* 35 (March):3–8.

Parade Magazine. 1987. Readers respond on capital punishment. *Parade* January 25:10.

Reckless, W. 1961. A new theory of delinquency and crime. *Federal Probation* 25 (December):42–46.

Remington, C. 1982. Restitution can work for serious offenders. *Change: A Juvenile Justice Quarterly* 5 (2):9–10.

Richards, C. E. 1972. *Man in perspective: An introduction to cultural anthropology.* New York: Random House.

Rosenbaum, D. P., Lurigio, A. J., & Lavrakas, P. J. 1986. *Crime stoppers—A national evaluation.* Washington, DC: National Institute of Justice.

Royko, M. 1985. Time to start shooting back. *Wichita Eagle Beacon* January 20:3B.

Ryan, B. 1980. Should delinquents be locked up? *Parade* October 12:21,23.

Safire, W. 1985. On language: Vigilante. *Emporia Gazette* February 11.

Sanders, W. B. 1981. *Juvenile delinquency: Causes, patterns, and reactions.* New York: Holt, Rinehart and Winston.

Sarri, R. 1974. *Under lock and key: Juveniles in jail and detention.* Ann Arbor: National Assessment of Juvenile Corrections, University of Michigan.

Seligson, T. 1986. Are they too young to die? *Parade* October 19:4–7.

Sherraden, M. W. & Downs, S. W. 1984. Institutions and juvenile delinquency in historical perspective. *Children and Youth Services Review* 6 (3):155–172.

Streib, V. L. 1987. *Death penalty for juveniles.* Bloomington: Indiana State University Press.

Time. 1982. Guardian Angels' growing pains. *Time* (January):21.

Tittle, C. R. 1974. Prisons and rehabilitation: The inevitability of disaster. *Social Problems* 21 (3):385–395.

Toby, J. 1965. An evaluation of early identification and intensive treatment programs for predelinquents. *Social Problems* 13 (Fall).

Toennies, F. 1887. 1961. Gemeinschaft and gesellschaft. In T. Parsons et al. (3rd ed.). *Theories of Society* (Vol. 1). Glencoe, IL: Free Press, pp. 19–201.

Tucker, W. 1985. *Vigilante: The backlash against crime in America.* New York: Stein and Day.

U.S. Department of Justice. 1987. *Sourcebook of criminal justice statistics—1986.* Washington, DC: U.S. Government Printing Office.

Vito, G. F. 1985. Probation as punishment: New directions and suggestions. In L. F. Travis III (Ed.), *Probation, parole, and community corrections: A reader.* Prospect Heights, IL: Waveland Press, pp. 73–79.

Webster's New World Dictionary. 1979. *Webster's New World Dictionary of the American Language* (Pocket-Size Edition). New York: Fawcett Popular Library.

Chapter 14

Treatment and Prevention Strategies

The reading of this chapter will help you achieve the following objectives:

1. Understand the treatment ideology in juvenile corrections.
2. Understand the prevention ideology in juvenile corrections.
3. Summarize some of the major juvenile treatment programs in the United States.
4. Summarize some of the major delinquency prevention programs in the United States.
5. Review the move toward deinstitutionalization and diversion in handling juvenile delinquents.
6. Develop a sociological perspective on the treatment and prevention of juvenile delinquency.

INTRODUCTION

Chapter 13 discussed the concept of social control. Social control involves societal intervention into an individual's life in an attempt to regulate social behavior. When a person's behavior is regarded as deviant, and the decision is made to formally or informally intervene, there are three overriding ideological approaches that society may take: punishment, treatment, and/or prevention. Chapter 13 primarily focused upon the punishment ideology, illustrating how societal members inflict social reprimands ranging from gossip and ridicule to imprisonment and death upon those who have violated social norms.

In this chapter, we focus on the treatment and prevention ideological approaches to delinquency. From the outset, it should be noted that these three different ideological approaches are not mutually exclusive. While proponents of one often view themselves as fundamentally at odds with the ideas of the others, there are marked similarities in the three approaches. All of them represent the attempts of society to regulate the behavior of its members. While these ideologies differ in their specific approaches to dealing with the problem of delinquency, more often than not, delinquency programs integrate aspects of all three to some extent.

The treatment and prevention ideologies are particularly compatible. While treatment programs are **reactive** in nature in that they are *implemented after a juvenile has been adjudicated delinquent*, they attempt not only to treat the juvenile delinquent, but also to prevent any future involvement in delinquent behavior. Prevention is a **proactive** strategy, based upon the assumption that if the underlying causes of delinquency can be identified and eliminated *before the delinquency occurs*, delinquent behavior can be prevented.

TREATMENT IDEOLOGY AND DELINQUENCY TREATMENT PROGRAMS

The **treatment ideology** *follows the rehabilitative philosophy of the juvenile court.* Treatment programs are usually based upon the assumption that delinquent behavior is the manifestation or symptom of some other deeper problem. The treatment ideology tends to apply the medical model approach to delinquency, which was introduced earlier in this book. Delinquency is viewed as analogous to disease, and treatment programs typically take on medical and clinical characteristics. Consequently, *symptoms* of delinquency are observed, in order to make a proper *diagnosis*, so that the appropriate *treatment* strategy can be pursued.

The treatment ideology tends to take an individualistic approach to delinquency, viewing delinquents as being socially and psychologically maladjusted or disturbed. Treatment programs attempt to readjust or remove what is disturbing the juvenile so that the youth can overcome the source of trouble, and go on to lead a normal life. Based upon many of the psychogenic explanations discussed in Chapter 5, psychiatry and psychology often dominate many of the current treatment strategies in juvenile delinquency.

Treatment programs can be undertaken either in conjunction with or apart from an institutional setting. Thus, just as treatment philosophies are compatible with the prevention ideology, they need not be totally at odds with the concept of punishment. Many juvenile institutions, particularly the state training schools and reformatories, often incorporate various treatment strategies into the process of rehabilitation. While utilizing confinement in an institution as a means of social control and punishment, various treatment strategies are often used to attempt to reform the juvenile and prevent any further delinquent or criminal activity. James Robison and Gerald Smith (1971) pointed out that what has often been viewed as the punishment versus treatment ideologies in corrections is not accurate, as these are not opposites. The two approaches are not mutually exclusive but can be used in conjunction with each other. Robison and Smith contended that it was more accurate to view the choice not as being between treatment or punishment, but between one type of treatment/punishment alternative and another.

A variety of strategies and techniques have been used in the treatment of juvenile delinquents. While it would be impossible (and pointless) to discuss them all, we will briefly describe some of the specific and representative types of treatment programs.

Behavior Modification

Behavior modification is based upon principles derived from research in experimental psychology, and is often associated with the work of the prominent psychologist, B. F. Skinner (1971). As the term implies, **behavior modification** is *a treatment technique which attempts to modify or change an individual's behavior*. Behavior modification operates on the principle that the consequences of an individual's actions play an important part in determining future actions. If an individual receives gratification, or *positive reinforcement*, from a particular act, the same or similar acts are likely to be repeated in the future. On the other hand, if an individual views the consequences of an act as undesirable, or experiences *negative reinforcement* from a particular behavior, that act or similar acts are unlikely to be repeated in the future.

Behavior modification, as a treatment technique, is compatible with the social learning theories of delinquency (see Chapter 6), and has been used in many juvenile correctional facilities. In a facility wherein the daily behavior of juveniles can be readily observed and evaluated, the principles of behavior modification have been used to reward approved actions, while punishing (or at least *not* rewarding) undesirable behavior. Different methods can be and have been used to provide the positive and negative reinforcement viewed as essential to behavior modification.

It is common for juvenile institutions to operate on some type of "level system" or to utilize a merit/demerit approach to encourage the incarcerated youth to obey rules and demonstrate acceptable behavior. Typically, level classifications are developed with different behavioral expectations required to move from one level to the next. As juveniles earn merits, or otherwise meet the requirements to move up to the next higher level, they are rewarded with more privileges, and higher status within the institution. For example, an institution which establishes five levels may set five curfews or "lights out" times for the various levels. Those who are on the lowest level might have to be in their rooms with lights out by 9:00 p.m., while those on the next highest level would be allowed to stay up until 9:30; whereas those on the highest level might not be required to be in their rooms until 11:00 p.m. Other rewards and privileges, such as time away from the institution to attend a movie, increased visitation privileges, or increased recreation time, can be utilized to motivate the youths to improve their behavior, and perhaps earn their release, or at least make their stay in the facility more palatable. Conversely, failure to meet behavioral expectations would lead to demerits or being moved to a lower level classification, with the loss of certain privileges.

It is difficult to evaluate the effectiveness of behavior modification in the treatment of delinquents, as different specific techniques of behavior modification can be utilized in a wide range of environments. Elery Phillips and his associates (1971) found the token economy system to be effective in dealing with adolescents, and Robert Rutherford (1975) reported case studies in which the use of behavioral agreements between supervising adults and juveniles was effective in modifying behavior in the home, the school, the community, and the institution. Token economies are utilized in many institutional settings, and can effectively reinforce (either positively or negatively) behavior through the use of tokens, coins, chits (institutional coupons), or some other tangible object which has monetary value within the institution. Behavioral contracts can be utilized in virtually any setting in which those in authority clearly delineate the rules and the appropriate behaviors expected from the youths for receiving certain desired rewards for fulfilling the contract (e.g., good grades, merits, money).

Some problems arise in the use of behavior modification with juveniles. One is that in order to be effective, almost constant monitoring and evaluation of behavior is required. If periods of time elapse when the juvenile's behavior goes unnoticed, hence unrewarded or unpunished, the principles of behavior modification are violated, and presumably, its effectiveness diminished. Another problem is that of determining appropriate positive and negative reinforcements for particular youths and specific behaviors. What is viewed as a reward by some, may be viewed with ambivalence or even negatively by others. Thus, appropriate punishment for one youth may only encourage the undesired behavior on the part of another. Either consciously or unknowingly, many teachers use the principles of behavior modification in attempting to maintain order in the classroom and to motivate students to perform academically and socially in desired ways. However, virtually every teacher has had the experience of singling out a student for verbal discipline in an attempt to embarrass the student in front of classmates, only to find that some students greatly enjoy the attention being granted them, and continue to misbehave in order to gain more of the same.

Another potential problem related to behavior modification resides in the use of punishment as negative reinforcement. While proponents of the treatment technique view it as humane, theoretically its implementation could take on cruel and inhumane proportions. For example, various forms of child abuse might be rationalized by the abusive parent as being appropriate punishment for undesirable behavior. Likewise, with available technology in drugs and equipment, the potential rewards and punishments for behavior are limited only by the imagination.

Finally, one of the problems with behavior modification involves the extent to which the desired behavioral changes continue once the environment is changed and the anticipated positive and negative reinforcements are not immediately forthcoming. The corrections literature is replete with examples of how the "ideal inmate" does not necessarily become the "ideal citizen" after release. It is difficult yet possible to constantly monitor a juvenile's behavior while institutionalized, but it is virtually impossible in the outside larger society. In society, seldom are all behaviors accompanied by a rigid structure that gives immediate rewards and punishments. Complicating the situation further is that in the larger social world, the juvenile has a variety of reference groups from which the potential rewards and punishments can come. As was discussed in Chapters 7 and 8, the family often must compete with the peer group in reinforcing the values and behavior of youths.

Transactional Analysis

Transactional Analysis is based upon the writings of Eric Berne (1961) and *focuses upon the interpretation of interaction between people.* According to Transactional Analysis theory, as people interact with one another, their **verbal exchanges,** described as *transactions,* reflect different **ego states** identified as either *parent, child,* or *adult.* The parent state arises out of an individual's identification with parents and is manifested in interactions reflecting or modeling the paternal or maternal role, while the child state reflects an individual's clinging to a past state of dependency. The adult state reflects the fully developed independent and mature self.

In his best seller, *Games People Play,* Berne (1964) described how people shift from one ego state to another in the course of social interaction, primarily through conversation, in an attempt to manipulate others and gain the desired outcome from the interaction. The goal of the therapist is to identify which ego state is the source of the problem for the individual and identify ways in which that person may resolve the problem through moving to another ego state.

In another best seller on transactional analysis, *I'm OK, You're OK*, Thomas Harris (1969) described the potential attitudinal outcomes of interaction. In any social encounter, four potential situations or "life positions" exist:

1. **I'm not OK, you're OK.** This life position reflects a situation typical of many children who, after continually being corrected by their parents and other adults, begin to believe that they are inherently wrong.
2. **I'm not OK, you're not OK.** Reflects a situation in which individuals still feel that their actions and ideas are wrong, but they also reject the ideas and actions of those who attempt to correct them.
3. **I'm OK, you're not OK.** Reflects a belief in one's self while rejecting the validity of others (a situation which may characterize the attitudes of many delinquents who feel that they have had adult values and norms imposed upon them and have been unjustly punished for their violation).
4. **I'm OK, you're OK.** Reflects the acceptance of one's own worth and validity while also accepting the validity of others (Harris, 1969:50–51).

It is the achievement of the fourth life position which is the goal of the therapist for the client. A variety of counseling techniques, conversations, role playing, and other devices are used in an attempt to develop this attitude in the patient.

Transactional Analysis gained a great deal of attention in the late 1960s and early 1970s, and as a result of the two previously mentioned best selling books, became a part of the "pop psychology" which was widespread in America during that period. However, in at least one study of a California state training school, Transactional Analysis was judged to be effective in the treatment of juvenile delinquents (Jesness, 1975).

Reality Therapy

Reality Therapy is primarily associated with the work of William Glasser (1965), and is *a treatment strategy which focuses upon the individual understanding the consequences of one's actions and accepting responsibility for them.* Unlike most psychotherapeutic techniques which tend to dwell upon a person's past in order to understand the causes of present behavioral problems, reality therapy focuses entirely upon the present. Glasser contended that concentrating upon individuals' past experiences was useless in effectively resolving present problems, and could potentially provide excuses and rationalizations which would exempt them from taking responsibility for their own actions.

As a technique for dealing with juvenile delinquents, reality therapy is much less concerned with *why* the juvenile committed the delinquent act, as with *what* can be done in order to ensure that the youth does not commit the same or similar acts in the future. In fact, why the act was committed is treated as irrelevant. Regardless of what problems the youth may have encountered in childhood—broken home, child abuse, inadequate socialization, poor environment, or other negative circumstances—the *reality* of the situation is that the youth has committed an act resulting in trouble with the law, and now must accept responsibility for that action. You may remember from Chapter 6 that Sykes and Matza (1957) contended that delinquent youths usually realize that they have violated society's norms, and experience a sense of guilt over having done so. However, they rationalize their actions through techniques of neutralization, one of which is *denial of responsibility*. Reality therapy directly attacks that neutralization technique, insisting that juveniles acknowledge that they are responsible for their behavior.

Reality therapy has been used widely with juveniles in both institutional and parole or probation settings. Glasser's research indicated that if the therapist develops an intimate relationship with the youth, gains the youth's trust, and genuinely cares about changing the individual's behavior, it can be very successful. Phillip Cole and Joseph Hafsten (1978) found that when reality therapy techniques were used during juvenile probation, they were effective in changing behavior. Interestingly, one of the elements of Cole and Hafsten's probation program included victim restitution. They believed that some form of restitution symbolically represented the juvenile's acknowledgment of responsibility for the offense. The Ventura Restitution Project specifically aims to make juvenile offenders understand the ramifications of their delinquent behavior by making it clear that they have direct responsibility for their actions (Remington, 1982). While it does not involve the intense individual approach that reality therapy demands, the project is based upon the primary assumptions of reality therapy—that individuals must accept responsibility for and the consequences of their actions.

Another program encompassing the reality therapy approach is "TOUGH-LOVE." Described as a "self-help program for parents, youths, and communities," TOUGHLOVE literature points out that the program deals in *behavior, not in emotions*. The program is one of crisis intervention to provide support groups for those whose lives are directly affected by the negative effects of delinquency. Avoiding the assignment of blame, the program emphasizes the need for responsible action on the part of all to alleviate the problem (see the Illustrative Anecdote at the end of this chapter).

Group and Individual Counseling

Many group and individual counseling techniques have been followed in treating juvenile delinquents, both inside and outside institutional settings. Transactional Analysis and Reality Therapy are but two examples of these counseling techniques. It would be impossible to delineate all of the counseling strategies that have been employed. Psychiatrists, psychologists, social workers, probation and parole officers, and virtually everybody else who has worked with delinquent youths have engaged in some aspect of individual and group counseling in an attempt to resolve the problems associated with delinquency.

The common elements shared by almost all programs which utilize counseling as part of their treatment strategy is that they tend to view delinquency from an individualistic perspective. Even group counseling techniques operate on the premise that the group can help the individual overcome a particular situation, and resolve the problems which caused the delinquent behavior. With few exceptions, counseling techniques, whether conducted individually or in a group context, are dominated by the psychogenic approach to delinquency and tend to ignore the sociological context in which juvenile delinquency occurs.

PREVENTION IDEOLOGY AND DELINQUENCY PREVENTION PROGRAMS

The **prevention ideology** is *based upon the assumption that the best way to deal with the problem of juvenile delinquency is to intervene early and prevent it.* Thus, whether the cause of delinquency is viewed as social, psychological, or physiological/biological, the preventive strategy attempts to identify the causal factors, and to intervene and alter those factors before delinquent behavior occurs.

Delinquency prevention strategies have been dominated by the psychiatric perspective. Michael Hakeem (1957–58) pointed out that even some sociologists working in criminology and corrections have tended to adopt the psychiatric approach to delinquency, viewing the problem of delinquent behavior as being rooted in the individual psyche. That is not to say that sociology has not played a role in delinquency prevention. In a later section of this chapter we illustrate how the sociological perspective has been successfully incorporated into some delinquency treatment and prevention programs.

Many delinquency prevention programs, however, have viewed delinquency as abnormal, and, like the treatment strategies just discussed, have tended to perceive delinquency from the medical model analogy. Delinquency was primarily viewed as an individual anomaly, and as such, early diagnosis, identification, and intervention were considered important for effective prevention.

Early Identification and Intervention

At the heart of the concept of delinquency prevention is the need to identify as early as possible the behaviors of children that are considered to be "warning signs" of impending delinquency. Prevention strategies assume that there are characteristics of "predelinquency" which, if caught soon enough, may be altered in time to prevent actual delinquency. In a pamphlet entitled "What Parents Should Know About Juvenile Delinquency and Juvenile Justice," Waln Brown (1983:12) provided a checklist for parents of what he considered to be a "partial list of delinquent acts and inappropriate childhood behaviors" for which parents should be on the alert, including behaviors ranging from being moody to actual law violations (see Figure 14–1).

A longer and even more exhaustive list of "predelinquency" symptoms was developed by a delinquency prevention project sponsored by the U.S. Children's Bureau in St. Paul, Minnesota. That list comprised virtually all sorts of childhood behavior, including bashfulness, crying, daydreaming, nailbiting, silliness, thumbsucking, and bedwetting (cited in Hakeem, 1957–58). Hyperactivity has also been identified as a "predelinquency" symptom, and Dan Hurley (1985) indicated that early detection and intervention could significantly reduce the likelihood of "high-risk" children becoming criminals.

The search for symptoms of "predelinquency" has underscored the psychiatric assumption that delinquency is a form of individual pathology that, like a disease, must be diagnosed early and treated before it consumes the person beyond hope of "cure." The important second phase in the prevention ideology is to intervene in the individual's life so as to alter a purported predisposition toward delinquency. This raises the question as to what type of intervention is most appropriate. No real consensus has arisen about this dilemma. Any and all of the treatment strategies discussed earlier in this chapter have been proposed

---

FIGURE 14-1
Partial List of Delinquent Acts and Inappropriate Childhood Behaviors

Alcohol use	Law violations
Bad temper	Losses or gains of large sums of money
Cheating	Lying
Complaints by neighbors	Moody
Cruelty to people or animals	Poor school grades
Destructive	Running away from home
Discipline problems in school	Regularly misses family meals
Discourteous	Secretive
Disobedient	Sexual misconduct
Drug use	Smoking
Fighting	Stays out late
Hanging out at places that have a bad reputation	Stealing
	Swearing
Inconsiderate	Threatens family members
Irresponsible	Truancy
Lack of friends	Verbally abusive

Source: Waln K. Brown, *What Parents Should Know About Juvenile Delinquency and Juvenile Justice*, The William Gladden Foundation, 1983. Reprinted by permission.

and tried, along with numerous other methods to prevent the juvenile from continuing on a path toward delinquency. Parents, churches, schools, and other social institutions have grappled with the problem of how to deal with the "troubled child" before that child becomes a delinquent. At least one publishing company has recognized this dilemma; it markets religious books and pamphlets, which are displayed in supermarkets with the message: "PARENTS: STOP JUVENILE DELINQUENCY BEFORE IT BEGINS," and "Your child needs *The Bible Story.*"

Interestingly, in at least one type of situation, early identification and intervention has apparently been successful, and that is youthful arson. Clifford Karchmer (1984) found five juvenile firesetter counseling programs, in San Francisco, Dallas, Los Angeles, Mesa (Arizona), and Prince Georges County (Maryland), in which firefighting personnel offered in-house counseling for young arsonists. A critical factor in the success of these programs apparently rests in the ability to diagnose potential juvenile firesetters as early as possible and begin intensive counseling as soon as possible.

Like the treatment strategies discussed earlier in this chapter, the prevention ideology and most prevention programs fail to put delinquency into its social context. Delinquency is viewed as an individual matter, and attempts to prevent it are primarily aimed at intervening into a person's life in order to alter future behavior. While morally uplifting, most of these preventive programs are sociologically bankrupt. As Alexander Liazos (1974) pointed out, virtually all programs based upon these assumptions have failed miserably.

Jackson Toby (1965) discussed the problems of early identification and intensive treatment of delinquency in regard to some of the problems related to accurate prediction, type of treatment, and its intensity. He analyzed the Cambridge-Somerville Youth Study and the New York City Youth Board Prediction Study. One of the studies (Cambridge-Somerville) employed the *extrapolation technique* of delinquency prediction, in which youths who had exhibited antisocial behavior are identified and treated. The other (New York City Youth Board) followed the *circumstantial vulnerability approach*, which is based more heavily upon sociological research and identifies those youths whose family and neighborhood characteristics have been linked with delinquency. The problem, according to Toby, was that both studies overpredicted delinquency, and he pointed out that the stigmatization of being identified as predelinquent may exceed or at least offset any benefits that might be derived from treatment. He summarized, "Early identification and intensive treatment, though probably not as erroneous as the flat-world theory, is more a slogan or a rallying cry than a realistic assessment of the difficulties that delinquency control programs must overcome" (Toby, 1965:160).

Another problem that arises with delinquency prevention is the legal and moral issues that accompany intervention into a person's life *before* the commission of an illegal act. The American judicial system and juvenile corrections are based upon intervening *after* a wrongful act has been committed. State intervention because of presumed future law violation is risky at best, and frightening at worse.

SOCIOLOGICAL APPROACHES TO DELINQUENCY TREATMENT AND PREVENTION

As previously mentioned, while most treatment and prevention programs traditionally have been dominated by the individualistic approach to delinquency, sociologists also have been concerned with dealing with delinquents and attempting to reduce the likelihood of their further involvement in delinquent behavior. Along these lines, there have been numerous sociological contributions to delinquency treatment and prevention, and sociologists continue to search for new and innovative methods toward this end. The sociological approach to delinquency treatment and prevention is distinctive in that it views delinquent behavior and the delinquent in their broader social contexts.

Rather than approaching the problem as being one of individual anomaly or pathology, the sociological approach takes into account the influence of society on the individual. Consequently, sociologically oriented programs which have attempted to "treat" delinquents and prevent (or at least reduce) further delinquency have approached delinquency as socially created and defined, and influenced by social groups, institutions, and the social and cultural environment. In this section we briefly examine some of the classic examples of programs that have approached the handling of delinquents from a sociological perspective. Then, we briefly describe some of the more recent attempts to apply a sociological perspective to the problem of delinquency treatment and prevention.

The Chicago Area Project

One of the first and most notable attempts to apply sociological principles to the treatment and prevention of juvenile delinquency was the Chicago Area Project. The Project began in the 1930s, and was developed out of the theoretical framework of Shaw and McKay (see Chapter 6) and what later became known as the Chicago School of Thought regarding delinquency.

Shaw and McKay (1942) identified several Chicago neighborhoods in which crime and delinquency were extraordinarily high (as were other forms of social deviance). They contended that any program to attempt to reduce delinquency in those areas would have to be developed in the communities themselves, utilizing human and institutional resources from within the neighborhoods, with only minimum guidance (and necessary funding) coming from external agencies (Shaw and McKay, 1942).

It was obvious that informal social control mechanisms were not working in the high delinquency neighborhoods in Chicago. Shaw and McKay believed, however, that some of those areas, such as the Russell Square neighborhood, known as "the Bush," had sufficient territorial and ethnic identity to effectively utilize local social institutions and some of the authority figures in the neighborhood to reduce and help prevent delinquency (Schlossman and Sedlak, 1983).

The Chicago Area Project was distinctively sociological in its approach. Rather than focusing upon individual delinquents (who were necessarily involved in the project), it focused upon the revitalization of meaningful social networks within the community. One of its first accomplishments was to establish organized recreational facilities for youths in the high delinquency areas. While recreation was not viewed as a resolution for delinquency, the formation of athletic teams and leagues required cooperative group efforts among juveniles and adults in the neighborhoods. In the Russell Square area, there were approximately 15 well-established gangs (Schlossman and Sedlak, 1983). Street workers were called upon to make contacts with the gangs, and help structure recreational activities in an effort to reduce involvement in delinquent activities. The workers were successful in organizing intramural basketball and baseball leagues and involving gang members in organized recreation. Soloman Kobrin (1959) assessed the general accomplishment of the Chicago Area Project as a success.

Shaw and McKay presented reports on official delinquency rates 10 years after the implementation of the Chicago Area Project that indicated substantial declines in official delinquency in the neighborhoods participating in the program. However, the success of the Chicago Area Project was not equal in all neighborhoods. As Steven Schlossman and Michael Sedlak (1983) pointed out, the key to success of the project was the involvement of indigenous leaders. Naturally, the same types of leaders and their abilities would not exist in all neighborhoods.

Kobrin's (1959) 25-year assessment of the Chicago Area Project was favorable. While delinquency was certainly not eradicated in the targeted neighborhoods of Chicago, it was apparently substantially reduced. Schlossman and Sedlak (1983) also viewed the project as generally successful, especially the work in the Russell Square area. The Project was not without criticism. Some residents of the community questioned whether workers in the project were too tolerant of delinquents. Because the streetworkers were willing to work with persistently and seriously delinquent youths, some critics charged that they were indirectly encouraging delinquency. Further, some of the private agencies in the area apparently resented the use of indigenous leaders and what they considered the rejection of their expertise (Schlossman and Sedlak, 1983). Nevertheless, the project stimulated the sociological imagination of scholars around the country, and other cities attempted to implement similar programs in their own communities.

The Mid-City Project

The Mid-City Project was developed in Boston in the early 1950s. The project operated between 1954 and 1957 in lower class slum neighborhoods and focused on executing "action programs directed at three of the societal units seen to figure importantly in the genesis and perpetuation of delinquent behavior—the community, the family, and the gang" (Miller, 1962:168).

The Mid-City Project used street workers to establish close ties with juvenile gangs in Boston. They helped the gangs establish organized recreational activities, club meetings, dances, fundraising dinners, and other acceptable social activities. They also helped gang members with problems related to employment, school, and obtaining legal counsel.

Though based upon the same sociological assumptions which underlay the Chicago Area Project, the Mid-City Project differed in some important ways. For one thing, the Chicago Area Project was envisioned and implemented as a long-term program designed to rehabilitate the community from within. The Mid-City Project, on the other hand, was designed as a 3-year program with three distinctive phases, primarily developed and overseen from outside the community. Another important distinction was that the Mid-City Project relied heavily upon psychiatric counseling techniques. Phase Two (Phase One was the Contact and Relationship Establishment phase, and Phase Three was the Termination Phase) involved the use of behavior modification, individual psychotherapy, and regular psychiatric counseling (Miller, 1962). Thus, while sociologically inspired, like many other treatment and prevention strategies, the Mid-City Project was dominated by the psychiatric model.

Sociologist Walter B. Miller evaluated the Mid-City Project. His final assessment of the program was mixed. Miller (1962) viewed much of the work of the streetworkers and gangs as successful; however, when he posed the important evaluation question, "Was there a significant measurable inhibition of law-violating or morally disapproved behavior as a consequence of Project efforts?" his answer, with minor qualifications, was "No." The project was not deemed a total failure, however, as some improvement was measured in school performance of participants, and the project played an important part in establishing and strengthening social organizations and institutions within the community, whose efforts at delinquency reduction might not be readily measurable over the short term, but might have some long-term impact.

Mobilization for Youth

Mobilization for Youth was begun in the early 1960s on the Lower East Side of Manhattan, and represented an attempt to apply Richard Cloward and Lloyd Ohlin's (1961) theory of differential opportunity structures in urban slum areas (see Chapter 6) to delinquency prevention in the community. The primary focus of the project was to organize the residents of the Lower East Side into social networks which would open channels of access to legitimate opportunities for achieving success in school, business, government, and other social institutions and agencies (Mobilization for Youth, 1961).

Unfortunately, the Mobilization for Youth project met with a great deal of resistance in the community, and fell far short of its ambitious expectations. Nevertheless, the project represented an attempt to apply sociological theory directly to a social problem, and even in its failure, gave credence to the sociological perspective that the nature of the problem of delinquency goes beyond the individual juveniles who commit deviant acts, and that consequently, any meaningful program to control or reduce delinquency must also reach beyond those individuals.

Minnesota Youth Advocate Program

The Minnesota Youth Advocate Program was a school-based program begun in 1971 designed to help youths who had been in correctional institutions readjust to school and the community. The program had four specific objectives: increased school persistence, improved school performance, reduced recidivism, and reduced reinstitutionalization (Higgins, 1978). This program represented the sociological perspective in attempting to effectively reintegrate institutionalized youths into the social institutions and networks of the community. This program required readjustment, not only on the part of the juvenile offender, but also upon the part of the school, the family, and the community.

Paul Higgins (1978) evaluated the program on its effectiveness in achieving its four specific goals. When he compared participants in the program with a control group of juveniles who had been released from institutions but not exposed to the program, he found no significant differences between the two groups on any of the four objectives.

Neighborhood Youth Corps

Neighborhood Youth Corps programs were developed during the 1960s and implemented in major cities throughout the United States. The thrust of the Neighborhood Youth Corps was to provide vocational training and better work opportunities for disadvantaged and delinquent youths. Like the Mobilization for Youth program, the Neighborhood Youth Corps attempted to afford delinquent youths access to legitimate avenues of opportunity.

Gerald Robin (1969) studied the programs of the Neighborhood Youth Corps in Cincinnati and Detroit. He compared stratified random samples of participants in the programs with control group subjects who had applied to the program but had not been accepted. In both cities, Robin found that participation in the Neighborhood Youth Corps program was unrelated to delinquency prevention or reduction. He concluded that the assumption that providing better occupational opportunities for youth in order to reduce delinquency has more theoretical than practical value. B. Dalia Johnson and Richard Goldberg's (1982) evaluation of a Massachusetts vocational rehabilitation program came to much the same conclusion.

The Highfields Project

Not all sociologically oriented treatment and prevention programs involved such ambitious attempts at mobilizing and focusing community resources as the aforementioned programs. One of the classic small group treatment programs in sociology was the Highfields Project begun in New Jersey in 1950.

Programs at delinquency treatment and prevention centers often involve local business people talking to youths about job opportunities available when they return to the community.

The Highfields Project took boys who had been placed on probation by the court and assigned them to a facility where they lived, worked, and played in a supervised small social group of other boys of similar circumstance. Viewing delinquency as a group phenomenon, the Highfields Project stressed guided group experiences, and the strengthening of conformity to social expectations of the group. The boys were allowed to go to town, attend movies, visit the drug store soda fountain, go skating, and participate in other social activities, but they returned to the facility by a specified hour. The project was limited to 16- and 17-year-olds who were beyond the age of compulsory school attendance. The facility did not provide formal education, but stressed vocational development and focused upon providing work for the boys for which they were paid. The expectation was that after experiencing the short-term treatment program, the boys would be much less likely to participate in further delinquency upon their return to their communities.

H. Ashley Weeks (1958) evaluated the Highfields Project by comparing the success rate of boys who went through the program to that of boys who had committed similar offenses but who were sent to Annandale Farms, the New Jersey State Reformatory for males. Weeks addressed three basic research questions:

1. Did delinquents who participated in the program show lower recidivism rates than boys in other kinds of programs?
2. Did delinquents in the program change their attitudes, values, and beliefs about their families, the law, and their perspectives on life?
3. Did delinquents in the program change their basic personalities or the behavior through which they demonstrated their personalities?

In answer to the first question, recidivism rates were lower for the High-fields participants, but not dramatically. The answer to the second and third questions was "No" (Weeks, 1958). Still, the project was viewed as having been effective with a large number of the boys.

The Provo Experiment

The Provo Experiment was begun in 1956 in Provo, Utah. It was based upon the subcultural and differential association theories of delinquency (see Chapter 6). The Provo Experiment insisted that delinquency is acquired from social groups and the only way to treat it is in a group context.

Habitual juvenile offenders between the ages of 15 and 17 were assigned to the Provo Experiment, which utilized the Pinehills Center for many of its activities. Boys lived at home, but participated in various group programs at the center during the day. The program was based upon the assumption that when boys are around other boys, peer pressure becomes the primary motivation for behavior. The Provo Experiment attempted to capitalize upon that peer influence by putting the boys into social situations in which pressure from within the group would lead to conformity to social norms. The experiment attempted to make conventional and delinquent alternatives clear to the participants; lead delinquents to question the value and utility of delinquent activities; and help conventional alternatives appear more positive to the boys (Empey and Rabow, 1961).

There was no specified length of stay in the program. Emphasis was placed upon developing good working habits and seeking to find meaningful employment for the boys in the community. Overall, Lamar Empey and Jerome Rabow (1961) viewed the Provo Experiment as successful. They suggested that changing the boys' attitudes and values toward work, while they experienced group encouragement and support for conformity to conventional norms, helped reintegrate them into the community in a way that was likely to reduce further involvement in delinquency.

While the Provo Experiment gained a great deal of attention in the sociological literature, the program was not widely adopted or followed in other areas. In many ways, the apparent success may have been related to the particular social circumstances of the Provo community. The strong Mormon influence, hence strong emphasis upon conformity, may have impacted upon the youths who participated in the program. In other words, juveniles raised in the Mormon tradition, although adjudicated delinquent, may have reacted differently and been more responsive to the programs offered in the experiment than would youths from the inner city slums of Detroit, Chicago, or other major cities.

Other Programs

Numerous other delinquency prevention programs based upon sociological underpinnings have been developed throughout the United States. A delinquency prevention program in an economically depressed urban community was based upon elements from both biological and social environmental theories of delinquency (Bass and Mandell, 1982). This program attempted to unify existing social agencies into a cooperative network intended to strengthen social ties between juveniles and social institutions, and to encourage nondelinquent behavior.

A community-based program was developed in North Carolina to provide additional educational, vocational, and social opportunities for juveniles. A study by the Governor's Advocacy Council (1983) indicated general satisfaction with the program among juvenile justice officials, school officials, and program practitioners.

Bruce Berg (1984) described an interesting program for juveniles tried in an eastern correctional facility which followed social scientific theory in delinquency prevention. This program included the clinical sociological technique of **sociodrama**, *a method involving role playing, intergroup relations and collective* *ideologies.* This program which was run by inmates was judged highly successful because of its flexibility, cost-effectiveness, and positive impact upon the participants.

The Millcreek Youth Correctional Facility for serious offenders, located in Ogden, Utah, emphasizes social responsibility in its rehabilitation efforts. The maximum security facility houses approximately 60 of the most dangerous and violent juvenile offenders in Utah (NBC News, 1987). Although monitored by closed-circuit television, kept behind locked doors, and surrounded by a high fence, the youths are encouraged and rewarded for contributing to the social group and environment to which they belong. Group counseling, intense social interaction with positive role models (workers and counselors in the facility), and positive reinforcement seem to make dramatic changes in the youths' behavior after release. When Barry Krisberg studied the Millcreek program, he found that released youths had fewer arrests, and, if arrested, had committed less serious offenses (NBC News, 1987).

An interesting and extremely controversial program in Ventura, California, Colorado Springs, Colorado, and Jacksonville, Florida is called S.H.O.D.I. (Serious Habitual Offender Drug Involved). Consistent with the assumptions of Control Theory, i.e., if an individual's inner containment is not strong enough to prevent deviance, societal measures of outer containment must be imposed, S.H.O.D.I. concentrates on monitoring the behavior of known juvenile offenders. Using computers, law enforcement personnel study arrest records to pinpoint the serious and habitual juvenile offenders in a particular area. Once identified, their names are placed on a list which is circulated to all law enforcement officers. If stopped, even for the most minor violation, these youths are arrested and taken to the police station. Social workers called "trackers" are assigned to these youths to monitor their behavior 24 hours a day if necessary. The trackers check to ensure that the youths are not violating curfew, skipping school, using drugs or alcohol, or committing any other infractions. While some of the youths' attorneys complain that the program amounts to little more than police harassment and unfair labeling of their clients, law enforcement officials are convinced that it is an effective way to reduce juvenile delinquent activities (NBC News, 1987).

The increased gang activities of the late 1980s spawned numerous juvenile prevention programs. Along with the increased efforts of law enforcement personnel to thwart the illegal drug trafficking and increased violence among juvenile gangs, other groups formed to help rid their neighborhoods of gangs and their activities. One such group called "Mothers Against Gangs" was organized to call increased media attention to the problem of teenaged gangs and their victims, in much the same way that MADD (Mothers Against Drunk Driving) did with the problem of drunk driving.

David Farrington (1985) explored the issue of delinquency prevention in the 1980s, and concluded that attempting to change basic social institutions (such as family, schools, and church), along with focusing on individuals, is a worthwhile effort. Similarly, Thomas Gullotta and Gerald Adams (1982) indicated that delinquency prevention must integrate theory and practice. They cited education, competency promotion, community organization, and natural caregiving as being the four important tools in delinquency prevention. A project in Louisiana designed to facilitate reentry into the community by adjudicated delinquents incorporated many of those elements into its program (Behre et al., 1982).

The family increasingly is being viewed as an important component in the treatment and prevention of delinquency. Brown (1983:13) provided a list of 21 family approaches to delinquency prevention. This list included some pragmatic strategies such as agreeing upon and following rules of conduct, spending more time together, and helping the child with homework. It also included some more abstract and subjective suggestions such as creating a more stable family environment, developing healthy family relationships, and parents setting a good example in their own behavior. "TOUGHLOVE", as mentioned before, is an innovative program which emphasizes the role of the parent (as well as schools and community youth groups) in dealing with troubled adolescents and delinquents. This program is discussed in the Concept Application at the end of this chapter.

The emphasis on educational strategies for resocialization is present in numerous delinquency prevention programs. In Chapter 10, we suggested some ways in which the schools could perhaps become more involved in delinquency prevention. Farrington (1985) also pointed to the school as potentially making meaningful contributions to the delinquency prevention effort. Murray Thomas and Paul Murray (1983) proposed that many children do not know enough about the law to make informed judgments about their behavior and the potential legal consequences of law violation. They proposed that schools should pursue strategies designed to better educate students about the law and its impact on their behavior, and get youths interested in the law before it gets interested in them. This is now being done in many schools across the country. For example, in one community, a 10-week course on Street Law is taught at night at the local high school by local attorneys (Horst, 1987). The course teaches criminal law and the consequences of its violation by youthful offenders. It was designed to reduce the number of juvenile complaints prosecuted by the juvenile court and to "influence youngsters to stay out of trouble with the law" (Horst, 1987:1).

While there is a lack of consensus as how best to attempt to prevent delinquency, a common trend in juvenile justice has been toward the deinstitutionalization of juveniles and diversion from the juvenile justice system. Consequently, communities and their various agencies are being viewed as playing an important role in delinquency prevention.

TREND TOWARD DEINSTITUTIONALIZATION AND DIVERSION

While the juvenile court was founded upon the philosophy of protection and rehabilitation, and viewed its foremost goal as preventing juvenile offenders from becoming adult criminals, many of the actions of the juvenile justice system have become viewed as punitive in nature. Consequently, as the treatment and prevention ideologies have gained support in juvenile corrections, we have experienced a noticeable trend toward deinstitutionalization and the diversion of youth from the formal juvenile justice system.

Deinstitutionalization

Deinstitutionalization simply means *avoiding the placement of juveniles in correctional institutions*. The Juvenile Justice and Delinquency Prevention Act of 1974 called for the development of a series of deinstitutionalization programs for status offenders (Rojek, 1982). Many of the community-based prevention programs discussed earlier in this chapter represented efforts to deinstitutionalize delinquents and return them to their communities for their correctional experience. Deinstitutionalization is most likely to be pursued for nonserious juvenile offenders.

Jerome Stumphauzer (1986:5) summarized the need for deinstitutionalization of juveniles by evaluating the imprisonment of youths in the following manner:

> A worse social learning program could not be designed: remove the youth from the very society to which he must learn to adapt, expose him to hundreds of criminal peer models and to criminal behaviors he hasn't learned (yet), and use punishment as the only learning principle to change behavior!

As an alternative to institutionalization and traditional institutional methods, Stumphauzer (1986:9–11) suggested using social learning techniques as follows:

1. **Institutional Programming.** If institutionalized, use token economies, positive rewards for conforming behavior, humane approaches to negatively sanction nonconforming behavior, and positive role modeling along with positive reinforcement;
2. **Behavioral Family Contracting.** Teaching and positively reinforcing nondelinquent behavior in the family setting;
3. **Social Skills Training.** Teaching the skills of problem solving and relating to authority figures;
4. **Probation Contracting.** Written agreements between juvenile probation

officers and juveniles on probation regarding acceptable and unacceptable behaviors and the attendant rewards and punishments for each;

5. **School Programming.** Using social learning techniques in the school to emphasize rewards for nondelinquent behavior, rather than focusing all attention on punishing rule-violating behavior;

6. **Clinical Behavior Therapy.** Training youths in techniques of self-control, anger control, and dealing with stress;

7. **Employment Skills Training.** Providing youths with necessary job skills, and the skills necessary for finding, applying for, and interviewing for employment;

8. **Group Treatment Homes.** Group homes using "teaching parents" as models, doing chores with emphasis upon positive reinforcement;

9. **Community Change and Prevention.** Instead of waiting for delinquency to occur and then making arrests, using positive reinforcement and social learning techniques in parks, recreation centers, housing projects, and so on, to acknowledge, reward, and encourage conforming behavior.

William Sheridan (1967) estimated that approximately 30 percent of all inmates in juvenile correctional institutions were there for committing **status offenses**—*acts that would not have been illegal if they had been committed by adults* (such as truancy and running away). He contended that placing these offenders in institutions pinned the "delinquent label" upon them and exposed them to the influence of more sophisticated delinquent peers, increasing the likelihood that they would continue their delinquency upon release. Richard Rettig (1980) argued that juvenile detention facilities were overpopulated with youths who did not belong in institutions. He contended that institutionalization has a place in juvenile corrections, and could provide a positive experience, if it is reserved for those youths who really need to be confined (those who pose a serious threat to the community).

Along with the philosophical arguments for deinstitutionalization, one of its strongest justifications has come from the lower costs. In 1984, the average cost of housing one juvenile in a public facility was $25,200 (U.S. Department of Justice, 1987:392). Paul Lerman (1968) pointed out that both private and public treatment centers experience high rates of failure, and suggested that it might be better to take some of the institutional allowances for food, clothing, supervisory personnel, and other expenses and allocate them to families of delinquents to be used to help the juveniles in their own homes. High costs and high failure rates indeed have led to the closing of juvenile institutions in some states.

Paul George and Patrick Mooney (1986) pointed out that the Miami Boys Club Delinquency Prevention Program serves approximately 120 hard-core male delinquents for approximately one-third the cost of the state training schools. A 1986 study by the California Youth Authority (reported on CNN Headline News, October 6, 1986) indicated that nearly one-half of the youths incarcerated in California's juvenile institutions were there because of property offenses. The average cost of housing a juvenile in California for 1 year was estimated at $25,000. Members of the California Youth Authority indicated that they believed that many youths are institutionalized who should not be, in response to a resurgent "get tough" attitude toward crime. Ira Schwartz (1984) acknowledged that attitude and pointed out that despite some gains toward more humane and less expensive programs, most states still lack sound programs like those suggested in the Juvenile Justice and Delinquency Prevention Act of 1971.

Diversion

Diversion refers to *an attempt to divert, or channel out, youthful offenders from the juvenile justice system.* Like deinstitutionalization, diversion primarily is intended for status and nonserious property offenders. There is some disagreement over the term "diversion." Dean Rojek (1982:316) pointed out that to some it means "simply the process of turning offenders away from the traditional juvenile justice system," while for others, it "connotes not only a turning away but also a referral to a community alternative." As a result, diversion and deinstitutionalization often are interrelated in community efforts to deal with less serious juvenile offenders.

Youth Service Bureaus
The President's Commission on Law Enforcement and Administration of Justice (1967) suggested the creation of Youth Service Bureaus to work with juvenile offenders in local communities. These bureaus primarily were designed to work with nonserious juvenile offenders, but, depending upon the particular community, provided a wide range of service to youthful law violators. The establishment of Youth Service Bureaus launched the move toward diverting youths, especially status offenders and other nonserious delinquents, from the juvenile court (Sherwood, 1972).

With the money and support provided by federal and state governments during the 1960s and 1970s for social programs aimed toward reducing poverty, crime, delinquency, and other social problems, Youth Service Bureaus gained widespread acceptance. Bureaus were established in virtually every community of any size, and programs were developed to aid juveniles in matters related to family, school, and the law. Although the 1980s brought severe cuts to numerous social agencies and programs, Youth Service Bureaus continue to exist in many communities, working closely with law enforcement, juvenile courts, schools, and other social agencies.

One of the criticisms leveled at the Youth Service Bureaus, and at similar diversionary programs, is that while well-intended, they may involve youths in the juvenile justice system who have committed very minor noncriminal offenses, which might be less problematic if ignored. Frederick Howlett (1973) criticized the Youth Service Bureau as being another manifestation of the "child saving movement". He suggested that rather than involving such minor offenders in the Youth Service Bureau, communities should redefine their concept of deviance, especially in regard to the types of behaviors they will and will not tolerate on the part of juveniles. We explore this issue in much more detail in Chapter 15, Rethinking the Delinquency Problem.

Scared Straight!

Diversion can take many directions. One of the best known diversionary programs is the *Scared Straight!* program begun by inmates serving life sentences at Rahway State Prison in New Jersey. In this program, juveniles are exposed briefly to the harsh realities of life in a maximum security prison. Small groups of juvenile offenders are taken to Rahway to spend the better part of a day inside the institution. The youths are shown the brutal side of prison life, highlighted by a session during which inmates serving life sentences for crimes such as murder, rape, multiple assaults, and other violent offenses, shout at and harass the juveniles through racial epithets, threats, and innuendoes about homosexual rape. While there is no actual physical contact between inmates and the youths, the threat of physical violence is ever-present. The program gained national attention when actor Peter Falk hosted an award winning television documentary on the subject. The program boasted impressive statistics regarding its success rate (90 to 95 percent) in deterring participants from involvement in later delinquency.

John Heeren and David Schicor (1984) analyzed the program and suggested that the documentary was perhaps more successful than the actual program. John Finckenauer (1982) concurred, and seriously questioned the alleged success rate of the *Scared Straight!* program. He conducted a study on youths who had completed the program at Rahway and compared them to a control group of teenagers who had committed similar offenses but who did not participate in the program. His findings indicated that the control group actually fared better in the first 6 months following their initial offenses (in terms of not committing subsequent offenses) than did the group who were exposed to *Scared Straight!* Finckenauer (1982:4) concluded that the *Scared Straight!* program, much like other delinquency prevention programs, is illustrative of what he calls the "panacea phenomenon"—the ". . . continuing search for a cure-all." This attempt to remedy a very complex social problem by means of a simplistic solution is not new, and as Finckenauer (1982:4) summarized, "The highway of delinquency prevention history is paved with punctured panaceas."

Nevertheless, the documentary appealed to public perception that crime was increasing at an alarming rate, but here was an innovative program that was playing a small part in alleviating it. Following the documentary, several states began steps to implement similar programs. While the Rahway program may not have been the "cure-all" hoped for by many, and its success rate was not the 90 to 95 percent claimed, to many people it seemed like a valid attempt to turn delinquent teenagers' lives around; and after all, perhaps doing something—anything—was better than doing nothing.

Place   A less dramatic diversion program developed at Syracuse University in 1984 is called PLACE. First-time offenders between the ages of 12 and 15 attend eight 90-minute classroom sessions in which they are involved in role-playing, mock trials, and discussions on the juvenile justice system and causes of delinquency. They talk to recent victims of property offenses. In one of the sessions they are booked, fingerprinted, and placed in a cell. A study conducted on more than 100 youths who had participated in the program during its first 2 years reported that only 11 percent of the participants had been rearrested (Horn, 1986:72).

VisionQuest   VisionQuest is a Tucson-based private program designed to rehabilitate "hard-core juvenile delinquents through positive experiences and physical challenges in the wilderness" (Gavzer, 1986:8). VisionQuest maintains wilderness camps in Arizona, Pennsylvania, and Florida. The program utilizes a practice involving a *rite of passage* similar to that used by the Crow and Cheyenne Indians. Juveniles in the program are expected to complete three "quests" which include working with wild horses and stubborn mules, a 6-month wagon train experience, and an 8-week program of training wild mustangs. The program is structured to teach the juveniles a strong sense of responsibility and a pragmatic understanding of the need to abide by social norms. After completing their quests, the youths experience a ritual ceremony signifying their accomplishments and marking their entrance into adulthood. One researcher who studied the program indicated that the youths were not merely ". . . playing cowboys and Indians . . . ," but were ". . . struggling to cope with real and difficult circumstances without the protection or cocoon of traditional institutional programs" (Gavzer, 1986:10). In addition to the wilderness experiences, the program includes daily schoolwork, the earning of a weekly allowance, counseling sessions, and immediate accountability to adult supervisors for behavior. Approximately 15 states send juvenile offenders to VisionQuest at a cost estimated to be approximately half that of traditional institutionalization. The program is considered to be relatively successful. According to one study, of the approximately 3,000 boys and girls who have gone through VisionQuest, only about one-third return to juvenile institutions (Gavzer, 1986:10).

EVALUATION OF DIVERSION

Several studies have been conducted in an attempt to evaluate various diversionary programs across the country, and have resulted in mixed findings. Mark Pogrebin and his associates (1984) reported moderate success in the Colorado diversionary programs they evaluated, as did Robert Regoli et al. (1985), although they pointed out some of the problems of using recidivism rates as a measure of success. William Selke (1982), on the other hand, assessed diversionary programs of the Youth Services Bureau in Michigan as being generally unsuccessful, and generally suffering from insufficient staffing.

Elizabeth Wilderman (1984) evaluated Colorado's diversionary program as reducing recidivism somewhat; but on the negative side, pointed out that it negatively labeled some juveniles simply on the basis of participation in it, whose offenses were so minor that they would have been better handled if ignored. This same theme has tended to dominate the critical assessments of many juvenile diversionary programs. For example, Bruce Bullington and his associates (1978) argued that the interest in diversion is faddish and that one of the major problems of diversionary programs is that while they were developed to divert juveniles from the juvenile justice system, they involve juveniles in diversionary programs who previously would have been ignored by the formal system. Hence, rather than bringing fewer youths into the system, diversion actually brings in more. Rojek (1982:321) registered the same criticism when he pointed out:

> In theory, diversion is perceived to be a process of deflecting offenders away from the traditional juvenile justice system. However, there is strong evidence that this deflection may result in another form of encapsulation.

Even the argument of reduced costs has come under scrutiny. Rojek (1982:318–320), for example, indicated that while diversion was being touted as more humane and cost efficient, its tendency to "widen the net" and identify more juveniles as delinquent represents a substantial investment of resources toward controlling "questionable acts of deviance." Anne Mahoney (1981) also pointed to the "net-widening" aspects of deinstitutionalization and diversion and raised concerns about increased costs to the families of delinquents who were brought into treatment programs. In a position paper, the National Advisory Committee for Juvenile Justice and Delinquency Prevention (1984) expressed similar concern when it noted that the wording of the Juvenile Justice Act of 1974 has caused federal money to be diverted to handling noncriminal acts of delinquency. The committee recommended that a new federal policy be developed focusing on serious juvenile delinquency. Charles Logan and Sharla Rausch (1985) concluded that efforts at diversion and deinstitutionalization are pointless unless they are accompanied by a movement toward decriminalization of status offenses.

Finally, constitutional and legal issues have been raised regarding diversionary programs. Bullington and associates (1978) argued against the widespread development of diversionary programs because they viewed them as violating the civil liberties that were assured by the Gault Decision (see Chapter 12). They viewed the biggest problem of diversion as involving disposition without adjudication. Bortner et al. (1985) found that there was differential treatment of blacks by the courts, with black females being more likely to be institutionalized for status offenses, while whites were more likely to be diverted and deinstitutionalized.

SUMMARY

This chapter examined the treatment and prevention ideologies in juvenile corrections and described some of the specific treatment and prevention strategies that have been used for juvenile delinquency. Clearly, traditional delinquency treatment and prevention programs have been dominated by the medical model and psychiatric approach. Hakeem (1957–58) indicated that the psychiatric approach focuses upon predelinquency, its causes, symptoms, and cures, and that while the psychiatric approach carries great prestige, its lofty status is not deserved. He charged that it is based on very little empirical verification and that the labeling of children as predelinquent is arbitrary and sometimes even whimsical. He urged that sociologists should turn to their own concepts and theories to develop programs for the treatment and prevention of delinquency. Likewise, the prominent sociologist and criminologist Donald Cressey (1955) lamented that when dealing with corrections, even sociologists have typically ignored sociological theories and reform techniques. He insisted that delinquents are products of social interaction and any attempt to reform them must focus upon social groups and group processes.

We then reviewed some of the treatment and prevention programs which have incorporated sociological theory into their strategies. Some of the classic delinquency programs were discussed and the evaluations of their relative strengths and weaknesses presented.

Recent trends in handling juvenile delinquents have turned toward the deinstitutionalization of offenders and the diversion of youths who have committed less serious acts from the juvenile justice system. Evaluations of deinstitutionalization and diversion have produced mixed conclusions. While generally viewed as more humane and less expensive than traditional court dispositions, questions of effectiveness, cost efficiency, needless stigmatization of participants, and possible violations of legal rights have been raised.

While it is important for society to develop new and innovative approaches to dealing with delinquents and delinquency, it is equally important that its members not get caught up in what Finckenauer (1982) called the "panacea phenomenon." As he pointed out, the search for a "cure-all" persists because of two rather naive and simplistic ideas: "doism" and "newism." "Doism" is the ". . . belief that it is better to do something than nothing," and "newism" is the ". . . appeal of approaches or programs because they are new" (Finckenauer, 1982:27).

From the sociological perspective, it is unrealistic to assume that society can eliminate a problem such as juvenile delinquency. Rather, social control mechanisms must be aimed at reducing the number of deviant acts, and, more importantly, at reducing their negative social impact. Many of the programs described in this chapter have shown evidence of providing meaningful social control, while others have been much less effective. Delinquency is such a complex phenomenon that any attempt to control, treat, or prevent it must take its complexity into account. As Hurley (1985:68) indicated, "There is no field of knowledge that does not apply to delinquency, barring perhaps Plate Tectonics." Similarly, Sheldon Rose and Jeffrey Edleson (1987:xiii) argued for the "multimethod approach" to dealing with delinquency which "draws upon problem-solving techniques, the modeling sequence, and an operant, cognitive change, relaxation, sociorecreational, small-group, relational, and extra-group methods of intervention."

In keeping with the theme of this book, it is our contention that juvenile delinquency is inherently social in nature and that any meaningful attempts to deal with it will have to approach it within the social context in which it occurs. In Chapter 15 we explore a sociological approach to rethinking the problem of juvenile delinquency.

CONCEPT APPLICATION

"TOUGHLOVE: A Program for Parents of 'Troubled Teens' "

TOUGHLOVE was founded in the late 1970s by Phyllis and David York, family therapists, who found that their professional training and numerous family counseling sessions could not help them control their own 18-year-old daughter:

> The culmination for us was when the police came to our house with shotguns and a warrant to arrest our daughter . . . she had stuck up a cocaine dealer (Brotman, 1982:15).

Upset and panic-stricken, the Yorks decided to try something different. They refused to post bond for their daughter, and later, when she was imprisoned, they refused to visit her or communicate with her. Instead, they urged friends to visit her. It was a difficult situation for the daughter, but when she realized that her parents would not step in to protect her as usual, she began to assume responsibility for her own behavior.

TOUGHLOVE programs began in 1978, and today there are well over 1,500 chapters nationwide and in Canada. According to its literature, TOUGHLOVE is:

... a self-help program for families and neighborhoods. It is a combination of philosophy and action which, together, can help families and neighborhoods change.

TOUGHLOVE is not a parenting program ... It is a crisis intervention program, structuring group meetings to support parents and spouses in demanding responsible cooperation from out-of-control family members (quoted from pamphlet by permission from TOUGHLOVE International).

TOUGHLOVE parents, school officials, and community workers establish rules that youths must obey if they are to continue to live at home, remain in school, or participate in community programs. For their own sake and the good of the youths, the adults involved in TOUGHLOVE respond on strict behavioral grounds: rewards for conforming behavior, and punishment for nonconforming, with advance warning and consistency. If the teenagers insist on disobeying, they lose certain privileges. Parents might severely limit or temporarily suspend the use of the telephone, television, or the family car. Teachers and school administrators might curtail any extracurricular activities; and community center workers might not allow the youth to participate in community recreation activities such as sports, dances, crafts, and others. The final underlying threat is expulsion—forbidding the child to live at home, attend school, and/or participate in community activities. On the other hand, when youths take responsibility for their own actions and conform to the rules established for home, school, and community, privileges are extended.

TOUGHLOVE is an interesting program in that it combines many of the treatment techniques and prevention strategies discussed in this chapter. It also acknowledges the individual problems which must be resolved by parents and teenagers, while placing the problem in its larger social context. Hence, a support network is established which includes the parents, teenagers, school officials, counselors, and youth workers in a given community.

* * * *

After reading the chapter and this Illustrative Anecdote, which specific treatment strategies do you see being applied by TOUGHLOVE? What elements of various prevention strategies are employed? What potential problems do you see with the TOUGHLOVE program?

CONCEPT INTEGRATION
QUESTIONS AND TOPICS FOR STUDY AND DISCUSSION

1. Explain the treatment ideology in juvenile corrections. What are some of its strengths? What are some of its weaknesses?

2. Explain the prevention ideology in juvenile corrections. What are some of its strengths? What are some of its weaknesses? How can this ideology be implemented from a sociological perspective?
3. Summarize some of the major treatment programs for juvenile delinquents in the United States. What are the major weaknesses of these programs? How might they be improved to overcome those weaknesses?
4. Summarize some of the major prevention programs for juvenile delinquents in the United States. What are the major weaknesses of these programs? How might they be improved to overcome those weaknesses?
5. Define deinstitutionalization. Give some examples of the deinstitutionalization of delinquents. What are some of the advantages of deinstitutionalization? Disadvantages?
6. Define diversion. Give some examples of the diversion of delinquents. Should efforts toward diversion be increased or decreased? Why?
7. How can the sociological perspective be applied to delinquency treatment and prevention programs? Devise a hypothetical plan utilizing sociological concepts for your own community which could treat and prevent delinquency.

References

Bass, S. A. & Mandell, F. 1982. Building networks in urban settings: An approach to delinquency prevention. *New England Journal of Human Services* 2 (Summer):20–25.

Behre, C., Edwards, D., & Femming, C. 1982. Assessment of the effectiveness of a juvenile transitional center for facilitating re-entry. *Journal of Offender Counseling, Services, and Rehabilitation* 6 (Spring):61–72.

Berg, B. L. 1984. Inmates as clinical sociologists: The use of sociodrama in a nontraditional delinquency prevention program. *Journal of Offender Therapy and Comparative Criminology* 28 (September):117–124.

Berne, E. 1961. *Transactional analysis in psychotherapy*. New York: Grove.
1964. *Games people play*. New York: Grove.

Bortner, M. A., Sunderland, M. L., & Winn, R. 1985. Race and the impact of juvenile deinstitutionalization. *Crime and Delinquency* 31 (January):35–46.

Brotman, B. 1982. Parents practice 'ToughLove' on child. *Tulsa World* July 10, 1982:15.

Brown, W. K. 1983. *What parents should know about juvenile delinquency and juvenile justice*. York, PA: William Gladden Foundation.

Bullington, B., Sprowls, J., Katkin, D., & Phillips, M. 1978. A critique of diversionary juvenile justice. *Crime and Delinquency* 7 (January):59–71.

Cloward, R. & Ohlin, L. E. 1961. *Delinquency and opportunity*. Glencoe, IL: Free Press.

CNN News. 1986. California youth authority study. October 6.

Cole, P. Z. & Hafsten, J. W. 1978. Probation supervision revisited: Responsibility training. *Journal of Juvenile and Family Courts* 29 (February):53–58.

Cressey, D. R. 1955. Changing criminals: The application of the theory of differential association. *American Journal of Sociology* 61 (September):116–120.

Empey, L. T. & Rabow, J. 1961. The Provo experiment in delinquency rehabilitation. *American Sociological Review* 26 (October):679–695.

Farrington, D. P. 1985. Delinquency prevention in the 1980s. *Journal of Adolescence* 8 (March):3–16.

Finckenauer, J. O. 1982. *Scared straight! and the panacea phenomenon*. Englewood Cliffs, NJ: Prentice-Hall.

Gavzer, B. 1986. Must kids be bad? *Parade* March 9:8, 10.

George, P. & Mooney, P. 1986. The Miami Boys Club delinquency prevention program. *Educational Leadership* 43 (Dec.–Jan.):76–78.

Glasser, W. 1965. *Reality therapy*. New York: Harper & Row.

Governor's Advocacy Council. 1983. Opening doors for children: A study of the North Carolina community-based alternative program. Governor's Advocacy Council on Children and Youth, Raleigh, NC. Chicago: John Howard Society.

Gullotta, T. P. & Adams, G. R. 1982. Minimizing juvenile delinquency: Implications for prevention programs. *Journal of Early Adolescence* 2 (Summer):105–117.

Hakeem, M. 1957–58. A critique of the psychiatric approach to the prevention of delinquency. *Social Problems* 5 (Winter):194–206.

Harris, T. A. 1969. *I'm OK—You're OK*. New York: Harper & Row.

Heeren, J. & Schicor, D. 1984. Mass media and delinquency prevention: The case of 'Scared Straight.' *Deviant Behavior* 5 (1–4):375–386.

Higgins, P. S. 1978. Evaluation and case study of a school-based delinquency prevention program. *Evaluation Quarterly* 2 (May):215–235.

Horn, J. C. 1986. A PLACE to go straight. *Psychology Today* 20 (July):72.

Horst, N. 1987. Young Emporia offenders offered an alternative. *Emporia Gazette*, March 30:1.

Howlett, F. W. 1973. Is the Youth Service Bureau all it's cracked up to be? *Crime and Delinquency* 91 (October):485–492.

Hurley, D. 1985. Arresting delinquency. *Psychology Today* March:63–68.

Jesness, C. F. 1975. Comparative effectiveness of behavior modification and transactional analysis programs for delinquents. *Journal of Consulting and Clinical Psychology* 43 (December):758–779.

Johnson, B. D. & Goldberg, R. T. 1982. Vocational and social rehabilitation of delinquents: A study of experimentals and controls. *Journal of Offender Counseling Services and Rehabilitation* 6 (Spring):43–60.

Karchmer, C. L. 1984. Young arsonists. *Society* 22 (November/December):78–83.

Kobrin, S. 1959. The Chicago Area Project—25 year assessment. *Annals of the American Academy of Political and Social Science* 322 (March):20–29.

Lerman, P. 1968. Evaluative studies of institutions for delinquents: Implications for research and social policy. *Social Work* 13 (July):55–64.

Liazos, A. 1974. Class oppression: The function of juvenile justice. *Insurgent Sociologist* 5:2–24.

Logan, C. H. & Rausch, S. P. 1985. Why deinstitutionalizing status offenders is pointless. *Crime and Delinquency* 31 (October):501–517.

Mahoney, A. R. 1981. Family participation for juvenile offenders in deinstitutionalization programs. *Journal of Social Issues* 37 (Summer):133–144.

Miller, W. B. 1962. The impact of a 'total community' delinquency control project. *Social Problems* 10 (Fall):168–191.

Mobilization for Youth. 1961. *A proposal for the prevention and control of delinquency by expanding opportunities.* New York: Mobilization for Youth, Inc.

NBC News. 1987. Crime, punishment, and kids. *NBC News Special* July 26.

National Advisory Committee. 1984. *Serious juvenile crime: A redirected federal effort.* National Advisory Committee for Juvenile Justice and Delinquency Prevention, Washington, DC: U.S. Government Printing Office (March).

Phillips, E. L., Phillips, E., Fixsen, D., & Wolf, M. 1971. Achievement place: Modification of the behaviors of predelinquent boys within a token economy. *Journal of Applied Behavior Analysis* 4 (Spring):45–59.

Pogrebin, M. R., Poole, E. D., & Regoli, R. M. 1984. Constructing and implementing a model juvenile diversion program. *Youth and Society* 15 (March):305–324.

President's Commission on Law Enforcement and Administration of Justice. 1967. *The challenge of crime in a free society.* Washington, DC: U.S. Government Printing Office.

Regoli, R. M., Wilderman, E., & Pogrebin, M. 1985. Using an alternative evaluation measure for assessing juvenile diversion programs. *Children and Youth Services Review* 7 (1):21–38.

Remington, C. 1982. Restitution can work for serious offenders. *Change: A Juvenile Justice Quarterly* 5 (2):9–10.

Rettig, R. P. 1980. Considering the use and usefulness of juvenile detention: Operationalizing social theory. *Adolescence* 15 (Summer):443–459.

Robin, G. D. 1969. Anti-poverty programs and delinquency. *Journal of Criminal Law, Criminology, and Police Science* 60 (Fall):323–331.

Robison, J. & Smith, G. 1971. The effectiveness of correctional programs. *Crime and Delinquency* 17 (January):67–80.

Rojek, D. G. 1982. Juvenile diversion: A study of community cooptation. In D. G. Rojek & G. F. Jensen (Eds.). *Readings in Juvenile Delinquency.* Lexington, MA: D. C. Heath, pp. 316–322.

Rose, S. D. & Edleson, J. L. 1987. *Working with children and adolescents in groups.* San Francisco: Jossey-Bass.

Rutherford, R. B., Jr. 1975. Establishing behavioral contracts with delinquent adolescents. *Federal Probation* 39 (March):28–32.

Schlossman, S. & Sedlak, M. 1983. The Chicago Area Project revisited. *Crime and Delinquency* 29 (July):398–462.

Schwartz, I. M. 1984. New moves in juvenile justice: Alternatives to getting tough are more humane and less expensive. *Public Welfare* 42 (Fall):28–31.

Selke, W. L. 1982. Diversion and crime prevention: A time-series analysis. *Criminology* 20 (November):395–406.

Shaw, C. R. & McKay, H. D. 1942. *Juvenile delinquency and urban areas.* Chicago: University of Chicago Press.

Sheridan, W. H. 1967. Juveniles who commit noncriminal acts: Why treat in a correctional system? *Federal Probation* 31 (March):26–30.

Sherwood, N. 1972. *The Youth Service Bureau: A key to delinquency prevention.* Paramus, NJ: National Council on Crime and Delinquency.

Skinner, B. F. 1971. *Beyond freedom and dignity.* New York: Knopf.

Stumphauzer, J. S. 1986. *Helping delinquents change: A treatment manual of social learning approaches.* New York: Haworth Press.

Sykes, G. & Matza, D. 1957. Techniques of neutralization: A theory of delinquency. *American Sociological Review* 22 (December):664–670.

Thomas, M. R. & Murray, P. V. 1983. Get kids interested in the law before the law gets interested in them. *Instructor* 92 (April):62–67.

Toby, J. 1965. An evaluation of early identification and intensive treatment programs for predelinquents. *Social Problems* 13 (Fall):160–175.

U.S. Department of Justice. 1987. *Sourcebook of Criminal Justice Statistics—1986.* Washington, DC: U.S. Government Printing Office.

Velasquez, J. S. & Lyle, C. G. 1985. Day versus residential treatment for juvenile offenders: The impact of program evaluation. *Child Welfare* 64 (March–April):145–156.

Weeks, H. A. 1958. *Youthful offenders at Highfields.* Ann Arbor: University of Michigan Press.

Wilderman, E. 1984. Juvenile diversion: From politics to policy. *New England Journal of Human Services* 4 (Summer):19–23.

Chapter 15

Rethinking the Delinquency Problem

The reading of this chapter will help you achieve the following objectives:

1. Briefly review the social nature of delinquency and the social processes involved in defining, treating, controlling and preventing juvenile delinquency.
2. Summarize some of the major recommendations that have been made for rethinking the problem of juvenile delinquency.
3. Reexamine various social values, norms, laws, institutions, and policies with an aim toward the reduction of some of the problems associated with juvenile delinquency.
4. Explore some imaginative and innovative ways of creating meaningful social change to help alleviate some of the social conditions which contribute to the problem of juvenile delinquency.
5. Explore the redefinition of juvenile delinquency and rethink the delinquency problem.

INTRODUCTION

In this final chapter, we underscore again the social nature of juvenile delin-quency and outline some of the suggestions and recommendations that have been made to help alleviate the problem. These suggestions have come from leading professionals in the fields of law, criminology, social work, and the social and behavioral sciences. Some of the recommendations have been attempted and implemented, at least partially, and some have been routinely ignored. As yet, none have seemed to make a great deal of difference.

Having done this, we have reached the point where most textbooks on juvenile delinquency, or any other social problem for that matter, usually come to a conclusion. The ending is usually highlighted by a typically nebulous summation—something to the effect of "now that we have defined, explored, and examined the nature of the problem, further research is needed in the areas that we have suggested in order to provide a more thorough understanding, . . ." As Haskell and Yablonsky (1978:543) noted:

> Sociologists are often reluctant to make recommendations for changes in the law, . . . the criminal justice system, or in correctional policies. The prevailing attitude . . . is that sociologists should maintain scientific objectivity in their studies, report the results of their research, and leave the conclusions to be drawn by others.

Perhaps it is the nature of their traditional scientific training that makes many sociologists reluctant to make suggestions for intervention strategies. Or, perhaps it stems from the fact that sociologists are essentially theoreticians and not practitioners. From a pragmatic standpoint, it may be that it is much easier to discern and describe the nature of a problem than it is to suggest ways of dealing with it. Whatever the case, one of the most frustrating experiences for students of sociology has been the tendency for sociologists to eagerly partici-pate in the exploration, discussion, and critique of social issues, only to rapidly retreat from any meaningful attempt to resolve them. We get excellent marks for asking probing questions, but seldom generate substantial answers. Our own backgrounds and experiences sorely tempt us to do the same thing. However, we agree with the assertion of Martin Haskell and Lewis Yablonsky (1978:544) that "sociologists with years of experience in the field of delinquency should freely present their opinions and recommendations, even though many of their assertions are not based on firm empirical evidence." For it is also an intrinsic part of our established perspective to exercise a *sociological imagination* (Mills, 1959) in which we seek to apply knowledge and expertise in creative and innovative problem-solving ways.

We should first acknowledge that not everybody believes that meaningful social changes are necessary in order to handle juvenile delinquency. There are those of the "traditional approach," who believe that all that is needed to curb delinquency is stricter rules, better law enforcement, and harsher punishments. This "get tough on crime/delinquency" attitude surfaces from time to time, as the social and cultural pendulum swings from the more liberal to the more conservative to the reactionary. We suggest, however, that any meaningful approach to the social problem of delinquency must go beyond the mere "tightening" of social control on youths. Rather, large-scale changes in cultural attitudes, values, and beliefs, along with changes in social institutions and practices, are necessary if the challenge of effectively dealing with juvenile delinquency is to be met.

Many of the suggestions and recommendations offered in this chapter represent a combination and synthesis of ideas that others previously have suggested. On the other hand, some of the recommendations set forth are uniquely ours. In either case, we challenge the reader to approach the chapter with an open mind and to explore the possibilities for social change presented herein.

THE SOCIAL NATURE OF JUVENILE DELINQUENCY

Adolescence is a social product that reflects the dominant attitudes, values, and beliefs of American culture. Largely as a result of urbanization and industrialization, Americans created the concept of adolescence and its accompanying normative expectations in an effort to regulate and to differentiate the social status, role, and legal treatment of people in this category from adult members of society. One of the results was the prolongation of the period of transition from childhood to adulthood. Another was the creation of a new form of social deviance—juvenile delinquency.

Prolonging the transition from childhood to adulthood in urban industrial America has been functional in many ways. For example, it has extended the length of time spent on formal education, delayed entry into the work force, delayed marriage (which in turn has had positive effects on reducing birthrates), and extended the period of time available for anticipatory socialization into future adult roles. On the other hand, it also has had some negative consequences. One of these is the marginality experienced by individuals who have biologically and physiologically matured into young adulthood, while socially and legally being denied access to meaningful adult roles.

Paul Goodman (1962), in *Growing Up Absurd,* laid the philosophical foundation for understanding the unique problems experienced by American youths. He pointed out that a youth subculture forms, in part, in response to the difficulty of growing up in a society that forces adult values upon juveniles, who are not allowed to fully participate in the social system. As Frank Musgrove (1965) pointed out, the creation of adolescence, and the fact that youths automatically experience that social "limbo," denies them the opportunity to acquire the basic skills, knowledge, and other attributes that are required in adult life. The marginal status arising from this temporary "no man's land," between child and adult, undoubtedly contributes to adolescent deviance. We thoroughly discussed and gave numerous examples of the problem in Chapter 8, "The Youth Subculture."

How to react to the social deviance of youths has been extremely problematic for American society. Ideologically floundering among the divergent philosophies of protecting, treating, rehabilitating, and punishing juveniles for their misbehavior, policies and programs have been developed which have attempted to do one or another, or all simultaneously. While there have been numerous individual successes, overall the result has been well over a century of ineffective and indecisive efforts toward alleviating the problem of juvenile delinquency.

A major element of the problem has stemmed from the inability or reluctance on the part of many to recognize and understand its social dimensions. Often viewed apart from its social context, delinquency has been approached as a discrete problem to be studied, analyzed, and treated. The consequence has been disjointed efforts at control and prevention aimed at specific individuals, or, in some cases, when viewed a bit more sociologically, at families, neighborhoods, gangs, and communities. The vast majority of these efforts, however, have ignored the broader societal context of juvenile delinquency almost entirely.

In harmony with this idea of changing the social milieu in order to reduce crime, delinquency, and other forms of deviant behavior, criminologists, sociologists, and behavioral scientists generally welcomed the urban renewal projects of the 1950s, 1960s, and 1970s. These projects cleared massive slum areas to make way for new apartment complexes and expanding central business districts. Endorsement of the projects was based upon the inaccurate hypothesis that slums have little or no social organization, and the premature conclusion that the lack of strong local social organization was responsible for the high incidence of crime and delinquency in such areas. It was assumed that environmental manipulation such as razing old tenements and clearing out urban blight would strike at a fundamental cause of juvenile delinquency and other social problems.

Unfortunately, the lessons learned from classic sociological studies such as William F. Whyte's *Street Corner Society* (1943) and Elliot Leibow's *Tally's Corner* (1964) were ignored. These works clearly indicated that while social organization in urban slums was different from that experienced by middle class society, it was far from nonexistent. The traditional urban renewal projects exemplify the failure to comprehend or incorporate the social dynamics of a neighborhood in dealing with social problems such as juvenile delinquency.

In a 1967 Presidential Task Force Report, Virginia Burns and Leonard

Stern (1967) pointed out the multifaceted nature of juvenile delinquency, and warned that the problem cannot be resolved through small or simple programs. Rather, they suggested that what was needed was a comprehensive effort to change the social system which produces conditions and strains conducive to the development of juvenile delinquency and other forms of youthful antisocial behavior.

We agree with Burns and Stern's assessment that a problem as complex as delinquency cannot be resolved through Band-Aid types of programs that treat symptoms rather than basic causes. In fact, we contend that if the social problem of juvenile delinquency is to be realistically approached, nothing short of major social and cultural change is necessary. This change must go beyond projects or programs aimed at individual delinquents, their families, and neighborhoods.

The Office of Juvenile Justice and Delinquency Prevention (1979) also acknowledged the significance of social reform in dealing with delinquency. It totally rejected delinquency prevention programs based upon delinquents' proposed biological differences, personality differences, or learning disabilities. It also rejected all programs based upon early identification and intervention which used criteria such as personality tests, socioeconomic status, broken or intact homes, or the criminal histories of parents. The accompanying risks of self-fulfilling prophecy were viewed as far outweighing any potential benefits of those programs. The Office of Juvenile Justice and Delinquency Prevention (1979) insisted that the programs with the most likelihood of producing long-lasting benefits were those that focused upon organizational change, especially those that utilized the school as one of the critical institutions for implementing social change.

It appears obvious from a sociological perspective that juvenile delinquency, like any other social problem, is inherently social in nature. From the cultural values which undergird the social norms defining delinquency, to the peers, parents, teachers, police, juvenile courts, and correctional institutions which react, reinforce, and respond to it, the social dimensions are ever-present. Consequently, if society is to deal effectively with the problem of juvenile delinquency, its members must evaluate the problem in its broadest and most fundamental social context. This necessitates totally *rethinking the problem of delinquency*—its definition, its social causes, social context, and its social consequences. In our view, this process of rethinking the problem necessitates eliminating or at least reducing the marginality experienced by juveniles. It also should include standardizing juvenile codes (or eliminating them altogether), decriminalizing status offenses, revising juvenile courts, and modifying juvenile corrections. Further, such an effort must include strengthening the family institution, changing the educational system to provide improved socialization, and totally redefining the concept of juvenile delinquency.

ELIMINATING THE MARGINAL STATUS OF JUVENILES

The marginal status of youths and the ambiguous normative expectations associated with their social positions may significantly weaken their social bonds with larger society. As control theorists point out, the weaker the social bond the stronger the likelihood of norm violation. It has been argued that one of the most significant steps toward delinquency reduction would be to more clearly define the social roles of the adolescent and to provide youths with greater status and power in society. For example, Haskell and Yablonsky (1978:546) indicated that society should "remove blocks to adult status," especially in regard to the legal and illegal discrimination in employment faced by youths. Roy Lotz et al. (1985:353) pointed out the importance of integrating youths into activities and decision making in the larger society:

> Quite simply, many youths do not feel that they belong to, or make any difference to, the communities where they live. And persons who behave irresponsibly may do so, in part, because they have few opportunities to be responsible (Lotz et al., 1985:353).

This position is confounded by the phenomenon of rapid social change in today's society. It is no longer easy to predict what the future will be as technology further impacts upon society, culture, and lifestyle. As Kenneth Keniston (1968) noted, it is virtually impossible for today's youths to foresee their future places in society, because due to rapid social change nobody knows exactly what that future society will be.

Nevertheless, in at least two ways society could meaningfully change in order to reduce or possibly eliminate the marginal status of adolescence and the resulting alienation and norm violation, rather than give up and accept the status quo. First would be to establish meaningful rites of passage into adulthood at about the onset of puberty. Second is to accompany those rites of passage with innovative and appropriate social expectations and the opportunities to fulfill important decision-making roles in society.

Rites of Passage

Throughout the life course, individuals move through a series of stages of development. Theoretically, the **life course** refers to *the successive role and status changes that each person occupies in society as a consequence of growing older.* Arnold Van Gennep ([1908] 1960) was one of the first to conceive of life as a series of passages or transitions from one stage to another and from one biological phase and social status to another. "Life is forever dynamic and anticipatory since there are always new thresholds to cross" (Van Gennep, [1908] 1960:189) and new adjustments to make. These adjustments are both biological and social, for while physical aging may be perceived as solely a biological/physiological process, how a person is viewed and treated at any particular age is based on sociocultural definitions. The life course is graphically illustrated in Figure 15–1.

You will note in Figure 15–1 that the upper horizontal line depicts the life course as the individual develops through the biological stages of childhood, adulthood, and old age. Each of these three stages is set apart and clearly delimited by the physiological events of birth, puberty, menopause (medical science indicates that males also experience a form of menopause), and death.

In many small and preliterate societies these natural events closely parallel the simple sequence of social roles and statuses that are imputed to people during their lifetimes. For example, in American Samoa, puberty is a time of family and community celebration and ceremony as children quickly and easily leave childhood behind and take on the rights and responsibilities of adulthood (Mead, 1928). Later, as the individual's physical strength and reproductive powers decrease, public acknowledgment and ceremony again implement the transition from adult worker to an honored social role associated with advanced age. Van Gennep ([1908] 1960) called these ceremonies linking age changes and other biological phenomena with changes in social status **"rites of passage."** Wendall Oswalt (1986:106) defined a **rite of passage** as *"ceremonial recognition of a major change in social status, one that will alter permanently a person's relationship with members of the greater community."*

In contemporary American society, we practice several ceremonies which serve as symbolic passage rituals. For example, christening and baptismal ceremonies, high school graduation exercises, college commencements, wed-

FIGURE 15-1
The Life Course

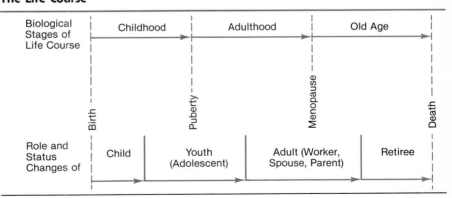

Source: Based on Arnold Van Gennep, *The Rites of Passage* (Translated by Monika B. Vizedom and Gabriel L. Caffee). Chicago: University of Chicago Press, 1960 [1908].

ding showers for brides-to-be, wedding ceremonies, baby showers for expectant mothers, and funerals all serve to ritualize the transition from one life stage and social status to another. However, many of these ritual events have little or no relationship to the biological stages of the life course. Again referring to Figure 15-1, you probably noticed that the lower horizontal line represents the sequence of different roles and status positions that most persons experience in contemporary American society. In contrast to the societies referred to earlier, in which the transition from childhood to adulthood is easy and natural, there is a rather uneven "fit" between many of the biological stages and the different social roles and status positions one is expected to occupy. Especially problematic is the artificial social stage of adolescence which cuts across the two naturally occurring biological life stages of childhood and young adulthood.

Passage ceremonies associated with puberty are much more likely to exist in preliterate and preindustrial societies than industrial societies like ours (Oswalt, 1986). However, social rituals held near the time of puberty are not unheard of in contemporary American society. For example, the "coming out" party of the upper class debutante marks her entry into adult society. Many middle class and lower class families provide their own version of this ceremony by giving their daughters a "sweet sixteen" birthday party. Still, these rituals come substantially after puberty or the biological onset of adulthood.

In our society, Jews probably provide the most clearcut rite of passage which most closely approximates the biological transition from childhood to adulthood. The *bar mitzvah* is held on the Jewish boy's thirteenth birthday and publicly acknowledges his assumption of adult religious responsibilities and duties. Although not as widely practiced, a similar ceremony, the *bat mitzvah*, for girls is observed by Orthodox Jews. Interestingly, several researchers have indicated that juvenile delinquency rates among Orthodox Jews is much lower than among other ethnic groups (e.g., Kvaraceus, 1945; Deardorff, 1955).

Why not develop and encourage meaningful social rituals to symbolize the rite of passage from childhood to adulthood which roughly coincides with the onset of puberty for all American youths? Surely such rituals and experiences are possible for an imaginative and creative society such as ours. Because of the pluralistic nature of American society, different racial, ethnic, religious, and social class groups could devise their own ceremonies which would be meaningful to them. For example, since Orthodox Jews already observe such a practice, there would be no need for them to change their ceremony. For other groups, the rite of passage need not have a religious connotation. A secular ceremony focusing upon rights and duties of adult citizenship or some similar topic would suffice. The significance would reside in the symbolic aspects of the ceremony which would signify to all that the young person participating in it was leaving childhood and entering adulthood. In order for such a ceremony to be successful, it would have to be institutionalized and internalized by everyone as being one of the most important rituals in our society. This ceremony could become a time of familial and community celebration and a time of fulfillment and

The bar mitzvah is a highly symbolic rite of passage from childhood to adulthood which eliminates for young Jewish males the marginal status experienced by most American adolescents.

achievement for youths. We have clearcut rites of passage to ease and announce the transition between other stages of the life course, for example, weddings, graduation exercises, and funerals. However, our culture includes no such standard or widely recognized device for moving our maturing children into adulthood. Why not?

Meaningful Social Participation

In a Presidential Task Force Report on delinquency prevention, it was emphasized that there is a strong need to involve young people in a much more meaningful and responsible way in the affairs of society that affect them (Burns and Stern, 1967). The Juvenile Justice Standards Project (1977:2) also insisted that juveniles "should have the right to decide on actions affecting their lives and freedom, unless found incapable of making reasoned decisions."

The Youth Development and Delinquency Prevention Administration (1972) specifically addressed the problem of lack of meaningful social roles on the part of adolescents. Among the suggestions made by that body were the following principles:

1. Delinquent behavior in the young has as its most general cause their exclusion from socially acceptable, responsible, and therefore personally gratifying roles.
2. Roles are made available to the young by the institutions in which they participate.
3. With respect to the problem of delinquency, the critical matter in institutional role allocation is the acquisition of roles imparting to the individual a legitimate identity.
4. Since roles are a product of institutional design and procedure, and since obstruction to a favorable course of youth development arises from failure to provide roles creating legitimate identity, a rational strategy of delinquency reduction and control must address the task of institutional change.
5. Among the institutions significant in the lives of young persons during the period of maximum vulnerability to delinquency and/or withdrawal, the school is of central importance.
6. The process through which illegitimate identities are formed and a commitment to delinquent activity arises among adolescents is best understood by contrast with the formation and maintenance of legitimate identity by adults.
7. The tie of the young person to the school as his 'institutional home' is maintained and reinforced by (a) the direct rewards of approval for valued academic and social performance; and (b) the indirect rewards of a credible promise of a desirable occupational future (Youth Development and Delinquency Prevention Administration, 1972:28–30).

There is no reason, other than cultural tradition, why juveniles cannot occupy more meaningful social roles which more thoroughly integrate them into larger society. For example, in Ramona, California, a group of youngsters formed Kidco, a successful corporation headed by a 12-year-old boy. The company, comprised entirely of children between 9 and 14 years of age, developed a secret formula for exterminating gophers. Unfortunately, their thriving business was shut down and criminal sanctions were threatened by the state government, because they did not have a license to do extermination work—a license for which applicants must be at least 18 years of age! The corporate head of Kidco, Dickie Cessna, summarized their dilemma:

We do not think it is fair or any good because we are just some little kids who want to do a good job killing gophers and selling manure instead of being out with a gang getting in dutch. Still we seem to be in trouble all the time thanks to some dumb laws (The Daily Tidings, 1977:3).

If a meaningful rite of passage is developed which signifies the movement into adult status, why not accompany that movement with the rights, responsibilities, and duties typically associated with adulthood? Young adults could serve on juries (especially in cases involving other young adults), compete for jobs for which their physical strength, educational background and training qualify them, and serve on school, community, state, and even national commissions, boards, and committees under the direction of older encouraging adults. It particularly makes sense to allow students to serve on local school boards.

In 1971, the Twenty-sixth Amendment was added to the U.S. Constitution which changed federal voting laws to allow 18-year-olds to vote. This change primarily came about in response to the complaint that young men aged 18 and over were being drafted to serve in military combat in Vietnam, but were not allowed to participate in the political process. Lowering the voting age

The elimination of marginality experienced by teenagers should be accompanied by the opportunity for more meaningful participation by them on local school boards, committees, commissions, and other decision-making bodies.

to 18 was opposed by some, but was considered to be a step in the right direction by most. Perhaps it was not a large enough step. Should the voting age be lowered even further? In some states, the legal age of criminal majority is as low as 17 or even 16 years of age. In many states, juvenile courts can relinquish jurisdiction of juveniles below that age to adult courts where they are held accountable for their criminal actions, especially in the case of serious felonies such as homicide. As indicated in Chapter 13, there are even inmates kept on "death row" for criminal offenses they committed while only 16 years of age. Clearly, in those cases, the individuals were considered legally responsible for their actions, and held accountable in the same way as adults. In less dramatic fashion, most states issue drivers' licenses to 16-year-olds (and some states offer permits or licenses to 14- and 15-year-olds), and hold them accountable for obeying traffic laws in the same manner as adults. We know that juveniles aged 14, 15, and 16 are physically capable of performing many adult functions. Their exclusion from meaningful adult roles is usually based on what is perceived as their emotional and psychological immaturity rather than their lack of physical abilities. Perhaps this so-called *emotional and psychological immaturity* is nothing more than **social retardation.** People in this age group are caught in the social paradox in which they are physically capable (and in some cases even physically superior) of performing virtually any of the roles occupied by their parents and other adults; yet, they are socially and legally prohibited from fulfilling that potentiality. Why? At least, we could eliminate the stereotype that all youths are disqualified and treat full societal participation as an individual matter. American society has moved in that direction at the other end of the life course by eliminating mandatory retirement at age 65.

Good judgment, social responsibility, and commitment to meaningful social roles do not magically occur when a person reaches a particular chronological age. Rather, individuals must learn them through effective socialization and the observation of exemplary role models. In addition, we learn to participate in meaningful social roles through actual experience in occupying them. Within the family, church, and school, juveniles must be provided greater access to full participation in social decision-making processes. Conformity to social norms probably would be more likely if juveniles participated in the norm creating and norm interpreting processes. As Schur (1973:167–168) commented, "There is some evidence that the most potent deterrent to delinquency lies in bonds of attachment to conventional society." Attachment to conventional society would no doubt be enhanced if juveniles were more realistically and meaningfully allowed to participate in it.

STANDARDIZATION OR ELIMINATION OF JUVENILE CODES

Juvenile law is statutory law. That means that each state legislature establishes the juvenile code for its state through the passing of statutes. It is possible that 50 different states may have fifty different juvenile codes. Theoretically, this is true for criminal codes which are also created through the statutory process. However, steps have been taken to standardize criminal codes across the United States. For example, the Federal Bureau of Investigation, which compiles official crime data for all 50 states, the District of Columbia, and Puerto Rico in its annual *Uniform Crime Reports*, sets forth standard definitions for criminal offenses. While state legislatures enact their own criminal statutes, most have simply reiterated the definitions for specific criminal offenses set forth by the FBI. Consequently the definitions of murder, forcible rape, aggravated assault, robbery, burglary, larceny-theft, auto theft, and arson are remarkably similar from state to state. While states may vary in what they classify as **misdemeanors**—*less serious crimes usually punishable by fine and/or imprisonment for less than a year*, as opposed to **felonies**—*more serious crimes punishable by fine and/or imprisonment for more than a year* (Siegal, 1986:34), the fact that all of these acts are classified as **criminal** to some degree standardizes the legal codes.

In Chapter 2, we highlighted the problems associated with defining juvenile delinquency. Much of the dilemma in defining delinquency stems from the lack of standardization of juvenile codes. One way to resolve this problem would be to standardize juvenile codes across the country by establishing uniform minimum and maximum ages for the jurisdiction of the juvenile court, perhaps ages 7 to 16. Sixteen might be the logical age cut-off between juvenile and adult, since, as Regnery (1985:1) noted, 16-year-old boys commit crimes at a higher rate than any other single age group, and "these are criminals who happen to be young, not children who happen to commit crimes." The remaining question would be whether there should be any circumstances under which an individual under the maximum age of jurisdiction should be remanded to the adult criminal court. If juvenile courts and juvenile corrections were significantly changed, this might not be as significant an issue as it is today. We discuss some possible revisions later in this chapter.

Once the age of jurisdiction is uniformly established, juvenile delinquency should be more clearly defined. Steven Cox and John Conrad (1987:11) pointed out:

> A basic difficulty with legal definitions of delinquency is that they differ from time to time and from place to place. An act that is delinquent at one time and in one place may not be delinquent at another time or in another place.

Most of the problems related to inconsistency in juvenile codes are associated with the age of jurisdiction of the juvenile court, and the second part of the two-fold legal definition of delinquency—that part of the definition which concludes that delinquency is *any act adjudicated as delinquent by a juvenile court*. One way to clarify the definition would be to limit the extent of delinquency to those acts which would be criminal if committed by adults. Thus, juvenile court would deal only with criminal behavior committed by juveniles. This would eliminate the time, energy, and effort currently focused upon juveniles who commit status offenses.

Another possible option for solving the problem of unstandardized juvenile codes would be to eliminate them altogether. If a meaningful rite of passage from childhood to adulthood were established which eliminated the marginal status of adolescence, it might be sufficient to simply treat those who have been granted adult status as *adults*. This would mean that those considered children would essentially be relieved of legal responsibility for law violating behavior (much of this legal responsibility could be transferred to their parents), and those considered adults would be held fully legally responsible for their actions. As previously mentioned, this type of change would require dramatic alteration of present cultural and social attitudes, values, and beliefs.

DECRIMINALIZATION OF STATUS OFFENSES

If the decision is made that states should retain separate juvenile codes, those codes should be as precise as adult criminal statutes. Schur (1973:169) recommended that "juvenile statutes should spell out very clearly just what kinds of behavior are legally proscribed, and should set explicit penalties for such violations (with perhaps some limited range of alternatives available to sentencing judges)." One way to do that would be to eliminate all status offenses. This does *not* mean that norms regulating adolescent behavior would be eliminated. Instead, these norms would be informal in nature, and their violation would be dealt with socially, rather than legally. Parents, school officials, clergy, and social workers would enforce these norms and impose sanctions, rather than the police, court officials, and correctional officers. This would limit juvenile delinquency to *only* those acts which would be criminal if committed by adults.

It is becoming evident that a very small number of youths account for an unusually large proportion of all serious juvenile crime (National Advisory Committee for Juvenile Justice and Delinquency Prevention, 1984). Longitudinal studies of large birth cohorts over a period of time have found that the assumption that most offenders progress through a delinquent career pattern from less serious to more serious offenses is highly questionable (e.g., Wolfgang et al., 1972). Rather, a fairly small number of persistent juvenile offenders tend to continue a career of crime into adulthood, committing more serious offenses as they get older (Wolfgang et al., 1987). Steven Lab (1984) found that the vast majority of his subjects were involved in victimless crimes and status offenses, such as truants, runaways, beer drinkers, and curfew violators, and that over two thirds (67 percent) ceased their delinquency before the fourth offense, regardless of whether or not they were apprehended and legally processed. Presently, those juveniles must be handled by the same court which handles abused, neglected, and dependent children, as well as muggers, robbers, rapists, and murderers. As discussed in Chapter 12, in an attempt to be "all things to all people," the juvenile court has been widely criticized as a failure.

The decriminalization of status offenses would greatly reduce the caseload of the juvenile courts. This would allow court personnel, judges, social workers, police, and others who work with juveniles to concentrate their efforts on serious juvenile offenders.

There appears to be widespread support for the decriminalization of status offenses. The Juvenile Justice Standards Project (1977) recommended that all status offenses be removed from juvenile court jurisdiction. Charles Logan and Sharla Rausch (1985) concluded that deinstitutionalization of status offenders is pointless unless it is accompanied by decriminalization of status offenses. This is not to say that the behaviors currently categorized as status offenses are not problematic, nor that they should be totally ignored. Rather, the point is that they need not be treated as *legal* problems. Truancy is essentially a school problem. Running away is a family problem. Many of the status offenses represent social problems that violate adult values about what is appropriate behavior for youngsters. If the prohibited behaviors are genuinely considered harmful or problematic, there is no reason why they cannot be handled by appropriate social agencies, family courts, departments of public welfare, and institutions outside the criminal justice system. Families, schools, churches, and social agencies in the community that have relinquished responsibility for youth to the legal system could reassert their significance in the socialization process.

REVISION OF THE JUVENILE COURT

The juvenile court has received widespread criticism from a variety of sources. These criticisms have ranged from assertions that the court is too lenient to claims that it is too harsh; from concerns about its devastating impact on youngsters who come before it, to the shocking realization that to many juveniles it is little more than a joke. Regardless of one's particular philosophical perspective, it appears almost unanimous that the juvenile justice system, most notably the juvenile court, is in serious need of revision.

Just as juvenile delinquency is part and product of the society which has created it, so is the juvenile court. Any attempt to revise the juvenile court must consider the social milieu in which it operates. As Krisberg and Austin (1978:569) noted:

> To state the obvious—the juvenile justice system operates within society. Its efforts and consequences are circumscribed and guided by the social arrangements of that particular historical, material, and cultural context which is *society* [italics in original].

In Chapter 12, we made some suggestions for the future direction of the juvenile court which included: limited jurisdiction, full implementation of due process, competent professional judges in every court, adequate and trained court personnel, and wider availability of a variety of dispositional alternatives. If a separate juvenile court is retained, we would like to underscore those recommendations.

The jurisdiction of the juvenile court should be limited to persons under the age of majority who have committed acts which violate criminal laws that would bring them before a criminal court if they were adults. Norval Morris and Gordon Hawkins (1970) included this suggestion as one of the effective elements of crime control. We have already elaborated upon this point in our argument for decriminalization of status offenders. Further, we contend that abused, neglected, and dependent children classified as in need of supervision should be handled in family courts rather than juvenile courts. This would accentuate the fact that these juveniles are *victims* and *not offenders*. These two revisions would substantially limit the jurisdiction of the juvenile court and allow it to focus its attention on dealing with youthful criminal offenders.

Once the juvenile court is limited to dealing with criminal law violations, the full constitutional rights of all who appear before it must be ensured. Schur (1973:168) insisted that "the juvenile justice system should concern itself less with the problems of so-called 'delinquents,' and more with dispensing justice." Limited due process has made its way into the juvenile court through important U.S. Supreme Court decisions, and an increasing number of juveniles are represented by attorneys when they appear before the court. However, the juvenile court is *not* a criminal court in which a clearcut adversarial relationship exists between the state and the accused. Consequently, all the rights guaranteed to an adult criminal offender are not necessarily granted to a juvenile who may have committed the same offense. This should be changed.

Competent judges who have extensive legal training, appropriate legal credentials, and actual courtroom experience are a "must," if juvenile cases are to be fairly and judiciously handled. Additionally, a variety of other trained court personnel are needed to adequately process juveniles through the justice system.

In 1977, a special conference on Juvenile Justice Standards convened in Washington, D.C. Members of that conference concluded their meetings with the following recommendations for revising juvenile courts:

1. Status offenses should be removed from juvenile court jurisdiction.
2. Visibility and accountability of decision making should replace unrestrained discretion and closed proceedings.
3. Juveniles should have the right to decide on actions affecting their lives and freedom, unless found incapable of making reasoned decisions.
4. Role of parents in juvenile proceedings should be redefined, especially when there is potential conflict between the interests of the juvenile and the parents.

5. Limitation should be imposed on detention, treatment, or other intervention prior to adjudication and disposition.
6. Strict criteria should be established for waiver of juvenile court jurisdiction to regulate transfer of juveniles to adult criminal court (Juvenile Justice Standards Project, 1977:2).

Numerous scholars have come up with similar recommendations in an attempt to salvage the juvenile justice system and allow it to regain (or gain for the first time, its most severe critics might contend) its credibility. Others contend that the juvenile court and the juvenile justice system that it represents should not be changed, but abolished altogether.

A MORE CONTROVERSIAL VIEW: THE ARGUMENT TO ABOLISH THE JUVENILE COURT

In a candid interview, prominent criminologist Ernest van den Haag asserted:

> I would abolish tomorrow all juvenile courts because they have been a terrible failure. I believe that anyone over thirteen should be dealt with in the adult court (cited in Bartollas, 1985:111).

While not everyone who favors abolition of the court would agree that age 13 would be the appropriate age for being legally treated as an adult, van den Haag is sounding a familiar refrain—frustration over the inability of the juvenile court to effectively handle serious juvenile offenders. Frances McCarthy (1977) contended that the legal concept of juvenile delinquency began to die with the Gault Decision of 1967. McCarthy (1977) went on to indicate that subsequent attempts to reformulate the legal concept of delinquency have failed, and concluded that delinquency jurisdiction should be removed from the juvenile court. Instead, it should be allowed to revert to the criminal courts, where the highly valued interests of society can be protected more fully.

If, as we have suggested in this chapter, society's concept of adolescence was eliminated, and maturing teenagers were effectively socialized to the responsibilities of adulthood, as well as socially acknowledged as holding full-fledged adult status, there might indeed be no need for a separate juvenile court.

The elimination of the juvenile court would not necessarily mean the end of juvenile corrections, however. Few would argue that teenaged offenders should be housed in the same jails and prisons as adult criminals. As van den Haag pointed out, while he believed that criminal offenders over the age of 13 should be handled by the adult criminal court, he also indicated that their punishment should take place somewhere other than adult prisons (cited in Bartollas, 1985:111–113).

MODIFICATION OF JUVENILE CORRECTIONS

Regardless of whether the juvenile court is kept as is, substantially revised, or eliminated altogether, there remains a need to dramatically modify juvenile corrections. Two necessary changes in juvenile corrections would begin with the disposition (or sentencing) phase of the correctional process. It has been suggested that juvenile sentencing should be **determinate** in nature, and **proportionate** to the seriousness of the offense (Juvenile Justice Standards Project, 1977: Mahler, 1977).

Determinate sentencing refers to *a disposition which specifies a definite period of time for the individual to be incarcerated, on probation, or otherwise supervised by the state.* In other words, rather than placing a juvenile under the auspices of an institution or court officer for an indefinite period of time, the length of sentence would be clearly delineated (e.g., 1 year, 2 years, or until the age of majority). This would eliminate the unreasonable power and unlimited discretion of probation officers, institution supervisors, and others who determine how long a juvenile is to remain under court supervision.

Proportionate sentencing simply means that *the severity of dispositions should be roughly equivalent to the seriousness of the offense committed.* A major problem with juvenile corrections has stemmed from the inappropriateness and inconsistencies of sentences imposed upon juvenile offenders. One reads with horror of a 16-year-old juvenile being sent to a detention facility for a period of 18 months for committing homicide, while another youth aged 13 is remanded to an institution for the remainder of his minority (5 years) for shoplifting. Remember, the case which stimulated the landmark *Gault Decision* involved a young boy who allegedly made an obscene phone call, and was sent to a detention facility for the remainder of his minority (6 years), whereas an adult would have received a maximum punishment of a $50 fine and/or 60 days in jail for the same offense. Mahler (1977) pointed out that in most states, juvenile dispositions are indeterminate and *not* related to the seriousness of the offense. He contended that juveniles should know where they are going, why they are going there, and for how long. Further, he suggested that a Case Assessment Bureau should be established to assess the gravity of the offense committed, and to prevent courts from imposing sanctions that are inordinately lenient or harsh.

If juvenile court dispositions are to be effective, there must be a wide range of dispositional alternatives available to the court. For juveniles who have committed serious criminal offenses, some type of maximum security correctional facility is necessary. The message must be sent out to youthful hoodlums who terrorize innocent citizens that they cannot hide behind their juvenile status. Cox and Conrad (1987) suggested that those juveniles who commit predatory offenses may have to be institutionalized for the good of society.

However, they warned that "the 'out-of-sight, out-of-mind' attitude should be eliminated through the use of programs designed to increase community contact as soon as possible" (Cox and Conrad, 1987:194).

In addition to maximum security facilities, there should be medium and minimum security institutions for less serious offenders. These centers also could be used to help ease the transition of even the most serious offenders back into the community prior to their release. Those incarcerated in the maximum security facility could be transferred to a medium security institution after a period of time, and if they successfully adapt to the increased freedom and responsibility there, they could eventually be transferred to a minimum security facility before being completely released. Thus, the offender would gradually experience increased freedom and responsibility while still under supervision. As Cox and Conrad (1987) indicated, assignment to these various facilities should not be made on a random basis or for convenience of vacancy or transfer. Rather, the seriousness of offense, prior offense record, age, and other pertinent factors should be taken into consideration in developing standard criteria for gradual return to the larger society.

This plan would necessitate major changes in existing juvenile institutions, and the creation of a number of new facilities. In addition to institutions, a number of community treatment programs would need to be implemented. Haskell and Yablonsky (1978) suggested that neighborhood and community correctional approaches should be applied to less serious offenses. They urged the expansion of community treatment programs such as halfway houses, work furlough, probation, and closely supervised parole. This has been attempted in many areas, but, unfortunately, because recent economic policies have severely limited the amount of federal and state money available to finance such programs, many of them have been drastically cut or eliminated altogether.

Haskell and Yablonsky (1978) went even further, and suggested that juvenile institutions should be closed entirely. They lamented that juvenile correctional facilities are primarily custodial in nature, promote future criminal careers, and experience recidivism rates that approach 70 percent (Haskell and Yablonsky, 1978:551).

Closing juvenile correctional institutions would indeed represent a workable approach to the problem if the decision was made to eliminate separate juvenile codes and to abolish the juvenile court. Under such a plan, juveniles who currently are institutionalized for status offenses would be handled outside the legal system by other social agencies. Those who committed criminal acts would be handled by the adult criminal court system. If convicted of a crime, they would be sentenced as adults. This does not necessarily mean that they should be placed in adult jails and prisons as they presently exist. It might be that society would like to establish age-graded correctional institutions and want to separate criminal offenders on the basis of age. For example, separate correctional institutions could be created for offenders ranging from 16 to 25 years of age, while other facilities could house those between the ages of 26 and 45. Still another institution could be designed to house offenders aged 46 and older.

Another possible approach to the corrections dilemma might be to segregate offenders by types of offense, and to separate first-time offenders from recidivists. This would address problems faced today in both juvenile and adult corrections, in that relatively nonserious first-time offenders now often must be housed in the same facilities (and sometimes even in the same cells) with hardened repeat offenders. Most 16-year-old nonviolent offenders share more in common with the 36-year-old property criminal than with the 16-year-old robber, rapist, or murderer. Type of offense and prior criminal record might be much more logical criteria for institutional segregation than mere chronological age.

A final suggestion related to juvenile corrections would be to minimize the stigma associated with adjudication and disposition. Along with being determinate and proportionate, sentences should also be finite. In other words, once a juvenile (or adult) is released from a correctional facility, or some other disposition (e.g., probation), the individual's "debt to society" should be erased. Haskell and Yablonsky (1978:557) recommended "amnesty upon completion of sentence" pointing out that once juveniles (and adults) have completed their restitution, it should be over. They suggested that arrest and sentencing records should not be publicly available, thus avoiding the stigma which denies equal access to schools, jobs, and other social activities.

Many researchers recommend more community-based delinquency correctional and prevention programs such as those discussed in Chapter 14 (e.g., Burns and Stern, 1967; Winslow, 1973; Haskell and Yablonsky, 1978; Krisberg and Austin, 1978; Cox and Conrad, 1987). However, as Krisberg and Austin (1978) indicated, not all communities have equal resources to provide adequate programs. They pointed out that the separation of delinquency prevention from basic human needs creates a false distinction. They insisted, "Reducing crime, improving the quality of education, promoting mental health, and supporting family life are several sides to a common, if complex, human service enterprise" (Krisberg and Austin, 1978:574). Acknowledging the social nature of delinquency, they pointed out that delinquency research indicates that we should encourage the full healthy development of all youths. Krisberg and Austin (1978:575) stated:

> Local centers . . . could offer educational and counseling programs in . . .
> health, nutrition, mental health, welfare, parent-effectiveness, and employment.
> Staffed by community people and professionals, neighborhood-based service
> centers could provide a vehicle for community organization efforts such as pub-
> lic forums on delinquency and related problems.

CHANGING THE EDUCATIONAL SYSTEM

Earlier in this chapter we emphasized the importance of providing meaningful social roles for juveniles which give them greater decision-making power, especially in areas which affect their lives. With the possible exception of the family, no social institution more directly influences the lives of young Americans than the educational system. In our opinion, if meaningful social change is to come about in an effort to reduce the problems currently associated with juvenile delinquency, the schools will need to play a very significant role.

In Chapter 10, we explored the social arena of the school and its relationship to juvenile delinquency and delinquency prevention. At the end of that chapter we suggested ways in which the schools might take a more active role in delinquency prevention. Those suggestions included: less emphasis upon identifying and labeling "predelinquents"; reeducating and resocializing parents, teachers, and students to the problems of the success-failure philosophy of the schools; a wider range of tolerance of nonserious rule violations on the part of students; and reducing some of the bureaucratization of the educational process.

Again, we must recognize the social context in which the schools exist and operate. Substantive changes in the educational process must be accompanied by widespread changes in the attitudes, values, and norms surrounding it. Since the Industrial Revolution, schools have tended to be modeled after the factory. Students entering the system are essentially viewed as "raw materials" to be shaped, formed, and molded into "finished products" upon graduation. The factory model revolutionized education, but not all of its results have been positive. The blue-ribbon panel of experts which produced the highly touted study *A Nation at Risk* (U.S. National Commission on Excellence in Education, 1983) enumerated some of the major problems related to education in America. Even that study, however, did not seriously question the attitudes, values, and norms which provide the foundation for the educational system. Rather, it primarily lamented declining test scores, lack of basic skills, and the failure of the teaching profession to attract and retain the "best and the brightest." While these are significant issues, they do not address the broader scope of the problem.

The schools are one of the most important elements in reducing the problems of delinquency, but dramatic changes need to be made in the educational system. For instance, Krisberg and Austin (1978:575) insisted that education must be more broadly defined with an expanded curriculum and a modified idea ". . . about who should be involved in the learning process and where education takes place." They suggested broader community involvement in all aspects of the schools.

In our view, broader community involvement should also include more meaningful participation on the part of juveniles. One of the ways to provide youths with more access to the power structure in education would be to include students on local school boards. This would give them direct input on budget, personnel, and curriculum decisions as well as enhance their identity and status as role models for other youths.

Most colleges and universities allow a degree of student participation in campus government. Students serve on committees, have a student government association, and usually participate in the evaluation of their professors. These same procedures generally have not been incorporated at the high school or lower levels. Why not? We are not advocating turning the schools over to the students. Rather, we are suggesting that students should be included in the decision-making process in the school system. J. David Hawkins and Joseph Weis (1980) also viewed the school as one of the potentially most effective sources of delinquency control. They suggested more thorough and broader vocational training, alternative education opportunities, education in civil and criminal law, and more student input into educational programs. We anticipate that more student input might lead to a stronger commitment by students to the common educational endeavor and objective.

Another change to be explored for the public schools would be the elimination of compulsory school attendance laws. School attendance is important as a democratic society demands an educated citizenry. Yet, as discussed in Chapter 10, many youths feel totally alienated, and experience nothing but frustration and failure in school. When truants are tracked down by police, processed as delinquent, and then forcibly brought back to school, it is not likely that positive educational results will occur. Once a person has undergone the rite of passage we have suggested denoting the transition into adulthood, the decision to attend school or drop out should rest with that person. If alternative vocational and training programs are made available, the stigma of dropping out of school could be greatly reduced. Those desiring to stay in school and further their formal academic education would not be hampered by having to share limited educational resources with those who really do not want to partake of them. Similarly, this should greatly reduce the vandalism and violence in the public schools from those who are "imprisoned" there against their will.

REDEFINING JUVENILE DELINQUENCY

The recommendations made in this chapter amount to nothing short of a total redefinition of the concept of juvenile delinquency. In our view, this redefining process is essential if society is genuinely interested in reducing the problems associated with delinquency. In general, this redefinition must reflect a serious assessment by societal members as to what youthful behavior can and cannot be tolerated. Frederick Howlett (1973:492) insisted that "the community clearly must redefine its limits of acceptable behavior." Our current laws prohibit many behaviors which society is actually willing to allow, and in fact, routinely does allow for many. Curfew violation, premarital sexual activities, smoking, truancy, and other status offenses are routinely ignored by some parents, teachers, and law enforcement officials. On the other hand, on occasion, the full force of the justice system may be exercised upon a youth who commits any one of these offenses. Such hypocrisy and random and selective enforcement helps create general disrespect toward the law and the legal process.

Narrowing the definition of delinquency as we have suggested would help reduce the problems of hypocrisy and disrespect. Only those behaviors that are considered beyond toleration by the larger society should be classified as illegal or delinquent. Schur (1973:154) suggested this approach in his concept of *radical non-intervention*, explaining:

> Basically, radical nonintervention implies policies that accommodate society to the widest possible diversity of behaviors and attitudes, rather than forcing as many individuals as possible to 'adjust' to supposedly common societal standards (Schur, 1973:154).

The basic public policy of radical non-intervention becomes *"leave the kids alone wherever possible"* [italics in the original] (Schur, 1973:155). We suggest that society must seek consensus on some basic non-negotiable standards of behavior. Those activities that do not seriously threaten the social order would be tolerated; however, those that were deemed beyond the range of tolerance by the larger society would be swiftly and appropriately sanctioned.

We have presented two possible ways in which society can broaden its range of tolerance and reduce some of the problems of juvenile delinquency. One solution is to redefine delinquency so as to standardize juvenile codes and eliminate status offenses. This standardization would include clearly specifying both the minimum and the maximum ages for juvenile court jurisdiction while retaining a sociological perspective on delinquency. Hence, the revised definition of delinquency would be: *all acts committed by individuals between the ages of 7 and 16 (or possibly 14) which would be considered criminal if committed by an adult, place the juvenile in the delinquent/criminal role, and result in society regarding the juvenile as intolerably deviant.* This new definition alone would resolve some of the problems of delinquency, especially those related to the ambiguity of its meaning. In order for this definition to be effective, however, it would need to be accompanied by some of the widespread modifications and revisions we have suggested in the operation of the juvenile court, and in juvenile corrections. This more concise and narrower definition would greatly reduce the quantity of what is considered delinquency, and allow available resources to be redirected in a more effective way toward implementing some of the proposed revisions in the court and correctional system. While the social problem of juvenile delinquency would not be eliminated, it would be significantly reduced. Further, the remaining juvenile delinquency which occurred could be more effectively handled.

A second, and perhaps more controversial way to approach the redefinition of juvenile delinquency, would be to "define it out of existence." You may remember that in Chapter 1, we pointed out that sociologists view deviance as a natural consequence of the normative system of society. When norms are created, so is deviance. Thus, as indicated in Chapter 13, society cannot hope to eliminate deviance, but must continually seek methods for effectively controlling it and minimizing its negative impacts upon its members. Consequently, defining juvenile delinquency out of existence will not actually eliminate the behaviors that currently constitute delinquency. Youngsters would still skip school, run away from home, steal, and even rape and murder. However, while redefining delinquency would not eliminate those behaviors, it would dramatically change our reactions to them. Truancy and running away from home would not be illegal acts. Consequently, they would be ignored by the criminal justice system—not ignored by society—but ignored by the legal system. Stealing, raping, and killing, on the other hand, would be crimes—not delinquent acts—but crimes, and society would still react with justified indignation.

This second alternative would require the most dramatic social changes. Undoubtedly, society would not want to invoke full legal sanctions upon children just because they had reached the age of 7. Instead, children aged 7 would be considered just that—**children.** Children would not be held legally accountable for their actions until they had gone through a formal rite of passage initiating them into adulthood. While this initiation is often directly associated with the onset of puberty in many societies, it could be adjusted slightly to fit society's consensually agreed-upon age. The rite of passage could be conducted at the age of 14, 15, or 16. From that point on, the individual would be accorded full adult status in society with all the normative expectations associated with adulthood attached—*rights* as well as *responsibilities.* Thus, any criminal violations would be handled through criminal courts.

There is ample research evidence to suggest that the midteens would be a logical point for legally differentiating between children and adults. For example, Barry Glassner et al. (1983) found that many youths sharply reduced their involvement in illegal activities after age 16. When asked, respondents indicated that they believed that there was a much greater probability of their being adjudicated as an adult, and actually going to prison if arrested after age 16. Their findings indicated that being held legally accountable for their actions as adults had a highly specific deterrent effect on the subjects. Similarly, the studies of Marvin Wolfgang et al. (1972) and Steven Lab (1984) suggested that many juveniles apparently "grow out" of their delinquency somewhere in their midteens. That being the case, perhaps lowering the age of legal accountability to 14 would achieve the same purpose. Youths would know that at age 14 they would socially and legally become adults. This might provide the same type of deterrent effect. In harmony with this idea, we know that, generally, young people in our society are reaching puberty at a younger age each generation. Therefore, rite of passage into adult social status would tend to approximate the biological onset of adulthood.

We concur with Jerome Stumphauzer's (1986) point that it is important to recognize and reinforce nondelinquency. Unfortunately, most of our attention is focused on punishing delinquents, not on rewarding nondelinquents. More public recognition of conforming and desired behavior by youths could serve to positively reinforce law abiding behavior.

We do not presume to know which direction society should take on this matter. Nor do we presume that these two possible directions in redefining delinquency are the only alternatives. We do believe, however, that it is essential that there be a careful and innovative rethinking of the delinquency problem by our entire society.

This would entail vigorous new directions in research and theory construction to develop theories which can be *applied* by public policy makers and practitioners. More attention must be focused upon social conformity as offering fresh insights into deviant and delinquent behavior. Most researchers and theorists have focused upon the more sensational and interesting deviants, almost to the exclusion of the vast majority of youngsters not involved in serious offenses.

Another dimension to our call for new research and theory emphasizes the need for genuine interdisciplinary studies. Sociologists can hardly continue to ignore the accumulating etiological insights from other disciplines. Likewise, other disciplines must not ignore the contributions of sociology.

SUMMARY

The best way to summarize this chapter is to present a list of suggestions and/or recommendations for possible changes that would alter the way Americans view young people, juvenile misconduct, and youthful crime. The goals of these changes would be to more effectively deal with the social problem of what constitutes juvenile delinquency, and to reduce and/or eliminate its negative impact upon society. Toward those ends, we suggest the following:

1. Delinquency is a social product and therefore must be viewed in its broadest sociological context. This requires societal members to seriously examine the values, attitudes, beliefs, and norms which surround the concept of juvenile delinquency.
2. Reduce or eliminate the marginal status of adolescence. This most effectively could be accomplished by establishing a meaningful rite of passage from childhood to adulthood which roughly coincides with or shortly follows the onset of puberty.

3. Provide meaningful social roles for individuals who have completed the rite of passage into adulthood. Eliminate barriers to reasonable employment based solely on age, and allow full participation in meaningful social roles and decision-making processes.

4. Standardize (or possibly eliminate) juvenile codes. If separate juvenile codes are maintained, there should be a uniform minimum and maximum age of juvenile court jurisdiction across the United States. Similarly, the definition of delinquency should be standardized, simplified, and clarified.

5. Decriminalize status offenses. Legal codes should narrow the concept of delinquency to include only those actions which would be crimes if committed by adults.

6. Revise (or possibly eliminate) the juvenile court system. If separate juvenile courts are maintained, they must be staffed with a wide variety of highly trained specialists. At the very least, all juveniles should be guaranteed the same access to full due process of law as adults.

7. Modify juvenile corrections. Incorporate determinate and proportionate sentencing into the disposition phase of juvenile justice. Segregate first-time offenders from repeat offenders and nonviolent offenders from violent offenders. Create minimum, medium, and maximum security institutions with emphasis upon community participation in the correctional process, and successful reintegration into the community as the ultimate goal.

8. Remove the stigma attached to having gone through the juvenile and/or criminal justice system. Punishment for law violations should be finite. Once restitution is made, it should be over.

9. Change the educational system. Deemphasize the process of identifying "problem children" and "predelinquents." Eliminate the success-failure philosophy which dominates education. Recognize the importance of vocational and technical education as well as traditional academic pursuits, and remove the stigma currently associated with many of those nonacademic programs. Eliminate the "factory model" philosophy of education. Create stronger ties between the community and the schools, and allow students to participate in the decision-making processes in their schools.

10. Redefine juvenile delinquency. Either: (a) standardize, clarify, and narrow the definition of delinquency to include only those acts that society clearly cannot and should not tolerate from youths; or (b) eliminate the concept of juvenile delinquency altogether by lowering the age of legal responsibility so that parents would be held responsible for law violations of children under the cutoff age, and youthful offenders over that age would be legally handled as adult criminals.

11. Apply new sociological and interdisciplinary approaches to research and theoretical explanations of youthful conformity and deviance.

12. Apply sociological and interdisciplinary theories to public policy and social practice.

The implementation of some or all of these suggestions would alter dramatically the way our society views juvenile delinquency. Many of the negative consequences of delinquency would be diminished, and perhaps some would even be eliminated. However, it would not eliminate youthful misconduct and law violating behavior. While youthful deviance might be reduced through implementation of our ideas, as long as we have social norms, we will have social deviance. No society can exist without norms. Therefore, deviance is inherently a part of every society. On the other hand, the way in which society chooses to define and react to deviance can be changed. Perhaps it is time that we do just that in regard to juvenile delinquency.

CONCEPT APPLICATION

"Treating Juveniles as Adults"

Item: In McAlister, Oklahoma, at Oklahoma State Penitentiary, a 17-year-old convicted of murdering a convenience store clerk and both his parents sits on death row awaiting his execution. At this writing, 32 other persons convicted of crimes committed while under the age of 18 share the same fate.

Item: In the summer of 1978, a police officer in Menlo Park, California recruited 10 teenagers to take responsibility for abandoned homes in or near their neighborhoods. The teenagers, called Junior Housing Inspectors, were paid $50 per week to supervise the houses in order to prevent what had become an endless series of very expensive break-ins and vandalism. The result was a dramatic decrease in the vandalism, a new sense of community pride, and a grant which brought federal money into the community to provide jobs for responsible hard-working youths who needed employment.

Item: In Clovis, New Mexico, teenagers sit on juries to hear the cases of first-time juvenile offenders. They make recommendations to the judge regarding the adjudication and disposition of the cases brought before them.

Item: In Odessa, Texas, Teen Court was developed to hear cases of defendants between the ages of 10 and 16 charged with traffic violations and misdemeanors such as public intoxication, shoplifting, running away, vandalism, and disorderly conduct. Six teenage jurors make a recommendation for sentencing to a retired district judge who presides over the court. If the youth successfully completes the sentence, all charges are dismissed and no criminal record is maintained.

Item: In Lockesburg, Arkansas, a 13-year-old was elected to serve on the City Park Committee. His membership was not an honorary position. Rather, he served as a full-fledged active member. During the summer months he devoted a great deal of time to working at the park. During the school year, he attended all meetings of the committee and worked weekends on park responsibilities.

What do all these items share in common? They all represent social situations in which teenagers have been treated as responsible citizens. Each of these items refers to actual cases in which individuals legally considered minors—"adolescents" or "juveniles"—have been judged to be mature enough to be held accountable for their actions in the same manner as adults. The first item represents the darker side of full accountability; the other items, the brighter side of meaningful social participation.

These items indicate that treating teenagers as adults is not totally unheard of in American society. Doubtless, there are numerous other specific examples which could be included here. However, that is not the norm. Typically, people under the age of majority are not granted the rights or the responsibilities commonly associated with adulthood.

Without question, treating teenagers as adults has mixed consequences. If society believes in trial by a jury of one's peers, teenagers should sit on juries. If society believes in policing its neighborhoods, teenagers may be recruited for the job. And, if society believes that it is just to execute its murderers, teenagers may be executed.

On the other hand, if society insists on treating teenagers as something other than adults, it can resign itself to innumerable social problems, not the least of which is juvenile delinquency. The choices are difficult, but they eventually must be made.

* * * *

Using your sociological imagination, can you think of other meaningful ways in which teenagers could take on adult responsibilities and fulfill meaningful statuses and roles in American society?

CONCEPT INTEGRATION

QUESTIONS AND TOPICS FOR STUDY AND DISCUSSION

1. Why is it important to view juvenile delinquency within a social context? What dominant values, attitudes, beliefs, and norms surround the

concept of delinquency? What social changes would have to occur for society's concept of juvenile delinquency to be significantly altered?

2. Should separate juvenile codes be retained? If not, why not? If so, should they be standardized? Should they be reinforced? Why? Why not? What revisions would you recommend?

3. Do you favor the elimination of status offenses? Why? Why not?

4. Should a separate juvenile court be retained? If not, why not? If so, what modifications should be made in the present juvenile justice system? How might the juvenile court be modified to more effectively deal with the problem of delinquency?

5. What changes would you recommend in the present educational system in an effort to reduce the alienation of youths and lessen or prevent youthful misconduct and law violation?

6. Do you favor redefining the concept of juvenile delinquency? Or legally eliminating the concept altogether? If redefined, what should be the new definition? If eliminated, how would you handle the problems which now constitute delinquency?

7. What rites of passage presently function in American society to ease the transition from childhood to adulthood? Can you think of any new ones which might make this transition easier and possibly alleviate some of the problems faced by today's youths?

References

Bartollas, C. 1985. *Juvenile delinquency.* New York: John Wiley.

Boyd, N. 1980. The circularity of punishment and treatment: Some notes on the legal response to juvenile delinquency. *Canadian Journal of Family Law* 3 (4):419–438.

Burns, V. & Stern, L. 1967. The prevention of juvenile delinquency. In *Task Force Report: Juvenile Delinquency and Youth Crime.* President's Commission on Law Enforcement and Administration. Washington, DC: U.S. Government Printing Office, Appendix S, pp. 361–364.

Cox, S. M. & Conrad, J. J. 1987. *Juvenile justice: A guide to practice and theory* (2nd ed.). Dubuque, IA: Wm. C. Brown.

Deardorff, N. R. 1955. The religio-cultural background of New York City's population. *Milbank Quarterly* 33 (April):152–160.

Glassner, B., Ksander, M., Berg, B. & Johnson, B. D. 1983. A note on the deterrent effect of juvenile vs. adult jurisdiction. *Social Problems* 31 (December):219–221.

Goodman, P. 1962. *Growing up absurd: Problems of youth in the organized society.* New York: Random House.

Haskell, M. R. & Yablonsky, L. 1978. *Juvenile delinquency* (2nd ed.). Chicago: Rand McNally.

Hawkins, J. D. & Weis, J. G. 1980. *The social developmental model: An integrated approach to delinquency prevention*. Seattle: Center for Law and Justice, University of Washington.

Howlett, F. W. 1973. Is the Youth Service Bureau all it's cracked up to be? *Crime and Delinquency* 91 (October):485–492.

Juvenile Justice Standards Project. 1977. *Juvenile justice standards*. Washington, DC: National Conference on the Proposed IJA/ABA Juvenile Justice Standards, October 30–November 3.

Keniston, K. 1968. *Young radicals: Notes on committed youth*. New York: Harcourt, Brace and World.

Krisberg, B. & Austin, J. (Eds.). 1978. *The children of Ishmael: Critical perspectives on juvenile justice*. Palo Alto, CA: Mayfield.

Kvaraceus, W. 1945. *Juvenile delinquency and the school*. Yonkers: World Book.

Lab, S. P. 1984. Patterns in juvenile misbehavior. *Crime and Delinquency* 30 (April):293–308.

Liebow, E. 1967. *Tally's corner: A study of Negro streetcorner men*. Boston: Little, Brown.

Logan, C. H. & Rausch, S. P. 1985. Why deinstitutionalizing status offenders is pointless. *Crime and Delinquency* 31 (October):501–517.

Lotz, R., Poole, E. D., & Regoli, R. M. 1985. *Juvenile delinquency and juvenile justice*. New York: Random House.

Mahler, J. M. 1977. *Rational approach to the reality of juvenile crime in America*. Rockville, MD: National Institute of Justice.

McCarthy, F. B. 1977. Should juvenile delinquency be abolished? *Crime and Delinquency* 23 (April):196–203.

Mead, M. 1928. *Growing up in Samoa*. New York: LW Morrow.

Mills, C. W. 1959. *The sociological imagination*. New York: Oxford University Press.

Morris, N. & Hawkins, G. 1970. *The honest politician's guide to crime control*. Chicago: University of Chicago Press.

Musgrove, F. 1965. *Youth and the social order*. Bloomington: Indiana University Press.

National Advisory Committee for Juvenile Justice and Delinquency Prevention. 1984. *Serious juvenile crime: A redirected federal effort*. Washington, DC: U.S. Government Printing Office.

Office of Juvenile Justice and Delinquency Prevention. 1979. *Delinquency prevention: Theories and strategies*. Washington, DC: Law Enforcement Assistance Administration, U.S. Department of Justice.

Oswalt, W. H. 1986. *Life cycles and lifeways: An introduction to cultural anthropology*. Palo Alto, CA: Mayfield.

Regnery, A. S. 1985. Getting away with murder: Why the juvenile justice system needs an overhaul. *Policy Review* 34 (Fall):1–4.

Schur, E. M. 1973. *Radical non-intervention: Rethinking the delinquency problem*. Englewood Cliffs, NJ: Prentice-Hall.

Siegal, L. J. 1986. *Criminology* (2nd ed.). St. Paul: West.

Sipila, J. 1985. Community structure and deviant behavior among adolescents. *Youth and Society* 16 (June):471–497.

Stumphauzer, J. S. 1986. *Helping delinquents change: A treatment manual of social learning approaches.* New York: Haworth Press.

The Daily Tidings. 1977. Kid corporation is in trouble again. *Daily Tidings,* Ashland, Oregon, November 3, 1977:3.

U.S. National Commission on Excellence in Education. 1983. *A nation at risk.* Washington, DC: U.S. Government Printing Office.

Van Gennep, A. [1908] 1960. *The rights of passage* (Trans. M. B. Vizedom & G. L. Caffee). Chicago: University of Chicago Press.

Whyte, W. F. 1943. *Street corner society: The social structure of an urban slum.* Chicago: University of Chicago Press.

Winslow, R. H. (Ed.). 1973. *Juvenile delinquency in a free society* (2nd ed.). Encino, CA: Dickenson.

Wolfgang, M. E., Figlio, R. M., & Sellin, T. 1972. *Delinquency in a birth cohort.* Chicago: University of Chicago Press.

Wolfgang, M. E., Thornberry, T. P., & Figlio, R. M. 1987. *From boy to man, from delinquency to crime.* Chicago: University of Chicago Press.

Youth Development and Delinquency Prevention Administration. 1972. *Delinquency prevention through youth development.* Youth Development and Delinquency Prevention Administration Pub. no. (SRS)73-26013. Washington, DC: U.S. Government Printing Office (May):28–30.

Name Index

Subject Index